The City

in

Newly Developing

Countries:

READINGS ON

URBANISM AND URBANIZATION

Prentice-Hall, Inc., Englewood Cliffs, N.J.

The City
in
Newly Developing
Countries:

READINGS ON
URBANISM AND URBANIZATION

Edited by G E R A L D B R E E S E Princeton University

Library of Congress Catalog Card No.: 69-11167

Current printing (last digit):

10   9   8   7   6   5   4   3   2   1

Printed in the United States of America

PRENTICE-HALL INTERNATIONAL, INC.
London

PRENTICE-HALL OF AUSTRALIA, PTY. LTD.
Sydney

PRENTICE-HALL OF CANADA, LTD.
Toronto

PRENTICE-HALL OF INDIA PRIVATE LTD.
New Delhi

PRENTICE-HALL OF JAPAN, INC.
Tokyo

WILBERT E. MOORE / NEIL J. SMELSER   Editors

Modernization of Traditional Societies Series

For ALICE JANETTE BAILEY BREESE

The twentieth century will be called many
things by future historians—the Age of Global
War, perhaps, the Age of Mass Society,
the Age of the Psychoanalytic Revolution,
to name a few possibilities. One name that
historians certainly will not fail to give
our century is the Age of the New Nation. For,
evidently, the convulsive emergence of
the colonies into independence and their
subsequent struggle to join the ranks of the
prosperous, powerful, and peaceful is the
most remarkable revolution of our time.
Taking the world as a whole, men are now
preoccupied with no subject more than they
are with the travail of the New Nations.
The world of the social sciences
has been studying the pace of social
change in these newly emergent areas,
and from time to time has been engaging in
technical assistance and even in the giving
of advice on high levels of social strategy.
Little of this effort has reached publicly
accessible form. Though technical treatises
abound, and isolated, journalistic reports
of distinctly exotic countries are not
wanting, college curricula have scarcely
reflected either the scientific endeavors or
the world-wide revolutions in technology
and in political affairs.
This series on "Modernization of
Traditional Societies" is designed to
inform scholars, students, and citizens about
the way quiet places have come alive, and
to introduce at long last materials on the
contemporary character of developing
areas into college curricula for

EDITORIAL FOREWORD

the thought leaders of the near future. To these ends we have assembled experts over the range of the social sciences and over the range of the areas of the underdeveloped and newly developing sections of the earth that were once troublesome only to themselves.

We are proud to be participants in this series, and proud to offer each of its volumes to the literate world, with the hope that that world may increase, prosper, think, and decide wisely.

WILBERT E. MOORE
NEIL J. SMELSER

Urbanism and urbanization in newly developing countries are enormously complex subjects. The phenomena are world wide, and complex partly for that reason. But they are also discernible in differing degrees and in differing contexts. They occur in their present forms as a result of varying histories from country to country, and even within countries. Such variation is embarrassing to the sociologist, but not disastrously so. The variations involve dimensions that are economic, psychological, sociological, political, and virtually every conceivable combination of these and other components. They are partly process and partly product. Perhaps it is presumptuous even to try to focus *one* reader on such diversity; doing so places a premium on what will be selected for inclusion.

Neither this nor any other such reader can be all things to all people. This one aims to provide the *newcomer* to the study of cities in newly developing countries with materials on aspects of the subject that the editor believes are among the most important. To be truly comprehensive would be to perpetrate a disastrous assembly of ill-sorted information.

The criteria for selection have included, among other considerations, the expertness of the author, a quality not easily come by in studying the new patterns of urbanization. The way in which the expert presented his material has been considered relevant to the task. The success with which the author from a particular discipline related his

PREFACE

materials to those of other disciplines seemed essential in dealing with a subject in which traditional limits of inquiry are inappropriate to the complexity of the field. Finally, the bizarre has been sacrificed for the typical or representative analysis of urbanization in newly developing countries.

If the variations are wide, they are not total. Not all of the selections used are equally qualified on these criteria; and criteria of judgment will differ. Nevertheless, any subsequent revision will inevitably include many replacements reflecting constantly improving resources from which to choose.

Only a few case studies of individual cities have been included; a reader comprised of such case studies is practicable, and would constitute still another approach to the subject. Space limitations have also precluded incorporating a formal bibliography, which to be of any real value would have to be annotated and classified, requiring another volume. However, selections for this reader were made partially on the basis of whether footnotes and internal references would provide a partial substitute for a full-scale bibliography. The interested user will find it possible to secure excellent substantive and geographical bibliographies. The more recent of the latter are for West African, Southeast Asian, and Latin American urban areas. It is impossible to condense this wealth to fit a modest table of contents.

It is regrettable that the majority of recent reporting of research dealing with cities in newly developing countries tends to be focused on large cities. The present reader reflects this focus, but reluctantly, in view of the very great importance of smaller urban centers in developing countries. Already research on such smaller urban areas is appearing in greater quantity and higher quality than before, and will eventually find its way into readers.

The organization of this reader is necessarily arbitrary, the divisions being made for convenience; there seems to be no practicable way of discussing everything simultaneously. Persons experienced in research on cities in newly developing countries do not jump to the conclusion that spatial separation in discussion implies lack of awareness of interrelationships, for on this subject, if anywhere, it is evident that although one sees the whole in its complexity, the presentation must perforce be in parts.

The inevitable dilemma of attempting to provide a reader touching on urbanism and urbanization in most newly developing parts of the world as against focusing on just one or two—say Latin America or Southeast Asia— was resolved, not without misgivings, in the direction of the former. As in the case of the editor's *Urbanization in Newly Developing Countries** the decision was made partly in view of the probable use by persons making their first exploration of the subject. Area specialists, and persons engaged in research on specific aspects of urbanism and urbanization in newly developing countries,

---

* (Englewood Cliffs, N.J.: Prentice-Hall Inc., 1966). The contents of this reader are selected to supplement other works, including the book just noted. The introductory section of each Part indicates the portions of *Urbanization in Newly Developing Countries* most closely related to the selections.

will seek more narrowly specialized compendia. The editor makes no apology for attempting to introduce a subject in a simpler form than heretofore has been available. There is nothing to prevent pursuing such study in more detail. The encouragement of further study, indeed, is one of the editor's main objectives.

Welcome to the field!

GERALD BREESE

It is a pleasure to express my appreciation
to the authors and publishers who have
granted permission to use the selections
in this reader. Specific acknowledgment
is made at point of use. I am particularly
indebted to those authors who have made it
possible to incorporate revisions, corrections,
and additions. The volume would obviously
have been impossible without the cooperation
of the scholars and editors involved.
Wilbert E. Moore and Neil J. Smelser
have been most patient and helpful in all ways,
especially through their constructive comments,
but they must not be saddled with responsibility
for the final product, roughly one-fourth
the length of the original version. That
responsibility clearly rests in the hands of
the volume's editor. I have appreciated the
help provided by the staff of Prentice-Hall, Inc.,
under the direction of James H. Clark,
Editor—Sociology. It is a pleasure to extend
special thanks for interest, professional skill,
and invariable cooperation to Barbara Clark,
Production Editor, and to Margaret G. McNeily,
for proofreading; various members of the
art staff ably surmounted many difficulties.
The dedication to Alice Janette Bailey Breese
can only feebly and imperfectly express my
thanks to her.
Dorothy E. Whiteman, a colleague at the
Bureau of Urban Research for several years,
and my Student Research Assistant, Joseph
R. La Torre, assisted in many ways for
which I am grateful. My own compensation
for the unexpectedly heavy investment

ACKNOWLEDGMENTS   required by this undertaking lies in the stimulation provided by an extensive survey of the literature on urbanism and urbanization in newly developing countries—phenomena destined to reach proportions and produce problems that may make those of Western counterparts seem minor and pale.

GERALD BREESE

Contents

The City

In

Newly Developing

Countries:

READINGS ON

URBANISM AND URBANIZATION

INTRODUCTION

Until data on the scale and pace of urbanization in newly developing countries are more generally and readily available, a substantial part of any reader must be devoted to presenting dimensions and trends.[1]

Despite expanding information on the world distribution of population, most people in Western countries suffer from somewhat provincial awareness of the extent to which urbanization is taking place outside Europe and in North America above the Rio Grande.

Accordingly, the first part of this reader begins with broad reviews of world population changes, with particular reference to urban areas. Kingsley Davis (1) presents a general picture of what is emerging, whereas the UN paper (2) will be found particularly useful as a reference source on trends during the period 1920–1960. It should be remembered that comparability of statistics is affected by the varying quality and frequency of censuses among nations of the world; these selections by Davis and the UN grapple with this problem and present what seem currently to be the most nearly reliable comparative data on a world-wide scale.

The major features and the dimensions of urban growth throughout the world are next discussed by large geographically defined areas. South, Southeast, and Southwest Asia are examined first in maps (3, 4, 5). Rhoads Murphey (6) provides a precise and penetrating consideration of Asian cities, including comparisons with non-Asian cities. His

[1] The readings comprising this part are most closely related to pp. 12-37 of Gerald Breese, *Urbanization in Newly Developing Countries* (Englewood Cliffs, N.J.: Prentice-Hall, Inc., 1966).

PART ONE

The Scale and Pace of Urbanization

paper is enhanced by a detailed bibliographical review providing ample sources for further study.[2]

A very short selection (7) on the ECAFE area is included to provide supplementary insight into other aspects of urbanization there.[3]

Morris Ullman (8) reviews the sparse data on cities of mainland China up to our own decades. The accompanying map provides the most recent picture of this urbanization. Such cautious analyses will have to suffice until more nearly reliable data become available.

Urban growth patterns in the Middle East are explored by Isis Ragheb (9), who notes details for an area that is continentally part Asia and part Africa.

The general African scene (10, 12—map) is partially reported statistically by an excerpt from an Economic Commission for Africa analysis (11) of recent demographic levels and trends in Africa. G. Hamdan's article (12) on "Capitals of the New Africa" examines these phenomena by means of a map, a table, and discussion. This is only one of scores of studies of African urbanization emerging in recent years and currently in progress. The richness of related literature, particularly in French and English, has already made it possible to prepare extensive bibliographies,[4] and current research promises to be even more fruitful.

Major features of Latin American urban development (13, 14) are presented by Durand and Peláez (15), supplemented by data from the UN *Economic Bulletin for Latin America* (16). Increasingly helpful materials on urban areas in Latin America are now becoming available.[5]

It is unfortunate that, to date, our most extensive and intensive knowledge of urban areas in newly developing countries is preponderantly based on studies of very large cities—metropolises.[6] Most countries with a primate city are expected to have some important supplementary urban areas in the future, but, except for a few monographs by geographers, even the numerous smaller centers in a country as large as India, for example, are still too seldom the subject of research scrutiny by professional students of the city. Some new insight into the importance of some of these smaller places is contained, for example, in conurbation-scale studies being completed for the Calcutta area.

Certain major features of the very largest cities in the world are reviewed in

---

[2] Monographic materials on particular segments of Asia are gradually appearing. See, for example, T. G. McGee, *The Southeast Asian City* (New York: Frederick A. Praeger, Inc., 1967).

[3] See also Leo Jakobson and Ved Prakash, "Urbanization and Regional Planning in India," *Urban Affairs Quarterly* 2(3): 36-65 (March, 1967).

[4] See, for example, both Ruth P. Simms, *Urbanization in West Africa: A Review of Current Literature* (Evanston, Illinois: Northwestern University Press, 1965), and P. Verhaegen, *l'Urbanisation de l'Afrique Noire: son cadre, ses causes et ses conséquences économiques* (Économique et Sociale Africaine, 1962).

[5] One recent example: Leo Schnore, "On the Spatial Structure of Cities in the Two Americas," in Philip M. Hauser and Leo Schnore (eds.), *The Study of Urbanization*, Chapter 10 (New York: John Wiley and Sons, Inc., 1965).

[6] A major exception, but still having many serious limitations, is the series of more than a score of studies of Indian cities of various sizes, sponsored by the Planning Commission, Government of India.

selections by Homer Hoyt and Jerome C. Pickard (17, 18), thereby providing limited comparative information on cities in developed countries.

No matter how refined our statistics and measurements become—and they are now at best rudimentary—they will never suffice to disclose the less readily quantifiable aspects of urbanization in newly developing countries. Parts II, III, and IV of this reader are therefore devoted to the changing role of the city, its inhabitants, and selected aspects of physical development.

World Population Changes

1. The Urbanization of the Human Population

KINGSLEY DAVIS

Urbanized societies, in which a majority of the people live crowded together in towns and cities, represent a new and fundamental step in man's social evolution. Although cities themselves first appeared some 5,500 years ago, they were small and surrounded by an overwhelming majority of rural people; moreover, they relapsed easily to village or small-town status. The urbanized societies of today, in contrast, not only have urban agglomerations of a size never before attained but also have a high proportion of their population concentrated in such agglomerations. In 1960, for example, nearly 52 million Americans lived in only 16 urbanized areas. Together these areas covered less land than one of the smaller counties (Cochise) of Arizona. According to one definition used by the U.S. Bureau of the Census, 96 million people—53 percent of the nation's population—were concentrated in 213 urbanized areas that together occupied only .7 percent of the nation's land. Another definition used by the bureau puts the urban population at about 70 percent. The large and dense agglomerations comprising the urban population involve a degree of human contact and of social complexity never before known. They exceed in size the communities of any other large animal; they suggest the behavior of communal insects rather than of mammals.

Neither the recency nor the speed of this evolutionary development is widely appreciated. Before 1850 no society could be described as predominantly urbanized, and by 1900 only one—Great Britain—could be so regarded. Today, only 65 years later, all industrial nations are highly urbanized, and in the world as a whole the process of urbanization is accelerating rapidly.

Some years ago my associates and I at Columbia University undertook to document the progress of urbanization by compiling data on the world's cities and the proportion of human beings living in them; in recent years the work has been continued in our center—International Population and Urban Research—at the University of California at Berkeley. The data obtained in these investigations are reflected in Figure 2 (p. 000) which shows the historical trend in terms of one index of urbanization: the proportion of the population living in cities of 100,000 or larger. Statistics of this kind are only approximations of reality, but they are accurate enough to demonstrate how urbanization has accelerated. Between 1850 and 1950 the index changed at a much higher rate than from 1800 to 1850, but the rate of change from 1950 to 1960 was twice that of the preceding 50 years! If the pace of increase that obtained between 1950 and 1960 were to remain the same, by

Scientific American, *213 (September 1965),* *40–53. The journal edition included aerial photographs. Reprinted by permission of author and publisher.* Copyright © *1965 by Scientific American, Inc. All rights reserved.*

1990 the fraction of the world's people living in cities of 100,000 or larger would be more than half. Using another index of urbanization—the proportion of the world's population living in urban places of all sizes—we found that by 1960 the figure had already reached 33 percent.

Clearly the world as a whole is not fully urbanized, but it soon will be. This change in human life is so recent that even the most urbanized countries still exhibit the rural origins of their institutions. Its full implications for man's organic and social evolution can only be surmised.

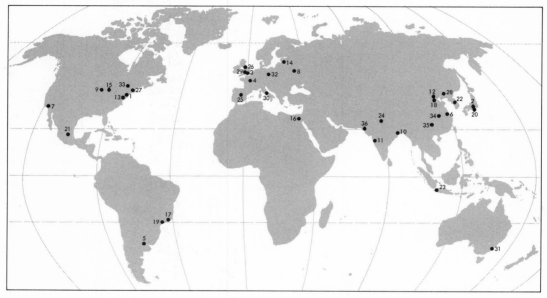

FIGURE 1

Major cities of the world are depicted as they rank in size according to data on "urban agglomeration" furnished to the United Nations by several countries. The data are intended to take into account not only the population within the political boundaries of a city but also that in the city's metropolitan area. The UN defines an urban agglomeration as the city proper and the "thickly settled territory...adjacent" to the city.

RANK	NAME	POPULATION	RANK	NAME	POPULATION	RANK	NAME	POPULATION
1	New York	14,114,927	13	Philadelphia	3,635,228	25	Madrid	2,443,152
2	Tokyo	10,177,000	14	Leningrad	3,552,000	26	Manchester	2,442,090
3	London	8,176,810	15	Detroit	3,537,309	27	Boston	2,413;236
4	Paris	7,369,387	16	Cairo	3,418,400	28	Shenyang (Mukden)	2,411,000
5	Buenos Aires	7,000,000	17	Rio de Janeiro	3,223,408	29	Birmingham	2,377,230
6	Shanghai	6,900,000	18	Tientsin	3,220,000	30	Rome	2,278,882
7	Los Angeles	6,488,791	19	Sao Paulo	3,164,804	31	Sydney	2,215,970
8	Moscow	6,354,000	20	Osaka	3,151,000	32	West Berlin	2,176,612
9	Chicago	5,959,213	21	Mexico City	3,050,723	33	Montreal	2,156,000
10	Calcutta	4,518,655	22	Seoul	2,983,324	34	Wuhan	2,146,000
11	Bombay	4,422,165	23	Djakarta	2,906,533	35	Chungking	2,121,000
12	Peking	4,010,000	24	Delhi	2,549,162	36	Karachi	2,060,000

In discussing the trend—and its implications insofar as they can be perceived—I shall use the term "urbanization" in a particular way. It refers here to the proportion of the total population concentrated in urban settlements, or else to a rise in this proportion. A common mistake is to think of urbanization as simply the growth of cities.

Since the total population is composed of both the urban population and the rural, however, the "proportion urban" is a function of both of them. Accordingly cities can grow without any urbanization, provided that the rural population grows at an equal or a greater rate.

Historically urbanization and the growth of cities have occurred together, which accounts for the confusion. As the reader will soon see, it is necessary to distinguish the two trends. In the most advanced countries today, for example, urban populations are still growing, but their proportion of the total population is tending to remain stable or to diminish. In other words, the process of urbanization—the switch from a spread-out pattern of human settlement to one of concentration in urban centers—is a change that has a beginning and an end, but the growth of cities has no inherent limit. Such growth could continue even after everyone was living in cities, through sheer excess of births over deaths.

The difference between a rural village and an urban community is of course one of degree; a precise operational distinction is somewhat arbitrary, and it varies from one nation to another. Since data are available for communities of various sizes, a dividing line can be chosen at will. One convenient index of urbanization, for example, is the proportion of people living in places of 100,000 or more. In the following analysis I shall depend on two indexes: the one just mentioned and the proportion of population classed as "urban" in the official statistics of each country. In practice the two indexes are highly correlated; therefore either one can be used as an index of urbanization.

Actually the hardest problem is not that of determining the "floor" of the urban category but of ascertaining the boundary of places that are clearly urban by any definition. How far east is the boundary of Los Angeles? Where along the Hooghly River does Calcutta leave off and the countryside begin? In the past the population of cities and towns has usually been given as the number of people living within the political boundaries. Thus the population of New York is frequently given as around eight million, this being the population of the city proper. The error in such a figure was not large before World War I, but since then, particularly in the advanced countries, urban populations have been spilling over the narrow political boundaries at a tremendous rate. In 1960 the New York—Northeastern New Jersey urbanized area, as delineated by the Bureau of the Census, had more than 14 million people. That delineation showed it to be the largest city in the world and nearly twice as large as New York City proper.

As a result of the outward spread of urbanites, counts made on the basis of political boundaries alone underestimate the city populations and exaggerate the rural. For this reason our office delineated the metropolitan areas of as many countries as possible for dates around 1950. These areas included the central, or political, cities and the zones around them that are receiving the spillover.

This reassessment raised the estimated proportion of the world's population in cities of 100,000 or larger from 15.1 percent to 16.7 percent. As of 1960 we have used wherever possible the "urban agglomeration" data now furnished to the United Nations by many countries. The U.S., for example, provides data for "urbanized areas," meaning cities of 50,000 or larger and the built-up agglomerations around them.

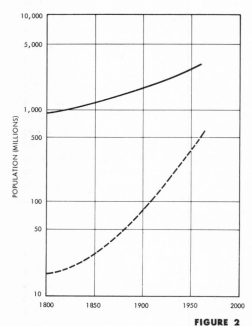

FIGURE 2

Rapid urbanization of the world's population is evident in this comparison of total population (*top curve*) with the population in cities of more than 100,000 inhabitants (*bottom curve*) over more than a century and a half. The use of cities of 100,000 or larger to define an urban population shows a close correlation with other definitions of urbanism.

The origin and evolution of cities are discussed by Gideon Sjoberg elsewhere. My concern is with the degree of urbanization in whole societies. It is curious that thousands of years elapsed between the first appearance of small cities and the emergence of urbanized societies in the 19th century. It is also curious that the region where urbanized societies arose—northwestern Europe—was not the one that had given rise to the major cities of the past; on the contrary, it was a region where urbanization had been at an extremely low ebb. Indeed, the societies of northwestern Europe in medieval times were so rural that it is hard for modern minds to comprehend them. Perhaps it was the nonurban character of these societies that erased the parasitic nature of towns and eventually provided a new basis for a revolutionary degree of urbanization.

At any rate, two seemingly adverse conditions may have presaged the age to come: one the low productivity of medieval agriculture in both per-acre and per-man terms, the other the feudal social system. The first meant that towns could not prosper on the basis of local agriculture alone but had to trade and to manufacture something to trade. The second meant that they could not gain political dominance over their hinterlands and thus become warring city-states. Hence they specialized in commerce and manufacture and evolved local institutions suited to this role. Craftsmen were housed in the towns, because there the merchants could regulate quality and cost. Competition among towns stimulated specialization and technological innovation. The need for literacy, accounting skills and geographical knowledge caused the towns to invest in secular education.

Although the medieval towns remained small and never embraced more than a minor fraction of each region's population, the close connection between industry and commerce that they fostered, together with their emphasis on technique, set the stage for the ultimate breakthrough in

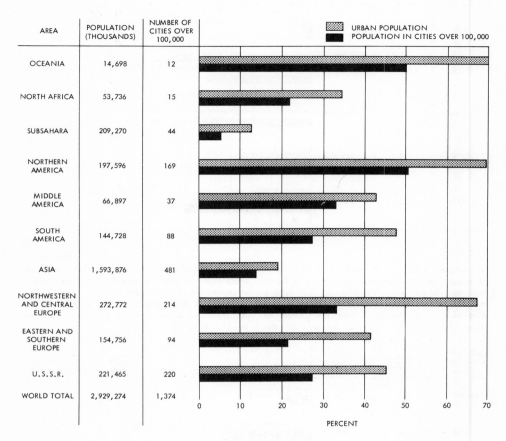

FIGURE 3

Degree of urbanization in the major regions of the world is indicated according to two different methods of classification. One uses the "urban" population as defined by each country of a region. The other uses the population in cities of 100,000 or more.

urbanization. This breakthrough came only with the enormous growth in productivity caused by the use of inanimate energy and machinery. How difficult it was to achieve the transition is agonizingly apparent from statistics showing that even with the conquest of the New World the growth of urbanization during three post-medieval centuries in Europe was barely perceptible. I have assembled population estimates at two or more

dates for 33 towns and cities in the 16th century, 46 in the 17th and 61 in the 18th. The average rate of growth during the three centuries was less than .6 percent per year. Estimates of the growth of Europe's population as a whole between 1650 and 1800 work out to slightly more than .4 percent. The advantage of the towns was evidently very slight. Taking only the cities of 100,000 or more inhabitants, one finds that in 1600 their combined

RANGE OF PERCENT URBAN	NUMBER OF COUNTRIES	POPULATION (THOUSANDS)	PERCENT
0-9	57	135,049	
10-29	62	1,480,604	
30-49	54	653,021	
50-69	24	269,604	
OVER 70	21	366,751	
WORLD TOTAL	218	2,905,029	

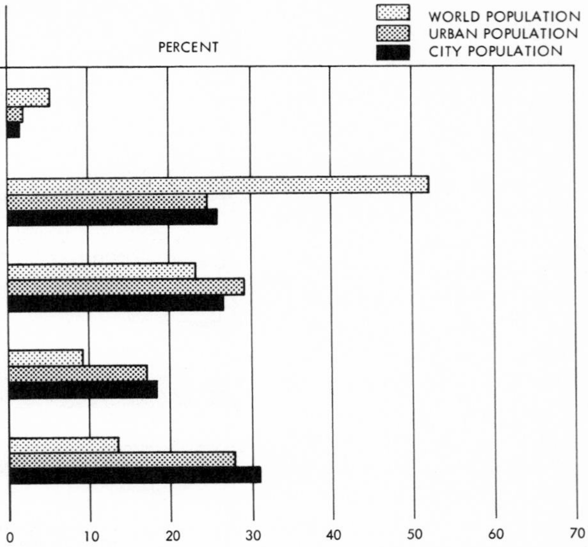

WORLD POPULATION
URBAN POPULATION
CITY POPULATION

0 10 20 30 40 50 60 70

FIGURE 4

a) Grouping of nations according to degree of urbanization shows that more than half are less than 30 percent urbanized and that 45 are more than 50 percent urbanized. The chart can also be read cumulatively from the bottom to show, for example, that 22 percent of the world's population live in countries that are more than 50 percent urbanized and that those countries have 45 percent of the world's urban people and 48 percent of its city people. The approximate date of the population statistics used is 1960.

PER CAPITA INCOME (DOLLARS)	NUMBER OF COUNTRIES	NUMBER OF CITIES OVER 100,000	PERCENT
UNDER 100	63	186	
100-300	89	303	
300-700	26	309	
700-1,500	18	194	
OVER 1,000	3	171	
NO DATA	19	178	
WORLD TOTAL	218	1,341	

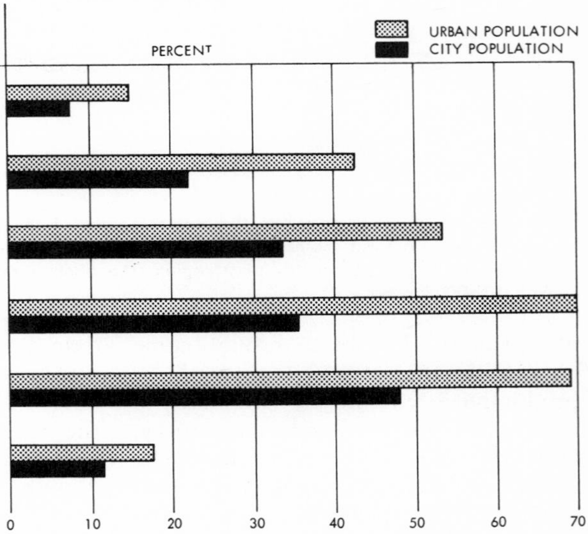

URBAN POPULATION
CITY POPULATION

0 10 20 30 40 50 60 70

b) Urbanization and income are compared. It is apparent that a linear correlation exists between per capita income and degree of urbanization. Thus the three countries with a per capita income of $1,500 or more a year have the highest degree of urbanization—and the 63 countries with per capita income under $100 a year have the lowest degree—by either of two classifications of urbanization: the urban population as defined by each country or the population living in cities of 100,000 or more inhabitants.

10

population was 1.6 percent of the estimated population of Europe; in 1700, 1.9 percent, and in 1800, 2.2 percent. On the eve of the industrial revolution Europe was still an overwhelmingly agrarian region.

With industrialization, however, the transformation was striking. By 1801 nearly a tenth of the people of England and Wales were living in cities of 100,000 or larger. This proportion doubled in 40 years and doubled again in another 60 years. By 1900 Britain was an urbanized society. In general, the later each country became industrialized, the faster was its urbanization. The change from a population with 10 percent of its members in cities of 100,000 or larger to one in which 30 percent lived in such cities took about 79 years in England and Wales, 66 in the U.S., 48 in Germany, 36 in Japan and 26 in Australia. The close association between economic development and urbanization has persisted; as shown in Figure 4b, in 199 countries around 1960 the proportion of the population living in cities varied sharply with per capita income.

Clearly modern urbanization is best understood in terms of its connection with economic growth, and its implications are best perceived in its latest manifestations in advanced countries. What becomes apparent as one examines the trend in these countries is that urbanization is a finite process, a cycle through which nations go in their transition from agrarian to industrial society. The intensive urbanization of most of the advanced countries began within the past 100 years; in the underdeveloped countries it got under way more recently. In some of the advanced countries its end is now in sight. The fact that it will end, however, does not mean that either eco-

nomic development or the growth of cities will necessarily end.

The typical cycle of urbanization can be represented by a curve in the shape of an attenuated S [see Figure 5a and 6]. Starting from the bottom of the S, the first bend tends to come early and to be followed by a long attenuation. In the United Kingdom, for instance, the swiftest rise in the proportion of people living in cities of 100,000 or larger occurred from 1811 to 1851. In the U.S. it occurred from 1820 to 1890, in Greece from 1879 to 1921. As the proportion climbs above 50 percent the curve begins to flatten out; it falters, or even declines, when the proportion urban has reached about 75 percent. In the United Kingdom, one of the world's most urban countries, the proportion was slightly higher in 1926 (78.7 percent) than in 1961 (78.3 percent).

At the end of the curve some ambiguity appears. As a society becomes advanced enough to be highly urbanized it can also afford considerable suburbanization and fringe development. In a sense the slowing down of urbanization is thus more apparent than real: an increasing proportion of urbanites simply live in the country and are classified as rural. Many countries now try to compensate for this ambiguity by enlarging the boundaries of urban places; they did so in numerous censuses taken around 1960. Whether in these cases the old classification of urban or the new one is erroneous depends on how one looks at it; at a very advanced stage the entire concept of urbanization becomes ambiguous.

The end of urbanization cannot be unraveled without going into the ways in which economic development governs urbanization. Here the first question is: Where do the urbanites come from? The possible answers are few:

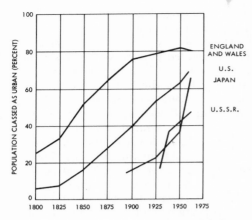

ENGLAND
AND WALES

U.S.

JAPAN

U.S.S.R.

FIGURE 5

a) Industrialized nations underwent a process of urbanization that is typified by the curves shown here for four countries. It was closely related to economic development. The figures for 1950 and 1960 are based on a classification that counts as urban the fringe residents of urbanized areas; that classification was not used for the earlier years shown.

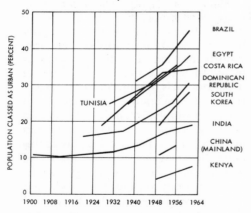

BRAZIL

EGYPT

COSTA RICA

DOMINICAN
REPUBLIC

SOUTH
KOREA

TUNISIA

INDIA

CHINA
(MAINLAND)

KENYA

b) Nonindustrial nations are undergoing a process of urbanization that is typified by these curves. The process started much later than in the industrialized nations, as can be seen by comparing this chart with Figure 5a, and is attributable more to the rapid rise of total population in these countries than to economic development.

The proportion of people in cities can rise because rural settlements grow larger and are reclassified as towns or cities; because the excess of births over deaths is greater in the city than in the country, or because people move from the country to the city.

The first factor has usually had only slight influence. The second has apparently never been the case. Indeed, a chief obstacle to the growth of cities in the past has been their excessive mortality. London's water in the middle of the 19th century came mainly from wells and rivers that drained cesspools, graveyards and tidal areas. The city was regularly ravaged by cholera. Tables for 1841 show an expectation of life of about 36 years for London and 26 for Liverpool and Manchester, as compared to 41 for England and Wales as a whole. After 1850, mainly as a result of sanitary measures and some improvement in nutrition and housing, city health improved, but as late as the period 1901–1910 the death rate of the urban counties in England and Wales, as modified to make the age structure comparable, was 33 percent higher than the death rate of the rural counties. As Bernard Benjamin, a chief statistician of the British General Register Office, has remarked: "Living in the town involved not only a higher risk of epidemic and crowd diseases . . . but also a higher risk of degenerative disease—the harder wear and tear of factory employment and urban discomfort." By 1950, however, virtually the entire differential had been wiped out.

As for birth rates, during rapid urbanization in the past they were notably lower in cities than in rural areas. In fact, the gap tended to widen somewhat as urbanization proceeded in the latter half of the 19th century and the first quarter of the 20th. In 1800 urban women in the U.S. had 36 percent fewer children than rural women did; in 1840, 38 percent and in 1930,

41 percent. Thereafter the difference diminished.

With mortality in the cities higher and birth rates lower, and with reclassification a minor factor, the only real source for the growth in the proportion of people in urban areas during the industrial transition was rural-urban migration. This source had to be plentiful enough not only to overcome the substantial disadvantage of the cities in natural increase but also, above that, to furnish a big margin of growth in their populations. If, for example, the cities had a death rate a third higher and a birth rate a third lower than the rural rates (as was typical in the latter half of the 19th century), they would require each year perhaps 40 to 45 migrants from elsewhere per 1,000 of their population to maintain a growth rate of 3 percent per year. Such a rate of migration could easily be maintained as long as the rural portion of the population was large, but when this condition ceased to obtain, the maintenance of the same urban rate meant an increasing drain on the countryside.

Why did the rural-urban migration occur? The reason was that the rise in technological enhancement of human productivity, together with certain constant factors, rewarded urban concentration. One of the constant factors was that agriculture uses land as its prime instrument of production and hence spreads out people who are engaged in it, whereas manufacturing, commerce and services use land only as a site. Moreover, the demand for agricultural products is less elastic than the demand for services and manufactures. As productivity grows, services and manufactures can absorb more manpower by paying higher wages. Since nonagricultural activities can use land simply as a site, they can locate near one another (in towns and cities)

and thus minimize the friction of space inevitably involved in the division of labor. At the same time, as agricultural technology is improved, capital costs in farming rise and manpower becomes not only less needed but also economically more burdensome. A substantial portion of the agricultural population is therefore sufficiently disadvantaged, in relative terms, to be attracted by higher wages in other sectors.

In this light one sees why a large flow of people from farms to cities was generated in every country that passed through the industrial revolution. One also sees why, with an even higher proportion of people already in cities and with the inability of city people to replace themselves by reproduction, the drain eventually became so heavy that in many nations the rural population began to decline in absolute as well as relative terms. In Sweden it declined after 1920, in England and Wales after 1861, in Belgium after 1910.

Realizing that urbanization is transitional and finite, one comes on another fact—a fact that throws light on the circumstances in which urbanization comes to an end. A basic feature of the transition is the profound switch from agricultural to nonagricultural employment. This change is associated with urbanization but not identical with it. The difference emerges particularly in the later stages. Then the availability of automobiles, radios, motion pictures and electricity, as well as the reduction of the workweek and the workday, mitigate the disadvantages of living in the country. Concurrently the expanding size of cities makes them more difficult to live in. The population classed as "rural" is accordingly enlarged, both from cities and from true farms.

For these reasons the "rural" population in some industrial countries never did fall in absolute size. In all the industrial countries, however, the population dependent on agriculture—which the reader will recognize as a more functional definition of the nonurban population than mere rural residence—decreased in absolute as well as relative terms. In the U.S., for example, the net migration from farms totaled more than 27 million between 1920 and 1959 and thus averaged approximately 700,000 a year. As a result the farm population declined from 32.5 million in 1916 to 20.5 million in 1960, in spite of the large excess of births in farm families. In 1964, by a stricter American definition classifying as "farm families" only those families actually earning their living from agriculture, the farm population was down to 12.9 million. This number represented 6.8 percent of the nation's population; the comparable figure for 1880 was 44 percent. In Great Britain the number of males occupied in agriculture was at its peak, 1.8 million, in 1851; by 1961 it had fallen to .5 million.

In the later stages of the cycle, then, urbanization in the industrial countries tends to cease. Hence the connection between economic development and the growth of cities also ceases. The change is explained by two circumstances. First, there is no longer enough farm population to furnish a significant migration to the cities. (What can 12.9 million American farmers contribute to the growth of the 100 million people already in urbanized areas?) Second, the rural nonfarm population, nourished by refugees from the expanding cities, begins to increase as fast as the city population. The effort of census bureaus to count fringe residents as urban simply pushes the definition of "urban" away from the notion of dense settlement and in the direction of the term "nonfarm." As the urban population becomes more "rural," which is to say less densely settled, the advanced industrial peoples are for a time able to enjoy the amenities of urban life without the excessive crowding of the past.

Here, however, one again encounters the fact that a cessation of urbanization does not necessarily mean a cessation of city growth. An example is provided by New Zealand. Between 1945 and 1961 the proportion of New Zealand's population classed as urban—that is, the ratio between urban and rural residents—changed hardly at all (from 61.3 percent to 63.6 percent) but the urban population increased by 50 percent. In Japan between 1940 and 1950 urbanization actually decreased slightly, but the urban population increased by 13 percent.

The point to be kept in mind is that once urbanization ceases, city growth becomes a function of general population growth. Enough farm-to-city migration may still occur to redress the difference in natural increase. The reproductive rate of urbanites tends, however, to increase when they live at lower densities, and the reproductive rate of "urbanized" farmers tends to decrease; hence little migration is required to make the urban increase equal the national increase.

I now turn to the currently underdeveloped countries. With the advanced nations having slackened their rate of urbanization, it is the others—representing three-fourths of humanity—that are mainly responsible for the rapid urbanization now characterizing the world as a whole. In fact, between 1950 and 1960 the proportion of the population in cities of 100,000 or more rose about a third faster in the underdeveloped regions than in the developed ones. Among the underdeveloped regions the pace was slow in eastern and southern Europe, but in the rest of the underdeveloped world the proportion in cities rose twice as fast as it did in the industrialized countries, even though the latter countries in many cases broadened their definitions of urban places to include more suburban and fringe residents.

Because of the characteristic pattern of urbanization, the current rates of urbanization in underdeveloped countries could be expected to exceed those now existing in countries far advanced in the cycle. On discovering that this is the case one is tempted to say that the underdeveloped regions are now in the typical stage of urbanization associated with early economic development. This notion, however, is erroneous. In their urbanization the underdeveloped countries are definitely not repeating past history. Indeed, the best grasp of their present situation comes from analyzing how their course differs from the previous pattern of development.

The first thing to note is that today's underdeveloped countries are urbanizing not only more rapidly than the industrial nations are now but also more rapidly than the industrial nations did in the heyday of their urban growth. The difference, however, is not large. In 40 underdeveloped countries for which we have data in recent decades, the average gain in the proportion of the population urban was 20 percent per decade; in 16 industrial countries, during the decades of their most rapid urbanization (mainly in the 19th century), the average gain per decade was 15 percent.

This finding that urbanization is proceeding only a little faster in underdeveloped countries than it did historically in the advanced nations may be questioned by the reader. It seemingly belies the widespread impression that cities throughout the non-industrial parts of the world are bursting with people. There is, however, no contradiction. One must recall the basic distinction between a change in the proportion of the population urban, which is a ratio, and the absolute growth of cities. The popular impression is correct: the cities in underdeveloped areas are growing at a disconcerting rate. They are far outstripping the city boom of the industrializing era in the 19th century. If they continue their recent rate of growth, they will double their population every 15 years.

In 34 underdeveloped countries for which we have data relating to the 1940's and 1950's, the average annual gain in the urban population was 4.5 percent. The figure is remarkably similar for the various regions: 4.7 percent in seven countries of Africa, 4.7 percent in 15 countries of Asia and 4.3 percent in 12 countries of Latin America. In contrast, in nine European countries during their period of fastest urban population growth (mostly in the latter half of the 19th century) the average gain per year was 2.1 percent. Even the frontier industrial countries— the U.S., Australia-New Zealand, Canada and Argentina—which received huge numbers of immigrants, had a smaller population growth in towns and cities: 4.2 percent per year. In Japan and the U.S.S.R. the rate was respectively 5.4 and 4.3 percent per year, but their economic growth began only recently.

How is it possible that the contrast in growth between today's underdeveloped countries and yesterday's industrializing countries is sharper with respect to the absolute urban population than with respect to the urban share of the total population? The answer lies in another profound difference between the two sets of countries —a difference in total population growth, rural as well as urban. Contemporary underdeveloped populations have been growing since 1940 more than twice as fast as industrialized populations, and their increase far exceeds the growth of the latter at the peak of their expansion. The only rivals in an earlier day were the frontier nations, which had the help of great streams of immigrants. Today the underdeveloped nations—already densely settled, tragically impoverished and with gloomy economic prospects—are multiplying their people by sheer biological increase at a rate that is unprecedented. It is this population boom that is overwhelmingly responsible for the rapid inflation of city populations in such countries. Contrary to popular opinion both inside and outside those countries, the main factor is not rural-urban migration. [See Figure 6.]

This point can be demonstrated easily by a calculation that has the effect of eliminating the influence of general population growth on urban growth. The calculation involves assuming that the total population of a given country remained constant over a period of time but that the percentage urban changed as it did historically. In this manner one obtains the growth of the absolute urban population that would have occurred if rural-urban migration were the only factor affecting it. As an example, Costa Rica had in 1927 a total population of 471,500, of which 88,600, or 18.8 percent, was urban. By 1963 the country's total population was 1,325,200 and the urban population was 456,600, or 34.5 percent. If the total population had remained at 471,500 but the percentage urban had still risen from 18.8 to 34.5, the absolute urban population in 1963 would have

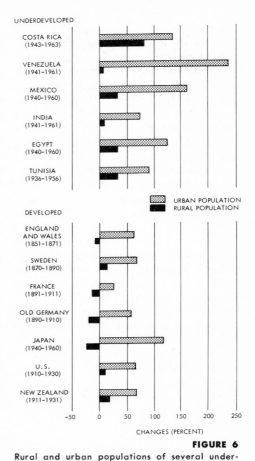

FIGURE 6

Rural and urban populations of several underdeveloped countries are compared with those in the currently developed countries at a time when they were undergoing rapid urbanization. It is evident that in the underdeveloped countries the rural population is rising in spite of urbanization, whereas in the earlier period it rose only slightly or dropped.

been only 162,700. That is the growth that would have occurred in the urban population if rural-urban migration had been the only factor. In actuality the urban population rose to 456,600. In other words, only 20 percent of the rapid growth of Costa Rica's towns and cities was attributable to urbanization per se; 44 percent was attributable solely to the country's general population increase, the remainder to the joint operation of both factors. Similarly, in Mexico between 1940 and 1960, 50 percent of the urban population increase was attributable to national multiplication alone and only 22 percent to urbanization alone.

The past performance of the advanced countries presents a sharp contrast. In Switzerland between 1850 and 1888, when the proportion urban resembled that in Costa Rica recently, general population growth alone accounted for only 19 percent of the increase of town and city people, and rural-urban migration alone accounted for 69 percent. In France between 1846 and 1911 only 21 percent of the growth in the absolute urban population was due to general growth alone.

The conclusion to which this contrast points is that one anxiety of governments in the underdeveloped nations is misplaced. Impressed by the mushrooming in their cities of shantytowns filled with ragged peasants, they attribute the fantastically fast city growth to rural-urban migration. Actually this migration now does little more than make up for the small difference in the birth rate between city and countryside. In the history of the industrial nations, as we have seen, the sizable difference between urban and rural birth rates and death rates required that cities, if they were to grow, had to have an enormous influx of people from farms and villages. Today in the underdeveloped countries the towns and cities have only a slight disadvantage in fertility, and their old disadvantage in mortality not only has been wiped out but also in many cases has been reversed. During the 19th century the urbanizing nations were learning how to keep crowded populations in cities from dying like flies. Now the lesson has been learned, and

it is being applied to cities even in countries just emerging from tribalism. In fact, a disproportionate share of public health funds goes into cities. As a result throughout the nonindustrial world people in cities are multiplying as never before, and rural-urban migration is playing a much lesser role.

The trends just described have an important implication for the rural population. Given the explosive overall population growth in underdeveloped countries, it follows that if the rural population is not to pile up on the land and reach an economically absurd density, a high rate of rural-urban migration must be maintained. Indeed, the exodus from rural areas should be higher than in the past. But this high rate of internal movement is not taking place, and there is some doubt that it could conceivably do so.

To elaborate I shall return to my earlier point that in the evolution of industrialized countries the rural citizenry often declined in absolute as well as relative terms. The rural population of France—26.8 million in 1846—was down to 20.8 million by 1926 and 17.2 million by 1962, notwithstanding a gain in the nation's total population during this period. Sweden's rural population dropped from 4.3 million in 1910 to 3.5 million in 1960. Since the category "rural" includes an increasing portion of urbanites living in fringe areas, the historical drop was more drastic and consistent specifically in the farm population. In the U.S., although the "rural" population never quite ceased to grow, the farm contingent began its long descent shortly after the turn of the century; today it is less than two-fifths of what it was in 1910.

This transformation is not occurring in contemporary underdeveloped countries. In spite of the enormous growth of their cities, their rural populations—and their more narrowly defined agricultural populations—are growing at a rate that in many cases exceeds the rise of even the urban population during the evolution of the now advanced countries. The poor countries thus confront a grave dilemma. If they do not substantially step up the exodus from rural areas, these areas will be swamped with underemployed farmers. If they do step up the exodus, the cities will grow at a disastrous rate.

The rapid growth of cities in the advanced countries, painful though it was, had the effect of solving a problem—the problem of the rural population. The growth of cities enabled agricultural holdings to be consolidated, allowed increased capitalization and in general resulted in greater efficiency. Now, however, the underdeveloped countries are experiencing an even more rapid urban growth—and are suffering from urban problems—but urbanization is not solving their rural ills.

A case in point is Venezuela. Its capital, Caracas, jumped from a population of 359,000 in 1941 to 1,507,000 in 1963; other Venezuelan towns and cities equaled or exceeded this growth. Is this rapid rise denuding the countryside of people? No, the Venezuelan farm population increased in the decade 1951–1961 by 11 percent. The only thing that declined was the amount of cultivated land. As a result the agricultural population density became worse. In 1950 there were some 64 males engaged in agriculture per square mile of cultivated land; in 1961 there were 78. (Compare this with 4.8 males occupied in agriculture per square mile of cultivated land in Canada, 6.8 in the U.S. and 15.6 in Argentina.) With each male occupied in agriculture, there are of

course dependents. Approximately 225 persons in Venezuela are trying to live from each square mile of cultivated land. Most of the growth of cities in Venezuela is attributable to overall population growth. If the general population had not grown at all, and internal migration had been large enough to produce the actual shift in the proportion in cities, the increase in urban population would have been only 28 percent of what it was and the rural population would have been reduced by 57 percent.

The story of Venezuela is being repeated virtually everywhere in the underdeveloped world. It is not only Caracas that has thousands of squatters living in self-constructed junk houses on land that does not belong to them. By whatever name they are called, the squatters are to be found in all major cities in the poorer countries. They live in broad gullies beneath the main plain in San Salvador and on the hillsides of Rio de Janeiro and Bogotá. They tend to occupy with implacable determination parks, school grounds and vacant lots. Amman, the capital of Jordan, grew from 12,000 in 1958 to 247,000 in 1961. A good part of it is slums, and urban amenities are lacking most of the time for most of the people. Greater Baghdad now has an estimated 850,000 people; its slums, like those in many other underdeveloped countries, are in two zones—the central part of the city and the outlying areas. Here are the *sarifa* areas, characterized by self-built reed huts; these areas account for about 45 percent of the housing in the entire city and are devoid of amenities, including even latrines. In addition to such urban problems, all the countries struggling for higher living levels find their rural population growing too and piling up on already crowded land.

I have characterized urbanization as

a transformation that, unlike economic development, is finally accomplished and comes to an end. At the 1950–1960 rate the term "urbanized world" will be applicable well before the end of the century. One should scarcely expect, however, that mankind will complete its urbanization without major complications. One sign of trouble ahead turns on the distinction I made at the start between urbanization and city growth per se. Around the globe today city growth is disproportionate to urbanization. The discrepancy is paradoxical in the industrial nations and worse than paradoxical in the nonindustrial.

It is in this respect that the nonindustrial nations, which still make up the great majority of nations, are far from repeating past history. In the 19th and early 20th centuries the growth of cities arose from and contributed to economic advancement. Cities took surplus manpower from the countryside and put it to work producing goods and services that in turn helped to modernize agriculture. But today in underdeveloped countries, as in present-day advanced nations, city growth has become increasingly unhinged from economic development and hence from rural-urban migration. It derives in greater degree from overall population growth, and this growth in nonindustrial lands has become unprecedented because of modern health techniques combined with high birth rates.

The speed of world population growth is twice what it was before 1940, and the swiftest increase has shifted from the advanced to the backward nations. In the latter countries, consequently, it is virtually impossible to create city services fast enough to take care of the huge, never ending cohorts of babies and peasants swelling the urban masses. It is even harder to expand agricultural land and capital fast enough to accommodate the enormous natural increase on farms. The problem is not urbanization, not rural-urban migration, but human multiplication. It is a problem that is new in both its scale and its setting, and runaway city growth is only one of its painful expressions.

As long as the human population expands, cities will expand too, regardless of whether urbanization increases or declines. This means that some individual cities will reach a size that will make 19th-century metropolises look like small towns. If the New York urbanized area should continue to grow only as fast as the nation's population (according to medium projections of the latter by the Bureau of the Census), it would reach 21 million by 1985 and 30 million by 2010. I have calculated that if India's population should grow as the UN projections indicate it will, the largest city in India in the year 2000 will have between 36 and 66 million inhabitants.

What is the implication of such giant agglomerations for human density? In 1950 the New York–Northeastern New Jersey urbanized area had an average density of 9,810 persons per square mile. With 30 million people in the year 2010, the density would be 24,000 per square mile. Although this level is exceeded now in parts of New York City (which averages about 25,000 per square mile) and many other cities, it is a high density to be spread over such a big area; it would cover, remember, the suburban areas to which people moved to escape high density. Actually, however, the density of the New York urbanized region is dropping, not increasing, as the population grows. The reason is that the territory covered by the urban agglomeration is growing faster than the population: it grew by 51 percent from 1950 to 1960, whereas the population rose by 15 percent.

If, then, one projects the rise in population and the rise in territory for the New York urbanized region, one finds the density problem solved. It is not solved for long, though, because New York is not the only city in the region that is expanding. So are Philadelphia, Trenton, Hartford, New Haven and so on. By 1960 a huge stretch of territory about 600 miles long and 30 to 100 miles wide along the Eastern seaboard contained some 37 million people. (I am speaking of a longer section of the seaboard than the Boston-to-Washington conurbation....) Since the whole area is becoming one big polynucleated city, its population cannot long expand without a rise in density. Thus persistent human multiplication promises to frustrate the ceaseless search for space—for ample residential lots, wide-open suburban school grounds, sprawling shopping centers, one-floor factories, broad freeways.

How people feel about giant agglomerations is best indicated by their headlong effort to escape them. The bigger the city, the higher the cost of space; yet, the more the level of living rises, the more people are willing to pay for low-density living. Nevertheless, as urbanized areas expand and collide, it seems probable that life in low-density surroundings will become too dear for the great majority.

One can of course imagine that cities may cease to grow and may even shrink in size while the population in general continues to multiply. Even this dream, however, would not permanently solve the problem of space. It would eventually obliterate the distinction between urban and rural, but at the expense of the rural.

It seems plain that the only way to stop urban crowding and to solve most of the urban problems besetting both the developed and the underdeveloped nations is to reduce the overall rate of population growth. Policies designed to do this have as yet little intelligence and power behind them. Urban planners continue to treat population growth as something to be planned for, not something to be itself planned. Any talk about applying brakes to city growth is therefore purely speculative, overshadowed as it is by the reality of uncontrolled population increase.

2. World Urbanization Trends, 1920-1960 (An Interim Report on Work in Progress)

POPULATION DIVISION
UNITED NATIONS BUREAU OF SOCIAL AFFAIRS

A. PROBLEMS OF SUBSTANCE AND METHOD

Comparability and Relevance

1. Internationally comparable statistics on urban population are not easily assembled. This in itself is an important observation. It compels us to recognize that urbanization is a process of both quantitative and qualitative change. In the process of growth, the characteristics and functions of localities, and particularly of towns and cities, are transformed, and this raises the question of the relevance of comparisons.

2. The two criteria which generally distinguish the urban element in a country's population are the quantitative in terms of population concentration, and the qualitative, such as the characteristics of the economy and modes of living which have "urban" rather than "rural" attributes. The correlations between these two criteria vary with time, location, and the "urban" features of the particular locality; hence the difficulty in determining criteria of general applicability. Many different census definitions are used among countries, and in addition it has been found necessary in recent censuses within countries to modify standards used earlier. There is also the great variation in urban and rural environments throughout the world to take into account.

3. Selection of criteria must therefore be made rather arbitrarily, frequently as a compromise between comparability, relevance, and the expediency of available statistics or methods of estimating them. An estimate of the world's urban population, at best, can so far only be derived from a patchwork of figures broadly selected, adjusted and interpolated.

4. The United Nations Population Division is now preparing a report on the growth of urban and rural population in the world.[1] The results so far are still preliminary in many respects and are undergoing revision. This paper presents a summary of the study to date, with many figures used tentatively and subject to further modification. Geographic settlement patterns are considered as a first step, leaving for examination at a later date their demographic, economic and social features.[2]

Inter-Regional Seminar on Development Policies and Planning in Relation to Urbanization, Organized by the United Nations Bureau of Technical Assistance Operations and the Bureau of Social Affairs in cooperation with the Government of the United States of America, Working Paper Number 6 (University of Pittsburgh, Pittsburgh, Pennsylvania, USA, October 24–November 7, 1966). Reprinted by permission.

[1] An earlier United Nations document on this topic is entitled "World Survey of Urban and Rural Population Growth" (Preliminary Report by the Secretary-General to the Population Commission), E/CN.9/187, 8 March 1965.

[2] Another approach is the study of interaction between changes in settlement pattern, viz. urbanization, and changes in economic and social circumstances, as affecting an entire population. That is the approach adopted in the companion paper at this Conference, "Urbanization and Economic and Social Change."

Methods of Delimiting Urban Localities

5. It scarcely need be said that the transformation of settlements into towns and cities has been accomplished according to the influence of the particular historic period. During the last century, the pattern of growth of urban localities in areas of recent European overseas settlement differed from that of the cities of Europe, South and East Asia and Africa founded much earlier, but by identification with their size and function the new localities assumed similar distinctions of "towns" and "cities."[3]

6. In general throughout the world, where a fundamental change in settlement pattern related to the modern growth of commerce and industry took place, some towns of minor importance expanded rapidly, outgrowing original administrative boundaries. Where boundaries were inflexible, the localities were re-defined as "agglomerations." The simultaneous growth of several towns within a small radius often caused them to merge into a "conurbation." In some cases, *de facto* conurbations became incorporated under a new combined urban administration, such as the cities of Wuhan in China, or Wuppertal in Germany. In others, the growth of large cities or "metropolises" absorbed adjacent towns, villages, or smaller cities without affecting their political autonomy, although certain services such as water, police, etc., were supplied under the administration of the agglomeration. With the increase in the number of large cities, the concept of "agglomeration" has gained more generalized use as an alternative to that of "city proper" in the statistics of many countries.

7. The more inclusive classification of "metropolitan area," as for Greater London, Greater New York, Greater Paris or Greater Tokyo, has evolved where a network of road and rail transportation has further expanded the confines of the settlement pattern. This broader concept has not been restricted to the largest cities, however.[4]

8. In comparing urban data, problems arise in connection with the adjustment of municipal boundaries. Where boundaries are flexible, "city proper" data may provide a realistic comparison of urban growth. Where boundaries have proved relatively rigid, the "agglomeration" is more meaningful provided it is re-defined at each census, a practice not followed in all countries. Also, there have been instances of drastic urban boundary adjustment which distort time comparisons. In Japan, *shi* have been suddenly widened from very constricted limits, particularly in the period 1950–1955 when they were enlarged to include a multiple of the previous area. This has occurred more recently in Peking and possibly also in other important cities in China.

9. It has proved practical to include in the agglomerations of large cities some rural areas serving the growing city for suburban residence and urban facilities. The growth of motor transport has made it reasonable for some countries to define "metropolitan regions" as including such rural or semi-rural territory.[5]

10. Entire belts or regions comprising cities, towns, their closely related rural

[3] For a comprehensive discussion, see L. Mumford, *The City in History*, New York, 1961, and P. M. Hauser, ed., "World Urbanism," a symposium, *The American Journal of Sociology*, vol. **60**, No. 5, March 1955.

[4] The most systematic attempt to define such areas comparably is that of Kingsley Davis, *et al.*, *The World's Metropolitan Areas*, International Urban Research, Berkeley and Los Angeles, California, U.S.A., 1959.

[5] See a discussion by A. W. Gilmore, *Transportation and the Growth of Cities*, Glenmore (Ill.) 1953.

areas, and connecting tracts with a mixture of features which cannot be described as either wholly "urban" or "rural," and having a recognizable pattern of inter-dependence, have thus emerged as a recent phenomenon.

The Standards Applied in This Study

11. It is recognized that typical villages in some countries are considerably larger than typical towns in others; also, that in some dominantly rural and agrarian regions, villages are so close and settlement so highly concentrated that average population densities over large areas are greater than those found elsewhere in large portions of urbanized territory within metropolitan agglomerations. But the rural settlement pattern is not a subject for consideration in this report.

12. Modest size limits are implied in the official definitions of "urban" population in the censuses of most countries, but a common international measure is more readily found when the limit is set relatively high. For the purpose of this study, therefore, "urban" population is defined as that of localities with 20,000 or more inhabitants, while the population of smaller localities or the open country-side is referred to as the "rural and small-town population."[6]

13. Tradition also suggests a distinction for localities with at least 100,000

[6] This definition has come into wide use in international research. It has at least the advantage that localities of a "rural," i.e., mainly agrarian, type, are thereby virtually excluded. True, it is also reported that many of the rural communes recently constituted in China comprise more than 20,000 persons, but there is little quantitative information concerning them, nor is it certain that the administrative arrangements have necessarily caused a coalescence in the settlement pattern of hitherto separate villages. An early use of 20,000 as a lower size limit in the study of urban population appears in Kingsley Davis and Hilda Hertz, "The World Distribution of Urbanization," *Bulletin of the International Statistical Institute*, vol. **33**, Part IV.

inhabitants. Earlier in the present century anyway, their functions seemed usually to differ sufficiently from those of smaller towns to justify their separate consideration.[7] The significance of the distinction at this level of size, however, has diminished where considerably bigger cities have become much more numerous, and also when the international scope of the study is widened. In this report, localities with 20,000–99,999 inhabitants will be referred to as "towns," larger localities as "cities."

14. The distinction of "urban" populations at the limits of 20,000 and 100,000 suggests the use of a multiplier of five to arrive at additional limits for a more detailed size classification.

Accordingly, the following combinations of "urban" population have been estimated for countries, regions, major areas, and the world:

20,000 and over:	"urban population";
100,000 and over:	" city population";
500,000 and over:	"big-city population";
2,500,000 and over:	"multi-million cities"; and
12,500,000 and over:	"metropolitan regions" (i.e., those of New York and Tokyo at the present time)

15. Towns and cities of up to 500,000 residents are so numerous that for many large countries their exact number could not be ascertained for the particular dates. Often only the combined populations comprising the group 20,000–99,999 could be interpolated, and sometimes this had to be done also for the 100,000–499,999 group. Since each town could not be investi-

[7] This distinction came into wide use especially in many German studies of urban population and geography. In those studies, localities with 100,000 and more inhabitants were generally referred to as "big cities" (Grosstaedte).

gated individually, and censuses are tabulated more often in terms of administrative limits than the geographic extent of urbanized territory, the definition in this report for these two size groups is mainly that of "city proper," in the administrative sense.

16. The attempt to measure and estimate the populations included in agglomerations, as variously defined, was restricted to big cities and multi-millions cities only, i.e., all those of at least 500,000 inhabitants. Their number is not formidable,[8] and in the period 1920–1960 their emergence could be recognized and the growth of each estimated, in the main. Additional cities and towns included in the agglomerations are considered as absorbed in the major agglomeration, and hence not counted again among cities and towns of smaller size.

17. One consequence of the more generous definition of big cities, in contrast with smaller ones, is a partial discontinuity in size distribution. Some "cities proper" (i.e. when more narrowly defined) have, say, 300,000 or 400,000 inhabitants but when defined more liberally are parts of agglomerations in excess of 500,000. Acknowledging disparity in definitions used here, such localities are then counted among the big cities, and not among the smaller ones, leaving a gap in the "cities" group. This affects particularly the estimates for Northern America.

18. No attempt has been made to go beyond the concept of agglomeration, or metropolitan region. The world's two largest cities have been defined liberally, so that the metropolitan region of New York includes northeastern New Jersey, and that of Tokyo comprises Yokohama. Consideration has not been given to the definition of even larger "megalopolitan" belts, whose demarcations would be indefinite in any event, though it is believed that their importance and relevance will become increasingly apparent in the future.

Types of Data Used

19. For the various parts of the world, the data differ in definition, period of coverage and number of observations, and recency; their approximation to accuracy and completeness is also unequal.[9] They have been dealt with in a number of ways, some still regarded as unsatisfactory from the standpoint of comparability. Most of the raw data are those of population censuses, variously interpolated to coincide with the selected dates, namely mid-year 1920, 1930, and so forth. A detailed account of the data and of the manner in which they have been used or adapted must be postponed until a more definitive report can be issued. Many of the provisional figures used in this report, and much of their comparison, are considerably affected by individual choices made in the use of data.

20. This makes it mandatory to draw the reader's attention to some of the principal decisions that were taken for the present purpose. For instance, in Northern America and Oceania the population of metropolitan regions has been estimated for past dates on an assumption that, with the early spread of networks of motor transportation, there had been a continuous geographic penetration of urban influence into the areas now recognized as metropolitan rings. No such assumptions have been made, on the other hand, in estimates

---

[8] Cities estimated as 500,000 or larger numbered 75 in 1920, 98 in 1930, 125 in 1940, 159 in 1950 and 232 in 1960.

[9] See also, on this problem, the United Nations document "World Survey of Urban and Rural Population Growth," *op. cit.*

for metropolitan regions in Europe or Latin America though there the networks of intensive transport have also widened conspicuously in recent years. It is evident that comparability cannot be established by such differing methods of estimation, and many of the estimating problems are still unresolved.

21. Figures are here presented for major areas and regions of the world as defined in a recent United Nations report on future world population,[10] with a few exceptions. These areas and regions are described in the Appendix to this report.

B. PROVISIONAL ASSESSMENT OF TRENDS

World-Wide Urban and Rural Population Growth

22. The severe shortcomings of the figures used in this provisional report

have been pointed out. It must be emphasized that the estimates are neither accurate nor comparable, and that many will be revised before a more definitive report can be published.

23. According to approximate determinations in other studies of total population growth, the number of the world's inhabitants has risen from about 1,860 million in 1920 to 2,069 million in 1930, 2,297 million in 1940, 2,517 million in 1950, and 2,994 million in 1960[11] (see Table 1). The estimated increases in successive decades were by 209, 228, 220, and 477 million, respectively. This recent sharp upturn in population growth has affected both the urban and the rural populations.

24. In terms of the present tentative estimates, the world's urban population (localities of 20,000 and more inhabitants) has grown from 253 million in 1920 to 753 million in 1960, a

Table 1

Distribution of World Population by Size of Locality, 1920–1960
(rough estimates, in millions)

Size of Locality (inhabitants)	1920	1930	1940	1950	1960
Total Population	1, 860.2	2,069.3	2.296.9	2.516.8	2.994.4
Under 20,000	1,607.3	1,741.2	1,869.9	1,985.3	2,241.0
20,000 and over	252.9	328.1	427.0	531.5	753.4
100,000 and over	160.0	216.6	287.6	360.0	525.5
500,000 and over	94.9	133.6	175.8	224.4	351.6
2,500,000 and over	30.3	48.8	66.5	84.3	139.4
12,500,000 and over	...	...	...	...	27.7[a]
20,000 – 99,999	92.9	111.5	139.4	171.5	227.9
100,000 – 499,999	65.1	83.0	111.8	135.6	173.9
500,000 – 2,499,999	64.6	84.8	109.3	140.1	212.2
2,500,000 – 12,499,999	30.3	48.8	66.5	84.3	111.7
12,500,000 and over	...	...	...	...	27.7[a]

a Metropolitan regions of New York (including northeastern New Jersey) and Tokyo (including Yokohama).

[10]*Provisional Report on World Population Prospects, as assessed in 1963.* United Nations, ST/SOA/Ser. R/7, 1965.

[11]Some of these figures differ slightly from those published in other sources, and are subject to further revision.

three-fold growth in forty years, or a net addition of roughly 500 million urban residents.

25. By subtraction, it can be seen that the world's rural and small-town population has apparently increased from about 1,607 million in 1920 to 2,241 million in 1960, hence more than 600 million have been added to the localities which have remained rural or small towns. This is rather more than an increase by one-third.

26. Absolute increases in urban population, in the successive four decades, were by an estimated 75, 99, 105, and 221 million, respectively. Absolute increases in rural and small-town population, in the same decades, are here estimated as 134, 129, 115, and 256 million. In the 1920's, 1930's and 1940's, the absolute increments in urban population rose gradually, and those in rural population diminished gradually, while in the 1950's, both in the urban areas and in rural areas and small towns the population gain was of twice the magnitude of the gains made in the preceding decade. Of the world's total population gain, as estimated, the urban percentage in the successive decades was 36, 43, 48, and 46; the rural and small town 64, 57, 52 and 54.

27. In relative terms, the world's total population grew by 11 per cent in the 1920's, 11 per cent in the 1930's, 10 per cent in the 1940's, and 19 per cent in the 1950's. Urban population in each of these four decades increased by 30, 30, 25, and 42 per cent; rural and small-town population by 8, 7, 6 and 13 per cent. Both urban and rural localities shared in the fluctuation of the world's population growth, its slight slackening in the 1940's and sharp acceleration in the 1950's. The fluctuation was more emphatic in the growth

of urban population, which slowed noticeably in the war-torn 1940's, and greatly accelerated thereafter. Acceleration in the growth of rural and small-town population in the 1950's was a striking reversal of a previously more stable trend.

28. In this report, no attempt is made to propose answers to the problems connected with urbanization. Its purpose is mainly to indicate with these tentative estimates the unprecedented magnitude and changing structure of the phenomenon and to mention certain repercussions resulting from similar growth trends in the two types of environments. A simple arithmetic exercise suffices to show that, with the accelerated growth in total population, rural population growth would have accelerated enormously if urban population had grown constantly at the 1920 rate throughout the period considered; similarly, had the growth in rural population continued merely at the rates of preceding decades, the number and size of towns and cities would have shown gains to an even greater degree.[12] In actual fact, both the urban and the rural areas shared in the accelerated population growth of the 1950's.

29. Of the world's total population, the percentage in urban localities rose from 14 in 1920 to 16 in 1930, 19 in

[12]Assuming urban population had grown by 30 per cent in the 1950's (as it actually did in the 1920's and 1930's), the accelerated growth in the world's total population would have caused rural population to grow from 1,985 million in 1950 to 2,302 million in 1960, that is by 317 million, or by 16 per cent. Assuming rural population had grown by 7 per cent in the 1950's (as it actually did on the average of the decades from 1920 to 1950), the accelerated growth in the world's total population would have caused urban population to grow from 532 million in 1950 to 870 million in 1960, that is by 338 million, or by 64 per cent.

1940, 21 in 1950, and 25 in 1960. Another illustration of the large environmental change is found in the ratio of rural and small-town population to urban population: 6.4 to one in 1920, 5.3 in 1930, 4.4 in 1940, 3.7 in 1950 and 3.0 to one in 1960. To consider another aspect, produce of rural areas was diverted in increasing, though not always adequate, amounts to the rising proportion of urban consumers, in addition to supplying a growing rural population. The terms of trade for marketing the increased surplus were not always beneficial to the rural economy. These changing quantities and balances in population and production naturally have an impact on investment and other elements of the economic structure, with effects extending beyond national boundaries.

30. Among the figures for urban population shown in Table 1, perhaps those for total urban (20,000 and over) are more nearly trustworthy. Less confidence can be placed in rural population estimates, particularly for East Asia and Africa. For the larger localities, total estimates are susceptible to increase or decrease depending on the criteria by which agglomerations are defined, or re-defined while their physical limits expand. The larger the cities, the more uncertain are their boundaries drawn for purposes of comparison. All these problems affect the comparison of the population estimates for the separate size groups.

31. According to the tentative estimates of Table 1, the size distribution within the urban population has undergone much change. It is possible that no less important structural changes have occurred in the rural population, but data have not been assembled to illustrate changing proportions of inhabitants of the rural categories of localities. Structural changes in both rural and urban sectors can have profound implications for the needs and potentialities of economic and social development.

32. As these figures indicate, the urban population (20,000 and over) grew in the four successive decades by 30, 30, 25 and 42 per cent; the city population (100,000 and over) increased by 35, 33, 25 and 46 per cent; the successive increases in big-city population (500,000 and over) were by 41, 32, 28 and 57 per cent; and those in multi-million cities (2,500,000 and over) by 61, 36, 27 and 65 per cent. While the shifts in structure were less in the economically depressed 1930's or the war-ravaged 1940's than in the 1920's and 1950's, their momentum was not interrupted.

33. Increasing numbers of previously smaller towns and cities which grow into the size-classification of larger localities partly contribute to the higher rates of growth of the latter. Although a large number of small towns must also have crossed above the lower size limit of 20,000 during the same periods, the accrued population has not been sufficient to permit rates of increase of the magnitude of those in the larger localities. In fact, an increase in "top-heaviness" has been under way in the urban population, for the urban population (20,000 and over) tripled in forty years while the big-city population (500,000 and over) quadrupled.

Urbanization, 1920-1960, in Eight Major Areas of the World

34. Urbanization varied considerably from one major world area to another. The provisional figures which are here being compared are shown in tables 2, 3, 4, 5 and 6. They differ from

Table 2

Urban Population (Localities of 20,000 or More Inhabitants) in Major Areas of the World, 1920–1960 (rough estimates, in millions)

Major Area	1920	1930	1940	1950	1960
World Total	252.9	328.1	427.0	531.5	753.4
Europe (ex. USSR)	104.4	123.3	140.1	147.6	173.8
Northern America	43.5	58.0	64.3	83.2	112.5
East Asia	39.1	56.6	81.6	105.8	160.5
South Asia	27.0	34.6	50.5	77.0	116.1
Soviet Union	16.0	24.0	47.0	50.0	78.0
Latin America	12.9	18.1	25.2	40.6	67.8
Africa	6.9	9.7	13.8	21.5	36.4
Oceania	3.1	3.8	4.5	5.8	8.3

Table 3

Population in Rural Areas and Small Towns (Smaller Than 20,000) in Major Areas of the World, 1920–1960 (rough estimates, in millions)

Major Area	1920	1930	1940	1950	1960
World Total	1,607.3	1,741.2	1,869.9	1,985.3	2,241.0
Europe (ex. USSR)	220.1	230.5	238.7	244.1	250.7
Northern America	72.2	76.2	80.0	82.9	86.2
East Asia	514.3	534.6	553.9	578.9	633.6
South Asia	442.8	494.4	559.6	619.7	741.8
Soviet Union	139.3	155.0	148.0	130.0	136.4
Latin America	76.6	89.4	104.7	121.8	144.6
Africa	136.0	154.1	177.7	200.0	239.3
Oceania	6.0	7.0	7.3	7.9	8.4

Table 4

Urban Population (20,000 and over) As a Percentage of Total Population in Major Areas of the World, 1920–1960 (rough estimates)

Major Area	1920	1930	1940	1950	1960
World Total	14	16	19	21	25
Europe (ex. USSR)	32	35	37	38	41
Northern America	38	43	45	50	57
East Asia	7	10	13	15	20
South Asia	6	7	8	11	14
Soviet Union	10	13	24	28	36
Latin America	14	17	19	25	32
Africa	5	6	7	10	13
Oceania	34	35	38	42	50

Table 5

Decennial Increases in Urban Population (20,000 and over) in Major Areas of the World, 1920–1960 (rough estimates, per cent)

Major Area	1920–30	1930–40	1940–50	1950–60
World Total	30	30	25	42
Europe (ex. USSR)	18	14	5	18
Northern America	33	11	29	35
East Asia	45	44	30	52
South Asia	26	46	52	51
Soviet Union	50	96	6	56
Latin America	40	39	61	67
Africa	41	42	56	69
Oceania[a]	22	19	29	42

a Percentage computed with unrounded data.

Table 6

Decennial Increases in Rural and Small-Town Population (Localities Smaller Than 20,000) in Major Areas of the World, 1920–1960 (rough estimates, per cent)

Major Area	1920–30	1930–40	1940–50	1950–60
World Total	8	7	6	13
Europe (ex. USSR)	5	4	2	3
Northern America	6	5	4	4
East Asia	4	4	5	9
South Asia	12	13	11	20
Soviet Union	11	—5	—12	5
Latin America	17	17	16	19
Africa	13	15	13	20
Oceania[a]	15	5	5	8

a Percentage computed with unrounded data.

estimates which have appeared in other sources[13] and, as explained in the introductory chapter, they may still have to be revised considerably before they can be published in more definitive form.

35. In 1920, Europe (i.e. without the Soviet Union) had 41 per cent of

[13]E.g., K. Davis *et al.*, *The World's Metropolitan Regions*, *op. cit.*; United Nations, "World Survey of Urban and Rural Population Growth," *op. cit.*; Homer Hoyt, *World Urbanization*, Urban Land Institute, Technical Bulletin No. 43; and numerous other sources.

the entire world's urban population, but while urban population in Europe has grown from 104 million in 1920 to 174 million in 1960, that is by two-thirds, Europe's share in the world's urban population has shrunk to an estimated 23 per cent. By contrast, East Asia's urban population, grown four-fold from 39 million in 1920 to 160 million in 1960, now approaches that of Europe and, given its steep trend, may soon surpass it. It must be admitted, however, that the comparison is dubious because of varied definitions and characteristics applying to the respective urban populations in those two major areas.

36. The urban population of Northern America in 1920 was second to that of Europe in size, amounting to nearly 44 million. This has grown 2 1/2-fold in forty years, to about 112 million by 1960. However, the urban population of South Asia, estimated as 27 million in 1920, and more than four times greater, namely 116 million, in 1960, now apparently surpasses it.

37. Approximately five-fold increases are estimated to have occurred between 1920 and 1960 in the urban populations of the Soviet Union, Latin America and Africa, while the smaller urban population of Oceania grew about 2 1/2-fold, as did that of Northern America.

38. The largest relative increase of urban population in a single decade, as here estimated, occurred in the Soviet Union in the 1930's, when it nearly doubled within only ten years. Increases of the order of two-thirds in a decade are estimated for Latin America in the 1940's and 1950's, and for Africa in the most recent decade. Increases of urban population by at least one-half are also estimated in the 1920's for the Soviet Union, in the 1940's for South Asia and Africa, and in the 1950's for East Asia, South Asia, and the Soviet Union.

39. By contrast, in each of the four decades Europe's urban population is estimated to have gained by less than one-fifth, and in the 1930's the urban gains in Northern America and Oceania were similarly moderate. Because of the destruction and disorganization caused by the war, only small urban increases occurred in the 1940's in Europe and in the Soviet Union and also in East Asia. It must be admitted that the urban population estimates for the Soviet Union and East Asia in

1950, also those for East Asia in 1940, partly depend on rather tenuous extrapolations of either the preceding, or the subsequent, trends. It is probable that accelerated urban growth in Europe, East Asia and the Soviet Union in the 1950's represents in part a compensation for the retardation of the 1940's. A different condition obtained in South Asia, where the fast growth of cities in the 1940's was followed by somewhat slower, though still very noticeable, growth in the 1950's; it is probable that the large refugee movements resulting from the partition of India and Pakistan reinforced the accelerated growth of cities particularly in the 1940's, but not so much in the 1950's.

40. Gains in estimated rural and small-town population were also diverse but did not fluctuate so much. Exceptions are the Soviet Union, where rural population diminished in the 1930's, and more substantially in the war years of the 1940's; and Oceania where the apparent gains in rural and small-town population of the 1920's have not recurred since then. In Europe and Northern America, perhaps also in Latin America, relative gains in rural and small-town population gradually slowed down between 1920 and 1950. In East Asia and Africa, they may have fluctuated without any decided trend, but the data are too uncertain to bear out such a contention. With the possible exception of Northern America, it is evident that rural and small-town population growth accelerated in all major areas in the 1950's; the acceleration was slight in Europe, Latin America and Oceania, but substantial in South Asia, Africa, and probably also in East Asia. Part of the resumed growth in rural and small-town population in the highly urbanized regions of Europe, Northern America, the Soviet Union and Oceania

may be attributable to the spread of improved means of transportation, permitting residence in small towns by workers and families who gain their livelihood in nearby cities.

41. The greatly varied rates of growth in rural and small-town population have made for very uneven gains in such population among the world's major areas. In the entire world, this population is here estimated to have increased by 634 million from 1920 to 1960; of that increase, nearly 300 million accrued to South Asia, 120 million to East Asia, 100 million to Africa, and 70 million to Latin America. In Europe, the rural and small-town population gained only about 30 million in forty years, and in Northern America about 14 million, whereas in the Soviet Union it is estimated to have been smaller in 1960 than in 1920.

42. Northern America, Oceania and Europe have been, and have remained, the world's most urbanized major areas, in terms of the percentage of total population contained in localities of 20,000 or more, while Africa, South Asia and East Asia have been, and still are, the least urbanized. Urbanization progressed most conspicuously in the Soviet Union and Latin America from levels in 1920 that

would now be regarded as low to levels in 1960 that would have ranked among the highest some forty years previously.

Growth of Big Cities and Multi-Million Cities

43. Proportions in distribution and increase during 1920–1960 are altered when the comparison is confined to big cities, i.e. agglomerations or metropolitan areas of at least 500,000 inhabitants (see tables 7, 8 and 9). The validity of the comparison is limited by the numerous difficulties of definition which have been encountered. In particular, there is cause to question whether the growth of cities in Europe and in Northern America has been traced comparably, and the reader is advised to refer to the notes in the Appendix.

44. Accepting the tentative estimates at face value, we may note that almost one-half the world's big-city population in 1920 was found in Europe, while in 1960 Europe had only one-fifth of the world's big-city residents. As compared with big cities of Europe in 1920, those of Northern America had only one-half as much population, and those of East Asia only one-third; in 1960, Northern America's big-city population equalled that of Europe, and that of East Asia surpassed it.

Table 7

Big-City Population (Agglomerations of 500,000 and More Inhabitants) in Major Areas of the World, 1920–1960 (rough estimates, in millions)

Major Area	1920	1930	1940	1950	1960
World Total	94.9	133.6	175.8	224.4	351.6
Europe (ex. USSR)	43.9	54.6	60.7	62.2	72.7
Northern America	21.8	31.0	36.4	50.0	72.0
East Asia	14.7	23.2	34.4	44.2	86.4
South Asia	4.6	6.3	13.4	26.1	42.4
Soviet Union	1.9	6.2	13.8	13.3	26.9
Latin America	5.4	8.4	11.8	19.6	35.2
Africa	0.9	1.8	2.9	6.0	10.8
Oceania	1.7	2.1	2.4	3.0	5.2

Table 8

Big-City Population (500,000 and Over) as a Percentage of Urban Population (20,000 and Over) in Major Areas of the World, 1920–1960 (rough estimates)

Major Area	1920	1930	1940	1950	1960
World Total	38	41	41	42	47
Europe (ex. USSR)	42	44	43	42	42
Northern America	50	53	57	60	64
East Asia	38	41	42	42	54
South Asia	17	18	27	34	37
Soviet Union	12	26	29	27	34
Latin America	42	46	47	48	52
Africa	13	19	21	28	30
Oceania[a]	54	55	54	51	62

[a] Percentages computed with unrounded data.

Table 9

Big-City Population (500,000 and Over) as a Percentage of Total Population in Major Areas of the World, 1920–1960 (rough estimates)

Major Area	1920	1930	1940	1950	1960
World Total	5	6	8	9	12
Europe (ex. USSR)	14	15	16	16	17
Northern America	19	23	25	30	36
East Asia	3	4	5	6	11
South Asia	1	1	2	4	5
Soviet Union	1	3	7	7	13
Latin America	6	8	9	12	17
Africa	1	1	2	3	4
Oceania[a]	18	19	21	22	31

[a] Percentages computed with unrounded data.

45. Except in 1940, Latin America's big cities at most dates had more inhabitants than did the big cities of the Soviet Union, though in the Soviet Union the combined urban population (including smaller cities and towns) always exceeded that of Latin America.[14] In Africa, only Cairo had more than 500,000 inhabitants in 1920, whereas by 1960 Africa's ten big cities comprised a population of appreciable size (10.8 million).

Regions of Varied Economic Development and Varied Population Density

46. Some of the major areas discussed in the foregoing contain regions of varied economic development. Thus,

[14]It is of interest to note the difference in the "top-heaviness" of urbanization in these two areas. This may be largely attributable to two circumstances. First, many of Latin America's big cities are the seats of separate national Governments, and these tend to grow large in a number of countries having few other sizable cities. Secondly, regional planning efforts in the Soviet Union have stimulated the growth of a number of widely distributed cities of considerable size, and thereby the tendency of urbanization to become concentrated in a small number of very large cities has been counter-balanced to a certain extent.

Table 10

Multi-Million Cities in Major Areas of the World, 1920–1960 (rough estimates, in thousands)

City	1920	1930	1940	1950	1960
World Total	30,294	48,660	66,364	84,923	141,156
Europe total	16,051	18,337	18,675	18,016	18,605
London	7,236	8,127	8,275	8,366	8,190
Paris	4,965	5,885	6,050	6,300	7,140
Berlin	3,850	4,325	4,350	3,350	3,275
Northern America total	10,075	13,300	17,300	26,950	33,875
New York	7,125	9,350	10,600	12,350	14,150
Los Angeles	(750)[a]	(1,800)[a]	2,500	4,025	6,525
Chicago	2,950	3,950	4,200	4,950	6,000
Philadelphia	(2,025)[a]	(2,350)[a]	(2,475)[a]	2,950	3,650
Detroit	(1,100)[a]	(1,825)[a]	(2,050)[a]	2,675	3,550
East Asia total	4,168	11,773	15,789	16,487	40,806
Tokyo	4,168	6,064	8,558	8,182	13,534
Shanghai	(2,000)[a]	3,100	3,750	5,250	8,500
Osaka	(1,889)[a]	2,609	3,481	3,055	5,158
Peking	(1,000)[a]	(1,350)[a]	(1,750)[a]	(2,100)[a]	5,000
Tientsin	(800)[a]	(1,000)[a]	(1,500)[a]	(1,900)[a]	3,500
Hong Kong	(550)[a]	(700)[a]	(1,500)[a]	(1,925)[a]	2,614
Shenyang	...[b]	(700)[a]	(1,150)[a]	(1,700)[a]	2,500
South Asia total	...	...	3,400	7,220	12,700
Calcutta	(1,820)[a]	(2,055)[a]	3,400	4,490	5,810
Bombay	(1,275)[a]	(1,300)[a]	(1,660)[a]	2,730	4,040
Djakarta	...[b]	(525)[a]	(1,000)[a]	(1,750)[a]	2,850
Soviet Union total	...	2,500	7,700	4,250	9,550
Moscow	(1,120)[a]	2,500	4,350	4,250	6,150
Leningrad	(740)[a]	(2,000)[a]	3,350	(2,250)[a]	3,400
Latin America total	...	2,750	3,500	12,000	22,300
Buenos Aires	(2,275)[a]	2,750	3,500	5,150	6,775
Mexico	(835)[a]	(1,435)[a]	(2,175)[a]	3,800	6,450
Rio de Janeiro	(1,325)[a]	(1,675)[a]	(2,150)[a]	3,050	4,700
Sao Paulo	(600)[a]	(900)[a]	(1,425)[a]	(2,450)[a]	4,375
Africa total	...	...	...	...	3,320
Cairo	(875)[a]	(1,150)[a]	(1,525)[a]	(2,350)[a]	3,320

(Slight discrepancies with figures shown elsewhere are the result of rounding.)

[a] Cities smaller than 2,500,000 are not included in totals.
[b] Smaller than 500,000.

Japan, Temperate South America, and Australia and New Zealand are economically more developed than other regions of East Asia, Latin America and Oceania. It is of interest, therefore, to differentiate the estimates of urban and rural population for the more developed regions and for the less developed ones. In addition, regions of greater average population density have been distinguished from those of less density. Comparisons are presented first for more developed and for less developed regions combined (types A and B), followed by additional comparisons for four sub-types of regions, as distinguished both by economic development and average density (sub-types 1 and 2 of A and B). The regions are grouped in the following manner:[15]

Type A-1.	More developed regions of high population density	All of Europe, and Japan
Type A-2.	More developed regions of lower population density	Northern America, the Soviet Union, Temperate South America, and Australia and New Zealand
Type B-1.	Less developed regions of high population density	East Asia without Japan, Middle South Asia, South-East Asia, and the Caribbean
Type B-2.	Less developed regions of lower population density	South-West Asia, Tropical South America, the Middle American Mainland, all of Africa, and Oceania without Australia and New Zealand

47. As shown in Table 11, from 1920 to 1960 total population grew by about 300 million in the more developed regions, and more than 800 million in less developed regions.

48. In both groups of regions in the forty years, urban population was augmented by about 250 million. But the urban population of the more developed regions, initially larger, increased by about 2.3 times while in the less developed regions urban population grew in the same period by 4.7 times.

49. Between 1920 and 1960, the rural and small-town population of the more developed regions had a net growth of only about 60 million, an increase of less than one-eighth the 1920 size. In the less developed regions, meanwhile, the addition to rural and small-town population was nearly 580 million, which is more than one-half its size in 1920.

50. The growth in big-city population, from 1920 to 1960, is estimated as 130 million in the more developed regions, and almost as much also in the less developed regions. But in the first type of regions big-city population was already of substantial size in 1920,

and in 1960 it came to about 2.7 times that size; in the less developed regions, by contrast, where big cities in 1920 were still rather few and not exceedingly large, the forty years' growth in big-city population was more than ninefold as estimated here.

51. In the more developed regions, the level of urbanization (percentage of total population in localities of at least 20,000 inhabitants) rose from 27 in 1920 to 44 in 1960, exceeding the rise in the percentage of urban population in less developed regions, where it increased from 6 per cent in 1920 to 16 per cent in 1960. From a relative point of view, however, it is correct to say that urbanization advanced more rapidly in the less developed regions, for there the level was initially low. Also, in the developed regions there was a comparatively slower growth in total population.

52. The concentration of urban population in big cities advanced relatively little in the more developed regions, namely from 43 per cent in 1920 to 49 per cent in 1960. In less

[15]The same regional groupings were used also in the United Nations *Provisional Report on World Population Prospects, op. cit.*

Table 11

Trends in Total, Rural, Urban and Big-City Population in Regions of Different Levels of Economic Development, 1920-1960 (rough estimates, in millions)

Group of Regions	1920	1930	1940	1950	1960
	Total population				
World total	1,860.2	2,069.3	2,296.9	2,516.8	2.994.4
More developed regions	672.3	757.8	821.6	858.0	976.5
Less developed regions	1,187.9	1,311.5	1,475.3	1,658.8	2,017.9
	Rural and small-town population				
World total	1,607.3	1,741.2	1,869.9	1,985.3	2,241.0
More developed regions	487.5	523.6	529.7	527.8	543.8
Less developed regions	1,119.8	1,217.6	1,340.2	1,457.5	1,697.2
	Urban population (20,000 and over)				
World total	252.9	328.1	427.0	531.5	753.4
More developed regions	184.8	234.2	291.9	330.2	432.7
Less developed regions	68.1	93.9	135.1	201.3	320.7
	Big-city population (500,000 and over)				
World total	94.9	135.6	176.8	224.4	351.6
More developed regions	80.1	111.2	133.8	149.8	212.4
Less developed regions	14.8	24.4	43.0	74.6	139.2
	Urban population as a percentage of total population				
World total	14	16	19	21	25
More developed regions	27	31	36	38	44
Less developed regions	6	7	9	12	16
	Big-city population as a percentage of urban population				
World total	38	41	41	42	47
More developed regions	43	47	46	45	49
Less developed regions	22	26	32	37	43
	Big-city population as a percentage of total population				
World total	5	7	8	9	12
More developed regions	12	15	16	17	22
Less developed regions	1	2	3	5	7

(Slight discrepancies with figures shown elsewhere are the result of rounding.)

developed regions, by contrast, the share of big cities rose from 22 to 43 per cent of the urban population during that time.

53. A further sub-division is introduced in Table 12, showing the changes in urban and rural population in the two regions of economic development for regions of high and low average population density. Until many geographic and other factors are weighed,

these density measures are of undetermined significance, and their consideration is included in this provisional report as a matter of interest for further research.

54. From reference to Table 12 it can be seen that the 1960 percentage distributions of the world's population among the four categories have a somewhat similar pattern for both total and rural and small-town population,

Table 12

Total, Rural, Urban and Big-City Population in Regions of Varied Development and Density for the World, 1920–1960 (rough estimates)

Group of Regions	Population (millions)					Percent of World Total				
	1920	1930	1940	1950	1960	1920	1930	1940	1950	1960
			Total population							
World total	1,860.2	2,069.3	2,296.9	2,516.8	2,994.4	100	100	100	100	100
A^a-1^b	379.9	417.7	451.3	474.9	517.9	20	20	20	19	17
A-2^c	292.4	340.1	370.3	383.1	458.6	16	16	16	15	15
B^d-1	948.8	1,036.5	1,149.5	1,269.7	1,519.8	51	51	50	50	51
B-2	239.1	275.0	325.8	389.1	498.1	13	13	14	16	17
			Rural and small-town population							
World total	1,607.3	1,741.2	1,869.9	1,985.3	2,241.0	100	100	100	100	100
A-1	262.5	275.9	283.7	296.1	301.2	16	16	15	15	13
A-2	225.0	247.7	246.0	231.7	242.6	14	14	13	12	11
B-1	898.8	965.9	1,047.7	1,122.0	1,294.8	56	56	56	56	58
B-2	221.0	251.7	292.5	335.5	402.4	14	14	16	17	18
			Urban population (20,000 and over)							
World total	252.9	328.1	427.0	531.5	753.4	100	100	100	100	100
A-1	117.4	141.8	167.6	178.8	216.7	46	43	39	34	29
A-2	67.4	92.4	124.3	151.4	216.0	27	28	29	28	29
B-1	50.0	70.6	101.8	147.7	225.0	20	22	24	28	29
B-2	18.1	23.3	33.3	53.6	95.7	7	7	8	10	13
			Big-city population (500,000 and over)							
World total	94.9	135.6	176.8	224.4	351.6	100	100	100	100	100
A-1	51.9	65.9	76.1	76.3	97.2	54	49	43	34	28
A-2	28.2	45.3	57.7	73.5	115.2	30	33	33	33	33
B-1	10.3	18.1	33.4	56.2	102.3	11	13	19	25	29
B-2	4.5	6.3	9.6	18.4	36.9	5	5	5	8	10

(Slight discrepancies with figures shown elsewhere are the result of rounding.)

---

[a] A. More developed regions.
[b] B. Less developed regions.
[c] 1. Regions of higher average population density.
[d] 2. Regions of lower average population density.

with about 50 per cent in the less developed higher density region and the remainder fairly evenly divided among the other three regions. The distribution of the world's urban population appears to be in nearly equal numbers among both regions of higher density and the more developed lower density region, while the proportion in the less developed lower density region is about half that of any of them.

55. In the period 1920–1960, for both total and urban population within each economic region, greater growth occurred in the less densely inhabited areas. For total population, increases amounted to 57 per cent for type A-2 region compared with 36 per cent for A-1, and 108 per cent for B-2 compared with 60 per cent for B-1. Urban population doubled in the type A-1 and tripled in the A-2 region, increased by 4–1/2 times in B-1 and by more than 5 times in B-2. The highest level of urbanization was registered in the A-2 region, technologically

advanced and possessing natural resources in great supply, increasing from 23 per cent in 1920 to 47 per cent in 1960. For type A-1, B-1 and B-2 regions, urbanization advanced by similar percentage points, from 31 to 42, 5 to 15 and 8 to 19, respectively.

56. Total population growth rates are, of course, closely linked to fertility levels, which are known to be higher in regions of lower population density.[16] The higher urban growth rates in these regions may in addition be related to the fact that urbanization occurred there more recently, advancing from a lower level in these regions as compared with Europe (see discussion in the following section).

Observations on Regions Grouped by Recency of Urbanization

57. Because world regions differ in pace of population growth as well as in levels, the element of time is here specifically examined in connection with the process of urbanization. Estimates for regions grouped according to attainment of 25 per cent urban in total population by specified years are given in the Appendix tables and summarized in Table 13. The groups are as follows:

I.	Regions at least 25 per cent urbanized by 1920	Western Europe, Northern Europe, Northern America, Temperate South America, and Australia and New Zealand
II.	Regions at least 25 per cent urbanized by 1960 but not by 1920	Southern Europe, Eastern Europe, Japan, Other East Asia, the Soviet Union, Tropical South America, the Middle American Mainland, Northern Africa, and Southern Africa
III.	Regions not yet 25 per cent urbanized by 1960	Mainland East Asia, Middle South Asia, South-East Asia, South-West Asia, the Caribbean, Tropical Africa, and Other Oceania

58. Urbanization is shown in Table 13 to progress fastest at the intermediate level, group II, but not so fast where the level is still low, or where it is already high.

59. In 1960, total population in group II was nearly twice that of group I, and total population in group III approximately twice that of group II. On the other hand, total urban populations in the three groups were nearly equal. The distribution of the world's rural population, accordingly, was all the more uneven: 9 per cent of the world's rural and small-town population, in 1960, was in group I, 24 per cent in group II, and 67 per cent in group III.

[16]See, in these respects, the United Nations *Provisional Report on World Population Prospects, ...op. cit.,* and also the introductory chapter in *Population Bulletin of the United Nations, with special reference to conditions and trends of fertility in the world,* New York, 1965.

60. Increases in urban and rural population proceeded unequally among the three groups of regions. Between 1920 and 1960, total population increased 52 per cent in group I, 61 per cent in group II, and 63 per cent in group III, comparatively slight differences in rates. During the same time, urban population doubled in group I, grew by 3 1/2 times in group II, and 4 1/2 times in group III; rural population grew by 17 per cent in group I, 28 per cent in group II, and 48 per cent in group III. In short, similar rates of total population growth have produced varied rates of urban and rural growth according to the levels of urbanization: where the level of urbanization was already high, only moderate rates of growth in both the urban and the rural populations occurred, but where the level of urbanization was low, both the urban and the rural populations grew with greatest

Table 13

Summary of Changes in Total, Rural, Urban and Big-City Populations in Regions of the World Classified by Recency of Urbanization, 1920–40 and 1940–60 (rough estimates, in millions)

Group of Regions	1920	1940	1960	1940 Per 100 in 1920	1960 Per 100 in 1940
Total population					
World total	1,860.2	2,296.9	2,994.4	123	130
Group I[a]	297.9	353.9	452.3	119	128
Group II[b]	503.9	648.0	813.6	129	126
Group III[c]	1,058.4	1,295.0	1,728.5	122	133
Rural and small-town population					
World total	1,607.3	1,869.9	2,241.0	116	120
Group I	176.6	187.5	206.4	106	110
Group II	426.9	493.6	545.0	116	110
Group III	1,003.8	1,188.8	1,489.6	118	125
Urban population (20,000 and over)					
World total	252.9	427.0	753.4	169	176
Group I	121.3	166.4	245.9	137	148
Group II	77.0	154.4	268.6	201	174
Group III	54.6	106.2	238.9	195	225
Big-city population (500,000 and over)					
World total	94.9	175.8	351.6	186	200
Group I	57.6	83.4	135.0	144	162
Group II	26.0	60.1	115.6	231	192
Group III	11.3	32.3	101.0	286	313
Urban population as a percentage of total population					
World total	14	19	25		
Group I	41	47	54		
Group II	15	24	33		
Group III	5	8	14		
Big-city population as a percentage of urban population					
World total	38	41	47		
Group I	47	50	55		
Group II	34	39	43		
Group III	21	30	42		
Big-city population as a percentage of total population					
World total	5	8	12		
Group I	19	24	30		
Group II	5	9	14		
Group III	1	2	6		

[a] Regions at least 25 per cent urbanized by 1920.
[b] Regions at least 25 per cent urbanized by 1960 but not by 1920.
[c] Regions not yet 25 per cent urbanized by 1960.

rapidity. Expressed in average annual rates, the phenomenon was as follows:

Type of Regions	Average Annual Rate of Population Growth, 1920-60		
	Total	Urban	Rural and Small-town
I. Early urbanized	1.0	1.8	0.4
II. Recently urbanized	1.2	3.2	0.6
III. Least urbanized	1.2	3.8	1.0

61. The recent acceleration of population growth in most of the world's regions, particularly the less developed ones, has merely intensified this phenomenon. Patterns are similar, but rates of growth in urban and rural populations diverged more widely.

62. The average annual rates for the 1950–1960 period are shown below.

Type of Regions	Average Annual Rate of Population Growth, 1950–60		
	Total	Urban	Rural and Small-town
I. Early urbanized	1.3	2.3	0.3
II. Recently urbanized	1.7	4.0	0.8
III. Least urbanized	1.9	4.5	1.5

63. If this analysis can serve to illustrate the nature of the momentum of urbanization, and if the distinctions made are relevant, the following general conclusions are suggested:

(a) With a given rate of growth in total population, and a low level of urbanization, both the urban and the rural populations are apt to grow rapidly, and yet the level of urbanization can advance only gradually;

(b) With a similar rate of growth in total population, and an intermediate level of urbanization, urban population can grow rapidly, and the level of urbanization can advance rapidly, without necessarily any rapid growth in rural population; and

(c) With a similar rate of growth in total population, and a high level of urbanization, both urban and rural population can grow at relatively moderate rates, while the level of urbanization progresses also at a moderate pace.

64. These dynamic considerations—in terms of rates of growth—must also be coordinated with a consideration of the resulting balance in absolute numbers and structural proportions. As compared with urban areas, the rural rates of growth are more moderate, but it should not be overlooked that those rates give large increases in numbers of rural inhabitants where the rural population is of large size. A comparison is made below of absolute increases in total, urban and rural populations in the three types of regions for the 20-year period from 1920 to 1940 and the 10-year period from 1950 to 1960. Both periods have been relatively undisturbed by war, and the world's total population has grown about as much in the recent decade as it did in the earlier two decades.

Type of Regions	Absolute Increases in Population (millions)		
	Total	Urban	Rural and Small-town
	1920–1940		
I. Early urbanized	56	45	11
II. Recently urbanized	144	77	67
III. Least urbanized	237	52	185
	1950–1960		
I. Early urbanized	56	50	6
II. Recently urbanized	129	87	42
III. Least urbanized	294	86	208

The Momentum of Urbanization and of Concentration in Big Cities

65. The analysis of changes in urban and rural population by each individual region and for each decade cannot yield or has not yet yielded much that is useful for purposes of broad generalization. First, the present estimates still suffer from many defects with respect to accuracy and comparability. Secondly, circumstances are differently combined in each region, causing an inter-action of factors impenetrable to any quick analysis. Finally, events of particular decades, such as wars, economic depression, and periods of rehabilitation affected regions diversely. Much remains to be learned from intensive regional studies.

66. The fluctuations caused by short-term interferences with normal regional developments are partly disposed of when the analysis is confined to long periods. The peculiarities of circumstances in particular regions are partly compensated for when regions are grouped. Salient features can then be deduced from data such as those brought together in Table 16. Quite obviously, on a world-wide scale, and over long periods, urbanization is characterized by a powerful momentum of its own. Similarly, it can be shown that the tendency of urban population to become increasingly concentrated in big cities also appears possessed of an inherent trend.

67. Big cities can become numerous and increase in size only where the urban population is already large. Part of the increase in big-city population is drawn from the surpassing of size-limits and the absorption of previously smaller cities and towns. In addition, individual big cities tend to grow in rough proportion with the general increase in urban population. It seems possible to consider that some average relationship might persist between levels of urbanization, general growth in population, and the emergence and growth of big cities. The possibility of such a relationship is suggested in a comparison of a few summary figures, given below:

Type of Regions	1940	1960	1920–40	1940–60
	Total population		*Gain in total population*	
World total	2,296.9	2,994.4	436.7	697.5
I. Early urbanized	353.9	452.3	56.0	98.4
II. Recently urbanized	648.0	813.6	144.1	165.6
III. Least urbanized	1,295.0	1,728.5	236.6	433.5
	Urban population (20,000 and over)		*Gain in big-city population (cities of 500,000 and over)*	
World total	427.0	753.4	80.9	175.8
I. Early urbanized	166.4	245.9	25.8	51.6
II. Recently urbanized	154.4	268.6	34.1	55.5
III. Least urbanized	106.2	238.9	21.0	68.7
	Urban population as a percentage of total population		*Gain in big-city population as a percentage of gain in total population*	
World total	19	25	19	25
I. Early urbanized	47	54	46	52
II. Recently urbanized	24	33	24	34
III. Least urbanized	8	14	9	16

68. As it happens—and no precise reason is known—in six of the eight sets of figures the percentages of urbanization and the percentages of total population gains accruing to big cities are within one point of each other. The two exceptions are found for 1940–60: in regions of type III (not yet highly urbanized), big cities appear to have grown slightly faster than indicated by the level of urbanization; in regions of type I (early urbanized), they appear to have grown somewhat more slowly. But these deviations are easily within the range of errors of the estimates. For instance, the metropolitan area populations in Europe have for the most part been estimated within constant boundaries, though the limits of urbanized territory probably were smaller at earlier dates.

C. A TENTATIVE LOOK AT THE FUTURE

A Crude Method of Projection

69. The dynamics of trends in total population have been studied in terms of fertility, mortality, international migration, and composition by age groups. Although unforeseen factors may affect them, trends in total population nevertheless can be projected into the future with some degree of plausibility. Use is made here of a recent set of regional and world projections of total population.[17]

70. Only crude methods are indicated at this time for projections of urban population derived from those of total population. The world-wide conditions attending urbanization are not clearly understood, and the factors which can modify them at any time are numerous

---

[17]*Provisional Report on World Population Prospects, op. cit.* The projections are for the same major areas and regions as used in the present study and set forth in the Appendix.

---

and complex. With the present information, it is unlikely that more refined methods can yield more trustworthy results. Based on the foregoing observations, two crude devices were used to obtain for the year 1980 estimates of urban (localities of 20,000 and over) and big-city (agglomerations of at least 500,000) population.

71. Comparing the magnitudes of increase in the percentages of urban population over the period 1920–1960, it can be seen from reference to Table 13 that the greatest increase accrued to the group intermediate in the scale of recency of urbanization, the least increase to the level of least urbanization, with the group of highest urbanization progressing at an intermediate rate. A logistic curve was fitted to the three series of group averages by assuming that together they may constitute a long time sequence, group II in 1920 being linked directly with group III in 1960, and being followed, after an interpolated time interval, by the sequence in group I. It was also assumed that urbanization would never exceed the level of 70 per cent in any world region. With this logistic curve, which fitted the data tolerably well, it was possible to estimate from a given percentage level of urbanization what might be—in conformity with the average of observed past trends—the percentage level of urbanization to be expected twenty years later. Of course this is an exceedingly crude method.

72. The second device is based on the observation made in the preceding section. For reasons which are unclear, a near coincidence has been observed between the percentage level of urbanization at the end of a twenty-year period, and the percentage of the absolute increment in total population during the twenty-year period which

is gained in the big cities. Big-city population can be tentatively projected on the crude assumption that this relationship will also hold true in the future.

73. The two crude assumptions, namely (a) a logistic curve for the extrapolation of the percentage of urban population, and (b) derivation from that percentage of estimates of growth in big-city population, have been applied, in rough calculations for a period up to 1980, to the estimates and projections of total population for each of the twenty-one regions. This was done indiscriminately, though it is unlikely that such crude assumptions can be applied with equal justification to regions where numerous other circumstances differ so much. Naturally, much study of the possible effects of various factors on urbanization is recommended as a basis for more realistic projections into the future, if these are to have any forecasting value.

74. The present projections should be regarded as not much more than a game in numbers, indicative perhaps of plausible orders of magnitude, but not as forecasts related to any detailed pertinent conditions. For whatever they may be worth, summary results of these calculations are shown in Table 14, together with estimates from 1920 onward, by twenty-year time intervals. The same calculations have also been used as the basis for the appended charts.

75. The projections suggest that, in the world as a whole, population may increase by as great an amount from 1960 to 1980 as it did in the forty years from 1920 to 1960. The 1960–1980 additions to the rural and small-town population may equal or slightly surpass those of the preceding 40-year period, and future increments to the urban

population may be considerably larger than those of the selected past period. It is possible that the population in the world's big cities (500,000 and more) may double between 1960 and 1980. This may happen though the several 1960–1980 increments in Europe, Northern America and Oceania may be smaller than have been those of the 1920–1960 period, and the 1960–1980 increments in East Asia and the Soviet Union may not be significantly larger. The acceleration of increments in total, rural, urban and big-city population is likely to become most conspicuous in South Asia, Latin America and Africa. At the same time, there will also occur a further re-distribution in urban population among different parts of the world.

The Possible Implications

76. The estimates and tentative projections for each region can also be brought together so as to distinguish the group of more developed and that of presently less developed regions (i.e., regions of types A and B, as previously described), and this is done for comparative purposes in Table 15. The percentage shares of the less developed regions relative to world totals are particularly noteworthy.

77. Of the world's total population, 64 per cent was that of less developed regions in 1920, 64 per cent in 1940, 67 per cent in 1960, and by 1980 it may be 72 per cent. Of the world's population increase from 1920 to 1960, 73 per cent accrued to the less developed regions, and of the increase projected from 1960 to 1980 the less developed regions may absorb 83 per cent.

78. In terms of rural and small-town population, the share in the less developed regions has risen from 70 per cent in 1920 to 72 per cent in 1940 and 76 per cent in 1960, and it may

Table 14

Crude Tentative Projections of Total, Rural, Urban and Big-City Population in Major World Areas, 1960–1980, and Estimates for 1920–1960 (millions)

Major Areas and Type of Settlement	1920 (est.)	1940 (est.)	1960 (est.)	1980 (project.)	Absolute Increment 1920–60	1960–80
World total						
Total population	1,860	2,298	2,994	4,269	1,134	1,275
Rural, small-town	1,607	1,871	2,242	2,909	635	667
Urban	253	427	752	1,360	499	608
(Big cities)	(96)	(175)	(351)	(725)	(255)	(374)
Europe (excluding USSR)						
Total population	324	379	425	479	101	54
Rural, small-town	220	239	251	244	31	−7
Urban	104	140	174	235	70	61
(Big cities)	(44)	(61)	(73)	(99)	(29)	(26)
Northern America						
Total population	116	144	198	262	82	64
Rural, small-town	72	80	86	101	14	15
Urban	44	64	112	161	68	49
(Big cities)	(22)	(36)	(72)	(111)	(50)	(39)
East Asia						
Total population	553	636	794	1,038	241	244
Rural, small-town	514	554	634	742	120	108
Urban	39	82	160	296	121	136
(Big cities)	(15)	(34)	(86)	(155)	(71)	(69)
South Asia						
Total population	470	610	858	1,366	388	508
Rural, small-town	443	560	742	1,079	299	337
Urban	27	50	116	287	89	171
(Big cities)	(5)	(13)	(42)	(149)	(37)	(107)
Soviet Union						
Total population	155	195	214	278	59	64
Rural, small-town	139	148	136	150	−3	14
Urban	16	47	78	128	62	50
(Big cities)	(2)	(14)	(27)	(56)	(25)	(29)
Latin Anercia						
Total population	90	130	213	374	123	161
Rural, small-town	77	105	145	222	68	77
Urban	13	25	68	152	55	84
(Big cities)	(5)	(12)	(35)	(100)	(30)	(65)
Africa						
Total population	143	192	276	449	133	173
Rural, small-town	136	178	240	360	104	120
Urban	7	14	36	89	29	53
(Big cities)	(1)	(3)	(11)	(47)	(10)	(36)
Oceania						
Total population	9	12	16	23	7	7
Rural, small-town	6	7	8	11	2	3
Urban	3	5	8	11	5	3
(Big cities)	(2)	(2)	(5)	(8)	(3)	(3)

(Slight discrepancies with figures shown elsewhere are the result of rounding.)

Table 15

Crude Tentative Projections of Total, Rural, Urban and Big-City Population in More Developed, and Less Developed Regions of the World, 1960–1980, and Estimates for 1920–1960 (millions)

Type of Settlement	1920 (est.)	1940 (est.)	1960 (est.)	1980 (project.)	Absolute Increment 1920-60	Absolute Increment 1960-80
			World total			
Total population	1,860	2,298	2,994	4,269	1,134	1,275
Rural, small-town	1,607	1,871	2,242	2,909	635	667
Urban	253	427	752	1,360	499	608
(Big cities)	(96)	(175)	(351)	(725)	(255)	(374)
			A. More developed regions			
Total population	672	821	977	1,189	305	212
Rural, small-town	487	530	544	566	57	22
Urban	185	291	433	623	248	190
(Big cities)	(80)	(134)	(212)	(327)	(132)	(115)
			B. Less developed regions			
Total population	1,188	1,476	2,017	3,080	829	1,063
Rural, small-town	1,120	1,341	1,698	2,343	578	645
Urban	68	135	319	737	251	418
(Big cities)	(16)	(41)	(139)	(398)	(123)	(259)
		Less developed regions as a percentage of world total				
Total population	64	64	67	72	73	83
Rural, small-town	70	72	76	81	91	97
Urban	27	32	42	54	50	69
(Big cities)	(16)	(24)	(40)	(55)	(48)	(69)

(Slight discrepancies with figures shown elsewhere are the result of rounding.)

attain 81 per cent in 1980. The remarkable observation can be made that of the world's increase in rural and small-town population in the past four decades 91 per cent occurred in the less developed regions, and the tentative projections suggest that almost 97 per cent of increments in the world's rural and small-town inhabitants may accrue there in the two decades to come.

79. Less developed regions have had a rapidly expanding share in the world's urban population, a trend that is likely to continue. Their share amounted to 27 per cent in 1920, 32 per cent in 1940, 42 per cent in 1960, and may rise to 54 per cent by 1980. One-half of the world's increase in urban population occurred there during 1920–1960, and more than two-thirds may occur there in 1960–1980. The less developed regions' share in the world's big-city population, initially low, has increased even more sharply.

80. Perhaps the following comparisons are most eloquent. In 1960, the more developed regions had a rural population of 544 million and an urban population of 433 million, of which 212 million [were] in big cities. As tentatively calculated here, in the presently less developed regions the net additions to the 1960 population may by 1980 amount to 645 million rural and 418 million urban inhabitants, of which 259 million [will be] in big cities. The *1960–1980 population increase*

in less developed regions, therefore, can exceed the *1960 total population in the developed regions*. According to this projection, an excess would appear in the big-city and rural and small-town populations, while the urban population would be nearly the equivalent of the 1960 urban population in the more developed regions.

81. Whatever the errors of estimate in so crude a projection, it is certain that the trend of urbanization will include far-reaching implications, many foreseeable and many as yet obscure.

82. Some of the foreseeable consequences of the momentum of urbanization cause much concern. To mention a few of the problems, there are those related to food production and distribution adequate for the dietary needs of city-dwellers and the economic needs of agriculturists; the equitable flow of capital and terms of trade between diversely endowed regions; the mental and physical health of the society; planning for housing, transportation networks and other physical needs for localities of all sizes and for the modes of exchange and inter-action between cities, towns and countryside, within and beyond country borders.

83. From another viewpoint, urban growth can be regarded as a power-house for development. Throughout history, towns and cities have been the crucible of a cultural, social and economic innovation and transformation permeating society. Urbanization, therefore, creates environments conducive to a quickened rate of progress. Certainly, the best possible use should be made of a process which, in any event, can hardly be circumvented.

84. It is also probable that further phases in the development process will affect the underlying population trends themselves and, by such "feedback" effects, cause them to differ from those that can be more directly projected.

85. As pointed out at the beginning of this study, the observed environmental changes are simultaneously quantitative and qualitative. Not only do cities grow, but in the process they become something different from what they have been. The traditional dichotomy between urban and rural areas is becoming increasingly blurred and new types of environment have begun to emerge under diverse conditions which can no longer be fittingly described as either "urban" or "rural." The process of urbanization may come to surpass itself and give rise to geographic and social forms of human settlement to which the current vocabulary can no longer be validly applied. Complementarity and mutual benefits may be generated among areas where at present only a conflict of local interests is most in evidence.

Appendix

I.   Major areas and regions of the world.
II. Charts of big-city, other urban, and rural and small-town population in major areas of the world:
   A. 1920 (estimated)
   B. 1940 (estimated)
   C. 1960 (estimated)
   D. 1980 (projected)
III. Tables of estimated population in world regions grouped by recency of urbanization, 1920–1960:
   A. Total population
   B. Urban population
   C. Rural and small-town population
   D. Urban population as a percentage of total population

MAJOR AREAS AND REGIONS OF THE WORLD[1]

The major areas are listed below in the order of size of the urban population (localities of 20,000 or more inhabitants) in 1920. Under each major area, regions and the countries comprised in them are listed according to the size of urban population in 1960,[2] and a brief account is given of methods of estimation insofar as these have a major bearing on the comparisons made further on.

Europe

Western Europe: German Federal Republic, France, the Netherlands, Belgium, Austria, Switzerland

Northern Europe: The United Kingdom, Sweden, Denmark, Finland, Norway, Ireland

Southern Europe: Italy, Spain, Yugoslavia, Greece, Portugal, Albania

Eastern Europe: Poland, Eastern Germany, Romania, Hungary, Czechoslovakia, Berlin, Bulgaria

Metropolitan areas have here been defined for many countries of Western and Northern Europe, also for Greece, Hungary and Portugal, but not for Germany and some other countries where it would have been relevant. The data on urban population in Italy and Spain refer to centres of municipalities, hence exclude towns not having such administrative status. Metropolitan areas have mostly been

[1] As defined in *Provisional Report on World Population Prospects, as assessed in 1963. op. cit.* In that report, West Berlin was included with Western, and East Berlin with Eastern Europe; considered as one city, and geographically contiguous with Eastern Germany only, Berlin is here placed with Eastern Europe. The regions of Western, Eastern and Middle Africa, used in that report, are here combined as "Tropical Africa"; and those of Melanesia, Micronesia and Polynesia appear here as "Other Oceania."

[2] For brevity, countries without a city of at least 100,000 inhabitants are omitted.

defined within constant boundaries though the extent of the urbanized area has probably expanded. The boundaries are usually those of a fairly recent census. Accordingly, "metropolitan" populations of an earlier date may sometimes be slightly overestimated, and their rate of growth underestimated.

Northern America

Northern America: The United States, Canada

For the United States, metropolitan areas have been defined in accord with censuses of 1950 (1951 in Canada) and 1960 (1961) where these constitute at least a population of 500,000, while for other urban localities the data are those for "city proper." Taking into account the increasing effect of motor transport, proportions of rings which have recently become parts of metropolitan areas have been included retroactively as seemed appropriate in the estimates for 1920, 1930 and 1940. The proportions were assumed to increase linearly from zero in 1900 to 100 per cent of areas included in the census in 1950.

East Asia

Mainland East Asia: China (mainland), Hong Kong, Macao, Mongolia

Japan: Japan

Other East Asia: Korea, China (Taiwan), the Ryukyu Islands

In this area, estimates of total population for China (mainland) are most uncertain, as are those for localities other than big cities. For most of China's big cities, population data and estimates could be found for three or more dates, permitting judicious interpolations. Data for all cities of at least 100,000 inhabitants are available from the 1953 census, and for cities of at least 200,000 from official estimates for end-1957. Estimates for all towns of at least 50,000 have been found in a compilation of the 1930's while other data have been extracted from reports of missionaries in 1918/1919, encyclopedias and geography textbooks of various dates, official sources for the 1940's, and a few very recent references to the largest cities. In these circumstances, the comparability of much of the data is questionable, and interpolations from selected data were substituted. The population of towns down to a size-limit of 20,000 had to be estimated from a comparison of data on the size distribution of towns and cities in China and in some other large countries, and the estimates for towns smaller than 100,000 are, accordingly, a very uncertain extrapolation. —In Japan, the geographic extent of administrative urban areas has probably expanded faster than that of the corresponding urbanized territory. Estimates of urban population have been made for 1920 and 1930 according to the administrative areas delimited in 1935, for 1940 and 1950 the administrative areas of the dates are used, but for 1960 use was made of data according to the new census concept of "densely inhabited districts." These irregularities inject much doubt as to the strict comparability of the figures. Comparability of the data and estimates for Korea, China (Taiwan) and the Ryukyu Islands may be similarly affected, as the systems of local administration at earlier dates were analogous to that of Japan, but have been modified in recent years.

South Asia

Middle South Asia: India, Pakistan, Iran, Ceylon, Afghanistan, Nepal
South-East Asia: Indonesia, the Philippines, Viet-Nam, Thailand, Burma, Singapore, the Federation of Malaya, Cambodia, Laos
South-West Asia: Turkey, Iraq, Syria, Israel, Saudi Arabia, Lebanon, Jordan, Kuwait, Aden

Urbanization of India and Pakistan is documented systematically, and with criteria comparable in time from the results of decennial censuses, including time series for metropolitan areas of large cities, as assembled in a recent census publication. For Burma, Ceylon, Israel, Malaya, Singapore and Turkey, series of data from censuses since 1920 have also been found. For Indonesia, it was necessary to interpolate 1930 and 1961 census data on cities and urban population. For several countries of South-East Asia, the administrative area to which urban populations are related is in doubt and data had to be selected by various rather arbitrary criteria. In the Philippines, for instance, the administrative divisions lead to an exaggerated measure of urbanization, while the opposite may be true for Thailand. For several other countries, e.g. Iran, Iraq, Nepal and Syria, there are only census returns for recent dates, and estimates for earlier dates had to be largely conjectured. To supplement gaps, recourse was had to estimates published at various dates in almanacs, encyclopedias, etc.

Soviet Union

Soviet Union: The Soviet Union

Estimates of the urban population of the Soviet Union in 1950, according to the lower size limit (20,000) here adopted, are not very firm since no census was taken between 1939 and 1959 and the official estimates of urban population include a great many smaller localities. To a lesser extent this applies to estimates for 1920, and it must be assumed that both in 1920 and

1950 the distribution of urban population by size of city was affected by the preceding periods of war. Since administrative boundaries of towns and cities are frequently re-adjusted, the estimates, at least for 1930, 1940, and 1960, are probably comparable.

Latin America

Tropical South America: Brazil, Colombia, Venezuela, Peru, Ecuador, Bolivia, British Guiana
Temperate South America: Argentina, Chile, Uruguay, Paraguay
Middle American Mainland: Mexico, Guatemala, El Salvador, Panama, Nicaragua, Costa Rica, Honduras
Caribbean: Cuba, Puerto Rico, Dominican Republic, Jamaica, Haiti

For most of Latin America, the estimates are well documented by censuses, but it is to be noted that in the two countries of largest urban population, a long time interval elapsed between successive censuses, none having been taken in Argentina from 1914 to 1947 and in Brazil from 1920 to 1940. Hence the interpolated estimates for 1930 and 1940 may be somewhat out of line. The metropolitan areas corresponding to the large cities have for the most part been defined within rather wide limits, mostly these adopted in the work of Davis.[3]

Africa

Northern Africa: United Arab Republic, Morocco, Algeria, Tunisia, the Sudan, Libya
Tropical Africa: Nigeria, Congo (Leopold-

[3] Kingsley Davis, *et al.*, *The World's Metropolitan Areas, op. cit.*

ville), Ethiopia, Ghana, Rhodesia, Kenya, Senegal, Madagascar, Angola, the Ivory Coast, Cameroon, Tanzania, Congo (Brazzaville), Mali, Sierra Leone, Guinea
Southern Africa: The Republic of South Africa

For Africa, estimates of past trends in total population are speculative, except in Northern and Southern Africa where national censuses have been taken repeatedly or periodically. Nevertheless, the documentation of urban population in Tropical Africa is not so unsatisfactory since estimates or enumerations of the population in towns and cities—which were then not so numerous—were often carried out in the colonial administrations, and the results have been published frequently enough to provide some basis for the present interpolations for particular dates.

Oceania

Australia and New Zealand: Australia, New Zealand
Other Oceania: (parts of Oceania other than Australia and New Zealand)

In Oceania, until quite recently, towns larger than 20,000 existed only in Australia and New Zealand, where censuses have been taken periodically, and metropolitan areas have been defined and could be estimated in a manner analogous with data and estimates for Northern America. Only recently a few towns elsewhere in Oceania have attained or surpassed 20,000 inhabitants, according to census data and official estimates. Hawaii is not included since it forms part of the United States.

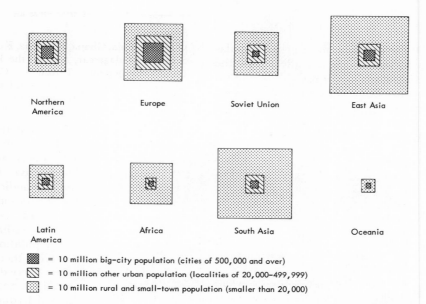

FIGURE 1

Big-City, Other Urban, and Rural and Small-Town Population in Major Areas of the World, 1920.

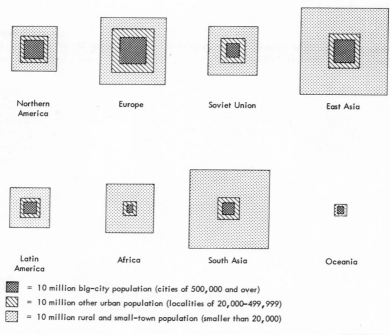

FIGURE 2

Big-City, Other Urban, and Rural and Small-Town Population in Major Areas of the World, 1940.

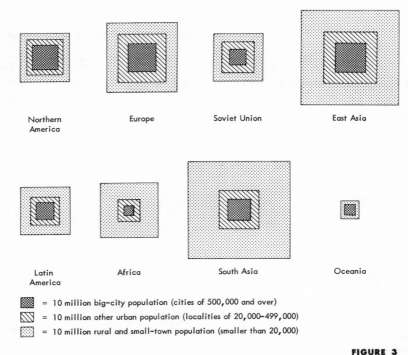

Northern America   Europe   Soviet Union   East Asia

Latin America   Africa   South Asia   Oceania

= 10 million big-city population (cities of 500,000 and over)

= 10 million other urban population (localities of 20,000–499,000)

= 10 million rural and small-town population (smaller than 20,000)

FIGURE 3

Big-City, Other Urban, and Rural and Small-Town Population in Major Areas of the World, 1960.

FIGURE 4

Big-City, Other Urban, and Rural and Small-Town Population in Major Areas of the World, as Projected to 1980.

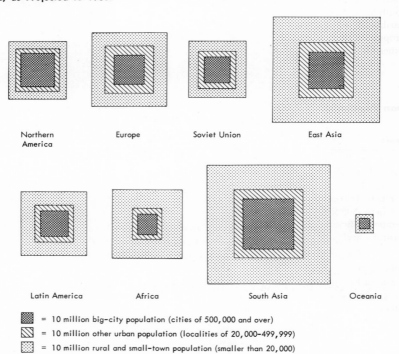

Northern America   Europe   Soviet Union   East Asia

Latin America   Africa   South Asia   Oceania

= 10 million big-city population (cities of 500,000 and over)

= 10 million other urban population (localities of 20,000–499,999)

= 10 million rural and small-town population (smaller than 20,000)

Table A.

Total Population in World Regions Grouped by Recency of Urbanization, 1920–1960
(rough estimates, in millions)

Region	1920	1930	1940	1950	1960
I. Regions at least 25 per cent urbanized by 1920					
Total of group	297.9	331.8	353.9	395.9	452.3
Western Europe	98.8	105.7	110.3	120.3	132.3
Northern Europe	62.0	65.0	68.3	72.5	75.8
Northern America	115.7	134.2	144.3	166.1	198.7
Temperate South America	14.8	18.9	22.3	26.9	32.8
Australia and New Zealand	6.6	8.0	8.7	10.1	12.7
II. Regions at least 25 per cent urbanized by 1960 but not by 1920					
Total of group	503.9	577.4	648.0	685.7	813.6
Southern Europe	82.7	92.6	102.5	108.5	117.4
Eastern Europe	81.0	90.5	97.7	90.4	99.0
Japan	55.4	63.9	72.5	83.2	93.4
Other East Asia	21.6	25.6	30.1	38.3	46.5
Soviet Union	155.3	179.0	195.0	180.0	214.4
Tropical South America	45.6	54.5	66.8	84.1	112.5
Middle American Mainland	19.4	22.5	26.9	34.7	46.8
Northern Africa	35.1	39.1	44.8	52.6	66.0
Southern Africa	7.8	9.7	11.7	13.9	17.6
III. Regions not yet 25 per cent urbanized by 1960					
Total of group	1,058.4	1,160.1	1,295.0	1,435.2	1,728.5
Mainland East Asia	476.4	501.7	532.9	563.2	654.2
Middle South Asia	333.1	370.9	422.2	479.0	579.9
South-East Asia	108.0	126.7	150.4	172.5	218.9
South-West Asia	28.7	31.4	37.5	45.2	59.1
Caribbean	9.7	11.6	13.9	16.7	20.3
Tropical Africa	100.0	115.0	135.0	155.0	192.1
Other Oceania	2.5	2.8	3.1	3.6	4.0

Table B.

Urban Population (20,000 and over) in World Regions Grouped by Recency of Urbanization, 1920–1960 (rough estimates, in millions)

Region	1920	1930	1940	1950	1960
I. Regions at least 25 per cent urbanized by 1920					
Total of group	121.3	148.3	166.4	196.0	245.9
Western Europe	37.9	43.6	49.8	52.5	62.9
Northern Europe	32.0	36.3	39.3	42.1	45.0
Northern America	43.5	58.0	64.3	83.2	112.5
Temperate South America	4.8	6.6	8.5	12.4	17.3
Australia and New Zealand	3.1	3.8	4.5	5.8	8.2
II. Regions at least 25 per cent urbanized by 1960 but not by 1920					
Total of group	77.0	105.0	154.4	182.2	268.2
Southern Europe	14.9	19.6	23.2	27.1	34.3
Eastern Europe	19.6	23.8	27.8	25.0	31.6
Japan	13.0	18.5	27.5	31.2	42.9

Table B. (Cont.)

Region	1920	1930	1940	1950	1960
Other East Asia	1.1	2.0	4.3	8.2	13.6
Soviet Union	16.0	24.0	47.0	50.0	78.0
Tropical South America	5.1	6.9	10.4	17.6	33.2
Middle American Mainland	2.0	3.0	4.1	7.3	12.5
Northern Africa	4.1	5.4	7.5	11.0	16.8
Southern Africa	1.2	1.8	2.6	3.9	5.7
III. Regions not yet 25 per cent urbanized by 1960					
Total of group	54.6	74.8	106.2	153.3	238.9
Mainland East Asia	25.0	36.1	49.8	66.4	104.0
Middle South Asia	18.2	23.6	34.5	52.6	76.6
South-East Asia	4.7	7.3	11.0	17.2	26.0
South-West Asia	4.1	3.7	5.0	7.2	13.5
Caribbean	1.0	1.6	2.2	3.3	4.8
Tropical Africa	1.6	2.5	3.7	6.6	13.9
Other Oceania	...	...	...	...	0.1

Table C.

Rural and Small-Town Population in World Regions Grouped by Recency of Urbanization, 1920–1960 (rough estimates, in millions)

Region	1920	1930	1940	1950	1960
I. Regions at least 25 per cent urbanized by 1920					
Total of group	176.6	183.5	187.5	199.9	206.4
Western Europe	60.9	62.1	60.5	67.8	69.4
Northern Europe	30.0	28.7	29.0	30.4	30.8
Northern America	72.2	76.2	80.0	82.9	86.2
Temperate South America	10.0	12.3	13.8	14.5	15.5
Australia and New Zealand	3.5	4.2	4.2	4.3	4.5
II. Regions at least 25 per cent urbanized by 1960 but not by 1920					
Total of group	426.9	472.4	493.6	503.5	545.0
Southern Europe	67.8	73.0	79.3	81.4	83.1
Eastern Europe	61.4	66.7	69.9	64.5	67.4
Japan	42.4	45.4	45.0	52.0	50.5
Other East Asia	20.5	23.6	25.8	30.1	32.9
Soviet Union	139.3	155.0	148.0	130.0	136.4
Tropical South America	40.5	47.6	56.4	66.5	79.3
Middle American Mainland	17.4	19.5	22.8	27.4	34.3
Northern Africa	31.0	33.7	37.3	41.6	49.2
Southern Africa	6.6	7.9	9.1	10.0	11.9
III. Regions not yet 25 per cent urbanized by 1960					
Total of group	1,003.8	1,085.3	1,188.8	1,281.9	1,489.6
Mainland East Asia	451.4	465.6	483.1	496.8	550.2
Middle South Asia	314.9	347.3	387.7	426.4	503.3
South-East Asia	103.3	119.4	139.4	155.3	192.9
South-West Asia	24.6	27.7	32.5	38.0	45.6
Caribbean	8.7	10.0	11.7	13.4	15.5
Tropical Africa	98.4	112.5	131.3	148.4	178.2
Other Oceania	2.5	2.8	3.1	3.6	3.9

Table D.

Urban Population (20,000 and over) As a Percentage of Total Population in World Regions Grouped by Recency of Urbanization, 1920–1960 (rough estimates)

Region	1920	1930	1940	1950	1960
I. Regions at least 25 per cent urbanized by 1920					
Total of group	41	45	47	50	54
Western Europe	38	41	45	44	48
Northern Europe	52	56	58	58	59
Northern America	38	43	45	50	57
Temperate South America	32	35	38	46	53
Australia and New Zealand	45	47	52	58	63
II. Regions at least 25 per cent urbanized by 1960 but not by 1920					
Total of group	15	18	24	27	33
Southern Europe	18	21	23	25	29
Eastern Europe	24	26	28	29	32
Japan	24	29	38	38	46
Other East Asia	5	8	14	21	29
Soviet Union	10	13	24	28	36
Tropical South America	11	13	16	21	30
Middle American Mainland	10	13	15	21	27
Northern Africa	12	14	17	21	25
Southern Africa	16	18	22	28	32
III. Regions not yet 25 per cent urbanized by 1960					
Total of group	5	6	8	11	14
Mainland East Asia	5	7	9	12	16
Middle South Asia	5	6	8	11	13
South-East Asia	4	6	7	10	12
South-West Asia	14	12	13	16	23
Caribbean	10	13	16	20	24
Tropical Africa	2	2	3	4	7
Other Oceania	0	0	0	0	2

Urbanization in Major Geographic Regions

3. Map—India, Ceylon, Pakistan, Nepal, Afghanistan: Urban Places Over 50,000

GERALD BREESE

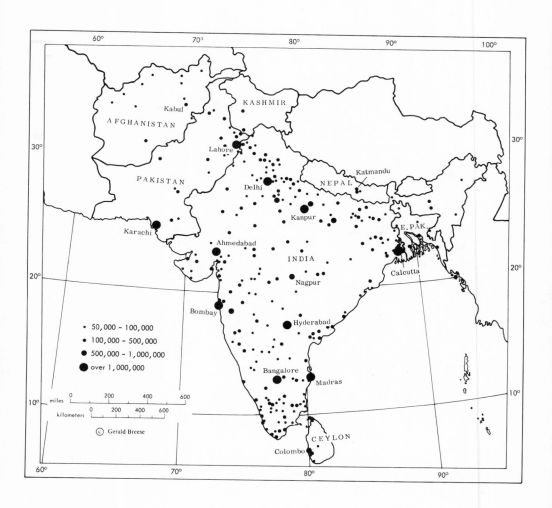

Note: *Certain cities are not shown for various reasons- Afghanistan (3), India (5). Source notes may be found on p. 555.*

4. Map—Southeast Asia: Urban Places Over 50,000

GERALD BREESE

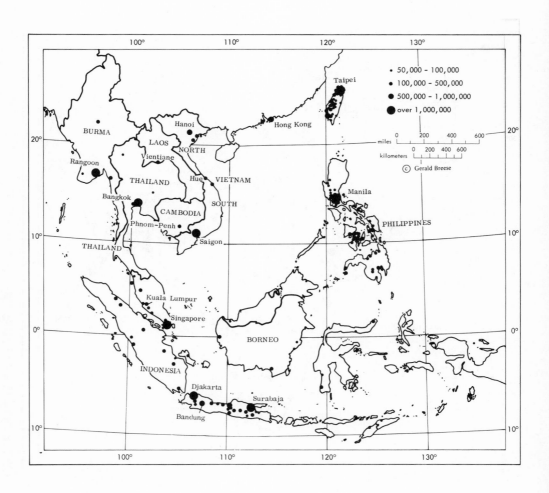

Note: *Some cities of Taiwan not shown (less than 10) for space reasons. Source notes may be found on p. 555.*

5. Map—Southwest Asia: Urban Population

GEORGE B. CRESSEY

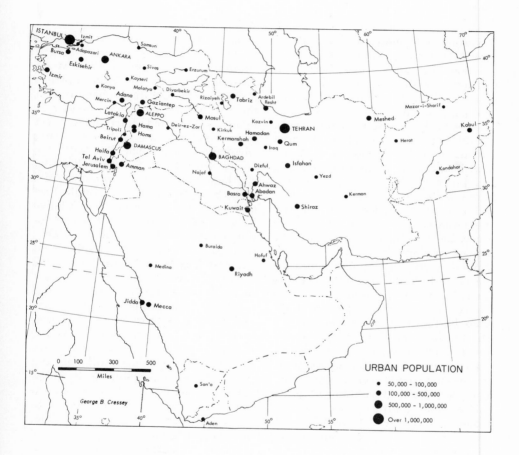

Reprinted by permission from Crossroads: Land and Life in Southwest Asia *by George B. Cressey, published by J. B. Lippincott Company. Copyright © 1960 by J. B. Lippincott Company.*

6. Urbanization in Asia

RHOADS MURPHEY

Throughout most if not all of recorded history, there seems little question that there have been and still are more people living in cities, and more cities, in Asia than in any other continent. Until about 1750 or 1800, it seems likely that Asia (used throughout this paper to refer only to the area sometimes called "monsoon Asia", from Pakistan on the west to Indonesia and Japan on the east, but excluding Soviet Asia) contained more cities and more city-dwellers than the rest of the world combined, a position which it may have regained by the end of the present century if current rates of population growth and of urbanization continue. Indeed one of the primary reasons for distinguishing the area referred to as "monsoon Asia" from the Arab-Turkish-Persian world of the Middle East and from the areas now included in Soviet Asia is the density of its population and the importance of an urban-centered "great tradition", in Robert Redfield's phrase. Monsoon Asia has had so little common cultural ground with the rest of the Asian continent that it is both arbitrary and misleading to lump them together in almost any analysis of human institutions. This is so despite the fact that

Ekistics, 21, No. 122 (January 1966), pp. 8–17. Reprinted by permission of publisher and author. This paper was delivered during a conference on International and Comparative Urban Studies held at Rutgers—The State University, in June 1965, under the auspices of the Rutgers Committee on International Education and the Urban Studies Center.

without much question the world's earliest true cities (as opposed to agricultural villages) arose in Asian Mesopotamia or in the Levantine uplands just west of it, and the probability that the rise of the first genuine cities in monsoon Asia owed something to direct or indirect contact with the earlier Mesopotamian model. But with the emergence of a civilized (literally, city-based) tradition in monsoon Asia, culture contact with the Middle East appears to have dwindled into relative insignificance (with the qualified exception of India) and the "great traditions" of south and east Asia matured and endured largely in isolation from the rest of the world. When external contact finally become of major importance, it was with the probings, colonialism, and traders of Europe and America, and it is this impact which has left the greatest marks on contemporary south and east Asia, most strikingly and perhaps most importantly in its cities.

Our knowledge of Asian urbanization is far from being proportional to its importance on the world scale. We cannot even measure with any precision what the total Asian urban population is, let alone delineate with assurance the factors responsible for its past and present growth or project its likely future shape. We are hampered both by inadequate data, reflecting imperfect census systems, and by a relative paucity of published studies. Present knowledge is, however, grossly uneven. Japan, with relatively complete and accurate data and with a history of detailed study by Japanese scholars, is in a class by itself in this as in so many other respects. Urbanization in India is more accurately measured and better analyzed and understood than in most other Asian countries apart from Japan. But China, which may currently contain more cities and more city-dwellers than any country in the world, is plagued by gross shortages of hard data of every kind, and has been given very little attention by students of urbanization. The same is true of Indonesia, the third most populous nation in Asia, with a total population well over 100 million—how much over, and how much of the total should be regarded as urban are not accurately known. China and Indonesia, in fact, illustrate particularly pointedly the data limitations which confront the student of Asian urbanization, especially by contrast with the relative wealth and reliability of census information in the West. It is not merely that precise population totals are often lacking, but that the' wide spread and variety of demographic information provided for at least the past several decades by many Western censuses is simply not available for most of Asia.

Nevertheless, it seems reasonably clear that at least a third of the present world total of urban population is now in Asia (as defined above), no matter how "urban" may be defined, but that the *degree* of urbanization in Asia is still considerably lower than in Europe or North America, since well over half of the world's total population is Asian. In neither respect—the total number of urban dwellers or the degree of urbanization—is there a reasonable correlation, by Western standards, with the absolute amount or the proportional share of industrialization, or

with per capita incomes. This suggests two apparently contradictory conclusions: that most of Asia is "overurbanized", and that urbanization in Asia is still in its early stages, with a much higher degree of urbanization clearly in prospect as industrialization and commercialization gather momentum and as the presently very high rates of urbanization continue. Indeed perhaps the most striking feature of Asian cities in the two decades since the end of World War II is their uniquely rapid growth, a phenomenon which has understandably led to both of the above conclusions. Their contradictory nature can, unfortunately, be rationalized only by assuming (as there are ample grounds for doing) that in most Asian cities living conditions will continue to deteriorate before they can improve. It may well be true that Asian urbanization has outrun its industrial-commercial base, which is the essence of the "overurbanization" argument, but this is not sufficient grounds for assuming either that this process will not continue, or that there is somehow a better viable alternative open to societies and economies which we fervently hope are already engaged in the inevitably painful process of economic growth and transformation. These and other general considerations will be discussed more fully below.

Apart from the simple shortage of reliable census figures in many Asian countries, the student of urbanization is also plagued by varying census definitions of "urban". This is of course a familiar problem even in the Western world, but it does grossly hamper comparability, and even within a single national unit may give rise to perplexing ambiguity. The varying definitions of "urban" are not however purely arbitrary, but reflect real and important differences. Probably the most important of these revolves around the nature of agricultural land use and settlement in Asia, which for the most part follow patterns distinct from any in the West. Many Asian settlements with populations well over 2000 (the lower limit of the "urban" category in the United States census) are almost exclusively agricultural in function and include or perform little or none of the functions commonly regarded as urban. In recognition of this, the Indian census sets the lower limit of the "urban" category in population terms at 5000, although it is recognized that some genuinely urban settlements may thereby be excluded. The Chinese census, on the other hand, in an attempt to adjust to a similar reality, stresses function as well as population size, setting a lower limit numerically at 2000 but including as urban many smaller settlements whose functions are clearly urban in nature—transport or small mining or manufacturing centers, for example—while excluding larger places which are primarily agricultural villages. But no census system except the Japanese takes account of another factor which also helps to distinguish Asian cities—the inclusion within the urban area —whether empirically or arbitrarily defined—of significant amounts of agricultural land and of agricultural workers. Such intra-urban land is, of course, worked extremely intensively and population densities associated with it may be at an urban or near-urban level, but it is nevertheless probably misleading to lump population figures from such areas with those from the functionally separate city.

There is the further problem of defining the spatial limits of a city for census purposes. Traditional Asian cities were relatively sharply distinct from surrounding rural areas in spatial

terms, and in probably the majority of the Asian cities of the present the rural-urban line is easier to draw than in almost any present Western city. But the tremendously high rate of urbanization characteristic of Asia especially during the past two decades, the beginnings of the kind of "transport revolution" which helped to transform Western cities, and the rise or further expansion of nearly thirty Asian cities in the million class have meant that "urban sprawl" is no longer a Western monopoly. It is at least as difficult now to make a neat census delineation of the largest Asian cities as it is for large Western cities. Tokyo and Calcutta represent the extremes; "greater Calcutta" and "greater Tokyo" are both in fact megalopolises, each including within a single contiguous urban area what were once several separate cities and making it really impossible to draw an unambiguous line around the spatial limits of either conurbation, or even around the limits of the "urban sprawl" at the peripheries, which tends increasingly to melt gradually into a rural-urban continuum along the Hooghly or around the shores of Tokyo Bay and the edges of the Tokyo basin. Such problems may be appropriate enough for Tokyo, as indisputably the world's largest city, or for Calcutta as an acknowledged urban giant, but they are beginning to be apparent or are already far advanced in many other Asian cities, notably Bombay, Karachi, Madras, Delhi, Singapore, Kuala Lumpur, Djakarta, Manila, and Osaka. In general, "urban" must be taken as what each national census says it is, while recognizing that this is not a uniform or necessarily accurate or reliable guide to reality.

One final difficulty which hampers the search for accurate and complete urban data in Asia is the very large and continuing role played by rural-urban migration. Almost every large Asian city has apparently owed half or more of its recent rapid growth to migration. But even so general a statement must be qualified, since the nature of migration makes accurate counting difficult and since in most Asian cities it is clear that many if not most migrants continue to maintain close ties with their rural origins and periodically return there; apart from this, there appears to be a significant though largely unmeasured amount of attrition which means that *net permanent* migration is less, to an undetermined extent, than gross migration as it might be revealed by a census or sample taken at any one time. As one illustration of the indeterminate or perhaps the qualified nature, both of rural-urban migration in Asia and of the completeness and validity of available data on it, one may cite the common Indian (and traditional Chinese) practice of giving one's ancestral village as place of origin or even of birth on the part of people who are unambiguously urban. At least in the Indian case, this is not entirely disingenuous since it is relatively common for urban women to go back to their villages to bear children and to return to the city domicile with their infants a few months after parturition. But uncertainties or ambiguities like these make it impossible to compile complete and accurate data on the role of migration in the growth of most Asian cities, and hence, given the admitted importance of that role, one is obliged to treat urban census figures with caution.

The reader should not, however, be left with the impression that there are no trustworthy data on Asian urbanization. Whatever their shortcomings, the data available afford students of urbanization ample opportunity to explore a field which Western scholars in particular have neglected in terms of its importance. The city has played an enormously significant role in both the traditional Asian societies of the past and in their current transformation, and any thorough understanding of the Asian half of the world must take full account of the urban factor. For students of urbanization per se, the Asian experience, past and present, offers an impressively wide and varied field which must be explored not merely for comparison with the Western experience but in order to understand the generic nature of cities. Through most of recorded history, Asia has bred more urbanism than the rest of the world. Its present rapid urbanization will not necessarily merely repeat the outlines of what has been called "the second urban revolution" in the West during the past two centuries; the urban revolution which now appears to be in progress in Asia is still in its early stages and will be shaped by Asian cultural and economic circumstances as well as by originally European innovations in manufacturing, trade, and transport.

The traditional Asian city was predominantly a political and cultural phenomenon rather than an economic one. The capitals and provincial administrative centers of the great Asian empires in China, India, Japan, and Southeast Asia functioned and were consciously intended as microcosms of the national policy—symbols of authority, legitimacy, and power, creators and molders of literate culture, seats of the dominant religious ideology, and resplendent thrones for the Great Tradition. Commercial and industrial functions were decidedly secondary, almost incidental, and were often in any case under varying degrees of control or manipulation by the state, whose chief monument was the city itself. Sites for such cities were chosen more with an eye to their administrative functions than to commercial advantage. Except for insular Japan (where productive and hence populous level land hugs the sea) and insular southeast Asia, traditional Asian cities were almost exclusively confined to inland locations from which they could best administer and control the territory of the state or best ensure its defense against incursion across what was regarded as the chief exposed frontier. Ch'ang An, Peking, and Delhi are classic examples of the former; Loyang, Nanking, Pataliputra, Ava, Ayuthia, Ankor, Polonnaruwa, and Jogjakarta of the latter. Cities were both sited and planned so as to ensure an appropriate symbolization of legitimate authority. In China and periodically in India the cities were walled (indeed the common Chinese word for *city* meant and still means also wall), not merely for protection but as a further mark of imperial or administrative sanction. City plans were in turn shaped by the great gates, one at each of the four cardinal points of the compass, from which major streets led to a center where some piece of monumental building—a drum tower, a temple, an array of government offices or troop barracks—further reinforced the symbol of authority. Commerce and manufacturing there certainly were, but although their absolute amounts were large, their relative importance rarely rivalled that of administration as the chief urban function, including the administration of trade; and commerce did not breed as in the West any significant group of independent entrepreneurs. In Japan, where cities were not walled, and in Southeast Asia where walling

was at best inconsistent, the traditional city nevertheless functioned primarily as an administrative, ceremonial, and symbolic center rather than as a base for trade.

Cities of the sort described contrast forcibly with the urban type which has been dominant in the West for most of the past two or three millennia. At the beginning of the Western tradition, the cities of classical Greece were sea-oriented and trade-oriented, as were the city colonies which the Greeks established elsewhere on the shores of the Mediterranean. Even Rome, although it became the capital of a huge empire and thus came to play both a real and a symbolic role as a center of authority and administration, was at best a hybrid in that trade remained one of its important functions through its maritime link with the port of Ostia and its incorporation of the commerce-centered Greek Mediterranean. But the greatest cities of medieval Europe were not the cathedral towns or the seats of royal power but the centers of trade—Venice, Genoa, Florence, Hamburg, Brughes—and London and Paris as commercial foci rather than as political capitals. The distinction has been preserved to the present in the case of London, where "the City", until the eighteenth century a geographically separate entity, is at least symbolically still set off from the seat of political authority at Westminster farther up the Thames. With the Age of the Discoveries, the accelerated revival of trade, and the coming of technological revolutions in agriculture, transport, and manufacturing, the Western city became and remains predominantly an economic phenomenon and with overwhelmingly economic functions.

In Asia, what was clearly a Western kind of city, derived directly from

Western experience, was in effect imported by the expanding Europeans who moved eastward in the immediate wake of the discoveries in search of trade. Their early accounts of what they observed in Asia, and of their dealings with Asian powers, have left us in fact with some of our most valuable material on the traditional Asian city, as well as on the early growth of the new kind of city which they, as entrepreneurs par excellence, began to construct on the maritime fringes of the Asian empires. They chose sites with an eye to commercial advantage in terms of overseas trade, sites which could best tap the parts of each country most productive of goods for export and which could at the same time be reached by ocean-going ships. They were interested, in other words, in the kind of access which had been of little or no concern to the builders of most traditional Asian cities; and from the nucleus of originally small trading factories, often with forts to protect them, there grew up on these sites the great majority of Asia's present large cities outside of Japan. Even in Japan, however, the growth and nature of Kobe and Yokohama link them generically to some degree with Bombay, Calcutta, Singapore, and the other foreign-founded or foreign-dominated port cities where almost all of Asia's urban growth has been concentrated during the past three centuries. Tokyo, Nagoya, and Osaka too, Japan's three urban giants, grew in considerable part along similar lines and for the same reasons: as booming centers of an expanding trade between Asia and the West, and increasingly as little urban islands of Europe-in-Asia. For it was in these port cities, from Karachi to Batavia to Dairen, that the basic institutions of post-Renaissance Europe were planted: the sanctity and freedom of private property, the virtues of free enterprise, the power and self-satisfaction of capital, and the battery of techniques which had burgeoned in Europe to carry on the business of the new urban-centered world—stock companies, agency houses, bills of exchange, banking and insurance facilities, legal safeguards and sanctions for the protection of enterprise and property, and the vastly improved means of transport which were necessary for the expanding trade which gave these cities life.

The functions which these cities performed, and the institutional structure on which they rested, were largely new to Asia, which had traditionally lacked both the economic and the institutional infrastructure for the kind of commercial enterprise which Europeans built. Physically and in their morphology the new port cities clearly revealed their Western and colonial origins. In most of them Westerners and Asians were spatially segregated for housing, with accompanying differences not only in street development and architecture but in levels of living and their spatial manifestations. Urban skylines came to be dominated by larger buildings in almost purely European or American style, and although the populations of all of them rapidly became and remained predominantly Asian, the look of at least the cities' centers was and remains unmistakably Western. The principal business of these new urban concentrations was overseas trade, and they were virtually all therefore port cities; but since they also needed to maximize access to their commercial hinterlands they often arose on or near the lower courses of navigable rivers. This in turn created increasing problems for many of them as the size of ocean-going vessels increased and as deltaic harbors became less and less adequate. But so long as ocean-going ships could reach them, with the help of assiduous dredging, the advantage of combined landward and seaward access and the commercial productivity of the areas which relatively easy access by water made tributary to each city were strong enough to offset the difficulties of their immediate sites. Only Bombay, Singapore, Manila, Hong Kong, Tsingtao, and Dairen, blessed with excellent natural harbors, escaped from such site problems, although in the cases of Bombay and Tsingtao at the sacrifice of easy access to their hinterlands. River valleys and their deltas are commonly productive places, in Asia as elsewhere, and the commercial opportunities which they presented were powerful attractions despite the navigational hazards.

There were of course important differences between the different port cities which arose as a result of the Western impact, and the list is extensive. But there is enough common ground between them to suggest that they do in fact belong to a single generic type. The largest cities in each Asian country now belong in varying degrees to this type in that they grew out of Western-founded ports and trading factories or in that they owe the bulk of their modern growth not merely to trade with the West but to the successful transplanting onto Asian urban soil of Western institutions and techniques, producing a city which was and is far more Western than traditional Asian. In most of the smaller Asian countries, the single dominant port became and remains not simply primate but the only genuine city in the national unit, in terms both of size and of what Westerners at least would regard as major urban functions. China, India,

and Japan continue of course to support a number of large older cities, once the seats of the Great Tradition, including their national capitals. But in most cases, the nature of these older indigenous cities has been transformed to such an extent that the past has been overwhelmed. So the city of Tokyo, in form and in function, has overwhelmed the old capital of Edo and its rather quaintly preserved castle in the middle of an exploding metropolis which is in many respects the heir of the Western impact rather than of the traditional *bakufu*. In all of the countries of Southeast Asia, sensitive new nationalism has still not prevented the originally colonial or foreign-influenced port city from becoming the national capital under independence. Not only was there no reasonable alternative, no other genuine city in any of these smaller countries with situational advantages and existing urban resources to rival those of the alien port, but the very origin and growth of nationalism took place in these foreign-dominated cities, where the Western model was planted for Asians to emulate.

There are now no Asian cities where the traditional form or function has been preserved unscathed. Indeed perhaps the major significance of the European-dominated port cities since the sixteenth century has been their role as centers of economic and institutional change which spread from them throughout the rest of each country and which has penetrated and altered even the urban citadels of the Great Tradition. Delhi and Peking are fully caught up in the process of revolutionary economic change, having abandoned their role as administrative guardians of the status quo. Ava, Pegu, Ayuthia, Polonnaruwa, Ch'ang An, and other inland capital cities of the past exist now only as archeological sites. "The Asian city" is now a hybrid, part Asian and part Western, not merely in terms of its origins but in terms of its present functions, its physical character, and its morphology. Distinct functional types may of course be discerned, as among cities in the West, but just as Western cities have grown more and more alike as economic and technological change [has] accelerated, so Asian cities become more like one another and more like commercial-industrial cities everywhere else in the world. In general, then, the similarities between Asian and Western cities have during the past century or two become more striking than the differences. There are nevertheless some differences remaining, and some which seem likely to endure.

Some of these have already been touched on at the beginning of this essay. It is by no means clear, for example, that the West's experience with the process of urbanization will be duplicated in Asia, nor even that it will necessarily go as far, in terms of the proportion of the total population living in cities. If we take a population figure of 20,000 as a safe urban minimum in any area, about 15 per cent of the present Asian population is urban, as against about 45 per cent in the United States and about 40 per cent in Europe. It is far from certain that most Asian economies (again with the exception of Japan) can produce or can tolerate the truly gargantuan urban population which would be represented by 40 per cent of population totals as they will be by the end of the present century. On the other hand, there is also inadequate basis for assuming that urbanization in Asia can or will continue only in the same proportion to industrialization and commercialization as in the Western experience. It has already, in the view of many,

dangerously exceeded that proportion, and yet there are still no significant signs of a major or permanent slowing of the urbanization rate. No one even superficially familiar with living conditions in large Asian cities can wholly disregard the argument that most of Asia is already seriously "overurbanized". But this perhaps over-glib term has never been more than vaguely defined, much less proven. Even the present frighteningly crowded cities, lacking in the bare minimum of what is referred to as "social overhead"— housing, water supplies, sanitation, public services,—let alone amenities, represent what are probably the most dynamic forces in the process of economic development and exert critically important productive and catalytic effects. Less urbanization would probably be worse than more, either as a symptom of lesser vigor in the economy or as a cause. It is, after all, in cities that economic growth concentrates, especially of the kind which Asia is currently seeking—industrialization. There are no cost-free solutions to the problem of economic development, and short-run misery for some may be an inevitable prelude to longer-run improvement for others, in Asia as in the past experience of the West. With some obvious exceptions, there are probably not more productive uses for capital or for labor in most Asian countries than in the cities, and investment there probably yields quicker returns and with a greater multiplying effect.

Even in the West, the rate and pattern of urbanization and its correlation with industrialization varied widely as between different countries and at different periods, and it is clearly doing so in Asia at present. Urbanization has been most rapid since 1945 in Japan, where Tokyo for example added an average of 300,000 to its population in each of the eleven years following the end of the war. (Tokyo Metropolitan Government, "Problems of an Excessively Growing City and the Development of a Capital Region", Tokyo, 1957, p. 2). This represented to some extent a recovery from the abnormal loss of urban population, especially from Tokyo, during the last years of the war, but more importantly it reflects an unprecedented rapid rate of economic growth, including industrialization. Japan as a whole has probably experienced the most rapid rate of urbanization in the history of the world, especially in the period since 1920. Hong Kong is obviously a special case which is hardly comparable with national units, but as a single city (including Kowloon and contiguous urban areas) its rate of increase in population since 1945 undoubtedly tops the list, and it also represents the peak of urban population density. Its growth, however, has rested on an equally high rate of industrialization. Malaya (including Singapore but excluding the rest of Malaysia) has also been characterized by very rapid urbanization, again in relation to a high rate of economic growth, and the same has been true of Taiwan. Urbanization rates since 1945 have been to varying degrees lower in Indonesia, the Philippines, South Korea, Vietnam, Thailand, Laos, Cambodia, Burma, Ceylon, India, and Pakistan, at least in part as a reflection of lower rates of economic growth than in Japan, Malaya, Hong Kong, and Taiwan, although with the possible exceptions of Laos and Cambodia urbanization rates for these countries were nevertheless high by world standards and especially in the cases of India, Pakistan, Thailand, and the Philippines. It is difficult or impossible to measure

overall urbanization rates in China since 1945 or since 1949 in the absence of complete or accurate census figures, especially for city populations even in the one modern census which has been taken in 1953. Reports in the Chinese press do, however, make clear that there has been a phenomenal growth of many cities, some of them virtually new, as a result of the government's policy of concentrating new industrial investment in areas previously neglected. Lanchow, Paotou, and Urumchi, for example, have grown exceptionally rapidly, while Shanghai, still the largest Chinese city, has had its growth controlled by government restrictions on in-migration and by forced removals of what were regarded as excess numbers for return to the countryside or for reassignment to new areas or urban construction and industrialization in the northwest or in Sinkiang.

Except for its larger scale, there does not seem to be anything about this process in Asia which differs significantly from the Western experience, where cities also grew, especially in the earlier stages of modern industrialization and urbanization, more through migration than through natural increase and where there was serious overcrowding ("overurbanization") before employment, housing, and municipal services began to catch up with booming city populations. The difference in Asia, in large part as a result of the much greater scale involved, may be that it will take longer for urban life to reach minimum acceptable standards, or that they may never attain current, let alone future, Western urban standards. Population densities in most Asian cities have already reached enormously high levels, and this may indeed be the most significant single respect in which Asian urbanism differs from urbanism in the West. In India, for example, there are an average of about 150,000 people per square mile in Old Delhi as a whole, at least three times the figure for the most crowded sections of American cities. The worst or most crowded wards of Delhi, Bombay, or Calcutta show almost incredible densities ranging from 300,000 per square mile to over 450,000. Such fantastic crowding of often illiterate city dwellers under slum conditions further increases the difficulties of accurate census taking.

BIBLIOGRAPHY

The foregoing article has attempted to summarize in very general terms some of the salient features of Asian urbanization, the general status of present knowledge of it, and some of the outstanding problems which confront the student. In what follows, an attempt will be made to summarize more specifically the work which has been done on and in the separate regions of Asia, principally from the geographical point of view.

Japan

Japan has been a relatively highly urbanized country for at least the past two centuries. Studies of Japanese urbanization have also been made both more appropriate and more fruitful by the relative abundance of reliable urban data, as one reflection of the sophistication of economic, educational, and technological growth in Japan. Unfortunately from the Western point of view, a great deal of the published material on Japanese urbanism is in Japanese, but some is also available in English and the total amount is rich and varied. The Association of Japanese Geographers established a Committee on Urban Studies in 1958, whose report titled *Research Materials on Urbanization* was published in 1959. (S. Yamaga, ed., *Toshika Kenyu Shiryo*. Tokyo, 1959.) The report is primarily an inventory and

bibliography, which has since been updated by S. Kiuchi, one of Japan's leading urban geographers, in an English-language article. (S. Kiuchi, "Recent Developments in Japanese Urban Geography", ANNALS, Assoc. of Amer. Geographers, 1963; 93–102). All but a few of the studies mentioned in these two accounts are in Japanese. They include analyses of functional urban types, urbanization rates, rural-urban migration, "metropolitanization", economic base, land use, morphology, urban spread and absorption, urban influences on rural areas, inter-urban communications and flow, wage rates, and land prices. Considerable work has also been done in central place studies, the use of gravity models, densities and intensiveness, industrial location, historical studies of specific cities and city regions, and physical studies of urban sites. Some attention has also been paid by Japanese urban geographers to cross-cultural comparison, and S. Kiuchi has in particular stressed the morphological differences between Japanese and Western cities. (S. Kiuchi, "Problems of Comparative Urban Geography", in *Tsujimura Taro Sensei Koki Kinen, Chirigaku Rombunshu* ("Geographical Essays in Honor of Prof. Tsujimura's Seventieth Birthday") Tokyo, 1961, pp. 557–73).

Urban planning has been increasingly emphasized in the literature on Japan, as a reflection of the virtual explosion of city populations and urbanized areas during the past two decades, and at least three Japanese journals are devoted to it: *Toshi Mondai, Toshi Mondai Kenkyu,* and *Shisei.* Most Japanese cities now have their own planning boards, many of which also carry out extensive studies of their own urban areas. (See for example the voluminous English-language report prepared for a U.N.T.A.B. mission to Japan titled *Basic Materials for the Comprehensive Development Plan of the Hanshin Metropolitan Region,* 2 vols., Osaka, 1960). The "castle-town" origins of many of

Japan's cities have been examined in a great variety of published studies, some primarily historical, others which focus on current urban morphology and structure as they have been influenced by earlier forms. (See for example J. W. Hall, "The Castle Town and Japan's Modern Urbanization", FAR EASTERN QUARTERLY, 1955; 37–56 (English); K. Tanabe, "The Development of Spatial Structure in Japanese Cities with Regard to Castle Towns", *Science Reports of Tohoku University* VIIth Series, Geography, No. 8, 1959, pp. 88–105 (English); T. Matsumoto, "The Structure of Modern Castle Towns", *Geog. Review of Japan*, 1962; 97–112 (articles in this journal are in Japanese, with short English summaries). But the bulk of Japanese urban studies has been concentrated on contemporary problems, especially on what the Japanese literature refers to as "metropolitanization", the process of big-city expansion, suburbanization, regional concentration, changes in urban structure and morphology as a result of growth and of changes in transport and industrialization, and adjustments in the urban hierarchy. (For a recent review and some general conclusions, see T. Ishimizu, "The Present Status of Urbanization Studies among Japanese Academic Geographers", *Geog. Review of Japan*, 1962; 362–73. See also the forthcoming biographical essay by N. S. Ginsburg, "Urban Geography and Non-Western Areas", to appear in P. Hauser and L. Schnore, eds., *The Study of Urbanization;* I am indebted to Prof. Ginsburg for most of the inventory and bibliographical material presented here, especially on Japan, for which his forthcoming work gives much greater detail).

Western-language studies by geographers on Japanese urbanism are still discouragingly few, especially in proportion to the wealth of data and the impressive contributions of Japanese geographers. J. D. Eyre and J. H. Thompson have studied urban food supply problems and agricultural land use (J. D. Eyre, "Sources of Tokyo's Fresh Food Supply", *Geog. Review*, 1959; 455–76; J. H. Thompson, "Urban Agriculture in Southern Japan", *Economic Geography*, 1957; 224–37) and Eyre has also analyzed the sources of migrants to Tokyo, Osaka, and Nagoya in a series of revealing maps. (Eyre, "Regional Variations in Japanese Internal Migration", *Papers of the Michigan Academy* XLIX (1964) 271–84). Older studies of urban origins, forms, and distribution by R. B. Hall and G. T. Trewartha are still valuable, (R. B. Hall, "The Cities of Japan; Notes on Distribution and Inherited Forms", *Annals*, Assoc. of Amer. Geographers, 1934; 175–200; G. T. Trewartha, "Japanese Cities; Distribution and Morphology", *Geographical Review*, 1934; 407–17.) and P. Scholler has more recently examined modern metropolitan growth. (P. Scholler, "Wachstum und Wandlung Japanischer Stadtregionen", *Die Erde*, 1962; 202–34). But of all of the areas of Asia, Japan offers the greatest opportunity to Western students of urbanization, and the least realized. The China field is proportionately much less extensively worked, but Japan is not only more highly urbanized but is equipped with a wide range of dependable data and an impressive body of knowledge as a result of the efforts of Japanese scholars over many years. Western sociologists and anthropologists have begun to make major contributions to our knowledge of Japanese urban life, (See most notably R. P. Dore, *City Life in Japan*, Berkeley, 1958; O. Shunsuke, "The Urban Phenomenon in Japan", *Journal of Asian Studies*, 1964; 122–29, and his many references; also T. O. Wilkinson, "A Functional Classification of Japanese Cities, 1920–1955", *Demography*, Spring, 1964) but for other Western students of urbanization this is still largely an untilled and potentially richly rewarding field.

China

While it is true that any study of modern urbanization in China must confront what amounts almost to a vast statistical void, traditional or pre-modern China accumulated without question the most immense body of detailed data on virtually every aspect of human experience that has ever been preserved from any culture. Much of traditional Chinese culture, and especially its literate aspects, centered in the city so that a great deal of the materials which have been preserved deal with urban phenomena. Very little use has yet been made of these data, and especially of the thousands of county (*hsien*) gazeteers. Some indication of their value for urban studies is provided by two revealing studies by S. D. Chang, which focus on the functions and distribution of the *hsien* (county) capitals as administrative centers through two thousand years of Chinese history. (S. D. Chang, "Some Aspects of the Urban Geography of the Chinese Hsien Capital", *Annals*, Assoc. of Amer. Geographers, 1961; 23–45; and "Historical Trends in Chinese Urbanization", *Ibid.*, 1963; 109–43). Some limited attention has also been paid to the capital cities and their symbolic role, particularly Peking but also Ch'ang An. (See for example A. Wright, "Symbolism and Function; Reflections on Ch'ang An and Other Great Capitals", forthcoming in *Journal of Asian Studies*, August, 1965; *Ibid.*, "Ch'ang An, 583–904", in *Historic Ages of the Great Cities*, London, 1964). The predominantly administrative consequences in institutional and locational terms are also considered and briefly contrasted with Western models, in an article by Murphey. (R. Murphey, "The City as a Center of Change: Western Europe and China", *Annals*, Assoc. of Amer. Geographers, 1954; 349–62). In more general terms, the traditional Chinese city remains largely unstudied, as the representative of what was clearly the major urban tradition in the world until a century or two ago. See however E. Balazs, "Les Villes Chinoises", *Receuils de la Soc. Jean Bodin*, Vol. 6, 1954; W. Eberhard "Data on the Structure of the Chinese City in the Preindustrial Period", *Ec. Dev. and Cultural Change*, April, 1956).

The treaty-ports have been given proportionately greater attention, but still relatively superficially, although for them as well there is a considerable body of data, principally in the records of the Maritime Customs, one of the oases in the statistical desert of modern China. Voluminous Western first person and secondary accounts from the nineteenth and early twentieth centuries are also available. There is as yet only one book-length geographical or specifically urban study of any of the treaty-ports, although it does treat the largest and most important of them, Shanghai, and attempts to generalize from the Shanghai case. (R. Murphey, *Shanghai: Key to Modern China*, Cambridge, Mass., 1953). Ginsburg, Spencer, and others have contributed smaller studies of other treaty-ports, including an example of those developed largely under the Japanese in Manchuria. (N. S. Ginsburg, "Ch'ang Ch'un", *Economic Geography*, 1949; 290–307; N. S. Ginsburg, "Ch'ing Tao", *Economic Geography*, 1948; 181–200; J. E. Spencer, "Changing Chungking; The Rebuilding of an Old Chinese City", *Geographical Review* 1939; 46–60; M. Hatch, "The Port of Tientsin", *Geographical Review*, 1935; 367–81; R. M. Hughes, "Hong Kong; An Urban Study", *Geogr. Journal*, 1951; 1–23; S. G. Davis, *Hong Kong in its Geographic Setting*, London, 1949). G. T. Trewartha's two articles on urban functions and distributions in pre-communist China are hampered by dependence on unreliable data and by superficial acquaintance with the Chinese setting. (G. T. Trewartha, "Chinese Cities; Origins and Functions", *Annals*, Assoc. of Amer. Geographers, 1952; 69–93, and "Chinese Cities; Numbers and Distribution", *Ibid.*, 1951; 331–47).

The great acceleration of urban growth in China since 1949 has unfortunately not been accompanied by increased scholarly attention, primarily because of data shortages. On the basis of the incomplete data available, a few tentative analyses have been attempted: (The most useful of these is probably M. B. Ullman, "Cities of Mainland China; 1953 and 1958", International Population Reports, Series P-95, Washington, 1961, which suggests a classification of cities according to both size and function. See also T. Shabad, "The Population of Chinese Cities", *Geogr. Review* 1959; 32–42, which relies mainly on Russian sources, J. S. Aird, "The Size, Composition, and Growth of the Population of Mainland China", International Population Reports, Series P-90, Washington, 1961, and J. P. Emerson, "Manpower Absorption in the Non-Agricultural Branches of the Economy of Communist China", *China Quarterly*, 1961; 69–84) but even the gross outlines of Chinese urbanization during the past decade are still largely unknown. Material available in enormous volume from the Chinese periodical and scholarly press, in Chinese and in selected translation, is seldom directly helpful, in part because accurate statistical data are not available domestically either, although there are frequent generalized references to new or rapidly growing cities, to migration patterns, to urban living conditions, and to the urban-related aspects of planned industrial location.

Contemporary Chinese geography concentrates virtually exclusively on regional resource development and on physical geography, and its journals publish almost nothing directly concerned with urban analysis. The relatively small volume of Chinese geographical publication before 1949 includes a small number of primarily descriptive accounts of individual cities, but their usefulness to Western scholars is further limited by the language barrier. In summary, our knowledge of urbanism and urbanization in China is extraordinarily slight, and especially so by contrast with the size of the problem and with its great historical depth. It seems particularly regrettable that we are at least for the present unable to see how in this outstandingly important case modern urbanization, with a significant industrial component, is grafted onto or transforms a pre-existing administrative urban structure of some completeness, and how the original treaty-ports are also to be integrated in what is already clearly becoming an expanded hierarchy heavily influenced by political considerations.

Southeast Asia

The existing geographical literature on urbanism in Southeast Asia appropriately reflects the relatively recent origin of any extensive urbanization, most of which has occurred during the last century and a half at most, and directly as a result of the colonial and commercial activities of Westerners and/or Chinese. The origins and nature of these cities which now in every case dominate each country in Southeast Asia are examined in three parallel articles which nevertheless duplicate one another surprisingly little. (D. W. Fryer, "The Million City in Southeast Asia", *Geogr. Review*, 1953; 474–94; N. S. Ginsburg, "The Great City in Southeast Asia", *Amer. Journ. of Sociology*, 1955; 455–62; and R. Murphey, "New Capitals of Asia", *Econ. Dev. and Cultural Change*, 1957; 216–43). More detailed work is seriously hampered by the shortage of adequate or reliable statistical data, especially for Indonesia, Thailand, Vietnam, and Burma. An account of these handicaps is given in an article by R. J. Neville, (R. J. W. Neville, "An Urban Study of Pontian Kechil, Southwest Malaya", *Journ. of Tropical Geog.* 1962; 32–56) which is however based mainly on work in Malaya where census and other relevant data are comparatively more abundant and dependable. As an understandable consequence, and also as a result of the presence of at least two major universities in Malaya (at Singapore and at Kuala Lumpur) with extensive research staffs and facilities, a disproportionate share of the published literature on urbanization in Southeast Asia deals with Malaya. (E. H. G. Dobby, "Settlement Patterns in Malaya", *Geogr. Review*, 1942; 211–32; *ibid.*, "Singapore, Town and Country", *Geogr. Review*, 1940; 84–109, D. F. Allen, *The Major Ports of Malaya*, Kuala Lumpur, 1951, and *The Minor Ports of Malaya*, Singapore, 1953; E. Cooper, "Urbanization in Malaya", *Population Studies*, 1951; 117–31; H. Sendut, "Patterns of Urbanization in Malaya", *Journ. of Tropical Geog.*, 1962; 114–30; T. G. McGee, "The Cultural Role of Cities; A Case Study of Kuala Lumpur", *Ibid.*, 1963; 178–96). Somewhat surprisingly, there has been relatively little attention paid by American geographers to urban phenomena in the Philippines, and in particular no adequate study of Manila, although one aspect of its commercial structure has been examined. (W. E. McIntyre, "The Retail Pattern of Manila", *Geogr. Review*, 1955; 66–80). Two other Philippine studies attempt to establish a wider set of constructs. Ullman's examination of the urban hierarchy and of inter-island trade movements provides important comparative analysis with actual and theoretical hierarchies in other parts of the world. (E. Ullman, "Trade Centers and Tributary Areas of the Philippines", *Geogr. Review*, 1960; 203–18) and Spencer attempts to supply a more reliable set of estimates for city sizes and for the structure of the urban hierarchy than the census figures alone suggest. (J. E. Spencer, "The Cities of the Philippines", *Journ. of Geog.*, 1958; 288–94). Wernstedt has also examined the important Philippino commercial

frame of inter-island trade in his study of Cebu. (F. L. Wernstedt, "Cebu; Focus of Philippine Inter-island Trade", *Econ. Geog.* 1957; 336–46). One of the few geographical studies of urbanism in Indonesia is also concerned with city sizes, and with the rank-size rule, which the author finds does not appropriately fit his Indonesian data. The article attempts in addition to measure the proportions of non-Indonesian population (mainly Chinese) in each of the several cities considered, a matter which is of course especially relevant to all Southeast Asian cities. (W. A. Withington, "The Kotapradja or "King Cities" of Indonesia", *Pacific Viewpoint*, 1963; 87–91). Urban structure and morphology are however probably the subjects of the largest single group of published studies on Southeast Asia, including the recent beginnings of a literature in the planning field, where attention has been focused in particular on Singapore (J. M. Frazer, "Town Planning and Housing in Singapore", *Town Planning Review*, 1953; 5–25; see also planning studies of Manila, Saigon, and Djakarta published in United Nations, *Public Administration Problems of New and Rapidly Growing Towns in Asia*, Bangkok, 1962). Earlier studies centering primarily on urban form include those by Spate and Trueblood on Rangoon (almost the only urban geographical study of Burma yet published in English), Dobby on Singapore (referred to above), and Withington on Medan. (O. H. K. Spate and L. Trueblood, "Rangoon; A Study in Urban Geography", *Geog. Review*, 1942; 56–73; W. A. Withington, "Medan; Primary Regional Metropolis of Sumatra", *Journ. of Geog.*, 1962; 59–67). The sociological/anthropological literature on the predominantly urban Chinese in Southeast Asia is relatively extensive, and a good deal of it deals directly with urbanism. (See for example G. W. Skinner, *Leadership and Power in the Chinese Community of Thailand*, Ithaca, 1958; Jacques Amyot, *The Chinese*

Community of Manila, Chicago, 1960; D. Willmot, *The Chinese of Semarang*, Ithaca, 1960; Barrington Kaye, *Upper Nankin Street, Singapore*, Singapore, 1960). Other perceptive analyses of the sociological aspects of urbanization in Southeast Asia include Geertz's recent study of the development of different forms of entrepreneurship in Javan towns, and Bruner's study of group identity. (Clifford Geertz, *Peddlars and Princes; Social Development and Economic Change in Two Indonesian Towns*, Chicago, 1963; E. M. Bruner "Urbanization and Ethnic Identity in North Sumatra", *Amer. Anthropologist*, Vol. 63; 508–21). The rapid mushrooming especially of Djakarta but also of Singapore, Kuala Lumpur, Manila, and Bangkok, accompanying urban sprawl, and the observable effects of local culture, national and political roles, and local economic realities on originally Western urban forms and functions have still to be examined in any detail.

India

Next to Japan, urbanization in India has received the greatest amount of research attention, but by both Indians and foreigners, and virtually all of the literature is in English. Probably its most important single theme is "over-urbanization", in a variety of forms including the implications for economic planning and investment, schemes for urban development or re-development ("urban community development"), the dimensions and nature or rural-urban migration, surveys of living conditions in the cities, the debate over industrial "decentralization", and the problems of both urban and rural unemployment and underemployment. Discussions of Indian urbanization have also had to confront an essentially Ghandian anti-urban and pro-village sentiment which is still expressed, although it has had little or no apparent effect on the urbanization rate or in particular on the massive scale of rural-urban migration.

The 1961 Census of India showed a slight slowing down of the rate of urbanization, as compared with the rate between 1941 and 1951, but this is not easy to account for beyond drawing attention to the possibility that living conditions and general economic opportunity in at least the larger cities may have been perceived by potential migrants from the rural areas as in balance slightly less favorable, a conclusion which almost certainly does accord with reality. Not only are the larger cities increasingly and dangerously overcrowded but the beginning of some improvement in levels of living, and perhaps of employment, are apparent in parts of the countryside. Continued concentration of industrial investment and of population growth in the already crowded larger cities is however argued as rational, even though some new investment may also be allocated to other urban centers such as the new or expanded steel towns under the third five-year plan. The Bombay and Calcutta conurbations combined now contain about 40 percent of all Indian industrial plants, but such a degree of concentration is probably economic and does not necessarily distinguish India from industrial countries in the West. In any case, planning decisions for the regional allocation of urban investment should be governed by economic cost-benefit analysis rather than by sentiment or political considerations. The biggest cities will probably continue to grow relatively rapidly, and will continue to generate both more overcrowding and more urgent planning problems. The Calcutta conurbation alone may include eighty million people by the end of the present century.

The best single guide to Indian urbanization is the volume edited by Roy Turner which resulted from a 1960 seminar in Berkeley, California. (Roy Turner, ed., *India's Urban Future*, Berkeley, 1962). Papers by Indians and Americans deal with urbanization rates and the role of migration, urban morphology and structure, sociological aspects of urban life, the economic implications of urbanization, the centralization-decentralization issue, and the role of the planner. A final paper by B. F. Hoselitz surveys the literature on urbanization in India and provides an excellent annotated bibliography. (An earlier version of the same paper appeared as "The Cities of India and Their Problems" in *Annals*, Assoc. of Amer. Geographers, 1959; 223–31). As Hoselitz points out, there are a large number of socio-economic studies of individual Indian cities, representing probably the largest single body of urban data, but fewer comprehensive analyses which succeed in providing an adequate spatial frame and which also consider urban structure and function, transport, hinterland relations, and planning problems. Outstanding among the latter are the two studies of R. L. Singh, on Banaras and Bangalore. (R. L. Singh, *Banaras: A Study in Urban Geography*, Banaras, 1955, and *Bangalore: A Study in Urban Geography*, Banaras, 1964. See also J. M. Datta, "Urbanization in Bengal", *Geogr. Review of India*, 1956; 19–23; E. Ahmad, "Origins and Evolution of the Towns of Uttar Pradesh", *Geographical Outlook*, 1956; 38–58; O. H. K. Spate and E. Ahmad, "Five Cities of the Gangetic Plain", *Geogr. Review*, 1950; 260–78). John Brush has provided in his article in the Turner volume a good survey of Indian urban morphology, necessarily with considerable historical reference, an approach which also characterizes most of the many studies of urban form in Indian journals. (John Brush, "The Morphology of Indian Cities", in Roy Turner, *op. cit.* pp. 57–70. M. N. Nigam, "The Evolution of Lucknow", *Natl. Geographic Journ. of India*, 1960; 30–46; R. V. Joshi, "Urban Structure in Western India", *Geogr. Review of India*, 1956; 7–19; C. D. Deshpande, "Cities and Towns of Bombay Province; Aspects of Urban Geography", *Indian Geogr. Journal*, 1941; 284–97;

P. P. Karan," The Pattern of Indian Towns; A Study in Urban Morphology", *Journ. Amer. Inst. of Planners*, 1957; 70–75; V. R. Prabhu, "Dhawar; A Study in Indian Urban Landscapes", *Bombay Geogr. Magazine*, 1953; 56–63). The work of the geographer N. R. Kar is also notable for its comprehensive approach to the urban phenomenon especially of Calcutta, and for its use of statistical models, structural theory, and other recently developed analytic techniques as well as more traditional methods. His several studies are valuable not only because they help to illumine the nature and problems of India's largest city but also because they specifically delineate the differences and the similarities between Calcutta and Western cities, while at the same time stressing the controlling importance of the Western impact, in the case of Calcutta and of the Bengali and Indian urban hierarchy more generally. (N. R. Kar, "Calcutta als Weltstadt", in J. M. Schultze, ed., *Zum Probleme der Weltstadt*, Berlin, 1959; *ibid.*, "Urban Characteristics of the City of Calcutta", *Indian Population Bulletin*, 1960; 34–67; *ibid.*, "Pattern of Urban Growth in Lower West Bengal", *Geogr. Review of India*, 1962; 42–59; *ibid.*, "Urban Hierarchy and Central Functions Around Calcutta, in Lower West Bengal, India, and Their Significance", in K. Norborg, ed., *Proceedings of the I.G.V. Symposium in Urban Geography, Lund, 1960*, Lund, 1962).

One of the few recent studies which also considers urban patterns before the British period is the paper by Robert Crane, (R. I. Crane, "Urbanism in India", *Amer. Journ. of Sociology*, 1955; 107–14) but the British impact, especially on urban morphology, is treated in almost all of the analyses of contemporary city forms. The alien origins of the great port cities have been given relatively extensive historical treatment, but the geographic implications have been for the most part examined only incidentally. (For a specific geographic study of the Indian prototype of the treaty-ports, however, see R. Murphey, "The City in the Swamp; Aspects of the Site and Early Growth of Calcutta", *Geogr. Journal*, 1964; 241–56, which stresses the essentially Western nature of the city, the parallel with Bombay, Madras, and the port cities of Southeast Asia and China, and the role which Calcutta was the first to play in spreading economic change). Bombay and Calcutta have been studied most extensively in the general urban literature, and especially in socio-economic terms. Bombay has received particular attention as the chief center of the cotton textile industry, and a recent volume deals in great detail with the widespread implications of the recruitment of an urban industrial labor force. (M. D. Morris, *The Emergence of an Industrial Labor Force in India: A Study of the Bombay Cotton Mills 1854–1947*, Berkeley, 1965); Socio-economic work on Calcutta (See especially S. N. Sen, *The City of Calcutta: A Socio-Economic Survey*, Calcutta, 1960) has more recently been overshadowed by planning research on a very large scale as part of the project to produce a comprehensive metropolitan plan for Calcutta, still in its relatively early stages and for the most part not yet available in print. The similarly ambitious Delhi Planning Project is outlined at the pilot stage by B. Chatterjee, and dealt with in greater and more current detail by Clinard. (B. Chatterjee, "Urban Community Development in India; The Delhi Pilot Project", in Roy Turner, *op. cit.* pp. 71–93; M. B. Clinard, *Urban Community Development and Slums*, Glencoe, 1965—nine chapters of this work are devoted to the Delhi Project, and one to a similar but smaller project in Dacca, East Pakistan). The establishment in 1958 of an Indian journal devoted entirely to planning, *Urban and Rural Planning Thought* (Delhi), is a further indication of the rapid increase of planning research and activity in recent years.

Marketing systems and city hinterlands have been the subject of several smaller studies. (See for example Robert Mayfield, "The Range of a Good in the Indian Punjab", *Annals*, Assoc. of Amer. Geographers, 1963; 38–49; S. N. Reddy, "Vegetable Markets and Regional Relationships of Hyderabad City", *Geog. Review of India*, 1961; 24–40; W. C. Neale, H. Singh, and J. P. Singh, "Kurali Market; A Report on the Economic Geography of Marketing in Northern Punjab", *Ec. Dev. and Cultural Change*, 1965; 129–68; F. K. Khan and M. H. Khan, "Delimitation of Greater Dacca", *Oriental Geographer*, 1961; 95–120). Functional classifications of cities, by employment, by size, and by population density have been attempted by Lal, Ahmad, and Learmonth, (A. Lal, "Some Aspects of the Functional Classification of Cities and a Proposed Scheme for Classifying Indian Cities", *Natl. Geog. Journ. of India*, 1959; 12–24; N. Ahmad, "The Urban Pattern in East Pakistan", *Oriental Geographer*, 1957; 37–39; A. T. Learmonth *et al.*, *Mysore State: An Atlas of Resources*, Calcutta, 1960, and *Mysore State: A Regional Synthesis*, Calcutta, 1962) and P. P. Karan has related industrial changes to urban growth. (P. P. Karan, "Changes in Indian Industrial Location", *Annals*, Assoc. of Amer. Geographers, 1964; 336–54).

India may present the clearest or at least the best known Asian example of the mixing of Asian and Western urban forms and of the long-term operation of Western-derived and Western-managed economic forces on existing and developing urban systems and on individual cities: What may make Indian cities particularly distinctive is their rapid growth at a time when the economy as a whole has not achieved substantial and permanent net gains of a self-perpetuating sort which can leave sufficient margin for basic "social investment", hence the arguments centering around "overurbanization". How far into the future such a pattern may extend, and to what degree Indian cities will become more reflective of Indian cultural and economic conditions and less reflective of Western influences are fruitful subjects for speculation. For the present, the amount and quality of published research on Indian urbanism, and its unique availability to Western scholars, plus the recent boost given to urban studies by the major planning efforts in Delhi, Calcutta, and elsewhere leave our understanding at a more satisfactory level than anywhere else in Asia outside of Japan, and suggest that it will continue to increase rapidly as the process of urbanization enters what may be a more distinctively Indian stage.

It remains to mention, and to acknowledge, some general works which deal with urban problems in Asia as a whole. By far the most valuable of these for the present essay is the long chapter by Norton Ginsburg titled "Urban Geography and Non-Western Areas", forthcoming in *The Study of Urbanization* and edited by Philip Hauser and Leo Schnore. Most of Ginsburg's chapter deals in fact with Asia and provides an excellent critical summary of the published literature. An earlier volume edited by Philip Hauser, *Urbanization in Asia and the Far East*, the proceedings of a joint UN/UNESCO/ILO Seminar on Urbanization in the ECAFE region in 1956 and published by UNESCO in Calcutta in 1957, is still useful both for its individual papers on a variety of social and economic aspects of urbanism and for the general summary by Hauser. "The City in the Asian Polity", Hugh Tinker's inaugural lecture of 1963 as Professor of Government and Politics at the School of Oriental and African Studies, University of London, published in pamphlet form in 1964, provides a graceful and stimulating survey of the character and significance of the traditional Asian city and contrasts it with the basically different kind of city which arose as a result of the Western impact. Gideon Sjoberg's *The Preindustrial City, Past and Present* (Glencoe, 1960) is an unreliable guide to traditional Asian urbanism, but the long critical review of Sjoberg's book by Paul Wheatley (*Pacific Viewpoint*, 1963; 163–88) titled "What the Greatness of a City Is Said to Be" helps to set the record straight and adds much additional material on the great Asian cities of the past.

In general, however, the study of urbanization in Asia must be regarded as only just begun, both in terms of the past and present scale of the problem and of its likely future dimensions. If, as seems probable, Asia and most of the rest of the world are still in the early stages of a process which may in the forseeable future make them as urban-centered as Europe and the United States, this is one of the most urgent fields of research for all students of human society.

7. The Demographic Situation and Prospective Population Trends in Asia and the Far East

UNITED NATIONS-ECAFE SECRETARIAT

IV. URBANIZATION

Information on the magnitude of migration from rural to urban areas is very limited in the ECAFE region. A clue to the size of the rural-urban movement, however, is given by the statistics of urban population growth, which are available for most countries, even though use of these data inevitably involves complicated problems of definition of urban and rural areas which differ from country to country, and may be changed from time to time.

Table 1 shows the proportion of urban to total population according

Table 1
Proportion of Urban Population to Total Population in Specified Countries, Around 1960

Country	Year	Percentage of Urban Population
ECAFE region		
Brunei	1960	43.6[a]
Cambodia	1958	12.8
Ceylon	1963	18.9[a]
China: Mainland	1956(E)	14.2
Taiwan	1955(E)	56.0
Hong Kong	1961	76.6[a]
India	1961	18.0[a]
Indonesia	1961	14.8[a]
Iran	1956	30.1

UN-ECAFE, Report on the Asian Population Conference and Selected Papers, *held in New Delhi, India, December 10–20, 1963 (New York: UN-ECAFE, 1964), pp. 80–83. Reprinted by permission.*

Table 1 (Cont.)

Country	Year	Percentage of Urban Population
ECAFE region		
Japan	1960	63.5[a]
Korea, Republic of	1960	28.6[a]
Malaysia:		
Federation of Malaya[c]	1957	42.7[b]
North Borneo[c]	1960	14.9[a]
Sarawak[c]	1960	15.0[a]
Singapore[c]	1960(E)	62.6
Nepal	1961	2.8[a]
Pakistan	1961	13.1[a]
Philippines	1960	29.9[a]
Thailand[c]	1960	12.5
Australia	1954	78.9
New Zealand	1959(E)	55.2
Economically advanced countries outside the ECAFE region		
England and Wales	1951	80.8
France	1954	55.9
United States	1950	64.0

(E) Estimates derived from *United Nations, Demographic Yearbook 1960.*

[a] Estimates derived from national census data.

[b] When gazetted areas having 10,000 population and over are taken as urban areas, the corresponding figure is 26.5 per cent in 1957. See *1957 Population Census of the Federation of Malaya* Report No. 14, p. 6.

[c] All municipalities recorded in the 1960 population census are taken as urban areas.

to the definitions used in the censuses of various countries of this region, compared with the situation in a number of industrialized countries outside the ECAFE region.

As stated above, the definition of an urban area is not uniform among the countries shown in Table 1.[1] For example, the Federation of Malaya takes as "urban" towns and villages of 1,000 or more inhabitants; India, localities (municipalities and towns) of 5,000 or more inhabitants, and having definite urban characteristics; Japan, municipalities usually having 30,000 or more inhabitants; and Korea, incorporated cities of 40,000 or more inhabitants.

Even with due regard to the variations in definitions, it is apparent that there are great contrasts in the proportions of urban population among countries in the ECAFE region. Percentages ranging from 3 per cent in Nepal and less than 20 per cent in China (mainland), India, Pakistan, Thailand, Indonesia and a number of smaller countries to well over 50 per cent in China (Taiwan) and Japan among the Asian countries (not to mention Hong Kong and Singapore) cannot be explained merely in terms of different definitions. The percentages of urban populations shown for Australia and New Zealand are in accord with the general pattern of economically advanced countries with varying degrees of industrialization. It is also apparent that the countries in the Asian part of the region are much less urbanized on the average than the economically advanced countries of the West.

The difficulties due to variations in definitions are lessened when attention is confined to the population in large cities. Table 2 shows percentages of population in cities having 100,000

Table 2
Percentage of Total Population in Localities of 100,000 Inhabitants or More

Country	Year	Percentage of Population in Localities of 100,000 Inhabitants or More
ECAFE region		
Burma	1958(E)	5.3
Cambodia	1959(E)	8.7
Ceylon	1963	5.9[a]
China: Mainland	1953	8.3
Taiwan	1959(E)	25.0
Fed. of Malaya	1957	10.8
Hong Kong	1961	75.9
India	1960(E)	8.0
Indonesia	1959(E)	9.4*
Iran	1960(E)	18.1
Japan	1960	40.5[b]
Korea, Republic of	1959(E)	22.8
Laos	1956(E)	6.3
Nepal	1952–54	1.3
Pakistan	1961	7.3*
Philippines	1960	9.9
Singapore	1959(E)	62.8
Thailand	1960	24.9[c]
Viet-Nam, Republic of	1959	10.8
Australia	1959(E)	57.4
New Zealand	1960(E)	32.2
Economically advanced countries outside the ECAFE region		
England and Wales	1958(E)	51.0
France	1954	16.8
United States	1950	29.5

Unless otherwise stated the percentages are derived from United Nations, *Demographic Yearbook, 1960.* (E) indicates an estimate of population, otherwise the data refers to national population census returns.
[a] Department of Census and Statistics. Population census results.
[b] 1960 Population Census of Japan, Volume 1.
[c] *Thailand Population Census, 1960,* Changwad Series, 1962–1963. Data refers to amphurs (districts) with 100,000 inhabitants or more.
* Provisional.

---

[1] For a detailed review of definitions of urban population used in countries of Southern Asia, see Chandrasekaran, C., and Zachariah, K.C., "Concepts used in defining urban population and data available on its characteristics in countries of Southern Asia", paper presented to the UNESCO Seminar on Urban-Rural Differences and Relationships, held in New Delhi, December 1962.

inhabitants or more for ECAFE countries and a few economically advanced countries outside the region.

Percentages of total population in localities of 100,000 inhabitants or more in most ECAFE countries are lower than 20 per cent and in about half of them lower than 10 per cent. Japan, China (Taiwan), the Republic of Korea, Thailand, Australia and New Zealand as well as the exceptional cases of Hong Kong and Singapore have higher percentages. It may be noted that Japan has by this definition a higher percentage of urban population than France, Germany and the United States.

Rural-urban migration movements in developing countries are typically characterized by a more rapid growth of the population in the "primate" or great city than of the total population. Table 3 shows the annual rates of population growth in selected large

Table 3

Annual Rates of Population Growth in Selected Cities and Countries of the ECAFE Region

City	Period	Annual Rate of Growth of City Population (per cent)	Country	Annual Rate of Growth of Total Population 1950–1960 (per cent)
Colombo	1953–63	1.7[a]	Ceylon	2.3
Taipei	1956–50	4.5	China (Taiwan)	3.4
Kuala Lumpur	1947–57	6.2	Fed. of Malaya	2.9
Bombay[b]	1951–60	3.3		
Delhi	1951–60	4.3	India	1.9
Madras	1951–60	2.0		
Djakarta	1955–59	10.8	Indonesia	2.0
Tehran	1956–60	5.0	Iran	2.2
Tokyo[c]	1950–60	4.9	Japan	1.2
Karachi	1951–61	4.2	Pakistan	2.1
Manila[d]	1948–60	1.3	Philippines	3.1
Bangkok/Thonburi	1947–60	6.9	Thailand	3.2

Except otherwise noted rates of population growth of cities derived from data in United Nations, *Demographic Yearbook, 1960*, Table 7. Population growth rate of each country based on United Nations, *Provisional Report on World Population Prospects* ..., *op.cit.*

[a] Department of Census and Statistics, Ceylon, from 1963 Census returns. The population of the "Greater Colombo" area grew 2.4 per cent during the same period, which is still a smaller rate than that in which the total population of Ceylon grew (2.7 per cent; 1953–63).

[b] According to a study of migration in Greater Bombay by S. N. Agarwala ("A method for estimating decade internal migration cities from Indian census data", *The Indian Economic Review*, Vol. IV, No. 1, February 1958, Table No. 4), it is suggested that net in-migration contributed about 45 per cent of the population growth in Greater Bombay during 1941–51.

[c] The role of migration in population increase in the Tokyo Metropolis is extremely important. More than 70 per cent of the population increase is ascribed to net in-migration. According to estimates the contribution of migration was 75 and 72 per cent during each of the quinquennia 1950–55, 1955–60. Consequently, the share of excess of births over deaths in population increase was less than 30 per cent. See Kuroda, T., "Population", Bureau of Resources, Agency of Science and Technology, 1963, Table 4 (mimeographed paper, text in Japanese).

[d] Refers to the City of Manila only. Rate of population growth per annum in metropolitan Manila (Manila and adjoining cities and towns) during the period 1948–57 was 4.5 per cent which is higher than that of the total population. See United Nations, *Population Growth and Manpower in the Philippines, 1960*, p. 11.

cities of Asian countries in the ECAFE region. The fact that these rates in most cases markedly exceed the rates of population growth of the countries in which the cities are situated, is some indication of the increasing degree of urbanization being brought about by large rural-urban migration.

So far as it is possible to judge by available data, there is apparently no great difference in the rate of natural increase between urban and rural areas in many countries of this region. It is therefore inferred that the increase in urban population is mostly attributable to migration into cities from rural areas. Population growth in all cities listed in Table 3 except Colombo and Manila was at a much faster rate than that of total population. While Thailand would double its total population in about 22 years at the present rate of growth of 3.2 per cent per annum, the Bangkok/Thonburi urban complex would double in less than 10 years if the present rate of growth [of] 6.9 per cent per annum should persist.[2]

In the Federation of Malaya, it is noted that the population growth in the states of Selangor, which contains the capital city, and Negri Sembilan, which is adjacent to Selangor, rose to remarkably high rates during the intercensal period, 1947–1957, that is, 3.6 and 4.3 per cent, respectively against the national growth rate of 2.8 per cent.

Recent disproportionate rates of urban growth are especially noteworthy in the case of Japan. During the intercensal period, 1955–1960, a rapid urbanward redistribution of population took place within this country. Twenty-

six out of a total of 46 prefectures experienced a decrease in population during this period. Three-fourths of 3,511 civil administration units, city, *ku*, town and village, showed population decreases; and in only one-fourth of them was there an increase of population. Nationwide, drastic changes in the distribution of the population are indicated in the pattern of increases and decreases in the population of various localities. For localities containing less than 30,000 inhabitants, the smaller the population, the larger was the rate of population decrease. In contrast, for localities having more than 30,000 inhabitants, the larger the population, the higher was the increase rate of the population, except in the biggest cities of more than one million population. More than 90 per cent (92.6) of the population increase during the intercensal period accrued in only six industrial, urbanized prefectures in which the six largest cities are located. About 40 per cent of the total increase of population in the same period occurred in the Tokyo Metropolis, which contains about 10 per cent of the total population of Japan.[3] Immigration

[3] Figures for Japan are based on the 1960 and 1955 population census data. Population growth rates by the size of localities during the period of 1955–60 are as follows:

Size of Localities	Population Growth Rate (per cent)
Total population	4.6
More than a million inhabitants	17.5
500,000 — 1,000,000	26.4
200,000 — 500,000	10.4
100,000 — 200,000	9.5
50,000 — 100,000	4.6
30,000 — 50,000	1.6
20,000 — 30,000	−1.7
10,000 — 20,000	3.1
5,000 — 10,000	−4.7
Less than 5,000 inhabitants	−5.6

Source: 1960 population census of Japan.

[2] The percentage of the population of Bangkok and Thonburi, combined, to total population continued to increase from 5.2 per cent in 1919 to 8.1 per cent in 1960, accelerating after 1947, *Thailand Population Census, 1960; Whole Kingdom,* 1962.

into the big industrial, urbanized zones has accelerated in recent years at a rate never experienced before in the history of Japan. This causes serious concern from the standpoint of regional socio-economic planning in the country.[4]

In connection with regional population growth in Japan, a remarkable change should be noted. The natural increase of population has recently played a more significant role in the growth of population in industrial, urbanized prefectures than in rural, agrarian prefectures due to a slight increase in the birth rates in the former against the continuous decline in the birth rates in the latter. The rates of natural increase, for example in Tokyo and Osaka prefectures, in 1961, have finally exceeded even the highest rates observed in some rural prefectures, resulting primarily from the opposite trends in fertility stated above.[5]

---

[4] The Population Problems Deliberation Council, Advisory Committee for the Minister of Health and Welfare, has been engaged for a few years in studies on the grave effects on regional development of tremendous migration flows into a few industrial, urbanized areas and has recently submitted a report to the Government (17 August 1963).

[5] See *Vital Statistics*, Division of Health and Welfare Statistics, Ministry of Health and Welfare, 1961, and *Population Estimates by Prefectures as of 1 October 1962*, Bureau of Statistics, Japan, 1963, Table 4 (Text in Japanese).

8. Cities of Mainland China: 1953-1959

MORRIS B. ULLMAN

This report is one of a series of studies of the population and labor force of various countries conducted by the Foreign Manpower Research Office of the Bureau of the Census. It brings together information from Chinese, Russian, and other sources on the population of urban places in Mainland China. Although some summary and analytical data are presented, the main emphasis has been placed on the assembly, adjustment, and presentation of data on the population of the individual urban places from sources not readily accessible to demographers and others who need data on the population of cities in Mainland China. The text discusses the nature of the sources, the relevant aspects of the urban administrative system, and the methods and assumptions involved in the compilation of the data, so that users may be advised of limitations which might affect applications of these data. Geographic, economic, and other supplementary information is also included to enhance the general utility of the report.

The bulk of the research was conducted under the direction of Mr. Morris B. Ullman, who prepared most of the tabular and appendix materials and wrote the first draft of the report.

After Mr. Ullman left the Bureau, Dr. John S. Aird undertook the preparation of the report for publication. Special credit is due to Mrs. Florence Yuan, whose handling of Chinese sources and mastery of detail were an invaluable help in assembling and preparing the materials upon which this report is based. Thanks are also due to Dr. Lawrence Krader, under whose direction the initial research was conducted, and to Dr. Ernest Ni for the development of some of the materials.

The Wade-Giles Romanization is observed for Chinese words and titles given in this report. Spelling of place names follows the usage of the U.S. Board of Geographic Names; authorized conventional spellings are used for names of provinces and some large urban places. . . .

Frequent use has been made of translations of Chinese sources published by the American Consulate General in Hong Kong. To simplify the footnotes, the following abbreviations are used in references to these materials:

Current Background (*CB*),
Survey of China Mainland Press (*SCMP*), and
Extracts From China Mainland Magazines (*ECMM*).

I. INTRODUCTION

Prior to the Communist era, information on the cities of China was subject to the same ambiguities and contradictions which affected other aspects of Chinese demography. Students of urban development in China differed not only in their estimates of the size of particular cities and the number of cities in various size-classes but also in their

U. S. Bureau of the Census, Foreign Manpower Research Office, International Population Reports, Series P-95, Number 59 (Washington, D.C.: Government Printing Office, August 1961), pp. 1–17, 35–36, 38–39 only. Reprinted by permission of author and publisher.

estimates of the proportion urban of the total population. Since the establishment of the present regime, there has been a greater degree of consistency among official reports as to the number and size of urban places.

The 1953 census, despite its limitations, should have made it possible to identify the major populated points in Mainland China and to determine their approximate size with sufficient uniformity of definition to assure comparability.[1] Instead of having to work with

[1] A critique of this census and discussion of its limitations is included in U.S. Bureau of the Census, *The Size, Composition, and Growth of the*

scattered fragments of information, it should have been possible to obtain data collected in essentially the same way throughout the country. Unfortunately, detailed census reports on the population of urban places are not yet available,[2] hence it is still necessary to assemble much of the needed information indirectly from secondary sources.[3]

The earliest general publication of the 1953 census results for urban places in China consisted of a list of population figures for places of 100,000 inhabitants or more given in a book by A. G. Shiger, published in 1957 in Moscow.[4] The population figures reported in this source (which did not distinguish rural from urban population living within city boundaries) were found to be generally in agreement with those given in other sources, principally the Chinese press and the *Great Soviet Encyclopedia*.[5]

A distribution of urban places by size-class and province presented in an

article describing the preparation of a wall map of population density afforded a further check and extension of the list given by Shiger. The map described in this article was based on 1953 census data and showed all places of 20,000 inhabitants or more by population size-class. It also gave the names of all places of 50,000 inhabitants or more. With the aid of other Chinese maps, urban places of 20,000 to 50,000 inhabitants were also identified by name. In the article on the population density map, as in Shiger, there is an indication that not all of the population of a "city" area is classed as urban. The article states that

. . . populations of cities are based on the administrative boundaries. Where the suburbs are too big, the agricultural population in these suburbs is subtracted when possible and included in the population density of the county (*hsien*).[6]

Comparison of Shiger's figures with the density map suggests that few population totals were much affected by these adjustments,[7] which probably means that the geographers who prepared the density map were unable in most instances to obtain separate figures for suburbs.

An additional check on city size

Population of Mainland China, by John S. Aird, International Population Statistics Reports, Series P-90, No. 15, 1961.

[2] An advertisement in a Chinese journal in 1958 indicated that a report containing this information had been published, but no copy of this report has yet been located outside China. The title advertised was as follows: State Statistical Bureau, *Chung-hua jen-min kung-ho-kuo 1953 nien jen-k'ou tiao-ch'a tzu-liao* (*Data on the 1953 Population Census of the Chinese People's Republic*), Peiping, 1958.

[3] However, since the information apparently is all based on the data from the 1953 census, figures for different urban places should be comparable.

[4] A. G. Shiger, *Administrativno-territorial'noye deleniya zarubezhnykh stran* (*Administrative-Territorial Divisions of Foreign Countries*), 2nd ed., Moscow, 1957.

[5] *Bol'shaya sovetskaya entsiklopediya* (*Great Soviet Encyclopedia*), 2nd ed., Moscow. Some additional population figures were obtained from this source, mainly for places of 50,000 to 100,000 inhabitants.

[6] I I-ch'ü, "Kuan-yü 'Chung-kuo jen-k'ou mi-tu kua-t'u'te shuo-ming" ("On the Explanation of the 'Wall Map of the Population Density of China'"), *Ti-li chih-shih* (*Geographical Knowledge*), November 1956, pp. 502–504.

[7] The major difference noted was for Foochow, in Fukien Province, for which Shiger gave the population as 553,000 but which was included in the 200,000 to 500,000 population group on the population density map. In addition, three other places for which population figures were given by Shiger and two others for which population figures were given in the *Great Soviet Encyclopedia* were shown in different size classes on the density map.

was provided by the 1957 *Atlas of the Chinese People's Republic*,[8] which indicated the population size-class for various urban places, based on 1953 census data. The maps of this atlas helped in the identification of some of the smaller places.

With the information obtained from these and other sources, an analysis of the urban and rural population totals reported by the census is presented in chapter II. This chapter also attempts to indicate the place of the municipality in the administrative system and to define the concepts "urban" and "rural" as used in Mainland China. Chapter III presents distributions of the estimated total and urban population of urban places by size of place. The exclusively urban population is shown by province, [and] by size class of urban place. Chapter IV points out the major factors affecting population growth in urban places and presents estimates of this growth between 1938 and 1958.

II. URBAN PLACES AND URBAN POPULATION

The Place of the Municipality and the Town in the Administrative Structure

The government of Communist China is highly centralized but its functions are performed through four levels of administration: (1) the central government; (2) the provinces; (3) the counties (*hsien*); and (4) the townships (*hsiang*).[9] The urban places of Mainland China, in a practical working sense, include the municipalities (*shih*) and towns (*chen*). (The

explicit definition of urban places is given on page 89.) The numbers of principal administrative divisions for various years are given in Table 1.

The municipality in China is an urban place which has been designated as a separate administrative unit. The "independent" municipality, of which there are now two (Peiping and Shanghai), is an administrative unit directly under the central government, hence at the same level as the provinces. Within the provinces there are municipalities administratively equivalent to counties.[10] Municipalities within counties (administratively equivalent to townships) were never numerically important, and apparently this designation is no longer used.

All urban agglomerations in China with 100,000 inhabitants or more are municipalities. An urban agglomeration of less than 100,000 inhabitants may also be a municipality if it is an important industrial or mining area, the location of an important provincial government agency, a comparatively large collection and distribution center, or a key urban center in a remote frontier area. In practice, the terms "city" and "municipality" are often used interchangeably in Chinese sources, the meaning in any given instance being discernible only from the context.

---

[8] *Chung-hua jen-min kung-ho-kuo ti-t'u chi* (*Atlas of the Chinese People's Republic*), Shanghai, 1957.

[9] A description of the administrative divisions can be found in several sources including Hsüeh I-yüan, "Chung-hua jen-min kung-ho-

kuo hsing-cheng ch'ü-hua te hua-fen" ("The Administrative Divisions of the People's Republic of China"), *Acta Geographica Sinica*, vol. 24, no. 1, 1958, pp. 84–97; and Ministry of Interior, *Chung-hua jen-min kung-ho-kuo hsing-cheng ch'ü-hua chien-ts'e* (*A Simplified Handbook of the Administrative Divisions of the Chinese People's Republic*), Peiping: Fa-lü ch'u pan she, 1957.

[10] In autonomous regions, which are minority areas, some of the municipalities are under the administration of subdivisions called "autonomous *chou*." In the Inner Mongolia Autonomous Region (I.M.A.R.) they may be under the corresponding units called "leagues."

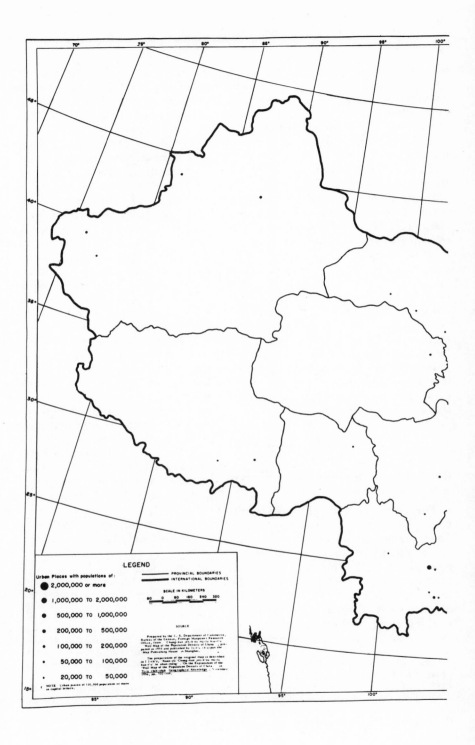

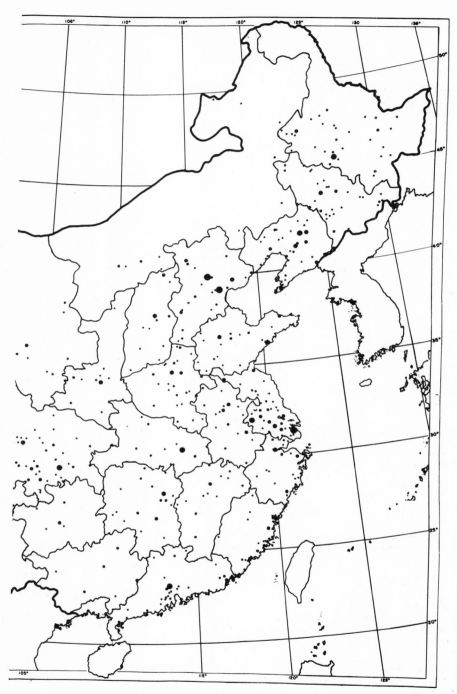

FIGURE 1

Urban Places of Mainland China with 20,000 Inhabitants or More: 1953
(based on data of June 1953 population census)

85

When the census began in the spring of 1953, there were 13 independent municipalities under central jurisdiction. By November 1954, at the time of the census report, all except three had been reduced to the level of provincial municipalities, and their populations included in the provincial totals. Later, Tientsin was made a provincial municipality, leaving only two municipalities directly under the administration of the central government. Though the num-

Table 1

Number of Administrative Divisions: 1947 to 1958[a]

Year	Provinces and Regions	Counties and Other Units at the County Level	Municipalities		Towns
			Independent	Provincial or Lower	
1958[b]	25	1,747	2	183	([c])
1957[d]	24	2,097	3	173	3,621
1956[e]	24	2,082	3	171	3,672
1955	24	[f]2,117	3	161	([c])
1954[g]	26	2,116	3	163	([c])
1953	30	[f]2,135	[h]14	152	[f]5,402
1952	30	[f]2,152	[h]13	[i]124	([c])
1951	[f]37	[f]2,182	[h]13	([c])	([c])
1950	[j]37	[f]2,204	[h]13	[j]122	([c])
1949	32	([c])	[h]12	([c])	([c])
1947[k]	[l]34	[m]2,063	12	46	([c])

[a] Excludes Tibet and the Chamdo Area. Numbers refer to the end of indicated year unless otherwise specified. Where no specific source is indicated, the number was derived on the basis of known changes as given in various sources.

[b] State Statistical Bureau, *Wei-ta te shin-nieh—Chung-hua jen-min kung-ho-kuo ching-chi ho wen-hua chien-she ch'eng-chiu te t'ung-chi (The Great Ten Years—Statistics on Economic and Cultural Construction Achievements of the People's Republic of China)*, Peiping: Jen-min ch'u-pan she, September 1959.

[c] Not available.

[d] Ministry of Interior, *Chung-hua jen-min kung-ho-kuo hsing-cheng ch'ü-hua chien-ts'e (A Simplified Handbook of the Administrative Divisions of the People's Republic of China)*, Peiping: Fa-lü ch'u-pan she, 1958.

[e] Ministry of Interior, *Chung-hua jen-min kung-ho-kuo hsing-cheng ch'ü-hua chien-ts'e (A Simplified Handbook of the Administrative Divisions of the People's Republic of China)*, Peiping: Fa-lü ch'u-pan she, 1957.

[f] Hsüen I-yüan, "Chung-hua jen-min kung-ho-kuo hsing-cheng ch'ü-hua te hua-fen" ("The Administrative Divisions of the People's Republic of China"), *Acta Geographica Sinica*, vol. 24, no. 1, February 1958, pp. 84–97.

[g] Chou En-lai, "Report on Government Work," *CB*, no. 296, September 28, 1954 (data probably as of September 1954), p. 14.

[h] Chang Li-man, "Special Features in the Changes of Administrative Areas in China," *Cheng fa yen-chiu (Political and Legal Studies)*, no. 5, 1956; translated in *ECMM*, no. 57, November 19, 1956, pp. 1–14.

[i] *Jen-min shou-ts'e 1952 (People's Handbook, 1952)*, 3rd ed., Shanghai, August 20, 1952 (data as of January 1952).

[j] *Jen-min shou-ts'e 1951 (People's Handbook, 1951)*, 2nd ed., Shanghai, February 10, 1951 (data probably as of November 1950).

[k] Ministry of Interior, Bureau of Population, *Ch'üan kuo hu-k'ou t'ung-chi (Population Statistics of China)*, 1947.

[l] Excludes Taiwan Province and the Inner Mongolia Autonomous Region which was created in May 1947 by the Communists in their occupied area.

[m] Excludes 24 banners and 2 leagues scattered in Suiyüan Province and in the northeast provinces.

ber of independent municipalities has declined, the number of municipalities of all levels has been increasing.

The larger municipalities are made up of city and suburban districts (*shih-ch'ü* and *chiao-ch'ü*). Additions to or reductions of municipal areas usually involve specific counties, townships, or sometimes towns. As a consequence, municipal boundaries today usually follow the boundaries of those townships or counties which have been absorbed.

The Rural Population of Municipalities and Towns

The total population of the 164 municipalities in 1953 was 52,354,000 (Table 4). However, since the urban population of the 164 municipalities was 43,523,000, it can be estimated that 83 percent of the total population was urban and 17 percent was rural.

There is little information on the proportion of rural population in individual municipalities. Peiping had 708,000 persons classified as rural at the time of the census and Tientsin had 365,000.[11] Nanking, with a total population of 1,092,000, had a rural population of over 270,000,[12] and Lan-chou's 397,000 population included 62,000 rural persons.[13] In other sources also there are references to "peasants" or to agricultural activities in the suburbs

[11] State Statistical Bureau, "Kuan-yü ch'eng hsiang hua-fen piao-chun jo-kan chu-yao wen-t'i te shuo-ming" ("Explanation of the Criteria Established for the Demarcation on Rural and Urban Areas"), *Hsin Hua pan-yüeh-k'an* (*New China Semi-Monthly*), no. 3, 1956, p. 8.

[12] Chou Li-san, "Nan-ching shih te ti-li" ("Geography of Nanking Municipality"), *Ti-li chih-shih* (*Geographical Knowledge*), no. 2, 1952, p. 35.

[13] "Lan-chou te kuo-ch'ü yü wei-lai" ("The Past and the Future of Lan-chou"), *Ti li chih-shih* (*Geographical Knowledge*), no. 6, 1957, pp. 243–247.

of municipalities, which would support the conclusion that the municipalities include both urban and rural population. Since the proportion of the total population classified as urban is known only for a few places, the total populations must be given here for individual municipalities, even though these totals include an unknown proportion officially classified as rural.

Statistically, the urban population of the municipality in Mainland China may be compared to the total population of the urbanized area in the United States and the total population of the municipality to the total population of the standard metropolitan statistical area. There does not seem to be any unit strictly comparable to our "city." The old walled city, which is the center of the typical Chinese city, usually includes an area similar to the older central section of the American city, but apparently it is different from the American "political" city.

[A] map of Peiping Municipality (Figure 2) illustrates the concept of the municipality. The city proper, the greater part of which is the old walled city, consists of the four city districts (*shih-ch'ü*) in the center. In the other districts, the numbered places are towns and county centers, each of which would be separately classified as urban or rural.

Usually the designation of a place as a town in official publications signifies urban status, but townships may also be considered urban. Towns are defined in a discussion by the State Council in 1955 as administrative units under the control of counties.

Towns may be established at locations of local or state agencies of the country level or above. Towns may also be established if necessary in areas with a total of 2,000 or more inhabitants if a considerable number of them are residents engaged in

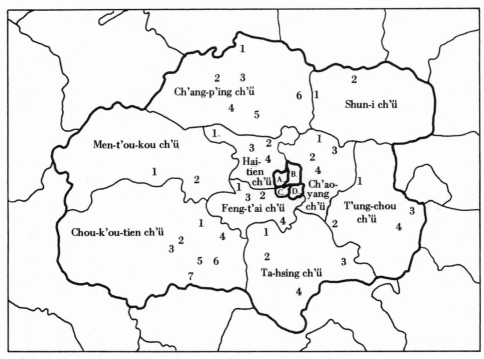

Prior to the annexation of four counties north of the area outlined.

A - Hsi-ch'eng ch'ü

B - Tung-ch'eng ch'ü

C - Hsüan-wu ch'ü

D - Ch'ung-wen ch'ü

Ch'ang-p'ing ch'ü

 1. Shih-san-ling
 2. Nan-k'ou
 3. Ch'ang-p'ing
 4. Yang-fang
 5. Sha-ho
 6. Hsiao-t'ang-shan

Men-t'ou-kou ch'ü

 1. Ta-t'ai
 2. Men-t'ou-kou

Chou-k'ou-tien ch'ü

 1. Tun-li
 2. Fang-shan
 3. Chou-k'ou-tien
 4. Liang-hsiang
 5. Tou-tien
 6. Chiao-tao-chen
 7. Liu-li-ho

Hai-tien ch'ü

 1. Wen-ch'uan
 2. Ch'ing-ho
 3. Ch'ing-lung-ch'iao
 4. Hai-tien

Feng-t'ai ch'ü

 1. Pei-hsin-an
 2. Feng-t'ai
 3. Ch'ang-hsin-tien
 4. Nan-yüan

Ta-hsing ch'ü

 1. Huang-ts'un
 2. P'ang-ke-chuang
 3. Ts'ai-yü
 4. Li-hsien-chen

Shun-i ch'ü

 1. Kao-li-ying
 2. Niu-lan-shan

Ch'ao-yang ch'ü

 1. Sun-ho
 2. Chiu-hsien-ch'iao
 3. Tung-pa
 4. Pa-li-chuang

T'ung-chou ch'ü

 1. T'ung-chou
 2. Ma-chü-ch'iao
 3. Hsi-chi
 4. Ma-t'ou

FIGURE 2

A Simplified Map of Peiping Municipality: October 1958

commerce or industry. In minority areas, towns may be established if necessary in areas with a total of less than 2,000 inhabitants if a considerable number of them are engaged in commerce or industry.[14]

The trend in the number of towns has been downward since 1953 (Table 1). The decline may be partly accounted for by a change in the method of classification, as another source suggests:

The reduction of the number of towns was due to the fact that the market towns in lumber and forestry areas and small industrial mining districts, where agencies of town administrative authority were not established, were included in the number of towns in 1953, whereas the 1956 figure includes only those in which town administrative authority was established.[15]

The Urban Population and the Urban Place

The total population of Mainland China, according to the census of June 1953, was 582,603,417. The urban population was reported as 77,257,282, or 13 percent of the total. Although this proportion is low compared with that for other countries, the total population of China is so large that, in absolute numbers, the urban population exceeds that of any other country in the world except the United States and the U.S.S.R.

The reported urban population included 43.5 million living in 164 municipalities, sometimes also referred to in Mainland China publications as large- and medium-sized cities. The remainder of the urban population, 33.7 million, lived in 5,404 towns. The latter included 7.8 million living

in 256 towns of more than 20,000 persons each, 24.7 million living in 4,228 towns of between 2,000 and 20,000 persons each, and 1.2 million living in 920 towns of less than 2,000 persons each. (See Table 4.)

According to the definition given in the 1955 resolution of the State council, urban places in China are those with 2,000 inhabitants or more of whom at least half are engaged in nonagricultural pursuits. Places of 1,000 to 2,000 population may also be classified as urban if not less than 75 percent of the population is nonagricultural, provided also that these places are industrial, commercial, rail, educational, or research centers, or are residential areas for workers. Places with sanitorium facilities in which patients constitute more than half of the local permanent population may also be classified as urban. Finally, the location of a municipal people's committee or of a people's committee of the county level or above is considered urban, except for mobile administrative units in the pastoral areas.[16]

A separate section of the resolution distinguishes the suburban areas of an urban place from the purely urban areas. An explanation published by the State Statistical Bureau notes that "in urban areas the population is more concentrated, commerce and industry are better developed, and the majority of the inhabitants are engaged in pursuits other than agriculture.[17] Since the proportions urban and rural in the reported and estimated figures on the population between 1949 and 1956 published by the State Statistical

---

[14]State Council Decision on the Establishment of Municipalities (*shih*) and Towns (*chen*) (passed at the 11th meeting of the State Council on June 9, 1953), *Chung-hua jen-min kung-ho-kuo fa-kuei hui-pien* (*Compilation of Laws and Regulations of the Chinese People's Republic*), July-December 1955, pp. 409–410.

[15]Hsüeh I-yüan, *op. cit.*, p. 97.

[16]"Kuo-wu-yüan kuan-yü ch'eng hsiang hua-fen piao-chun te kuei-ting" ("State Council Resolution on the Criteria for Demarcation of Urban and Rural Areas") (adopted November 7, 1955), *T'ung-chi kung-tso t'ung-hsün* (*Statistical Work Bulletin*), no. 12, 1955, p. 4.

[17]From the source indicated in note 11.

Table 2

Urban and Rural Population: 1949 to 1957

(Data refer to end of year. Absolute figures in thousands)

Year	Total[a]	Urban[b]		Rural	
		Number	Percent	Number	Percent
1957	642,000	92,000	14.3	550,000	85.7
1956	627,800	89,150	14.2	538,650	85.8
1955	614,650	82,850	13.5	531,800	86.5
1954	601,720	81,550	13.6	520,170	86.4
1953	587,960	77,670	13.2	510,290	86.8
1952	574,820	71,630	12.5	503,190	87.5
1951	563,000	66,320	11.8	496,680	88.2
1950	551,960	61,690	11.1	490,270	88.9
1949	541,670	57,650	10.6	484,020	89.4

[a] As reported in the sources noted below.

[b] Includes those living in market places and towns in the suburbs of urban places, but excludes those living in villages in such suburbs. The annual average urban population of 74,650,000 for 1953, based on these data, is 2.6 million persons less than the reported census total of 77,257,000. The difference cannot be accounted for with the information available at present.

Source: 1949–1956: "China's Population from 1949 to 1956," *T'ung-chi kung-tso (Statistical Bulletin)*, no. 11, June 14, 1957; translated in *ECMM*, no. 91, July 22, 1957, pp. 23–25.

1957: Wang Kuang-wei, "How to Organize Agricultural Labor," *Chi-hua ching-chi (Planned Economy)*, no. 8, 1957, pp. 6–9; translated in *ECMM*, no. 100, September 23, 1957, pp. 11–14.

Bureau show no abrupt change in 1953 or 1954 (Table 2), it is probable that the definition observed in tabulating the urban totals for the 1953 census was essentially the same as that used for other years. Apparently, in planning for the 1953 census, a list of urban places was prepared before the enumeration which was to have been revised after the census results were reported. However, in the report of the Russian expert who helped plan the census it is stated that the list was used as originally prepared, since the pressure of time after the data were gathered did not permit revision.[18]

It is not possible, however, to determine how the definition was actually applied in practice, since, to the best of our knowledge, the State Statistical

[18]S. Krotevich, "Vsekitayskaya perepis' naseleniya 1953 g." ("The All-China Population Census of 1953"), *Poslevoyenniye perepisi naseleniya (Postwar Population Censuses)*, Moscow: Moscow Economic Statistical Institute, 1957, pp. 80–122.

Bureau has not published any list of Chinese cities and their populations as of the census of 1953. A note in the article "Data on China's Population from 1949 to 1956" states that the figures for the urban population include urban residents in suburban areas but exclude the rural residents in these areas.[19]

III. THE POPULATION OF URBAN PLACES

Population by Size of Urban Place

Population totals for urban places in Mainland China are usually published singly in newspaper articles on the development of particular places. Figures assembled from such a variety of sources are frequently not comparable. The figures themselves often appear to be estimates. They are seldom accom-

[19]*T'ung-chi kung-tso (Statistical Work)*, no. 11, 1957; translated in *ECMM*, no. 91, July 22, 1957, pp. 22–25.

panied by explanations as to the method by which they were originally obtained, the precise dates to which they pertain, or the definition of the population included. It is sometimes impossible to tell, even in comparing a number of alternate figures for the same city, whether a particular figure refers to the total population under the city administration, to the population within the city proper, or only to the urban population of the city. The definition can seldom be inferred from the context in which the figure was cited.

Nevertheless, for the analysis of the development of city populations in Mainland China it is necessary to compile the available information on the size, rates of growth, and distribu-

tion of urban places and to supplement this information with estimates as required. Table 3 presents the basic information obtained from various sources on the urban population and the number of urban places in Mainland China in June 1953.

The data given [in Table 3] are not identical with those given in the State Statistical Bureau source noted [in note b to Table 3]. In 1955, two urban places in Yünnan Province, Ma-li-p'o and Ho-k'ou, lost their municipal status. The population of Ma-li-p'o in 1953 was given by A. G. Shiger (*Administrativno-territorial'noye deleniye zarubezhnykh stran* [*Administrative-Territorial Division of Foreign Countries*], 2nd. ed., Moscow, 1957, pp. 142–144) as 196,300. The 1953 population of Ho-k'ou is not known.

Table 3

Data Available on the Number of Urban Places and the Urban Population, by Size of Place: June 1953
(Population figures in thousands)

Size of Place	Number of Urban Places			Urban Population		
	All Urban Places	Munici-palities[a]	Other Urban Places	All Urban Places	Munici-palities	Other Urban Places[b]
Total	5,568	164	[c]5,404	[d]77,257	[e]43,523	33,734
1,000,000 or more	9	9	. . .			. . .
500,000 to 999,999	16	16	. . .			. . .
200,000 to 499,999	28	28	. . .			. . .
100,000 to 199,999	49	49	. . .	51,313	[e]43,523	. . .
50,000 to 99,999	71	50	[f]21			
20,000 to 49,999	247	12	[f]235			7,790
2,000 to 19,999	4,228	. . .	[b]4,228	24,699	. . .	24,699
1,000 to 1,999	727	. . .	[b]727	1,108	. . .	1,108
Less than 1,000	193	. . .	[b]193	137	. . .	137

[a] Table 7. (It should be noted that the distribution given here differs slightly from that in the source cited in note c.)

[b] Derived from figures given in State Statistical Bureau, "Kuan-yü ch'eng hsiang hua-fen piao-chun jo-kan chu-yao wen-t'i to shuo-ming" ("Explanation of the Criteria Established for the Demarcation of Rural and Urban Areas"), *Hsin Hua pan-yüeh-k'an* (*New China Semi-Monthly*), no. 3, 1956, pp. 7–8.

[c] Hsüeh I-yüan, "Chung-hua jen-min kung-ho-kuo hsing-cheng ch'ü-hua te hua-fen" ("The Administrative Divisions of the People's Republic of China"), *Acta Geographica Sinica*, vol. 24, no. 1, February 1958, p. 97.

[d] "Communique of Results of Census and Registration of China's Population," NCNA, Peiping, November 1, 1954, translated in *CB*, no. 301, November 1, 1954, p. 2.

[e] Derived from figures in sources cited in notes b and d.

[f] Derived from Table 7 and figures in source cited in note b.

In 1947 the population of Ho-k'ou County was reported as 25,107, and that of Ma-li-p'o County as 118,824 (Ministry of Interior, *Ch'uan kuo hu-k'ou t'ung-chi* [*Population Statistics of China*], 1947, p. 59). There is reason to believe, therefore, that the 1953 "municipality" populations assigned to these two places were actually county populations. The withdrawal in 1955 of their municipality status returned their largely rural population to the county authority and reduced the county seats to small urban places. In a Chinese atlas for 1957 they are shown as under 5,000 population each.

It was assumed in Table 3 that the population of these places was 3,500 each in 1953, the midpoint of the class interval 2,000–5,000 within which they fall. It was also assumed that the large rural populations included in the two municipalities before 1955 were excluded from the total urban population reported in the census, as was the case with other municipalities. Hence, in preparing this table, the total urban population of municipalities given in the State Statistical Bureau source was reduced by 7,000, and that of the "other urban places" was increased by the same amount. This change also reduced the number of municipalities from the reported 166 to 164 and increased the number of "other urban places" from 5,402 to 5,404.

The individual figures for the 164 municipalities were purportedly 1953 census figures and included rural population in suburbs and outlying sections of the municipal areas. The total population, including both urban and rural residents, in the municipalities was 52,354,000;[20] however, of

the national urban population of 77,257,000, the 5,404 smaller urban places had an urban population of 33,734,000, which would leave a residual total of 43,523,000 urban residents in the municipalities. Subtracting this latter figure from the total municipal population of 52,354,000 leaves a residual of 8,831,000, or about 17 percent, which is presumably rural according to the definition used in the census compilation. For many local administrative purposes the combined urban and rural figures for municipal populations probably have the greater utility, but for analysis of the growth of urbanism the figures for the urban population undoubtedly are more meaningful.

But the distinction between urban and rural population in urban places poses a number of problems. In the first place it is not possible to say for certain whether the population figures given for smaller urban places represent only the urban component or whether the whole population of such places was considered urban. The definition of what places were to be counted as urban implies that as much as 50 percent of the population in some instances could be engaged in agriculture. When the urban totals were compiled for the census release, was the entire population of these places included or was only the 50 percent nonagricultural population counted? No answer is obtained from the materials presently available from Mainland China. In the absence of any clear indications to the contrary, it is here assumed that smaller urban places were considered to be wholly urban; no attempt was made to distinguish between urban and nonurban population within urban places of less than 20,000 inhabitants.

Table 4 gives the total and urban population in urban places by size of

[20]Excluding Ma-li-p'o and Ho-k'ou in Yünnan Province. See [comments on] Table 3 in original source.

Table 4

Number of Urban Places and Estimated Total and Urban Population in Urban Places, by Size of Place: June 1953
(Absolute population figures in thousands)

Size of Place	Number of Urban Places			Total Population				Urban Population			
	All Urban Places	Munici- palities	Other Urban Places	All Urban Places		Munici- palities	Other Urban Places	All Urban Places		Munici- palities	Other Urban Places
				Number	Percent			Number	Percent		
Total	5,568	164	5,404	87,669	100.0	52,354	35,315	77,257	100.0	43,523	33,734
1,000,000 or more	9	9	...	21,020	24.0	21,020	...	17,474	22.6	17,474	...
500,000 to 999,999	16	16	...	11,279	12.8	11,279	...	9,377	12.1	9,377	...
200,000 to 499,999	28	28	...	8,492	9.7	8,492	...	7,060	9.1	7,060	...
100,000 to 199,999	49	49	...	7,201	8.2	7,201	...	5,986	7.8	5,986	...
50,000 to 99,999	71	50	21	5,497	6.3	3,925	1,572	4,570	5.9	3,263	1,307
20,000 to 49,999	247	12	235	8,236	9.4	437	7,799	6,846	8.9	363	6,483
2,000 to 19,999	4,228	...	4,228	24,699	28.2	...	24,699	24,699	32.0	...	24,699
1,000 to 1,999	727	...	727	1,108	1.3	...	1,108	1,108	1.4	...	1,108
Less than 1,000	193	...	193	137	0.1	...	137	137	0.2	...	137

Source: Calculated as indicated in text.

93

place as of the census of June 1953. In this table, the total population figures for all municipalities of 100,000 inhabitants or more were presumably census figures except that for Liao-yang, in Liaoning Province, to which the average figure for its size class, 147,000, was arbitrarily assigned in the absence of a census figure. Municipalities in size-classes 50,000 to 100,000 and 20,000 to 50,000 persons for which no specific population figures were available were assigned the average population figure for cities of known population in the same size classes. The estimated urban population of municipalities was obtained by applying the proportion of urban to total population in all municipalities (83.13 percent) uniformly to all size classes.

The urban population in urban places other than municipalities was given or could be derived from given figures for all size classes, except that the urban population for the 256 urban places in the two size-classes 20,000 to 50,000 and 50,000 to 100,000 was not subdivided. To allocate this population to these two component size classes it was necessary to assume a ratio between the average size of urban place in each of the two size classes which would yield the announced total of 7,790,000. This was done by applying to the Chinese data the average ratio between the mean size of city in these two size classes as reported in recent censuses for four other non-Western countries with large agrarian populations: India, Pakistan, Burma, and Turkey. These calculations yielded an average population of 27,389 for urban places in the 20,000 to 50,000 class and of 61,421 for places in the 50,000 to 100,000 class.

According to Table 4, one-third of the urban population of China in 1953 lived in places of less than 20,000 inhabitants, and nearly one-fourth lived in places of 1,000,000 inhabitants or more. Slightly more than half of the urban population lived in places of 100,000 inhabitants or more; these urban dwellers in larger urban centers constituted nearly 7 percent of the total population of the country.

The estimated distribution of the urban population by province is summarized in Table 5, which gives the proportion of the urban population of each province living in urban places of 100,000 inhabitants or more and the proportion living in urban places of less than 100,000 inhabitants as of 1953. The three northeast provinces were the most highly urbanized. The inclusion of Peiping and Tientsin in Hopeh Province and of Shanghai in Kiangsu Province raises the proportions for these provinces well above the national average. All other provinces fall below the national average of 13.3 percent of the population classified as urban in 1953.[21]

IV. POPULATION GROWTH IN URBAN PLACES

Information on the growth of Chinese cities since 1953 is meager. For lack of better data, use is made here of fragments of information from various sources on the total population of particular cities for recent years. Some inferences are also drawn from the still more limited data available on rural to urban migration, the extension of municipal boundaries, and natural increase rates in urban areas.

[21]For a further discussion of the distribution of the urban population by province see U.S. Bureau of the Census, *Distribution of the Urban and Rural Population of Mainland China: 1953 and 1958,* by Ernest Ni, International Population Reports, Series P-95, No. 56, October 1960.

Table 5

Urban Population as a Percent of Total Population, by Size of Urban Place in 1953 and Province: June 1953
(Provincial boundaries as of 1957)

Province	Total Population (in Thousands)	Percent Urban		
		Total	100,000 or More	Under 100,000
Mainland China	582,603	13.3	6.9	6.4
Northeast				
Heilungkiang	11,897	31.1	12.6	18.5
Kirin	11,290	29.0	12.3	16.7
Liaoning	20,566	42.0	24.4	17.6
I.M.A.R.	7,338	10.7	3.4	7.3
North				
Hopeh	43,348	23.2	13.9	9.3
Shansi	14,314	12.9	6.5	6.4
Northwest				
Kansu	12,928	8.6	2.6	6.0
Shensi	15,881	9.9	4.8	5.1
Sinkiang	4,874	10.8	4.2	6.6
Tsinghai	1,676	7.0	4.7	2.3
East				
Anhwei	30,663	6.7	2.9	3.8
Chekiang	22,866	9.8	4.6	5.2
Fukien	13,143	12.0	5.6	6.4
Kiangsu	47,137	29.1	17.9	11.2
Shantung	48,877	6.9	3.5	3.4
Central-South				
Honan	44,215	6.5	2.8	3.7
Hunan	33,227	7.0	3.3	3.7
Hupeh	27,790	8.6	4.6	4.0
Kiangsi	16,773	7.6	2.0	5.6
Kwangsi	17,591	4.8	2.9	1.9
Kwangtung	36,740	12.2	5.4	6.8
Southwest				
Kweichow	15,037	3.9	1.5	2.4
Szechwan	65,685	9.7	5.0	4.7
Yünnan	17,473	7.4	4.1	3.3
Tibet and Chamdo	1,274	12.7	. . .	12.7

Source: U.S. Bureau of the Census. *Distribution of the Urban and Rural Population of Mainland China: 1953 and 1958,* by Ernest Ni, International Population Reports, Series P-95, No. 56, October, 1960, Tables 1, 2, and 4.

Migration

From the nature of official actions and newspaper accounts, it is clear that a considerable movement of population from rural areas to the cities took place between 1953 and 1957 and that numerous official attempts were made to reverse this movement.[22] To what extent the migrants have been included in the published estimates of the population of various urban places is not known. Since this migration was not sanctioned, it is likely that many rural migrants living in cities avoided registration in order to escape the attention of the authorities.

Some estimates of the extent of the urban influx have appeared in Chinese publications, and there are a few figures on the number of temporary residents in particular cities. The Deputy Mayor of Wu-han reported that, by the end of 1957, the "temporary and floating" population in China's cities numbered more than 2,200,000.[23] According to the Tientsin Municipal Public Security Bureau, a total of 205,000 peasants came to Tientsin

during 1956 and 1957, including some 100,000 women. Only a small number of these became permanent workers. It is explained that there were "many reasons" for the migration:

Flight from calamities is only one of them. Most of the peasants involved were not happy with the jobs of agricultural production they had and admired urban life. As far as urban work is concerned, the high level of pay and welfare for unskilled and ordinary workers and apprentices, the denial to these of vacations to visit their domiciles in countryside, the recruitment, without authorization, by industrial and commercial enterprises, farms and handicraft industries, of help in the rural district, the relaxed control of household registration and of unlicensed peddlers and lenient supply of food grains are factors responsible for the influx.[24]

Even if the announced population of cities includes the registered migrants with the permanent population, in view of the confusion in urban registration that prevailed during the period from 1953 to 1957, it is unlikely that any complete estimate of unregistered in-migrants was possible. Hence, it is probable that the actual population for any given date was larger than that indicated by official reports and estimates.

Expansion of Municipal Boundaries

Another factor in the growth of the population of certain cities is the extension of the boundaries to include additional territory. A list of the known increments to areas of cities between 1953 and 1958 is given in Appendix D [not reproduced here].

[22]"GAC Directive on Dissuasion of Peasants from Blind Influx into Cities," New China News Agency, Peiping, April 17, 1953, in American Consulate General, *SCMP*, no. 554, Hong Kong, p. 24. Sun Kuang, "Urban Population Must be Controlled," *Jen-min jih-pao (People's Daily)*, Peiping, November 27, 1957; translated in *SCMP*, no. 1668, December 10, 1957, pp. 3–7. "Joint Directive of the CCP Central Committee and State Council on Prevention of Blind Exodus of Rural Population," New China News Agency, Peiping, December 18, 1957; translated in *SCMP*, no. 1682, January 2, 1958, pp. 2–4. "Stop Blind Rural Exodus," *Jen-min jih-pao (People's Daily)*, Peiping, December 19, 1957; translated in *SCMP*, no. 1682, January 2, 1958, pp. 4–7.

[23]A speech by Wei Ting-huai, Deputy Mayor of Wu-han, at Municipal People's Congress, reported in Hankow, *Ch'ang-chiang jih-pao*, February 27, 1958; translated in *SCMP*, no. 1764, May 5, 1958, p. 39.

[24]"Peasants in Cities Should be Urged to Return to Production in Village," *Jen-min jih-pao (People's Daily)*, Peiping, December 16, 1957; translated in *SCMP*, no. 1682, January 2, 1958, p. 7.

... these extensions seem to have become more numerous in 1958. They probably represent an attempt to increase the control of the municipality over its own food supply and over local transportation. Since transportation facilities are still not well developed, the movement of food to the cities has been an increasingly acute problem. Enlarging the rural area within the municipal boundaries permits the municipal authorities to exert more influence on the types of crops planted, to reduce the dependence of the municipality on food supplies from other areas, and to control local distribution of food more effectively.

The extension of municipal areas is usually reported in terms of whole administrative units, such as counties, townships, or towns. Occasionally the actual land area involved is reported, but seldom is there any indication of the number of people in the newly acquired area. This number can sometimes be estimated from the increase in the reported total population. Such an estimated figure, however, cannot be related directly to the increase in the urban population of the municipality as a result of annexation. Since there is reason to believe that the proportion of the population in the annexed areas classified as rural is much higher than that within the original municipal boundaries, the proportion of population of municipalities which was rural in midyear 1958 may thus have been well above the 17 percent indicated for 1953.[25]

[25]The determination of the urban population of the municipality is further complicated by the fact that the total urban population of the expanded municipality may embrace more than one formerly discrete urban place. Tientsin, for example, acquired within its new boundaries two urban places which were

The policy of expanding municipal jurisdictions has been carried further since midyear 1958. In the latter part of 1958 the groupings of counties known as "administrative districts," formerly under the control of the provincial governments, were abolished in the vicinity of some of the larger municipalities, and their areas "placed under the jurisdiction of" the municipalities. This meant that extensive areas with extremely large populations were nominally included in the territory of a single municipality. The new limits of Shanghai embraced a total population of 10 million; Tientsin had 11.4 million. The area included under Peiping's authority was 17,000 square kilometers; Tientsin's authority covered a total of 20,000 square kilometers. (See Appendix D.)

What precisely this jurisdiction consists of is nowhere specified, not even in the resolution of the Standing Committee of the National People's Congress, passed somewhat belatedly in September 1959, authorizing the urban expansion:

With a view to coping with the rapid development of the socialist construction of our country, especially since last year's big leap forward in industrial and agricultural production and the people's communes in the rural areas, promoting mutual support between industry and agriculture, and facilitating the assignment of man-

municipalities in their own right. Hence, in studying the growth of population of municipalities by size-class, special care is required to distinguish the population of the municipality proper from that of other urban places in the new municipal area. Otherwise, estimates of urban growth based on composite figures for specific municipalities are liable to double count the urban population of smaller urban places enveloped in the enlarged municipal boundaries.

power, it has been resolved that municipalities under direct Central authority and relatively large municipalities may have jurisdiction over *hsien* and autonomous *hsien*.[26]

The purposes of the move as described in this resolution are primarily economic. In the case of the two "independent" municipalities, Peiping and Shanghai, the administrative districts, which had been the purveyors of provincial authority in the counties absorbed by these municipalities, have been abolished. Hence, these municipalities now exercise full political control over their extensive rural hinterlands. In the case of the other expanding municipalities, however, the former administrative districts have not been superceded by the municipal authority. In their hinterlands the change may amount to little more than a paper transfer of jurisdiction.

Natural Increase

Information on births and deaths in Mainland China is limited to a few national rates and data for several large cities. There is some doubt as to how the data were compiled, what areas they cover, and the extent of underregistration.

Official birth and death rates for seven large cities for the period 1953–1956 were published in an article by Pressat,[27] who obtained them from the State Statistical Bureau during a visit to Peiping. In presenting the rates, Pressat mentions the possibility of underregistration of births and deaths. Nothing is said, however, about changes in boundaries, though it is known that the areas of at least three of the seven

[26]New China News Agency, Peiping, September 17, 1959.

[27]Roland Pressat, "La Population de la Chine et son Économie," *Population*, October-December 1958, vol. 13, no. 4, pp. 569–590.

cities were expanded during the period covered. These data must therefore be regarded as approximate.

However, comparison of the expected and reported increase in the population of these cities between 1953 and 1956 suggests that natural increase contributed substantially more to urban growth than did migration. In several cities natural increase exceeded total growth, implying a net loss of population by migration. Actually these years witnessed the restriction of rural-to-urban migration and the expulsion of migrants from some of the larger centers during 1955. Still, the magnitude of natural increase was so great (usually in excess of 3 percent per year) that it is doubtful whether migration could have exceeded natural increase even had no restrictions been imposed.

Trends in Population Growth of Urban Places by Size-Class

Any attempt to observe the growth of China's cities in a longer historical perspective than that afforded by the current official figures runs into serious problems due to the fact that data from different sources and periods are not comparable. Most of the earlier figures were crude estimates. Some of them implied an urban population for the country as a whole of more than 20 percent as compared with 13 percent according to the 1953 census. Figures for the larger cities may be more comparable than the estimates of the total urban population; however, even these comparisons should be regarded as suggestive of general trends only.

Table 6 summarizes the growth of the total population of 95 of the largest urban places in Mainland China, by size-class in 1938. Of the 95 places classed as municipalities as of the 1953 census, and for which population data are available, 89 had increased in

Table 6

Growth of Population of Selected Places Classed as Municipalities in 1953, by Size-Class in 1938[a]

Item and Date	All Size-Classes	1,000 or More	500 to 999	200 to 499	100 to 199	50 to 99	Less than 50
Number of places:							
1938	95	5	5	20	32	25	8
1953	95	9	16	26	35	8	1
1958	95	15	19	32	26	3	0
Population:							
(by size-class in 1938)							
1938	24,856	8,656	3,104	6,250	4,621	1,938	287
1953	46,241	14,692	6,578	10,807	9,203	4,088	873
1958	60,225	18,496	8,096	14,059	12,324	5,925	1,325
Population increase:							
(by size-class in 1938)							
1938 to 1953							
Number	21,385	6,036	3,474	4,557	4,582	2,150	586
Percent	86.0	69.7	111.9	72.9	99.2	110.9	204.2
1953 to 1958							
Number	13,984	3,804	1,518	3,252	3,121	1,837	452
Percent	30.2	25.9	23.1	30.1	33.9	44.9	51.8
1938 to 1958							
Number	35,369	9,840	4,992	7,809	7,703	3,987	1,038
Percent	142.3	113.7	160.8	124.9	166.7	205.7	361.7

[a] The data included here are for the 95 places classed as municipalities in 1953 for which population figures are given in Table 7. Population data and size-class categories in thousands.
Source: Municipal status: Table 1 [in original article]. Population: Table 7.

population during the period 1938 to 1958. During these 20 years, the population of these 95 places had increased from 24.9 million to 60.2 million, or 142 percent. In general, the smaller the place was in 1928, the higher the rate of growth both during the period 1938 to 1953 and during the period 1953 to 1958. The population of the eight places of less than 50,000 inhabitants in 1938 grew more than three times as rapidly in the next 20 years as did the population of the five places of 1 million or more. Although there was some concentration in growth among the smallest places, population increase was broad in scope in the sense that places of each size-class more

than doubled their populations in the 20 years.

All places which were municipalities in 1953 or in 1958 are included in Table 7. The order of arrangement is by province and, within the province, by population size in 1958.

The midyear 1938 estimates mainly were derived by extrapolating the data presented by Trewartha on the population of Chinese cities for various dates between 1922 and 1937. Most of the midyear 1948 estimates were derived by interpolation and extrapolation of the 1947 and 1948 estimates given in *The Columbia Lippincott Gazetteer of the World*. The 1953 data are as shown in [a table not reproduced here] and

Table 7

Population of Municipalities, by Province: 1938, 1948, 1953, and 1958

(The urban places included here are those classified as municipalities in 1953 or 1958. Except as otherwise indicated, these places were classified as municipalities at both time periods. Data refer to midyear and are in thousands. (...) indicates data not available and no estimate made.)

Province and municipality	1938	1948	1953	1958	Province and municipality	1938	1948	1953	1958
Kwangtung					**Shantung—(Con.)**				
Canton	1,022	1,414	1,599	1,867	Chefoo	166	227	116	140
Hai-k'ou	...	60	135	402	Chi-ning	...	...	86	...
Swatow	196	215	280	250	Liao-ch'eng [j]	...	...	20-50	...
Chan-chiang	245	271	166	170	Lin-ch'ing [m]	...	...	20-50	...
Fo-shan	135	96	122	120	Lin-i [j]	...	...	20-50	...
Chiang-men	...	...	85	110	T'ai-an [j]	...	...	20-50	...
Ch'ao-chou	152	60	101	*101	Te-chou	...	...	20-50	...
Shao-kuan	176	73	82	...	Wei-hai	194	175	20-50	...
Pei-hai	...	36	80	...	Chang-chou [p]	...	...	50-100	...
Shih-ch'i	81	84	93	...					
Hui-chou					**Shensi**				
(Hui-yang) [j]	...	35	20-50	73	Sian	218	503	787	1,368
Chao-ch'ing [j]	...	...	...	70	Pao-chi	...	56	130	180
					Han-chung	...	60	70	...
Kweichow					Hsien-yang	...	16	70	...
Kuei-yang	145	240	271	530	T'ung-ch'uan [j]	...	...	20-50	...
Tsun-i	72	72	...	200					
Tu-yün [j]	...	10	...	60	**Sinkiang**				
An-shun [j]	...	41	20-50	...	Urumchi	45	88	141	320
					Kashgar	...	...	91	100
Liaoning					I-ning	...	...	108	85
Mukden	772	1,121	2,300	2,423	Karamai [j]	...	...	...	43
Dairen	504	544	766	[n]1,590	So-ch'e [b]	...	...	80	...
Fu-shun	215	513	679	1,019					
An-shan	120	166	549	833	**Szechwan**				
Pen-ch'i	66	321	449	*449	Chungking [q]	528	1,000	1,772	2,165
Chin-chou	105	148	352	400	Ch'eng-tu	458	727	857	1,135
An-tung	211	271	360	370	Tzu-kung	176	223	291	280
Fou-hsin	160	180	189	290	Nan-ch'ung	55	60	165	*206
Liao-yang	90	110	147	169	I-pin	78	80	178	190
Ying-k'ou	160	159	131	*161	Nei-chiang	...	32	190	180
Port Arthur	133	25	126	([n])	Wu-t'ung-ch'iao	...	...	199	*140
					Lu-chou	68	50	289	130
Shansi					Ya-an	...	...	55	...
T'ai-yüan	177	200	721	1,053	Ho-ch'uan [q]	...	40	50-100	...,
Ta-t'ung	70	80	228	*243	Wan-hsien	...	...	50-100	...
Yang-ch'üan	...	...	177	200					
Ch'ang-chih	...	...	98	180	**Tsinghai**				
Yü-tz'u	...	...	60	100	Hsi-ning	...	59	94	150
Hou-ma [j]	...	...	...	...					
					Yünnan [r]				
Shantung					K'un-ming	184	300	669	900
Tsingtao	592	788	917	1,144	Ko-chiu	...	16	160	180
Tsinan	472	575	680	882	Hsia-kuan	...	...	26	...
Tzu-po [p]	...	...	184	875	Tung-ch'uan [j]	...	...	...	...
Wei-fang	98	134	149	190					

* Represents an estimate made where the latest information available was 1953. For the basis of the estimate, see appendix A.
[a] Established as a new municipality in 1956.
[b] Municipal status abolished in 1954.
[c] Established as a new municipality in 1957.
[d] Municipal status abolished in 1958.
[e] Population prior to March 1958 annexation. (See also footnote 9.)
[f] Hsüan-hua municipality abolished in 1955; area incorporated with Kalgan municipality.
[g] Feng-feng municipality, established in 1955, was abolished in 1956 and area incorporated with Han-tan municipality.
[h] Municipal status, established in 1958, was abolished in December 1958.
[i] Municipality placed under the administrative control of Peiping municipality in March 1958.
[j] Established as a new municipality in 1958.
[k] Municipal status, established in 1956, was abolished in November 1958.
[l] Established as a new municipality in 1955.
[m] Established as a new municipality in 1954.
[n] Population is that given for Lu-ta municipality, which includes the Dairen and Port Arthur municipalities and the Chin and Ch'ang-hai hsien.
[o] Municipal status, established in 1956, was abolished in 1957.
[p] Chang-chou municipality abolished in 1955; area incorporated with Tzu-po municipality.
[q] Ho-ch'uan municipality abolished in 1957; area incorporated with Chungking municipality.
[r] Ho-k'ou and Ma-li-p'o were shown as municipalities in Chung-hua jen-min kung-ho-kuo fen-sheng ti-t'u (Provincial Atlas of the Chinese People's Republic), 6th ed., Shanghai, December 1953. Their municipal status was abolished in 1955.

Source:
  Municipal status: Table 1 and Appendix C [not reproduced here.]

Table 7 (cont.)

Province and municipality	1938	1948	1953	1958
Anhwei				
Ho-fei	94	153	184	360
Pang-fou	136	201	253	330
Huai-nan	...	...	287	280
Wu-hu	168	204	242	240
An-ch'ing	117	109	105	*129
Ma-an-shan[a]	...	...	...	...
T'ung-kuan-shan (T'ung-ling)[a]	...	...	...	...
T'un-ch'i	...	...	50-100	...
Chieh-shou[b]	...	...	20-50	...
Chekiang				
Hangchow	575	570	697	794
Ningpo	247	210	238	280
Wenchow	237	157	202	210
Shao-hsing	149	92	131	*160
Chia-hsing	92	53	78	132
Hu-chou	66	45	63	120
Chin-hua	34	23	46	...
Fukien				
Foochow	343	331	553	623
Amoy	177	158	224	308
Ch'üan-chou	57	121	108	110
Chang-chou	56	62	81	...
Nan-p'ing[a]	82	29	20-50	...
Heilungkiang				
Harbin	468	760	1,163	1,595
Ch'i-ch'i-ha-erh	97	175	345	704
Chi-hsi[l]	...	...	20-50	253
Mu-tan-chiang	100	200	151	251
Chia-mu-ssu	71	168	146	232
Ho-kang	20	53	90	200
I-ch'un[c]	...	...	20-50	200
Shuang-ya-shan[a]	...	...	20-50	110
Honan				
Cheng-chou	197	150	595	785
Lo-yang	73	60	171	500
K'ai-feng	303	300	299	*318
Chiao-tso[a]	...	...	20-50	250
Hsin-hsiang	...	...	170	203
Shang-ch'iu	73	70	134	*165
An-yang	94	115	125	*153
P'ing-ting-shan[c]	...	...	...	70
Ho-pi[c]	...	...	...	...
San-men-hsia[c]	...	...	...	...
Hsü-ch'ang	51	55	58	...
Hsin-yang	...	...	50-100	...
Lo-ho	...	...	50-100	...
Nan-yang	50	...	50-100	...
Chou-k'ou[d]	141	104	86	...
Chu-ma-tien[d]	...	...	20-50	...
Hopeh				
Peiping	1,574	1,603	2,768	[e]4,148
Tientsin	1,223	1,686	2,694	3,278
T'ang-shan	146	137	693	812
Shih-chia-chuang	194	198	373	623
Kalgan[f]	146	151	229	480
Han-tan[g]	...	30	90	380
Pao-ting	216	130	197	250
Ch'in-huang-tao	47	100	187	210
Ch'eg-te	43	60	93	120
Hsüan-hua[f]	...	...	114	...
Han-ku[d]	...	...	50-100	...
Hsing-t'ai[d]	...	...	50-100	...
Ts'ang-hsien[h]	...	...	50-100	...
T'ung-chou[i]	...	...	50-100	...
Feng-feng[g]	...	...	20-50	...
Po-t'ou[d]	...	...	20-50	...
Hunan				
Ch'ang-sha	464	396	651	709
Hsiang-t'an	103	133	184	247
Heng-yang	122	184	235	240
Chu-chou	...	7	127	190
Hunan—(Con.)				
Shao-yang	83	106	118	170
Ch'ang-te	85	50	95	...
Ching-shih	...	...	50-100	...
I-yang	...	...	50-100	...
Hung-chiang	...	...	20-50	...
Hupeh				
Wu-han	1,242	910	1,427	2,226
Huang-shih	...	28	110	*135
Sha-shih	104	91	86	...
Hsiang-fan	...	...	...	73
I-ch'ang	...	...	50-100	...
I.M.A.R.				
Pao-t'ou	70	82	149	490
Huhehot	94	104	148	320
Chi-ning[a]	...	19	30	100
Hailar	22	16	43	60
Ulanhot	...	10	51	...
Man-chou-li	7	6	30	...
Ch'ih-feng	40	47	49	...
T'ung-liao	40	...	40	...
Pa-yen-hao-t'e[k]	...	...	...	...
Kansu				
(Including Ninghsia)				
Lan-chou	122	204	397	732
Yü-men[l]	...	...	...	200
Yin-ch'uan	58	41	84	91
Pai-yin[j]	...	...	5-20	50
P'ing-liang	58	59	60	...
T'ien-shui	59	50	63	...
Lin-hsia	...	...	50-100	...
Chang-yeh[j]	...	...	20-50	...
Chiu-ch'üan[j]	...	...	20-50	...
Wu-chung	...	...	45	...
Te-wu-lu[j]	...	...	5-20	...
Kiangsi				
Nan-ch'ang	275	267	398	520
Ching-te-chen	125	87	92	266
Kan-chou	58	59	99	...
Chiu-chiang	93	121	65	...
Chi-an	...	69	53	...
Shang-jao	...	31	50-100	...
Fu-chou[m]	...	18	20-50	...
Kiangsu				
Shanghai	3,595	4,423	6,204	6,977
Nanking	440	1,230	1,092	1,455
Süchow	205	340	373	710
Soochow	388	381	474	651
Wu-hsi	272	273	582	616
Ch'ang-chou	125	239	296	300
Nan-t'ung	155	226	260	240
Hsin-hai-lien	...	125	208	210
T'ai-chou	81	131	160	*200
Chen-chiang	213	179	201	190
Yang-chou	127	127	180	160
Ch'ang-shu[d]	94	64	101	*101
Ch'ing-chiang	73	47	77	...
Kirin				
Ch'ang-ch'un	360	630	855	988
Kirin	132	247	435	583
Liao-yüan	32	185	120	177
T'ung-hua	42	80	129	*158
Ssu-p'ing	56	76	126	130
Yen-chi	36	43	70	80
Kung-chu-ling[a]	34	...	20-50	60
Pai-ch'eng[j]	...	...	...	...
Kwangsi				
Nan-ning	101	200	195	260
Liu-chou	...	194	159	190
Kuei-lin	88	131	145	170
Wu-chou	103	207	111	120
P'ing-hsiang[a]	...	...	...	7

are from the sources identified there. Where a population figure was not available the limits of the population size-class are given.

The 1958 data on the total population of municipalities of 500,000 inhabitants or more in 1958 are extrapolations to midyear 1958 of the 1953 data and the year-end 1957 data given in *The Great Ten Years*. Except for the 15 municipalities marked with an asterisk [in Table 7], 1958 figures for other municipalities were either reported figures or estimates based on the rate of growth between the 1953 census and a subsequent date for which a figure was available. Population figures for various dates since 1953 were assembled from a number of different sources—mostly from speeches and newspapers. They were checked against each other and, in case of inconsistency, the decision as to which figure to use was based on reasonableness and agreement with other information. Some additional figures were obtained from atlases and journal articles. Figures quoted in technical journals, such as *Ti-li chih-shih* (*Geographical Knowledge*) were accepted in preference to alternative figures of more uncertain origin. The specific source of each figure is not given here, but this information is available for specific municipalities on request from the Foreign Manpower Research Office of the U.S. Bureau of the Census.

The 1958 figures for 15 municipalities are marked with an asterisk to indicate that these are estimates made without any information on the population since 1953. Of these, three places, K'ai-feng in Honan Province, Pen-ch'i in Liaoning Province, and Ta-t'ung in Shansi Province, were in the size-class 200,000 to 500,000 in 1953, and the other 12 were in the size-class

100,000 to 200,000. For K'ai-feng, Ta-t'ung, and nine of the places of 100,000 to 200,000 inhabitants, the 1958 estimate was based on the average increase rate between 1953 and 1958 for places of the same size-class for which more substantial estimates or announced figures as of 1958 were available. Separate average increase rates were used for places of 100,000 to 150,000 inhabitants and 150,000 to 200,000 inhabitants in 1953, since there were enough cases on which to compute separate average increase rates and since the rates differed significantly. For the remaining four municipalities other procedures were followed. In the case of Pen-ch'i, use of the size-class average rate of increase would have put the city well over 500,000 by 1958; however, Pen-ch'i was not included in the list of cities with populations in excess of 500,000 as given in *The Great Ten Years*, hence it was assumed that the population in Pen-ch'i was the same in 1958 as in 1953. In the case of Ch'ang-shu in Kiangsu Province, Ch'ao-chou in Kwangtung Province, and Wu-tung-ch'ao in Szechwan Province, the 1958 estimate took into account a change in their political status. Within the 1953–1958 period, the designation of these places as municipalities was withdrawn. This action may be taken to mean that their populations had probably declined to less than 100,000 by 1958. In the absence of other information, Ch'ang-shu and Ch'ao-chou were considered as having had no change in population from 1953 to 1958. Wu-tung-ch'ao was considered as having decreased in population to 140,000 in 1958, a figure reported for 1957.

In addition, the estimate of population made for one other urban place requires an explanation. Liao-yang, in Liaoning Province, was the only urban place of 100,000 population or more for which the specific population in 1953 was not known. In the absence of other information it was assumed that Liao-yang had 147,000 inhabitants in 1953, the average size for places in the 100,000 to 200,000 size-class in 1953, and that it grew at the average rate for places of its size-class between 1953 and 1958.

No attempt was made to estimate the 1958 population of places having less than 100,000 inhabitants in 1953 and for which there was no information as to the population since 1953.

9. Patterns of Urban Growth in the Middle East

ISIS RAGHEB (SOUTHALL)
FOR THE UNITED NATIONS,
BUREAU OF SOCIAL AFFAIRS

I. INTRODUCTION

A. Purpose and Scope of the Paper

Comparatively little up-to-date information is available in a systematized form on the structure and functioning of population concentrations in the Middle East, taken as separate economic, social and physical entities. Most available data and considerations published by operational experts either focus on technical aspects of town planning or deal only from a national-aggregate point of view with other problems relevant to urban development, such as for example national policies of industrialization. Even fewer reports on the Middle East seem available which cover in some logical coherence the widely diverse aspects of recent shifts in population distribution over wide geographical areas.

The present paper reflects this lack of readily available facts and figures on historical trends and projected programmes. On the basis of a rather limited range of data it attempts however to discuss recent shifts in population distribution in the Middle East and

in particular: general migratory patterns and their causes; problems resulting from the present pattern of migration especially as regards the cities; and finally the measures taken, both at the local and national level, in response to these vast changes in patterns of settlement and population distribution.

This paper presents in varying degrees data on the following countries: Iraq, Israel, Jordan, Kuwait, Lebanon, Syria and Turkey. Unless otherwise stated the term Middle East as used in this paper, refers to this group of countries, stretching from the Black Sea to the Red Sea and from the Mediterranean to the Persian Gulf.

B. General Characteristics of the Middle East Area

With few variations, this region can be classified as a region in transition, occupying geographically as well as in levels of development a position between the countries of Western Europe and the majority of those in Asia and Africa.

Throughout the region, spatial distribution of the population is uneven, so that nearly 99 per cent of the people earn their livelihood from about one fifth of the land area, the rest being either desert or arid mountainous zones. Agriculture, the mainstay of many economies, has to support a fast growing population which has almost doubled in the last three decades. In some countries annual rates of popula-

Inter-Regional Seminar on Development Policies and Planning in Relation to Urbanization, Organized by the United Nations Bureau of Technical Assistance Operations and the Bureau of Social Affairs in co-operation with the Government of the United States of America, Working Paper No. 8, *University of Pittsburgh, Pittsburgh, Pennsylvania, USA, October 24–November 7, 1966. Reprinted by permission. Short-form footnotes refer to items in Bibliography*, infra.

tion growth have reached the 3 per cent mark,[1] the population of the region as a whole growing faster than that of any other major region, except Latin America.

Employment problems, both in rural and urban areas, confront the governments, the effective labour force having been estimated at only 30% of the population.[2] Underemployment is widespread in view of the long dead seasons in the agricultural cycles, and the excessive numbers employed in "tertiary" occupations such as commerce, communications, transport, utilities and services.

Agriculture, which employs nearly three quarters of the labour force, yields about two fifths of the national product in Iraq, Syria and Turkey; in Lebanon the proportions are one half and one sixth correspondingly. *Per capita* income in agriculture is thus one half or less of that in the economy as a whole. Land reform as well as agricultural improvement programmes have been introduced in some countries.

The proportion of economically active population in industry is much the same throughout the region, but the content of this sector and the income derived from it vary. In Jordan, for example, industry—including also handicrafts, represents about one-tenth of the economically active population and one-tenth of national product. In Iraq on the other hand where the oil industry provides the main source of income, handicrafts and oil extraction and refining employ less than one tenth of the active population (one per cent in oil itself) but provide together three-tenths of the income. Where handicrafts are supplemented by larger-scale manufacturing, industry

may still occupy only one tenth of the population, but produce one sixth of the national income, as in Syria.[3]

Aside from problems of an economic and demographic nature, the area has been passing through a phase of political upheaval and instability. This has sometimes resulted in vast dislocations of population affecting population settlement, especially in urban areas.

II. POPULATION MOVEMENTS

A. Causes

Population movements in the area have been of two magnitudes. The first movement has been in the shape of vast dislocations of population due to political wars and has involved over a million persons. The second has been a centrifugal rural-urban shift which is still in process and involves large segments of the population.

1. *Dislocation of populations.* The population movements of the past 15 to 20 years have equalled in scope those which the region underwent as a result of the dissolution of the Ottoman Empire. Between 1946 and 1960 one half million Jews from Europe and the Americas, and an equal number from Africa and Asia were settled in Israel. Correspondingly, a million Palestinian refugees are now assisted by the United Nations Relief and Works Agency (UNRWA). It is estimated that another million Arab refugees settled in the neighbouring Arab countries. Jordan alone received a mass of migrants estimated at 600,000; about 50,000 went to Kuwait, others to Lebanon, Saudi Arabia and Syria.

The majority of these migrants settled in towns where employment prospects seemed good. Many of them, the

---

[1] United Nations, *1963 Report on the World Social Situation*, 63. IV. 4. p. 142.

[2] *Op. cit.*, p. 142.

[3] *Ibid.*, p. 143.

educated and those who already had a skill, were assimilated into the working population. Needless to say they formed a heavy burden on the host countries, in housing, particularly.

In Israel the immigrants were for the most part professionally and technically trained persons from Europe and represented a valuable technical and managerial manpower, settling primarily in urban areas, while rural migrants from Africa and Asia needed training and education in order to be assimilated effectively into the new economy. This population movement has almost exhausted itself, although migrants continue to arrive in Israel. Over 150,000 Turks from Bulgaria migrated to Turkey in 1950–51.[4]

2. *Rural-urban migration.* Population movements from rural to urban areas are not recent phenomena in the region, though in recent years they seem to be gathering momentum. Several factors account for this trend:

a) *Discovery and exploitation of oil resources:* This fact has brought thousands of workers into the new urban settlements in search of employment. In Saudi Arabia, Kuwait and Iraq new oil-towns have sprung up with incredible rapidity. These workers are not necessarily from the oil-producing countries themselves but from neighbouring countries as well. In Kuwait the 1961 census disclosed that of a total population of 321,621 only 50.4% were Kuwaitis, the remaining 49.6% being non-Kuwaiti citizens. These included Jordanians (9.6%), Iraqis (8.4), Iranians (5.7), Egyptians (6.2), Lebanese (5.0), Omanis (4.3), Indians (2.4), Pakistanis (2.2), Palestinians (2.0), Saudi Arabians (1.4), British (0.8), Yemenis (0.4), and others.[5]

b) *Flow of capital from oil revenues:* With 135 wells producing 800,000 barrels of oil

daily, Kuwait's annual income from oil amounts to $150,000,000. The flow of part of this Kuwaiti income to neighbouring countries has made a direct impact on the rate of growth of the cities in these countries. Lebanon and more specifically, Beirut has been the outstanding beneficiary.

c) *Population explosion:* The annual rate of population growth is 3.3% in some countries, this has caused greater pressure on land.

d) *Growing difficulty in finding additional land for cultivation and the implementation of agricultural policies which make labour redundant in rural areas:* Turkey's mechanization of agriculture in the decade between 1948 and 1957 has displaced about 200,000 families. Of those some 160,000 families moved to the urban areas, adding to the population of these places.[6]

e) *Accessibility of the towns* due to improved methods of transport between village and town.

f) *Attraction of the city* to the rural dweller as the main centre for education, health, employment, entertainment, and a totally different way of life.

The strength of these "push" and "pull" factors varies from region to region, and also changes over time. Each country has its unique social and economic situation.

For example, according to an ILO study published in 1960, in Iraq the "push" factors in migration were extremely strong; the earnings of cultivators were at subsistence level by reason of the low yields and the high proportion of the crop claimed as share-rent by the landowner; health conditions were extremely bad, and, the majority of the fellaheen suffered from diseases of acute malnutrition. This ILO study went on to state that pull factors were also strong; although the oil industry itself employed only

[4] U.N., *1963 Report on the World Social Situation.*

[5] Government of Kuwait, Central Statistical Office, *Statistical Abstract, 1965.*

[6] Robinson, Richard D. "Turkey's Agrarian Revolution and the Problem of Urbanization," *Public Opinion Quarterly, Vol. 22, 1958.*

small numbers, the volume of employment created by new public expenditure was large; most of the new employment was on construction, water control projects, roads and urban building.

3. *Age and sex composition of migratory flows.* In the three countries for which comparable data are available, the ratio between males and females in urban areas is a more or less balanced one. In Iraq it is 1,284,744 males to 1,201,699 females; in Syria 868,454 males to 816,502 females and in Turkey 3,978,939 males to 3,328,877 females. This is to a large extent explained by the migratory pattern in these regions. It is a family pattern, which implies that the population movement is in one direction and that the rural migrant to the city intends to stay. In Iraq it was reported that 95% of the migrant

peasants left the rural areas with their families,[7] and in Turkey it is estimated that the mechanization of agriculture had resulted in the movement of some 160,000 families to urban areas in search of employment.[8]

A different sex ratio, on the other hand, obtains in Kuwait, and probably to a similar degree in Saudi Arabia, where the oil industry has attracted a large migrant labour force from outside the country. Males, mostly between 15–50 years of age account for the largest part of this group. Unlike the native migrants, these alien labourers are transient migrants who come without their families to whom they remit part of their salaries.[9] Their aim is to earn a sufficient amount of capital and return home. This different sex ratio is illustrated in the following figures:

Urban/Rural Population, by Sex and Nationality 1957[10]

	Kuwaiti			Non Kuwaiti			Grand Total
	Male	Female	Total	Male	Female	Total	
Kuwait City	30,143	29,436	59,579	36,722	8,250	44,972	104,557
Suburbs	5,347	4,863	10,210	9,253	1,915	11,168	21,378
Towns, villages, etc.	23,664	20,169	43,844	26,929	9,782	36,711	80,544
Total	59,154	54,468	113,622	72,904	19,947	92,851	206,473

While the ratio of females to males among the Kuwaiti population is fairly balanced i.e., 30,143 males to 29,436 females, among non-Kuwaitis it is highly unbalanced, being 36,722 males to 8,250 females.

In Jordan the male/female ratio in major urban districts is as follows:

[7] El Madfai, in United Nations, ST/TAO/ M/21 (see Bibliography, item 13, *infra.*)
[8] Robinson, *Ibid.*
[9] Estimated at $120,000,000 a year by F. Shehab, "Kuwait, the Super Affluent Society," *Foreign Affairs*, April 1964.

Population of Jordan by District and Sex, 1958 (in thousands)[11]

District	Male	Female	Total
Ajlun District	134	128	262
Amman District	127	118	245
Balqa District	57	53	110
Hebron District	77	74	151
Jerusalem District	179	177	456
Karak District	37	34	71
Maan District	17	15	32
Nablus District	193	186	379
Total Districts	821	785	1,706

[10]Shiber, *Ibid.*
[11]Berger, M., *Ibid.*

...in the three countries[12]—Iraq, Syria and Turkey, the 5–15 years age group contains about one fourth of the urban population varying between 24.6% in Iraq, 25.7% in Syria and 21.8% in Turkey. It cannot be determined with accuracy what proportion of this population might be classified as "dependent" in the conventional sense of the word, or as economically active. School attendance is not rigorously enforced in the countries of the region; moreover in spite of legislation on minimum age of employment, it is not unusual for children to be employed as apprentices. The bulk of the population is in the 20–60 age bracket, with a dwindling number in the 60–70 bracket. Thus, the urban population is young and fairly balanced in its sex ratio.

B. Patterns of Urban Growth

As a result of these combined factors, as the table below shows, a relatively high proportion of the population lives in towns and cities in the region.

Percent of Total Population Living in Localities of 100,000 and More Inhabitants[13]

Country	Census Year	Percent
Iraq	1957	14.5
Jordan	1952	8.1
Kuwait	1957	50.6
Lebanon	1958	33.2
Saudi Arabia	1954	8.4
Syria	1955	28.9

Two aspects of population movements in these countries are of interest,

[12]Table A, giving age breakdowns, is not reprinted here (Editor).
[13]U.N., *Administrative Problems of Rapid Urban Growth in the Arab States*, New York, 1964 (ST/TAO/M/21).

i.e., their spatial, and time dimensions. Spatially, population concentrations occur usually in and around the main towns or urban conurbation; in terms of time, the urban populations seem to be growing at an accelerated rate. For example by the end of 1958 the population of the conurbations of Tel Aviv included 30% and of Haifa, 12% of the total population of Israel. Moreover, the total population of Tel Aviv-Jaffa, Haifa and Jerusalem expressed as a percentage of the total Israeli population rose from 17.5 in 1922 and 23.5 in 1931 to 35.5 in 1959.[14] Israel has the "privilege" of holding third place in the world in ratio of urban population to total population (75.9%).

Turkey's urban population, distributed among its six largest cities, more than doubled in less than thirty years, rising from 1,085,942 in 1927 to 2,380,833 in 1955. Similarly in the last three decades, the population of Aleppo has doubled, rising from 218,289 in 1930 to 465,960 in 1959. Official statistics estimate an annual growth of 20,000 over the next twenty-five years. In 1961, Amman District had a population of 441,000 or 26% of the total population, compared with 218,000 or 17% in 1952.

A large proportion of the inhabitants of Lebanon live in Beirut (450,000 out of a total of 1,626,000 population). The problem of urban over-concentration in Lebanon is likely to become more severe, since the annual rate of population increase is estimated at 2.3%. It is estimated that the urban population, including Beirut, Tripoli, Sidon, [and] Zahleh, will constitute 65% to 75% of the total population by 1978.

[14]Amiran and Shabar: "The Towns of Israel," *Geographical Review*, Vol. 51, July 1961.

Projected Population Distribution[15]

	1959	1968	1973	1978	Rate of Increase
Beirut and Suburbs	450,000	526,000	573,000	625,000	+39 %
Mt. Lebanon	372,000	467,000	529,000	600,000	+61
North Lebanon Including Tripoli	338,000	416,000	468,000	526,000	+56
South Lebanon	238,000	299,000	339,000	384,000	+61
Al Beka'a	228,000	286,000	324,000	368,000	+61
Total	1,626,000	1,994,000	2,233,000	2,503,000	+54 %

In Iraq, the four main cities contain almost half the urban population of the whole country, which accounts for over one third of the total population. In 1957 city population figures were as follows:

Baghdad	847,062
Mosul	179,646
Basrah	174,586
Kirkuk	120,593

By 1959 the population of Baghdad Liwa (province) had increased to 1,306,604. The degree of population concentration in Iraq is reflected in the fact that Baghdad city with towns and rural areas within its administrative boundaries had a population of 1,056,604, just under one sixth of the total population. Urban growth rate has been accompanied by a decline in rural population as follows:

	1947	1957
Rural	64%	61%
Urban	36%	39%

III. PHYSICAL GROWTH AND CHANGING STRUCTURE OF CITIES

A. Change in Size of Built-Up Areas

Within the Middle East region, the modern metropolis with few exceptions has come into being within the last three to four decades. The uncontrolled growth of what were for the most part medieval towns, has led to their mushrooming over surrounding areas at a rapacious rate.

Most cities have at least doubled in size over a decade or two, while some cities like Beirut have incorporated surrounding towns. "Greater Baghdad" and "Greater Kuwait" have spilled outside their city walls. In Israel almost the whole coastal plain, from Haifa in the North down to Tel Aviv, is gradually evolving into one metropolitan area. The intermediate and surrounding agricultural settlements are losing their former rural character and are becoming urban centres with a population of 200,000 or more, either in their own rights or in conjunction with the two big cities. Thus a single metropolitan area with a population of over one million is being formed.

The urban area of Aleppo has expanded from 33 sq. kms. in 1949 to 76 sq. kms. in 1960. A zone of 225 sq. kms. has been established as a safety margin all around the enlarged area. A master plan for Greater Aleppo is in preparation as part of a major master plan for all cities in Syria. Population density in the old city has reached 750 persons per hectare, and it is estimated that, in order to meet the needs of the

[15]ST/TAO/M/21, p. 111.

growing population and to alleviate a density problem living quarters should cover approximately 5,000 hectares.[16]

Beirut, by the nature of its ecology has spread out only to the East, being bounded by the sea to the north and west. Its 525 square miles accommodate about one third of the country's population in addition to 120,000 daily commuters from neighbouring suburbs. The special problem presented by the suburbs of Beirut lies in the fact that though they form one built-up area with Beirut they lie outside the political boundaries of the city, and hence are completely independent from it and do not come under any "Greater Beirut" plan. In a country whose very existence has depended on its laissez-faire policy, each suburb has grown as an independent agglomeration with its own residential, commercial and industrial sectors, but they continue to rely for many services—government, business, etc. on the metropolis. Thus they form satellites which are physically part of greater Beirut, but are classified under the province of Mount Lebanon.

What is considered today as "greater" or "metropolitan" Kuwait has grown so fast as to encompass the original germinal nuclei of population settlement. A process of conurbation and coalescence is still going on. Broadly speaking, the original settlements comprised:

1. Jahra, an oasis slightly removed from the sea, settled because of the presence of sweet water.
2. Old Kuwait, originally known as "Koot" meaning arsenal or fortress.
3. Salmiya, comprising seven or eight settlements growing around the waterfront.
4. Parts of the desert hinterland.
5. Later came Ahmadiya, the oil-company-town which was annexed to Greater Kuwait.

[16]Chehade, N., "Aleppo," in M. Berger (ed.), *op. cit.*, p. 91.

In the process of metropolitan growth, Old Kuwait was partly dismembered. Old traditional quarters were torn down to make way for modern type "urban renewal." Great vistas were opened for the huge cars brought in by the new "super-affluent society." In addition the surrounding desert was used for haphazard development. In this process of metropolitization, the city of Kuwait has quadrupled in size.

The development of Tel Aviv as the primate city in Israel (its conurbation more than doubled in population between 1945 and 1957) can best be explained by the recent historical events in the country. Together with Haifa, Jaffa and Gaza it formed a complex of the larger cities along the coast. Haifa has a major harbor which has always played a leading part in the urban economy. Gaza lost its position after the 1948 annexation to Egypt. Tel Aviv, the largest and economically most important city, added its political importance to these benefits.

Tel Aviv was founded in 1909 as a Jewish "garden city" away from the Arab municipality of Jaffa. The influx of a large number of immigrants prior to the partition of Palestine enabled it to build a reservoir of technical and managerial manpower and a considerable amount of capital—conditions which favoured the development of industrial and commercial enterprises. Today the industrial labour force of Tel Aviv conurbation is more than two and a half times greater than that of Haifa.

Since 1948, the increasing primacy of Tel Aviv has been concomitant with the changes in the political situation of the whole region. Over the last 15 years, the metropolitan area of Tel Aviv has grown by absorbing 10 surrounding towns. The conurbation of Tel Aviv lies adjacent to other urban agglomerations in the central coastal plain of Israel. These extend to Herzlia and Kfar Saba in the North, to Petah Tikva in the East, to Lod and Ramle in the South East and to Rehovot in the South. All these urban agglomerations are located within a circle, the radius of which is only 20 kms. from the centre of Tel Aviv.

Today less than one km. of rural land separates the fringe of the built-up area of Tel Aviv and that of Petah Tikva and the same is true of other borders. Thus in an area amounting to 5% of the total area of the country more than 40% of the population is concentrated. All these towns are within one hour's reach of Tel Aviv by bus. All contribute as well to the increasing urbanization of the surrounding area, bringing an increasing number of towns into the Tel Aviv conurbation.[17]

Beyond a certain point in the development of a metropolis, economies of scale give way to diseconomies. Rocketing land values, congestion, [and] scarcity of housing propel industrialists and entrepreneurs towards the open countryside. Population movements outside the urban areas begin to occur, residential suburbs form a ring around the metropolis, or satellite towns appear according to the availability of space. Hopefully the metropolis acts as a centrifugal force vis-à-vis the surrounding areas. The backwash effect is matched by a spread effect which further expands the area and the domination of the metropolis. In the Middle East, Beirut, Baghdad, Kuwait and the urban conurbation of Tel Aviv-Jaffa-Jerusalem-Haifa represent an open system in their urban growth.

[17]Amiran and Shabar, *Ibid.*

They continue to feed on the surrounding areas. Beirut reaches up to the mountains; Baghdad has engulfed a perimeter nearly 50 kms. wide and Kuwait spreads out into the desert. Perhaps Kuwait is an illustration of the open system par excellence.

B. Change in Internal Physical Structure

Most Middle Eastern towns, in their modern growth are characterised by a land use admixture which makes it difficult to trace a clear pattern in their spatial arrangement. No residential area can be kept strictly residential, small workshops or even larger industries find their way wherever space is available. And even where land use legislation exists it has not been strictly adhered to. Industrial areas are infiltrated with slums and run-down residences; and commercial zones, as in Beirut, are half commercial and half residential with the business office located on the main floor and the other six or eight occupied by middle class tenants.

Kuwait and Beirut, because of their physical location have been able to develop concentrically. Situated on the sea, Kuwait could only expand inland. The central business centre remained located in the old city of Kuwait. By 1952 a first concentric ring (in the inland direction only) was attached to it and comprised new residential areas. By 1962 a third ring had been added following the coast line in a "curvilinear" pattern. Plans for a fourth ring inland are envisaged which will bring the inland village settlements closer to the metropolis of greater Kuwait.

Similarly the city of Beirut could only stretch inland into the mountains where the well-to-do businessmen keep summer homes, commuting daily to the city during the summer months. In Beirut the commercial zone is located near the harbor, and is completely built up with an admixture of commercial, residential and small industrial buildings. Concentric to the port area is a semi-residential commercial zone. This area contains the schools and some industry as well as apartment houses and the shopping centre. On the fringe of the second zone and up to the city limits are residential areas. Thus Beirut's physical pattern is concentric-linear, as imposed by its natural surroundings.

Aleppo's development in the 19th and 20th centuries occurred mostly to the West of the old city, but there was expansion to the East as well. In the centre the business zone within the old city area includes local markets and the central food markets. Surrounding it is a mixed-industrial zone including mechanical repair shops, garages, textile workshops as well as apartment houses, hotels, cafes and restaurants. This is a sizable quarter near the vital centre of the city. Housing is old and in bad condition. A commercial zone with multi-family dwellings forms a third concentric ring. On the street level are the stores, shops or warehouses, and on the upper floors are modern apartments occupied by business offices as well as by private tenants. Buildings are bordering on the main roads and arteries of the city. Two residential zones exist. An older one which is on the East side of the old city is known as the Eastern Residential zone. It lies half within the old city walls and half outside the walls in modern extensions. The Western Residential zone forming the last concentric ring is composed mainly of modern villa-type dwellings surrounded with gardens.

Baghdad's pattern of growth has been primarily determined by the river Euphrates which crosses the city, hence its development has followed a linear pattern. Its central business district lies on both sides of the river, where the ancient market complex existed. Industrial areas of two types exist: one downtown area with workshops on both sides of the business area and the other on the edges of the city to the east and south. This area includes factory districts, the railways workshops, the government oil refinery and other manufacturing industries. Around both areas, but especially on the outskirts of the town is a ring of slum dwellings, reaching sometimes a width of five kms. Higher income housing is to the North of the city in the new city of Al-Mansur.

IV. FUNCTIONS OF THE CITY

Theories on the origin of the metropolis tend to ascribe its specific location to economic considerations. Other factors, however, such as strategy, defence, political expediency, religious significance, climate and the like cannot be discounted. Whatever the combination of factors affecting the spatial location of cities, a certain specific role or function attaches to urban agglomerations.

Perhaps the best way to look at the city is as a set of administrative, trading, industrial and socio-cultural sub-systems in the overall national system.

A. The City as an Administrative Sub-System

[The city] is the seat of government and public organizations ruling not only the city but also perhaps the larger regions surrounding it and the nation as a whole. City government will vary according to the type of central government, i.e., whether it is highly centralized or fragmented. The existence of the central government, its military forces, its legislative and executive branches and the host of civilian administrators and public officials and employees all create certain demands which can best be met in the city. Employees make the city the nexus of administration and the main supplier of all the demands created by this administrative network. The city presents, therefore in this sense the administrative sub-system which is part of the network of national development.

B. The City as a Trading Sub-System

As a centre of population the city assumes the nodal trading position in the national system. Products of rural areas pour into the city to service city dwellers, while finished goods are sent back to the villages in a network of trade transactions. As a result of trading activities of the city, the administration taxes the traders for a portion of its income.

Aleppo's location as a commercial link between the Middle East and Europe gives commerce an important role in its economy. Beirut has acquired added importance as an international business centre, especially since the Suez crisis in 1956. Aviation companies, commercial houses, banks and oil companies tend to locate their overseas offices in Beirut. In addition, its favourable location on the Mediterranean and cool mountains have attracted an increasingly important tourist industry.

Relations with the hinterland. The metropolis can be viewed not only as the outcome of economic forces, but also as an agent of economic change for the country as a whole.

In most developing countries, however, the metropolis tends to suck the elements of economic development away from the hinterland. This is no less true for the Middle East, except perhaps in the case of Israel, Syria and Lebanon, where agriculture plays a less pronounced role. The metropolis attracts capital, labour, and entrepreneurship. Savings accruing in the countryside are spent in the city where investment opportunities are greater and more varied. Skilled and unskilled workers leave their agricultural employment for the city where wages are higher and job opportunities more extensive, e.g. 36.4% of a group of rural migrants to Beirut gave better employment opportunities as a reason for moving to the city. Both quantitatively and qualitatively the metropolis acts as a centripetal force on the surrounding hinterland.

This process is further intensified by the unfavourable rate of exchange between urban and rural products. Especially in countries trying to industrialize, prices of industrial products, protected by legislation, tend to rise while agricultural products are subject to national or international price controls. In the long run the terms of exchange for the farmer weigh heavily against him.

C. The City as an Industrial Sub-System

It may be appropriate to examine the city both as a locus of production and of consumption activities.

1. *The city as a locus of production.* As a production centre the city is the nexus of industrial activity in the country, i.e., before industry seeks cheaper zones outside the city boundary proper. However, modern industry is based primarily on two factors: scientific and technical discoveries and the growing demand for manufactured goods. Both have their origin in the city. Scientific and technical discoveries take place in institutes in the city, and the training of specialized manpower is accomplished in cities. The existence of power and water supplies, transport facilities, in addition to industrial labour skills are important factors in making cities the

centre of industrial development. It is now common practice for such installations as atomic and nuclear energy centres and space research stations to locate in areas which develop into urban centres. These serve the scientific needs of all the country.

In the process of production several factors come into play—such as raw materials, skilled and unskilled labour, power and water—to produce the finished product. To these, transportation adds a vital element both in assembly and in distribution. In this connection the problem of optimum location arises, and the city seems to form the most suitable locus for transport-oriented industries. Aleppo because of its key geographical position in Syria, has the role of a collection and distribution centre for (a) the produce of neighbouring lands, (b) the industrial and agricultural products of Northern Syria such as cotton, grains, fruits and vegetables, (c) all local products among which textiles are increasing rapidly. About 2,000 trucks [and] 300 inter-urban buses (with 1,200 entries and exits daily) pass through the city traffic.

But the industries themselves, and also the population, must be housed, consequently, the next type of industry drawn to the city is that of building and construction. In an area like the Middle East where skilled labour is still at a premium and where the building industry has not been mechanized, construction and its allied side-industries provide employment for a large number of unskilled workers.

Soon the metropolis becomes the source of external economies. The presence of a large number of enterprises services the newcomers. The metropolis develops a gravitational pull serving as the most favourable locality for the production of a large array of commodities. Greater Baghdad counted 4,573 industrial establishments in 1954; 4,449 of which each employed no more than twenty persons, and, mostly of the workshop type which employed 11,726 workers. The remaining 124 were larger establishments and employed 21,641 workers. These latter ranged from wool and textile factories, to construction material production and the workshop of the State Railways, followed in importance by food, drink, clothing, furniture, metallurgy and repair works.[18]

Service industries such as banking, insurance, brokerage, packing, storage and a host of other services become indispensable. These service industries are in effect vital to the survival of modern production. The cities of the Middle East are primarily service centres, offering the opportunity of odd jobs or year-round work to under-employed migrants from the country-side. Government policy has fostered the role of the city as a service centre. Public hospitals, dispensaries, schools, are first located in the cities, and the associated service personnel concentrate in the cities as well. All these economic activities need labour, and act as a magnet for population drifts from the surrounding hinterland. Since the discovery of oil, Kuwait's labour market has drawn heavily on outside labour, technicians and professionals from the surrounding countries. In return, its oil revenues have been invested in real estate, banking, commerce and industry in the neighbouring Arab States. The Kuwait Development Bank finances projects throughout the area, providing badly needed foreign exchange. Surrounding capitals like Beirut, Amman in Jordan and Damascus in Syria have greatly benefited from Kuwait's revenues.

Though industrial activity in the

[18]Al-Madfai, K. H. J., "Baghdad," in M. Berger (ed.), *op. cit.*, p. 51.

Middle East is mainly concentrated in the cities, and though a few cities are in fact industrialized, total factory employment in the region was estimated at below one million in 1963.[19] A few employment figures help illustrate this point.

In Iraq, over half the working population is employed in agriculture. (some one and a half million). Outside agriculture, employment in Iraq was divided as follows in 1958.[20]

Manufacturing industries (including construction)	90,000
Oil Fields and refineries	14,000
Railways and Port	20,000
Road transport	29,000
River transport	5,000
Trade and other forms of business	200,000
Hotels and catering	20,000
Professions	5,000
Education	13,000
Civil Service	37,000
Police	21,000

In 1963, Kuwait's labour force employed in government industrial establishments amounted to 6,062, divided as follows:[21]

Stone quarrying	2
Miscellaneous food preparation	531
Saw milling	408
Printing, publishing and allied industries	588
Manufacture of salt, chlorine, and caustic soda	63
Brick making	10
Metal products manufacture	580
Repair of machinery (except electric machinery)	678
Repair of motor vehicles	2,524
Electricity and water	678
Total	6,062

Employment in Israel, on the other hand, showed the following pattern:[22]

Service industries (including commerce, banking, service in government, public and business services)	44.0%
Industry, mining and quarrying	20.9%
Agriculture, forestry and fisheries	17.0%
Unemployed	7.4%

More than 70% of Turkey's population, about 10 million, are employed in agriculture. The number of people employed in industry, including handicraft, on the other hand amounted in 1955 to 784,000; those in mining and quarrying 45,000 and 174,000 in transport.[23]

Industry of the light manufacturing type (except in oil producing countries like Iraq, Kuwait and Saudi Arabia), commerce and transport provide in varying degrees employment for a large number of the urban population. Except in Turkey, industries are clustered around the cities. Only a few towns—like the oil-company towns—are of industrial origin or have become essentially industrialized. When the city is also the national capital, government service is added to the list of occupations.

Israel, meanwhile, exhibits a unique picture of urbanization in relation to other countries in the region. Towns in Israel grew not as centres for the surrounding countryside, but as centres of foreign immigration, which gave urban characteristics to the economy of the whole country. The urban economy was then based mainly on capital imports and the know-how of individual immigrants. Private initiative and capital in addition to middle class

[19]U.N., *1963 World Social Situation.*

[20]Longrigg, Stephen and Stoakes, Frank, *Iraq*, Praeger, 1958.

[21]Government of Kuwait, Development Board, Statistical Abstract, 1965.

[22]Weinryb, Bernard D. "Impact of Urbanization in Israel", *Middle East Journal*, Vol. XI, Winter 1957.

[23]F.A.O., *Mediterranean Development Project: Turkey, Country Report*, Rome, 1959.

immigrants with an urban occupational background helped develop the country more along the lines of an urbanized than a rural society. Industrial production increased 18 times between 1922 and 1937, with the numbers of persons employed in industry rising from 4,750 in 1922 to 27,260 in 1937; 67,000 in 1947 and 120,000 in 1952. While the Israeli population grew 16 times in the period 1922–52, the number of industrial workers rose 25–26 times.

2. *The city as a locus of consumption.* Production in the metropolis is directly related to consumption. The greater the volume of production the greater the flow of income and consequently of effective demand. The occupational distribution of the population in the metropolis reflects the pattern of demand. Consumption services such as restaurants, theatres, hotels, and cinemas are mostly centralized in larger towns and employ a large proportion of the working population. The taste for luxury items, often imported, can best be satisfied in the metropolis so that it acts as the natural outlet for high quality highly differentiated foreign goods.

A significant aspect of the metropolis is the per capita income of its inhabitants. Data on this subject show that per capita income is significantly higher in the city than in other parts of the country. Per capita income in Baghdad Province is almost double the average for the country (excluding oil industry income).

D. The City as a Socio-Cultural Sub-System

Urbanism is characterised, among other things, by an increase in specialization both in ordinary crafts and techniques and in the higher spheres of cultural and creative activities. Educational and scholarly institutions flourish in cities, and university cities have been known to exist since the Middle Ages. The city acts as a market place for cultural and creative activities. Social movements and innovations as well as political parties and ideologies have their origin in cities. Finally, sports, amusement and recreational facilities develop in the city for the higher income leisure groups.

V. PROBLEMS OF URBAN GROWTH

A. Traffic and Transport

The continuous flow of migrants into the cities and the resulting urban growth poses many economic, social and physical problems.

The superimposition of a modern metropolis on the preexisting medieval-type towns has often resulted in a conflict of functions and existence. A common problem in some cities is the continuing use of animal transport and the habit of driving herds of cattle through city streets on the way to the abattoirs or slaughter houses. Narrow winding streets as in Jerusalem, Beirut or the Old City of Kuwait are inadequate for modern transport. Traffic congestion is a common phenomenon in those cities. In Lebanon for instance there has been almost a tripling of private car registration between 1952 and 1959, most of them in Beirut. In Damascus there are more than 45,000 tram passengers daily in five different lines. In addition there are over 120 private buses carrying about 200,000 passengers daily. And in Baghdad the bus service operated a fleet of 326 buses in 1957 on thirty routes.

In the Old City of Kuwait many buildings and quarters have been demolished to create large vistas and avenues, adequate for modern transport. Lacking a public transport system, private car and taxi ownership have reached a very high mark. The area of worst traffic congestion is the "Safat Square" lying in the centre of the Central Business District. Traffic there is generated both from within the Old City itself and from the suburbs. The creation of an underpass is being envisaged to divert some of the traffic load.

B. Water

Water: The availability of water for domestic and industrial use has been one of the main factors affecting the growth of cities. Water requirements of the modern metropolis have put a heavy strain on the available resources. In some cities, e.g. in Iraq and Syria, water is abundant and modern water systems exist; while in others the lack of water seems to be one of the most crucial development problems. In Amman, for example, water shortage has been an acute bottleneck. Relying mainly on rain for its drinking supply, the amount of water in Amman fluctuates from summer to winter, and a dry year creates serious difficulties. The present system of water pumping is operating at 50% efficiency with complicated manoeuvres of opening and closing valves to supply various neighbourhoods. At the present rate of 700 cubic meters pumped per hour, water reaches each section of the city only every second or third day. Some individual houses do not receive water for a week or longer. In the poorer slum areas, thousands of refugees obtain their water from community hydrants. No water-system master plan has yet been developed so that water sources remain inadequate and subject to infiltration from polluted ground water and surface run-off. Treatment by hand-operated gas chlorinators provides inadequate protection against

contamination. In Jerusalem the main source of water is one which goes back to Biblical times. Rain water is stored in private storage wells during the rainy season. Kuwait's water is obtained by a desalination process at the cost of $140 per inhabitant and $250 a shrub or tree per year.[24] The daily shortage of water in Ankara is between 30,000 and 40,000 tons. Water rationing is necessary all over the city, mains being opened only a few hours a day to each locality. A similar situation obtains in Istanbul.

C. Waste Disposal

Closely linked to water supply is the problem of sewage and waste disposal. The general picture is one either of total absence or inadequacy of existing systems of sewage and waste disposal. In Beirut, storm water and general sewage disposal are combined in some parts of the city. In other sections there is a separate system for storm-water run-off, while a minor portion of the city has no system at all. Sewage flows through outlets to the sea contaminating the water near the city. In Baghdad there is no sewage system except for a small downtown area. A refuse dump with the city's only open sewage disposal canal has become the headquarters of one of the city's biggest slums. A canal made up of pools of dirty water and lagoons of black liquids has been recently replaced by a closed channel. Contracts have been drawn up, however, and a new sewage disposal system is under construction.

Amman has no system, except in minor areas for run-off of rain water. Some of the sewage is discharged directly into the Amman river which crosses the town and from which some people take water directly for domestic

[24]Shehab, F., *Ibid.*

purposes. The present open dumping of garbage and other refuse on the outskirts of the town in an uncovered area constitutes a health menace. In Ankara and Istanbul, garbage disposal and the sewerage system are reported as "hopelessly inadequate." In Jerusalem the system of sewers constructed by the Romans, and consisting of wide underground tunnels, is still used in the old city. These have now been connected with the new city system which empties in the Silwan valley, south of the old city. Damascus and Aleppo both have adequate sewage systems covering 90% and 100% of these cities, respectively.

D. Housing and Shanty Towns

Urbanization is most closely related to housing problems since the population movement means the abandonment of dwellings in one area with concomitant demand and overcrowding in the other. Attempts to meet this demand both by the private and public sectors have been dispersed and unconnected. In the private sector, rural migrants to the city have brought with them their skill at constructing, quickly and cheaply, one-room houses without any amenities, which quickly deteriorate into delapidated unhealthy slums. City dwellers, on the other hand, have shown a great tendency to invest in luxurious reinforced-concrete apartment houses which have served the needs of the well-to-do population. The greater bulk of the population, under these circumstances, have looked to the governments to devise middle-income housing which would meet both their needs and finances.

The proliferation of housing programmes in the region has not succeeded in checking the growth of slum areas within certain pockets of the cities. Shanty towns inhabited by the rural migrants and set up in a hurry to accommodate the refugees have plagued several towns. The rural migrants quickly establish pockets of rural-type dwellings devoid of any sanitation or modern facilities, very difficult to dislodge. Or, if dislodged, they appear in another vacant plot. Slums around Beirut have been in existence for over forty years. Amman's problem in absorbing tens of thousands of Palestinian refugees is far from being solved.

In many parts of Kuwait, migrant workers have managed to build all types of shelter without municipal sanction. As a result, areas on the fringes of Kuwait, as well as many of the villages surrounding it have mushroomed in an unplanned fashion. Two such areas grew near the modern International Airport. It is estimated that they contain a population of 70,000. Another problem facing the Kuwaiti government is that of "urbanizing the bedouin." The bedouins emigrating to the city form the major part of transient or seasonal workers who sometimes become relatively more stable by engaging in construction work. They settle in shack-towns. A "laborers' town" composed of dormitory-type accommodation has naturally not succeeded in attracting that element in the population. It is now proposed under the Bedouin Urbanization Scheme to build 7,000 units in the vicinity of the Laborers' Town to house some 15,000 persons.

Similarly Baghdad has been confronted with the "sarifa" or immigrant shanty town. The "sarifa" is a one-room house constructed mainly of reed matting. Its roof is covered in a semi-circular shape with an independent matting supported at the two ends. The walls are often covered with mud during the winter. One distinguishing feature of the "sarifa" is that it can be removed easily to another site without need of any tools to remove the roof. Family members can themselves remove the "sarifa" and re-erect it in a new location. Two "sarifas" are sometimes attached to each other and occupied by one family. It is estimated that there are 44,000 "sarifas" in Greater Baghdad, nearly 45% of the total number of houses. Their inhabitants are estimated at 250,000—more than a quarter of the population of the city. Sarifas exist both around the city, where they are five kilometers deep in places, and inside the city.

"Sarifa" dwellers have all the characteristics of migrant workers. Unskilled for the most part they earn on an average $28 per month and live under the most unhealthy conditions. About 99% of the shacks have no latrines. 63% of the dwellers work as unskilled labourers, the rest engaging in desultory occupation as peddlers, office servants, night watchmen, sweepers, gardeners, etc. The luckier ones join the police force or the army.

E. Land Speculation

The real estate business, or "real estate craze" as it has been called, has dominated the economic scene in the region during the last two decades. Traffic in land and building—mostly urban—for quick speculative profit, has been the major direction in which the economic vitality of the speculators has been channelled. Population influx resulting from both the rural/urban migrations and from the refugee influx has put large masses of population at the mercy of real estate manipulators. The first spurt of real estate development took place in Palestine as a result of the influx of Jews from all over the world. This influx caused both Arab and Jew to engage in the development of cities; Tel Aviv, Haifa, Jaffa and Jerusalem gained appreciably in population. The Jews built many types of new settlements and communities. In 1948 the influx of Palestinian refugees into Amman and Beirut produced population pressures which led to an increase in building activity and hence in number of land transactions. Today Lebanon has become the focal point for real estate commerce. Owners of empty plots hold on to them, forcing prices up. Religious foundations, both Islamic Waqfs and Christian religious foundations have joined the group of speculators. It has been estimated that one-third of down-town Beirut is in their hands.

Land prices in Ankara have boomed under the manipulation of profit seekers. In an urban upper class residential section in Ankara prices rose from 10 lira per square meter in 1952, to 20 in 1953, 30 in 1954 and between 80 and 100 lira in 1955. By 1958 it had risen to 150 lira. A similar rise has occurred in the price of other urban real estate.

Similarly in Kuwait land values have reached excessive levels in some areas. In 1961 some U.S. $270,000 was paid by the government to acquire pieces of land for the accommodation of public toilets and a small transformer station! In the early years of urban growth, control over land was overlooked by the government. But as the economy developed, large tracts of desert land were fenced by those who foresaw the future prospects. In the re-acquisition of this land for public uses, the cost to the Treasury was substantial. Within the city proper the government reversed its policy. It purchased land in excess of what was actually required for public projects and sold the surplus back to the public at a fraction of its cost. (Sometimes as low as 4%.) Enormous private fortunes were amassed by both selling to and buying from the Treasury. In the old city, the government paid large sums to owners of areas to be demolished and helped them resettle outside the city walls.

A type of land speculation is sometimes engaged in by squatters organized under a leader. A group of families will settle in an unused lot. When the owner goes to court to evict them, their appointed leader acts as a go-between, collecting extralegal rent to pay the landlord, but also charging the families for illicit tapping of electric power and water lines. In return he acts as their intermediary in dealing with public authorities. In the absence of effective legislation, shanty towns are allowed to grow on vacant lots both inside and around the city.

VI. MEASURES TAKEN IN RESPONSE TO RAPID URBAN GROWTH

A. Measures to Cope with Problems of the Individual City

1. *Housing*. Government and private efforts to deal with housing problems have been along the following lines:

a) Low cost housing projects for industrial workers, provided by oil companies or by governments out of revenue from oil.

b) Middle-income housing to be paid for by employees over a certain period of time.

c) Provision of cheap land and credit through Real Estate and Credit Banks.

d) Planned "neighbourhood units" for large groups, combined into a "community" type settlement.

e) Private housing, at government expense, for foreign personnel.

f) Private, multi-family apartment houses of the luxurious type to meet the demand of higher income groups and the foreign international community.

In most countries of the region a combination of these programmes exists to cater to the various income groups of the population.

Although public low-cost housing has reached more than token proportions, governments have been unwilling in general to spend scarce capital on projects judged not to be directly productive. Such programmes as there have been, remain at a scale unrelated to the size of the housing shortage. Moreover, most governments have not tried to use the building capacities of the urban population themselves, owing perhaps to lack of the necessary technical and supervisory personnel. Governments which possess large revenues from oil, however, such as Iraq and Kuwait, have used some of this income to provide accommodation and amenities for the different categories of employees.

In Beirut, up to 1945 housing conditions seemed under control with prices of land and rents at a reasonable level. In the wake of World War II a boom in construction started as a result of the population movement toward the city. The upsurge of economic activity following the Second World War saw the replacement of the three-storey two-apartment walkup by de-luxe apartment houses much in demand by staff of foreign firms working in Lebanon. High prices encouraged speculators and builders to erect seven to nine storey buildings. Capital invested in this type of building yielded as much as 15 per cent interest.

Consequently a complete halt occurred in low and medium cost construction. Average and low income groups took to old buildings; slum areas abandoned by the speculator grew at a rapid pace. The working class has been left to rely on government programmes to improve their housing conditions. Yet government proposals to erect low cost housing in open space suburbs have been unsuccessful, since such a policy would move the workers away from industrial sites.

Kuwait's housing programme has been financed from oil resources, and has catered to various income groups according to their needs. For those persons dislocated by the expansion of the new city, the authorities have allocated building plots at cost price within "neighbourhood units" reserved only for Kuwaiti citizens. A 600 house development is under construction by private enterprise on land belonging to the government. Around the neighbourhood units, a vast area has been created for residential buildings for non-Kuwaitis who constitute an estimated 51% of the present total population. Housing on this site has been of the Western style private villa type. A number of government officials were provided with free housing in this area.

The government has built a considerable volume of housing consisting of "Eastern" and "Western" type models for middle income group Kuwaitis. Some 2,300 such houses are planned for 10,000 persons in this category.

Since World War II Iraq has been facing an acute housing problem, which private enterprise could not solve alone. Construction material prices and a high level of rent have weighed heavily on family budgets. Rents have sometimes appropriated half the family income. Various government departments, mainly the Ministry of Social Affairs and later the Ministry of Housing, have co-ordinated their efforts under a national programme for housing. Between 1950–60, 8,500 houses were built for sale to government officials and other persons capable of paying for them over a period of years. In addition, larger industrial concerns

have been encouraged to follow the example of the port, railways and oil companies in making provision for their labourers. Building societies through which families can have houses built to their own design and pay for them in instalments have been established by banks, such as the Real Estate Bank, and by oil companies.

Under legislation which permits it to control a proportion of the privately registered land, the Iraqi government is offering building sites at low cost. Provision is also being made for the peasants who have drifted from the rural areas and have formed "sarifa" shantytowns especially around Baghdad. Land is to be levelled and streets cut; water, electricity and sewage facilities installed; and the foundations to be laid for houses which the owners will build themselves. The success of these enterprises, will, of course, depend to a large extent on the availability of skilled workmen and on the development of suitable building material.

The housing situation in Turkey has led to the creation of a Ministry of Reconstruction and Settlement in 1958. 22% of Turkey's urban families lived in single rooms, and 34.5% in two-room houses. Between 1950 and 1955 construction permits for 23,438 dwelling units were issued in Ankara. During that period the population of the city increased by 174,624 persons.

The Bank of the Provinces and the Real Estate and Credit Bank devote a large share of their resources to housing and urban facilities. Between 1950 and 1957 the latter invested around $260 million in housing for 70,000 persons. A housing project financed by this Bank provided 4,200 cheap dwelling units at a cost to the dweller of between $2,900 and $3,600, to be paid over 20 years.

In Syria, Aleppo's municipality does

not construct housing for the city's population since it has been proved that government construction costs are 40% more than private construction costs. Experience has shown that the housing shortage and high rents have resulted from lack of allotted land and the high price of land in general. There is a large number of building workers, masons and private construction companies. There is no shortage of liquid assets as the middle classes represent 50% of the city's population. It is judged that by guaranteeing land for construction and advantageous financial conditions, and by allowing some flexibility with regard to building permits, together with tax exemptions, that people will be encouraged to build their own homes. For the working class which represents another 40% of the population, land should be acquired at low price and capital made available on a long-term basis with a moderate interest rate from a land bank.

2. *Physical planning.* Physical planning has been implemented in the sense that most governments have a "master plan" for the capital city and a townplanning office. However, most cities in the region, if not all, had grown to unmanageable proportions before master-plans were prepared, so that the effectiveness of these plans is greatly restricted. Damascus, Amman and Tel Aviv have had effective townplanning which facilitated orderly growth. Kuwait has now a "master plan" covering both Kuwait city as well as the surrounding regions, though due to ten years of unrestricted growth, rapid and chaotic expansion following the oil boom has resulted in the wastage of nearly 50% of urban land. Baghdad suffers from the lack of a comprehensive overall plan. A former plan, amended later, is being carried out piecemeal and haphazardly, depending on the personal wishes of municipal officials. The plan has been interpreted as a mere street-and-road system with little attempt at staging of the main building activities in the city. Until 1960 the municipality employed only one townplanner, with a few assistants.

The master plan of Beirut is a synthesis of many previously conceived plans which were never implemented. Until 1952 Beirut had no officially approved master plan, and no zoning laws.

Since the formulation of its first city plan in 1932, the expansion and development of Aleppo have been haphazard. Expansion necessitated the drawing up of a new plan in 1952 which was not put into effect until three years later. During that period the municipality stopped all construction by refusing to give building permits on empty lots. This only gave real estate agents and builders a good chance to engage in fraudulent construction and private illegal building, without any sanitary facilities and without any plan.

In the Master Plan of Kuwait provision has been made for the development of eight neighbourhood units to accommodate 48,000 people. Each unit is to include a limited population, to have supporting facilities and amenities such as shopping areas, schools, a clinic and a mosque, as well as recreation facilities. Five to six such units will form a "community" with such amenities as higher schools, an auditorium etc.

3. *Land use legislation.* Most cities suffer from a high degree of land use admixture unsuited to the modern functions of the metropolis. The city of Beirut provides a good example of this facet of "urban abandon." Zoning regulations have had little effect in restricting arbitrary land use in most cities. Residential buildings are interspersed throughout the city following

an income pattern rather than land use legislation.

Legal controls over land use have been of two types: zoning ordinances and licensing procedures. The former have succeeded in keeping new industry to specific restricted zones away from residential districts. But licensing laws have not always succeeded in keeping cheap housing units from mushrooming around these industries.

Within the cities themselves, urban development programmes are frustrated by inflated land prices, due to speculation. This has led governments to enact legislation both to acquire land for public use and to impose building restrictions in areas within city planning programmes.

In Lebanon public authorities may acquire lands needed for any public project upon issuance of a public decree, and after paying adequate compensation to the owner. If construction of certain projects raises the value of the land the authorities can acquire part of the land, without any compensation if the part taken does not exceed 24% of the land. If more is taken, compensation is paid for the additional amount.

Moreover, municipalities have the right to consolidate fragmented holdings in order: (a): to ameliorate certain areas or to expand towns and villages; (b): to re-divide slums and blighted areas for improvement and sanitation areas; (c): to reconstruct devastated areas; (d): to construct public roads and (e): for physical planning purposes. After consolidation, each landowner is given a piece of land, equivalent in value to what he owned before consolidation, and the authorities acquire 25% of the land free.

Real estate pools—or syndicates—for land acquisition can be formed in Lebanon for the development of land in certain areas by a decree from the Council of Ministers. The members of the pool are the landowners, the State, and the municipalities concerned. The total value of the land is then estimated and the owners given shares the value of which is equal to the current value of the land. The State allocates itself 25% of the shares free of charge. After developing the area, the land is sold in a public auction and the returns are distributed to the shareholders according to the shares they hold.

Another device used to discourage speculation is legislation requiring landowners to build on vacant land within two years of its acquisition. If the owner fails to do so he is either forced to sell the land, or to pay double taxes on it. Special government committees establish fixed prices for the lands used for building purposes so that landowners cannot exploit others and engage in real estate speculation.

In Jordan, the law enables the municipality to acquire land for a public project after paying compensation for it. In developing the new town of Aqaba on the Red Sea, a Government committee drew a plan for the new town showing the building facilities required by new industries. Private owners were compensated for land acquired from them for the execution of the plan.

In Kuwait, no legislation concerning the acquisition of land for public uses existed until 1961. Freezing of building permits was imposed in the Old City in order to ease the already existing congestion. A minimum of 500 sq. meters required for residential plots caused landowners to make property readjustments among themselves.

Rent control legislation is in existence, both to protect the tenants and to discourage real estate owners by making the real-estate business less lucrative. However, when not strictly enforced, such legislation has had the effect of raising the "key money" demanded by owners from tenants or by tenants among themselves.

B. Measures Influencing the National Pattern of Population Distribution

1. *Industrial location.* A close correlation exists between industrial location and population settlement. Industry seeks a supply of labour, and labour is magnetised to industrial sites. In recognition of this fact some governments in the region, notably in Turkey and Israel, have attempted to decentralize new industries. In Iraq and Kuwait new agglomerations have grown around oil towns.

Much of Turkish state-owned industry is located partly to provide alternative employment to those agricultural workers who would be displaced from the land as a result of the mechanization of agriculture. Often such location is far away from either markets or sources of skilled labour. However, the financial cost to industry is compensated by holding the population to the rural areas.

Likewise the Iraqi government plans to locate state industrial enterprises in provincial capital towns.

In Kuwait, the oil-company town of Ahmadi has been located in an area close to the oil fields, but at the same time close to the harbour and to the old Kuwait city. A new industrial complex is envisaged at Shei'be' in an attempt at regional development. Endowed with natural gas, Shei'be' will house an electric power station, a water distillation plant and a new port. When developed it will complete the urban matrix of the tri-town area of Ahmadi-Fahaheel-Shei'be'.

Israeli government efforts for a consciously planned diffusion of population have met with little success. Spontaneous urban growth, however, has tended to spread out to surrounding agricultural villages which have gradually become urbanized. These now constitute intermediate cities ranking in size between the big metropolitan centres and small settlements in rural areas.

2. *Promotion of administrative unity in metropolitan regions.* In most of the major cities of the region urban growth has extended outside legal city boundaries. Municipalities do not extend their services outside their boundaries, and the smaller administrative units on their outskirts are usually unable to give the inhabitants the services needed, especially when overcrowded with migrants. Thus the problem of shantytowns is sometimes aggravated by the inability of the municipality to deal with them legally, and the inability of the local administration to assist them technically.

Various solutions have been sought to this situation. Within the metropolitan area of Beirut, for example, there are eleven municipalities, aside from Beirut itself. They formed a union to develop better municipal services. This attempt at "metropolitan government", has not yet been successfully implemented. In Jordan a new system of local boundary lines is being contemplated to make municipal administration consonant with the modern distribution of population.

In other instances, as in Baghdad, the city government has had its boundaries extended to include the entire metropolitan area. This was done for the twofold purpose of increasing municipal revenue and to provide for the development of vacant land for new housing.

Greater Baghdad, with a population

of over one million, has annexed to its metropolitan area five settlements surrounding it. These include (a) the agricultural settlement of Abu Ghraib which specializes in dairy and meat products and feeds the city. The 15 kms. separating it from the city are being steadily built up; (b) the ancient site of Ktesiphone with a population of 2,000 which acts as a tourist center; (c) the town of Mahmoudiya, 50 kms. southwest of Baghdad. This town acts as a market centre for the agricultural villages in the district, but because of its administrative affiliation to the city and because of its location on the main highway, it is part of the metropolis; (d) Khan Beni Saad, 35 kms. east of the city is envisaged as a future industrial site; (e) the military settlement of Al Taji, 30 kms. on the northern road to Mosul.

3. *Physical planning in relation to overall planning.* Most countries in the region are strongly committed to national planning and balanced development. If national planning means the simultaneous development of economic, social and political as well as administrative conditions in the country, the attainment of this aim is bound to affect the physical, economic and social setting of cities.

One of the main problems in balanced development is to set a proper balance between the development of rural and urban areas. National planning encompasses both the future picture of industrialization in the country and the transformation of agricultural production. It involves changes in trade patterns and levels of income, in transport and in communication, in population growth, literacy, culture and many detailed aspects of economic and social life.

From this viewpoint, the city is a sub-system which, ideally, should be integrated both economically and culturally within the national system.

As previously mentioned, city planning in the countries of the region has been haphazard, incomplete or even absent. Most of the plans are inspired by transport and traffic requirements rather than by an overall objective of improving the conditions of urban living. Sometimes each housing project has been treated as an independent project with no co-ordination with a long term plan for the locality as a whole. Master plans have not gone far enough in placing the urban agglomerations within a wider national framework. The main obstacle to comprehensive planning for metropolitan areas is that national and local government agencies do not conceive them as a problem of national concern. Several municipalities exist within one metropolitan area and act separately each within its local boundaries. In some cases steps have been taken to promote the consolidation of such separate entities under some system of area-wide administrative unity.

City planning, to be realistic and effective, must draw on the knowledge and experience of many disciplines, such as the demographers in arriving at estimates of future population, on social welfare experts in ascertaining future needs in health, recreation, education and social facilities. City planners need to know about projections in industrial growth and commercial development. They need to consider the administrative importance of the city in relation to the rest of the country. Family patterns, growth and distribution of income, working relations and size of the labour force—all are important factors in comprehensive city planning.

It is difficult to estimate the growth in the future population of a city in isolation of the rest of the country. It is well nigh impossible to determine the income and wealth, industrialization and commerce, except insofar as they develop as part of the general development in the country as a whole. Hence the close relation between city planning and national planning.

BIBLIOGRAPHY

1. United Nations, *1963 Report on the World Social Situation*, 63. V. 4.
2. SJOBERG, GIDEON, *The Pre-Industrial City, Past and Present*, New York, 1960.
3. BERGER, MORROE (ed.), *The New Metropolis in the Arab World*, Allied Publishers, 1963.
4. AMIRAN, D.H.K., and SHABAR, A., "The Towns of Israel, the Principles of their Urban Geography," *Geographical Review*, Vol. 51, July 1961.
5. SHIBER, SABA GEORGE, *The Kuwait Urbanization*, Kuwait, 1964.
6. von GRUNEBAUM, G. E., "Islam," *The American Anthropologist*, Vol. 57, No. 2., Part 2, April 1955.
7. LONGRIGG, STEPHEN, and STOAKES, FRANK, *Iraq*, Praeger, 1958.
8. State of Kuwait, Planning Board, Central Statistical Office, *Statistical Abstract, 1965*.
9. WEINRYB, BERNARD D., "Impact of Urbanization in Israel," *Middle East Journal*, Vol. XI, Winter 1957.
10. F.A.O., *Mediterranean Development Project, Turkey, Country Report*, Rome, 1959.
11. CHURCHILL, CHARLES W., *The City of Beirut, A Socio-Economic Survey*, Beirut, 1954.
12. ROBINSON, RICHARD D., "Turkey's Agrarian Revolution and the Problem of Urbanization," *Public Opinion Quarterly*, Vol. 22, 1958.
13. United Nations, *Administrative Problems of Rapid Urban Growth in the Arab States*, New York, 1964 (ST/TAO/M/21).
14. SHEHAB, FAKHRY, "Kuwait the Super Affluent Society," *Foreign Affairs*, April 1964.

10. Tropical Africa: Urban Population

A. L. MABOGUNJE

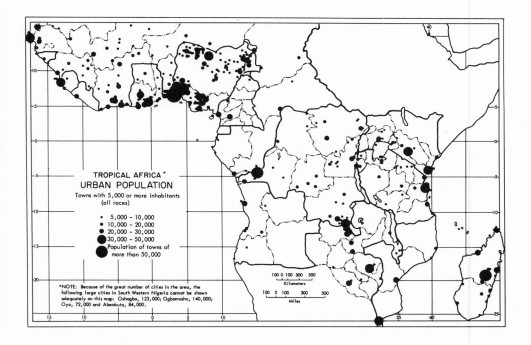

Yoruba Towns (*Ibadan, Nigeria: Ibadan University Press, 1962*), *Figure 1. Reprinted by permission of author and publisher.*

11. Size and Growth of Urban Population in Africa

UNITED NATIONS ECONOMIC COMMISSION FOR AFRICA

The knowledge of the size of the urban population in an area and its rate of growth is of great importance in planning for both economic and social development. Although Africa is the least urbanized of the major world regions, the rate of growth of the urban population has recently been, and is estimated to continue to be, the most rapid in the world.[1]

This aspect of the African population dynamics has to be considered in any economic survey. With a rate of growth of population higher than the world average, Africa is at present contributing 8 million to the world's population increase of over 60 million per year. The urban population increases not only by the balance of births over deaths, i.e., by the natural increase, but also by the net migration from the rural areas and from one town to another. According to the United Nations revised estimates, the population in towns of 20,000 or more inhabitants increased at an annual rate of 5.4 per cent between 1950 and

1960 in Africa (from $21\frac{1}{2}$ to $36\frac{1}{2}$ million), compared to the rate of 5.3 per cent in Latin America; and the projections made at the United Nations suggest that the urban population would increase to 89 million in 1980 (growing at an annual rate of 4.6 per cent, compared to the rate of 4.1 per cent in Latin America during the same period), and would constitute 20 per cent of the total population in Africa.[2]

Considering only the cities of 100,000 or more inhabitants in Africa, which contain at present about 30 million persons, the rate of growth is estimated to be 3 million annually. The magnitude of this increase of the city population is highlighted on a comparison with that in India, whose total population is about one and half times that of Africa: during 1951–61, the city population increased by 11 million (from 24 to 35 million) in India, but during the same time, the corresponding increase in Africa is estimated to be 14 million.[3]

For Africa, this unprecedented increase of the urban population in the recent past, and the prospects for further increase in the near future, have immediate economic and social implications concerning employment, housing, education, health, etc.;[4] unless positive planning measures are taken, this

United Nations Economic Commission for Africa, Demography and Social Statistics Section, Statistics and Demography Division, Preliminary study, final version to appear in 1968 in Economic Survey of Africa, 1967 (Revised October 24, 1967). Reprinted by permission of United Nations Economic Commission for Africa, Tables 4, 7, 8, 9 and Annex I omitted.

[1] United Nations, *World Urbanization Trends, 1920–60* (An interim report on work in progress), paper prepared for the United Nations Urbanization Seminar, 24 October–4 November 1966, Pittsburgh.

[2] *Ibid.*

[3] United Nations Economic Commission for Africa, *Economic Survey of Africa, 1966*, "Some demographic indicators for Africa" (draft).

[4] *Ibid.*

rapid growth of urban population in Africa is likely to aggravate the present urban pathology, expand the "bidonvilles," slums and shantytowns, and lead to considerable discontent and unrest.[5]

In the present paper, the size and growth of urban population in Africa are studied, with occasional references to other demographic aspects of urbanization.

PREVIOUS STUDIES OF THE UNITED NATIONS

The United Nations studies on the urban and rural population of the world were presented at the United Nations Interregional Seminar on Development Policies and Planning in Relation to Urbanization, held in Pittsburgh in 1966[6] and at the meeting of [the] *Ad Hoc* Committee of Experts on Programmes in Demographic Aspects of Urbanization, in Sydney in 1967,[7] and summed up in the United Nations document, *World Demographic Survey: Urban and Rural Population, 1920–80,*[8] presented at the Fourteenth Session of the Population Commission.

Aspects of urbanization in Africa were studied at the Workshop on Urbanization in Africa in Addis Ababa in 1962[9] and at the Seminar on Population Problems in Africa in Cairo also

in 1962,[10] and in the document "Recent Demographic Levels and Trends in Africa."[11] The problems associated with the rapid growth of the urban population in Africa were discussed and attention drawn to the need for economic and other measures to mitigate the urban hypertrophy.[12] The social implications of urbanization in Africa have also been examined in the United Nations document, *Urban Growth and Social Development in Africa.*[13]

DEFINITIONS AND LIMITATIONS OF DATA

Considerable variations obtain in the definition of urban areas in different countries which make international comparisons difficult: some recent African practices are detailed in Annex I [not reprinted here].

The statistical delimitations of "localities" constitute another problem in definition. For example, the city of Cairo, which in 1960 had over 3.3 million people within the city proper, does not appear as one entity in the distribution of the localities by size for the United Arab Republic.[14]

Attempts have also been made to relate the occupational distribution of the population to evolve a measure of urbanization.

For the purposes of this paper, and to preserve uniformity, the following

[5] United Nations, *Urban Growth and Social Development in Africa*, paper prepared for the United Nations Urbanization Seminar, 24 October–4 November 1966, Pittsburgh, Working Paper No. 5.

[6] *Report of the United Nations Interregional Seminar on Development Policies and Planning in Relation to Urbanization*, Pittsburgh, 24 October–4 November 1966 (ST/TAO/SER.C/97).

[7] United Nations document E/CN.9/218.

[8] United Nations document E/CN.9/209.

[9] United Nations Economic Commission for Africa, *Report of the Workshop on Urbanization in Africa*, Addis Ababa, 26 April–5 May 1962 (E/CN.14/170).

[10] United Nations Economic Commission for Africa, *Report of the Seminar on Population Problems in Africa*, Cairo, 29 October–10 November 1962 (E/CN.14/186).

[11] United Nations, *Economic Bulletin for Africa*, Vol. V, January 1965 (Sales No.: 65. II. K. 6), Chapter B.I.

[12] *Report of the Workshop on Urbanization in Africa, op. cit.,*

[13] *Inter-regional Seminar on Development Policies and Planning in Relation to Urbanization*, Pittsburgh, 1966 (Working Paper No. 5).

[14] United Nations, *Demographic Yearbook 1965.*

definitions have been adopted, in line with recent United Nations studies:[15]

(a) Urban population = Population in towns with 20,000 and more inhabitants;
(b) City population = Population in cities with 100,000 and more inhabitants;
(c) Big-city population = Population in "big cities" with 500,000 and more inhabitants;

Note that both "city population" and "big-city population" are included in the "urban population," and that the "big-city population" is also included in the "city population."

The proportions of urban-, city-, and big-city population are computed on dividing the respective populations by the total population of the area.

In addition, the concentration of the urban population in the cities is measured by the proportion the city population constitutes of the total urban population.

Even when definitions are standardized as above, comparison of the urban population and its components has an added constraint. The urban population can grow either by the growth of the population within the same limits or by the addition of population due to accretion of areas to the previous urban area or by both. For computation of the rates of growth of the urban population in the African countries, no attempt was made to separate the two components. On the other hand, a simplified approach was adopted, viz., to compute the rates of growth on [the] basis of

[15] *World Demographic Survey: Urban and Rural Population, 1920–80, op. cit.*; United Nations, *Statistical Concepts and Definitions of Urban and Rural Population: National, Regional and World-wide*, Ad Hoc Committee of Experts on Programmes in Demographic Aspects of Urbanization, Sydney, 29 August–2 September 1967 (E/CN.9/AC.7/L.9), etc.

the population defined as urban at the two specific points in time.

The figures on which the computations of urbanization and rates of growth are based are themselves subject to errors and biases that occur in all processes of data collection, whether on a sample or a complete enumeration basis. Regardless, the basic trends are clear and could not generally be explained by errors in the data.

URBANIZATION IN AFRICA AND OTHER WORLD REGIONS

Table 1 gives estimated percentages of urban population for the world regions in 1950 and 1960. It can be seen that Africa has a lower proportion of its population (13 per cent) in localities of 20,000 and more inhabitants than any other region, and hardly more than half the world average (25 per cent). Even compared with the other developing regions—Asia (17 per cent) and Latin America (32 per cent)—the degree of urbanization in Africa is very low.

The percentage in cities of 100,000 and more inhabitants is also the lowest in the world (9 per cent): presently, there are about 100 such cities in Africa.

Perhaps the most significant figure in the Table for Africa is that denoting the urban concentration—68 per cent of the people living in towns with 20,000 and more inhabitants are found in the cities (those of 100,000 and more). The fact that this figure is above the world average (64 per cent), coupled with the low rate of actual urbanization, indicates that there are too few towns of intermediate size in the region.

The proportion of "big-city" population to the total population is also the least in Africa, about 5 per cent

Table 1

Urbanization in Africa and Other World Regions, 1950 and 1960

Region	Percentage of the Population in Localities of 20,000 and More Inhabitants[a]		Population in Localities of 100,000 and More Inhabitants as a Percentage of:			
			(i) Total Population		(ii) Population in Localities of 20,000 and More Inhabitants	
	1950	1960	1950[b]	1960[c]	1950[b]	1960[c]
World Total	21	25	13	16	62	64
Africa	10	13	5	9	51	68
Asia	13	17	8	11	63	66
Latin America	25	32	16	25	66	77
North America	50	57	29	28[d]	69	60[d]
Europe (ex. U.S.S.R)	38	41	21	24[d]	60	59[d]
U.S.S.R.	28	36	18	24	58	67
Oceania	42	50	41	43	87	81

[a] From United Nations, *World Urbanisation Trends 1920–1960*, (Interim Report on Work in Progress) (67–46528).

[b] From K. Davis and H. Hertz "The World distribution of Urbanisation," *Bulletin of the International Statistical Institute*, Vol. 33.

[c] E.C.A. estimates.

[d] Percentages for population in cities proper only.

around 1960, as compared to the world average of 12 per cent; at present there are 12 such big cities in Africa.

Comparing the figures with those for 1950 (also given in Table 1) it can be seen that whereas the concentration in most world regions has increased slightly over the ten-year period, and has even lessened in Europe, North America and Oceania, in Africa it has increased by one third.

The implications of the scarcity of medium-sized towns are serious. It seems likely that people will continue to flock to the cities, and the gap between these and the small and medium towns (population 20,000–100,000) will become even wider than it is at present.

In general, the larger the town, the more it will differ from the former environment of the people coming to live there, and consequently, the greater will be the problems of employment, housing, education, health and adaptation to the new social conditions.

URBANIZATION IN THE AFRICAN COUNTRIES AND SUB-REGIONS

The degree of urbanization and rate of growth of urban population in Africa vary considerably from country to country and from one sub-region to another. The sub-regions are therefore treated separately, and wherever possible, comparisons made between different sub-regions and countries.

Table 2

Urbanization in Individual African Countries

Country and Sub-region	Year	Percentage of Total Population in Towns of 20,000 & More Inhabitants[a]	Population in Cities of 100,000 and More Inhabitants as a Percentage of:	
			(i) Total Population	(ii) Population in Towns of 20,000 and More Inhabitants
North Africa				
Algeria	1948	14.1	6.6	46.8
	1960	21.6	16.4	68.6
	1966	. . .	13.9	. . .
Libya	1954	18.3	11.9	65.0
	1964	. . .	22.5	. . .
Morocco	1960	23.7	18.9	79.7
Sudan	1956	5.2	2.5[b]	47.2
	1962	3.9	1.7	44.6
Tunisia	1956	20.7	10.8[b]	52.4
	1966	22.9	10.4	45.4
U.A.R.	1947	28.9	20.0	69.2
	1960	36.6	27.1[b]	74.0
	1966	38.2	29.6	77.2
Total, North Africa	1960	24[b]	18[b]	72[b]
West Africa				
Dahomey	1955	5.5	—	—
	1961	8.3	—	—
Gambia	1951	—	—	—
	1964	8.9	—	—
Ghana	1948	5.0	3.3	66.0
	1960	12.3	9.5	77.7
Guinea	1955	5.1	—	—
	1960	6.6	5.7	86.6
Ivory Coast	1956	6.8	5.1	75.0
	1960	7.0	5.6	79.3
Liberia	1960	7.9	—	—
Mali	1956	1.8	—	—
	1962	4.7	2.3	70.5
Niger	1956	—	—	—
	1963	1.3	—	—

[a] Including cities of 100,000 and more inhabitants.
[b] E.C.A. estimates.
[c] African population only.
[d] Unofficial estimate.
[e] Excluding Mozambique, for which data are not available.
[f] U.N. estimate.

Source: United Nations Demographic Yearbook 1962, '63, '64, '65 and National publications. Ellipsis dots indicate that data are not available. Dash indicates a magnitude of 0.

Country and Sub-region	Year	Percentage of Total Population in Towns of 20,000 & More Inhabitants[a]	Population in Cities of 100,000 and More Inhabitants as a Percentage of:	
			(i) Total Population	(ii) Population in Towns of 20,000 and More Inhabitants
West Africa (Cont'd)				
Nigeria	1952–53	11.4	4.1	36.0
	1963	14.0	8.7	61.8
Senegal	1956	19.0	9.9	52.1
	1960–61	22.5	12.6	55.9
Sierra Leone	1962	7.1	5.9	82.8
Togo	1958	4.5	—	—
	1961	5.9	—	—
Upper Volta	1956	2.3	—	—
	1960	3.1	—	—
Total, West Africa	1960	12[b]	8[b]	61[b]
Central Africa				
Burundi	1965	2.6	—	—
Cameroon	1962–64	6.6	4.4	66.7
Central African Republic	1950	10.0	10.0	100.0
Chad	1963	2.8	—	—
Congo (Brazzaville)	1955–56	26.4		. . .
	1961–62	. . .	16.0	. . .
Congo (Dem. Rep.)	1957	7.1	3.5	49.3
	1959	9.1	5.9	65.1
Equatorial Guinea	1960	26.3	—	—
Gabon	1963	10.1	—	—
Total, Central Africa	1960	8[b]	4[b]	50[b]
East Africa				
Ethiopia	1965	4.7	3.4	73.5
French Somaliland	1963	58.0	—	—
Kenya	1948	3.8	2.2	58.4
	1962	5.9	5.2	87.9
Madagascar	1959	7.9	4.7	59.0
	1962	9.0	5.2	57.6
Malawi	1962	2.0[c]	—	—
	1966	5.3	5.3	100.0
Mauritius (excluding dependencies)	1952	—	—	—
	1962	30.1	—	—
Réunion	1954	45.0	—	—
Somalia	1962–63	7.7[d]	5.7[d]	75.0
Tanzania	1948	1.7[c]	—	
	1957–58	2.5	1.4[c]	57.0[c]

Country and Sub-region	Year	Percentage of Total Population in Towns of 20,000 & More Inhabitants[a]	Population in Cities of 100,000 and More Inhabitants as a Percentage of:	
			(i) Total Population	(ii) Population in Towns of 20,000 and More Inhabitants
East Africa (Cont'd)				
Tanganyika	1948	1.2	—	—
	1957	1.9	1.5	77.2
Zanzibar	1948	17.1	—	—
and (Pemba)	1958	19.4	—	—
Uganda	1948	0.4	—	—
	1959	1.2	—	—
Zambia	1963	16.5[c, e]	5.9[c, e]	35.9[c, e]
Total, East Africa	1960	5[b]	3[b]	60
Other African Countries				
Angola	1950	4.1	3.4	82.9
	1955	5.8	4.25	73.3
Botswana	1964	18.0	. . .	. . .
Mozambique	1960	. . .	2.7	. . .
Southern Rhodesia	1965	15.9	12.9	81.3
South Africa	1951	30.8	23.1	75.1
	1960	35.1	26.5	75.5
South West Africa	1951	4.7	—	—
	1960	6.8	—	—
Total Other African Countries	1960	26[b, e]	15[b]	59[b]
Total, Africa	1960	13[f]	9[b]	69[b]

There was relatively little growth in urban centres in Tropical Africa until the Second World War; since then, an increasing expansion of towns and cities has occurred in West, Southern and Eastern Africa. But in the North African countries bordering on the Mediterranean, centres of trade and civilization which had passed through varying periods of growth and decline experienced a high rate of growth during the recent past. Indigenous urban centres have also been in existence for a long time in Western Africa, lying on the trade route between north and south of Sahara, and also later serving as centres of slave trade; in Eastern Africa, development of urban centres is generally a more recent phenomenon.

North Africa

The most urbanized sub-region in Africa is the North, where about 24 per cent of the total population in 1960 were living in towns and cities with 20,000 and more inhabitants, compared with 13 per cent in the whole of Africa. The proportion in towns and cities with

100,000 and more inhabitants is 18 per cent in 1960 whereas it is only about 10 per cent for Africa as a whole.

Of those for which data are available, the individual country recording the highest percentage of its population in towns with 20,000 and more inhabitants is UAR (38.2) (see Table 2), closely followed by Morocco (23.7), Tunisia (22.9), and Algeria (21.6).

In fact, the only sizeable country in the sub-region with a proportion of urban population less than the average for the African region is the Sudan (3.9 per cent in 1962).

The greatest proportion of population in the cities (100,000 and more inhabitants) is observed in UAR (29.6 per cent), and this is indeed the highest proportion in any African country save possibly South Africa (the recorded proportion there is lower, but is for an earlier date). The second highest is Libya (22.5 per cent) and three other countries, namely Morocco (18.9 per cent), Algeria (13.9 per cent) and Tunisia (10.4 per cent) have proportions above that for the African Region as a whole.

The maximum concentration in the cities occurs in Morocco, where 79.7 per cent of the urban population is in towns of 100,000 and more inhabitants; in UAR the proportion is 77.2 per cent, in Algeria 68.6 per cent, in Libya 65.0 per cent, in Tunisia 45 per cent, and in Sudan 44.6 per cent.

In North Africa there are 34 cities with population greater than 100,000. Almost half (16) are located in UAR, and there are 8 in Morocco, 4 in Algeria, 3 in the Sudan, 2 in Libya and 1 in Tunisia. Cairo is the most populous city (4.2 million in 1966), in the sub-region, and in the whole of Africa. It is followed by Alexandria (1.8 million in 1966), Casablanca (965 thousand in 1960), Alger (884

thousand in 1960), Giza (571 thousand in 1966) and Tunis (463 thousand in 1966). These are the only 6 cities having more than 400,000 inhabitants in North Africa.

West Africa

The degree of urbanization in Western Africa is less than that in North or South Africa, but greater than that in the Eastern and Central Sub-regions. The proportion of the population living in towns or cities with 20,000 and more inhabitants is 12 per cent in 1960, which is slightly less than the proportion for Africa as a whole; 8 per cent of the total live in cities with populations of 100,000 and more, and again this proportion is less than that for the whole of the region.

Among the individual countries, the highest urban population is found in Senegal (22.5 per cent of its total in 1960/61) followed by Nigeria (14 per cent in 1963) and Ghana (12.3 per cent in 1960). The countries showing the lowest numbers of persons in Urban Areas are Mali (4.6 per cent in 1962), Upper Volta (3.1 per cent in 1960) and Niger (1.3 per cent in 1963); the remaining seven countries all have proportions between 5 per cent and 10 per cent.

Of those for which data are available, the country with the greatest proportion of its population living in towns or cities with 100,000 and more inhabitants is again Senegal (12.6 per cent). The second highest is Ghana (9.5 per cent) and the third Nigeria (8.7 per cent).

The maximum concentration of population in the cities occurs in Guinea, where 86.6 per cent of the urban population are resident in cities with 100,000 and more inhabitants. The concentration is also high in the other countries for which data are available, and the concentration for the whole Sub-region is 61 per cent.

There are 32 cities in Western Africa with 100,000 or more inhabitants . . . . Over 75 per cent (23) of them are in Nigeria, and 3 are in Ghana; Dahomey, Guinea, Mali, Senegal, Sierra Leone and the Ivory Coast have one each. The city with the greatest population is Lagos (665 thousand), and Ibadan is a close second with 627 thousand; seven of the remaining thirty cities have populations greater than 200,000.

Central Africa

The urbanization level in Central Africa as a whole is low, only 8 per cent of the population living in towns of 20,000 and more inhabitants. There is, however, a wide diversification amongst the individual countries. Both the Congo (Brazzaville) (26.4 per cent) and Equatorial Guinea (26.3) have high proportions of their populations in such towns, whereas in all other countries in the Sub-region, the percentage is less than the total for Africa and in two countries, Chad (2.8) and Burundi (2.6), it is extremely low. Neither Rwanda nor the Islands of São Tomé and Príncipe have any town with as many as 20,000 inhabitants.

Only four countries in the Sub-region have cities with population greater than 100,000, namely Cameroon, the Central African Republic, and the Congos. The Congo (Brazzaville) has the highest proportion of its population (16 per cent) living in these cities, the Central African Republic has 10 per cent, the Democratic Republic of the Congo has 5.9 per cent, and the Cameroon 4.4 per cent. The proportion for the whole of Central Africa is 4 per cent which is less than half that for Africa as a whole.

The concentration of population in the cities is highest in Cameroon, where 66.7 per cent of the urban population are in cities with more than 100,000 inhabitants; in the Democratic Republic of Congo the proportion is 65.1 per cent. Taking the sub-region as a whole, 50 per cent of its urban population live in the cities of 100,000 and more inhabitants, a lower percentage than in any other sub-region.

Of the seven cities in the sub-region four are located in the Democratic Republic of the Congo, and this country also has the city with the biggest population, viz., Kinshasa, which has 402,500 inhabitants. The second biggest is Douala in Cameroon (187,000) and third is Brazzaville (136,200).

The situation in the sub-region as a whole is similar to that in West Africa, in that the population is unevenly spread. In a few countries the urban population is high, whereas in others it is low, and in some cases even non-existent by our definition, though this latter is partly due to overall small populations in the countries concerned.

East Africa

East Africa has the lowest urban population relative to its total population in the region, only 5 per cent overall, though, as in Western Africa, urbanization is high in some individual countries. The highest is in French Somaliland, where 58 per cent of the population is found in localities having 20,000 or more inhabitants, second is Réunion (45 per cent) and third Mauritius (30.1 per cent); then there is a big gap, the next highest being Zanzibar (19.4 per cent). At the other end of the scale are Ethiopia (4.7 per cent), Tanganyika (1.9 per cent) and Uganda (1.2 per cent).

The percentage of the population living in cities of 100,000 and more is very low in all countries of the sub-region. Zambia has the highest (5.9) followed by Somalia (5.7), Malawi (5.3), Kenya (5.2) and Madagascar (4.7). Only two other countries have cities, Ethiopia, where they hold about 3.4 per cent of the population, and Tanzania, where the proportion is 1.4 per cent. Of the whole population of East Africa, only 3 per cent live in such cities, less than one-third the average for Africa as a whole.

In the countries of the Sub-region that do have cities of 100,000 and more inhabitants, the concentration of the urban population in these cities is high. In Malawi it is 100 per cent, in Kenya 87.9 per cent, in Tanganyika 77.2 per cent, in Somalia 75 per cent, in Ethiopia 73.5 per cent, and in Madagascar 57.6 per cent. Only in Zambia (35.9 per cent) does less than half the urban population live in the cities, and in most of the countries it is three-fourths or more; for the whole sub-region, the proportion for 1960 is about 60 per cent.

There are ten cities in East Africa having 100,000 or more inhabitants, and these are located in seven countries. Ethiopia, Kenya and Zambia have two each, and the others are in Madagascar, Malawi, Somalia and Tanzania. The city having the greatest population in the sub-region is Addis Ababa in Ethiopia (637 thousand) and the only other cities having more than 200,000 inhabitants are Nairobi in Kenya (315 thousand) and Tananarive in Madagascar (254 thousand).

Other African Countries

The combined population of the remaining African countries is far below that of any of the sub-regions we have discussed. Nevertheless a large proportion of this population is found in towns having 20,000 or more inhabitants. The bulk of this population is, however, concentrated in two countries, Southern Rhodesia, (15.9 per cent in 1965) and South Africa, (35.1 per cent in 1960), and to a large extent, only in the latter.

In addition to the two countries mentioned above, Angola and Mozambique also have each a city of more than 100,000 inhabitants. South Africa has 26.5 per cent of its population living in the cities, and Southern Rhodesia 12.9 per cent. In the other two countries the proportion is much lower, 4.2 per cent in Angola and 2.7 per cent in Mozambique. The overall proportion in these countries is around 15 per cent, exceeded in Africa only by the North.

The concentration of the urban population in the large cities is very high in each of the four countries having such cities. The proportion in Southern Rhodesia is 81.3 per cent; in South Africa it is 75.5 per cent, in Angola 73.3 per cent and in Mozambique 47.5 per cent.

Of the 15 cities in these countries having populations greater than 100,000, eleven are in South Africa; two are in Southern Rhodesia and Angola and Mozambique have one each. Johannesburgh in South Africa (1.2 million) is one of the three African cities with populations in excess of one million (Cairo and Alexandria are the others) and South Africa also has the four next most populous cities in the Southern part of the region, —Capetown (807 thousand), Durban (681 thousand), Pretoria (423 thousand), and Port Elizabeth (291 thousand).

The present positions of the African

Table 3

Distribution of the African Countries According to the Percentage of Total Population in Towns of 200,000 and More Inhabitants Around 1960/65

Percentage of Total Population in Towns of 20,00 or More Inhabitants	Sub-regions				
	North	West	Central	East	Other
Over 40				Réunion French Somaliland	
30–40	UAR			Mauritius	S. Africa
20–30	Algeria Libya Morocco Tunisia	Senegal	Congo (B) Equatorial Guinea		
10–20		Ghana Nigeria	Gabon	Zambia	S. Rhodesia Botswana
5–10		Dahomey Gambia Guinea Ivory Coast Sierra Leone Togo	Cameroon CAR Congo (K)	Kenya Madagascar Somalia	Angola S.W. Africa
Less than 5	Sudan	Mali Niger Upper Volta	Burundi Chad	Ethiopia Malawi Tanzania Uganda	Mozambique

Source: Table 2.

countries concerning the level of urbanization and the concentration of the urban population in the cities are also summarized in Tables 3 and 4 respectively.

RATE OF GROWTH OF TOTAL AND URBAN POPULATION IN AFRICA

The estimated annual rate of growth of population in Africa in the decade 1950–1960 is second only to that of Latin America among the world regions (Table 5). This rate can be expected to remain constant, or even to increase in the near future due to reduced mortality rates. Although Africa is not at present over-populated as far as actual space is concerned, this trend could cause problems, both social and economic, unless it is considered in future plans for development.

Of even greater implication is the speed at which urbanization in Africa is occurring. Although at present the least urbanized amongst the world regions, Africa's rate of urban growth

Table 4

Distribution of the African Countries According to the Concentration of the Urban Population in the Cities Around 1960/65

Percentage of Urban Population in the Cities	Sub-regions				
	North	West	Central	East	Other
Over 90			C.A.R.	Malawi	
80–90		Guinea Sierra Leone		Kenya	S. Rhodesia
70–80	Morocco U.A.R.	Ivory Coast Ghana Mali		Ethiopia Somalia	Angola
60–70	Algeria	Nigeria	Cameroon Congo (K)		S. Africa
50–60		Senegal		Madagascar Tanzania	
40–50	Tunisia Sudan				Mozambique
30–40				Zambia	

Source: Table 2.

(5.4 per cent) is the highest in the world, and is almost double the world average (3.2 per cent). This is, of course, understandable, since the degree of urbanization is currently low compared with other regions, and Africa is, in a sense, catching up.

As pointed out previously, it is the large cities which create the biggest problems, and [it is a] fact that these cities are also growing faster than the smaller urban areas . . .; the rate of growth of localities in Africa having more than 100,000 inhabitants is 8.6 per cent—more than four times the annual rate of population growth between 1950 and 1960, and over one and half times the rate of increase of the smaller towns. This percentage is by far the highest amongst the world regions, double the world average, and 1.4 per cent and 3.4 per cent respec-

tively greater than the rates for Latin America and Asia, the other developing regions.

The position in individual African sub-regions and countries is examined below.

When considering the individual countries of the region, some of the recorded rates of growth will seem improbable. This is due to the questionable reliability of some of the official estimates from which these rates are computed. Even when the results of full population censuses have been used, the rates are often unrealistically high, because of under-enumeration in the earlier census.

The rate of natural increase of population is obtained from the balance of the birth-rate over the death-rate and does not take account of the migration factor. There are two sources of data

Table 5

Rate of Growth of Total and Urban Population in World Regions 1950-1960

Region	Total Population[a]			Population in Localities of 20,000 and More Inhabitants[b]			Population in Localities of 100,000 and More Inhabitants		
	Number in Millions		Annual Rate of Growth (%)	Number in Millions		Annual Rate of Growth (%)	Number in Millions		Annual Rate of Growth (%)
	1950	1960		1950	1960		1950[c]	1960[d]	
World Total	2,515	2,998	1.8	531.5	753.4	3.2	327	474	3.8
Africa	222	273	2.1	21.5	36.4	5.4	11	25	8.6
Asia	1,381	1,659	1.9	182.8	276.6	4.2	110	183	5.2
Latin America	162	212	2.7	40.6	67.8	5.3	26	52	7.2
North America	166	199	1.8	83.2	112.5	3.1	48	55[e]	1.4[e]
Europe (ex. U.S.S.R.)	392	425	0.8	147.6	173.8	1.6	82	100[e]	2.2[e]
U.S.S.R.	180	214	1.7	50.0	78.0	4.5	32	52	5.0
Oceania	13	16	2.1	5.8	8.3	3.6	5	7	3.4

[a] From United Nations, *World Population Prospects as Assessed in 1963* (ST/SAO/Ser A/41), 1966.
[b] From United Nations, *World Urbanisation Trends (1920–1960)*, Interim Report on the Work in Progress, (67-46528).
[c] From K. Davis and H. Hertz, "The World Distribution of Urbanisation," *Bulletin of the International Statistical Institute* Vol. 33.
[d] E.C.A. Estimates.
[e] 1960 Percentages for population in cities proper only.

on births and deaths, civil registration and demographic sample surveys. Of these, the latter is generally more reliable, and the former is, in any case, non-existent in some countries of the region. Even the results of Sample Surveys tend to be unsatisfactory, and the rates . . . have been adjusted further, to help minimize the effect of different types of errors and biases. Despite these inaccuracies, there is no doubt that rates of population growth are very high in Africa.

North Africa

The overall annual rate of population growth in North Africa is about 2.9 per cent which is above the rate for the region as a whole. Amongst the individual countries, fairly high rates are recorded in Libya (3.7 per cent), Sudan (3.1 per cent), Ifni and Morocco (both 2.8 per cent) and UAR (2.4 per cent). Spanish North Africa has the least growth (only 0.8 per cent) but this could possibly be due to emigration from the country.

Data on the rate of natural increase are available for only three countries. In both Morocco (2.7) and the Sudan (2.5–3) the estimated rate is high, but in Spanish North Africa it is much lower.

Estimates of the growth rate of the urban population are available for only four countries in the sub-region. The highest recorded rate is in Algeria (5.8 per cent) followed by UAR (4.4 per cent), Morocco (3.1 per cent) and Tunisia (2.7 per cent).

For the cities, data are a little more easily obtainable. Here the fastest recorded rate of growth is in Libya (10.5 per cent). It is also high in the Sudan (5.5 per cent), Morocco (4.6 per cent), and in the UAR (4.4 per cent); in Algeria, however, the city population decreased during 1960–66,

when one town went below the 100,000 line.

West Africa

Many of the recorded rates of population increase for the countries of Western Africa can be regarded as too high. This is particularly true of Dahomey (4.2 per cent), Upper Volta (4.7 per cent) and Togo (5.0 per cent) from each of which emigration is known to have taken place during the period under consideration. Likewise, the rates in Senegal (6.0 per cent), Nigeria (5.8 per cent) and Ghana (3.2 per cent) are higher than seems reasonable, even allowing for immigrants from neighbouring countries. Despite the errors, however, the rate of population increase in the sub-region still seems to be higher than the African average in all but three countries—Gambia (1.1 per cent), Guinea (0.5 per cent) and Sierra Leone (also 0.5 per cent).

The rates of natural increase are also high, those of only two countries, Gambia and Upper Volta (both 1.8 per cent) being less than 2 per cent and those of the Cape Verde Islands and Mali (3.0 per cent and 3.1 per cent respectively) being exceptionally high.

The highest rate of growth in urban population is recorded in Dahomey (24.4 per cent) and this is followed by Mali (23 per cent), Liberia (18.3 per cent), Nigeria (16.5 per cent), and Upper Volta (15.5 per cent). In most countries of the sub-region, the rate of growth of urban population is four to five times that of the total population, and even in Gambia, where the rate is only 3 per cent, it is still almost three times that of the overall population increase.

The cities with 100,000 and more inhabitants are also growing fast. The highest rate (15.1 per cent) is recorded in Senegal; in Nigeria it is 13.8 per cent, in Ghana 9 per cent, in Ivory Coast 6.9 per cent, and in Sierra Leone 6.3 per cent. All these are at least twice the rates of increase of total population in the countries concerned.

Central Africa

Excepting Burundi (2.7), Rwanda (3.1), and the Democratic Republic of Congo (2.6), the rates of population growth in Central African Countries are generally low, 2 per cent or less in all except Equatorial Guinea (2.2 per cent).

The rate of natural increase is likewise low, 2 per cent or less in all countries save Rwanda (3.8 per cent), Burundi (2.9 per cent), the Islands of São Tomé and Príncipe (3.3 per cent), and the Democratic Republic of Congo (2.3 per cent). These low rates of increase are due to high mortality in the countries of the sub-region.

Although urbanization in Central Africa has not yet reached a high level, Table 2 shows that in those countries for which data are available, it is increasing substantially. This is especially so in Gabon, where the population in towns of 20,000 and more inhabitants increased by 13.9 per cent per annum in the period 1961–64, and in Chad, where the annual rate of increase in the period 1958–63 was 12.9 per cent. Other high rates are observed in Burundi (8.1 per cent), Democratic Republic of Congo (7.5 per cent) and Central African Republic (5.6 per cent).

Only four countries in the sub-region have towns or cities with population over 100,000, and of these, only two have data on the increase in population of these towns. In the Democratic Republic of Congo, the estimated rate in the interval 1955–59 is 15.2 per cent and in Cameroon, it

is 1.5 per cent for a slightly earlier period.

East Africa

Excluding the small territories and islands, the rate of population growth is less than 2 per cent in only two countries in East Africa, namely Ethiopia (1.6 per cent) and Tanzania (1.8 per cent), and in several sizeable countries it is 2.5 per cent or over— Malawi 3.3 per cent, Kenya 2.9 per cent, Zambia 2.8 per cent and Uganda 2.5 per cent. These figures are indicative of a generally high rate of growth for the whole sub-region in the near future, for it is probable that the countries with low rates of increase are subject to exceptionally high mortality, which can be expected to decrease.

In those countries for which data are available, the rates of natural increase are high, too, less than 2 per cent only in Zanzibar.

There is very little available information on the rate of growth of the urban population in Eastern Africa, but it is known that the number of people living in towns of 20,000 and more inhabitants has increased by a yearly average of 6.6 per cent in Kenya, by 4.4 per cent in Mauritius, by 5.4 per cent in Tanzania, and by 12 per cent in Uganda, so the urban centres of the sub-region are certainly expanding rapidly.

The growth of the cities (100,000 and more inhabitants) has been even faster in the countries for which data are available. In Ethiopia the rate is 6.0 per cent, in Madagascar 6.9 per cent, and in Kenya 9.7 per cent, in each case more than twice the rate of population increase of the country concerned.

Other African Countries

The rates of population growth of the remaining African countries are varied, but in all except Angola and Mozambique (about $1\frac{1}{2}$ per cent per annum), they are high. There are only two available estimates of natural increase, 1.7 per cent for Lesotho and 3.0 per cent for Southern Rhodesia.

There are not many data on the rate of growth of the urban population in these countries. Of the rates that are available, Botswana has the highest (23.2 per cent), followed by Angola (9.0 per cent), South West Africa (4.5 per cent), and South Africa (4.1 per cent).

The highest rate of increase in the population in the cities (100,000 and more inhabitants) is observed in Southern Rhodesia (9.3 per cent) with South Africa (4.2 per cent) second and Angola (3.4 per cent) third.

Overall it can be seen that although the total population in African countries is increasing fast, the urban population in all sub-regions is increasing at least twice, and in some cases three or four times as fast. In many countries the population in the cities (100,000 and more inhabitants) is increasing at a higher rate than that in the small and medium towns (population between 20,000 and 100,000).

To sum up the present levels and the trends for the future, the very low level of urbanization in the African countries shows prospects of a rapidly accelerating rate of growth in the near future.

The other characteristic of urbanization in Africa is the existence of primary cities, a feature also observed in much of Latin America.[16] Excluding the highly urbanized South Africa, many countries of Africa south of Sahara have more than half of their urban population in the principal city: this was mainly due to the development

of one centre to serve administrative (including liaison with the metropolitan powers) and commercial interests. Many of these countries again have no city of as many as 100,000 inhabitants.[17]

The concentration of the urban population in the cities is also noted in the African countries; excluding Tunisia, Sudan, Mozambique, Zambia, and Congo (Brazzaville), the African countries have over half of their urban population residing in cities of 100,000 inhabitants (Table 4).

In the discussion on the respective rates of growth of urban and rural populations, the magnitudes of absolute growth involved should also be considered: this depends also on the level of urbanization in the region. For Africa as a whole, of the total annual increase of 8 million persons, about 2 million or 25 per cent are absorbed in the urban sector. On the other hand, in East Africa where urbanization is very low, the corresponding figure is 10 per cent, only 166 thousand of the total annual increase of 1.75 million being absorbed in the urban areas.

FACTORS OF URBANIZATION

The "push and pull" theory has general currency in explaining the phenomenon of urbanization. According to this theory, the push comes from deteriorating conditions in rural areas forcing migrants to seek a livelihood in towns, and the pull is exerted by the towns to attract rural migrants because of desired and increasing opportunities. A widespread general view is that the earlier urbanization of the industrially advanced countries in America and Europe had been mainly activated by the pull factor, whereas the current urbanization in the less-developed countries is activated mainly by the

---

[16] United Nations, *World Survey of Urban and Rural Population Growth*, Population Commission, Thirteenth Session (E/CN.9/187).

[17] *Ibid.*

push. However, the actual interplay of factors is more complex;[18] and the planned economic and social development, being undertaken by a large number of African countries, introduces an exogenous element in the situation.

As has been noted earlier, migration plays a more important rôle in the growth of urban population than the natural increase. For the urban areas in African countries during 1950–60, the contribution to the growth of the population by migration is estimated to be over 60 per cent, and for the cities over 75 per cent.

Given the artificial frontiers bequeathed by colonization, migratory movements across frontiers in the pre-independence days in Africa were commonplace, at least among people belonging to the same tribal groups. However, the swiftly changing ideological currents and the political ordeals and turbulence that have followed in the wake of independence and even much later, have conspired to dam these inter-country migrations. Internal migrations within a country are, on the other hand, estimated to have increased, leading to the rapid growth in the urban and city population, subject again to internal instabilities in some cases.

Migration has several demographic patterns. The first is the distortion of the general sex-ratio of the population: this is observed in urban areas of rapid growth. On the other hand, in older towns as also in cities where there are good prospects for work for women, as in some areas in North and Western Africa, the adult female population tends to be comparable in number to

males of corresponding age.[19] The other is the overwhelming proportion of the non-indigenous population in the urban areas. In South Africa, the policy of apartheid prohibits the settlement of African families in the towns; in the other countries, the disparity evolved as a historical process, due to economic and social factors.

DEMOGRAPHIC DIFFERENTIALS

The important demographic differentials in the rural and urban populations are the fertility and mortality measures. The available data show that fertility in Africa is generally lower in urban than in rural areas, in keeping with the situations in other parts of the world: mortality was invariably lower in the urban areas than in the rural.[20] That fertility differential is not due to different sex-age distribution of population has been demonstrated in the case of Ghana, where half the differential was attributed to a general rural-urban differential and the [other] half to socioeconomic differential within the towns.[21]

PROJECTIONS OF THE URBAN POPULATION

Projection of the urban population is, by its very nature, more tentative than that of the total population. Such projections have been made by the

[18] *Report of the United Nations Inter-regional Seminar on Development Policies and Planning in Relation to Urbanization, op. cit.*

[19] United Nations Economic Commission for Africa, *Demographic Factors and Trends*, Workshop on Urbanization in Africa, Addis Ababa, 1962 (SEM/URB/AF/4).

[20] *Recent Demographic Levels and Trends in Africa, op. cit.*

[21] J. C. Caldwell, "Fertility Differentials as Evidence of Incipient Fertility Decline in a Developing Country. The case of Ghana," *Population Studies*, Volume XXI, No. 1, July 1967.

United Nations on the assumption that in every region, urbanization levels (percentage of population in towns of 20,000 and more) would rise according to one logistic curve,[22] and are presented in Table 8 [omitted here] for the rural and small-town populations, the urban and the big-city population for the world regions for 1980; the figures for Africa are also presented in Table 9 [omitted here], with the additional projection of the city population. Recently, another set of projections has been made on the assumption that the urban population would increase at twice the rate of total population in each region, except that at high levels of urbanization where this assumption would have led to a decline in rural and small-town population, the modification was introduced that there would be no such decline; to project the population of the big cities, it was assumed that they would continue to absorb one-half of the absolute increase in urban population, as suggested by the observations over the past forty years.[23]

The projections presented in tables 8 and 9 show that the growth of the urban population will be the most rapid in Africa; the total urban population will increase from 36 million in 1960 to 89 million in 1980, the city population from 25 to 75 million, and the big-city population from 11 to 47 million during the period, over two-, three- and four-fold increases respectively.

IMPLICATIONS OF URBANIZATION

The economic and social implications of the rapid growth of urbanization in the African countries are obvious. The economic implications relate to investment needs for housing, schooling, public health, etc.; the social stabilization of the urban population, uprooted from normal rural and small-town environments would also be called for.[24]

However, since at all times the cities have served as promoters of necessary change, the growth of cities need not be viewed as an entirely negative phenomenon.[25] The helpful consequences of urbanization are generally seen in the lowering of fertility and mortality rates, changed occupational composition of the population, acquisition of literacy and skills, and changed consumption patterns. In order that urbanization may turn out to be more a positive, constructive phenomenon, it would however be necessary for the African countries not merely to treat urbanization as an exogenous factor to be taken into account in their planning, but to make it the subject of a deliberate and comprehensive policy in planning for economic and social development.

---

[22] *World Urbanization Trends, 1920–1960, op. cit.*

[23] United Nations, *Urban and Rural Population Growth 1920–1960 with Projections,* Population Division Paper No. 15.

[24] United Nations, *Urban Growth and Social Development in Africa, op. cit.*

[25] *Report of the United Nations Inter-regional Seminar on Development Policies and Planning in Relation to Urbanization, op. cit.*

12. Capitals of the New Africa

G. HAMDAN

The political capital in Africa has, possibly more than in any other continent, an extraordinarily vital importance in the continent's life. Not only is it the culminating point of the cultural evolution of this "Newer World," but it also represents the greatest embodiment of the all-pervasive process of culture contact and is the truly tangential point between two worlds. The African capital is, in Spengler's phraseology, a "pseudomorph"[1] that epitomizes the hybrid nature of contemporary Africa at large. As such, the capitals are the most evident fingerprints of Europe on African life and the most solid palimpsests of colonial history. Indeed, more than any other western bequest, they are "Europe in Africa." If such means of overseas communication as maritime lines, submarine cables, etc., be the umbilical cord which has linked the culturally nascent continent to the mother culture of Europe, the umbilicus itself is surely none other than the political capital; hence its critical role in the life of the new continent. A front of collision between dissimilar heritages; a melting pot of culture if not of color; a dominant focus of cultural transmission and dissemination and a hot bed of political fermentation—to this has come the evolution of the average African capital.

Economic Geography, 40, No. 3 (July 1964), pp. 239–253. Reprinted by permission of author and publisher.

[1] Oswald Spengler. Des Untergang, des Abendslandes, Munich, 1927.

But how far fitted is it for these responsibilities and particularly for the new obligations brought about by independence? How fully does it express the newly-forged nationalisms and national lives? In what direction is it likely to develop? These and other questions this paper attempts to answer systematically. Three main topics are discussed: first a historical perspective surveys the evolutionary background of African capitals and classifies them into distinct types; a study of location viewed in terms of centrality as well as of nodality follows; finally metropolitan size is treated: its categories, patterns, and controlling factors.

HISTORICAL PERSPECTIVE

Like the nation state, the political capital in the greater part of Africa is a very recent introduction. The regional differential in the age and historical perspective of African capitals represents, therefore, an important element in their character and structure. From the viewpoint of origins and historical evolution four types of political capitals can be distinguished in the continent, viz., historic, native, colonial, and post-colonial. [See Figure 1.]

Historic Capitals

Historic (or ancient) capitals are confined to Arab Africa which, from the dawn of history, has known one form or another of the nation state and with it witnessed the rise of the national

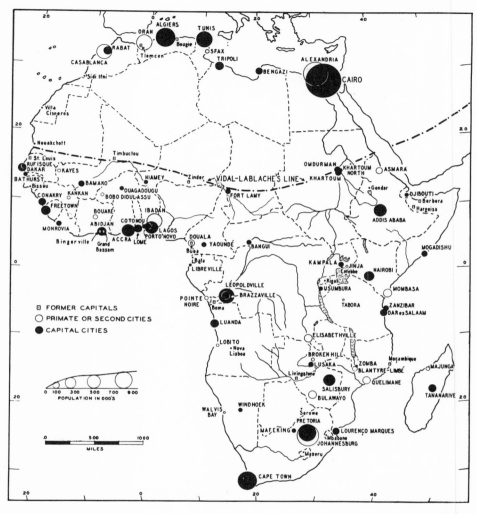

FIGURE 1

Capital Cities in Relation to Certain Other Cities in Africa

historic capital. Some of these capitals attained relatively huge sizes and importance and so deeply expressed the national life that they became immortal capitals despite some passing discontinuities in their legal status. This millennial history gives them today considerable momentum and prestige. Whether as Pharaonic Memphis and Heliopolis or as Arab Fustat or Cairo proper, Cairo is easily the most ancient of historic capitals in the continent. If Damascus claims to be the oldest continuously inhabited city in the world,[2] Cairo is probably older though less continuous. The total age of Cairo as capital easily exceeds the combined ages of all the political capitals of tropical Africa or sub-Saharan Africa. As to size, more than once in her history she was the biggest city in the world; at least a millennium ago she had reached the million mark.[3]

Since Carthage, Tunis too has been a major historic capital and in the Middle Ages was a serious rival of Cairo. Algiers, on the other hand, is relatively more recent; although of Berber origins, as a capital, it was begun by the Turks in 1519 and has since remained the capital of Algeria. Rabat is an older city, founded by the Almoravides as one of their characteristic "ribats" (religious strongholds) which punctuated the Maghrib in the Middle Ages. It is an old, particularly successful ribat, but was chosen capital only under the French.[4]

Native Capitals

"Native" (or medieval) capitals are in fact a transitional type between the historic and colonial capitals. Historically, they are medieval in origin, the greater majority of them having started in the later centuries of the Middle Ages while a few originated a little earlier. Culturally, they are universally associated in one way or another with intrusive, alien influences, mainly Arab and generally Asian. Geographically, they are scattered throughout a belt describing a right angle around tropical Africa with one arm along the savanna-saharan borders and the other along

the east coast all the way from the African Horn to Madagascar. Strongly permeated with Arab influence whether from north or east, this belt is in more than one sense the "penumbra of the Arab World." Here developed a rather modest type of capital city. They may conveniently be called "native" capitals. They were not particularly strong, stable capitals, nor indeed were their states anything like clearly defined or areally settled. Prominent among them were Timbuctou, Gao, Mali, and Kano in the western Sudan, and some of them now reach a full thousand years of age. Of a greater importance, though by far the latest native capital in West Africa, is Ibadan. It was the first truly forest city in tropical Africa and startled the early European colonists with its unusual magnitude and architecture.

In the eastern Sudan the Gezira triangle in particular abounded in thriving capital cities including Sennar, seat of the Fung dynasty, El-Damer, Shendi, and finally Omdurman.[5] In the African Horn, Berbera, Gondar, and Addis Ababa were at one time or another native political capitals. Contrary to a common belief, Addis Ababa is not an ancient city; it was founded at a relatively recent date.[6] In the Zanj coast, native capitals were essentially coastal, Arab creations. Zanzibar (= Coast of the Negroes), Dar-es-Salaam, Mombasa, Malindi, and Sofala (a corruption of its homonym Zofar of Oman and sometimes called Zofar of the Negroes[7]) were already thriving capitals when the Portuguese arrived in the 16th century.

[2] Benjamin E. Thomas, "North Africa and the Near East," in *World Geography*, Otis Freeman and John Morris, Eds., 1958, p. 419.

[3] G. Hamdan, "The Pattern of Medieval Urbanism in the Arab World," *Geography*, Vol. 47, Part 2, No. 215, April, 1962, p. 128.

[4] *Ibid.*, pp. 130–131.

[5] G. Hamdan, "The Growth and Functional Structure of Khartoum," *Geogr. Rev.*, Vol. 50, 1960, p. 21.

[6] G. H. T. Kimble, *Tropical Africa*, N.Y., 1960, Vol. 1, p. 100.

[7] A. H. Keane, *Africa*, London, 1895, Vol. 2, p. 520.

To the same category should be added Tananarive in Madagascar which was founded in the Middle Ages by the Merina immigrants of southeast Asia to be their seat of power in the island.[8]

Few of all these native cities are today political capitals; colonial capitals have come to inherit their role and to seal their fates. Thus Dakar has inherited all the inland capitals of western Sudan in (the former) Afrique Occidentale Française, while Lagos has replaced Ibadan in Nigeria. In the east, Khartoum displaced Omdurman, while in British Somaliland the capital shifted from Berbera to Hargeisa. Only Dar-es-Salaam and Tananarive were adopted by the colonial powers as starting points for their capitals.

Colonial Capitals

Colonial capitals are entirely the creation of the new masters of the continent. An absolutely novel introduction in an entirely virgin land insofar as urbanism was concerned, they were necessary as centers of control and administration.[9] Their range practically covers tropical Africa or more precisely Africa south of the Sahara, that is to say the colonial capital is areally and numerically the dominant type in the continent. Three major characteristics distinguish the colonial capital. First, absolute youth; the majority do not exceed a bare century in age, indeed few antedate the "scramble" of the eighties of the last century. This minority usually goes back to the beginnings of the colonial era in the 16th to 17th centuries and is, therefore, strictly coastal in distribution, e.g., Lourenço Marques (1545), Luanda (1576), and Cape Town

(1652). On the contrary, the latest colonial capitals are those situated inland—indeed the relationship between inland situation and young age seems almost direct. Thus Pretoria was founded in 1855, Mafeking in 1885. Farther north the dates are more recent; both Salisbury and Kampala date from 1890, Buluwayo and Entebbe from 1893, while Nairobi and Khartoum come together in 1899. Still younger are Fort Lamy (1900) and Livingstone (1905).[10] In short, most colonial capitals in Africa are the product of the last century if not of the present one.

The second salient feature of the colonial capitals is their pronounced instability, essentially an earmark of the pioneer fringe in which they were planted and denoting the experimental stage of trial and error. Thus quite often these capitals shifted from one location to another, occasionally even to a third, in such a way as to suggest that they were sometimes hasty, improvised geographical adventures or unsuccessful urban speculations. In all this, they strongly remind, on a vaster scale, of the well-known experience of Brazil in this respect.[11] Hence the striking profusion of dead or "fossil" capitals in young tropical Africa. The shifts of the colonial capital were usually prompted by physical or political factors or by the changes in means of communications. Thus in Portuguese Guinea the capital underwent three shifts: until 1890 it was Geba, so central but so malarial that it had to be moved to Bolama whence it was again moved in 1942 to Bissau on a densely-populated

[8] Kimble, *op. cit.*, p. 101.
[9] Pierre George, *La Ville. Le Fait urbain à travers le Monde*, Paris, 1952, pp. 311–315.

[10] For these dates, see: *Statesman's Yearbook*, 1960–1961; A. Gordon-Brown, *Yearbook and Guide to East Africa*, London, 1961; *Year Book and Guide to Southern Africa*, London, 1961.
[11] Maurice Le Lannou, *La Géographie Humaine*, Paris, 1949, p. 178.

island in the Geba estuary commanding the economic heart of the country. Similarly, in the Ivory Coast the capital remained in Grand Bassam until 1900 when, after a series of epidemics and plagues, it moved to Bingerville from which it again trekked to Abidjan in 1934.[12] In French West Africa, St. Louis was initially the capital but was eventually replaced by Dakar.[13] In most of these cases the shifts in trade routes and the substitution of railways for inland waterways were factors in re-location.[14]

Until 1926 Zinder was capital of Niger, but its desert location, though central, necessitated its replacement by extremely marginal, but riverine, Niamey.[15] Again in the Cameroon, Buea, a health resort and a "hill station" inland, was the capital under the Germans until the seat of administration was moved to Douala whence it again migrated back inland to Yaoundé where it has remained so far.[16] Likewise, the capital in neighboring (French) Congo was moved from coastal Point Noire to Brazzaville. A somewhat parallel move took place in (Belgian) Congo in 1929 when the capital was transferred from Boma to Léopoldville. Since 1926 Nova Lisboa on the plateau heights, the "planalto," of the interior, has been capital-designate of Angola and has since been prepared to replace unhealthy, low-lying, coastal Luanda. Farther east, Livingstone remained capital of Northern Rhodesia until 1935 when it was succeeded by Lusaka. Again,

since 1907, Lourenço Marques in Moçambique has replaced the earlier capital of that name.[17] From this account, it will be noticed, first, that West Africa in particular is a vast cemetery of dead capitals, second that Portuguese capitals in Africa have been the most unstable and this despite—or is it because of?—the fact that Portuguese colonization is the most ancient in the continent.

Finally, some colonial capitals in Africa betray certain rather abnormal features which may well be a manifestation of political anomaly. One such feature is the dualism or multiplicity of capitals in the same country. Until recently, Libya had two capitals, Tripoli and Bengazi—a direct result of the split of the habitable sector into two discrete "islands," Tripolitania and Cyrenaica. But the Maghrib is unique in having five capitals between which the government periodically moves:[18] besides Rabat, the political capital proper, Casablanca is the economic capital, Marrakesh the historic capital, Fez the religious capital, while very recently Tangier has been officially added as the summer capital. In Sudan, Khartoum is sometimes considered the modern capital and Omdurman the native capital. Besides Entebbe, strictly the political capital, Kampala is the real economic metropolis of Uganda. The Union of South Africa, a strongly centralized unitary state,[19] let it be remembered, has officially two political capitals: Cape Town is the seat of Parliament, Pretoria that of the executive government. This dualism is a direct reflection

---

[12] R. J. Harrison Church, *West Africa*, London, 1960, p. 349.

[13] Pierre George, *op. cit.*, p. 315.

[14] Derwent Whittlesey, *The Earth and the State*, Washington, 1944, p. 67.

[15] Church, *loc. cit.*, p. 266.

[16] R. J. Harrison Church, *Modern Colonization*, London, 1950, p. 61.

[17] L. D. Stamp, *Africa. A Study in Tropical Development*, N.Y., 1953, pp. 373 and 447.

[18] *Statesman's Yearbook*, 1960–1961.

[19] Nelson E. Mustoe, "South Africa Today," in *The Africa of Today and Tomorrow*, Royal African Society, London, 1959, p. 89.

of the well-known Afrikaner-Briton dichotomy. It is not often so well known that, in South-West Africa, Swakopmund is considered a summer capital to which the Government moves from Windhoek for a few months every year.[20]

As a result of all this, Africa has more capitals than states. Of the latter there are 50 (including the pocket states and enclaves but excluding Zanzibar, Mauritius, and Comoro) while the political capitals proper number 52. Apart from number, a striking anomaly in Africa is that of the "borrowed capital." Until very recently, there were two cases where the state "borrowed" her capital from another political unit across the borders—a state of affairs unknown almost anywhere else in the world. Thus Mauritania was administered from St. Louis in Senegal while Bechuanaland's capital was Mafeking in the Union. It will be noticed that both countries are mere "boxes of sand," lacking any real economic base.

Post-colonial Capitals

Post-colonial, or post-independence, capitals are in general the inherited colonial capitals, only with some modifications related to the abrupt changes in the political map in the liberation period. The instability of the contemporary political landscape as represented in movements of unification and separatism is also a factor now controlling the fates of many capitals. Thus the sudden creation of many new states has engendered the overnight promotion to political capitals of previously mere administrative centers. Many such "fiat capitals" were not fitted for the new function—some

indeed were no more than glorified villages—but there was no alternative: they are "necessity capitals." Examples particularly abound in the successor states to the former Afrique Occidentale Française. The latest capital created by political fissioning is at present Kigali in Ruanda. The previously capital-less states of Mauritania and Bechuanaland are now facing the problem of developing new capitals of their own: Mauritania, with French aid, is already creating Nouakchott literally from nothing,[21] while with the withdrawal of the Union of South Africa from the Commonwealth, Bechuanaland must either create a new capital or adopt one of her midget towns as capital— Serowe perhaps.[22]

A few of the states of Africa are lucky in that they have inherited the capitals of vaster political units, e.g., Senegal has inherited Dakar, capital of the whole A.O.F., and the Congo republic that of A.E.F., Brazzaville. On the other hand, the few political mergers and annexations that have taken place in the continent have proved a catalyst that has naturally engendered the "demotion" of certain capitals. Asmara has lost its former status as capital since the annexation of Eritrea as "Northern Ethiopia." Similarly, Hargeisa has become an administrative sub-capital since the formation of unified Somalia. In the now dissolved Central African Federation it was natural that Salisbury, capital of Southern Rhodesia, the "nuclear core"[23] of the Federation, should be the federal capital, while Lusaka, capital of Northern Rhodesia, began relatively to stagnate.

[20] Gordon-Brown, *Yearbook & Guide to Southern Africa*, pp. 462–463.

[21] R. J. Harrison Church, "Mauritania," *Focus*, Vol. 12, No. 3, Nov., 1961, p. 2.

[22] A. G. Hodgkiss and R. W. Steel, "The Changing Face of Africa," *Geography*, Vol. 46, Part 2, No. 211, April, 1961, p. 159.

[23] Whittlesey, *op. cit.*, p. 2.

But whether promoted or demoted, most of these capitals face a common problem: the stigma of their colonial ancestry and the often incongruous maritime orientation imposed by the colonial powers. Such problems had equally faced the Asian states at their independence a decade earlier and defeated all their attempts to originate fresh, fully "nationalist" capitals free from the memories of the past and affording genuine symbols of national pride. The reason is that the existing capitals are about the only place in a backward country where the economic potential of the state has been accumulated to guarantee a reasonably decent cultural climate necessary for a modern capital, and it is no easy proposition to duplicate them anew or forsake them for "raw," poor, and incompetent centers. In addition, if these capitals symbolize the colonial past, they equally symbolize the nationalist movement, since they were the seats of the struggle for liberation and independence.[24]

It is for all these reasons that the present inherited capitals will in all likelihood remain unreplaced. If certain states are now searching for new capitals, this is simply because of physical or domestic reasons. Thus Libya, vexed by her capital dualism, has, after prolonged hesitation between many sites including el-Shahat and El-Beida in Cyrenaica, opted for the latter and has already begun developing it as the new federal (now national) capital. Ethiopia, too, is lately contemplating moving the capital from Addis Ababa, where excessive elevation and rarified air make its climate unhealthy, to Gondar, an ancient regional capital situated to the north of Lake Tana at a moderate elevation from sea level.

Even in such few cases, the shift to the new capital is likely to meet, as the example of distant Brazilia has recently shown, with staunch resistance from the vested interests of the inhabitants of the previous capital. In Libya many, especially Tripolitanians, have resented Beida on the grounds of "extravagance and its eccentric position."[25]

LOCATION

Two main themes will be considered here: first, centrality will refer only to "geometric" location within the political area of the state; and, second, nodality will view location in physiographic terms, i.e., with reference to the lineaments of the physical landscape.

Centrality

The cardinal fact about the location of African capitals is undoubtedly their excessively marginal situation within the political framework, so much so that we can safely say that Africa is the continent of eccentric capitals. Very few capitals are centrally situated. It is needless to emphasize the resulting difficulties of political control and administration, the weakened grip of the capital on the distant provinces and its failure to strike a balance between the component regions of the state. This is all the more true of those vast, wide-flung countries, especially with the backward, almost primitive, state of transport and communication in most of the continent. No less serious is the fact that the peripheral capital, especially when young, as indeed most African capitals are, tends to acquire a "regional" rather than a truly national character. Perforce most of the population is recruited from the immediate

---

[24] R. L. H., "New Capitals of Asia," *Geogr. Rev.*, Vol. 48, 1958, pp. 435–436.

[25] John I. Clarke, "Oil in Libya: Some Implications," *Econ. Geog.*, Vol. 39, 1963, p. 49.

local surroundings or regional cadre. This is very likely to cause regional interests to prevail and to override the national interests, a state of affairs bound in ethnically heterogeneous and tribal states, as are most African countries, to make the capital the subject of protest and contention instead of being a factor of harmony and integration between the regions of the state.

Thus Khartoum, standing as she does at a ratio of 1 : 2 from north to south within the political framework, is essentially a "northern" capital at a time when the country is threatened by the cessionist separation of the southern minority.[26] Similarly Lagos, in loosely knit federal Nigeria, is not much different from the traditional Yoruba-capital Ibadan in that the dominant element in her population is, as a result of her marginal position in the Western Region, the Yoruba. Indeed, the very eccentric position which precludes the equal representation of all the elements of the state in the capital at the same time tempts foreign elements from bordering states to immigrate for work there. A clear example is Brazzaville where a native population of mostly local extraction competes with an unusually large proportion of foreign Africans drawn from all the adjoining countries of Central Africa.[27]

Two or three main factors account for the eccentricity of African capitals. There is, first, the marginality of the "ecumene," i.e., the habitable and productive part of the state.[28] In all African countries the ecumene represents a very small fraction of the total area, and more often than not this tiny core tends to be located along one side or another of the political area. Even when the capital occupies a central position in this core—which is not often the case in Africa—it remains peripheral with reference to the total political area. The second control is political and comes from without, namely colonial orientation whereby the location of most capitals is determined, as in Asia, by the nature and interests of maritime colonization. Whether in the earlier "foothold" stage or in the later penetration stage, they were necessarily coastal—from the standpoint of the maritime powers a location essentially central between the "hinterland" of the colony on one side and on the other the invisible metropolitan "foreland" overseas.[29]

This coastal selection was not confined to the colonial capitals proper but also involved the historic and native capitals as well. Having reoriented the continent and "turned it inside out," this areal preference moved many interior capitals to the coast, e.g., from Marrakesh and Fez to Rabat in Morocco and from Timbuctou, Gao, and Ibadan to Dakar, Accra, and Lagos in West Africa. Surely, the extreme of peripheral coastal capitals was reached in the anomalous situation of A.O.F. and A.E.F., which, before their dissolution, were governed respectively from Dakar and Brazzaville, that is each some 2000 miles away from the farthest borders of its territory, and that under an intensely over-centralized system of "direct rule."[30]

Does climate play a part in locating capitals in Africa, a continent suffering

---

[26] G. Hamdan, "Some Aspects of the Urban Geography of the Khartoum Complex," *Bull. Soc. Geog. d'Egypte*, Vol. 32, 1959, pp. 90–91.

[27] *Aspects Sociaux de l'Industrialisation et de l'Urbanisation en Afrique au Sud du Sahara*, ed., Daryll Forde, Unesco, Paris, 1956, p. 120.

[28] Whittlesey, *op. cit.*, p. 2.

[29] Guido Weigend, "Some Elements in the Study of Port Geography," *Geogr. Rev.*, Vol. 48, 1958, p. 195.

[30] Whittlesey, *loc. cit.*, p. 381.

badly from an oppressive tropical climate? It may plausibly be suspected that in states possessed of extreme climates capitals tend to seek the optimum margins, that is the most temperate sectors of their areas.[31] It is certain that the coastal situation in most African states, besides meeting the needs of colonial policy, realizes this desideratum. Thus in the tropical states, it is at least a guarantee of a refreshing waterfront and a modified meso- or micro-climate. In extra-tropical countries like the Maghrib states and South Africa it *ipso facto* locates the capital on the more temperate side of the territory (i.e., the farthest from the equator). The poleward bias of the capital is manifest in interior Cairo and Khartoum which strongly tend to the northern sectors of their countries, that is, those farthest from the equator. Similarly, but in the opposite direction, the capitals of the Central African Federation cling to the extreme south. In Moçambique, just as in Brazil where the Portuguese capital had earlier moved along the coast from Bahia well in the north to Rio in the extreme south, the capital moved early in this century fully ten degrees of latitude from Moçambique in the far north to Lourenço Marques in the extreme south—in fact in the sole extra-tropical pocket of the territory.

The end product of all these controls is the marginal capital, whether coastal or internal. Thus with few exceptions all the coastal countries have their capitals on the coast. Of 36 coastal states (including pockets and enclaves but excluding Zanzibar, Mauritius, and Comoro) 27 have coastal capitals. The coastal capital is thus the rule in

Africa. Eccentricity becomes magnified in particularly extensive territories like Libya, Algeria, Mauritania, Nigeria, Angola, and Moçambique. The dualism of capital in Libya is no remedy, while in Algeria some 1200 miles (i.e., the distance between Paris and the Black Sea) separate Algiers from the southern border. In Mauritania the new capital is not even central with reference to the coastal strip, while in Nigeria, Lake Chad is some 850 miles distant from Lagos. The British realized this gross marginality and at one time Kaduna was almost chosen by Lugard to be capital of Nigeria in view of its unique centrality as well as its moderate climate. The project, however, did not come to fruition. So, too, was the fate of a French project to choose fairly central Meknes instead of Rabat in Morocco.

In Angola, on the other hand, Nova Lisboa is already the capital-designate, though Luanda is still the actual capital. Even with regard to the coast alone, neither Mogadishu nor Lourenço Marques is anything like central. In the Union the dualism of the capital compensates for pronounced marginality and strikes a balance between north and south, between Boer and British; Pretoria and Cape Town stand on the horns of the "Fertile Crescent" of South Africa. Spanish possessions show a special case of marginality of capitals; often the mainland pockets are ruled from offshore islets or at least from other pockets. Thus although Sidi Ifni is capital of the Ifni enclave, the seat of government is Cabo Juby in "Southern Morocco" in Spanish Sahara.[32] Again, although Bata is capital of Rio Muni, the capital of Spanish Guinea, which

---

[31] G. Hamdan, *Urban Geography* (in Arabic), Cairo, 1960, p. 247.

[32] Nevill Barbour, *A Survey of North West Africa (The Maghrib)*, London, 1959, p. 189.

includes the islets of Fernando Po, Annobon, Corisco, in addition to Rio Muni, is Santa Isabel on Fernando Po.

Of coastal countries with interior capitals, only 10 cases are found in Africa. The inland situation is explained either by the magnetism of an arterial river, as in the case of Léopoldville and Brazzaville on the Congo and of Cairo and Khartoum on the Nile, or by the attraction of an elevated site [for] "hanging capitals" in tropical latitudes as in the cases of Addis Ababa, Nairobi, Yaoundé, Windhoek, Pretoria, and Tananarive. The internal situation, however, is not necessarily a guarantee of political or ecumenical centrality: Yaoundé, Pretoria, and Nairobi are more or less marginal, while Léopoldville and Brazzaville fall right on the frontiers. On the other hand, Windhoek, Addis Ababa, and Tananarive are to a great extent central. Khartoum, too, though politically rather marginal, is ecumenically at the very hub of Sudan; she stands at the apex of the Gezira triangle which, being the central core of the savanna "middle belt" (the really inhabited third of the country)[33] is the economic heart of modern Sudan. *Prima facie*, Cairo would also seem far from central within the ecumene; the Delta is only 170 kilometers long against some 800 kilometers for Upper Egypt. The fact, however, is that the Delta is twice as big in area and productivity, while in population the two sectors are nearly equal. Furthermore, Cairo, like the peak of a stepped pyramid, tops the densest sector of the whole valley and is thus the best harmonizer and welder between north and south. As Stamp

rightly says, "From the point of view of modern Egypt, Cairo is perhaps the most rationally situated capital in the world."[34]

Finally, the inland countries, of which Africa has 14 (including the various enclaves and pockets), have surprisingly marginal capitals. Fort Lamy and Bangui are on the borders outright; Bamako, Niamey, and Salisbury almost; while even in tiny Basutoland, Maseru nearly abuts the western border, not to mention Bechuanaland where the capital falls entirely beyond the border. In the Sahara-Sahel-Savanna states of the western Sudan, the explanation of this pronounced marginality is the eccentric position of the narrow habitable strip along the southern frontiers. The sole exception is Ouagadougou in Upper Volta, a small territory with but an unusually tiny desert sector. In the three units of British South Africa, the marginal capital is a deliberate choice meant, in keeping with the tenets of "indirect rule," to keep the European headquarters as far removed as possible from the bulk of the native population.[35]

Nodality

Where the major lineaments of the physical landscape create, by convergence or divergence, conspicuous foci, the resulting nodalities are bound to be constants of everlasting attraction despite such variables as sequent occupance and political vicissitudes. This is why certain colonial capitals have in fact inherited ancient native nodalities in Africa.[36] "Site," to be sure, may differ, in general to guarantee geographical and cultural segregation be-

---

[33] William A. Hance, Vincent Kotschar, and Richard J. Peterec, "Source Areas of Export Production in Tropical Africa," *Geogr. Rev.*, Vol. 51, 1961, p. 494.

[34] *Africa*, p. 213.
[35] Whittlesey, *op. cit.*, p. 391.
[36] Daryll Forde, *loc. cit.*, p. 28.

tween black and white, but the general geographical setting, "situation," remains essentially the same. Modern Rabat follows the general setting of old Rabat; Khartoum and Omdurman are two discrete sites in one and the same situation; Kampala is but a natural extension of Mengo, the old capital of the native kingdom of Buganda, and was directly determined by its location, while Entebbe, the strictly political capital and residence of the European community, is not far away.[37] In West Africa the siting influence of old native cities on colonial capitals is rather strong, while it is entirely lacking in southern Africa.[38]

Although "portality" is the key to the nature and function of most African coastal capitals, river-mouth nodalities are very rare, almost lacking, in Africa. In fact, as in the whole of the Mediterranean basin,[39] such natural nodalities are decidedly shunned by major cities. Most African rivers end with deltas[40] which, with their malarial marshes and tropical, insalubrious mud flats, are no magnets for population. Thus Tunis is not situated on the Mejerda but away from its mouth, while Dakar is sited on the Cape Verde peninsula and not on the Senegal—indeed the capital was moved from St. Louis to Dakar only to correct an ill-sited riverine situation. Again, Accra is not on the Volta, but is well removed from it. So it is with regard to the marshy Niger delta, with Lourenço Marques with regard to the shallow, malarial delta of the Zambezi, and with Dar-es-Salaam with respect to the Rufiji. On the other hand, the rare rivers ending in tidal estuaries are prized locations as in the case of the Gambia, the best navigable river in West Africa (Bathurst), the Geba (Bissau) and the Congo where two capitals stand astride Stanley Pool (*villes à cheval*)[41] not far from the coast. All along the African coast, headland and promontory nodalities assume particular importance as urban seats, presumably to compensate for the dispersive effect of river deltas. Tunis, Dakar, and Cape Town—the last is Mackinder's World Promontory[42]—are prominent examples, while Libreville and Luanda are secondary cases.

In the interior, dominant natural nodalities are more characteristic of the northern half of the continent, no doubt because nurtured and crystallized for far longer stretches of time. The natural nodality of Cairo is unique: "a diamond button clipping the fan of the Delta,"[43] her focality is due not only to the Y-shaped hydrological nodality drawn by the river; she is equally the convergence point of the Fayum cup-oasis from the left and the valley of Wadi Tumailat from the right, while the difficulty of crossing the canal-studded Delta compels the coastal and desert east-west routes to swing south to Cairo.[44] As much as she is the "waist" of the Nile Valley, she is also the waist of the surrounding desert. Similarly, Tunis possesses an outstanding nodality: besides being the waist of the Mediterranean she is the rendezvous and center of gravity of all Tunisia, the effective Tunisia (*la Tunisie "utile"* of the French). Thither point and end the three major digits of the natural

---

[37] A. W. Southall, in *Aspects Sociaux de l'Industrialisation etc.*, Unesco, p. 593.

[38] *Ibid.*, p. 536.

[39] Andre Siegfried, *The Mediterranean* (trans.), London, 1948, pp. 168–172.

[40] Stamp, *Africa*, p. 13.

[41] Jean Tricart, *Cours de Géographie Humaine*, Fasicule II, Habitat Urbain, Paris, 1958, pp. 225–226.

[42] H. J. Mackinder, *Democratic Ideals and Reality*, Pelican Books, 1944, p. 46.

[43] M. Clerget, Le Caire. *Étude de Géographie Urbaine*, Cairo, Vol. 1, 1934.

[44] Benjamin H. Thomas, *World Geography*, loc. cit., p. 414.

landscape: "Friguiya" or the Tunisian Tell from the west, the Mejerda valley from the southwest, and the "Sahel" from the south.[45]

In Algeria natural nodality is less well developed. As in Chile, the broad lineaments of the natural landscape are but a long, attenuated strip strangled between mountain and sea and in which no prominent node can be overriding. Directly because of this pattern, the capital historically swung, as according to circumstances, between the extreme east and the extreme west, between, that is, Bougie and Tlemcen.[46] This may also explain why Algiers had relatively such a late start as capital. Despite some physical nodality inherent in the Metija plain which the capital occupies, the real attribute of Algiers is relative centrality (within the coastal strip) rather than absolute nodality. It is interesting that in Morocco the situation is midway between the supreme nodality of Tunisia and the relative disorientation of Algeria. The intricate inter-digitation of lowlands and mountains here assumes a roughly circular pattern and within this circumference not only one but many nodes emerge. Therefore, if the historic movement of the capital in Algeria has been strictly "linear," it has here been "circular." This also explains the unusual "Pentapolis" nature of the capital in Maghrib.

Moving south, the next prominent nodality is that of Dakar, not only because of its promontory site on the "African Bulge" but also because it is the first outpost of the Sudan ecumene after a dead, desert coast, the first green spot—mark the name Cape Verde—after a dreary yellow sandsea

not unjustly named the "Bone-Yard" of Africa.[47] In fact, the nodality of Dakar stems from the fact that it is the most strategic point along the Savanna-Sahara fusing line. The latter is nothing other than the African sector of Vidal—La Blache's famous circum-desert urban line which beads together the whole series of the Sudan capitals from Dakar in the west to Khartoum in the east and including Bamako, Ouagadougu, Niamey, and Fort Lamy in between. Specific location along this plane of intersection between "the steppe and the sown" is determined either by riverine, lacustrine (Fort Lamy), or caravan route nodalities. Besides heading the richest and most productive "inland delta" in tropical Africa, Khartoum in particular is doubly fortunate with her hydrological nodality describing an inverted Y.

South of the Sahara, few striking nodalities have yet developed. The Léopoldville-Brazzaville twin represents an "estuary-head" nodality which has replaced the less naturally endowed "estuary-mouth" nodality of Boma-Matadi. Lacustrine nodalities are fairly well represented in the "Lakeland" of East Africa, e.g., Kampala-Entebbe, Usumbura, and to some extent Zomba. Many of the "hanging capitals" perched on the highlands of the continent have at best local nodality; Nairobi, for example, started with an artificial nodality represented in its break-of-bulk location on the Mombasa-Uganda railway then under construction.[48]

SIZE

Although the African capital varies within a very wide range of size, reaching 1000 at its lowest (Villa Cisneros) and nearly 4,000,000 at its highest

[45] J. Klein, *La Tunisie*, Coll. Que Sais-Je? Paris, 1939, pp. 14–17.

[46] Hamdan, "Pattern of Medieval Urbanism in the Arab World," *loc. cit.*, p. 131.

[47] W. M. Macmillan, *Africa Emergent*, Pelican Books, 1949, p. 97.

[48] W. Fitzgerald, *Africa*, London, 1955.

(Cairo), Africa is easily the continent of modest, if not of midget, capitals. Fully 16 cases are pygmy capitals (−50,000), some of which are surely but modest villages (e.g., Niamey). Many, especially in the Western Sudan, are fiat, that is artificial capitals, in this respect probably an extension of the nature of their states. Figuratively, it may be said that we are here dealing with "capital-less states." This, however, is true in the literal sense of Mauritania and Bechuanaland. Another 18 cases range between 100,000 and 250,000 and may be considered the backbone of African capitals. Addis Ababa is probably the biggest tropical capital, though not the biggest tropical city, in Africa. The latter place goes to Ibadan. Ibadan, however, includes, in truly West African tradition, a very substantial element of rural population which may render the comparison illusory; indeed, some consider Addis Ababa to be bigger even irrespective of the rural component in Ibadan.

Only four capitals in the continent surpass the 500,000 mark but alone total together 5,253,000 inhabitants, i.e., nearly half the total metropolitan population of Africa. Significantly, they are all extra-tropical and almost all are ancient, historic capitals (generally Arab). Although three are coastal, Cairo, the leading capital and city in Africa, is inland. It is the only African capital that surpasses the million mark, and comes seventeenth in the order of leading cities in the world. It is not often realized that Cairo is the largest city not only in Africa or in the Arab world, but also in an area including Eurasia south of the Alps-Carpathians-Caucasus belt and west of the Indus. Clearly, then, the largest capitals in Africa are extra-tropical; the tropical capital hardly averages one-fifth their mean size. It is interesting to note that

the whole metropolitan population of Africa (barely some 10,860,000 or 0.45 per cent of the total population of the continent) is hardly equal to any such major world conurbation as New York, Tokyo, or London.

With regard to their respective national populations, African capitals betray a very wide range of ratios. While in some cases the ratio drops to 0.5 per cent (Nyasaland), in others it soars up to 50 per cent, nearly half the country's population (Fr. Somaliland, 46.5). Undoubtedly, this extremely wide range is less a function of the sizes of capitals than of the sizes of their national populations. It is for this reason that we find that most of the larger-sized countries in population (excepting Egypt and Algeria) fall in the lowest ratio orders while the greater number of the cases with very high ratios are in fact but those pygmy states and tiny pockets or enclaves. This at once means that capitals are more uniform in their sizes than are the national populations and that there is no completely proportionate correlation between metropolitan size and national size. But this apart, three definite types of size are recognizable (Col. 4, Table 1).

First, the very low ratios would point to almost "capital-less states," like Niger, Ruanda, Burundi, and Togo. Second, the extremely high ratios, on the contrary, might denote no more than nearly "capitals without states" as in the case of islet and enclave countries, etc. Thus in Zanzibar, Mauritius, Réunion, and French Somaliland, the "state" is hardly anything more than a city, a head without a body as it were. These political curios are in a sense "city states" which remind of the medieval, feudalist State-Rei, only with a different origin and in a different setting, that of imperialism. They are

Table 1
Capital Cities in Relation to Hierarchy

Primate City		Second City (2)		Percentage (2/1)	Percentage of Metropolitan Population out of National Population
Casablanca	700	Rabat	160	23.0	1.7
Blantyre-Limbé	46.1	Zomba	17.7	38.3	0.6
Douala	118.8	Yaoundé	54	45.4	1.6
Cotonou	56.2	Porto Novo	31.5	57.0	1.5
Ibadan	600	Lagos	364	60.6	1.3
Johannesburg	1,096	Cape Town	732	66.7	2.4
Quelimane	144	Lourenço Marques	100.2	70.0	1.5
Omdurman	113	Khartoum	93	82.3	0.9
Ouagadougou	47.5	Bobo Dioulassu	41.7	87.0	1.2
St. Denis	42	St. Paul	29	69.0	16.9
Salisbury	270.5	Bulawayo	178.0	65.8	8.6
Kampala	46.7	Jinja	29.4	63.0	0.7
Lusaka	75	Broken Hill	46.8	62.4	3.0
Nairobi	250	Mombasa	152	60.8	3.8
Brazzaville	99	Pointe Noire	57	57.5	7.1
Léopoldville	355	Elisabethville	183.8	51.7	2.6
Algiers	806	Oran	389	48.2	7.7
Cairo	3,035	Alexandria	1,416	46.6	15.0
Tripoli	184	Bengazi	80	43.4	16.7
Bamako	68.6	Kayes	29.5	43.0	1.4
Abidjan	177	Bouaké	70	39.5	5.7
Windhoek	38.5	Walvis Bay	14	36.3	6.8
Fort Lamy	70	Moundou	25	35.7	2.7
Addis Ababa	400	Asmara	130	29.0	2.2
Conakry	112.5	Kankan	29.1	25.5	4.5
Tananarive	206.3	Majunga	51.7	25.0	4.0
Dakar	234	Rufisque	50	21.0	9.0
Luanda	189.6	Lobito	31.6	16.6	4.2
Dar es-Salaam	129	Tabora	15.3	11.8	1.4
Tunis	680	Sfax	65	9.5	17.0

also reminiscent of the contemporary oil city-states which oil has recently created around the Persian Gulf. The raison d'être is a universally strategic situation either as a free port (Djibouti),[49] a transit depot (Zanzibar), or as a naval base (Mauritius). Between the two extremes of low and high ratios

exists a third type characterized by a big national population and an equally high capital ratio. Under this heading comes Cairo, but Tunis is surely a most flagrant case. No country in Africa other than Tunisia has a population of some millions with at the same time as high a capital-to-state ratio as 1:5. This may not yet be the stage of "the capital is the state," but is surely not far from it.

[49] Francis I. Schadegg, "Central and Southern Africa," in *World Geography, op. cit.,* p. 459.

To turn to the place of the capital in the hierarchy of the cities of the African state, this can be detected by means of the "primate city" technique devised by Mark Jefferson.[50] It will be recalled that the "normal" hierarchy as defined by Jefferson for the three leading cities is in the ratio of 100: 30: 20, but for our purposes it will suffice to consider only the two leading cities. Table 1 is based on figures mostly for 1957–1961. At once, three major types make themselves manifest, viz., the inferior capital, the weak capital, and the dominant capital.

The "inferior capital" is one which is not the primate city in its country.[51] Outstanding cases in Africa are Lagos, Pretoria, Cape Town, Rabat, Porto Novo, Yaoundé, and Nouakchott. Until recently, Bobo Dioulassu in Upper Volta was bigger than Ouagadougou, the capital. Sudan would join the list if distinction is made between Khartoum and Omdurman as separate cities. If the inferior capital does not signify some political or cultural anomaly, it is at least not the general rule. Some African examples remind of American and Commonwealth capitals, but others actually represent a deliberate attempt on the part of the colonial powers to keep the political center away from those hotbeds of nationalism and foci of political fermentation and agitation —the indigenous metropolises; witness the cases of Lagos, Khartoum, and Rabat with regard respectively to Ibadan, Omdurman, and Casablanca. It is, however, almost certain, especially since independence, that the capitals will soon overtake their rivals in size to become the undisputed primate cities.

The present rate of growth of Khartoum vis-à-vis Omdurman is a good pointer in that direction.[52]

The "weak capital" does not usually exceed the second city very considerably; they normally stand at a ratio of 100: 70. In this category come St. Denis in Réunion, Salisbury, Ouagadougou, and Niamey. Until recently Conakry was a weak capital (38,000 against 24,000 for Kankan—a ratio of 63 per cent). In these cases, the capital is often either so newly founded or chosen that it has not had time to gather enough momentum and prestige to outstrip its nearest rivals appreciably. Likewise it means that the capital has not matured enough to fully represent national spirit and life. The example of Conakry points to the enhanced primacy that awaits the weak capital with the new political changes.

The "dominant capital" dominates the urban scene in its country, completely overpowering its nearest rivals and often, but not always, symbolizing a satisfactory crystallization of the body-politic. In most cases this stage is reached when the capital is twice or thrice the size of the second city. The type is fairly frequent in Africa. Dakar, Conakry, Abidjan, Léopoldville, Bamako, Tananarive, Addis Ababa, Fort Lamy, Algiers, Tripoli, Mogadishu, and the Triple Capital (taken as a whole) are all dominant capitals, while Cairo and Tunis are over-dominant. Many of these cases belong to the larger-sized countries which are relatively rich both economically and culturally. They are also mostly ancient capitals—they include all Arab capitals—and have thus much historical weight and momentum

[50] Mark Jefferson, "Law of the Primate City," *Geogr. Rev.*, Vol. 29, 1939, pp. 226–232.

[51] Egon E. Bergel, *Urban Sociology*, New York, 1955, p. 68.

[52] Hamdan, "Some Aspects of the Urban Geography of the Khartoum Complex," *loc. cit.*, p. 93.

behind them enough to carry them far above their rivals. When, however, this supremacy goes unbridled, as in the case of Tunis, it may well imply a pathological condition. Tunis is in fact unique in the continent in that it is ten times as big as its immediate follower, representing thus an extreme monopoly of power and wealth, looking almost like a "macrocephal from Lilliput" and threatening to turn the country into a merely vast suburb of the capital. As Gautier rightly says, "Toute la Tunisie est accroché à cette ville monstre."[53]

Considering the small size of the average African capital, the widespread frequency of the dominant capital in the continent really means that most African countries possess only one fairly big city followed after a wide chasm by a number of midget or microscopic ineffective towns. Such urban scatter is in fact so typical of most backward, colonial countries that it can safely be called the "colonial urban pattern."

[53] George, *La Ville, op. cit.*, p. 274.

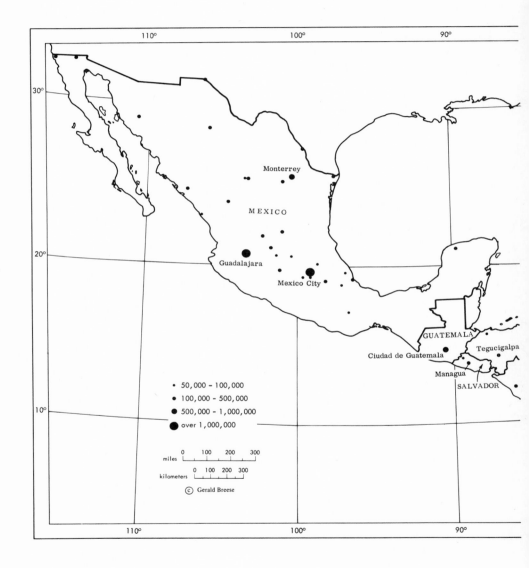

MEXICO

Monterrey

MEXICO

Guadalajara

Mexico City

GUATEMALA

Ciudad de Guatemala

Tegucigalpa

Managua

SALVADOR

· 50,000 - 100,000

● 100,000 - 500,000

● 500,000 - 1,000,000

● over 1,000,000

miles | 0 100 200 300 |

kilometers | 0 100 200 300 |

© Gerald Breese

13. Mexico, Central America and the West Indies: Urban Places Over 50,000

GERALD BREESE

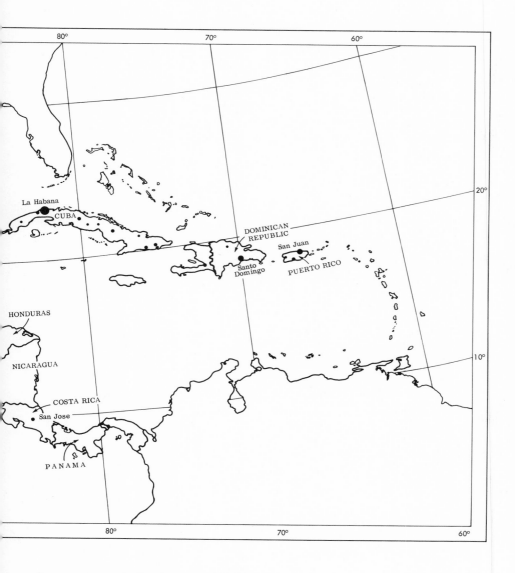

Source notes may be found on pages 555–56.

•	50,000 - 100,000
●	100,000 - 500,000
●	500,000 - 1,000,000
●	over 1,000,000

miles 0   200   400   600   800
kilometers 0   200   400   600   800

ⓒ Gerald Breese

14. South America:
Urban Places Over 50,000

GERALD BREESE

The following sources were used in preparing selection 14.

Argentina: U.N. Demographic Yearbook 1966, *Table 6 for 1960 Census; used for places of 100,000 plus. Note: all references to Yearbook are Table 6, below.*
 Pan American Union, America en Cifras 1965, *for 1947 census for places of 50,000 to 100,000.*
Bolivia: *Pan American Union,* America en Cifras 1965, *for 1965 estimate.*
Brazil: U.N. Demographic Yearbook 1966, *for 1965 and 1966 estimates, places of 197,000 and over. Brazilian Census 1960, for places 50,000 to 197,000.*
Chile: U.N. Demographic Yearbook 1966, *1965 estimate for places 1,000,000 & over. Pan American Union,* America en Cifras 1965, *for 1960 census 50,000–100,000.*
Colombia: U.N. Demographic Yearbook 1966, *for 1964 census, 100,000 and over except Santa Marta. Pan American Union,* America en Cifras 1965, *for 1964 census, cities of 50,000–100,000 and Santa Marta.*
Ecuador: U.N. Demographic Yearbook 1966, *for 1965 estimates, places 100,000 & over. Pan American Union,* America en Cifras 1965, *for 1962 census, 50,000–100,000.*
Guyana: U.N. Demographic Yearbook 1966, *for 1960 census, Georgetown only.*
Paraguay: *Pan American Union,* America en Cifras 1965, *for 1962 census.*
Peru: *Peruvian Census 1961.*
Surinam: U.N. Demographic Yearbook 1966, *for 1964 estimate, Paramaribo only.*
Uruguay: Statesman's Yearbook 1965–1966, *for 1964 estimate (incomplete?).*
Venezuela: U.N. Demographic Yearbook 1966, *for 1966 estimate, places 100,000 over. Venezuelan Census 1961, for 50,000–100,000.*
 Note: About 7 cities not shown, 4 in Brazil and 1 each in Argentina, Colombia, and Peru.

15. Patterns of Urbanization in Latin America

JOHN D. DURAND

AND

CÉSAR A. PELÁEZ

This paper presents some provisional results, for the Latin American region, of a world survey of urban and rural population growth since 1920, which is being conducted by the United Nations Secretariat. Demographic aspects of urbanization in Latin America were analyzed in an earlier United Nations study, with reference to data from censuses taken around 1950 and in earlier decades.[1] Measures of the principal dimensions and trends of urbanization are brought up to date here with more recent census data for most of the countries. Pertinent data from censuses taken in 1960 or later were found, in sources available at United Nations Headquarters at the time this paper was written, for 15 of the 22 Latin American countries having 1 million or more inhabitants.[2] These 15 countries con-

tained over 80 per cent of the estimated 1960 population of the region, which was defined as including all countries in the Americas south of the United States.

THE MEASURE OF URBAN POPULATION

For the purpose of this study, urban population is defined as the population in localities reported in the census of each country as having 20,000 or more inhabitants. This measure has been used widely for international comparisons, in United Nations studies and others. Although it is not ideal, it has the great advantage of eliminating effects of differences in the definitions of urban areas applied in the censuses of different countries, so far as the minimal number of inhabitants qualifying a locality as urban is concerned. It also eliminates much of the effect of differences in other criteria of urban status applied in the censuses of some countries, such as the legal status of municipalities, density of the population, occupational composition of the labor force, pattern of settlement, and provision of certain public utilities and services. Most localities having 20,000 or more inhabi-

From Components of Population Change in Latin America, *Proceedings of the 60th Anniversary Conference of the Milbank Memorial Fund, New York, April 5–7, 1965,* ed. Clyde V. Kiser, Milbank Memorial Fund Quarterly, *43,* No. 4, part 2 *(October 1965), 166–96. Reprinted by permission of authors and publisher.*

[1] United Nations Population Branch, Demographic Aspects of Urbanization, in Hauser, Philip M. (editor), *Urbanization in Latin America,* Paris, UNESCO, 1961. *See also* Geographical Distribution of the Population of Latin America and Regional Development Priorities, *Economic Bulletin for Latin America,* 8, 51–63, 1963.

[2] Countries with 1 million or more inhabitants in 1960 for which full returns of recent census data suited to the purposes of this study were not found are: Bolivia, Colombia, Cuba, Guatemala, Haiti, Paraguay, and Uruguay. Censuses have been taken since 1960 in Colom-

bia and Uruguay but the pertinent data were not available at United Nations Headquarters when this paper was in preparation. For Argentina, 1960 census statistics of the population in cities of 100,000 or more inhabitants and the metropolitan area of Buenos Aires were available, but the population in cities of 20,000 to 99,999 had to be estimated.

Table 1

Percentage of Urban Population (in Localities with 20,000 or More Inhabitants), by Regions of World, 1950 and 1960

Regions	Estimated Averages for All Countries		Averages for Countries Having 1950 and 1960 Data	
	1950	1960	1950	1960
World total	21	24–25[a]	27	30
Less developed regions	14	17–18[a]	18	22
Africa	10	13	14	18
North Africa	21	26	25	31
Sub-Sahara Africa	6	9	8	11
Asia	14	16–18[a]	19	21
excluding China (mainland)	17	19	19	21
China (mainland)	10	10–15[a]	—	—
Latin America	25	32	28	36
Argentina, Chile, Uruguay	47	56	48	57
remainder of Latin America	21	28	21	29
More developed regions	37	41	38	41
North America	43	46	43	46
Europe (excluding USSR)	37	40	37	40
northwestern	52	54	52	54
central	37	40	37	40
southern	23	27	23	27
USSR	31	36	31	36
Oceania	46	53	56	64
Australia and New Zealand	58	65	58	65
remainder of Oceania	—	3	—	15

[a] Range of estimated values corresponding to alternative estimates for China (mainland).

tants are also likely to qualify as urban by such criteria.

An obvious shortcoming of this measure is the omission of the population in localities with less than 20,000 inhabitants, which exhibit essentially urban characteristics as seen from economic and sociological points of view. The consequent understatement of the size of the urban population is likely to be greater in proportionate terms in countries that are relatively little urbanized (i.e., where the fraction of total population in localities of 20,000 or more inhabitants is relatively small) than in more urbanized countries. Therefore, the measure used here tends somewhat to exaggerate differences in degrees of urbanization of the Latin American countries.

Another shortcoming results from the fact that the criteria used in defining limits of urban localities are not the same in the censuses of different countries. Three types of definitions have been distinguished:[3]

Type a—agglomerations of population without regard to fixed boundaries;

Type b—localities with fixed boundaries, commonly under the jurisdiction of local or "urban" forms of government;

[3] Demographic Yearbook, 1962, New York, United Nations, pp. 35–36.

Type c—relatively small or the smallest administrative subdivisions having fixed boundaries and, in sum, comprising the entire country.

The types of definitions underlying the data for the Latin American countries considered in this study are designated by the codes, a, b, and ab in Table 2; *ab* refers to a mixture in which a definition of *type a* is used to delimit certain urban areas (particularly the larger metropolitan districts) and one of *type b* for other areas. *Type c*

definitions were not found in the statistics of the countries considered here. *Type a* statistics are the most satisfactory measures of urban population if the areas are defined as comprising the whole of each urban agglomeration which makes a demographic, economic, and sociological unit. *Type b* statistics tend to understate the urban population inasmuch as they exclude parts of the population belonging to such agglomerations but living outside the legal or administrative boundaries of the corresponding muncipalities.

Table 2

Population of Localities in Latin American Countries Classified by Number of Inhabitants, by Results of Censuses Since 1920 (Figures in 1000s)

Country	Census Year	Total Population	Rural Population (Localities of Less than 20,000)	Urban Population (Localities of 20,000 or More)				Type of Definition
				Total	20,000–99,999	100,000 or More	Largest City[a]	
Middle America								
Costa Rica	1927	472	381	91	91	—	91	a
	1950	801	622	179	—	179	179	a
	1963	1,325	1,007	318	—	318	318	a
Cuba	1919	2,889	2,186	703	278	425	425	ab
	1931	3,962	2,867	1,095	361	734	633	ab
	1943	4,779	3,313	1,466	514	952	833	ab
	1953	5,829	3,760	2,069	731	1,338	1,064	ab
Dominican	1920	895	864	31	31	—	31	b
Republic	1935	1,479	1,374	105	105	—	71	b
	1950	2,136	1,898	238	57	182	182	b
	1960	3,014	2,450	564	197	367	367	b
El Salvador	1930	1,434	1,305	129	129	—	89	b
	1950	1,856	1,616	240	78	162	162	b
	1961	2,511	2,067	444	188	256	256	b
Guatemala	1950	2,791	2,479	312	28	284	284	b

[a] *Costa Rica:* Total population of the San José metropolitan area. *Cuba:* metropolitan Havana including Havana, Marianao, Guanabacoa y Regla. *Jamaica:* Kingston–St. Andrew metropolitan area. *Puerto Rico:* San Juan including Rio Piedras. *Argentina:* Gran Buenos Aires. *Chile:* Gran Santiago. *Paraguay* (1962): Asunción plus Lambaré. *Peru:* Lima metropolitan area. *Venezuela:* Caracas metropolitan area.
[b] Estimates.

Ellipsis dots indicate that data are not available. Dash indicates a magnitude of 0.

Country	Census Year	Total Population	Rural Population (Localities of Less than 20,000)	Urban Population (Localities of 20,000 or More)			Largest City[a]	Type of Definition
				Total	20,000–99,999	100,000 or More		
Haiti	1950	3,097	2,939	158	24	134	134	b
Honduras	1940	1,108	1,040	68	68	—	47	b
	1950	1,369	1,275	94	94	—	72	b
	1961	1,885	1,667	218	83	134	134	b
Jamaica	1921	858	770	88	88	—	88	ab
	1943	1,237	1,035	202	—	202	202	ab
	1960	1,610	1,210	400	24	376	376	ab
Mexico	1940	19,654	16,103	3,551	1,549	2,002	1,448	b
	1950	25,791	19,586	6,205	2,305	3,900	2,235	b
	1960	34,923	24,571	10,352	3,840	6,512	2,832	b
Nicaragua	1950	1,057	896	161	52	109	109	b
	1963	1,480	1,139	341	115	226	226	b
Panama	1930	467	360	107	107	—	78	b
	1940	623	457	166	44	121	121	b
	1950	805	589	216	52	164	164	b
	1960	1,076	720	356	83	273	273	b
Puerto Rico	1920	1,300	1,181	119	119	—	77	b
	1930	1,544	1,326	218	90	128	128	b
	1940	1,869	1,518	351	162	189	189	b
	1950	2,211	1,613	598	241	357	357	b
	1960	2,350	1,692	658	111	547	432	b
South America								
Argentina	1947	15,894	8,212	7,682	1,777	5,905	4,722	ab
	1960	20,006	8,506	11,500[b]	2,396[b]	9,104	6,762	ab
Bolivia	1950	3,019	2,426	593	272	321	321	b
Brazil	1920	30,636	27,161	3,474	799	2,675	1,158	b
	1940	41,253	34,934	6,319	1,906	4,413	1,519	b
	1950	51,944	41,451	10,493	3,620	6,873	2,303	b
	1960	70,967	51,045	19,922	6,613	13,309	3,223	b
Chile	1920	3,730	2,687	1,043	353	690	507	b
	1930	4,287	2,895	1,392	503	889	696	b
	1940	5,024	3,194	1,830	668	1,162	952	b
	1952	5,933	3,394	2,539	850	1,689	1,350	b
	1960	7,374	3,342	4,032	1,580	2,452	1,907	b
Colombia	1938	8,702	7,583	1,119	499	620	326	b
	1951	11,548	8,981	2,567	868	1,699	639	b
Ecuador	1950	3,203	2,633	570	101	469	259	b
	1962	4,581	3,348	1,233	367	866	511	b
Paraguay	1950	1,328	1,109	219	—	219	219	a
	1962	1,817	. . .	. . .	. . .	305	305	a
Peru	1940	6,208	5,327	881	360	521	521	ab
	1961	9,907	7,046	2,861	1,033	1,828	1,436	ab
Uruguay	1963	2,556	. . .	. . .	. . .	. . .	1,173	b
Venezuela	1936	3,364	2,819	545	200	345	235	ab
	1941	3,851	3,155	696	243	453	332	ab
	1950	5,035	3,430	1,605	584	1,021	680	ab
	1961	7,524	3,975	3,549	1,296	2,253	1,333	ab

DEGREE OF URBANIZATION

A crude measure of the degree of a country's urbanization is the percentage of urban population in its total population. For Latin America as a whole in 1960, this figure is estimated provisionally at 32 per cent. For the purpose of this estimate, in countries lacking recent census data, the increase in the urban population percentages since the dates of earlier censuses have been estimated provisionally by considering available information on the past trends of urbanization in these countries as well as the recent trends in other Latin American countries.

Latin America, on the whole, is considerably more urbanized than the average of the world's regions (*see* Table 1). It is much more urbanized than either Africa or Asia and somewhat more urbanized than southern Europe, although in industrialization and economic development generally, Latin America is considerably less advanced than southern Europe. Latin America is not a great deal less urbanized than the Soviet Union or Central Europe. Only North America, northwestern Europe, Australia, and New Zealand are very far ahead of Latin America in urbanization.

But the countries of Latin America differ greatly in degrees of urbanization. Among those for which recent data are available, the percentages of population in localities with 20,000 or more inhabitants, as shown in Table 3, range from 11.6 in Honduras (1961) to 57.5 in Argentina (provisional estimate for

Table 3

Measures of Degree of Urbanization and Urban Concentration in Latin American Countries at Each Census Since 1920

Country	Census Year	Per Cent of Total Population in Localities of Specified Number of Inhabitants			Per Cent of Urban Population in Localities of Specified Number of Inhabitants	
		20,000 or More	100,000 or More	Largest City	100,000 or More	Largest City
Middle America						
Costa Rica	1927	19.3	—	19.3	—	100.0
	1950	22.3	22.3	22.3	100.0	100.0
	1963	24.0	24.0	24.0	100.0	100.0
Cuba	1919	24.3	14.7	14.7	60.4	60.4
	1931	27.6	18.5	16.0	67.0	57.8
	1943	30.7	19.9	17.4	64.9	56.8
	1953	35.5	22.9	18.3	64.7	51.4
Dominican	1920	3.5	—	3.5	—	100.0
Republic	1935	7.1	—	4.8	—	67.6
	1950	11.1	8.5	8.5	76.5	76.5
	1960	18.7	12.2	12.2	65.1	65.1
El Salvador	1930	9.0	—	6.2	—	69.0
	1950	12.9	8.7	8.7	67.5	67.5
	1961	17.7	10.2	10.2	57.6	57.6
Guatemala	1950	11.2	10.2	10.2	91.0	91.0

Ellipsis dots indicate that data are not available. Dash indicates a magnitude of 0.

Country	Census Year	Per Cent of Total Population in Localities of Specified Number of Inhabitants			Per Cent of Urban Population in Localities of Specified Number of Inhabitants	
		20,000 or More	100,000 or More	Largest City	100,000 or More	Largest City
Haiti	1950	5.1	4.3	4.3	84.8	84.8
Honduras	1940	6.1	—	4.2	—	69.1
	1950	6.9	—	5.3	—	76.6
	1961	11.6	7.1	7.1	61.5	61.5
Jamaica	1921	10.3	—	10.3	—	100.0
	1943	16.3	16.3	16.3	100.0	100.0
	1960	24.8	23.4	23.4	94.0	94.0
Mexico	1940	18.1	10.2	7.4	56.4	40.8
	1950	24.1	15.1	8.7	62.8	36.0
	1960	29.6	18.6	8.1	62.9	27.4
Nicaragua	1950	15.2	10.3	10.3	67.7	67.7
	1963	23.0	15.3	15.3	66.3	66.3
Panama	1930	22.9	—	16.7	—	72.9
	1940	26.6	19.4	19.4	72.9	72.9
	1950	26.8	20.4	20.4	75.9	75.9
	1960	33.1	25.4	25.4	76.7	76.7
Puerto Rico	1920	9.2	—	5.9	—	64.7
	1930	14.1	8.3	8.3	58.7	58.7
	1940	18.8	10.1	10.1	53.8	53.8
	1950	27.0	16.1	16.1	59.7	59.7
	1960	28.0	23.3	18.4	83.1	65.6
South America						
Argentina	1947	48.3	36.8	29.7	76.2	61.5
	1960	57.5	45.5	33.8	79.2	58.8
Bolivia	1950	19.6	10.6	10.6	54.1	54.1
Brazil	1920	11.3	8.7	3.8	77.0	33.3
	1940	15.3	10.7	3.7	69.8	24.0
	1950	20.2	13.2	4.4	65.5	21.9
	1960	28.1	18.8	4.5	66.8	16.2
Chile	1920	28.0	18.4	13.6	66.2	48.6
	1930	32.5	20.7	16.2	63.9	50.0
	1940	36.4	23.1	18.9	63.5	52.0
	1952	42.8	28.5	22.7	66.5	53.2
	1960	54.7	33.3	25.9	60.8	47.3
Colombia	1938	12.9	7.1	3.7	55.4	29.1
	1951	22.2	14.7	5.5	66.2	24.9
Ecuador	1950	17.8	14.6	8.1	82.3	45.4
	1962	26.9	18.9	11.2	70.2	41.4
Paraguay	1950	16.5	16.5	16.5	100.0	100.0
	1962	...	16.8	16.8	...	...
Peru	1940	14.2	8.4	8.4	59.1	59.1
	1961	28.9	18.4	14.5	63.9	50.2
Uruguay	1963	...	...	45.9	...	...
Venezuela	1936	16.2	10.3	7.0	63.3	43.1
	1941	18.1	11.8	8.6	65.1	47.7
	1950	31.9	20.3	13.5	63.6	42.4
	1961	47.2	29.9	17.7	63.5	37.6

171

1960). The actual range may be wider, since Haiti (for which recent data are lacking) may be less urbanized than Honduras. Haiti, with only 5.1 per cent of its population in localities of 20,000 or more inhabitants in 1950, was the least urbanized of Latin America's major countries.

In the southern part of South America, Argentina, Chile, and Uruguay make up a group of the world's most urbanized countries; more than half of their population is found in localities with 20,000 or more inhabitants.[4] Elsewhere the only major countries with urban population of more than 50 per cent in 1960, according to this measure, were the United Kingdom, Australia, New Zealand, and the Netherlands. Two other Latin American countries are also highly urbanized, namely, Venezuela and Cuba. Venezuela, with 47.2 per cent of its population in localities of 20,000 or more inhabitants at the 1961 Census, was on a par with the United States in this respect. Up-to-date statistics are lacking for Cuba, but at the 1953 Census 35.5 per cent of this country's population was urban according to the definition used here—a higher percentage than that of Venezuela in 1950. Several other Latin American countries, though less urbanized than the regional average, are slightly, if any, less urbanized than some European countries that are much more advanced in industrialization and economic development. Brazil and Mexico, for example, with urban populations of 28.1 and 29.6 per cent, respectively, in 1960, are only slightly less urbanized than Switzerland, and more urbanized than Czechoslovakia.

[4] Although full returns of the 1963 Census for Uruguay were not available at the time this paper was written, Montevideo was reported as having 45.9 per cent of the total population of the country.

Although a comparative analysis of degrees of urbanization and indices of economic and social development was ruled beyond the scope of this study because of the limitations of time and space, it is apparent that Latin America, on the whole, is more urbanized than it is industrialized or developed in other respects. In degree of urbanization, several Latin American countries are equal or superior to countries in Europe and North America, that would rank much higher on the scales of such indices as the proportion of labor force engaged in nonagricultural employment, per capita energy consumption, per capita income, level of education, etc. These discrepancies reflect generally lower levels of development of the Latin American countries, both in agricultural and nonagricultural sectors of the economy and in the rural and urban sectors of the society. Another factor accentuating the discrepancies is a more polarized urban-rural division of Latin American societies. As yet, Latin America has seen comparatively little suburban development, commutation between rural communities and cities, and other forms of the extension of urban ways of life into the countryside, which have been blurring dividing lines between the urban and rural sectors in the more developed countries of North America, Europe, and Oceania. In other words, the rural sector is, on the whole, more purely rural in the Latin American countries. The same can be said of developing countries in Africa and Asia.

SIZE OF CITIES

As a measure of the degree of urbanization, one of the failings of the simple percentage of population in localities with any given minimal number of inhabitants is that it does not discriminate between different sizes of cities.

A great metropolis is more intensely urban than a small town, five urban areas with 20,000 inhabitants are not equivalent to one with 100,000, nor are 10 cities of 100,000 equivalent to one with 1 million inhabitants. If variations in intensity of urbanization according to city size could be represented on a numerical scale, a refined index of the degree of a country's urbanization could be calculated by applying the appropriate values on this scale as weights to the percentages of population in different size-classes of cities. Actually, it is difficult to find a satisfactory basis for such weighting in international comparisons; it would require a synthesis of data on the variations of a number of economic, social, and demographic indices according to the size of cities in various countries.[5] Without attempting this, it is still worth while to compare degrees of urbanization of countries in terms of proportions of the population in larger cities as well as those in localities with 20,000 or more inhabitants. Pertinent data for Latin American countries are given in Tables 2 and 3.

In terms of population in cities with 100,000 or more inhabitants, Latin America appears no less urbanized in comparison with other regions of the world than it does when comparisons refer to localities of 20,000 or more. Argentina, with 45.5 per cent of its population in cities of 100,000 or more in 1960, is second in this respect only to Australia among major countries in other regions. The percentage for Uruguay is even higher (45.9 per cent of

the population are residents of the city of Montevideo). Chile, with 33.3 per cent, and Venezuela, with 29.9 per cent, in cities of this size, are at a comparable level with such highly developed European countries as the United Kingdom, the Netherlands, Denmark, the Federal Republic of Germany, and Belgium, and surpass the level of the United States. The majority of other Latin American countries, for which recent census data are available, have 15–25 per cent of their populations in cities of 100,000 or more. In this range are such European countries as Finland, Eastern Germany, Norway, Sweden, Hungary, Poland, Switzerland, and Italy. An interesting feature of the percentages of population in cities with 100,000 or more inhabitants in Latin American countries is their historical trend; this has been constantly upward in all the countries without exception. So far, there is no indication that this trend will be reversed. Actually, the increase of the percentages has accelerated during the last intercensal period in several countries.

Latin America also has a good share of its population in major metropolitan agglomerations. Ten cities now have more than 1 million inhabitants in their metropolitan areas, and the aggregate population of these 10 cities or metropolitan areas amounts to about 25 million, or 12 per cent of the total population of the region. The latest census figures on their population are shown on the next page.[6]

Urbanization in the majority of Latin American countries is megalo-

[5] Some of the kinds of indices that would be pertinent are exemplified by Otis Dudley Duncan's study of the United States Census data for 1950 in his Community Size and the Rural-Urban Continuum, in Hatt, Paul K., and Reiss, Albert J., Jr. (editors), *Cities and Society: The Revised Reader in Urban Sociology*, Glencoe, Ill., The Free Press of Glencoe, 1957.

[6] Figures are for metropolitan areas, except those for Rio de Janeiro, São Paulo, and Montevideo. In the case of Mexico City, the figure used here to represent the population of this metropolitan area is the total for areas in the Federal District classified as urban according to the definition used for the Mexican census.

Metropolitan Area	Census Year	Population (thousands)	Percent of Country's Total Population
Buenos Aires, Argentina	1960	6,762	33.8
Rio de Janeiro, Brazil	1960	3,233	4.5
São Paulo, Brazil	1960	3,165	4.5
Mexico City, Mexico	1960	2,832	8.1
Santiago, Chile	1960	1,907	25.9
Lima, Peru	1961	1,436	14.5
Caracas, Venezuela	1961	1,333	17.7
Bogotá, Colombia	1964	1,679	–
Havana, Cuba	1953	1,064	18.3
Montevideo, Uruguay	1963	1,173	45.9

cephalic, that is, concentrated to a large extent in one principal city. Sixteen of the 22 countries, for which data are shown in Tables 2 and 3, had half or more of their urban population concentrated in one city or metropolitan area at the latest census, and a seventeenth country (Chile) was only slightly below this ratio (47.3 per cent of the urban population in 1960 being concentrated in the Santiago metropolitan area). In two countries (Costa Rica and Paraguay), the capital cities were the only ones qualified as urban under the definition used here, and the capitals of these countries were not small towns. San José, Costa Rica, had over 300,000 inhabitants in its metropolitan area at the 1963 census; Asunción, Paraguay, had over 300,00 in 1962. Other examples of extreme megalocephalism in Latin America are Jamaica, Guatemala, and Haiti—with more than 80 per cent of their urban population at the latest censuses concentrated in the area of the capital—and Panama, where the corresponding ratio in 1960 was 76.7 per cent.

High degrees of concentration of urban population in principal cities are also found in many less developed countries elsewhere in the world, especially in Africa and to a lesser extent in Asia. In the more developed countries of Europe, North America, and Oceania, on the other hand, the pattern of urbanization is typically less concentrated.

Latin American countries with less than half of their urban populations in a single city or metropolitan area at the latest census were Ecuador (41.4 per cent), Venezuela (37.6 per cent), Mexico (27.4 per cent), Colombia (24.9 per cent), and Brazil (16.2 per cent). Ecuador is an example of marked bicephalic concentration, as two cities, Quito and Guayaquil, together account for 70 per cent of the total urban population of this country. Brazil also exhibits a bicephalic pattern of concentration, but to a much less marked degree. Brazil's two great cities, Rio de Janeiro and São Paulo, were nearly equal in population at the 1960 Census and together made up nearly one-third of the country's urban population. But Brazil had 29 other cities of 100,000 or more inhabitants at the 1960 Census.

When urban concentration is measured by the percentage of each country's urban population found in cities of 100,000 or more inhabitants, instead of the percentage in the largest city, the Latin American countries are found to be more homogeneous. Eleven of the 22 countries listed in Tables 2 and 3 had 60 to 70 per cent of their urban populations in cities of this size. The United States and a number of European countries are in the same range of values of this index, although deviations above and below this range are common in European countries. Latin American countries with higher percentages of urban population in cities of 100,000 or more are Argentina, Uruguay, and Puerto Rico, in addition to the six highly megalocephalic countries already mentioned (Costa Rica, Haiti, Paraguay, Guatemala, Jamaica, and Panama). Countries with lower percentages of urban population in such large cities were Bolivia (54.1 per cent in 1950) and El Salvador (57.6 per cent in 1961).

GROWTH OF URBAN POPULATION AND INCREASE OF URBANIZATION

The mushrooming growth of cities is a conspicous feature of recent population trends in less developed countries. Nowhere is it more in evidence than in Latin America. According to present provisional estimates for the decade 1950–1960, the population in localities of 20,000 or more inhabitants increased by approximately two-thirds during the 10 years, or at an annual rate of about 5 per cent. The growth rate of the total population in Latin America was also high, estimated at an average of 2.7 per cent annually for the decade; this exceeds the estimated rates of growth in all other regions of the world. It appears, though, that the rate of growth of the urban population in Latin America was nearly twice that of the total population. The difference was due chiefly, if not entirely, to migration from the countryside to the cities. As a result, the regional average percentage of urban population rose

from about 25, in 1950, to 32 per cent in 1960, according to the provisional estimates.

While increased urbanization was general throughout the world during the 1950's, Latin America surpassed all other regions in the rate of growth of its urban population and all except Oceania in the magnitude of the increment to the percentage of urban population. In Oceania, the most urbanized region in the world, the increase in urbanization was similar to that in Latin America.

Among Latin American countries where the urban population grew at the dizziest rates during the 1950's were the Dominican Republic, with a 9.0 per cent annual rate of increase in localities of 20,000 or more, and Honduras and Venezuela, with rates of approximately 8 per cent (Table 4.) The growth rate of 8 per cent compounded annually doubles the population in only nine years.

The typical range of urban population growth rates for the majority of other Latin American countries in the 1950's was from 4.5 per cent (Costa Rica) to 6.6 per cent (Ecuador). Lower rates were recorded in Jamaica (4.0 per cent for 1943–1960), Argentina (provisional estimate of 3.2 per cent for 1947–1960), and Puerto Rico (1.0 per cent for 1950–1960). The low rate for Puerto Rico is explained mainly by emigration to the United States which drains off much of the population that would otherwise have accumulated in the Puerto Rican cities. In spite of this, the urbanized area in and around San Juan had a substantial population gain but some other urban centers in Puerto Rico lost population during the 1950's. Emigration also explains the relatively moderate growth rate of the population in Jamaica's cities, though the scale of emigration from

Table 4

**Rates of Total, Urban, and Rural Population Growth
and Rate of Urbanization in Latin American
Countries in Intercensal Periods Since 1920**

Country	Period	Annual Per Cent Rate of Population Growth			Rate of Urbanization $r = 100 \left(\dfrac{(u) - (t)}{100 + (t)} \right)$
		Total (t)	Urban (u)	Rural	
Middle America					
Costa Rica	1927–50	2.3	2.9	2.2	0.6
	1950–63	4.0	4.5	3.8	0.5
Dominican	1920–35	3.4	8.5	3.1	4.9
Republic	1935–50	2.4	5.5	2.2	3.0
	1950–60	3.5	9.0	2.6	5.3
El Salvador	1930–50	1.3	3.1	1.1	1.8
	1950–61	2.8	5.8	2.3	2.9
Cuba	1919–31	2.7	3.8	2.3	1.1
	1931–43	1.6	2.5	1.2	0.9
	1943–53	2.1	3.7	1.3	1.6
Honduras	1940–50	2.2	3.3	2.1	1.1
	1950–61	3.0	8.1	2.5	5.0
Jamaica	1921–43	1.7	3.9	1.4	2.2
	1943–60	1.5	4.0	0.9	2.5
Mexico	1940–50	2.7	5.6	2.0	2.8
	1950–60	3.1	5.2	2.3	2.1
Nicaragua	1950–63	2.6	5.9	1.9	3.2
Panama	1930–40	2.9	4.5	2.4	1.5
	1940–50	2.6	2.6	2.6	0.1
	1950–60	2.9	5.1	2.0	2.1
Puerto Rico	1920–30	1.7	6.2	1.2	4.4
	1930–40	1.9	4.9	1.4	2.9
	1940–50	1.7	5.5	0.6	3.7
	1950–60	0.6	1.0	0.5	0.3
South America					
Argentina	1947–60	1.8	3.2	0.3	1.3
Brazil	1920–40	1.5	3.0	1.3	1.5
	1940–50	2.4	5.3	1.7	2.9
	1950–60	3.1	6.5	2.1	3.3
Chile	1920–30	1.4	2.9	0.7	1.5
	1930–40	1.6	2.8	1.0	1.2
	1940–52	1.4	2.8	0.5	1.4
	1952–60	2.8	5.9	−0.2	3.1
Colombia	1938–51	2.2	6.7	1.3	4.4
Ecuador	1950–62	3.0	6.6	2.0	3.5
Peru	1940–61	2.2	5.7	1.3	3.4
Venezuela	1936–41	2.7	5.0	2.3	2.2
	1941–50	3.0	9.7	0.9	6.5
	1950–61	4.0	8.1	1.4	3.9

Jamaica was much smaller than from Puerto Rico. Argentina's comparatively low rate of urban population growth conforms to the typical pattern of recent trends in European and North American countries which, like Argentina, are relatively highly urbanized and have relatively moderate rates of natural increase.

In a number of Latin American countries, the rates of urban population growth were distinctly higher in the 1950's than in earlier intercensal periods since 1920. The data for Brazil, Chile, Costa Rica, the Dominican Republic, El Salvador, Honduras, and Panama conform to this pattern, although in the cases of the Dominican Republic and Panama the data for the last three intercensal periods show an irregular trend. On the other hand, the urban population in Venezuela and Puerto Rico increased at lower rates during the 1950's than during the 1940's. In Venezuela, the urban growth rate dropped from the extraordinarily high level of 9.7 per cent in 1941–1950 to the still very high level of 8.1 per cent in 1950–1961. In Puerto Rico, the rate fell from a moderately high 5.5 per cent in 1940–1950 to a very low 1.0 per cent in 1950–1960, mainly as a result of the emigration that was also primarily responsible for cutting Puerto Rico's total population growth rate down from 1.7 per cent annually for the earlier period to 0.6 per cent for the 1950's. The data for Mexico show a slight slackening of the rate of urban population growth in 1950–1960 compared with 1940–1950, while those for Jamaica indicate only a slightly higher rate for 1943–1960 than for 1921–1943. In view of these variations and the lack of data to represent the trends in other countries in the region, it would be risky to attempt any generalization

about the trends of urban population growth rates during recent decades in Latin America as a whole.

The increase of urban population between the dates of successive censuses is due, in most cases, partly to the increase in number of localities qualifying as urban and partly to natural and migratory growth of population in the localities that were urban at both censuses. In the Dominican Republic, for example, the population in localities of 20,000 or more inhabitants increased from 238,111 in 1950 to 564,416 in 1960, and about one-third of this increase can be attributed to the fact that five towns with less than 20,000 inhabitants in 1950 had more than that number by 1960. Likewise in Chile, El Salvador, and Peru, one-third or more of the increase of the urban population during the latest intercensal period was due to additions to the list of localities qualifying as urban. This factor was somewhat less important in other countries for which pertinent data are available.

Variations in the component of urban population growth due to natural and migratory increase in the cities are measured by the rates shown in Table 5, which refer to the population in localities having 20,000 or more inhabitants (classified by population size) at the date of the latest census. The growth rates calculated on this basis have a narrower range of variation than those shown in Table 4, but follow a generally similar pattern.

The rate of growth of the urban population is not the same as that of urbanization—i.e., the pace at which the shift in rural-urban distribution of a country's population proceeds. The latter depends, of course, on the relative rates of population change in the urban and rural sectors. Several different indices may be used to measure the rate of urbanization; the index shown in Table 4 has been calculated by relating the annual per cent rates of growth of urban (u) and total (t) population according to the following formula:[7]

$$r = 100 \left(\frac{(u) - (t)}{100 + (t)} \right)$$

The data shown in Table 4 permit a comparison of this index of the rate of urbanization in the 1950's with corresponding values for earlier intercensal periods since 1920 in 11 Latin American countries. In seven of these countries, the rate of urbanization was higher in the 1950's than in the earlier periods, and in four countries it was lower. These four countries are Puerto Rico, Venezuela, Mexico (where the rate of urban population growth was lower in the 1950's than in the next earlier intercensal period), and Costa Rica. In Costa Rica, although the growth of the urban population accelerated in the 1950's as compared with 1927–1950, the growth of the total population accelerated more, so that the pace of increase in the degree of this country's urbanization slackened.

GROWTH OF RURAL POPULATION

The rates of growth of the rural as well as the urban population accelerated during the 1950's in a majority of Latin American countries for which data are available to compare the trends during this decade with those of earlier periods. It appears that the increasing flow of migration to the

[7] This is equivalent to the annual per cent rate of increase in the ratio of urban population to total population.

cities was not enough, in most cases, to offset the rising rates of natural increase in the rural communities due to falling death rates and steady, high birth rates. In fact, in spite of rural out-migration, rates of rural population growth in the 1950's averaged higher than 2 per cent annually in 10 of the 17 countries (Table 4) for which recent data are available, and in one country —Costa Rica—the population in localities of less than 20,000 inhabitants increased at the extraordinary annual rate of 3.8 per cent between 1950 and 1963.

The four countries where the rural population grew less rapidly during the 1950's than during the preceding intercensal period were Jamaica, Panama, Puerto Rico, and Chile. In Chile there was a slight decrease of rural population from 1952 to 1960, due to the sharp acceleration of the movement to the cities. In Jamaica and Puerto Rico, as already mentioned, emigration to other countries was a major factor.

In Argentina, the rural population grew little between 1947 and 1960, the provisional estimate of the growth rate being only 0.3 per cent for the rural sector. In this respect, the trend in Argentina was similar to that in European and North American countries where levels of urbanization are high and rates of natural increase are relatively low.

TRENDS OF URBAN CONCENTRATION AND DISPERSION

A trend toward decreasing importance of principal cities is apparent in the majority of Latin American countries where measures of changes in distribution of urban population by

Table 5
Average Annual Rates of Population Increase in Recent Intercensal Periods, in Cities of 20,000 or More at Latest Census, Classified by Population Size of Locality, For Selected Latin American Countries

Country	Intercensal Period	Population Size of Locality			
		Total, 20,000+	20,000— 99,999	100,000 and Over[a]	Largest City
Costa Rica	1927–50	3.0	—	—	3.0
	1950–63	4.6	—	—	4.6
Cuba	1931–43	2.1	1.9	1.7	2.4[b]
	1943–53	3.2	3.9	3.4	2.6[b]
Dominican Republic	1935–50	4.6	2.8	—	6.3
	1950–60	6.1	4.2	—	7.3
El Salvador	1930–50	2.2	1.3	—	3.0
	1950–61	4.0	3.6	—	4.3
Honduras	1940–50	3.4	1.8	—	4.4
	1950–60	6.5	7.6	—	5.9
Mexico	1940–50	...	...[c]	4.9	5.6[d]
	1950–60	...	...[c]	5.3	4.9[d]
Panama	1940–50	2.8	2.2	—	3.0
	1950–60	4.4	2.1	—	5.2
Puerto Rico	1940–50	5.1	3.1[e]	—[c]	6.6
	1950–60	1.3	0.2[e]	—[c]	1.9
Brazil	1940–50	...	...[f]	4.4	4.6[g]
	1950–60	5.2	6.4[h]	5.5	3.9[g]
Chile	1940–52	2.6	2.7	1.4	3.1
	1952–60	4.4	5.1	3.0	4.2
Colombia	1938–51	5.7	5.0	6.1	6.2
	1951–64	...	...	...	6.7
Ecuador	1950–62	...	...	...	5.2
Peru	1940–61	4.6	4.6	3.7	4.9
Venezuela	1941–50	7.6	7.1	7.2	8.3
	1950–61	6.5	6.5	6.2	6.8

[a] Except the largest city.

[b] Includes those parts of metropolitan Havana (as officially defined in 1953) for which comparable data could be obtained at earlier censuses.

[c] Individual listings for cities in this size-class are not available in the 1960 Census reports thus far issued. For 1940–50 Durán gave figures for 19 cities in this size-class showing a lower growth rate than that for cities of 100,000+; see Durán Ochoa, Julio, POBLACION, Mexico City, Fondo de Cultura Económica, 1955.

[d] Figures relate to the Federal District.

[e] Ponce, with slightly more than 100,000 inhabitants in 1960, is included here in the size-class of 20,000–99,999.

[f] It is not possible to trace in the 1940 Census tabulations many of the cities which reached the 20,000+ size-class only during 1950–60. An average rate of increase of 4.17 was computed for 88 cities with 20,000–99,999 population in 1950.

[g] For the combined population of Rio de Janeiro and São Paulo which had nearly equal populations in 1960.

[h] Excludes Vila Velha (population 31,027 in 1960) and Paranavai (population 22,141 in 1960) which could not be located in the 1950 Census tabulations.

Ellipsis dots indicate that data are not available. Dash indicates a magnitude of 0.

city-size classes are available for successive intercensal periods since 1920 (see Table 3). The percentage of the total urban population found in the largest city was smaller at the latest census than at any earlier census since 1920 in 14 of the 17 countries where such comparison can be made. The exceptions are: Costa Rica where the capital remained as the only city qualified as urban by the criterion of having 20,000 or more inhabitants; Panama, where the capital city's share of the total urban population increased gradually from 1940–1960; and Puerto Rico, where it decreased from 1920–1940, but increased after 1940 and slightly exceeded the 1920 percentage by 1960.

Where the percentage of total urban population in the largest city diminished, the cause in some cases was a shift in the prevailing directions of migration in favor of smaller cities and, in other cases, the appearance of additional localities qualified as urban in view of their numbers of inhabitants at successive censuses. In the Dominican Republic, for example, the latter factor was responsible for a decrease between 1950 and 1960 in the share of total urban population concentrated in the capital, although the rate of growth of the capital city exceeded the average rates of natural and migratory increase in the smaller urban places (*see* Table 5.) The situation in El Salvador and Venezuela was similar.

In some countries where the principal city's share of the urban population was decreasing, the gainers were cities in the class of 100,000 or more inhabitants, and in other cases smaller cities, of 20,000 to 99,999, were the ones to increase their share of the urban population. No consistent regional pattern is apparent in the trends of

urban population distribution between cities of *more and less* than 100,000 inhabitants. However, as already noted, there has been a general trend of increasing percentages of the total population of Latin American countries in cities of 100,000 or more.

COMPARISON OF RECENT TRENDS OF URBANIZATION IN LATIN AMERICA WITH PAST TRENDS IN THE UNITED STATES

It is instructive to compare the increases of urbanization in recent censuses in Latin American countries with the experience of the United States at comparable stages in the history of its urbanization. For this purpose, an approximate series of percentages of United States population in urban areas of 20,000 or more inhabitants at the decennial censuses since 1790 has been prepared (Figure 1), together with a fitted long-range trend curve.[8]

The highest rates of urbanization in the United States occurred during the first half of the nineteenth century. The rates of urbanization (as defined above), implied in the long-range trend curve of urban population percentages, rose from about 3 per cent annually around 1810 to 5 per cent in the 1830's, and have since declined

[8] The basis of this chart is the historical series of estimated percentages of the United States population in urban areas of 25,000 or more inhabitants (according to the definition used in the censuses of 1940 and earlier) shown in: United States Bureau of the Census, 1960 *Census of Population*, Vol. I, Part I, pp. 1–14. These percentages were multiplied by a constant factor of 1.05631 to make the series coincide in 1960 with the percentage of population in urban areas of 20,000 or more inhabitants. The smoothed long-range trend curve was obtained by fitting a polynomial of third degree to the original series of percentages and multiplying the calculated values by the same factor 1.05631.

PERCENT

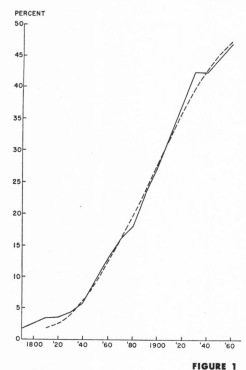

FIGURE 1

Percentage of Population in Urban Areas of 20,000 or More Inhabitants, United States, 1790–1960

progressively to about 0.4 per cent in the 1950's. Against this background, it appears that recent urbanization rates in some Latin American countries have been at levels comparable to or above the highest rates in the historical experience of the United States. In this category are the rates for the Dominican Republic, 1920–1935 (4.9) and 1950–1960 (5.3); Honduras, 1950–1961 (5.0) and Venezuela, 1941–1950 (6.5). Urbanization rates in the range of 2 to 4 per cent, experienced recently in a considerable number of Latin American countries (Table 4), are comparable to those experienced in the United States between the 1840's and 1870's.

In Figure 2, trends in the percentages of urban population recorded in various Latin American countries since 1920 are compared with segments of the smoothed long-range trend curve for the United States, selected to show how the recent experience of the Latin American countries resembles or differs from that of the United States at a time when it was at a corresponding level of urbanization.[9]

For example, in Venezuela in 1936, about 16 per cent of the population were residents of urban areas. This level of urbanization was attained in the United States about 65 years earlier: that is, about 1871. After 1941, Venezuela experienced urbanization at a very high rate, far exceeding that of the United States in the corresponding period (after 1876). As a result, Venezuela by 1960 was slightly more urbanized than the United States (47.2 vs. 46.9 per cent). In other words, in 24 years, Venezuela advanced in urbanization as much as the United States did in 89 years.

Peru, in 1940 with about 14 per cent urban population, was at the level reached by the United States about 1865. Between 1940 and 1961, Peru's urban percentage rose to about 29, whereas the percentage in the United States, during the corresponding period (1865–1887) increased only to about 22. In 1961, Peru was at a level of urbaniza-

[9] The comparison is incongruous in that the figures used for the United States are from a fitted long-range trend while those for Latin American countries are unadjusted figures, affected by short-term deviations from the secular trends. Therefore, relatively minor, temporary differences—like those shown in the chart for Honduras and Jamaica, for instance— have little significance. However, great and persistent divergences, like those shown for Venezuela and Peru, represent highly significant differences of trend.

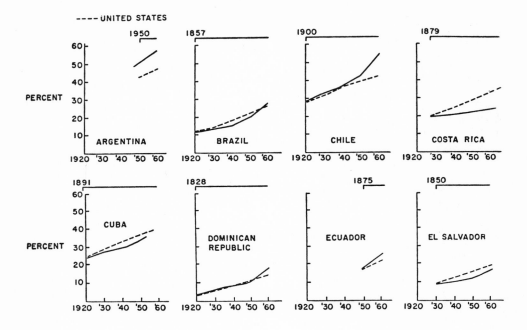

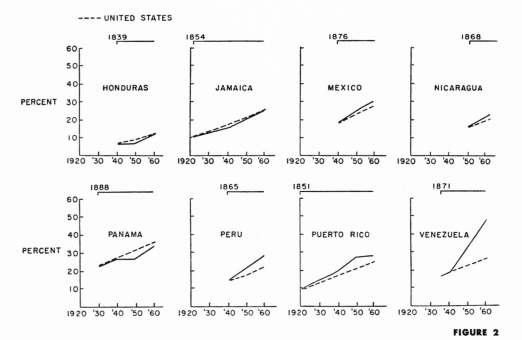

FIGURE 2

Percentages of Population in Localities of 20,000 or more Inhabitants in Latin American Countries Since 1920, Compared With Long-Range Historical Trend in the United States.

tion which it would have reached only about 1979 if the trend from 1940 onward had conformed to the long-range historical trend in the United States.

To cite one more example, Chile in 1920 had 28 per cent of its population in urban areas—the percentage reached in the United States about 1900. Between 1920 and 1940, Chile's trend of urbanization closely paralleled the long-range trend in the United States with a 20-year lag. After 1940, and especially after 1950, the advance of urbanization in Chile accelerated sharply, far outpacing the long-range United States trend. By 1960, with nearly 55 per cent of the population urban, Chile was at a level which the United States would not attain before the year 2000 if the long-range historical trend should continue in the future.

In only six of the 16 countries included in the chart—namely, Brazil, Costa Rica, Cuba, El Salvador, Panama, and Puerto Rico—has the increase of urbanization during any intercensal periods since 1920 lagged significantly behind what would correspond to the long-range past trend in the United States. In Puerto Rico, such a lag has occurred only since 1950. As already mentioned, this is a peculiar situation, owing to the effects of emigration. Costa Rica is also peculiar in that the population considered as urban is confined to a single metropolitan area which is very extensive and includes a good deal of only slightly urbanized territory.[10]

[10] Another peculiarity is that four localities in Costa Rica outside the San José metropolitan area were just under the limit of 20,000 inhabitants at the 1963 census. Thus, at the next census, a considerable increase in the number of places qualified as urban may be expected, and this may give an appreciable impetus to the increase of the urban population.

Nevertheless, the lag of urbanization in this country since 1927 is a significant deviation from the typical pattern for Latin America, as well as from historical experience in the United States. In Brazil, the lagging trend of urbanization during 1920–1940 gave way to an accelerating trend during 1940–1950—and especially from 1950–1960—with the result that by 1960 Brazil's percentage of urban population was above the level it would have reached by following the long-range historical trend of the United States from 1920 on. Brazil's example is suggestive of what may occur in the 1960's in El Salvador and Panama, where an earlier lag was partly compensated for by an upturn of the urbanization trend during the 1950's.

The general conclusion to which this analysis points is that, while trends of urbanization in Latin American countries in recent decades exhibit a considerable diversity, on the whole the progress of urbanization, especially since 1950, appears rapid against the background of past experience in the United States as well as contemporary experience in other regions of the world.

SUMMARY

This paper presents some provisional results, for the Latin American region, of a world survey of urbanization since 1920, which is being conducted by the United Nations Secretariat.

Latin America, on the whole, is considerably more urbanized than the average of the world's regions. It is much more urbanized than either Africa or Asia and somewhat more urbanized than southern Europe. Only North America, northwestern Europe, Australia, and New Zealand are very far ahead of it in urbanization. But the countries of Latin America differ greatly in degrees of urbanization. In terms of population in cities of 100,000 or more, Latin America appears no less urbanized in comparison with other regions of the world than it does when comparisons refer to localities of 20,000 or more. Latin America also has a good share of population in major metropolitan agglomerations.

Urbanization in a majority of Latin American countries is megalocephalic. Sixteen of 22 countries for which data were available had half or more of their urban population concentrated in one city or metropolitan area. If urban concentration is measured by the percentage of each country's urban population found in cities of 100,000 or more, then 20 of the 22 countries considered had more than 60 per cent of their urban population in cities of this size. A trend of decreasing dominance for principal cities is apparent in the majority of the Latin American countries where this measure of concentration is available; on the other hand, there has been a general trend of increasing percentages of the total population of Latin American countries in cities of 100,000 or more inhabitants.

The growth rate of the total population in Latin America during the decade 1950–1960, estimated at an average of 2.7 per cent per annum, exceeds the estimated rates of growth in all other regions of the world. It appears, however, that the rate of growth of the urban population in Latin America was nearly twice that of the total population. While an increase in urbanization was general throughout the world during the 1950's, Latin America surpassed all other regions except Oceania, both in the rate of growth of its urban population and in the magnitude of the increment to the percentage of urban population.

In view of the variations observed in the trends for several countries of the region, it would be risky to attempt any generalization about trends of urban population growth rates during recent decades in Latin America as a whole.

The rate of urbanization was higher in the 1950's than in earlier intercensal periods in seven of the 11 countries for which a comparison could be made.

In spite of the increasing flow of migration to the cities, the rate of growth of the rural population was higher during the 1950's than in the immediately preceding intercensal period in a majority of Latin American countries for which data are available.

A comparison was made between the increases of urbanization shown by recent censuses in Latin American countries, and the experience of the United States at comparable stages in the history of its urbanization. The general conclusion to which this analysis points is that, while the trends of urbanization in Latin American countries during recent decades exhibit a considerable diversity, on the whole the progress of urbanization in the region, especially since 1950, appears rapid against the background of past experience in the United States as well as contemporary experience in other regions of the world.

DISCUSSION

Dr. Dorothy Thomas: This is a magnificent paper, in the tradition established by other reports from the Population Branch of the United Nations. We look forward to the publication of the complete report which will give similar details for other regions of the world and presumably will develop some of the correlations suggested by the present paper.

In this paper the Latin American countries are, in a summary manner, put in regional and world perspective. The paper gives insights that should lead to further research. One of the important substantive findings is the extent to which the Latin American rural population tends to be much more "rural" than we are accustomed to find in more developed countries. Correspondingly, the urban population is, in general, far less "urbanized" and also less "developed" from the economic standpoint than in the more industrialized countries.

There is very little to criticize in the main presentation. On the technical side, however, I shall raise two questions. First, why was it necessary to proceed beyond simple comparisons of urban growth rates with total or with rural growth rates to an index based on ratios of rates of increase? These ratios are not easy to interpret, and they could lead to absurd results. If we look at the matter of weighting that occurs for, say, Argentina, Chile, and Venezuela, where there are high urban proportions, and compare these ratios with those countries where there are low urban proportions (e.g., Honduras, El Salvador, etc.) a somewhat different picture emerges in respect to direct comparisons versus ratio comparisons.

My second question relates to the matter of trend determination for the urban series of the United States. I like the idea of taking segments of a long-time series of urban proportions in a highly developed country during the course of its development and seeing how these shorter term trends of recently developing countries correspond to segments of the model. I am, however, not convinced about the desirability of utilizing a third-degree parabola to express this trend. The very interesting chart (Figure 1) of the Durand-Peláez paper strongly suggests that the authors would have approached reality more closely by utilizing a simpler technique of trend determination—for example, a three-date moving average centered at each middle date. I noted also that the authors themselves apparently had little confidence in their parabolic trend for the earliest dates,

perhaps because such a trend yields absurd results for terminal dates. I was, therefore, somewhat shaken by the extrapolation of the trend into the future and by the authors' suggestion that Chile, with almost 55 per cent of the population in urban areas of 20,000 or more inhabitants in 1960 "was at level which the United States would not attain before the year 2000 if the long-range historical trend should continue in the future."

Despite these criticisms of technique, I compliment the authors of the paper and also the Population Branch of the United Nations, and I look forward to the publication of the complete report in a forthcoming Bulletin.

Mr. Robert O. Carleton: I, too, should like to congratulate the authors of this paper. Before I did my paper, I tried to do one on this subject—and threw up my hands in despair. It is tricky because the boundaries and data are not always comparable.

I wanted to stress one difficulty I experienced, the difficulty of interpreting data of this kind without an intimate knowledge of each country. In this connection, I was struck by a reference to Puerto Rico, the one country I know well in Latin America. It was observed that the population in some of the urban centers of Puerto Rico actually decreased in the past decade. This decrease is explained by emigration to the mainland of the United States.

This explanation is correct, but it is not the most important one. I have firsthand knowledge of what happened in Puerto Rico. The urban growth in the decade 1950–1960 took place outside the legal urban centers. It was a suburban growth that was technically rural because the urban limits were not changed to keep pace with changing population movements. Before the 1960 Census was taken, no one thought to change these boundaries.

When the first census results became known, we discovered that the urban population of Puerto Rico had not changed, despite the tremendous urbanization. We realized what had happened, and we made a panicky call to the Census Bureau in Washington which sent a geographer down. We explained the problem to him. So that he could see for himself, I personally took him around to about 10 of the *municipios* which we thought were the most flagrant cases. The preferred solution of changing the urban boundaries encountered insuperable legal obstacles except in the case of one *municipio* (Arecibo). The solution adopted by the Census Bureau geographer was to introduce the concept of urban fringe into Puerto Rico and to apply this concept to the urban growth outside the city limits in the *municipios* we visited.

But the remaining *municipios* were left as they were. As a consequence, the final census report shows that in 35 of the 76 *municipios* the urban population as a percentage of the total population actually *decreased*. This, of course, does not mean a trend toward ruralization in Puerto Rico. It is just that population growth took place in legally rural areas.

I mention the case of Puerto Rico in order to raise the general problem of changing urban boundaries in countries where the analyst does not have firsthand knowledge. The introduction of census publications generally carries information about the boundary changes that have been made since the last census. What they do not tell, and really cannot be expected to tell, is which urban boundaries should have been changed and were not changed. It is difficult to have firsthand knowledge of all the countries of a region in order to make comparisons. But how else can one acquire this information?

Dr. Leona Baumgartner: I will speak, but remember that I am not a specialist in this field of migration.

It seems to me quite obvious that people move for a reason. We have been talking about boundaries and certain other important factors—but have not talked about reasons for moving. Let me take Puerto Rico as an example. What was happening in its economic development? What of its efforts to decentralize industry and to develop services for people in rural areas or on the fringes of its larger cities? What of its re-housing schemes? Could the relationships between people moving and the reasons why they moved have been examined more carefully in these studies?

I am anxious to have these other factors studied more carefully because, it seems to me, if there is to be any social engineering in this world today, we need to get at some of these human factors and not stop with recording the facts about people moving.

Dr. Lee: I don't think anyone would quarrel with Dr. Baumgartner's contention that we need more information as to why people move. The fact is that the data presented here do not permit the authors to make such inferences. Such studies should be made, but they are studies of an order different from those we are now discussing.

Dr. Baumgartner: That is true, but there are many important findings which could be recorded, perhaps in future research. One paper discussed movement of people in Argentina, Chile, and Santiago. If I remember correctly, the years that were discussed were the years in which there was a very large economic development in the area of Guayaquil. I don't know if there was a similar economic growth in Santiago. It seems to me that these studies could begin to take notice of environmental activities as well as the mere movement of the people.

I am sure people move for jobs and for other reasons. I have just been in Nepal and seen an influx of people into a previously relatively unpopulated rural area. Why? Because malaria was conquered in that area; some water was found; a road was built. People moved from surrounding areas and moved there because they can now grow food there.

These environmental factors do not seem to be too difficult to take into account at the same time these excellent studies are undertaken. Of course, I thoroughly approve of them in any event, Mr. Chairman.

Mr. César Peláez: I shall start with Dr. Thomas' questions. She referred first to the index we used to measure the "acceleration" of urbanization. This formula may appear to be rather strange, but actually it has a clear meaning. If we consider the degree of urbanization as a percentage, this formula provides the rate of increase of that percentage. Instead of the usual formula for geometric rate of growth we used this one because the calculations are less complicated, since we had already calculated the percentages for other purposes.

The index we have used to measure the tempo of urbanization gives us a clearer picture of this process than the mere consideration of the changes in the percentages of urbanization in the different periods of time. I feel that it is more appropriate to talk about variations in this index, rather than merely saying that the percentage of urbanization was so much at one time, and that it decreased or increased to so much at another time. This type of description, I think, does not give a clear picture of the process of urbanization.

As to the irregularities, I agree that another procedure, such as moving averages, could have been used. Some kind of smoothing of the data had to be done; otherwise, the irregularities would have impeded the comparisons.

It is important to point out that these comparisons are in a way relative since the data for the Latin American countries refer to comparatively short periods of time and nothing could be done to correct their irregularities. Let us assume, for instance, that we do not have the information for

Brazil in 1920, and that the comparison begins in 1940. In this case, the trend curve for the United States would be below the curve for Brazil whereas, if we consider data for 1920, the trend curve for the United States will be above the curve for Brazil.

Our purpose was to compare the long-range trend in United States urbanization with the available data for Latin American countries. We should not overestimate the reliability of the results of these comparisons. They are suggestive, but they have not been completely proved.

We needed a deeper analysis of the existing conditions in different countries and the United States at these different periods of time. This is one of the main shortcomings of this type of study; we try to draw national comparisons, but, in the way we have done it, we have evidently sacrificed depth in the analysis of specified causes and specific considerations in every country.

As to the statement we made that in 1960 Chile achieved a level of urbanization which the United States would not attain before the year 2000, I think that it should be considered in the framework of our basic premise, that is, that the curve we fitted to the data for the United States represents the long-range historical trend of urbanization in that country. We have taken a premise, and from that premise we have drawn our conclusion. We could also have said that the validity of the basic premise is not the same for all the segments of the curve; that the curve may be more representative of the central part of the period covered by the original data than of the extremes of this period, and, finally, that the figure for the year 2000, being a mathematical extrapolation of the historical trend, should be considered with extreme caution. Dr. Lowell J. Reed, who is here with us, has had an important part in developing these curves, and his studies have contributed to an understanding of the possibilities and risks of this type of extrapolation.

As to the statement that the survey should include other aspects of these problems, I think that somebody has already answered for me. We have tried to analyze and study trends and levels of urbanization without consideration of their relationships with other social phenomena. This does not necessarily mean that we underestimate the importance of studying those relationships; we feel that these studies are very important and useful. Many of the delegates at the recent meeting of the Population Commission of the United Nations stressed the need for research in this field with due consideration of ecological and sociological variables. However, we think that the type of study we have presented here is also very important and, perhaps, a prerequisite to more detailed and deeper studies. We have spoken of the need for a socio-economic approach in research on urbanization. But this type of research will require much more sophisticated and complete data than those currently available in most countries of the world.

16. Urbanization and Distribution of Population by Size of Locality

UNITED NATIONS COMMISSION FOR LATIN AMERICA

The implications of the distribution of population among regions within countries differ according to the degree and kind of urbanization; it has already been suggested that the concentration of population in small areas of Latin America now depends much more on the growth of large cities than on increases in density of rural and small-town settlement. Let us next examine the distribution of population first between urban and rural areas and then among "inhabited localities" of varying sizes.

The difficulties of establishing a satisfactory dividing line between urban and rural localities are well known. The arbitrary figure of 2,000 inhabitants will here be used as the bottom limit for urban localities, although this criterion undoubtedly exaggerates to some extent the size of the population with truly urban traits. Two other difficulties that limit the comparability of data must be kept in mind: first the countries (and regions within countries) differ in the extent to which "urban" functions predominate in settlements of a given size. Villages devoted entirely to agriculture may have larger populations in some countries (e.g. Mexico) than do many local commercial centres in others (e.g.

Pages 50–60 from "Geographic Distribution of the Population of Latin America and Regional Development Priorities," United Nations Economic Bulletin for Latin America, 8, No. 1, (March 1963), 51–63.
Reprinted by permission of publisher.

Argentina). Also the general growth in population combined with improvements in transport and communications may mean that localities of a given size are less likely to have urban characteristics than in the past; strictly rural settlements may grow above 2,000 people without becoming more "urban" in their functions, and small towns may lose their commercial and other urban activities to the larger centres now become more accessible. (Conversely, of course, the improvement of communications is likely to bring about a diffusion of some urban traits into very small localities.) Present demographic data throw very little light on these important questions. In its later stages the present study will attempt to explore more deeply the functions and characteristics in different countries of the localities on the borderline between urban and rural, with their changes over time.

For present purposes, however, the fixing of a dividing line between "urban" and "rural" localities is of less interest than the patterns of distribution of population through the whole range of localities by size. Further difficulties arise in the comparison whether between countries or over a period of time, of populations in localities of varying sizes, and these difficulties are greatest with respect to the largest and the smallest localities. Only in a few countries of Latin America do the censuses distinguish "localities" within boundaries defined by strictly geographical criteria such as extent of definitely urbanized territory, rural nuclei of population grouped in physical proximity, and dispersed points of habitation in the countryside. In most cases, localities are delimited by administrative boundaries.

The smallest unit of administration in the majority of Latin American countries is the *municipio*, usually made up of an administrative centre or *cabecera* with its own boundaries, plus surrounding territory that may contain a number of population nuclei but is not further subdivided for administrative purposes. Since there are few large centres that are not *cabeceras*, the distribution of *cabeceras* by size within certain maximum and minimum size limits, is nearly equivalent to the distribution of all inhabited places by size. For smaller localities this system becomes increasingly unreliable because of the existence of centres without any administrative status that are larger than the smallest *cabeceras*. Nor do census tabulations distinguishing only between the population of the *cabecera* and that of the remainder of the *municipio* throw any light on the general character of the rural habitat, i.e., whether the people are grouped in villages or smaller nuclei or live mainly dispersed.

On the other hand, once a *cabecera* attains a respectable size its administrative boundaries may no longer correspond to the continuous urbanized area within the *municipio*. At a further stage of growth, this urbanized area may cover the entire *municipio* and expand beyond its bounds. The resulting city may eventually come to engulf other nearby towns, throw out solidly urbanized tentacles along the major highways, and establish such a dominance of its own economic, residential and recreational needs over peripheral towns and rural areas, possibly across the country's major administrative boundaries, that the whole may best be considered a single metropolitan region. To the extent possible the present study deals with some of the largest cities in terms of such geographic rather than administrative boundaries, but this could be done only through rough approximations, at the cost of some loss of comparability among cities of nearly equal size, and also of some loss of comparability over time, since metropolitan areas expand over more and more territory, incorporating cities and towns previously enumerated separately.

The most recent estimates indicate an increase in the urban population of Latin America—i.e., that in localities with 2,000 or more inhabitants from 61 million in 1950 to 95 million in 1960, or at an average annual rate of growth of 4.5 per cent. Rural population—i.e. the remainder—meanwhile grew from 95 million to 111 million, or at an average annual rate of about 1.5 per cent. [See Table 1.] In 1950, only Argentina, Chile, and Uruguay had urban majorities, while in eleven countries the urban population was less than 30 per cent of the national total. In 1960, more than half the population was urban also in Cuba, Mexico, and Venezuela, while only in the Dominican Republic, Haiti, and Honduras is the urban population believed to be still below the 30 per cent mark. The rapid rises in percentage of urban population in Brazil, Mexico, Peru, Venezuela, and the Dominican Republic are now documented by new census data, as are the more modest increases in Argentina, Chile and El Salvador. On the whole, the per-

Table 1

Urban and Rural Population, in Thousands, 1950 and 1960, Urban Population Being Defined as That of Localities with 2,000 or More Inhabitants[a]

Country	1950				1960			
	Urban	Rural	Total	Per Cent Urban	Urban	Rural	Total	Per Cent Urban
Uruguay[b]	1,893	514	2,407	79	2,313	514	2,827	82
Argentina	11,038	6,151	17,189	64	14,161	6,795	20,956	68
Chile	3,513	2,560	6,073	58	4,801	2,826	7,627	63
Venezuela	2,430	2,544	4,974	49	4,521	2,810	7,331	62
Cuba	2,713	2,795	5,508	49	3,709	3,088	6,797	55
Mexico	11,826	14,000	25,826	46	18,740	16,248	34,988	54
Colombia	4,253	7,426	11,679	36	7,134	8,334	15,468	46
Panama	287	510	797	36	433	622	1,055	41
Brazil	16,021	35,955	51,976	31	27,800	42,800	70,600	39
Costa Rica	232	569	801	29	443	728	1,171	38
Peru	2,388	6,133	8,521	28	3,890	6,967	10,857	36
Ecuador	885	2,312	3,197	28	1,499	2,818	4,317	35
Nicaragua	298	762	1,060	28	501	976	1,477	34
Paraguay	388	1,009	1,397	28	597	1,171	1,768	34
El Salvador	517	1,351	1,868	28	795	1,647	2,442	33
Guatemala	674	2,131	2,805	24	1,167	2,598	3,765	31
Bolivia	778	2,235	3,013	26	1,104	2,592	3,696	30
Dom. Republic	458	1,673	2,131	21	872	2,142	3,014	29
Honduras	247	1,181	1,428	17	438	1,512	1,950	22
Haiti	340	3,040	3,380	10	523	3,617	4,140	13
Total	61,179	94,851	156,026	39	95,431	110,815	206,246	46

[a] Estimates of urban and rural population for mid-year 1950 and mid-year 1960 were first published in the November 1960 issue of the Statistical Supplement of the *Economic Bulletin for Latin America,* and in partly revised form in the November 1961 issue. The present table contains more extensive revision based largely on new data from censuses carried out in ten countries during 1960 and 1961. Further revisions will be needed when the results of other censuses become available.

[b] For lack of a recent population census, the "urban" population of Uruguay was estimated as that of localities having schools of an "urban" type.

centage of urban population rose fastest in countries at intermediate levels of urbanization, more slowly both in countries already predominantly urban and in those very little urbanized. If present trends continue, regional urban population will exceed rural from about 1966.

For the twenty Republics combined, the estimates show an absolute ten-year gain of 34 million in urban population and of 16 million in rural population. Had there been no transfers of population from rural to urban sectors, urban population would have gained only about 20 million while the rural population would have grown by 30 million, hence a net transfer of 14 million persons over ten years appears to have occurred. Actually, the transfer may have been somewhat larger and rising over the years in relation to general growth of population.[1]

Moreover, available statistics show that the more strictly urban centres with 20,000 or more inhabitants have been growing more rapidly than the urban population as a whole, even when comparisons are made in terms of a fixed number of urban places, so as to eliminate localities that have moved from a lower to a higher-size class between 1950 and 1960. [See Table 2.] It follows that smaller towns between 2,000 and 20,000 in population must have been growing with relative slowness. Unfortunately, the variations in census definitions are severe impediments to an internationally comparable presentation of trends in the growth of population centres of the different size classes. The trends must be studied separately for each country with methods modified in accordance with the available statistics.

The most striking advances have been made in the numbers and size of cities—or metropolitan areas—which surpass one million inhabitants each. Buenos Aires was Latin America's only "million" city until 1930, when Mexico City passed this mark, soon to be followed by Rio de Janeiro and São Paulo. By 1950, Havana, Lima and

[1] The calculation assumes equal rates of natural increase in urban and rural population. In practice, because of higher rural birth rates, natural increase tends to be higher in rural areas. On the other hand, some previously "rural" localities must have entered the "urban" category simply by growing above the 2,000 population limit. It is probable that the numerical effect of the first phenomenon has been greater than the offsetting effect of the second. Accordingly, the roughly calculated transfer of 14 million persons represents a minimum estimate.

Santiago were also above one million, bringing the number of such cities to seven. By 1960, Bogotá, Caracas and Montevideo were added. If present trends continue there may be sixteen "million" cities by 1970 and twenty-six by 1980.

The rising number of "million" cities contained 8 million people in 1940, 16 million in 1950, and 27 million in 1960. If their combined population continues to rise at 6 per cent annually, it will reach 48 million by 1970 and 90 million by 1980.

The high proportions of total urban population concentrated in a single city, usually the national capital, have long been one of the characteristic features of urbanization in the majority of Latin American countries; there are only two countries (Brazil and Colombia) in which the leading city does not contain at least one quarter of the total urban population. In the majority of countries recent population trends are confirming this concentration. Calculations, some of which depend on rather rough estimates, show that between 1950 and 1960 the percentage of urban population increase absorbed by the leading cities in a majority of countries exceeded their previous share of the urban population.

Can the Latin American urban population, with its obviously high degree of concentration, be measured against any objective standard for the "normal" distribution of cities by size? A number of scholars have examined such distribution patterns in other regions in the course of their studies of inter-community equilibrium in economic activities. They have commonly made use of the so-called "rank-size rule" as a theoretical model of the distribution of cities by size to which actual observations conform

Table 2

Population (in Thousands) of Largest City (in Brazil and Ecuador, Two Largest Cities), Relationship to Total Urban Population, and Percentage of 1950-1960 Increase in Urban Population Absorbed by Largest City

Country	City	Population		Per Cent of Urban Population of Country		Population Increase of Largest City as Percentage of 1950-1960 Increase in Urban Population
		1950	1960	1950	1960	
Argentina	Buenos Aires[a]	5,100	7,000[b]	46	49	61[c]
Bolivia	La Paz	320	450[c]	41	41[e]	40[c]
Brazil[d]	Río de Janeiro	2,303	3,200	14	12⎱	18[e]
	São Paulo	2,017	3,250	13	12⎰	
Chile	Santiago[f]	1,275	1,900	33	40	49
Colombia	Bogotá	620	1,118	15	16	17
Dom. Republic	Santo Domingo	180	365	39	42	59
Ecuador	Quito	210	314	24	21⎱	48[e]
	Guayaquil	259	450	29	30⎰	
Paraguay	Asunción[g]	219	311	56	53	44
Peru	Lima-Callao[h]	1,075	1,875	45	48	50
Uruguay	Montevideo[i]	935[c]	1,150[c]	49[c]	50[c]	51[c]
Venezuela	Caracas[g]	694	1,250	29	28	27
Costa Rica	San José[g]	140	250[c]	60	56[c]	52[e]
Cuba	Havana[j]	1,080	1,600[c]	40	43[c]	52[c]
El Salvador	San Salvador[g]	162	248	31	31	31
Guatemala	Guatemala	284	400[c]	42	34[c]	24[c]
Haiti	Port-au-Prince	134	240[c]	39	46[c]	57[c]
Honduras	Tegucigalpa[g]	100	180[c]	41	41[c]	42[c]
Mexico	Mexico[k]	2,884	4,666	24	25	26
Nicaragua	Managua	110	210[c]	37	42[c]	49[c]
Panama	Panama	175[l]	265	56[l]	61	61

[a] Metropolitan region as defined for censuses of 1947 and 1960, respectively.

[b] Estimate very rough; 6,763,000 according to probably incomplete census data; between 7,206,000 and 7,341,000 according to alternative estimate.

[c] Estimate very rough.

[d] Cities not defined as metropolitan regions.

[e] Combined percentage for the two leading cities.

[f] Metropolitan region as defined in 1952 census.

[g] Metropolitan region as defined in 1950 census.

[h] Urban population of the Provinces of Lima and Callao.

[i] *Departamento* of Montevideo.

[j] Metropolitan region as defined for censuses of 1943 and 1953.

[k] Urban population of *Distrito Federal*.

[l] Within new administrative city limits; census figure for 1950, within then narrower city limits, is not comparable.

more or less closely.[2] According to the rank-size rule, the population of each city tends to be in inverse proportion to its rank by order of size. Thus, the second, third, and fourth largest city might be expected to have one-half, one-third and one-quarter the population of the largest city, and so forth.

The theoretical implications of the rank-size model and the interpretation of observed departures from it in the actual distribution of cities in a given country are matters on which agreement has not been reached. Cities specialize to varying degrees in their functions and differ in the territorial radius within which these functions are effective. For many of these functions, concentration and dispersal of the urban population offer competing advantages and drawbacks, e.g., proximity to sources of raw materials and local markets vs. internal economies of scale and availability of a large and varied labour force. It is not obvious that the most advantageous distribution of cities must conform to the rank-size rule; the size, geographical configuration and level of development of the country may explain considerable deviations from it. Nevertheless, very wide deviations from the model distribution, or very marked discontinuities therein—unless explicable in terms of some known special features peculiar to the country —are presumptive evidence of some

[2] The rank-size rule is virtually equivalent to the "Pareto curve." Authors who have used these tools to study size distribution of cities have been cited in *The Determinants and Consequences of Population Trends* (United Nations Publication, Sales No. 53.XIII.3), pp. 175–176. See also Walter Isard, *Location and Space Economy, A General Theory Relating to Industrial Location, Market Areas, Land Use, Trade and Urban Stucture* (Massachusetts Institute of Technology, 1956), particularly Chapter 3, "Some Empirical Regularities of the Space Economy."

structural anomaly within the country's urban system. This view is plausible, even if one refrains from accepting any doctrinaire interpretation of the matrix of interrelations which might account for the observed approximate conformity of city distribution in many countries to the rank-size rule.

If nothing more, the rank-size rule can be used as a yardstick in relation to which the city distribution of different countries can be compared and time-changes in the structure of each urban system can be noted. This has been done in certain studies referring to industrialized countries: it was observed that, from an initial relative dominance of the largest city, closer conformity of city distribution to the rank-size rule was progressively attained in the course of industrialization. The interpretation of this phenomenon, in terms of "forces of concentration" and "forces of dispersal," admittedly remains controversial.

The distribution of cities by size in the majority of Latin American countries does, in fact, show large deviations from the rank-size rule. The degree of deviation can be indicated by a table comparing the populations in groups of cities which, by the rank-size rule, ought to be equal. These groups are defined as follows:

Group   I: the largest city.
Group II: cities 2 and 3 and a fraction of . city 4.
Group III: cities 5–10, and fractions of cities 4 and 11.
Group IV: cities 12–30, and fractions of cities 11 and 31.
Group V: cities 32–82, and fractions of cities 31 and 83.

The relative sizes of these five groups, expressed in index numbers whose inter-group geometric average equals 100, show up as [in Table 3].

Unfortunately, not all the countries that have conducted censuses since 1960 have as yet issued tabulations permitting the use of the most recent urban population figures in [Table 2].

Detailed study of the figures [Table 3] indicates that neither the size of the country nor the size of its urban system has any systematic influence on its pattern, except in the case of Brazil, where, evidently, in a very large territory, the distribution of urban functions may be quite different from that of the other countries. If Brazil is excepted, the following features emerge from a comparison of the urban systems:

(a) As was to be expected, the first city towers above the other groups in almost every country. In most instances, first-city dominance is even more striking when group I is compared with group II (the second and third cities, plus two-thirds of the fourth). Group I is 7.2 times the size of group II in Peru; it is more than 5 times the size of II in Uruguay, Guatemala and Paraguay; more than 4 times in Argentina; more than 3 times in Cuba, Mexico, Chile and Panama; more than twice in Haiti, Costa Rica and the Dominican Republic; and between 1.8 and 1.4 times in El Salvador, Nicaragua, Venezuela, Bolivia and Honduras. Group II equals or surpasses group I only in Ecuador, Colombia and Brazil.

(b) While there is considerable variation in the relative sizes of the different groups, groups II and III tend to be the weakest, with combined populations increasing from group III to group V quite markedly in several countries.

(c) There is a positive correlation between the first feature and the second; that is, the more disproportionate the size of the largest city, the

	Date of Census	Group I	Group II	Group III	Group IV	Group V
Argentina	1947	370	77	71	65	77
Bolivia	1950	182	112	103	68	70
Brazil	1960	95	128	91	87	84
Chile	1952	232	70	67	97	93
Colombia	1951	101	121	99	92	88
Costa Rica	1950	194	71	111	86	...
Cuba	1953	257	69	77	93	77
Dom. Republic	1950	171	82	85	83	...
Ecuador	1950	152	159	76	80	69
El Salvador	1950	150	84	79	96	103
Guatemala	1950	263	46	59	95	144
Haiti	1950	187	65	93	93	93
Honduras	1961	145	98	77	88	...
Mexico	1950	237	66	69	87	106
Nicaragua	1950	163	94	88	91	81
Panama	1960	328	90	63	58	74
Paraguay	1950	289	55	59	88	120
Peru	1961	396	56	67	81	83
Uruguay	1908	271	47	78	...	...
Venezuela	1961	164	95	82	93	85

Table 3

more regressive the distribution of population in smaller cities and towns from the third group onward tend to be.

The relatively small size of groups II and III suggests a kind of structural discontinuity, which may have originated in disproportionately rapid growth of the first city or disproportionately slow growth of those next in rank, or both. Data on time-changes in city distribution, to the extent that they exist, have yielded no conclusive evidence on this point, although in a number of countries it appears that marked regressivity in the size of the groups of cities of lower rank has preceded rather than followed the increase in relative dominance of the first city.

Incomplete data from the most recent censuses suggest that in a majority of the countries in which first-city dominance is particularly pronounced the gap between the first city and those of the second and third rank continues to widen. Among the countries in which the largest city (group I) stands above 200 in the table, this appears to be true of Argentina, Chile, Panama, and Peru, while information is lacking or inconclusive for Cuba, Guatemala, Paraguay, and Uruguay. Mexico is the only known exception in this class of countries; although metropolitan Mexico City is rising more rapidly than the urban population as a whole, it is being outdistanced in rate of growth by some vigorous cities in groups II and III. On the other hand, of the two countries in which first-city dominance is absent, Brazil shows rates of growth rising from group I to group V, while Colombia has its highest rates of growth in groups II and III. Venezuela, with a relatively even initial distribution in the five groups, shows remarkably even, although very high, rates of growth from group I to group V.

The cases are too few, the comparability of the data too limited, and the special factors influencing each case too many and too imperfectly known to permit this analysis to be carried much further. In particular, the causal relationship, if any, between first-city dominance and regressivity in size-distribution of the smaller cities cannot be determined at present. Two alternative hypotheses might be formulated: (i) where populations among all except the first few cities are initially rather evenly distributed, none of the smaller cities provide sufficiently strong points of attraction for urban growth, so that a disproportionate part of it flows into the one or two leading cities; or, (ii), where one city has become dominant at an early stage, it inhibits particularly the growth of the second and third rank cities that compete with it most directly, while not affecting the growth of smaller cities and towns to such an extent. Or one might hypothesize that both causal relationships exist and reinforce each other. Present evidence is clearly insufficient to confirm them or to trace in what manner—through bottlenecks in transportation, administration, distribution of goods, capital or skilled labour force—the present distribution of urban population has been influenced.

One might expect the kind of discontinuity in the urban system that has been noted to have unfavourable implications for economic and social development. The functions of cities of the second and third rank as regional centres are presumably not being adequately carried out; urbanization taking place largely through migration concentrated upon the largest cities implies a maximum break in cultural and occupational continuity for the migrant, with a likelihood of multiple maladjustments. Various kinds of evidence other than demographic support such conclusions. It is interesting, however, that the table shows no correlation between first-city dominance with accompanying small-city regres- sivity and either the level or the rate of economic development attained by the different countries, measured by their *per capita* national incomes.[3]

---

[3] A recent statistical study of 95 countries also concludes that "different city size distributions are in no way related to the relative economic development of countries," although correspondences can be detected between the size distribution and certain characteristics or degrees of specialization in the national economies. (Brian J. L. Berry, "City Size Distributions and Economic Development," *Economic Development and Cultural Change*, July 1961, pp. 573–587.)

17. The World's Million-Population Metropolises

HOMER HOYT AND JEROME P. PICKARD

London was the first occidental city to attain one million population in the modern era, having surpassed Paris as the largest city of Europe about the beginning of the 18th Century. In 1801, the London urban area contained 864,035 population and the city and county of London had 959,310. Within the first decade of the 19th Century the great British metropolis exceeded a million inhabitants. Tokyo, metropolis of the Orient, probably reached one million inhabitants before 1800 due to the concentration of population induced by the powerful Shogun.

Paris, a great city even in the middle ages, reached the million level in 1850. New York City entered the million class after the Civil War. The city of Chicago, founded in 1833, spread out rapidly in territory. It entered the charmed circle by 1890, and was hailed as the fastest growing city of the 19th Century.

In Europe, Moscow and Leningrad both became members of the million population club in 1900, while Berlin had reached that level in 1880. At the close of the nineteenth century, there were only 13 cities in the world with a population of approximately one million or more.[1]

DRAMATIC INCREASE

In the 20th century there has been a dramatic increase in the number of great metropolises. Prior to 1900 suburban populations were relatively small and census data emphasized the population of central cities. However, when urbanized area and metropolitan area population figures for 1950 were tabulated, it was found that there were 83 metropolitan areas in the world with a population of a million or over;[2] by 1962 this number had increased to 133.

In 1962, a total of 335 million people or 11 percent of the earth's population were living in these huge metropolitan areas, compared with 232 million twelve years earlier. Most of the earlier census data are for the years 1950 or 1951, but in mainland China, there was no census before 1953, and in the U.S.S.R. the census prior to the most recent one was in 1939.[3] Consequently time comparisons in these countries cover a longer span than in most other nations.

Using comparable data for the period 1950 or 1951 to 1962, it will be observed in Table 1 that the South American metropolises led all the rest, with a gain of 72 percent in this period com-

Urban Land. 23, No. 8 (September 1964), 2, 7–10. Reprinted by permission of authors and publisher.

[1] W. S. and E. S. Woytinsky, *World Population and Production—Trends and Outlook*, New York: The Twentieth Century Fund, 1953, pp. 20–22. Philadelphia, Vienna, Istanbul and Peking had reached one million popula-

tion by 1900, in addition to the cities already named.

[2] *Ibid.*

[3] This total is derived from data by International Urban Research *The World's Metropolitan Areas*, Berkeley and Los Angeles: University of California Press, 1959.

pared to 32 percent for the United States, 62 percent for four great African centers and 46 percent for the two Australian metropolises. The rate of growth was the slowest in England and Scotland where the first great urban expansion took place in the 19th Century, having now slowed down to 2 percent gain in the 11 years from 1951 to 1962, partly as a consequence of planned decentralization.

While the population data on China relates back to an earlier period of 1922 to 1939, the gain in the one million or over city population is impressive with an increase from 18 million to 36.6 million or over 100 percent in 23 to 40 years. Likewise the increase in the population of the great metropolises of the U.S.S.R. from 15 million in 1939 to 23 million in 1962, despite the destruction of World War II—a recovery and growth of 52 percent—is significant. Three Indonesian cities made a spectacular gain from 1,042,000 in 1930 to 5,050,000 in 1962, for an average growth of 64 percent per decade over 32 years.

Outstanding in their rates of growth in the 20th Century were the Miami-Ft. Lauderdale complex in Florida, which grew from 2,000 in 1900 to 1,397,000 in 1962; São Paulo, Brazil, which increased from 240,000 in 1900 to 4,900,000 in 1962; Mexico City with a gain from 345,000 to 5,150,000 in the same period; Buenos Aires, which grew from 236,000 in 1880 to 7,175,000 in 1962; Djakarta, Indonesia which shot up from 533,000 to 2,950,000 between 1930 and 1962. Spectacular also was the growth of the Johannesburg metropolitan area in South Africa, where population increased from 3,000 in 1886 to 2,100,000 in 1962. These gains matched the remarkable growth of Chicago in the 19th Century and of Los Angeles, which increased its num-

bers from 102,000 in 1900 to 7,185,000 in 1962. The growth in the numbers and population increase of the great metropolises has been world-wide.

VARIATION IN GROWTH RATES

Table 2 reveals that there is a great deal of variation among the continental regions in the occurrence of great metropolises and their relative size. The proportion of population found in these great centers is highest in the newly-settled countries with advanced technology: Australia (40 percent) and Northern America—essentially the United States (36 percent) and Canada (23 percent). These two regions possess one-fifth of the world's great metropolitan centers though they contain only 7 percent of world population.

The proportion of really large metropolitan areas in the population of Europe is perhaps surprisingly low (only 20 percent). Despite its long period of settlement, Europe is divided physically and politically into many regions and there are a vast number of small towns and villages which, along with medium-sized cities, contain the bulk of European population.

The developing countries of Latin America contain a population slightly greater than Northern America, but both the number of "million-cities" and their included population are less than one-half that of their northern neighbors—the proportion is 15 percent of total population. The U.S.S.R. is very close to the world average in terms of proportion of population in large cities but the majority of these centers have recently arrived at this size and had from 1.0 to 1.7 million population in 1962. This is a consequence of regional planned development and the spreading of urban population and resource

Table 1

Population Increase in Metropolitan Areas with Million Population or Over 1950-1962

(population in thousands)

	Cities	(Earlier Year) 1950	(Recent Year) 1962	Percent Increase
United States	22	50,594	67,002	32.43
Canada	2	2,774	4,010	44.56
Total	24	53,368	71,012	33.05
Middle America				
Mexico and Cuba	2	4,200	6,700	59.52
South America				
South America	9	15,259 (1950)	26,165	71.47
Asia				
Japan	5	18,389 (1950)	27,955	52.02
India	7	15,005 (1951)	19,995	33.25
China	17	18,008 (1922–1939)	36,615	103.32[a]
Pakistan	2	1,975 (1951)	3,375	70.88
Indonesia	3	1,042 (1930)	5,050	384.64[a]
South Korea	2	1,920 (1949)	3,785	97.13
Hong Kong	1	850 (1930)	2,875	238.23[a]
Philippines	1	1,657 (1948)	2,650	60.00
South Vietnam	1	1,600 (1951)	1,700	6.25
Iran	1	1,531 (1956)	2,025	32.26
Singapore	1	938 (1947)	1,720	83.36
Thailand	1	1,179 (1947)	2,250	90.83
Taiwan	1	607 (1953)	1,075	77.10
Total Asia	43	64,701	111,070	71.66
Africa (1947–1951)				
Egypt, South Africa, Algeria	4	5,366 (1947–1951)	8,705	62.22
Oceania				
Australia	2	2,902 (1951)	4,225	45.59
Europe				
England	7	21,831 (1951)	22,330	2.29
West Germany	8	13,011 (1950)	15,010	15.36
Berlin	1	4,200 (1950)	4,000	−4.77
France	1	6,069 (1946)	7,750	27.70
Italy	4	6,030 (1951)	7,855	30.27
Spain	2	3,190 (1950)	4,500	41.06
Poland	2	2,975 (1950)	3,440	15.63

[a] Period longer than 15 years.

Sources: For 1939–1950, International Urban Research, op. cit.
For 1962, Richard L. Forstall, Rand, McNally & Co. (see footnote 4).

		(Earlier Year)	(Recent Year)	
	Cities	1950	1962	Percent Increase
Portugal	1	1,043 (1950)	1,350	29.43
Greece	1	1,379 (1951)	1,890	37.06
Austria	1	1,862 (1951)	2,005	7.67
Romania	1	1,042 (1948)	1,375	31.96
Czechoslovakia	1	933 (1950)	1,060	13.61
Netherlands	2	1,773 (1947)	2,650	49.46
Belgium	2	2,030 (1947)	2,930	44.33
Sweden	1	946 (1950)	1,140	20.50
Denmark	1	1,220 (1950)	1,365	11.88
Hungary	1	1,590 (1949)	2,150	35.22
Istanbul	1	1,024 (1950)	1,900	85.55
Total Europe (Except U.S.S.R.)	38	72,088	84,700	16.51
U.S.S.R. (Including Asia)	11	15,075 (1939)	22,990	52.50[a]
Total World	133	233,019	335,567	44.0

development over a large national territory.

In spite of the impressive number of "million-population metropolises" in the world—133 in 1962—there are still only a dozen which have attained five million or more population. Their estimated populations in 1962 were:[4]

New York	15.8 million
Tokyo-Yokohama	14.7 ″
London	10.9 ″
Osaka-Kobe	8.4 ″
Moskva (Moscow)	8.2 ″
Shanghai	7.8 ″
Paris	7.8 ″
Buenos Aires	7.2 ″
Los Angeles	7.2 ″
Chicago	7.0 ″
Calcutta	6.4 ″
Mexico, Ciudad	5.2 ″

[4] These data and data for 1962 in Tables 1 and 2 are derived from a published table, "Largest Metropolitan Areas and Cities of the World, 1962," in Rand McNally, *Commercial Atlas and Marketing Guide* (Ninety-fourth Edition, 1963), p. 489, prepared by Mr. Richard L. Forstall, Senior Research Editor. The latest Rand McNally published list for 1964 contains

These twelve "spots" on the globe contain over 100 million people—or about $3\frac{1}{2}$ percent of the entire human race!

Metropolitan centers of two to five million population each numbered approximately 43 in 1962, and contain a population of over 120 million (see Table 2). If these centers (or some smaller ones) grow rapidly to the end of the twentieth century, it appears that the number of great metropolises of five million or more population in the world might number fifty by that time—this prospect, more than any other—indicates the true dimension of the world's "metropolitan population explosion."

If present trends continue, it is estimated that the population living in metropolitan areas of one million or more population will increase from 335 million in 1962 to at least 496 million in 1975 and to 1285 million in the year

139 metropolitan areas. Total populations of nations and the world for January 1, 1962 are based upon data in the United Nations *Demographic Yearbook 1962*.

Table 2

Population in World's Great Metropolises, by Continental Regions January 1, 1962

Number of Great Metropolises and Total Population in Millions

Region and 1962 Population	Over 5 Million		2–5 Million		1–2 Million		1 Mill.+ Metro Total		% of Region
Northern America 203 million	(3)	29.9	(8)	22.7	(13)	17.8	(24)	70.4	34.7
Middle America 70 million	(1)	5.2		—	(1)	1.5	(2)	6.7	9.6
South America 151 million	(1)	7.2	(4)	14.0	(4)	5.0	(9)	26.2	17.4
Europe (excluding U.S.S.R.) 432 million	(2)	18.6	(11)	30.1	(25)	36.0	(38)	84.7	19.6
Asia (excluding U.S.S.R.) 1,750 million	(4)	37.3	(16)	43.1	(23)	31.2	(43)	111.6	6.4
Africa 265 million		—	(2)	6.1	(2)	2.6	(4)	8.7	3.3
Australia 10.6 million		—	(1)	2.2	(1)	2.0	(2)	4.2	39.9
Rem. of Oceania 6.5 million		—		—		—	(0)		0
U.S.S.R. in Europe and Asia 220 million	(1)	8.2	(1)	3.9	(9)	10.9	(11)	23.0	10.5
World 3,110 million	(12)	106.4	(43)	122.1	(78)	107.0	(133)	335.5	10.8

2000.[5] This vast expansion will be accompanied by the merging of existing metropolitan areas which is even now taking place, and the formation of megalopolises.

MEGALOPOLISES OR URBAN REGIONS

The merging of metropolitan areas located at no great distance from one another, and the coalescence of several metropolitan areas into a highly urbanized region, with many transportation links between its centers and great diffusion of urban activities, has given rise to the modern "megalopolis."[6] Constant improvement in technology and the shortening of effective distances and travel-times in the advanced countries will increase the

[5] Homer Hoyt, *World Urbanization*, Urban Land Institute Technical Bulletin No. 43, April, 1962, p. 50.

[6] Megalopolises in the United States are defined and described in "Urban Regions of the United States," by Jerome P. Pickard, *Urban Land*, Volume 21, No. 4 (April 1962).

spread of megalopolitan development at an accelerating rate in the next several decades. At the present time, we can identify at least seven great megalopolises in the world, with populations of 10 million or more.

The World's Great Megalopolises, 1964

Atlantic Seaboard (U. S.) (New York, Philadelphia, Boston, Washington, Baltimore)	40 million
Lower Great Lakes (U. S. and Canada) (Chicago, Milwaukee, Detroit-Windsor, Cleveland, Pittsburgh, Buffalo, Toronto)	30 million
Keihin (Japan) (Tokyo-Yokohama)	15 million
Midlands (England) (Liverpool, Manchester, Leeds-Bradford, Birmingham)	10–15 million
Central Japan (Osaka–Kobe, Kyoto)	10–15 million
Rhine-Ruhr (W. Germany) (Köln, Düsseldorf, Ruhrgebiet)	10–15 million
Southern California (U. S.) (Los Angeles, San Diego)	11 million

Together, these seven megalopolises contain 24 million-population metropolises and about 130 million population, though two great North American megalopolises have more than one-half of this total. The concentration of population in such gigantic clusters puts a great strain on regional resources for water supply and sewage disposal, and presents many difficult problems of accommodation in terms of land use planning, transportation needs, and living amenities including recreational and open space areas to provide some occasional "decongestion" for residents of these super-metropolises.

Since the anticipated new growth of 950 million in the population living in cities of a million and over between

Table 3

Population in Million-Population Metropolises, Leading Nations, 1962

Population		Number Met. Areas 1 Million+	1 Million+ Total Met. Pop.	Percent of Nation
185.0	U.S.A.	(22)	66,359	36.0
715.0±	China[a]	(19)	41,375[a]	6.0
94.5	Japan	(5)	27,955	30.0
220.0	U.S.S.R.	(11)	23,025	10.5
53.1	U.K.	(7)	22,330	42.0
446.0	India	(7)	19,800	4.5
73.6	Germany (W. & E. + Berlin)	(9)	19,010	26.0
1,787.0	Seven leading nations	(80)	219,854	12.3
74.0	Brazil	(3)	10,900	15.0
10.6	Australia	(2)	4,225	40.0
1,236.0	Rest of world	(48)	100,585	8.0

[a] Including Taiwan and Hongkong in geographical definition of China.

now and the year 2000 will necessitate the construction of more than twice as much living space, shopping centers, parks, industrial plants, transportation facilities and offices in these future cities of a million population as are now in existence, a vast field of work exists for planners, builders, and engineers who will plan and carry out extensions to the world's present metropolitan areas and design entirely new cities that will come into existence in the next 36 years.

18. Growth and Structure of Twenty-One Great World Cities

HOMER HOYT

PART ONE: GROWTH OF CITIES

The great surge in growth of cities throughout the world from 1800 to 1960 is shown by the fact that the number of cities with a population of 100,000 and over increased from 36 in the year 1800 to 678 in 1930 and to 1128 in 1960, and that the population residing in these cities shot up from 11.5 million in 1800 to 243 million in 1930 and to 590 million in 1960.[1]

To analyze the factors of growth and structure in all of these cities would require years of effort on the part of numerous specialists in many nations and would necessitate a work of many volumes. As a beginning, I have in this article summarized some of the more important factors of growth and structure of twenty-one great world cities which were described by the authors in *Great Cities of the World*. These cities are Bombay, Calcutta, Buenos Aires, Chicago, Copenhagen, London, Los Angeles, Manchester, Montreal, Toronto, Moscow, New York, Paris, Rio de Janeiro, Rome, Stockholm, Sydney, Cologne, Johannesburg, Tokyo, Osaka.[2] I have brought the population figures down to the year 1960 and 1961, the latest years for which comparable census data are available.[3] For the years 1800, 1850, 1880, 1900, 1920 and 1940 I have used the figures compiled by W. S. and E. S. Woytinsky.[4]

Of these 21 cities, 15 were in existence in 1850 and they had then a total population of 4,325,000. By 1880 all 21 cities were in existence and their aggregate population was approximately 14,400,000. In 1900 these 21 cities contained approximately 23,000,000 persons within the city limits. At the beginning of the 20th Century the suburban population was relatively small but, as cities grew rapidly and filled up their old boundaries and with the increasing use of automobiles and mass transit, the central cities absorbed villages on their peripheries into the urban mass.

The population increase in central cities slackened from 1950 to 1960, as the increase was only from 52 to 60 million, a gain of 15.3 per cent. Four great central cities—London, New York, Manchester and Copenhagen— lost population in this period. (See tables 1 and 2.) Meanwhile the suburbs were gaining in nearly every metropolitan area with an increase of 32 per cent in numbers in the same period. In 1960 the total population of the 21 metropolitan areas was 105 million, of which 45 million lived outside of the central city.

Land Economics, *42 (February 1966), 53–64.*
Reprinted by permission of author and publisher.

[1] Homer Hoyt, "The Growth of Cities from 1880 to 1960 and Forecasts to the Year 2000, *Land Economics*, May 1963, p. 170.

[2] William A. Robson, Editor, *Great Cities of the World* (New York: Macmillan Company, 1957).

[3] *United Nations Demographic Yearbook 1962.*

[4] W. S. and E. S. Woytinsky, *World Population and Production-Trends and Outlook*, (New York: Twentieth Century Fund, 1953), Part I, Chapter 4, pp. 120–122.

Table 1

Population of Twenty-One Selected Great Cities: 1800–1960

(thousands)[a]

City	1800	1850	1880	1900	1920	1940	1950	1960
Bombay	200	—	773	776	1176	1490	2840	4152
Buenos Aires	40	76	236	821	1320	1720	2457	2967
Calcutta	600	—	580	802	886	2070	2549	2927
Chicago	—	30	503	1699	2702	3397	3621	3550
Cologne	50	97	145	373	643	772	731	809
Copenhagen	101	129	235	401	561	600	762	721
Johannesburg	—	—	3	100[c]	300[c]	500[c]	632	594
London	959	2363	3830	4537	4485	2320	3348	3195
Los Angeles	—	2	11	102	577	1504	1970	2479
Manchester	77	336	462	544	736	766	693	661
Montreal	—	—	155	268	619	1140	1021	1191
Moscow	250	368	612	989	1028	4137	5000	6262
New York[b]	79	696	2273	4130	6710	8567	9010	8836
Osaka-Kobe	350	—	400	996	1253	3092	2555	3085
Paris	547	1053	2269	2714	2906	2800	2725	2790
Rio de Janeiro	43	76	236	821	1720	2457	2377	3223
Rome	153	175	300	423	660	1368	1652	1829
Stockholm	76	93	169	301	419	530	740	808
Sydney	—	44	100	100	100	88	207	181
Tokyo-Yokohama	800	—	1000	2145	2596	4076	6530	9118
Toronto	—	—	96	208	522	667	668	672
Total	4325	—	14388	23310	31919	44061	52087	60050

[a] Cities only—not metropolitan areas.
[b] Includes central cities in New York and Northeastern New Jersey.
[c] Estimated.

Decline in Population of Some Great Cities

This spectacular growth in the population of great cities in the past 160 years has created an impression that the population of every metropolitan area in modern times increases steadily from year to year and never declines. This is by no means true. Bombing raids in World War II destroyed large sections of great cities and caused sharp population declines. The population of the metropolitan area of Tokyo dropped from 7,800,000 in 1942 to 3,060,000 in August 1945 after the city was literally reduced to ashes by bombing raids. The population of Osaka, Japan as a result of air raids fell from 3,250,000 in 1940 to 1,030,000 in August 1945.[5] The population of Cologne fell from 772,000 in 1939 to 40,000 in 1945. Warsaw, with a pre-war population of 800,000, was almost completely destroyed by bombing and by systematic dynamiting of its remaining buildings by Hitler's orders, until it had virtually no population in 1945. All of these cities have recovered and, after rebuilding, have gained all or more of the pre-war population level.

Not all population declines of great cities are the direct result of war-time

[5] Masamichi Royama, "Tokyo and Osaka," in Robson, op. cit., p. 724.

Table 2
Population (thousands) of Metropolitan Areas, Twenty-One Selected Great Cities: 1950, 1960 and Latest Projected Estimates

City	1950	1960	Percent Increase or Decrease	Latest Projection (Estimates)[a]
Bombay	3387	5741	69.50	b
Buenos Aires	4603	7000	52.07	b
Calcutta	4578	4340	−5.20	4580 (1964)
Chicago	5580*	6795	24.86	7491 (Oct. 1965)[c]
Cologne	1060*	1300	22.64	b
Copenhagen	1168	1262	8.04	b
Johannesburg	1607	2000	24.45	b
London	8346	8172	−2.10	8187 (1964)
Los Angeles	4368	6742	54.34	8100 (Oct. 1965)
Manchester	2423	2427	0.17	2449 (1964)
Montreal	1395	2110	51.25	2205 (1963)
Moscow	5600	6824	21.86	8075*(1963)
New York	12912	14759	14.30	16000 (Oct. 1965)[c]
Osaka-Kobe	5348	6405	19.76	8050*(1963)
Paris	6068	6524	7.51	7369 (1962)
Rio de Janeiro	3052	3974	30.20	b
Rome	1757	2161	22.99	2329 (1963)
Stockholm	980	1161	18.47	1162 (1964)
Sydney	1626	2183	34.25	2256 (1963)
Tokyo-Yokohama	9049	11374	25.57	12018 (1963)
Toronto	1117	1824	63.29	1925 (1963)

[a] Data from *United Nations Demographic Year Book 1964*, Table 7, for metropolitan areas outside the United States.

[b] No recent estimate of population of this metropolitan area.

[c] Estimate by Homer Hoyt for population in October 1965.

* Represent author's corrections to previously published table (Ed.).

bombing. The population of Moscow declined from 1.7 million in 1918 to one million in 1920.[6] The population of the metropolitan area of Calcutta declined from 4,578,000 in 1951 to 4,340,000 in 1961.

Central areas even of rapidly growing metropolitan areas have declined in population in recent decades. The population of the administrative County of London fell from its peak of 4,536,237

in 1901 to 2,320,000 in 1941,[7] and had recovered only to 3,195,000 by 1961. The population of Manhattan Island in New York fell from a peak of 2,331,542 in 1910 to 1,698,281 in 1960. The population of five central wards of Tokyo in 1955 had only 70 per cent of the population of 1940.[8] Even in rapidly growing Los Angeles, central census tracts have declined in population.

[6] Roger Simon and Maurice Hookham, "Moscow," in Robson, *op. cit.*, p. 384.

[7] Robson, *ibid.*, "London," p. 261.

[8] Masamichi Royama, "Tokyo and Osaka," in Robson, *op. cit.*, p. 723.

Declining Density of Population in Great Cities

As a result of the exodus to the suburbs there has been a thinning out of the density in large cities. The average number of persons per square mile in Manhattan declined from 106,000 in 1910 to 77,000 in 1960. Average population densities in Calcutta and Bombay were still high in 1950—106,000 to the square mile in Calcutta and 97,000 to the square mile in Bombay. Densities in some closely packed residential areas have risen far above these averages—454,000 per square mile in the highest density area of Bombay in 1941 and 291,000 per square mile in the highest density area of Calcutta in the same year. In 1910 there was a population of 500,000 in the 1,000 acres of the Lower East Side of Manhattan, or 320,000 to the square mile.

In calculating densities for a city or metropolitan region allowance must be made for the areas devoted to parks, schools, industries and shopping centers where there is no residential population. It is possible to have high population densities and also open spaces and ample light and air in every room in the residential buildings consisting of tall elevator apartments. The Parkchester high-rise apartments in New York City house 40,000 people in 12,200 apartments on 141 acres, a density of 284 persons per acre or 182,000 to the square mile, yet the land coverage of the buildings is only 25 per cent. Westmount, in the Montreal area, is planning to build six 20-story apartment buildings containing 1,900 units housing 3,000 people on five acres of land. This would be a density of 600 persons to the acre or 384,000 to the square mile, yet the land coverage would be only 36 per cent, leaving 64 per cent of the land in open areas.

However, the spreading of the city to suburban areas where single-family houses predominate has greatly reduced metropolitan densities. The average number of persons per square mile in the London metropolitan area of 722 square miles is only 11,400. In 1950 the average density of population in 157 central cities in the United States was 7,788 persons per square mile and in 157 urban fringes 3,200 persons to the square mile. In New York City in its entirety, with a high proportion of apartments, there was an average of 25,046 persons to the square mile, and in the urban fringe only 4,066 to the square mile. In Los Angeles City, on the other hand, with a predominance of single-family homes, there was an average density of only 4,253 persons to the square mile. Baltimore City, with its row houses, had a density of 12,067 per square mile and Philadelphia, also with many row houses, had a density of 16,286 to the square mile. Central Boston also had a density of 16,767 a square mile but its urban fringe had a density of 4,822.[9]

There has been a marked decline in density in urbanized areas in the United States from 1950 to 1960. The urbanized population used 44 per cent more land per person and twice as much in the aggregate in 1960 than had been used by the urbanized population in 1950. The total land use in 1960 for 95.8 million persons in urbanized areas was 25,544 square miles, compared to the 12,804 square miles for 69.3 million persons in urbanized areas in 1950. (Part of this increase is due to change in definition of urbanized areas in 1960 compared to 1950.) Average densities in urbanized areas declined from 5,412 persons per square mile in 1950 to 3,750 persons per square mile in

⁹ *United States Census of Population 1950*, Vol. 1, Table 17, pp. 1–26, 29.

1960.[10] However, the recent trend toward suburban and central apartments will increase densities in many urbanized areas in the decade from 1960 to 1970.

Sources of Population Increase in Great Cities

Most of the population increase of the great cities has been the result of net in-migration. Thus, in the Tokyo metropolitan area, of the increase in population from 3,942,479 at the end of 1945 to 8,037,084 in 1955 (a gain of 4,094,605 in 10 years) 3,220,841 represented in-migration, or 70.8 per cent, and 873,584 or 29.2 per cent represented natural increase.[11] In Rome, from January 1, 1939 to December 31, 1949 there was an excess of births over deaths of 160,819, but an in-migration of 240,481.[12]

Causes of Population Growth of Great Cities

The chief cause of the population growth of great cities was the expansion of manufacturing in these cities during the 19th and the first half of the 20th Centuries. It is often not realized that the capital cities, noted for their palaces, museums, art treasures, etc. are sustained chiefly by a concentration of industry within their borders or suburbs. In regard to Moscow, Roger Simon and Maurice Hookham said:

Before the 1917 revolution Moscow was mainly a centre for light industry, and the textile, leather and food industries accounted for three-quarters of its total output. But the industrial character of the city was funda-mentally transformed in the course of the first-year plan (1928–1932); it became a great engineering centre, producing machine tools, a wide variety of instruments, motor-cars and lorries, electrical equipment for the mining and oil industries, while important metallurgical and chemical plants were erected as well. A great range of consumer goods are produced, clothing and footwear, motor cycles, radio sets, watches and household utensils, and Moscow is the biggest source of supply of fabrics, footwear and clothing in the Soviet Union. Small scale industry, organized in industrial cooperatives, also produces considerable quantities of clothing, furniture, china and other articles. Moscow has been the scene of an unparalleled increase in production during the past twenty years. Already by 1940 the city was producing twenty-one times more than it produced in 1913, and twice as much as the entire industrial output of Russia in 1913.[13]

In regard to London, Robson says:

London is a great industrial city. The county of London contains 30,000–40,000 factories and workshops and there are many others in outer London. Most of the factories within the County are on a small scale.[14]

Masamichi Royama thus describes the importance of manufacturing in Tokyo: "Tokyo has thus become the largest consumer city as well as the greatest manufacturing centre in Japan. In 1953 there were in Tokyo 42,000 factories employing 670,000 employees. The amount of goods shipped out of Tokyo in that year was 820,000 million yen."[15] Osaka was an even greater industrial city than Tokyo, measured in number employed. In 1954 there were 150,000 industrial units in the city employing 1,150,000 workers.[16]

---

[10] Robinson Newcomb, "Urban Land Use Shifts to Low Gear," *The Appraisal Journal,* July 1964, p. 376.

[11] Masamichi Royama, in Robson, *op. cit.,* p. 724.

[12] Guiseppe Chiarelli, "Rome," in Robson, *ibid.,* p. 523.

[13] Simon and Hookham, in Robson, *ibid.,* p. 384, citing Ranevsky, *Moscow Industry,* 1947, p. 32.

[14] Robson, "London," *ibid.,* p. 263.

[15] Royama, in Robson, *ibid.,* p. 721.

[16] *Ibid.,* p. 728.

In regard to Manchester, Shena D. Simon says: "Manchester, the third largest city in England (population 715,000) is the core and pivot of one of the most highly industrialized regions in the world, that of south-east Lancashire. It includes a population of 10 million people within a radius of fifty miles, and the proportion of the total population employed in manufacturing is nearly double that so employed nationally."[17]

Paris is not only the intellectual and political capital of France; she is also its greatest industrial and commercial center. As Brian Chapman says:

From the Ville de Paris and the Department of the Seine are collected 50 per cent of all the taxes paid in France. Some 30 per cent of all the industrial and commercial activity of the whole of France is carried on in the metropolitan area. . . . Industrial activity in the Department of the Seine far surpasses that of any other area; nearly a third of all persons concerned with metallurgical industries in all France work here, and two-thirds of all the national automobiles and aircraft industries are in this area. Heavy industries, electrical engineering, the chemical industry and paper production, as well as specialized luxury trades such as crystal, glass, ceramics, fabrics, tapestries, precious metals, printing, and book production, all have very important centres in or near Paris.[18]

In regard to Cologne, Lorenz Fischer and Peter Van Hauten say: "The economic structure of Cologne and its ring of agglomeration is best reflected in the relative numbers of persons gainfully employed in agriculture, trade and public or other services. In 1950 agriculture and forestry accounted for 4 per cent, trade, commerce, industry and handicrafts for 77 per cent, public administration and public or other services for 19 per cent of the gainfully employed in the entire agglomeration."[19]

M. Venkatarangaiya points out the importance of industry in Bombay and Calcutta: "Both cities are busy centres of industry. Bombay is the home of the cotton and Calcutta of the jute industry of India. These industries expanded rapidly with the development of railways and other quick means of transport for which these cities became converging points."[20]

Chicago has always been known as a great manufacturing center as well as a great railway, financial and wholesale center. Employment, first in meat packing and agricultural machinery and then in electrical machinery was one of the greatest causes of its growth.

It has been a matter of surprise to many that New York City, noted for its financial center in Wall Street, its theater district and its Port, was also a great manufacturing center with 35,496 different industrial establishments employing 1,357,876 persons. Apparel, with 311,000 workers, was the largest single industry, but it also had 50 per cent or more of the total national employment in pencils, tobacco, pipes and scientific instruments.[21]

Los Angeles, the noted home of the movies, is chiefly sustained by manufacturing, which is the main cause of its remarkable population growth. Its manufacturing employment rose from 387,100 in 1947 to 771,800 in 1957. More defense contracts have been awarded to this area than to any other region in the United States.

[17] Shena D. Simon, "Manchester," in Robson, *ibid.*, p. 325.
[18] Brian Chapman, "Paris," in Robson, *ibid.*, p. 452.
[19] Lorenz Fischer and Peter Van Hauten, "Cologne," in Robson, *ibid.*, p. 654.
[20] M. Venkatarangaiya, "Bombay and Calcutta," in Robson, *ibid.*, p. 139.
[21] Homer Hoyt, *The Economic Status of the New York Metropolitan Region in 1944.*

While manufacturing is thus of outstanding importance in the rapid growth of the great cities, industry has been supplemented by other basic economic factors. London, Paris, Moscow, Rome, Stockholm, Copenhagen and Tokyo are capital cities, and have grown with increase in government employment. London, New York, Stockholm, Copenhagen, Tokyo, Rio de Janeiro and Sydney are great ocean ports. Chicago is the world's leading railroad center. London, New York, Chicago and Tokyo are great financial and commercial centers. London, Paris, Rome, Copenhagen, Los Angeles, Stockholm, Tokyo and Rio de Janeiro attract great throngs of tourists. The Washington, D.C. metropolitan area has grown rapidly as a result of expansion of the functions of the Federal Government, with very little manufacturing. Johannesburg, the youngest great city, having been founded in 1886, is the largest city that has mining as its chief economic base. In 1962, the Witwatersrand gold mining area of which Johannesburg is the center, had a population of 2,100,000 and its mines have produced in the past $20 billion in gold and are now producing two-thirds of the free world's gold output.

PART TWO:
STRUCTURE OF GREAT CITIES

I have thus far discussed the growth and causes of growth of entire metropolitan areas, without seeking to describe changes in the internal structure of the cities caused by this growth, such as the location of industries and areas occupied by different racial, social and economic classes.

Factory Location

In the old cities, factories were located close to the homes of workers because means of transportation were not available. This is still true in many cities. In New York City the garment industry is in the center of Manhattan. In London, as Robson says:[22]

In the period between the two world wars a vast industrial expansion took place in London. Many new factories were set up in the metropolis, and many firms migrated there from provincial towns and the areas where unemployment was most severe, in order to be near the nation's biggest market or to avoid high local taxes. . . . The east end of London is occupied by factories, workshops, and the vast paraphernalia of docks, wharves, quays and warehouses associated with the port.

In Paris there is a concentration of workers' homes near the automobile and aircraft industries to the south and east of Paris.[23]

Small industries in London, Tokyo, Manchester, Paris and other cities are often scattered throughout central city areas.

In Moscow:

. . . industries are mainly concentrated in the east and southeast, although they are distributed irregularly throughout the town. This is not considered a disadvantage, as it enables people to live near their work, and the best of the big Moscow factories are spaciously laid out and surrounded by gardens and apartment houses for their workers, each factory having its own club, children's playground, nursery, health centre, night sanitorium, and so forth. Moreover, as the principal sources of power are gas and electricity, Moscow is a remarkably clean city, free from smoke and grime.[24]

As to Manchester, England, the Regional Plan Commission said: "As in most northern industrial regions, the intermingling of factories, mills, business

[22] Robson, *op. cit*, pp. 263–264.
[23] Chapman, in Robson, *ibid.*, p. 482.
[24] Simon and Hookham, in Robson, *ibid.*, p. 403.

premises and dwelling houses, without any semblance of order, results in a lack of light, air and good working conditions."[25]

Heavy industries were early located on ocean ports or rivers where there was water transport, as along the Thames in London, or at docks for ship building such as Belfast, Glasgow, London and Hamburg. Steel industries have located on the shores of Lake Michigan at South Chicago and Gary. The railroads at first and the automobiles and trucks later, permitted industries to leave central areas.

The Union Stock Yards was established in Chicago in 1865 and the Central Manufacturing District in 1908—at locations four miles from the center of the city. When more ground was available separate districts were established, zoned for industry, in which a number of industries of complimentary or non-nuisance character located in the same district, with rail and trucking facilities. One of the first of these districts was the Clearing District in Chicago, three miles long, begun in 1914.

The construction of belt highways around cities, and increased reliance on truck transportation, with most workers in the United States having their own automobiles, enabled industries to be established on these belt highways even without railroad connections as, for example, the electronics plants on Highway 128 around Boston. New types of non-nuisance industries, in park-like settings, are located in residential areas, such as Melpar in Fairfax County, Virginia, near Washington, D.C. Increased ownership of automobiles in Europe will probably cause the same outward movement of industries there. Garden cities, with homes for

workers, will also enable industries to be established in suburbs. Some plants early established model towns for their workers, as Pullman in Chicago and many mill villages in southeastern United States.

Residential Areas—Social Classes

In early cities the homes of the poor and the well-to-do were often close together. Thus, in Stockholm prior to 1900, as Gunnar Heckscher and Per Holm say:

As a rule, the well-to-do occupied the larger and more elegant quarters which fronted towards the watercourses and centrally-located thoroughfares. Low income groups lived in those flats which faced away from the street and towards the courtyards. However, the housing of this period did not involve a distribution of social classes to different parts of the city. Labourers, white-collar workers and executives mingled on the same streets, and lived in the same blocks throughout the whole city. Only the locations of houses and floors separated them. As a result, Stockholm never acquired the pronounced slum areas or working-class districts which often characterize the chief cities of other countries.[26]

In Chicago and New York City in the 1800's and 1890's the higher income groups lived on separate streets or boulevards apart from the poorer classes. But the distance between the richest and poorest was a matter of only a few blocks. It was only three or four blocks from Prairie Avenue, the most fashionable street in Chicago in the 1880's, to the vice area and the poorest slums west of State Street. In New York City, Fifth Avenue, the home of the millionaires, was only two blocks west of Third Avenue and the Lower East Side.

However, as cities expanded in size,

[25] Shena D. Simon, in Robson, *ibid.*, p. 326.

[26] Gunnar Heckscher and Per Holm, "Stockholm," in Robson, *ibid.*, pp. 560, 561.

the different social areas were separated by greater distances. In Paris, the better residential areas are on the west side of the city in Arrondissements I, VIII, IX, XVI, and XVII, but they are not far from Arrondissements XVIII, XIX, XX on the north, XIII to the southeast and XIV on the south, where there is overcrowding, lack of sanitation, juvenile delinquency, high infant mortality and tuberculosis.[27]

In London there is a greater separation. As Robson says:

Immediately south of the Thames, in places like Southwark, Battersea, Balham, Brixton, Peckham, Camberwell, Lewisham, are vast areas of lower middle class housing. There are similar areas north of the river in such places as Finsbury, St. Pancras, Islington, Hackney and Stoke Newington. Further South, as one approaches the lovely grass-covered rolling hills of the North Downs, the character of the buildings changes and the standard of housing improves. Here are the homes of the better-off Londoners who have escaped from the noise and hustle of the town. A similar trend occurs to the north and northwest of outer London. The most favoured residential districts in the central area are to be found in Chelsea, situated near an attractive stretch of the river, and in Westminster, Marylebone, Kensington, all within easy reach of the magnificent parks which are the finest of inner London. Hyde Park, Kensington Gardens, St. James' Park, Green Park and Regents' Park are 'royal' parks. . . .[28]

However, as Robson continues, there are areas in London where there is a complete mixture of all income groups in the same block:

Fortunately for the material, mental and moral health of Londoners, poverty and wealth are not segregated as completely as the preceding remarks might suggest. Over-crowded tenements and slums sometimes exist within a stone's throw of modern blocks of luxury flats; one can often find a lovely eighteenth-century Georgian house in an old-world garden standing amid dreary rows of monotonous nineteenth-century dwellings built for low-paid artisans and clerks.[29]

In practically all cities of the United States, however, where single-family homes predominate, the higher income groups live in certain sections of the city or suburbs, such as the North Side of Chicago and the northern suburbs along the Lake Shore, the north side of Dallas, the west side of Houston, the west side of Philadelphia, the south side of Kansas City and the Beverly Hills district of Los Angeles.[30] The same is true of Latin American cities, as families move into single family homes on the periphery. Some great cities have a separation of neighborhoods or districts based on race. In Johannesburg and other South and East African cities, the native Africans live in separate quarters or villages, the Colored and Asians (from India) likewise have their own districts, as do the Europeans their own residential sections. In Montreal there is a cleavage between families of British origin, all of whom speak English and some of whom speak French. In Chicago, from 1860 to 1900, the Irish lived on the South Side, the Germans on the North Side and after 1880 the Italian, Polish and Jewish immigrants all lived in separate sections of Chicago. The second and third generations of these immigrants have tended to move to all parts of Chicago and the old national origin districts in older sections of Chicago are being cleared away. The Negroes, who came in large numbers to

---

[27] Chapman, "Paris," in Robson, *ibid.*, p. 482.
[28] Robson, *ibid.*, p. 264.
[29] *Ibid.*
[30] Homer Hoyt, *Structure and Growth of Residential Neighborhoods in American Cities*, Federal Housing Administration, 1939.

northern cities of the United States after 1914, nearly all lived in segregated areas in the older sections of the city but this racial separation may gradually disappear.

The Form of City Growth

Early cities in Europe were built in a circular form behind walls erected for defense. As cities expanded new areas were set up outside the walls. In the United States, cities like Chicago, with a network of suburban railways, spread out like fingers along the railroad lines, leaving open spaces between. Copenhagen grew in a similar fashion along radial railroad lines.[31] The Year 2000 Plan for Washington, D.C. would establish this radial pattern for future growth of the national capital area.

After centuries of unplanned growth of cities, planning commissions have endeavored to pass laws opening up the city and widening narrow streets. One of the most dramatic and effective of these plans was that of Baron Georges Haussmann for Paris, who carved the broad boulevards through the congested streets of Paris from 1853 to 1869. In Buenos Aires wide streets were created in central areas by demolishing houses in one entire narrow block between two streets. In New York City the large Central Park area in midtown Manhattan was purchased in 1856. In Chicago a system of parks and boulevards was created in 1869.

The first zoning law regulating the height and bulk of buildings and the boundaries of different types of land uses was adopted in New York City on July 25, 1916. Following the example of New York, hundreds of American cities and counties adopted zoning regulations after 1916, until today every large city in the United States

[31] Axel Holm, "Copenhagen," in Robson, *op. cit.*, p. 252.

except Houston, Texas has zoning regulations.

The efforts of social control over city growth were exerted in three directions: (1) the rebuilding of central blighted or slum areas; (2) the control of new housing and industrial development on the urban fringe or in vacant areas beyond the central built-up area, and (3) the limiting of population of the city. Urban redevelopment laws were adopted in the United States in 1948. These laws provided for the condemnation and clearing of slum areas and resale of the cleared land to private builders with the federal government contributing two-thirds and the local government one-third of the difference between the acquisition cost and the resale price. In Moscow, where the land is owned by the state, the redevelopment authorities had to pay only for the cost of demolishing the existing buildings.

Under the redevelopment laws in the United States, the midtown area in Baltimore, Charles Center, has been rebuilt, and the Bunker Hill area in the center of Los Angeles is being rebuilt with office buildings, apartments and motels. Mid-Town Plaza in Rochester, New York has been developed with private funds. Other urban renewal projects are under way in Boston, Washington, D.C., San Francisco and many other cities. Outstanding developments already accomplished are the office buildings in Penn Center, Philadelphia, the Golden Triangle of Pittsburgh, the redevelopment of the Near South Side of Chicago with apartments and the new shopping center in downtown New Haven, Connecticut.

Progress on urban renewal in the United States has been slow. In May 1964, 15 years after the law was passed, 29,200 acres have been planned for acquisition, 22,000 acres having been acquired by June 1963. Redevelopers have been selected for 12,700 acres of the land acquired but redevelopment is completed on only 4,200 acres and is under way on another 2,000 acres.[32] In Europe the bombed out areas of Hamburg, Cologne, Warsaw, London and other cities have been rebuilt.

The second form of control in city growth has been the attempts to regulate unplanned urban sprawl or subdivisions of homes beyond the city built-up areas. One form of control in the United States has consisted of restriction of the number of houses to one or two to the acre, which makes construction of low-priced houses not economically feasible because of the high cost of extending utilities over thinly settled areas.

In Europe completely planned garden cities have been developed. There is a similar trend in the United States in the recent planning of separate towns or cities with homes, recreation areas and industries in suburban areas. One of the most outstanding projects of this kind is the Reston development on 7,000 acres near Washington, D.C. Fairfax County, Virginia authorities favor a cluster-type development with groups of houses and apartments adjoining golf courses or green belts separated from other clusters by open areas of lower density.

Another method of preventing an unbroken settlement of areas is the acquisition of public land in a belt around cities to be kept as a green area or park and not built upon. This has been adopted in Ottawa, the capital of Canada, and is proposed for Moscow and a number of other cities.

The Year 2000 Plan for Washington, D.C. (previously referred to) provides for a series of radial bands of growth

[32] *Nation's Business*, May 1964, p. 92.

served by fast transportation lines, with vacant areas between. A similar plan is proposed for Copenhagen. These bands of growth originally followed suburban railroad lines in Chicago but the open spaces between have been filled in, as a result of the automobile which enabled population to move away from mass transit lines. In Swedish and Russian cities, where the state owns or controls areas of land, it is possible to direct population growth in a definite path which is served by subways to the center of the city.

In the United States 8,300 shopping centers with free parking for automobiles have been built in suburban areas since 1946. This has required rezoning in thousands of cases because this new type center requires depths of 600 feet or more instead of the old strip zoning with lot depths of 100 to 150 feet.

The third method of control of future city growth is to limit the size of cities. In Russia it is proposed to limit Moscow to a population of 5 or 6 million, which can be done by controlling the location of new industries. Many new cities of 100,000 population and over have been built in Russia since 1917. Where the state owns all of the land and operates all of the industries, as in Russia, it is possible to allocate given industries to any city, new or old. This cannot be done easily in the United States, where private industries are free to move to the location offering the maximum advantages in markets and production costs. However, the United States can exercise control over industrial location by awarding defense contracts to depressed areas or to other cities where there is room for population growth.

If estimates of the growth of the world population from over 3 billion in 1964 to 6.3 billion by the year 2000 are realized, and if increase of the population of cities continues to outstrip the gains in rural areas, then the urban population may be expected to increase from one billion in 1960 to 3.4 billion in the year 2000.[33] This would mean that urban population growth in the next 30 years will be two-and-a-half times as great as the total urban population of today. The population of metropolitan areas of a million and over is expected to rise from 285 million in 1960 to 1285 million by the year 2000, an increase of three-and-a-half times.[34]

In this period of urban growth, great metropolitan areas will merge in megalopoli, forming, in the United States, continuous unbroken bands along the Atlantic Seaboard from Boston to Washington, D.C., along the shores of lake areas, or along the Pacific Ocean from San Francisco to San Diego, California. It may be necessary to build entirely new cities to take care of urban population growth but the trends of population growth so far have been for people to congregate in the long established urban centers. New capital cities such as Brasilia, Canberra and the new capital cities of Pakistan may set the pattern for a new type of planned city built in undeveloped regions. The control of this vast urban expansion will be the greatest challenge of the last 35 years of the 20th Century.

There will be urgent need for new mass transportation systems, new sources of potable water, extensions of sewer systems, new radial and belt highways, which will be determined by the form in which this urban growth takes place. Will this vast growth be in the form of urban sprawl, new garden cities, clusters in the suburbs or radial bands of growth separated by open areas? Will blighted areas be rebuilt with tall apartments or will entirely new cities be established far from existing urban agglomerations? It is probable that there will be a combination of all these forms of growth. Planning and social control on a scale hitherto undreamed of will be necessary if urban chaos is to be avoided.

There is accordingly, more reason now than ever before, to analyze the internal structure of our cities upon which new growth will be superimposed or attached, in order that the coming generation will understand how our cities can be renewed and expanded by removing worn-out elements and directing new growth into the most desirable channels.

[33] Homer Hoyt, *World Urbanization* (Washington, D. C., Urban Land Institute) Technical Bulletin 43, April 1962, p. 50.
[34] *Ibid.*

Even if it is not likely that urban areas in newly developing countries will replicate Western urbanism,[1] it remains true that they must be studied in the context of origins of urbanization, the role of cities vis-à-vis economic growth and social change in the larger societies of which they are a part, the range and variations of urbanization, and whether urban growth is presently out of scale with the national and cultural development of the area.[2]

Each of these subjects has frequently been examined in articles, monographs, and entire books of readings, so it is impossible to explore them fully here. It *is* possible, however, to call attention to the major aspects of these matters as background for understanding the issues and their resolution.

Gideon Sjoberg (19) and Bert F. Hoselitz (20) investigate, in one case, the major questions relating to the origin and subsequent fate of early urban development, and in the other, the crucial role of cities in national economic growth.

The focus of the readings then shifts to social change and urbanization in the item by A. L. Epstein (21), whose discussion identifies a wide range of implications of urban growth in Africa; their applicability to other newly developing areas will be apparent.

The relatively small size and other existing characteristics of many newly developing countries, together with their histories as influenced, for example, by colonialism, have often resulted in the phenomenon of primate cities. The ramifications of primate city growth for national and regional urbanization are explored by Arnold S. Linsky (22) and S. K. Mehta (23). The issues

[1] Cf. Rhoads Murphey (6).
[2] The readings in Part II are most closely related to pp. 38–72 in Breese, *Urbanization in Newly Developing Countries.*

PART TWO

THE CHANGING ROLE
OF THE CITY

that will continue to be debated for a long time are succinctly detailed here.

Much interest attaches to the relationship between urbanization and techno-logical level, organization of industry, and related matters. Some international patterns of these phenomena are presented by J. Gibbs and Walter T. Martin (24).

Finally, the intriguing but complex question of whether, when, and to what effect overurbanization exists is reviewed by N. V. Sovani (25). Differences in detail will exist, but the changing role of the city crucially affects the national future as well as its own—whether the scene be Asia, Africa, or Latin America.

19. The Rise and Fall of Cities: A Theoretical Perspective

GIDEON SJOBERG

The extension and contraction of city life is a central feature of social change in civilized societies. This can readily be perceived even through a casual reading of man's struggles against the centuries. It might even be averred that recorded history, at least prior to the Industrial Revolution, is a catalogue of the successes and failures of urban living (and of the concomitant expansion and shrinking of empires); for in the last analysis the political, religious, and intellectual elites, the primary subject matter of traditional historical writings, have typically been urban, rather than rural, in their residence and commitment.

The prime purpose of this essay is to provide a theoretical orientation for explaining (1) the expansion of cities in size and number, (2) their diffusion into previously nonurbanized and lightly urbanized regions, and (3) their disappearance or decline and occasional resurgence throughout history in divergent cultural settings.[1] Although we can discern little or no current interest in the problem of the rise and fall of cities in history, the matter was treated by such early social theorists as Ibn Khaldūn[2] (in the 14th century) and Giovanni Botero[3] (some centuries later). Both recognized that the fortunes of cities were closely associated with the strengths and weaknesses of the supporting political structure. However, neither of them developed his original insights in any systematic way, nor has this been accomplished by other scholars in the intervening centuries.

We hypothesize, as did Ibn Khaldūn and Botero, that the patterns of urban development, dissemination, and decline result mainly from like changes in the political (or power) structure on the societal level—especially the rise and fall of empires. However, as in most matters social and cultural, the relationships between social power and city-building are complex. Indeed, we can not properly evaluate the impact of political power upon the shifting tides of urban life unless we also consider the effects thereon of "technology," in particular, along with "cultural values" and even "natural disasters." Nor can we understand the way the political organization influences the development and decline of cities unless we examine the functions of cities in empire-building.

International Journal of Comparative Sociology, 4, No. 2, September 1963, pp. 107–120. Reprinted by permission of author and publisher.

[1] This essay is an elaboration and modification of certain ideas that I set forth in *The Preindustrial City* (Glencoe: The Free Press, 1960), especially pp. 64ff. This book also contains a discussion of some of the controversies which surround terms such as "urban" and "city."

[2] Ibn Khaldūn, *The Muqaddimah, An Introduction to History*, trans. by Franz Rosenthal, 3 vols. (New York: Pantheon Books, 1958).

[3] Giovanni Botero, "The Greatness of Cities" (trans. by Robert Peterson, 1606) in Giovanni Botero, *The Reason of State and The Greatness of Cities* (London: Routledge and Kegan Paul, 1956).

As for the meaning of certain terms: For us a "city" or "urban community" (as distinguished from a village, or rural community) is characterized by larger size, greater density and heterogeneity, and the presence of a significant number of full-time specialists, including a literate group, engaged in a relatively wide range of nonagricultural activities. Concerning industrial vs. preindustrial technology, this distinction rests upon the kinds of tools, energy, and know-how employed. Unlike the preindustrial type, the industrial technology involves the use of exceedingly complex tools, inanimate (rather than animate) energy sources, and a know-how stemming from the scientific method. What is significant is that these different technological bases are associated with quite distinctive types of societal (as well as urban) social structures. We therefore distinguish among preindustrial civilized, transitional, and industrial orders—and their respective cities.

With this background in hand, we proceed to sketch a theoretical orientation for explaining the rise and fall of cities—providing in the process certain illustrations which suggest the kind and range of data supporting our argument.

I

Growth in Size and Number

At any given stage of technological development, the grander the empire the grander the size and number of its cities. Bear in mind that when technology (and social organization) were still at a relatively simple stage of development, both the territorial base of the empire and the size and number of its cities were decidedly limited. Such was clearly the case in the Mesopotamian riverine valley where cities first emerged. But, over time, a larger number of urbanites could be supported. As the technology advanced, more food could be produced and empires could expand territorially (other conditions permitting). If we compare the early empires with the Roman and the later British one, we discover that a much improved technology was essential if these former were to exert control over their vast territorial domain. Still, our argument holds, in any given historical period the dominant political system (or systems) —for example Rome and Britain in their prime—is able to marshall the technology (and other resources) to create the most highly developed urban complex.

Also, before we examine the specific impact of political power upon urban growth we must consider the functions of the city in maintaining an empire's social organization. In this regard the concentration of population into a relatively small space makes possible certain kinds of protection that are usually unavailable to ruralites. People scattered about the countryside or living in small villages, lacking as they do the economic resources and technical skills to build fortifications like the walls that have surrounded most preindustrial centers, have been more exposed to invading armies and especially to local marauders. Nor can the village population take full advantage of the society's military power, which is most effectively employed within limited areas—as, say, around cities. More significant still, the concentration of peoples into urban communities serves to maximize communication and to facilitate the exchange of goods and services among the various categories of specialists. The rise of cities, then, made possible more intensive kinds of commercial activity. Conversely, the more effective the commercial enterprise the more viable is urban living for the nonagriculturalist. And most important of all, the leaders of the political, educational, and religious organizations have, by residing in the city, been able to maximize communication with one another and thereby sustain the system, as well as their sense of group identity, which in turn has reinforced their own social power.

When evaluating the city's role in furthering communication,[4] we discover that many bureaucratic functions apparently are most effectively carried out when the leaders, and even employees in the lower echelons, are able to maintain personal face-to-face contacts with one another. Personal communication plays a vital part in delicate negotiations involving struggles for power and helps the leaders to sustain an intimate knowledge of trouble spots in the organization. Under these circumstances, officials who consult with one another can interpret the gestures and other nonverbal indicators that convey information in tension-laden situations. Even in the wake of the vast expansion of modern communication media—the telephone, radio, television, and such duplicating machines as typewriters and printing presses—the managerial group, and the supporting functionaries, tend to concentrate within limited sectors of the city, as well as in certain cities of the society. Evidence from such industrial cities as New York and London reveals that, despite the recent massive decentralization of certain industrial, commercial, and residential establishments, numerous managerial activities continue to concentrate in the downtown area.[5] Furthermore, New York is said to contain office space exceeding that in all other large cities of the United States combined.[6]

The need for personal communication among organizational personnel, especially the leadership, is even more vital in the preindustrial-urban context, where the absence of an industrial technology makes individuals almost completely dependent upon personal contacts if the goals of the organization are to be attained. Some communication in preindustrial civilized societies occurs via the written word, but most of it is on an oral basis. The elite, therefore, tend to cluster in the city and typically have their primary residence in the city's center. In this sector the key governmental, religious, and intellectual activities (and buildings) are concentrated as well. With transportation limited to animal-drawn vehicles or human carriers, such an ecological arrangement is essential to maximize personal contacts in the ruling group.

Not only has the elite historically resided near the city's center, but the most powerful elements of this group have congregated in the political capital. In the preindustrial order, particularly, the capital city has been the hub of almost all major political decision-making and often of the most significant intellectual and religious activities as .well. And because the capital has been the chief residence of the ruling group it has included within

[4] For a discussion of other facets of the relationship of the city to communication, see various essays in Lloyd Rodwin (ed.), The Future Metropolis (New York: George Braziller, 1961).

[5] E.g. Edgar M. Hoover and Raymond Vernon, Anatomy of a Metropolis (Cambridge: Harvard University Press, 1959) and The Paper Metropolis (London: Town and Country Planning Association, 1962).

[6] Harry C. Kenney, "Manhattan: Office Buildings Climb," Christian Science Monitor, December 28, 1962, p. 1.

its confines the large merchants whose trade is inter-urban or inter-societal in nature; often the luxury goods prized by the rulers must be imported from distant lands. This conspicuous consumption in turn has enabled the ruling group to rationalize its authority to the broader populace.

Furthermore, the capital has usually been the prime locus of the cultural arts, for this activity typically has been subsidized by the ruling element. The most eminent of the artists and entertainers have been retained by the royal court itself. Thus the very existence of the elite in the capital has attracted thereto other groups, for considerable prestige has attached to residence in the capital city. Little wonder that these urban centers have so frequently been more or less "equated" (by historians and others) with the empire or nation they have served: Rome as the command post of the Roman empire, Constantinople as the heart of the Byzantine and later the Ottoman empire, Peking off and on as the focal point of numerous dynasties, including that of the Mongol conquerors, and more recently London as the nucleus of the once-vast British empire. Although today the capitals of the great industrial powers are perhaps not as dominant as they were in the preindustrial setting, cities like Washington, D.C.[7] and Moscow still loom large on the societal and world scene.

The lower ranks of the ruling elite have often resided in the lesser cities scattered about the realm—so that the hierarchy of cities has reflected, albeit crudely, the status system in the society as a whole. These lesser cities have been situated astride the principal communi-

[7] The "dominance pattern" of Washington, D.C. (relative to other cities) in American society is in some respects a special case that deserves detailed attention.

cation routes; thus the local or provincial rulers could maintain contact with the control center—the capital—and the key political functionaries.

Our thesis that the ruling element has been urban rather than rural in residence runs counter to the views of some social scientists. They have been led astray by the fact that in preindustrial civilized orders—such as traditional China or India—the elite has included the large landowners. However, most of the landlords have typically had the city as their base and have resided therein at least part of the year. Also, some historians writing on medieval Europe have seen the cities as havens for the commercial interests, which stood in opposition to the nobility (or traditional rulers) whose residence was rural. Such a proposition, if valid, holds for only a limited expanse in space and time, and even then is open to serious question. We must recognize that throughout history the main political leaders have been urban based.

The central role of cities in sustaining empires or nations helps to explain the impact of the political structure on urban growth. The political organization, to perpetuate itself, must provide a favorable climate for the development of cities. Conversely, cities can not survive without the support of a stable, viable political system, for they are, after all, only partial systems which must import food and raw materials to sustain their population. But the producers of these items—especially farmers—have not always relinquished their "surplus" willingly. Therefore, the political leaders must, through taxes or a system of tribute, or more subtle forms of political coercion that find support in the religious-political ideology, siphon off a food supply sufficient to underwrite the urbanites. Even today, particularly in developing societies, a major problem facing those occupying seats of power is how to create a social organization that can supply sufficient food for the rapidly expanding urban population.

Control of the agricultural surplus has been furthered by the elite's direct ownership of land or its ownership by the political apparatus the elite controls. In preindustrial orders not only has land usually been the most stable form of investment, but it has provided the ruling group with direct control over the peasant and the fruits of his labor.

The political structure has also served to sustain the lines of communication so essential for commerce—and urban living. Without a sufficiently effective system of power to repress banditry or piracy, ever-recurrent problems in the preindustrial order, large-scale trade could not have flourished. Moreover, the rulers have provided the leadership necessary to synchronize the work of laborers on large-scale public projects, such as roads, that have made long-distance commerce more feasible. And as industrialization proceeds, the bureaucracy of the state is more and more extending its controls over the commercial (and industrial) sectors in order to further urban growth and stability.

It is the primacy of political power in providing the social stability necessary for the maturation of commerce and manufacturing that is responsible for our de-emphasis of the role of purely economic or commercial factors in the rise (and diffusion and decline) of cities. These forces are significant on their own account; yet they can operate only under the aegis of a broader societal power structure.

As an example, the numerous trading centers of the Phoenicians along the Mediterranean littoral are almost invariably described as commercial cities; but it is less frequently realized that this widespread commercial organization could not have developed and been sustained had not the Phoenicians also been a significant military (here, naval) power. Similarly, the so-called city-states of Greece, e.g. Athens, or those that arose in Italy in the period just following the Dark Ages, were able to establish outposts at various points around the Mediterranean because they were little empires exhibiting sufficient military (i.e. naval) power to overcome any opposition. For example, the flowering of Venice was fostered by this city's military conquests.[8] And the revival of cities like Genoa and Pisa in the 10th and 11th centuries was associated with their expanding controls over Sardinia, Corsica, and other areas to the south.[9]

In more recent times the Spanish and British empires developed commerce (and commercial centers) throughout the world because of their dominant military position. Trading cities like Singapore and Hong Kong[10] have flourished because they have been protected by, and have actually served as bases for, the British fleet. As for the Spanish empire, at least one historical work, drawing upon a vast body of empirical data, has demonstrated that even the fluctuations in trade over time

[8] See Gino Luzzatto, *Studi di storia economica veneziana* (Padova: Casa Editrice Dott. Antonio Milani, 1954).

[9] Gino Luzzatto, *An Economic History of Italy*, trans. by P. Jones (New York: Barnes and Noble, 1961), pp. 53–55.

[10] Hong Kong today represents a "broker" type city which has existed in other eras as well. Although Hong Kong is under British control, the Chinese, if they were determined, could perhaps capture it, or by cutting off all flow of goods and people with the mainland, they could readily reduce its size and effectiveness.

between Spain and her colonies were directly related to the security of the trade routes.[11] And we can with reason assume that urban growth in the mother country was affected by the vagaries of commercial activity.

Implicit in our argument is the theorem that the more extensive the territorial base a political system controls (either directly or indirectly through its colonial outposts), the more likely is the society to have available the necessary diversity of resources for city-building. Undoubtedly, the city-states that emerged in Greece, a rather poorly endowed region in terms of natural resources, could never have achieved prominence had they not been able to draw upon the food and raw materials of the Mediterranean area. Even though by modern standards this trade was meager, it was sufficient, along with the local resources, to support cities of considerable size for that era.

The need for political controls over broad territorial expanses has been even more strikingly apparent in recent centuries. For such countries as Britain and Japan, containing as they do relatively limited natural resources, colonialism was required for the construction of an industrial-urban complex.[12] The large industrial cities that subsequently arose have depended

upon the importation of critical raw materials; such could not have been secured without the exercise of some political power over other peoples. Nations like the United States and the U.S.S.R., because of their vast territory containing most of the essential raw materials, have had to rely less upon colonial outposts for their urban development. But then it could be argued that to a considerable extent both the U.S. and the Soviet Union originally grew to their current size through the incorporation of territory via military conquest.

Although at any given level of technology the politically dominant social orders are those most likely to be the most highly urbanized, we must recognize that the extent of urban development has been dramatically accelerated by the shift from the preindustrial to the industrial level of technology. The Industrial Revolution, by vastly increasing the surplus of food and raw materials, has permitted the formation of full-fledged urban societies. A reasonable guess is that cities of preindustrial societies embraced 5 to 10 percent of the total societal population. Compare this with the situation today in highly industrial-urbanized systems, where well over half the population is urban and where cities over a million have become almost commonplace. Actually, many of the famous cities of the past were relatively small by modern standards: few numbered over 100,000. Though some writers continue to refer to earlier cities of a million—for instance, ancient Rome at its height, or some "medieval" cities of Japan and China—the trend among historians has been to downgrade the population estimates for cities before the Industrial Revolution. Certainly this is the case

[11]For a summary discussion of the work by Huguette and Pierre Chaunu, *Séville et l'Atlantique* (1504–1650), see Robert S. Smith, "Seville and the Atlantic: Cycles in Spanish Colonial Trade," *Journal of Economic History*, 22 (June, 1962), pp. 253–59.

[12]See e.g. George W. Barclay, *Colonial Development and Population in Taiwan* (Princeton: Princeton University Press, 1954) and K. Berrill, "International Trade and the Rate of Economic Growth," *Economic History Review*, 12 (1960), pp. 351–59.

in recent writings on preindustrial cities in the Western world.[13]

As industrialization had magnified the scale and tempo of urbanization, the latter's dependence upon the political power structure has not diminished —it may, in fact, have become intensified. We have already suggested that Britain's and Japan's empire-building may well have been both a necessary and a sufficient condition for the industrial-urbanization of these countries. Moreover, today a pattern quite different from any in the past has emerged: forced and planned urban growth. First in the Soviet Union and now in China, the political organization has been purposively engaged in a massive, at times ruthless, marshalling of human and natural resources so as to extend the urban base and, in turn, the nation's political might, for nowadays industrial-urbanization is the basis for sustaining power on the international scene.

The Diffusion of Cities

Another dimension to city-building is the diffusion of urban life into non-urbanized or lightly urbanized regions. If one examines the historical record in Asia, North Africa, and the Americas, one is struck by the close association between the diffusion of cities and the expansion of the political system. Actually, cities as such were invented in at most only a few times and places; in all other situations that complex of traits we call urban living has developed via diffusion from one people to another.

[13]See e.g. Roger Mols, *Introduction à la Démographie Historique des Villes d'Europe du XIVe au XVIIIe Siècle* (Louvain: Université de Louvain, 1955), and J. C. Russell, "Late Ancient and Medieval Population," *Transactions of the American Philosophical Society*, 48 (Philadelphia: American Philosophical Society, 1958).

As for the reasons for the diffusion of urban forms, we must recognize that the civilized societies to which we refer have possessed the organizational and technical knowledge essential for constructing and maintaining cities in their imperial domains. At the same time, the diffusion of urban living has been necessary for the maintenance of the political structure. For one thing, cities are useful for sustaining hegemony in the newly won areas. Many of these centers, often arising on the sites of existing villages, started primarily as military bases, though obviously this function had to be supplemented by others. Food and other vital supplies must be acquired through commerce; therefore, these bases have also served as trading centers. In some cases cities whose primary role is commercial have arisen on the frontier. Then too, the military forces have been buttressed by an administrative apparatus which has sought to organize the territory as a viable political entity—hence the rise of some urban communities with extensive administrative functions.

Aside from their role in sustaining political control over the annexed territories, the frontier cities have been the media through which the ruling order has exploited the fruits of conquest. Through these centers have flowed the luxury goods (including slaves) that provide the societal ruling group, particularly in the capital, with its *raison d'être*.

The frontier cities have also been a primary medium for civilizing preliterates or, in the case of already civilized peoples, socializing them into the lifeways of the dominant group. It is in the cities, not in the small villages, that the potentiality for interaction and diffusion of ideas is greatest. (This is highly significant for our discussion in the section below.)

Here are some illustrations of this diffusion process. It was during the Ch'in and Han dynasties, for example, that city life disseminated into many nonurbanized areas of what is China today—to the south, west, and north. In northern India the Maurya empire, through its conquests, gave impetus to the rise of cities in the previously nonurban south and in Ceylon. The Persian Achaemenian empire was responsible for transporting into Central Asia that complex of traits we associate with urbanization, thereby stimulating the civilization of various nomadic Turkic groups in the region, most prominent among whom have been the Uzbeks. More familiar is the Roman empire with its diffusion of urban forms into previously nonurban regions in much of Europe—France, England, the Low Countries, southern Germany and Austria, and parts of the Balkans. The Romans also built and refurbished cities in areas where civilizations once flowered—e.g. in North Africa, the Near East, and beyond.

Nor did this urbanization process end with the demise of these and other empires of antiquity: it has continued to the present day. Certainly, in more recent centuries the Spanish empire introduced cities into much of South America and the Antilles (formerly inhabited by preliterates) and vastly accelerated the rate of urban development in parts of Middle America that had already given rise to small indigenous urban communities. Still more recently the British, French, Belgians, and other European empire-builders were responsible for creating urban centers in Africa south of the Sahara—e.g. Johannesburg, Capetown, Leopoldville, Elizabethville, etc.—in a vast area where the inhabitants had not yet developed true cities. Moreover, these and other colonialists like the Dutch transported the traits we associate with industrial cities into much of preindustrial civilized Asia—the Near East, India, Southeast Asia, the East Indies, and so on. One result of this colonialism has been that the cities of transitional (or underdeveloped) countries in Asia today exhibit a semi-preindustrial, semi-industrial character, industrial traits having been superimposed upon an already existing urban social structure.

The Decline and Resurgence of City Life

At this juncture we should remind ourselves that cities have always led a precarious existence. In the preindustrial era they were subject to all manner of natural catastrophe, ranging from destruction by volcanoes (e.g. Pompeii) to the periodic obliteration of large sectors of their population (e.g. medieval European cities) by plagues.[14] But far more devastating to the city's permanence have been socio-cultural forces—above all, war. In the modern age, technological advances have afforded industrial cities far more protection against the adverse forces of nature; yet the threat of social disaster looms larger today than ever before. Manmade methods of wiping out urban communities via nuclear warfare are a threat to the veritable foundations of the industrial-urban order. This leads us back to our central theme—the dependence of urban living upon the vagaries of political power. Armed conflict is simply the most dramatic instance of the struggle for power among social systems.

Our hypothesis is that urban decline is largely the result of built-in contradictions in the administration of such

[14]E.g. Mols, *op. cit.*

political systems as empires. As we noted previously, a society that extends its borders by virtue of military prowess comes to acculturate within the context of its frontier cities some elements among the conquered. For the motherland usually is unable or unwilling to supply all the personnel necessary for governing and exploiting the incorporated territories. The rulers therefore must rely upon members of the "native" population to perform certain vital functions. Particularly is this true where the governing element and the alien groups use different languages or exhibit markedly divergent cultures.

Moreover, if the dominant power structure is to legitimize its activities in the eyes of the native populace, it must encourage emulation of its lifeways. An unanticipated consequence of this is that some subject peoples do more than acquire the superior skills and knowledge of the conquerors; they also adopt the latter's values, including the emphasis upon political dominance and elite status.

To state our argument more sociologically, a large-scale political system (e.g. an empire) often is confronted by contradictory functional requirements that in turn give rise to contradictory structures.[15] Thus the very actions that may be mandatory if one is to reap the rewards of conquest can, in the long run, contribute to the downfall of the conquerers.[16]

What are some of these administra-

tive practices by which subject peoples become acculturated into the values and organizational techniques of the dominant system? For one thing, empires, to gain personnel for the military establishment, must recruit volunteers or mercenaries and/or employ force to press individuals into service. Often, to fill the ranks of the militia they must draw upon the conquered group. But in the process the latter acquire knowledge of the rulers' superior weapons and the military tactics that made the conquest possible. Such is accentuated when, as has occurred at various points in history, some "natives" in the system are placed in charge of their own people, within or without the military establishment, to ensure greater cooperation from the latter. They are in an ideal position to lead the troops that eventually seek to overthrow their masters.

Similar patterns develop within the nonmilitary sector of the government. Some personnel are recruited from among the subject peoples and trained in the techniques of administration— procedures for collecting revenue, and so on. A few persons acquire, along with this technical knowledge, formal education in the literary heritage of the dominant group. As a result the frontier cities may sprout "native" intellectuals who provide the rationale for the "native" leadership's counterattack against the established order.

Still another group—those who engage in commerce and the production of goods and services—is nourished in these frontier cities. The expansion of an empire is a strategic means of diffusing commercial knowledge and improved production techniques, the more so as the empire strives to take full economic advantage of the territory under its control. Thus, in the wake of the Industrial Revolution, European empires

---

[15]For a more detailed analysis of the theoretical position adopted herein, see Gideon Sjoberg, "Contradictory Functional Requirements and Social Systems," *Conflict Resolution*, 4 (June, 1960), pp. 198–208.

[16]For a discussion of the internal contradictions within empires that bears directly upon our analysis, see S. N. Eisenstadt, "The Causes of Disintegration and Fall of Empires—Sociological and Historical Analyses," *Diogenes*, No. 34 (1961), pp. 87–112.

have transmitted to their preindustrial colonies the new technological and scientific knowledge, which has laid the basis, especially in the cities, for an entirely new system of production. The process is continuing today in principle, if not in form, as Americans and Russians, in particular, export their advanced industrial system to developing societies and their cities.[17]

We can now re-state and sharpen our argument. It is the subordinate peoples —preliterate or civilized—who become socialized into the dominant power's superior skills that are most likely, and able, to spur a countermovement against their overseers (at times with the tacit cooperation of local representatives of the latter who come to identify more with the local populace than with their superiors in the homeland). Furthermore, the urban outposts of empire are the rallying points for the constitution of a new empire or separate nation. Of course, at times even systems beyond the outermost boundary of the dominant political system acquire, because of extensive social contacts, the knowledge, skills, and values essential for attacking the established power structure.

In any event, loss of the conquered realms, especially in the preindustrial past, has had grave consequences for the cities in the empire's heartland. If the emerging political system not only breaks away from the mother territory but overcomes it, some of the latter's cities may be destroyed, never to rise

again. Others may shrink for a time but later revive as they attach themselves to a new power complex. This is especially true of cities lying along important trade routes and those possessing such symbolic significance (e.g. former religious and educational centers) that even the new empire wishes to preserve or rebuild them.

Obviously, armed conflict itself may directly affect the fortunes of cities. Although from one perspective cities have been strongholds against invaders from without, they have also, because of their political significance, been highly vulnerable to enemy attack. Above all, capture and/or destruction of the capital has often symbolized the empire's (or nation's) defeat.

As a result of these struggles the fortunes of many cities have radically shifted on numerous occasions. Some like Antioch and Jerusalem have been destroyed and rebuilt many times.[18] Here, the refurbished city has been linked with its predecessors primarily through tradition (including special institutions) and on the basis of approximate site, for at times there may have been little continuity of the population itself.

Several illustrations from the history of empires should further clarify our thesis. First, the Roman empire. The Germanic groups who swept over Rome have traditionally been termed "barbarians." And somehow the notion that these barbarians were simply preliterates has been perpetuated in the literature. But were they? Actually, the leaders of these groups—Visigoths, Ostrogoths, Burgundians, etc.—had, within the frontier cities established by

[17]Some modern scholars believe that empires continue to persist but in a different form. Certain industrial-urban powers today sustain economic controls over less-developed regions without direct political control. See the writings of the German scholar Adolf Grabowsky and of the American historian William Appleman Williams. E.g. the latter's book, *The Tragedy of American Diplomacy* (Cleveland: World Publishing Co., 1959).

[18]See e.g. Glanville Downey, *A History of Antioch in Syria* (Princeton University Press, 1961) and Martin Noth, *The History of Israel*, trans. by Stanley Godman (London: A. & C. Black, 1958).

the Romans, acquired many of the religious, administrative, and military trappings of Rome, as well as its literary tradition. Some had even achieved exalted political positions in the Roman empire.[19]

Ponder for a moment how difficult it would have been for preliterates, with their simple economic organization, rudimentary technology, and poorly developed administrative skills, to overrun a flourishing empire such as Rome. The attempt to account for the latter's fall by, say, the too-facile argument that moral degeneracy of the populace led to its easy conquest overlooks the significant social and technical transformations that had long been occurring beyond the frontiers (especially in the cities).

The effects upon urban life of the fall of Rome were profound. To the north and west—e.g. Gaul—cities experienced a marked decline as the political structure in these regions became fractured and divided. Here the conquerors were simply unable to re-establish a political system that could support large cities. At the same time,

not all urban life disappeared.[20] To the east a quite different pattern emerged. Here, within the Eastern Roman empire, cities flourished, with Byzantium (Constantinople) the leading city of the Western world. Still, a few cities did shrink markedly after Rome's decline. The case of Athens is instructive. After the collapse of the Athenian power structure and the incorporation of Athens into the Roman empire, it persisted—because of its exalted intellectual and cultural heritage—as a community of considerable significance. But after the collapse of Roman power Athens sank to the size of a small town, to re-emerge as a city of importance only recently as the capital of modern Greece.

A second cogent, though more controversial, illustration is the Mongol empire.[21] Many historians tend to assume that the Mongols who conquered the civilized Chinese during and after the time of Genghis Khan were a nomadic people without an urban civilization. No doubt the Chinese, like the Romans, viewed their conquerors as "uncivilized". But it was the Chinese who had in the preceding centuries, directly or indirectly, urbanized and civilized several of the Mongol groups. For as the Chinese colonizers moved westward into what are today Mongolia and Chinese Turkestan,

[19]Data that support the views expressed herein can be found in such works as Samuel Dill, *Roman Society in the Last Century of the Western Empire* (2nd ed. rev., London: Macmillan, 1910); J. B. Bury, *History of the Later Roman Empire*, II (London: Macmillan, 1923); M. Rostovtzeff, *Social and Economic History of the Hellenistic World*, II (Oxford: Clarendon Press, 1959); and Ferdinand Lot, *The End of the Ancient World*, trans. by Philip Leon and Mariette Leon (New York: Alfred A. Knopf, 1931).

Also such recent articles as E. A. Thompson's "Christianity and the Northern Barbarians," *Nottingham Mediaeval Studies*, I (1957), pp. 3–21. Thompson's articles in succeeding issues of this journal are relevant as well.

For a summary of various theories regarding the fall of Rome (views that differ from our own) see Chester G. Starr, "The History of the Roman Empire, 1911–1960," *Journal of Roman Studies*, 50 (1960), pp. 149–60.

[20]E.g. Ferdinand Lot, *Recherches sur la population et la superficie des cités remontant à la période Gallo-Romaine*, I (Paris: Librairie Ancienne Honoré Champion, 1945).

[21]B. Vladimirtsov, *Le régime social des Mongols*, trans. by Michel Carsow (Paris: Adrien-Maisonneuve, 1948); W. van Ruysbroek, *The Journey of William of Rubruck to the Eastern Parts of the World, 1253–55*, trans. and ed. by William W. Rockhill (London: The Hakluyt Society, 1900); S. V. Kiselev, "Iz rabet Mongol'skoi arkheologicheskoi ekspeditsii instituta istorii material'noi kul'tury AN SSSR" in *Mongol'skii Sbornik, Ekonomika, istoriiā, arkheologiiā*, 24 (1959), p. 201.

they constructed cities that were the basis for some degree of urbanization of the Turkic and Mongol peoples in the region. The failure to recognize that the Mongols may have acquired their administrative and military skills via the urbanizing effects of the Chinese conquest is apparent even in the writings of such renowned specialists as Lattimore.

The evidence seems clear that the Mongols who swept over much of Asia and into Europe did have an urban-based leadership. Their first major settlement—Karakorum—had the basic ingredients of an urban center. Though small by modern standards, it had some important permanent structures—palaces and temples—and the physical remains and extant written accounts of eyewitnesses during its heyday suggest that there was a literate elite who kept genealogical records, as well as slaves, and attracted a wide variety of merchants and guildsmen to supply its wants.[22] The fact that many persons lived in tents (yurts) does not mean Karakorum was not a city. Rather, it had a special flavor of its own. The point is that the Mongols had acquired a complex social organization, and the evidence indicates that this was adopted, directly or indirectly, mainly from people they later conquered—the urban Chinese.

Our final example is of more recent vintage. The Europeans, notably the British, Spanish, French, Dutch, and Portuguese, who spread over vast areas in the 15th and ensuing centuries, transported urban forms to both nonurban and little-urbanized (i.e. preindustrial civilized) regions. But consider the consequences of this. The

cities the Europeans fostered in their colonies later became the foci of the anti-colonial or independence movements that have typified the 20th century. In such divergent societies as Algeria, Nigeria, India, Burma, Indonesia, to mention only a few, it was the very group who were educated (and/or Westernized), either in the frontier cities of the empire or in the universities of Europe, that did most to foment rebellion against their overlords. For the Europeans, like colonists before them, to make fuller use of their colonies' resources and to justify their rule, provided some of the native peoples with advanced administrative and technological skills.

As we indicated, education of colonial peoples into the rulers' administrative skills and values (above all nationalism) has meant teaching them not only to want independence but also how to achieve it. Many Europeans were caught unawares when their subjects began to rise up against the mother country, for they had misguidedly believed that by training Africans or Asians to be like themselves, they could count on these people's loyalty.

The similarities among independence movements over time are apparent enough, but some differences emerge as well, particularly in the impact of these independence movements on urban centers in the homeland. Although the shallowness of the historical period about which we are generalizing makes speculation hazardous, we should recognize that the urban centers of highly industrialized countries in Europe (and Japan as well) have in recent decades suffered few adverse affects from the loss of their colonial holdings. In fact, during the greatest period of decolonization, following World War II, many European nations

---

[22]Vladimirtsov, *op. cit.*, pp. 54–55, has noted the existence of irrigation agriculture near Karakorum.

were expanding their industrial-urban complex at a marked pace.[23] This resulted in part from the fact that during the transition period the economic and political power structure of the United States underwrote many of these European nations, especially via the Marshall Plan. Also, we are witnessing a realignment of the industrial-urban nations with respect to one another. There is a growing political-economic integration of western Europe into some larger whole (although the specific future form remains in doubt). Apparently, industrial-urban societies find it more advantageous today to sustain close political (and economic) ties with one another than with underdeveloped countries.[24] Thus, although political power and urbanization remain closely associated with one another, some new dimensions in this relationship are emerging.

II

We have outlined a theoretical orientation that we believe accounts for the shifting fortunes of urban centers over much of history. We have, in other words, sought to formulate a set of generalizations having *cross-cultural* validity. In the process we have stressed the *form*, rather than the specific cultural content, of various relationships.

One of our primary assumptions is that if we are to understand the rise and fall of cities over time we must examine these urban centers in their broader societal context. Thus, we hypothesize that the political power structure is the main variable in explaining the growth and decline of city life. Not that we ignore other variables—especially the role of the city in sustaining large-scale political structures such as empires —but the political factor deserves priority.

We could go on to consider the ups and downs of city life in relatively self-contained empires or nation-states over shorter time-periods—shifts that involve changes in the internal rather than the external power arrangements. For example, the level of urbanization in the United States by regions has been closely associated with a general realignment in the power structure of the broader society. Moreover the rise, or occasional decline, of individual cities is becoming increasingly dependent upon the community's (or region's) ability to funnel federal support to various undertakings within its confines.

Whatever the final verdict concerning the adequacy of our formulation, we are convinced that sociologists must devote far more attention than they have in the past to analyzing the changing course of city life over time and space.

---

[23]See, e.g., J. Frederic Dewhurst, John O. Coppock, P. Lamartine Yates and associates, *Europe's Needs and Resources* (New York: Twentieth Century Fund, 1961).

[24]For materials that bear at least indirectly on this problem, see Karl W. Deutsch and Alexander Eckstein, "National Industrialization and the Declining Share of the International Economic Sector, 1890–1959," *World Politics*, 13 (January, 1961), pp. 267–99.

20. The Role of Cities in the Economic Growth of Underdeveloped Countries[1]

BERT F. HOSELITZ

At its twenty-seventh meeting the Institute of Differing Civilizations discussed the problem of urbanization and economic growth, and in the general report summarizing the economic aspects of the problem R. W. Steel listed nine general propositions which, he believed, met with general approval by the participants of the conference. The second proposition listed by Steel and the explanatory comment appended by him run as follows:

The growth of population in urban and industrial centers appears to be inevitable if there is economic development, whether by industrialization, by the development of mining, or by the commercialization and improvement of agriculture. If governments desire economic development, they must be prepared to face the consequences and to attempt to mitigate the effects of the concentration of people in restricted built-up areas. Not every town, of course, is an indication of commercial development. There are everywhere historic centers, established centuries ago for religious, social, administrative or other reasons; even these have often grown considerably as a direct result of the economic progress of the present century.[2]

Journal of Political Economy, *61* (*1953*), 195–208. Reprinted by permission of author and publisher.

[1] I gratefully acknowledge the assistance given by my colleagues, E. C. Hughes, M. B. Singer, Sylvia Thrupp, and R. R. Wohl, who made extensive comments on an earlier draft. None of them is, of course, responsible for the text as it appears here.

[2] R. W. Steel, "Economic Aspect: General Report," in International Institute of Differing Civilizations, *Record of the XVIIth Meeting Held in Florence*, (Brussels 1952), p. 120.

This proposition is quite widely accepted, and many persons, notably when they think of industrialization as a means of economic development, tacitly assume that this is bound up with increasing urbanization. But, although there is much talk of industrialization and urbanization as two processes which are apparently closely and necessarily related, the whole array of forces making for urbanization in developing economies is often left unexamined, various types of urban centers are left undistinguished, and the moral and social-psychological, as well as economic and political, consequences of urbanization are left unexplored. This short paper will attempt to suggest the various problem areas that arise in probing somewhat more deeply into the process of urbanization and the study of towns and cities in underdeveloped countries.

The study of urbanization in relation to economic development has several points of interest. In the first place, it offers a field for the testing of hypotheses on the theory of location. The precise location of new cities may, therefore, be planned, and the findings of the theory of location may be applied to the development of a net of urban settlements in new countries (or new parts of old countries).

Second, and this is also still primarily a problem area in economics, a city may be studied from the point of view of the mobilization of manpower for industrial and other economic development. It is well known that one of the crucial problems in the study of economic development is the determination of conditions under which human resources will be forthcoming for the new productive tasks which the developing economy sets itself. Now it may be said with a good deal of confidence that in underdeveloped countries, notably in those with population pressure on existing agricultural resources, there has been little difficulty, in the past, in obtaining unskilled laborers in sufficient number for new enterprises. The bottlenecks and shortages that existed were due to the limitations of native individuals with adequate training for some complex tasks or to the lack of industrial discipline in a population still little used to factory work. Though from the standpoint of efficient resource allocation labor may be more redundant, and hence cheaper, in the open country than in cities and towns, urban areas are, nevertheless, the most suitable places for the establishment of factories, since they are the centers in which a potential industrial labor force is concentrated. From the standpoint of the laborer the city provides the possibility of shifting to other industrial jobs, often—especially in large industrial towns—in the same industry. From the standpoint of the entrepreneur it makes it unnecessary to select his force from a group of peasants whom he may have to drill and accustom to industrial discipline and for whom he often may have to provide housing and other services. Instead, he can select from a generally floating population that is looking for work in industrial and other nonagricultural enterprises and, in some cases, even from a skilled work force that he can attract by offering higher wages or better working conditions than those prevailing in the industries in which his prospective workers are now employed. In other words, in the town or city—

and only in the town or city—a labor force can be found that is finally committed to industry and does not tend to float back regularly to the land, and this fact makes the labor contract more impersonal, functionally specific, and tends to endow it with universalistic criteria in the selection of individuals for industrial jobs. Labor comes to be regarded more and more as a commodity, and in the allocation of tasks, status considerations, kinship ties, and similar noneconomic variables tend to be more and more disregarded. This in turn leads to a more rational (in Max Weber's sense of "*Zweckrationalitaet*") allocation of human resources.

But the town, and especially the large city, has still another advantage for the location and expansion of nonagricultural enterprises in the greater variety of skills and occupational specialties which can be found there. This factor has the tendency of minimizing bottlenecks due to shortages of certain skilled persons and of facilitating horizontal and vertical expansion of existing nonagricultural enterprises.

All these factors appear to be commonplace, but together they explain why in underdeveloped countries industries tend to concentrate in a limited number of cities, why these cities often grow to very great size, and why many countries entering the path of industrialization have vast agricultural regions with very few industrial islands in them. These factors have the result of sharpening the contrast between city and country, and it is perhaps not inappropriate to regard the cities in underdeveloped regions even as exhibiting a different culture from that of the countryside.

This fact, in turn, leads to a very important question. To what extent is the growth of an urban culture in underdeveloped countries a vehicle for changing the values and beliefs of the society so as to make it more inclined to accept economic growth? It is generally acknowledged that one of the chief barriers to rapid economic advancement in many parts of the world—in spite of the widely prevalent aspirations for economic betterment—is the traditionalism in the social values on the part of the bulk of the population. Using Robert Redfield's terminology, a characteristic of many underdeveloped countries is the relatively high degree of prevalence of a folk-like society which is usually opposed to rapid change and unable to adapt itself quickly enough to the pressures exerted on it by the increasing integration of underdeveloped countries into the world economy. But the cities, even in underdeveloped countries, are modeled, at least in some significant aspects, after the urban centers of the West. They exhibit a spirit different from that of the countryside. They are the main force and the chief locus for the introduction of new ideas and new ways of doing things. One may look, therefore, to the cities as the crucial places in underdeveloped countries in which the adaptation to new ways, new technologies, new consumption and production patterns, and new social institutions is achieved. The main problem remaining is the nature of this adaptation in the various underdeveloped countries and the degree to which the changed culture of the urban centers affects the surrounding "sea" of traditional folk-like ways of life.

So far we have treated urbanization as though it were a process set in motion only by industrialization. But, as already stated in the passage quoted from Steel's paper, this is by no means the case. Although there is a high correlation between industrialization and urbanization, the development of towns and cities is not dependent upon the previous establishment of industries, nor must all industrial establishments be located in cities in order to flourish. Historically, cities have been the seats of learning and education, they have been the centers of governmental and administrative organizations, and they have performed the function of religious or cultural rallying points. In these ways their importance for the survival of a given culture has proved to be much greater than could be assigned to them merely on the basis of population.

Even though often only a small percentage of a country's population inhabited its cities, among this small group could be found the principal carriers of its cultural and intellectual values and the chief holders of its political and economic power. This is probably the most outstanding aspect of cities, and the one most often commented upon. It finds expression as early as the late medieval works which stand at the very beginning of urban sociology. Ibn Khaldūn, writing in the fourteenth century, stressed particularly the view that the city as the seat of a central or provincial government also exhibits economic patterns significantly different from those of the surrounding countryside. Since the proceeds of taxation are accumulated in the cities, and, since governmental and educational functions are concentrated there, new patterns of demand arise. These tend to affect, in turn, the patterns of production and supply, bringing about profound economic differences between country and city. Similar views were expressed some two hundred years later by another "forerunner" of urban sociology, Giovanni Botero. The main difference between the theories of these two writers is the relative emphasis placed on political and on economic factors. Ibn Khaldūn, who lived in Spain and North Africa, places primary emphasis on the fact that cities are centers of government and political power; Botero, who lived in Italy, places more stress on the commercial and industrial features of cities.[3]

Modern writers on urban sociology have reiterated these aspects of cities in a more sophisticated and scientific manner, but they have added relatively little to the identification of the essential distinctive features of urban aggregations. This literature, however, points to urban developments in the West as a model by means of which the interaction between urbanization and economic growth can best be studied.[4]

One way of exploring differences in urban function and the effects of different types of towns and cities upon the economic and cultural development of the surrounding regions may be through a historical study of the development of the cities of western Europe and their interaction with the economic development of the part of the world in which they were situated.

It is well known that, beginning with the early eleventh century, western Europe underwent a process of economic development which was accompanied by growth of towns and urban institutions. This development reached its peak in the late thirteenth and early fourteenth centuries. Many of the old Roman *municipia* in Italy and Gaul had lost vigor and importance first during the barbarian invasions and later due to the control of Mediterranean trade by the Arabs but had never completely ceased to exist. In the course of this process of development they were revived and began a renewed period of growth. At the same time entirely new towns were founded, and some of them, notably in Flanders and along the North Sea, became of great importance and power and grew to considerable size.

In considering the role played by medieval cities, we may follow the general lines of argument developed by Alfons Dopsch and Henri Pirenne. Few men have been concerned so consistently with this problem, and, although fully aware of the legal and constitutional problems inherent in the history of urban development in medieval Europe, they attached major importance to the economic aspects of urbanization.[5]

Like its forerunner in antiquity, the medieval town was a fortified place in which the surrounding rural population could find shelter during periods of war or invasion. But those medieval towns that survived the great Norman raids of

[3] See Ibn Khaldūn, *Prolégomènes* (composed between 1375–78), edited and translated by M. G. de Slane (Paris, 1936), II, 238–41, 277–82, and 294–313; and Giovanni Botero, *Delle cause della grandezza e magnificenza delle città* (first published in 1588), reprinted in an edition prepared by Carlo Morando of Botero's *Della ragion di Stato* (Bologna, 1930), pp. 315–82. An English translation of this work by Robert Peterson appeared under the title *A Treatise, concerning the causes of the Magnificencie and greatnes of Cities* (London, 1606). For Botero's views on "urban sociology" see especially pp. 322–25 and 346–72 of the Italian edition cited and pp. 9–14 and 41–86 of the English translation.

[4] See, for example, Adna Ferrin Weber, *The Growth of Cities* ("Columbia University Studies in History, Economics and Public Law," Vol. XI [New York, 1899]); and especially Max Weber, *Wirtschaft und Gesellschaft* (3d ed.; Tübingen, 1947), Part III of *Grundriss der Sozialökomomik*, II, 514–44.

[5] See Alfons Dopsch, *The Economic and Social Foundations of European Civilization* (London, 1937), pp. 303–57; Henri Pirenne, *Medieval Cities* (Princeton, 1925), and many other writings. All of Pirenne's works on medieval urban life have been brought together in the collection *Les Villes et les institutions urbaines* (2 vols.; Paris, 1939).

the ninth century, or that were founded afterward, had still another function. They were places which had either a special economic or a special political function. The city with a primarily political function Pirenne calls the "Liége" type and the city with a primarily economic function the "Flemish" type. Liége was the seat of an archbishop who ruled over an extended territory. His court, at which were employed a considerable number of officials and administrators and which was supplemented by institutions designed to train priests, administrators of church property, and other "intellectuals," formed the nucleus of the city. Pirenne describes Liége in the following words:

Until the middle of the 14th century Liége was essentially a city of priests, bristling with church towers and cut up by great monastic precincts. As its clerical population increased and the court of the bishop developed, the number of artisans necessary for the maintenance of this community grew proportionately.[6]

In other words, Liége was a town of administrators, bureaucrats, teachers, and students, to whom were added an appropriate number of artisans and servants supplying them with finished goods and services. Economically, it was of little importance up to the fifteenth century, but as a center of political power and a capital of education it was unequaled for many leagues around. Such cities as Liége existed in many parts of medieval Europe. Reims and Laon in France, Utrecht in the northern part of the Low Countries, and Worms, Mainz, and Speyer in

Germany are other examples. In Britain the political and educational functions were separated, and Oxford and Cambridge developed independently of Westminster. But many important centers maintained a primary political or educational function not only throughout the Middle Ages but beyond. Examples of this can be found among the cities which formed the capitals of later German states, such as Karlsruhe or Weimar, or which attained new political importance because of the consolidation of states, such as Bern, which became the capital of the Swiss confederation.

In contrast to the Liége type of city, there developed in medieval Europe a city which had primarily an economic function. In fact, when we think of the typical medieval city, we have in mind the great emporiums which developed along the Mediterranean and the North Sea; we think of Bruges or Ghent rather than Liége, of Marseilles or Rouen rather than Laon, of Lübeck, Venice, or Genoa rather than Worms or Speyer. In other words, we think of the medieval city as an institution responding to the economic rather than the political, educational, or religious needs of European society.

Yet we must not exaggerate the number of large commercial and financial centers that existed. In the territory which in the late nineteenth century formed Germany there were altogether some twenty-three hundred "cities."[7] It is not necessary to point out that many of these places, although endowed with special rights (*Stadtrecht*), were not cities in the same sense as Cologne, Frankfurt, or Augsburg. They were small places, with not more than

[6] Henri Pirenne, *Belgian Democracy, Its Early History* (Manchester, 1915), p. 101. Dopsch, although he does not use the concepts "Liége" and "Flemish" type, makes the same distinction (*op. cit.*, pp. 318–26).

[7] Karl Bücher, "Die Grosstädte in Gegenwart und Vergangenheit," in Th. Petermann (ed.), *Die Grosstadt* (Dresden, 1903), p. 21.

two to five thousand inhabitants, which had significance for the immediate neighborhood in which they were established but whose radius of effective influence was strictly limited. The overwhelming majority of medieval cities, not only in Germany but all over Europe, was of this kind.

Among the larger towns we may distinguish two kinds: the city with primarily commercial and financial functions and the industrial city. By far the majority of medieval cities seem to have had commercial and financial functions. These were the towns whose power and wealth were based upon their being the home base of a group of important merchants engaging in international trade or which were places in which great banking houses were domiciled. In many instances merchants and financial families were so closely related that it is often impossible to distinguish between those towns which were primarily centers of trade and those which were primarily banking centers. Examples of cities that performed mercantile and financial functions are Genoa, Venice, Milan, Marseilles, and Barcelona in the Mediterranean and Hamburg, Bremen, Lübeck, Cologne, and later Augsburg and Antwerp in the region north of the Alps.

These cities all present a series of special features, some of which might be worth enumerating. Their government was composed of a small and progressively less open group of wealthy patrician merchant and financial families. Since they had little industry, they had no proletariat comparable to that of the industrial towns. Their social structure was made up of three main classes: the wealthy families, who, as a rule, formed the political elite; artisans and their journeymen, who

were usually organized in guilds and thus assured of a standard of life appropriate to their status; and a mass of floating rabble—poor persons, servants, and recent immigrants from the country who found occasional or regular employment but who did not yet form a relatively homogeneous working class such as existed in Europe later in the eighteenth and nineteenth centuries.[8]

The few industrial centers exhibit some different features. They are the towns to which Pirenne refers when he speaks of a Flemish type, for the cities of Flanders and a few towns in northern Italy and upper Germany were the only ones before the fifteenth century which were centers of sizable industries. In the large towns of Flanders and in Florence we find a textile industry; in upper Germany we find some textile produc-

[8] It should be noted that the discussion in the text relates primarily to the cities on the continent of Europe. Sylvia Thrupp has shown that the degree of social mobility in medieval London was very high and that the merchants, above all, formed a class with exceptional social fluidity (see *The Merchant Class of Medieval London* [Chicago, 1948], *passim*, esp. chap. v). As Miss Thrupp indicates, there may be a significant difference between London and the cities of the Continent (*ibid.*, p. 191), and the descriptions which we have of some great commercial-financial cities of Italy and Germany seem to confirm the statement of the limited possibilities of ascent to the uppermost social group made in the text. Cf., for example, for Cologne, Gustav Schmoller, *Deutsches Städtewesen in älterer Zeit* (Bonn, 1922), p. 74; for German medieval cities in general, Georg von Below, *Das ältere deutsche Städtewesen und Bürgertum* (Bielefeld, 1898), pp. 118 ff.; for some cities in France, Ch. Petit-Dutaillis, *Les Communes françaises* (Paris, 1947), pp. 150 ff.; for Venice, Charles Diehl, *Une république patricienne: Venise* (Paris, 1931), pp. 81–119; and for the cities of Flanders and Italy in general, J. Lestoquoy, *Les Villes de Flandre et d'Italie sous le gouvernement des patriciens* (Paris, 1952).

tion; and in Milan and Brescia we find metallurgical industries. In Venice, in addition to the production of woolen cloth, there was the manufacture of ships and shipping equipment in the large Arsenal of the Republic.

The demand for labor was considerably greater, other things being equal, in an industrial town than in a financial-mercantile center. This demand was met in part by providing more regular employment opportunities for immigrants to the city and, in part, by drawing within the economic compass of the city the inhabitants of villages near it. Here is an instance of the direct impact of the city on changing or "co-ordinating" the economic activity of the region in which it is located. Whether or not the workers within and around these industrial cities may be regarded as a distinct social class is still disputed, but there is no doubt that all groups engaged in industry acquired a political education the hard way, as well as new ambitions. The history of these industrial cities differed from that of mercantile centers probably because of the strong and unified front which the industrially employed population could present. The oligarchy in these cities was broken, or at any rate made insecure, and the result was recurring revolt or the approach to democratic government and a broadening of political power. The war of the textile workers of Bruges against the patrician Leliaerts and the king of France associated with them in the period 1301–28, the struggle of the weavers of Ghent in the 1370's and 1380's against the French crown, and the violent strike of the Florentine *ciompi* in 1378 (crowning a movement of social unrest which had lasted for over a century) led to a democratization of urban government and a greater participation of the popular classes in

the legislatures and hence the destinies of their towns.[9]

The main new sets of ideas and practices which were developed by medieval cities may be grouped as follows. On the one hand, there were towns with predominantly political and intellectual functions. New forms of administration, new bureaucracies, new methods of legislation and of international negotiations, and new forms of political behavior on the part of the rulers and their servants were developed. At the same time the town was a center of learning. Knowledge, science, and philolophy were pushed forward in the universities located in larger cities. The town population was more literate than the country population. The town was the place in which a nascent intelligentsia was formed, at first composed exclusively of clerics, but later, even before the Reformation, it gradually became more and more secular, culminating in the group of rationalist humanists of the sixteenth century.[10]

---

[9] An adequate history of medieval social revolutionary and social reform movements is yet to be written. On the "heroic" period of Bruges see, e.g., J. Parneel, *Une page détachée de l'histoire de Flandre: 1301–1328* (Bruges, 1850), and, above all, H. Pirenne, *Le Soulèvement de la Flandre Maritime de 1323–1328* (Brussels, 1900), pp. i–lxx. On the revolutions in Florence see, for example, Niccoló Rodolico, *La Democrazia fiorentina nel suo tramonto (1378–1382)* (Bologna, 1905), esp. Part I, chaps. i and iii; Part II, chaps. i–iii. The underlying sociological differences between oligarchic-aristocratic and popular-democratic medieval towns have been described by Max Weber (*op. cit.*, pp. 544–83), who designates the two types of towns as "*Geschlechterstadt*" and "*Plebejerstadt*." The latter he also regards as the prototype of the modern industrial city.

[10] An interesting connection between the medieval businessmen and the intellectuals of the Renaissance is drawn by Yves Renouard, *Les Hommes d'affaires italiens du Moyen Âge* (Paris, 1949), esp. pp. 171 ff.

Apart from their political and intellectual function, cities had a predominant economic function. They were the places in which new forms of economic activity and new types of economic organization were evolved. They were the places not merely in which new commodities were traded and whence new markets and sources of supply were explored and conquered but in which appeared the first signs of new class relations based on alterations in the division of social labor. And, for all the differences in national temperament, religious beliefs, customs, and historic circumstances, Bruges and Ypres are are the true forerunners of Manchester and Bradford; they are the textile towns of medieval Europe.

This sketch of the kinds of medieval towns and the functions of urban centers contains an enumeration of culture complexes for whose change the existence of sizable towns or cities appears to be an indispensable requirement. The impact of cities in these fields has been felt in the Western world in an enhanced fashion in the period since the end of the Middle Ages. Especially with the growth of manufacturing industries in the seventeenth and eighteenth centuries, the industrial city has been given a powerful impetus, and we have come to associate industrialization and urbanization as part and parcel of one and the same process. But even while the new industrial cities of Lancashire and the Ruhr mushroomed, the consolidation of national states in Europe aided the growth of political capitals, commercial centers, and port towns. The medieval dichotomy between Liége and Bruges has its modern counterpart in the dichotomies between The Hague and Amsterdam, Rome and Milan, Bern and Zurich. At the same time such giants as London, Paris, and Berlin, and other cities of

similar size elsewhere, exhibit a multitude of aspects. The capitals of many European countries are urban areas in which commercial, financial, industrial, intellectual, and political functions are combined, so that it would be difficult to "type" a place like London or Paris. But this is the outcome of the high degree of coordination made possible by modern administrative techniques and a business technology facilitating the most minute division of labor. It is also due to the large concentration of many millions of persons in a relatively small space made possible by the development of transportation facilities and new technology in housing and city planning. The multifunction city, such as London or Paris, is clearly a modern phenomenon, although some vestiges of this type of city can be found as far back as the sixteenth century.

This suggests several different problems which might be elucidated by a closer study of urbanization and economic growth in their historical dimensions. On the one hand, we may discern a growing diversification of urban functions with advancing technology which makes feasible communication within a city and between it and an increasingly larger surrounding region. Just as modern technology permits the development of vast and complex businesses, so it permits the development of vast and complex multi-function cities. At the same time, and I believe as a consequence of the more conscious application of principles of the theory of location, we witness an increasing specialization of cities in the kinds of products they supply and often in the type of economic function they fulfil. An example is the establishment of specialized cities in the U.S.S.R. during the last twenty years. Thus we may witness two opposing trends, one affecting chiefly the very large metropolitan centers which tend to give up specific urban functions and to adopt many different functions; the second affecting smaller cities which tend to develop new forms of specialized functions—for example, the university town, the resort town, the steel town, the port, the railroad center.

In view of this, the problems which we discovered in studying medieval urban development are repeated in part in presently underdeveloped countries. I have given this sketch of the forms and functions of medieval cities, not because I believe that precisely the same forms and functions can be found in the underdeveloped countries of today, but to show, by means of an example, how the study of the development and growth of towns in an economically underdeveloped area (such as medieval Europe) can shed important light on the over-all conditions and processes of economic development.

There exist, as I hope will be admitted, many parallels between the European Middle Ages and presently underdeveloped countries. For example, in many parts of the world we have the functional division between political-intellectual urban centers and economic centers. Delhi and Bombay, or Quito and Guayaquil, and to some extent even Rio de Janeiro and São Paulo, or Peiping and Shanghai, are instances of this difference. At the same time, however, large urban settlements are so sparse in many underdeveloped countries that many of those that have developed are multi-purpose cities. Jakarta, Rangoon, and most capitals of Latin-American countries are examples.

But these distinctions have been made not to obtain criteria by which towns and cities can be classified but rather to obtain a series of variables important for economic development which require for their full unfolding an urban environment. Commerce, financial institutions, industrial establishments, governmental bureaucracies, and advanced educational and intellectual training facilities all require an urban climate to develop and flourish. Our first problem is to see whether we can discern significant differences in the occupational structure and social composition of different cities in underdeveloped countries and to try to determine whether any regularities can be ascribed to such differences. Benares and Ahmedabad are both cities of several hundred thousand inhabitants in India. Yet I am convinced that a careful sociological survey of the two would show considerable differences between them. If these differences can be ascertained, let us then proceed to make hypotheses concerning the characteristics of different cities which are relevant to different aspects of economic development. In some instances an industrial environment may be wanted, but in others the impetus for the formation of a critically minded intelligentsia or an impersonal, honest, efficient bureaucracy may be just as important preconditions of economic development. In our preoccupation with the close association between industry and urbanization we often tend to forget that underdeveloped countries need not only industries but also other social, political, and intellectual innovations which may be fostered more effectively in nonindustrial urban centers.

Posing the problem in this way leaves open the question of the relation between industrialization and the development of efficient governmental services. Historically, the two trends appear to have been closely associated, although it would probably be difficult to say which exercised the determining influence. In Prussia modern forms of public administration preceded industrialization. In Britain and, to a lesser extent, in France they lagged behind. But, regardless of the precise historical sequence, the net effect in all cases was an increase in average real income, which also strongly affected the non-urban regions located near the centers of development. This process has recently been described by T. W. Schultz.[11] His essay, though addressed explicitly to another problem, contains a set of theoretical generalizations of the first importance for the study of the interrelations between urbanization and economic growth. The problems raised by Schultz form a bridge to the questions discussed in the succeeding paragraphs.

Our second task is to investigate the over-all impact which urban centers have under modern conditions of economic development. Two men whose social views are diametrically opposed both testify to the overwhelming importance of the difference between town and country. Marx pointed to this "antithesis" in many of his works and, in *Capital*, even went so far as to state that "the whole economical history of society is summed up in the movement of this . . . separation between town and country."[12] M. I. Rostovtzeff, who, as is well known, was and is an ardent anti-Marxist, introduced a course of lectures he gave in 1922 with the following words:

What is my purpose in giving this short introduction to your work? It is to interpret one of the main problems of modern economic and social life. . . . The problem I mean is the problem produced by the existence in our social life of two different types of men, the country people and the city people. Of course, these two types exist in this country also, but, as far as I know, there is no such sharp antagonism, so sharp a contrast between these two types as there is, for example, in Russia and to a lesser extent in Western Europe.[13]

Both Marx and Rostovtzeff had in mind, above all, differences in the typical form of economic organization characteristic of urban and rural economic activity. The city, the factory with its proletarian labor force, and the sharp distinction between workers, middle class, petty bourgeoisie, and entrepreneurial groups (enhanced in pre-World War I Russia and strongly marked in nineteenth-century Europe) were contrasted with the economic and social order of the countryside. There the typical productive unit was small and normally required the participation of the members of only one family, and the landlord was opposed to the small owner-farmer or tenant farmer. The middle class and, above all, the intelligentsia were not indigenous to the countryside; and whatever officials, teachers, or other intellectuals resided there had migrated from urban areas.

The economic organization of the city represented the predominant form of capitalist economy; that of the countryside still contained many elements of precapitalistic economic forms. On the purely economic level, therefore, differences were clearly discernible in institutions, forms of productive organization, occupational specialization, and social structure as it related to economically differentiated groups. Within

[11]Theodore W. Schultz, "Reflections on Poverty within Agriculture," *Journal of Political Economy*, 58, No. 1 (February, 1950), 1–15.

[12]See Karl Marx, *Capital* (Chicago, 1903), I, 387.

[13]Michael I. Rostovtzeff, "Cities in the Ancient World," in Richard T. Ely (ed.), "Urban Land Economics" (Ann Arbor, 1922), p. 18 (mimeographed).

limits, these contrasts could be interpreted as representing an aspect of a dual economy, such as has been found to exist in some underdeveloped countries. The difference between Marx's analysis of nineteenth-century western Europe and Rostovtzeff's analysis of early twentieth-century Russia, on the one hand, and the picture of the urban-rural contrast in medieval Europe outlined in this paper, on the other hand, does not lie in the fact that the contrast had disappeared. Rather the difference is that in the Middle Ages the cities were still struggling for recognition, and urbanism as a way of life was as yet the exception, whereas in the later period capitalism centered on urban areas was the predominant form of socioeconomic organization, and the way of life of the city had won out over that of the country.

But the contrast between city and country is not confined to economic organization alone. Although they do not expressly state it, all the writers who note this contrast imply that it is more far-reaching than is reflected merely in differences in productive organization and forms of economic activity. When Marx says that the antagonism between town and country is one of the main forces in history and when Rostovtzeff says that there are two different types of men, the city people and the country people, they have in mind two cultural types which are opposed to each other. I have mentioned earlier the cultural dichotomy between countryside and city in non-Western societies. This difference is confirmed by observers in many parts of the world. For example, Boeke notes it in Indonesia (where he discusses it as an important aspect of what he calls the "dual society"), Steel mentions it for Africa, and Redfield has described cultural differences between localities exhibiting different degrees of urbanism in Yucatán by applying to them a yardstick derived from the typological contrast between folk and urban culture.[14]

Redfield's typology has proved very fruitful for his analysis of the different forms of cultural integration found in urban centers and rural villages, but it suffers from a shortcoming of which he is by no means unaware. Rather than working out the independent determination of two contrasting ideal types, Redfield developed only the type of the folk society and assigned to the urban society all those characteristics which are nonfolk-like. In other words, in Redfield's schema, the urban society is really the nonfolk society.

Redfield would not deny that differences exist between urban centers, but his schema does not penetrate them, because it was not designed to do so. From what has been said earlier, it will be clear that I do not suggest that working out a model of a unique urban culture is easy or even possible. The difficulty in constructing even an ideal-type model of urban culture is due to that fact that its outstanding characteristic is its heterogeneity and that, therefore, sets of culture traits found in the urban centers of one country need not be repeated in those of another country. Urban cultures may vary with differences in geographical location or with differences in the general level of advancement of the countries in which different cities are located. Hence, if it is our aim to stipulate a single type of urban culture,

[14]See J. H. Boeke, "Oriental Economics" (New York, 1947) (mimeographed), *passim*, esp. chap. i; Steel, *op. cit.*; Robert Redfield, *The Folk Culture of Yucatán* (Chicago, 1941), chap. ii, and "The Folk Society," *American Journal of Sociology*, 52, No. 4 (January, 1947), 293–308.

as contrasted to a single ideal-typical folk culture, the only possible procedure is to choose the path which Redfield used and to describe the urban culture as exhibiting a series of traits which are the opposite of related traits found in the folk culture. Thus, the method chosen imposes by necessity our constructing the urban culture as a nonfolk culture.

For our problem, that is, the determination of the relationship between urbanism and economic development, it is, however, not necessary to stipulate a single type of urban culture. In fact, I believe that this would be a wrong procedure altogether. Whereas Redfield was interested in determining the forces which made for cultural stability and integration, economic development provokes social and cultural change, and our primary attention is directed, therefore, to forces which may disturb (temporarily or even permanently) cultural homogeneity and close integration of fairly uniform folkways. The analysis of the role of cities in the Middle Ages shows that there appear to be several points of vulnerability of traditional action patterns and that cities which have different primary functions are the principal places where the critical changes occur. But there is one important difference between medieval cities and cities in contemporary underdeveloped countries. The former were indigenous adaptations to new forms of economic activity and new types of productive organization. In this way their social structures and over-all functions were, in general, fairly uniform and simple. But the cities of contemporary underdeveloped countries are hybrid institutions, formed in part as a response to the indigenously developing division of social labor and in part as a response to the impact made upon less advanced coun-

tries by their integration into the world economy. The urban areas of underdeveloped countries are the chief centers of cultural contact, and the different degree of interpenetration of diverse cultural traits in the cities of different underdeveloped countries, or sometimes even in different cities of the same underdeveloped country, is the chief reason why the characteristics of urbanism (and hence the models for an ideal-typical urban culture) vary from country to country.

In view of the fruitfulness of Redfield's typology for analyzing the characteristics of the folk society, some suggestions he has made for the analysis of different types of urban cultures should be followed up. The modern urban community, as opposed to the folk society, is perhaps more clearly defined as "an aggregate of populations and institutions in civilizational arrangement," whereas the recently formed, rapidly growing city emerging now in many underdeveloped countries may be regarded as "a recent assemblage of folklike societies."[15] This already established two, perhaps focal, types of urban culture. It is an empirical question to determine the extent to which features characteristic of one type are present in the other. Even in our most modern cities folklike traits may be found in the relationships existing in certain ethnic or linguistic neighborhoods, religious communities, or other institutions. At the same time, some of the characteristic features of Western urban centers culturally furthest removed from the folk society, such as interpersonal relations based purely on

[15]These two definitions are taken from an unpublished seminar outline by Professor Redfield. Needless to say, the concept "civilization" in the first definition relates to the characteristic aspects of modern Western culture.

an economic nexus or anonymity between members of productive or political associations, can be found in many cities of underdeveloped countries. These complexes, as well as differences in the relations of different cities with their hinterland, are variables which must be considered in working out a more definitive typology of urban cultures relevant for the study of the impact of cities on economic growth.

Since our uncertainties and doubts about these problems are due mainly to the scarcity of data, the first and chief task in the study of the role of urbanization in economic growth is the need to initiate a number of surveys of urban institutions and the social and occupational composition of different urban centers in underdeveloped countries. Only a few such surveys exist, and many of these are inadequate.[16] On the basis of data on the occupational and social structure of cities in a variety of underdeveloped countries, with different social functions (ports, railroad centers, industrial centers, administrative and governmental centers, and multifunction cities), further hypotheses on the relation between economic growth and urbanization could be formulated. Such surveys should include also an analysis, wherever possible,

of the changing aspects of observed economic variables with changes in the size of the city and changes in its overall social function, if such change has occurred.

The second set of problems which these surveys of the cities of underdeveloped countries should cover is the nature of their growth. Are cities a melting pot for rural populations coming from many parts of their countries? To what extent do immigrants into the city tend to remain there and permanently adopt an urban way of life? What contacts do they maintain with their original home, and what impact do they exert on the places from which they came? Do they tend to migrate to the larger urban areas directly from the villages or by stages through temporary residence in smaller provincial towns? What changes in family structure, religious views, political affiliations, and class or caste status are associated with these migrations? These are a few of the questions which appear important in learning more about the social and cultural changes to which persons gaining contact with urban areas become subjected and in determining the dimensions of the cultural differences between city life and rural life in the various underdeveloped countries.

The third area of study which might produce fruitful results is the comparative study of urbanization processes in currently underdeveloped countries and similar processes in the history of advanced countries, especially in western Europe. This is not a plea to relearn the "lessons of history," and I am fully aware that the conditions under which, for example, the mining region in South Wales was peopled and developed economically in the later eighteenth and nineteenth centuries differ in many ways from the related process in the Rand mining region in South Africa.

[16]Among surveys of cities in underdeveloped countries which have come to my attention are S. D. Gamble, *Peking: A Social Survey* (New York, 1921); Richard M. Morse, "São Paulo in the 19th Century: Economic Roots of the Metropolis," *Inter-American Economic Affairs*, Vol. 5, No. 3 (Winter, 1951); Lucila Herrmann, "Clase Media em Guaratinguetá," in Theo R. Crevenna (ed.), *Materiales para el estudio de la clase media en la América Latina* (Washington, 1950), III, 18–59; N. V. Sovani, *Social Survey of Kolhapur* (3 vols. [Nos. 18, 23, and 24 of the "Publications of the Gokhale Institute of Politics and Economics"]; Poona, 1951–52); and Roger Le Tourneau, *Fès avant le protectorat* (Casablanca, 1949); Horace Miner, *The Primitive City of Timbuctoo* (Princeton, 1953).

The study of urbanization processes in Europe may, however, draw attention to a series of social and economic facts which are often obscured in the underdeveloped countries because of differences in speed of urbanization and because of the contrast between the culture of the immigrant from a remote village and that which he meets in an already partly "Westernized" city. There are many problems which play a significant part in the process of transforming peasants and primitives into city people. Among them are the need to overcome forces fostering *anomie* on the part of the immigrant who is torn loose from an environment in which he felt secure and thrown into a city where impersonal forces predominate and primary groups outside the immediate family are scarce or absent; the problems of adjustment of these immigrants, who may be regarded as culturally marginal, to a new form of life; and the intermingling of ethnic or linguistic groups which often provokes the establishment of new quasi-caste relations.[17] These are among the important factors making for the vulnerability to radical social and political programs to which workers in newly formed industrial centers are often subject. They are among the main background forces at work determining the forms of social organization that will prevail in the urban centers of a culture—centers which tend to impress their characteristics on the rest of the society as it undergoes economic growth.

On the basis of these studies a series of more detailed theoretical generalizations could probably be made about the impact exerted by processes of urbanization on economic growth and the problems of the emergence of urban culture and its association with economic change. Whether we shall be able to stipulate some unique set of culture traits as characteristic of urban culture is uncertain. It might be possible to do so, if those traits were stated in such general terms as to be of little usefulness to practical research. We may find that the urban cultures of the underdeveloped countries in South Asia differ from those in, say, Latin America or the United States; we may find that the culture of industrial cities, such as Monterrey or Ahmedabad, differs from that of administrative centers, such as Delhi or Quito; or we may find that the culture of some of the multifunction capitals in underdeveloped countries differs from that of some of the smaller towns with one primary function. But, even if we find these diversities, we shall still be able to judge more accurately what impact is exercised by urbanization and its different forms on the progress and destiny of the peoples in the less advanced parts of the world.

[17]On this problem see the very stimulating remarks by Everett C. Hughes, "Queries concerning Industry and Society Growing Out of Study of Ethnic Relations in Industry," *American Sociological Review*, 14, No. 2 (April, 1949), 211–20.

21. Urbanization and Social Change in Africa

A. L. EPSTEIN

The achievement of political independence in so many African countries and their emergence into nationhood are spectacular and dramatic expressions of the great contemporary upheaval of society throughout the continent. While from some points of view these developments might seem to have been extremely rapid, they have not, however, occurred overnight. They are rather the end-product of very complex economic, social, and political processes that have been at work over many years. Among the many factors contributing to these developments has been the growth of large modern towns and cities, in themselves both a striking index of change and a stimulus to further change.

The importance of the towns in social change has not gone unobserved amongst students of African affairs. Thus Hodgkin, a political scientist, has commented (1956: 18) that "it is above all in these new urban societies that the characteristic institutions and ideas of African nationalism are born and grow to maturity." Hodgkin remarked the parallels between urban growth in Africa today and that in England in the early phases of the Industrial Revolution. Gluckman (1960: 56–57), from a more specifically anthropological point of view, has written in somewhat similar terms:

Current Anthropology, Vol. 8, No. 4 (1967), 275–96. Reprinted by permission of author and publisher. Notes omitted.

... modern industrial towns have everywhere produced specific types of associations arising from the needs of urban life.... We must expect these associations inevitably to develop in Africa.... An African townsman is a townsman, an African miner is a miner.

Most of the detailed studies of urbanization and urbanism in Africa to date have been made by social anthropologists. Gluckman's aphorism was in fact the developed expression of a point of view he first advocated in his Seven Year Research Plan of the Rhodes-Livingstone Institute (1945). The standpoint he adopted there provided an invaluable corrective to earlier studies which tended to assess urban phenomena against a rural-tribal model, and it heavily influenced the work of a number of younger scholars in the field, including myself. Such approaches as those of Hodgkin and Gluckman marked a big advance in thinking about these problems by their emphasis on the positive features and functions of urban life. Yet, as our knowledge of African urbanism accumulates, it also becomes clear that such formulations do less than justice to the complexity of the phenomena, and can lead to an obscuring of certain important problems calling for analysis. Thus, for example, the connection which Hodgkin postulates between the growth of towns and the rise of African nationalism seems, on the face of it, straightforward and indisputable. On the other hand, we must face the fact that the countries of tropical Africa where nationalism has been most advanced have sometimes had very small proportionate numbers engaged in wage labour, surely a primary mark of modern urban life. Clearly, urbanization in modern Africa has gone hand in hand with a number of other processes —industrialization, Westernization, the growth of settler communities, etc.—all of which have to be kept analytically distinct if we are to make valid generalizations.

Consideration of Gluckman's position also points up the increasing need for sharper and more varied conceptual tools. Thus if, as he has argued, every African is "detribalized" as soon as he leaves his tribal area to come to town, what meaning is to be given to the term "urbanization" itself, and how can we decide whether one African or one population is more "urbanized" than another? It is of course true, as Gluckman remarks, that the man who comes to town finds himself involved in different kinds of grouping from those which obtained in the village; he also earns his livelihood in a different way and comes under different authorities. But none of this can tell us anything of what Mitchell and Shaul (1963) have called "the degree of commitment to urban residence," still less of the connection between urban commitment and the development of new patterns of behavior and sets of values and attitudes. For example, discussing the role of the African urban courts in towns on the Copperbelt of Northern Rhodesia (Zambia), I have drawn attention to an inconsistency in the attitudes of Africans towards these bodies (Epstein 1953a, 1953b). This assessment was based on evidence of a wholly qualitative order. In a later study of power and prestige among urban Africans, the use of quantitative methods threw

further light on the position of the court members within the urban community (Mitchell and Epstein 1957). The respondents in this experiment were divided into three categories in terms of the number of years they had resided in town: (1) under two years; (2) between three and seven years; and (3) eight years and over. The data showed that the court members were ranked higher by respondents in the second category than by those in the first or the third. In short, what Mayer (1962) has called Gluckman's alternation model disregards the very process of becoming a townsman; it does not take sufficient account of the fact that urbanization, in at least one of its dimensions, involves a process of growth and change.

A further difficulty of Gluckman's formulation is that while it correctly invites us to set our studies of African urbanization in the context of studies of urban life elsewhere, it does not enable us to handle so readily the problem of variation in urban social systems. As studies of modern urban Africa accumulate, it becomes increasingly plain that the patterns of migration and urban growth are far from uniform throughout the continent: in particular, there appear to be a number of important respects in which the West African situation differs markedly from that obtaining in South and Central Africa (see, e.g., Banton 1966). While it is possible to detect certain general patterns in African urbanization, the deeper understanding of this phenomenon and its role in social change requires not only that we pay closer attention to the problem of variation, but that this diversity be handled within a single conceptual framework.

What, then, are we to understand by urbanization? In an immediate sense, it refers, of course, to living in towns as against living in rural settlements, and it is on this basis that simple, quantitative indices of urbanization are sometimes constructed: for example, the proportion of a population resident in towns of a given population size at a given moment. Such indices are useful for certain limited purposes, for example, as a measure of demographic change, but in other respects the results they give are not always very helpful, particularly in the African context. What, for instance, is to be made of a measure which is based on the number of cities with a population of 100,000 or more and gives Nigeria an index of urbanization of 4.3, whereas Zambia, whose Copperbelt constitutes a large, modern industrial and urban complex, does not even register (see Appendix in Almond and Coleman 1960)? There are parts of Nigeria where Africans have lived traditionally in large, densely populated settlements, but where the contemporary drift to the towns has been relatively slight. A number of Yoruba towns, for example, have populations in excess of 100,000 but between 1921 and 1952 Yoruba country had the lowest rate of urban growth in Nigeria, and the population of these cities remained fairly homogeneous (Coleman 1958: 75). In Zambia, by contrast, during this same period, about 250,000 Africans, from every part of the country and beyond, came to live and work in the towns of the Copperbelt. It seems more meaningful to me therefore to regard urbanization as involving a process of movement and change; its essence is that it creates the possibility of discontinuity with some pre-existing set of conditions. This may be contrasted with urbanism, which is the way of life in the towns themselves. In this way it may be possible to speak, for example, of

Yoruba urbanism without necessarily implying Yoruba urbanization, though it is clear that this process too is now occurring on an increasing scale (Schwab 1966). It follows also that urbanization cannot be treated as a unidimensional phenomenon: it has demographic, social structural, and cultural aspects, each of which poses separate analytical problems, but which also have to be studied in their interrelations. There are now available studies of a fair number of African towns and cities, so that some attempt at synthesis may be useful at this stage, even though there are still vast lacunae in our knowledge. The main emphasis here, however, will be on the structural aspects of urbanization: in what follows, therefore, I have set out to examine some of the variables that shape the structure of social relations in modern African towns. And since towns are not self-contained social entities, but have their place within a wider field of social relationships, I shall also discuss the relations of these towns to other towns and to the rural areas, and consider briefly the role of the towns within the developing nation.

THE DETERMINANTS OF URBAN SOCIAL STRUCTURE

Many writers nowadays remind us that towns were known in Africa long before the onset of the modern period, particularly in West, and parts of Central, Africa. Many of the famous urban centres of the past have declined, however, and those that have remained important have done so only by undergoing a transformation. The towns with which we are chiefly concerned, then, are new, and in most cases have seen their most rapid growth in the decade or two following the Second World War. During this period the population of many centres more than doubled. Unlike the tratitional towns and cities, these new centres are the product of colonialism: as Dresch (quoted in Balandier 1956: 497) puts it, "they are towns built by whites and occupied by blacks." This factor alone has been of great importance in stamping the towns with a number of general characteristics: great racial and ethnic diversity, accompanied by wide differences between the groups in economic and social status, technical skills, and way of life. In general terms, the dichotomy of rich and poor has correlated closely with that of white and black, between whom a third "colour group" of Asiatics or Levantines frequently intervenes.

These contrasts and divisions within the community are at once reflected in the physical lay-out of the town. The physical separation of the races and of ethnic groups finds its most rigid expression in the principle of *apartheid* in the Union of South Africa, but the tendency for African urban-dwellers to be housed on their own separate estates was almost universal in pre-independence days. Thus as Pons (1965) has recorded of Stanleyville:

The physical lay-out of the town could be seen as both an expression and a symbol of the relations between Africans and Europeans. European residential areas were situated close to, and tended to run into, the area of administrative offices, hotels, shops and other service establishments, while African residential areas were strictly demarcated and well removed from the town centre.

Pons notes too how the location of the African areas contributed to their "suburban" or dormitory character: from early morning until the night curfew which prohibited African entry to the "European town" and European entry to the African areas, there was a large volume of movement between the two. The African area (*centre extra-coutumier* or "municipal location") has indeed some affinities with a suburb, or more often perhaps with a slum in, say, a Western city, but its legal status is quite different. Moreover, the effect of social convention and administration has been to set a barrier round the location and thus effectively to exclude the residents from full participation in the life of the town and the enjoyment of its amenities. Africans in what is now Zambia used to sum it up succinctly: tarred roads always stop at the entrance to the location. In the countries of West Africa, physical segregation was not built into the legal code, but the social pattern has often been broadly similar. In some cases, indeed, the town includes a number of areas which belong to different ethnic or tribal communities. Thus in Monrovia, the capital of Liberia, the Vai, the Kru, and the Bassa each corporately owns and administers its own area (Fraenkel 1964: 52).

The impact of the colonial regime on the physical structure of the town is to be seen in other ways. Of Tanzania's capital, Dar-es-Salaam, for example, it has been remarked that an air of Bavaria still dominates much of its architecture (Bates 1962: 401); while a comparison of Elizabethville with the Copperbelt towns of Zambia will leave no doubts about the national origins of the architects of each. However, the "colonial experience" itself has not been uniform, and other variables which touch more immediately the process of urbanization and the system of social relations that build up within the town need to be brought into the analysis. Three factors in particular appear to merit attention: (1) the "industrial structure," that is, the organizational framework through which the town seeks to achieve those economic aims and purposes that brought it into existence, or give it its present importance; (2) the "civic structure," which derives from the policies and practices of its administration; and (3) the "demographic imperative" (Mitchell 1959), which affects in a variety of ways the social composition of the town and the degree of urban commitment.

As I noted earlier, all the indications in the available literature point to important differences between the patterns of West African urbanization and those encountered further to the south. There are a number of reasons for this, but a major one clearly relates to differences in "industrial structure." The wealth of many of the West African countries has been based on various cash crops: palm-oil, cocoa, or ground nuts. Hence, as Hodgkin has remarked (1956: 78) many of the larger towns have been relatively feeble as centres of production and have developed rather as centres of import and export and, increasingly, of administration. This, I suggest, immediately gives them a character that contrasts sharply with that of more purely industrial towns. In my own work on the Copperbelt, I have drawn attention to the different ways in which urban associations and the patterns of political leadership develop in a mine township as compared with a municipality (Epstein 1958, 1961). The company town, built up around the mine, tends to develop a markedly paternalistic regime providing for and controlling most aspects of the social life of the workers and their families. By contrast, the commercial township, with its hundreds of small firms offering many different forms of employment, is much more diversified in its structure, and its people tend to develop a more independent outlook. Interesting confirmation of this view is to be found in Powdermaker's study (1962) of the impact of mass-communications on Africans in Luanshya, where she was able to show that Africans in the municipal location there bought many more magazines and newspapers and read much more widely than their fellows on the mine. On this argument, it is therefore in the ports and great commercial centres rather than around the mines that variegated interest groups may be expected to emerge and political associations and trade unions to develop and flourish. Certainly this was the case with the Industrial and Commercial Workers Union, one of the first great experiments in African trade unionism: the I.C.U. had its beginning in 1920 among the African dock-workers of Cape Town, then spread to the seaports of Port Elizabeth and East London, and only in 1925 moved its headquarters to Johannesburg (Roux 1948). The growth on the Copperbelt of the African Mine-Workers Union, perhaps the most successful example of African unionism on the continent, might appear to controvert this argument. However, the A.M.W.-T.U. developed in particularly favourable circumstances, and the mine-workers were among the last African workers in what was then Northern Rhodesia to be organized in a union. The mine-workers indeed tended to be held in rather low esteem within the wider African urban community and, it was said, were commonly regarded by the shop-assistants and others as being too "primitive" ever to comprehend the principles of trade unionism (Epstein 1958: 90). It is not enough, then to regard modern urban centres in Africa simply as towns: if we are to understand the systems of social relations developing within them and their implications for social or political change, we have to think of them too in terms of industrial structure—as administrative centres, as market-places, as sea-ports or railway junctions, and as centres of production, or as various combinations of these.

Towns differ not only in the patterns of their economic activities, but also in the institutions and practices through which they are governed. These may relate in some measure to those factors just previously considered, but they are also affected by broader administrative policy, for example the idea of stabilization of the urban population. Thus stabilization was the policy favoured in the Belgian Congo, and its result was the development of the *centre extra-coutumier*, a self-contained residential and administrative unit under the close supervision of a European administrative officer, within which Africans could establish a stable family life in their own homes. The situation that obtained in Stanleyville, where a team of investigators found they had a convenient sampling frame available because all dwelling compounds were officially recorded by number (Pons 1956: 244), contrasts sharply with that in Lagos, where the fieldworker's task was more difficult, partly because the records were inadequate, partly because the household itself was so puzzling to define. Marris notes (1961: vii) that people who shared the same room might be unrelated and live entirely independent lives; on the other hand, a wife might live several streets away from her husband, though she would cook for him every day and depend upon him for support.

Such differences of policy and practice in regard to the housing of African urban-dwellers are usually the expression of basic differences in the approach to urban administration. Other such differences appear in policy in regard to the acquisition of land rights within the township area; in the presence or absence of measures for "influx control"; in the different forms of machinery of urban local government; and in the extent to which Africans participate in civic affairs or in the administration of justice. An interesting illustration of the latter point is to be found in the part played by "tribal" authorities in urban administration in different places. In some cases, for example, the system of local administration has been built up around the principle of tribal representation. In Freetown, Sierra Leone, tribal headmen were officially recognised and played an important part in maintaining law and order (Banton 1957), while on the Copperbelt tribal elders fulfilled similar functions. Moreover, on the Copperbelt and in other towns of Northern Rhodesia, as well as in the *centres extra-coutumiers* of the Belgian Congo, African urban courts had been established by Government where disputes (mainly matrimonial) involving Africans could be settled in accordance with African customary law. By contrast, in Dar-es-Salaam there was no urban court, and the magistrates' courts interfered in such matters hardly at all (Leslie 1963: 220). It is interesting to note, however, that what Leslie calls tribal associations seem to have developed spontaneously in Dar-es-Salaam at quite an early date. Leaders of these associations became the acknowledged spokesmen of their people before the German government, and they appear to have fulfilled many of the functions described for tribal headmen in Freetown and tribal elders on the Copperbelt. In West Africa, so far as I am aware, there were no such urban courts, and, Sierra Leone apart, nothing corresponding to the position of tribal elder within the formal administrative framework. On the other hand, there are frequent references in the West African literature to the existence of large numbers of tribal associations of varying types and degrees of importance (Little 1965), a feature of African urban social life that has been only of marginal significance on the Copperbelt. It seems reasonable to assume therefore that the form of associational life that develops within the towns is closely connected with their civic structure.

The approach to urban phenomena illustrated above also provides a means of ordering within a single framework the material accumulated in numerous studies of urbanization and urbanism in Africa. For example, if the forms of local administration are an important source of variation between towns, then we can classify the towns of Africa by the positions they occupy along a continuum defined in terms of civic structure. At one end of such a scale would be the towns and cities of the Union of South Africa, where the civic structure is marked by segregated housing areas and a tightly administered policy of influx control. At the other end would be the situation of relative laissez-faire that seems characteristic of West Africa. The towns and cities of West Africa have never been the "place of the white man" in the same way as Cape Town or Johannesburg or the urban centres of the Rhodesias. They have commonly grown up around the sites of long-established indigenous settlements, and many features of the old towns have been incorporated in the new (Lloyd 1959). Often, indeed, they are syntheses of villages in which each village, though absorbed in the growing town, has preserved its identity (Hodgkin 1956: 72). Clearly such centres have a much more organic character

than those in which African town-dwellers are required to live in municipal locations or mine compounds. It follows that in the West African countries there has been a much less rigid approach to matters of urban administration: not only is there less direct control over housing and housing conditions, but there is not that same insistence on maintaining public standards of hygiene and sanitation that is one of the hallmarks of the settler-dominated city to the south. In Lagos, we are told, the visitor who explores the immediate environs of the large department stores and office blocks must still pick his way amongst rams and chickens rummaging among the garbage, as he seeks a dry foothold beside the open drains (Marris 1961: vii): in Johannesburg the down-town slum yards like Rooiyard (Hellmann 1948) were systematically demolished long ago and their populations removed to considerable distances from the city centre. Between these two extremes was the former Belgian Congo. There, as we have seen, theoretically "tight" urban administration went hand in hand with a policy of urban stabilization. Within the *centres extra-coutumiers* Africans were encouraged to establish their own homes and were granted loans to acquire a plot of land and build on it. This had a number of important implications; for while on the one hand the organization and control of the *centre* suggest many parallels with the locations of Central and South Africa, its residents enjoyed in certain respects an area of choice unknown in the locations. On his plot a man could gather around him a small body of kin and so create a unit somewhat similar to that of the traditional village. In this respect Congo urban patterns of residence seem a little closer to those of certain West African towns than to those of southern Africa. A further point is that the Congolese were also permitted to use their plots as business premises. Many established small shops (see, e.g., Pons 1961). While this did not produce a new bourgeoisie on the West African model, it did mean that men who were no longer able or willing to seek wage employment (and also divorced women and elderly widows) were able to support themselves in the town and did not have to return to the village as in South Africa or Zambia.

African towns may also be classified from the standpoint of their "industrial structure," and here again we find the same broad geographical pattern of contrasts. As noted, the wealth of West Africa has been built up around the export of cash crops. The economy remained essentially land-based, but wealthy Africans frequently built themselves town-houses and increasingly sent their children to be educated overseas. Moreover, European personnel was often unobtainable, and the commercial firms had to offer posts to Africans which elsewhere would have been reserved for Europeans. The road was thus opened up for the earlier emergence of a better-educated and more numerous class of African businessmen, lawyers, and junior officials. By contrast, in the centres of South Africa and Zambia, built around extractive industries, the African urban population has been made up predominantly of manual workers, and a commercial or professional class has been both numerically and politically insignificant.

A classification of towns in terms of industrial structure does not coincide completely with that based on civic structure; at a number of points, the industrial classification appears to cut across the other, which was mainly an expression of the settler/non-settler cleavage. For example, it is my impression that in (Southern) Rhodesia, whose main cities have been manufacturing rather than marketing centres, more scope has been allowed to African business enterprise. A number of Africans in Salisbury and Bulawayo have emerged as wealthy businessmen and store-keepers. Many of these seem to have been associated with the African nationalist movement, but it may not be without significance that African merchants in Rhodesia have been noticeably more "accommodationist" (Coleman 1960: 273), and the nationalist movement itself, at least until quite recently, less militant than elsewhere. Secondly, a number of important mining centres have developed in West Africa, and it would be interesting to learn whether they have more in common with, for example, the towns of the Copperbelt than with other towns within the West African region. A study of one of these townships, for instance of Enugu in Nigeria, would be of great interest. In particular, it might tell us a great deal more about the development and role of trade unions in these countries, whose leaders now stress the changed character of trade unionism under independence (Friedland 1964).

Southall (1961: 6) has distinguished two types of town: type A, the old, established, slowly growing town, found mostly in West Africa, Tanganyika (Tanzania), and Uganda; and type B, the new town of mushroom growth, primarily found in the Union of South Africa, the Rhodesias, Kenya, and the Belgian Congo. Examination of the data from the standpoints of industrial and civic structure leads to a refinement of Southall's categories; it counteracts any tendency to view urbanization too simplistically, for example in terms of broad contrasts between geographical regions; and it raises issues for further inquiry.

The third factor which needs to be considered here is the demographic. Many observers have drawn attention to the imbalances which occur when rural people seek work in towns. Typically, the structure of the urban population is marked by an excess of men over women and an over-all predominance of people aged 20–40. These factors relate to the patterns of migrancy and to the continuing relations between the town and the areas from which it draws its supply of labour: all have profound implications for the system of social relations developing within the town.

The drift to the towns is the universal concomitant of early industrialization, but the way in which it occurs is not everywhere the same. In 19th-century England, for example, the expansion of the industrial towns was achieved by the flow of labour into them from the smaller rural towns in their immediate hinterland. In Africa a few instances of progressive migration have been reported (e.g., Doucy and Feldheim 1956), but in the main urbanization has proceeded, not by a series of stages, but by a sharp leap from small village to distant urban centre, from *kisendji*, the ancient way of life of the tribe, to *kizungu*, the "civilized" way of life of the towns (Pons 1956: 250). But if in Africa the transition to the town has been somewhat sharper, paradoxically, the break with the village has been less radical. The new African urban labourer remained bound by social, political, and even religious ties to his kinsmen in the rural areas so that, as Mitchell observes (1961: 232), it is the circulation of labour rather than its migration which has become its characteristic feature. In this context

physical distance becomes a factor of considerable importance, the response to urban living amongst different groups being related, at least in part, to the ease with which they can return to their rural homes. So in the East African sea-port of Dar-es-Salaam, whose main sources of labour are not too remote, the agricultural seasons still have immediacy, since "indebtedness is relieved for many by a capital sum accruing from the rice harvest in June/July, mainly from fields in their home districts" (Leslie 1963: 7). Similarly, the fact that East London in South Africa is able to meet most of its labour requirements from the reserves of the Ciskei and Transkei, which lie on its very door-step, accounts for the relative tribal and linguistic homogeneity of its African population (Reader 1961). More important, the ease with which large numbers of East London labourers are able to move back and forth between town and country at week-ends puts the Xhosa migrant in a very different position from that, say, of the "Blantyre" in Johannesburg, who, some thousands of miles from his home in Malawi, is necessarily less amenable to the pressures of incapsulation. Indeed, even within East London itself, the factor of distance may have some relevance to the cleavage of "Red" and "School" migrants described by Mayer (1961), for it is the districts which immediately surround the city which are predominantly "Red," while the majority of "School" Xhosa come from further afield.

It is not simply a matter of distance, however; there is also the question of the *situation* of the home area, giving rise to what Leslie has called "the community of the route." Leslie describes how, when Dar-es-Salaam was a very small town, and most of the immigrants came by foot, the earliest entrants naturally set down their loads at the first opportunity, on the side of town nearest to the direction of their coming. As others followed them, and went to the address of those already there, and then "hived off" and built themselves houses nearby, there was a perceptible polarization of tribes, each group tending to inhabit the quarter nearest its place of origin. Though increasingly blurred as the town grew, the original pattern of geographical groups survived and is still perceptible even today. Similar processes have been at work on the towns of the Copperbelt (Mitchell 1953) and elsewhere. Pons (1965), for example, has noted how in Stanleyville the physical distribution of different tribal groups around the different areas of entry to the town offsets the implications of the high degree of heterogeneity in the population at large and emphasizes the significance of each township as a distinctive locality of fellow-tribesmen. With time and the increasing flow of people to the town, the populations of these localities become ethnically more mixed, but their character, deriving from the pattern of original settlement, is never wholly obscured. Such grouping emphasizes too the very different patterns of incorporation of various tribes into the life of the town and widely differing sets of urban-rural relations.

THE SOCIAL STRUCTURE OF THE TOWN

Wirth (1938) has offered a sociological definition of the city as a relatively large, dense, and permanent settlement of heterogeneous individuals, and from these postulates has sought to deduce its major identifying characteristics. Urban social relations are dominated, on this view, by the cash nexus and the labour market, and the contacts of the city tend to be impersonal, superficial, transitory, and segmental. Diversification allows for a greater degree of variability in personal behaviour, and, as primary groupings decline in significances, there is a corresponding emphasis on formal procedures of social control and on the development of associations. The towns of modern Africa with which we are mainly concerned satisfy the criteria of Wirth's definition of the city, and there is much in his analysis which has an immediate relevance to African urbanism. Indeed, many of those who have written of the African towns in terms of their poverty, the break-down of family life, the rise of prostitution, juvenile delinquency, and crime, and the problems of psychic maladjustment are describing phenomena that are fully accounted for in Wirth's theory. All of these are undoubtedly facts of the African urban situation, no less than they were of Chicago when studied by Wirth and his colleagues in the 1920's, or of Manchester nearly a century earlier, which presented itself to Engels as "the dissolution of mankind into monads." Nevertheless, the picture is still curiously lopsided and leaves out of account many of the more positive features of urban life. The Africans who flock into the urban centres are not monads in a "world of brutal indifference where it occurs to no man to honour another with so much as a glance" (Engels 1950: 24). Quite to the contrary, what is so universally striking about the life of African towns is its ebullience and gusto, its camaraderie, and the casual ease with which social contacts are established (Wilson and Mafeje 1963; Sampson 1956; Ekwensi 1954). Nor is this simply a reflection of "the peculiar *humaneness* in African social relations" of which African intellectuals frequently speak (Worsley 1964: 127). The point is that the African who comes to town rarely arrives as a complete stranger. The situation described by Leslie (1963: 33) for Dar-es-Salaam probably has universal application:

It would be difficult to find a single African who arrived in Dar-es-Salaam knowing not a soul.... Almost every African who decides to come [there] comes to a known address, where lives a known relation; this relation will meet him, take him in and feed him and show him the ropes, help him seek a job ... until he considers himself able to launch out for himself and take a room of his own.

Every African urban-dweller tends therefore to be involved in a complex network of social relations, composed of ties with neighbours, work-mates, friends, and acquaintances. At the core of the network, however, are those who are readily fitted into the elastic categories of kinship provided by a classificatory system of terminology and those who count as fellow-tribesmen (Epstein 1961). These ties clearly introduce an element of stability into an extremely fluid situation: they link together large numbers of individuals not only within the one town, but between one town and another, and between town and country. More than this, they provide the basis for a more elaborate scheme of organizing social relationships in the new environment. I refer here to what has been variously termed "urban tribalism" (Mitchell 1956a; Epstein 1958), "supertribalism" (Rouch 1956), or "ethnicity" (Wallerstein 1960). As Mitchell has so clearly demonstrated, the "tribalism" that is so prevalent a feature of African urbanism is a phenomenon of a quite different order from the "tribalism" of the rural areas: in the latter it refers to a particular kind of social regimen in which social relationships are organized within a distinctive

structural and cultural framework; in the former the tribe is no longer an organized political and social unit, but serves rather as a means of classifying a heterogeneous urban population into a limited number of meaningful social categories. Tribalism in this sense operates in a number of different urban contexts or fields of relationship. Most immediately, it offers a guide to behaviour in situations of casual interaction amongst relative strangers; it provides the primary badge of identity, to which even the smallest child is able to respond. Tribalism again tends to be important in the sphere of domestic relationships and leisure time activities: wives tend to be sought most frequently within the tribe or wider "ethnic group," and it is within this category also that a man most frequently finds his friends and drinking companions. Then very frequently, too, the "tribal principle" provides the basis for the formation of associations which serve a variety of functions as mutual aid or burial societies, political pressure groups, and the like. The significance of these associations seems to vary from place to place, and since their character and functions are not always carefully distinguished in the literature, the matter may perhaps be usefully considered here.

Tribal associations have sometimes been spoken of as an adaptive mechanism, easing the adjustment of migrants to the strange surroundings of the town. Thus, according to Little (1957: 593), the association facilitates this adjustment by substituting for the extended group of kinsmen a grouping based upon common interest which is capable of serving many of the same needs. Balandier seems to be making a similar point when he notes of Brazzaville (quoted in Wallerstein 1960: 478) that the early emergence of ethnic associations tends to indicate a high degree of uprootedness among the ethnic group and is to be found particularly in small minorities. Support for this view is perhaps to be found in the fact that where a particular tribe is dominant in the town, or enjoys a special relationship to it, as in the case of the Ganda in Kampala, its members are unlikely to form a separate tribal association (cp. Leslie 1963: 40).

Associations, then, are of different types, cater for different social categories, and serve different ends. The form of tribal association in Dar-es-Salaam referred to earlier seems to have had its origin in the insistence of the German Administration that the dead from the hospital be buried by their particular tribes. Recognized leaders of each tribe were appointed to see that this was done and to report all deaths for entry in the register. In addition, these leaders organized funeral parties and also periodic dances. They also seem to have acted as arbitrators in disputes. Indeed, as noted earlier, the arrangement corresponded closely to the institutions of tribal eldership and tribal headmanship which were to develop on the Copperbelt and in Freetown. All three served similar purposes, none of which required any attempt at incorporation: there was no constituted group with a formal membership and no set of rules to which all were required to subscribe. In short, to apply the term tribal association to such an arrangement can be very misleading. Certainly, they represent a very different form of organization from such groups as the Temne *compins* described by Banton (1957), variants of which seem to flourish in West and East Africa. These represent, in a sense, a later phase in the process of urbanization. No longer dominated by the conservative elders, they tend to have a formal

membership drawn mainly from amongst the ranks of the young men aspiring to prestige and status in the urban world. This aspect of the groups is at once evident in the number of officeholders and the proliferation of titles as well as in the patterns of their activities. The young men of the Temne *compins* believed in "civilization," by which they meant the adoption of certain European and Creole practices. (Banton [1957: 175, 173] remarks that the food served up at some of their social events resembled the sort fashionable at European cocktail parties.) Since tribe remained the primary category of interaction and therefore a ready means of mobilizing support, leaders in these groups could use them as a stepping stone to political office at the local or national level. Yet another kind of development has been the emergence of large-scale Tribal Unions such as those of the Kenya Luo or some of the Nigerian groups. Of a much higher order of organizational complexity, they constitute in some cases pan-tribal federations providing, as Coleman observes (1960: 319), the infrastructure for comprehensive nationalist movements and competitive political parties. A fourth type of grouping approximates more to the type of exclusive social club. These emerge typically amongst small immigrant groups whose members enjoy a much higher social and economic status than other sections of the urban African community.

All of these various forms of organization have their basis in tribalism, but it is equally clear that they cannot be adequately understood as simple manifestations of the "tribal principle." As the towns have grown, their African populations have been increasingly diversified in terms of occupation, formal education, and style of life.

This does not necessarily imply the emergence within the towns of a class structure on the Western model. On the other hand, a number of studies do attest to the development of systems of social stratification defined in terms of status groups in the Weberian sense (Xydias 1956; Michell and Epstein 1959; Schwab 1961). For many years it was a commonplace in the literature of urban sociology that associations have an overriding importance in the social organization of the town, but this view has come to be increasingly challenged. Various empirical studies in the United States (e.g., Komarovsky 1946; Dotson 1951) and Britain (e.g., Bottomore 1950; Stacey 1960) have shown a close connection between membership of associations and socioeconomic status: the lower one's position on the scale, the fewer the associations to which one belongs. My own evidence from the Copperbelt presents a similar picture, and I suspect it is equally valid elsewhere in Africa. The vast majority of recent immigrants to towns are not "joiners," and it seems to me to be an obscuring of the sociological issues to argue, as Little has recently done (1965: 24), that the growth of voluntary associations represents the newly arrived migrants' response to urban conditions, "a spontaneous adjustment to their environment." I would argue rather that tribal associations have to be understood in their relationship to associations of other types and to the over-all status system that has developed within the community. A recent study carried out in Kampala (Parkin 1965) brings out the close relationship between membership in various associations (tribal and otherwise), residence in different urban neighbourhoods and localities, and the total status system. Accounts of Kampala (e.g., Southall 1956a; South-

all and Gutkind 1956) suggest closer affinities with the urban centres of West Africa than with those of Central or South Africa. Similar detailed studies in one or other of the great West African cities might go a long way to explaining the "exuberant growth" of voluntary associations there and at the same time help to provide a more adequate picture of West African urbanism.

RELATIONS BETWEEN TOWNS

We have seen that circulation of population between town and country is a characteristic feature of social life in much of contemporary Africa. There is also considerable movement between towns. For example, Mitchell (1953) has shown that newcomers to the Copperbelt move about a good deal in the first five years of their residence, and then settle down in one town. This raises at once important questions about the spatial distribution of urban centres within a country, the relations that develop between them, and the implications that variation in these regards has for social change, particularly in the political field. Curiously enough, these topics find little mention in the anthropological literature, but they are touched upon by Coleman, a political scientist (1960: 273). Many countries of Africa are, in effect, "one-city states," and the single major city, also the territorial capital, often dominates such a country's political life. Coleman develops the argument that this circumstance permits concentration of political activity in one place and thus facilitates the mobilization of political strength. By contrast, in those countries having two or more major cities, such as Zambia (Lusaka vs. the Copperbelt), Rhodesia (Bulawayo vs. Salisbury), or the Congo (Leopoldville vs. Elizabethville), African political leadership has been dispersed, if not competitive, and it has been far more difficult to organize a comprehensive nationalist party on a territorial basis. This argument has considerable merits, but it seems to me to miss a point that is very relevant for the understanding of urbanization: what is important here is not so much the number of different foci of interest, but how the different centres are involved with one another. Zambia and the Congo present an interesting contrast from this point of view. The Congo centres were not only physically distant from one another, but their industrial structures were also quite different. In addition, they tended to draw their African populations from quite different areas. In short, there appears to have been little convergence between them and it would be interesting to know what kind of communication took place between the major Congo cities. By comparison, in the towns of the Copperbelt, while there were frequently concentrations of particular tribes in any given town, in the main all the principal urban centres drew on the same territorial population. The number of the towns and their close physical proximity to one another meant that they stood out in opposition to one another *as towns*. Each in time developed its own subtle distinctiveness, so that it used to be said, for example, that some of the Copperbelt towns had characteristic styles of drumming and dress. Opposition between the towns was expressed through the football league and other forms of competition. There were also links which cut across these divisions: members of opposing football clubs from different towns were drawn from the same tribal groups; citizens of different towns were yet members of the same trade unions; and all townsmen, the "sugarboys," contrasted themselves with the rural bumpkins. In short, for an understanding of the role of urbanization in developing new sets of identities, a key question would seem to be to what extent the growth of towns gives rise to a system of cross-cutting ties and allegiances.

TOWN, COUNTRY, AND NATION

The process of urbanization thus has several aspects. One, the demographic, involves the redistribution of population as people move from rural to urban areas. A second refers to participation in social relations in town and the changes in behaviour patterns which such participation involves. These are closely related processes, though, as Mitchell reminds us (1956b: 694), they need to be kept analytically distinct. The third aspect of urbanization is a "feed-back" process; it is concerned with the influence of town on country and the implications of urban growth for social change. Wilson (1941–42) has analyzed brilliantly the concomitants of a system of migrant labour, showing how instead of stimulating an agricultural revolution in the reserves to match the industrial revolution in the towns, it led to rural deterioration. Circulation of population between town and country did something to ameliorate these conditions, since a certain amount of wealth did filter back in this way to the tribal areas. Circulation of the population was, as Wilson noted, "the keystone of the unstable arch of present day Northern Rhodesia economy." This, however, is only one aspect of the impact of town and country. The towns are the locus of the new civilization: here are to be found new concentrations of economic and political power, and the new avenues of communications along which the influences of the towns may reach out into the countryside in varied and subtle ways. The important questions to be asked here are therefore: What are the relations of town and country? More specifically, since we are concerned with countries most of which have only recently attained nationhood, what implications do the varying features of urban social systems have for national integration?

Two assumptions commonly underlie much discussion of this aspect of urbanization: (1) that towns inevitably act as instruments of social transformation; and (2) that change is uniformly in the same direction and of the same character. Both seem to derive from the fact that the model of urban-rural relations has frequently been constructed around the response of a single tribe or area, which was deemed to be typical. Wilson's study of Broken Hill, where the analysis concentrated on the experience of the Bemba, is a case in point. Had he examined the position of the neighbouring Mambwe, Wilson might well have been led to modify his conclusions (cf. Watson 1958). More recent studies suggest that both assumptions may need to be qualified. In some parts, for example, far from bringing about a transformation in the countryside, the pull of the towns becomes, paradoxically, a means by which the traditional system in the reserves is perpetuated. Here rural-urban relations are in a state of relatively stable equilibrium. Thus amongst the Pedi and other South African groups, where land is critically short, the export of surplus man-power to the towns does not merely prevent the disintegration of the rural social system, but positively reinforces that system (Sansom 1965). The network of rural ties is maintained in the towns, where kinsmen and others assist one

another in getting jobs, frequently with the same firm, and finding accommodation. Moreover, individuals who achieve influential positions in the towns can translate them into positions of prestige within the tribal system when eventually they return home. It is against this kind of background that one has to understand the remarkable persistence in East London, a city that has been established for more than a hundred years, of the division between "Red" and "School" Xhosa. Incapsulated within their *amakhaya* cells, "Red" Xhosa may spend many years in town and yet apparently remain carefully insulated from the typical diversions and blandishments that the city has to offer; they are in the town, but never of it (Mayer 1961).

The response, then, of different groups to the pull of the towns is not uniform. Some groups, for example the Ila of Zambia or the Masai of Kenya, have (for reasons which are still imperfectly understood) consistently rejected town life. The responses of others have been conditioned by features of the indigenous culture and social structure, or even in some cases by special constitutional arrangements, such as those once enjoyed by the Barotse of Zambia (which from time to time created difficulties between the Barotse and other tribes in the towns). Such differences are reflected in different patterns of incorporation into the life of the town. In Lunsar, Sierra Leone, for example, the traditionally slave-owning and Muslimized Fulbe (Fula) seek to minimize their involvement with other groups, and they do this by avoiding manual occupations or others which would involve status inferiority: they work as tailors or as petty traders and the like (Butcher 1965). (Yao on the Copperbelt, also traditionally slave-owners and Muslims, are also to be found predominantly in the category of the self-employed.) In his study of Stanleyville, Pons (1965) has examined in some detail the strikingly different patterns of urban incorporation of the Babua, Lokele, and Topoke.

None of this, of course, is to be taken to mean that we are dealing with a simple transplantation of the tribal system into an urban context. As Wallerstein points out (1960: 477), the emergence of modern ethnic groups is a function of the urban social situation. On the other hand, unless we take into account the different constellations of rural-urban relations, we cannot hope to understand the significance that ethnicity comes to assume in the wider political field. Wallerstein argues indeed that ethnicity serves to aid national integration in a number of ways. Yet if the towns are new focal points of integration, they are also a fertile source of conflict, so that ethnicity may come to play an important part in shaping, in some cases perhaps even dominating, the character of national politics. Thus it has been said of the Congo that ethnic nationalisms were born in the large urban centres, where Congolese of different origins, speaking different languages, intermingled. These contacts, far from "bringing their hearts close together," only made them more conscious of their differences and strengthened their feelings of mutual alienation (van Wing, quoted in Lemarchand 1964: 99). Yet this development has not been universal, even in the Congo, and clearly a number of different factors are at work. There is the question of the number of different tribes represented and the relative positions of strength or influence they have been able to achieve in the new setting. The dominance of a single group, for numerical or other

reasons, is likely to stimulate ethnic particularism among the other tribes. The converse of this proposition is illustrated in Stanleyville where, according to Lemarchand (1964), the ethnic diversity of its population was the main reason for its conspicuous indifference to the appeals of ethnic nationalism. There were, as one of Lemarchand's African informants observed, too many tribes in Stanleyville, and none of them had any striking predominance. A second relevant factor is the emergence of an urban class structure. One might expect that the relationships of social class that build up in towns would tend to cut across the divisions of tribe. This does happen, but what also seems to occur frequently is that the lines of an incipient class structure correspond with tribal or ethnic differences (e.g., McCulloch 1956).

Once again, if ethnic particularism is a product of the towns, it also has to be understood in the context of perduring rural-urban relations. The differential response to, and participation in, the life of the town amongst the tribes may also be an expression of different regional interests. For example, Mitchell and I have shown that while "tribalism" is a primary category of social interaction amongst Africans in the towns of the Copperbelt, the tribal nexus is frequently cross-cut by membership in trade unions, staff associations, and other bodies. On the other hand, there are some groups which do not appear to become involved in the urban "melting-pot," a notable instance being the Ila of the Southern Province of Zambia, a group with a long-established reputation for aggressive independence and preoccupation with their cattle. (The African opposition party in contemporary Zambia, the African National Congress, whose leader is a Muila, draws its main support from the Southern and Central Provinces amongst the congeries of people known as the Bantu Botatwe.) Again, regional interests seem to lie behind the formation of large tribal unions in Nigeria and the intense struggles that have gone on over the years between the Ibo and Yoruba (Mercier 1965: 490–93; Coleman 1958). When emergence of different political parties expresses the diversity of regional interests rather than more purely ideological differences, there may be much less room for the operation of cross-cutting ties. Presumably these factors I have just been outlining weigh heavily on political leaders striving to create a new nation: perhaps from this point of view they may contribute something to our understanding of the emergence of one-party states in Africa and of the opposition in some parts between the new national leadership and the tribal chiefs.

SITUATIONAL CHANGE AND CULTURAL PERSISTENCE

The African who leaves his village to come to town at once enters a new world whose symbols are increasingly, in Louis Wirth's words, the factory whistle and the traffic light. The town has its own physical structure; but more than this, it has its own structure of social relations. Viewed against the background of tribal life, urban existence involves changes—what Mitchell (1966) has recently suggested we should call "situational" as distinct from "processive" or historical change —in almost every department of social life: in family and kinship relations, in types of association and grouping and forms of leadership, in the use of leisure, and in patterns of speech

(Epstein 1959). Indeed, given the common technological base of modern urban society, claims such as that "the social structure of urban Africans is increasingly tending . . . to approximate more closely to Western institutions" (Hellmann 1956: 743) might appear at first sight as self-evident. However, two points need to be noted. First, the processes of urban social growth in Africa are not automatic or pre-determined. African urbanism, as I have repeatedly stressed, is not characterized by uniformity, and Hellmann's delineation of the South African situation has clearly less immediate relevance to West Africa. Secondly, as Hellmann herself argued on an earlier occasion (1937: 432), the Africans are not a supine people, and their incorporation into the wage-earning economy of the towns has not involved the complete submergence of their indigenous culture. Mitchell (1965) shows how Africans in Salisbury continue to interpret their experience of personal misfortune in the urban world in terms of categories and assumptions that have their roots in tribal culture and society. I would argue from this that in the study of urban social relations we need to pay attention to content as well as to form. For example, the African trade union leader may be expected to have much in common with his English counterpart; to be successful, he must be able to organize, to hold and sway an audience, and to negotiate. The character of his leadership will also be shaped, however, by his own conception of his role and the expectations which his followers have of him, and these may be very different from those of a typical British trade unionist. Thus for many Africans on the Copperbelt the union leader takes on many of the attributes of the tribal chief and is expected to behave like one in certain contexts. African urban institutions, even when most closely fashioned on an alien model, do not become a mere mirror-image of the prototype; they become infused with elements that derive from African tribal culture. As I mentioned at the outset, urbanization and Westernization often go closely together in modern Africa, but analytically they must not be confused. It was this point which presumably Hodgkin had in mind when he spoke of the capacity of African townsmen to create a new indigenous civilization. All the studies I have cited in this paper refer, unfortunately, to the "colonial past." As studies come to be made of urbanization and urbanism under conditions of independence we may hope to see such questions as these explored much further.

Comments[1]

by Edward M. Bruner

The strength of this paper is that it summarizes a series of empirical findings that have emerged in recent studies of African urbanization, and it presents them in terms of a theoretical position that takes off from the views advanced by Max Gluckman. Epstein goes beyond Gluckman, but my comment is that he does not go far enough. I agree with Epstein's conclusions but suggest that he is still operating within a Gluckman-type framework, which somewhat befuddles our understanding of the urbanization process, particularly in larger comparative perspective. Gluckman and his colleagues, despite their outstanding contributions to the study of towns and, of course, to social anthropology in general, are Africa-bound.

[1]The original article was submitted to 34 scholars. The comments of those who responded, along with the author's reply, follow.

Gluckman tells us to view urban data in an urban context rather than against a village-tribal-rural background. He says we cannot explain social relations in the city simply by reference to the forms of social relations that exist in the village, and that we must take full account of the urban situation in which these relations have developed and in which they are expressed. All students of urbanization, I believe, would agree with Epstein that Gluckman's views, at the time they were expressed, served as an "invaluable corrective" to earlier excesses. Urbanization had long been seen rather negatively, as progressive disintegration from a pristine "tribal" system.

Epstein is critical of Gluckman's position because it does not shed light on the process of becoming a townsman nor on the degree of commitment to urban life and to urban behavior patterns. We know that residence in an urban center does not automatically make a man urbanized. Epstein also states that Gluckman treats all towns as if they were alike, and he points up the importance of dealing with variations in urban social systems. These are valid points.

When Epstein deals with rural areas and the village background, he does so in the limited sense of considering rural-urban relations; but he still does not take into account the larger societal context in which these relations are embedded. He writes about the rural and the urban as if they were two separate and partially autonomous systems. In the Copperbelt region and in the areas of Africa studied by anthropologists associated with the Rhodes-Livingstone Institute, there may have been a legal, political, and social separation between the village and the city. Elsewhere in Africa, there is less discontinuity between the rural and the urban; and in countries like Japan and Mexico with a long urban tradition and an established state organization, rural and urban areas have become even more similar. Here a rural migrant to the city confronts people very much like himself. We are in effect dealing, in parts of Africa, with temporary labor migration rather than with more permanent urbanization and with a tribal-colonial situation rather than with a developed indigenous civilization. These aspects of the larger context make a vast difference in the nature of the urbanization process.

The less discontinuity there is between rural and urban areas, the less applicable is the Gluckman viewpoint. The rural and the urban are never completely independent and autonomous; they are invariably related in many diverse and subtle ways. Epstein's major weakness in this paper is that he does not take account of the diversity, but sees urbanization processes almost entirely as a function of factors intrinsic to the city itself.

The industrial structure, for example, is seen as an aspect of town organization; but degree of industrialization, one of the key variables in the urbanization process, cannot be localized within the boundaries of a city. Industrialization is a function of a larger region and influences the nature of social life for all who reside within the region, whether they live in a city, town, or hamlet. The fact that Urbana, Illinois, is not an industrial town is less important for understanding the quality of social relations within Urbana than the fact it is located in the American Midwest. Again, Epstein relates the forms of associational life to the civic structure of the town, and his observations here are very suggestive; but administrative services provided through the city government, such as welfare services, are more dependent upon national-level institutions than upon local urban ones.

Epstein makes some excellent comments on ethnicity and tribalism which I have found to be applicable to many areas of Indonesia as well as to the African cases cited. It is clear that tribalism in the village is not the same as tribalism in the city.

But again, the nature and extent of "urban tribalism" [are] not entirely dependent upon local characteristics of specific cities. [They are] a function of the nation or region. In countries with many different ethnic groups in which no one group has a majority, we may find the same degree of urban tribalism in a wide variety of different towns, irrespective of variations in industrial or civil structure.

All of us working in this field are interested in how people live in cities and in how social life changes as a consequence of urban residence. We must be careful, however, not to assume too firm or direct a connection between where one lives and how one lives. Culture patterns are not so dependent upon locality or place of residence, nor does the city influence all aspects of life to the same extent. Family life in an administrative city such as Washington, D.C. may not differ at all from family life in Gary, Indiana, particularly for those whose occupations are not linked to the administrative or industrial structure of their respective cities.

In any case, Epstein is moving in the right direction. He has made a number of insightful comments and has presented us with a fine summary of recent research in Africa.

by Peter C. W. Gutkind

As early as 1931, Julian Huxley predicted in his *Africa View* that "Towns will certainly be the crux of the native problem in the tropics;" and if the recently launched *African Urban Notes* is a reliable guide to research currently in progress, clearly a large number of social scientists have decided that urban life in Africa is an important feature of the general transformation of the continent. It is quite clear that we have come a long way since Epstein (1958: 224) wrote: "As a field of study, African urbanism is still largely virgin territory, in which much of the preliminary spade-work has yet to be done." The days of the generalized urban survey are over; we are moving into more structured investigations. Thus Epstein's helpful summary of some, but by no means all, of the literature and his critique and suggestions for alternative lines of investigation are appropriately timed.

Epstein states his main theme as the examination of "some of the variables that shape the structure of social relations in modern African towns." Contributions are badly needed, however, not only from social anthropologists, but also from political scientists, economists, historians, and others who might not cast their conceptualization in such a framework. We must be more eclectic. The study of urban systems provides scope for many disciplines, and we still need solid empirical studies judiciously blended with fresh theoretical approaches. For one thing, we have tended to concentrate on the large urban areas at the expense of the smaller centers and townships. Thus we have often learned a good deal about the main features of the capital city, as these have crystallized by the time research got under way, but little about the processes of urban growth and urbanism in its early phases. We have often concentrated on the atypical urban structure. Particularly in West Africa, where there are many small towns and even more small townships under 5,000 in population, much interesting work on the lines of the Lunsar (Sierra Leone) study must be undertaken.

We also need to put some order into the large number of variables, many of which we have not yet rigorously isolated and controlled, which many researchers have suggested as anchorages for controlled comparative research. Without such research we cannot hope to arrive at general explanations. This in turn might suggest that we need to pay more attention to the specific methodologies required in African urban research. It is possible that we social anthropologists, reared on the "rural tradition of the tribe," lack the techniques (particularly in the field of demography) to work in societies less homogeneous and larger-scale than those we are used to. We may be led to take too structural an approach, ignoring the enormous range of personal behaviour and institutional arrangements to be found in urban Africa. No clear and consistent model of African urban life has yet developed. Individuals and groups are all engaged in a battle to keep their heads above water. Each African urbanite manipulates the social, economic, and political order to such an extent, and in such a variety of ways, that at times there appear to be as many adaptations to urban life in Africa as there are Africans living in the new and older towns on that continent. Of course, this is not the case. African urban society is not an indeterminate, amorphous mass. Rather, its coherence is based upon characteristics of social organization which we have not always seen in this light.

In order to understand this coherence, it is probably wise to select relatively small units for observation. Even the smaller urban areas in Africa have developed an internal complexity which calls for a comparative study of specific neighbourhoods, particular occupational and political groupings, and special interest groups of all sorts. If the urban areas of Africa are composites of a large number of discrete and/or overlapping subsystems, then micro—rather than macro—studies should have priority. Many West African towns are of such a size now that we find towns within towns and a wide variety of neighbourhoods; within the towns of Eastern and Southern Africa, housing estates may differ markedly one from the other. I doubt very much that we have reached the stage in which we can order "within a single framework the material accumulated in numerous studies of urbanization and urbanism in Africa." A single framework will lead invariably to the very tendency which Epstein deplores: the "tendency to view urbanization too simplistically." We simply do not know enough yet about urbanization in Africa in general terms.

I cannot share Epstein's or Mayer's criticism of Gluckman's formulation, for it seems to me that Gluckman helped us specifically to look for the very particular processes of becoming a townsman when he wrote: "An African townsman is a townsman, and an African miner is a miner." This is *the* point of theoretical articulation. What Mayer calls Gluckman's "alternation model" does not preclude insight into the processes of growth and change. Besides, the fact remains that urban Africans do often, although less so today, move from town to country and back again. What I would like to see (and Epstein hints at this) are a number of exploratory studies showing how urban Africans—of whatever length of urban residence—view the urban areas in which they live, or why they move from one town to another or from one neighbourhood in the same town to another. I think that studies like these might help us to sort out how particularistic perception is crosscut by universalistic characteristics of organization. Epstein himself has carried out such a study (see Epstein 1961). We need many more studies of the activities of individuals and groups if we are to find out how Africans interpret, and handle, their urban experiences. We will then be able to show why some urban Africans maintain their ties with tribal culture while others become new urbanites.

We should also pay greater attention to the study of the social problems which are increasingly manifest in the urban areas of Africa. Poverty, vice, and the predicaments of unemployment, now faced by millions of Africans, present an endless variety of social situations which open up important features of social organization of African urban life.

Finally, we need far more time perspective in African urban studies. Thus far our studies have been almost wholly synchronic, although most of us have felt the need to give a little historical depth. What we need are more diachronic studies whereby we keep under observation the older and the newer African towns and townships over considerable periods of time. Demographers tell us that some towns grow in population by as much as 10% per year. If this is so, we must look at each of these towns at least once every three years. This calls for coordinated research.

by Michael M. Horowitz

In this very welcome paper, Epstein properly insists on a conceptual distinction between the culture of cities and the processes of their development, and makes a useful division of the process of urbanization into demographic (and ecologic?), structural, and cultural aspects. I shall limit myself to a brief comment on ethnic organization.

Once Whyte (1943) had documented the social organization of an urban slum, shortly after the publication of Wirth's article referred to by Epstein, there was little reason to continue in the belief that urban social relationships "tend to be impersonal, superficial, transitory, and segmental." The phenomenon of "urban tribalism" is recurrent wherever cities receive migrants from diverse ethnic backgrounds.

Where mobility is severely restricted, or possible only in terms of a whole group advancing its interests against some other group, "urban tribalism" seems to be quite durable, and the city has the features of pluralism. The towns of the classic Sudanic states had these characteristics: economic activities were distributed among ethnic segments, and all were subject to the political domination of one of them. Superficially, at least, this resembles the colonial situation in many places.

In the modern town, ethnic segmentation is probably transitional. The individual may see his advantage either in identification with an ethnic segment or in membership in some other association. Choosing the latter can involve risking the security of an ordinary life among kinsmen and neighbors for the chance of greater rewards among strangers. The rewards of ethnic association are more immediately intelligible to the migrant; those of other associations are more remote. Where there are encouragements for individual mobility through the sequential acquisition of statuses, we expect the ethnic association to have a less enduring appeal. This has been the experience, of course, of many European immigrants to American cities. The migrants were met by relatives and countrymen, who found for them housing, employment, membership in the *landsmenschaften*, and even a burial plot. The ethnic group became politically organized, facilitating the entry of members into positions of power. In the long run, however, individuals found greater advantages in other contexts (e.g., the trade union, political party, church, corporation, school, army, etc.), and the "tribe" as a socially functional unit declined, to survive principally in cultural identifications such as the preference for certain foods, or clothing, or women.

by Kenneth L. Little

The growing number of students interested in African urbanization will derive great benefit from Epstein's informative and well-balanced critique of research done in this field. His essay provides a remarkably succinct analysis of many of the sociological issues involved.

I welcome in particular the distinction he makes between "urbanization" and "urbanism," and I am glad that he draws attention to the problem of variation in urban social systems. Thus, in West Africa, not only is there less discontinuity between rural and urban social behaviour than in the central and southern parts of the Continent, but Africans participate freely at every level of society. Epstein's article throws less light on the structural implications of the latter phenomenon than it does on the effects of tribal migration. Admittedly, he wrote before the appearance of some relevant publications, but a good deal of work was available by Mercier, as well as by other French and British authors. In particular, much has been written about new types of marriage and of the family, and also about the function in urbanization of new religious movements and cults. In the West African context these matters are fundamental to the theoretical orientations that Epstein considers.

Epstein rightly casts doubt on the assumption that towns inevitably act as instruments of social transformation and that change is uniformly in the same direction and of the same character. Epstein contrasts Wilson's (1941–42) conclusions about the Bemba with the response to social change of the neighbouring Mambwe reported by Watson (1958); but he does not explain in this regard that the urban/rural relation may depend partly on government policy. Van Velsen's (1961) study, for instance, makes it very plain that Tonga migrants continue to adhere to their rural villages largely because the administration of their home territory is based upon "tribal integrity."

I accept, however, Epstein's stricture on my own simplification of associational growth. It is true that many recent immigrants to towns are not "joiners." Consequently, to speak of the growth of voluntary associations as a "spontaneous adjustment" to urban conditions obscures the sociological issue. On the other hand, the migrant, if illiterate and unskilled, generally does depend upon "practises of mutuality" even though the group concerned may not become institutionalized in the sense that one *formally* joins it. I agree, therefore, with Epstein that we need much more detailed information about the larger West African towns. This would include the informal networks which involve interaction not only between fellow migrants but between established urbanities. Such knowledge, in turn, would throw light upon the associational structure.

by Daniel F. McCall

At the risk of oversimplification of each, I shall attempt three comments in the allotted space:

1) For several years Mitchell and Epstein and others have reiterated that mere residence in towns is an index of urbanization in demographic terms but tells nothing of change of attitudes. Sociologists who have studied immigrant groups in the U.S.A. have long known that peasant attitudes persisted long after transplanting of European rural families to American cities. Neither African urban anthropologists nor American sociologists have worked out any measures for the psychological aspects of urbanization.

Could the concept of "scale" put forward by Wilson (1954) be useful here? If urbanization constitutes a change of scale for the new town-dweller, then his mental horizons must be stretched. Content analysis of samples of newspapers, radio programs, union officials' speeches, etc. coupled with a check of informants' frequency of exposure to the media and an observation of behavior, including verbal, ought to yield an index of attitude change if the contrasting traditional pattern has been recorded. A great deal of time and work would be involved in the analysis of several media and much more in projecting a reasonable sized sample of informants against the resultant. Also, there is obviously not one traditional pattern, but several, and each must be as rigorously established as the "urban" pattern.

2) The "emergence of African businessmen" in West Africa . . . is not the consequence of cash crops. The diary of Antra Duke (see Forde 1956) attests to the existence of businessmen in the 18th century. Businessmen trading wih Europeans were also common in the 17th century, as is clear from many published accounts, and, at least in the interior, the prototype had already been well known for centuries.

"Double-towns" in Western Africa were always the indication of a continuous turnover of strangers, coming and going on the stimulus of commerce and enjoying while temporarily resident a kind of extraterritoriality. The state system in this region was a network of city-states competing for trade; empires were but the military control of many city-states by one. The continuity of urbanism in Africa is not to be obscured by the sharp increase in size and numbers of cities as a consequence of industrialization, for the same distinction between the preindustrial and the industrial city is to be seen in Europe. The idea that urbanism was previously only characteristic of the Yoruba (see e.g., Gibbs 1965: 547) indicates familiarity with Bascom's studies and a tendency to put others (e.g., Miner 1953; Monteil 1900) in another category. Hausa and Mende people were at least as urban as the Yoruba.

3) A typology of associations is needed. The type observed in the Gold Coast prior to independence was different from that of Nigeria and Sierra Leone. Headmen of "strangers' communities" were elected, and their office followed an attenuated pattern of chieftaincy in the home area.

by Philip Mayer

Epstein's paper seems to me to serve two purposes admirably: to draw attention to the fast-accumulating material on African urbanisation and to indicate some of the areas of chief theoretical interest. Possibly it sometimes leans towards the near-obvious (e.g., in stressing that African towns vary greatly, that urbanisation is not uni-dimensional, or that it is analytically desirable to distinguish between urbanism and urbanisation, or between urbanisation and westernisation), but it also offers much stimulus to thought.

Epstein proposes a typology which is

intended to refine the distinction between "old-established" indigenous towns and "new" mostly European-created towns (Southall's type A and type B). He shows that African towns differ from each other both in regard to their industrial structures and in regard to their civic structures. This seems to me a useful way to deploy material. I am not sure, however, that the analysis materially advances our understanding of urbanisation, or that it is correct to single out the industrial and civic aspects as "determinants of" urban social structure. Are they not simply intrinsic to it, along with many other things? Granted that one can "classify the towns of Africa by the positions they occupy along a continuum defined in terms of civic structures," why is this continuum necessarily more significant than the many others that could be constructed—e.g., between towns with rapidly circulating population and with relatively stable population; monotribal and multitribal towns; towns with more christianised and less christianised population, or more moslemised and less moslemised population, etc.? It seems to me that different criteria of classification will assume importance according to the problems being investigated and that there cannot be a master key.

Epstein rightly points out that tribal associations in town "are of different types, cater for different social categories and serve different ends," and he proposes a distinction of three types. Again, I have some reservations about his criteria. He does not distinguish, for instance, associations that are based on the bond of a common home place (outside the town) from those based on a more general categorical similarity of "tribal interest." This distinction is important if one wishes to ascertain whether a tribal association mainly reflects cultural and tribal oppositions within the town or also reinforces its members' extra-town ties (Mayer 1964). It may be because Epstein does not make this distinction that he takes exception to Little's proposition that the growth of voluntary associations represents the newly arrived migrants' response to urban conditions. ("The vast majority of recent immigrants to town are not joiners," Epstein thinks.) I would say that where tribal associations are based on the home-place principle they are very likely to attract newcomers, as Little has proposed, though they may not do so where they are based on other principles.

Epstein poses the question "What, then, are we to understand by urbanization?" but here neither offers an effective answer nor gives sufficient consideration to previous models. He postulates a distinction between "social structural and cultural" aspects of urbanisation (cf. my analyses of East London, South Africa [Mayer 1961, esp. Chapters 1 and 18]) but does not follow this up in detail. In these respects, then, the article whets the theoretical appetite more than satisfies it. It would be good to have an expanded version, with Epstein's own theoretical standpoint set out more explicitly.

by Horace Miner

The main thrust of Epstein's discussion lies in his attempt to discern the more significant causes of social change in Africa as evidenced in studies of its towns and cities. His essay at theoretical synthesis cannot be evaluated simply in terms of its coverage of the literature. Instead, his propositions should be judged largely in terms of their internal logic, their conformity with the evidence, and their adequacy in the light of other theoretical systems. As his synthesis is to some extent an elaboration of Southall's earlier one (1961), we may seek part of Epstein's distinctive contribution in the differences between the two, particularly in his "determinants of urban social structure."

Southall conceives urban social change in Africa as being influenced by factors which are extrinsic to social relationships in the local situation. His use of "extrinsic" is not further specified, but the factors are listed roughly as follows: demography; the nature of urban-rural (tribal) links; degree of ethnic diversity; extent of industrialization; occupational characteristics and income distribution; housing policy and administration; the strength of missions and world religions. Southall recognizes the interrelated and overlapping nature of many of these.

In general, Epstein has moved in the direction of reducing the overlap among Southall's factors by collapsing some into single variables and by eliminating the religious ones. He has also moved toward a more formally scientific statement of relationships. Southall's "factors" which "affect" social relationships have become "variables" which "shape" or "determine" social structure. Epstein's three determinants are clearly to be regarded as independent variables in the urbanization process. What is not clear is his basis for selection of the independent variables, two of which, like the dependent variables, are aspects of the social structure. He does not (as does Southall) characterize his factors as "extrinsic," which term at least suggests their distinctive nature. Nor does he provide any theoretical scheme to show how the determinants are interrelated or why they should have the effects he describes.

There is little to say about his treatment of the demographic variable, in which he follows Mitchell, except perhaps to add reference to the principal summary of the subject by Lorimer, Brass, and Van de Walle (1965). Turning to the economic variable, the results of Epstein's outstanding research on African towns contributed to Southall's formulation of economic factors. Epstein's "industrial structure" points to a more generic variable than Southall's. The "industrial" part of a town's social structure is said to be that "through which the town seeks to achieve those economic aims and purposes that brought it into existence, or give it its present importance." Such purposes include industrial production, transshipment, trade, and governmental administration. Regarding the last item, his anthropomorphic description of a city's economic aims tends to blur the fact that administration has political as well as economic functions. His deterministic attribution of urban origins to economic purposes also disregards those non-economic functions of cities to which the growth of capitals, holy cities, and university towns has been attributed. It may be useful, therefore, to indicate a theoretical position being elaborated elsewhere (Miner 1967) which brings the two frames of reference together in the present context.

Sharing Epstein's dissatisfaction with the basic characterization of the city in terms of population size and density, with or without Wirth's "heterogeneity," I have found it fruitful to focus, as Epstein does in another context, on the relationship of the urban community to the wider social structure. In these terms, a universally recognized attribute of cities is their dominance over hinterlands. This control is to a great extent economic, but also derives from such institutionalized power systems as those of government, religion, and education. That which brings cities into existence and gives them their distinctive character is the control function they perform for the society at large. Most urbanites engage in community maintenance occupations, but the mix of externally oriented functions of any town determines much of its internal social structure, as Reiss (1956) had demonstrated for the United States. Similar effects are indicated in the research literature on African occupational and status differentiation, which receives rather scant attention from Epstein despite his contributions in this area.

His delineation and discussion of "civic structure" is not as successful as Southall's treatment of the same phenomena. Neither the nature of civic structure nor the way in which it is a "determinant" of social structure is made clear. We are told that the civic structure of a town "derives from the policies and practices of its administration." His examples indicate that civic structure is a variable embracing the degree to which discriminatory control is exerted by whites over African movement, housing, and living conditions, although Epstein is strangely loath to put it in so many words. Perhaps this is because his description of the "scale" of civic structure is peculiarly tied to the African scene, rather than being expressed in more general terms. In any case, we are not informed what civic structure causes, unless it is particular local forms of discrimination, which would appear to be redundant. He seems to say that the implementation of administrative policies of discriminatory white control over African living brings about discriminatory patterns of urban life; but are not the administrative policies the very thing we need to explain? The most relevant theoretical considerations would appear to concern minorities, race relations, and pluralism as dealt with by such scholars as Leo Kuper, Balandier, Van den Berghe, and M. G. Smith.

Finally, anyone interested in the history of ideas, or in what is still the clearest conceptual treatment of the phenomena involved in Epstein's determinants, should refer to Mitchell's "external imperatives" (1960, 1966), which preceded Southall's "extrinsic factors."

by Leonard Plotnicov

The grand scope of Epstein's paper, and the clarity and logic of its design, merit much praise. The author is to be commended for his daring attempt to relate the variables of industry, administration, and demography to processes of urbanization and systems of urban social relations. While we cannot expect him to give equal consideration to all the factors each of us might personally consider relevant, I do feel that he did not sufficiently stress history. In my opinion it is not possible to under-

stand African urban social relations without taking into account the histories of ethnic groups and regions. For example, the fact that southern Nigerians came into early and prolonged contact with Europeans and acquired Western education and skills before other Nigerians has a direct bearing on political and economic behavior and ethnic relations in Nigeria today.

Epstein's introductory section points to the rapid maturation of anthropological inquiry in contemporary African urbanization since the days of Gluckman's stimulating concepts not so very long ago. We have reached a stage where it is realistic to call for the application of "sharper and more varied conceptual tools". . . . Sharper and more varied conceptual tools will increase our methodological sophistication and aid us with particular research problems; but I do not believe they will be of much utility in answering the question of what African urbanization basically is. For this question we need a single conceptual framework, as Epstein points out . . . and, I would add, one that is at a high level of generalization. Such a framework should not only handle diversity within Africa; it should also have universal applicability. We cannot begin to develop such a framework without employing some concept of modernization as an integral aspect of analysis. Modernization may well turn out to be more profitable a focus for analysis than urbanization per se. For example, it helps us to recognize the far greater resemblance in social institutions and in the "way of life" between a town of 5,000 and a city of 500,000 in America today than between a traditional Yoruba city of over 100,000 and a modern town of 50,000 on the Nigerian Plateau. These latter are examples of very different species. The traditional Yoruba city (cf. Bascom 1955, 1958, 1962) is an overgrown town, representing a special response to historical conditions in Yorubaland during the 18th and 19th centuries. It makes no sense to conceive of the traditional Yoruba city in a framework that includes modern towns of comparable size.

Epstein mentions "degree of urbanization"; I would like to know what it is we should be measuring. Other disciplines may stress quantitative indexes of urbanization, but anthropology has the special task of dealing with those qualitative aspects that appear to be the necessary concomitants of the high degree of population size and density that mark urban settlements. Furthermore, we must also attempt to understand urbanization as a phenomenon associated with a wider social system that has, as Epstein points out, demographic, social structural, and cultural aspects. . . . The single conceptual framework should be, I think, the wider social system, which may be pre-industrial or, as is the case today in Africa, developing modern industrial in nature. The framework must also include the evolution of that system.

Epstein should have defined for us what is meant by Mitchell's "demographic imperative" . . . since it is one of three factors mentioned as important for the analysis of urbanization and the development of urban social relations, and since the reference cited (Mitchell 1959) is unpublished.

The concept of the stabilization of African urban populations and, related to this, the question of the extent to which Africans are developing a commitment to an urban way of life have long been theoretical problems. Mayer (1961) addressed himself to the latter problem specifically, and Mitchell reflects this concern in his work on lengths of urban residence. Implicit in these inquiries, I think, is the assumption that the development of an urban way of life, from a sociological perspective, depends on a basic transformation of personal attitude—that so long as African town residents conceive of themselves as committed to returning to their rural homes, the complete development of urban

social systems is somehow inhibited. If my view is correct, then this assumption should be made explicit; and if there is a direct relationship between attitudes of temporary urban residence and the kind of social life developing in the cities, then Epstein should have dealt more extensively with the implications of the circulation of labor migration and the degree to which there is a commitment to live in the rural homelands. It is now quite clear that while many tribesmen may consider themselves as migrants, only temporary urban residents, their actual condition is that of permanent town-dwellers (cf. Pons 1956: 669, Plotnicov 1965, 1967: Chap. IX). Even target workers may find their urban sojourn prolonged because they are unable to return home with money as quickly as they initially intended (Sofer and Sofer 1955: 603–04). Despite professed rural orientations, people remain in the cities, and they do something about making their urban existence more secure and more satisfying. Precisely what they do about it is represented by the developing urban systems. As I have tried to show elsewhere (Plotnicov 1967), individuals may disclaim a commitment to permanent urban residence while at the same time participating in the building of (from their point of view) enduring urban social institutions.

This discussion is intimately related to two important problem areas raised by Epstein: urban-rural communications and the extent to which (and under what conditions) traditional systems are perpetuated and perhaps even strengthened. The persistence of the traditional appears to us, as Epstein aptly calls it, a paradox (cf. Van Velsen 1960). The author has provided some notable situations (Sansom 1965; Mayer 1961) in which commitments to traditional systems are total. We should also examine the more numerous instances of partial retentions. For example, during recent years there has been an efflorescence of traditional title-taking among urban Ibo, and they are hardly unique among southern Nigerians who seek traditional offices and titles as if thereby to validate high status achieved in a modern social context. In addition to the rejuvenation of traditional values and parts of cultural systems, we commonly find the kinship institutions of traditional social systems remaining strong while other aspects decline. Family members continue to offer each other loyalty and support, manifesting these in behaviors appropriate to the modern context, in spite of the fact that they may be dispersed among several cities and the family rural base. I view this manifestation of family solidarity as both a possible and necessary result of conditions of modernization. Modern communications systems (post, road, rail) have developed to a point where easy contact (in the transmission of persons, messages, and money) is now the norm for most places in West Africa, thus making it possible for traditional kinship structures to remain viable. Also, the kinship group continues to perform traditional support and aid functions because modern welfare institutions have not yet developed sufficiently to meet town-dwellers' needs (Plotnicov 1966). Further anthropological investigation will uncover many such paradoxes and increase our knowledge of those we are already aware of.

Epstein's remarks on another of these paradoxes, "tribalism" in the cities, are instructive and help clear a murky area. He is quite right in pointing out that groups which come under the general rubric of tribal associations can have very different forms of organization, goals, and functions. The variations among such groups represent, as Epstein says, different phases in the process of urbanization, as well as the relations of members of ethnic groups to other types of associations "and to the over-all status system that has developed within the community." These aspects are well illustrated in the case of the Opobo Town Ijaw who, although highly sophis-

ticated in Western education and holding elite occupations, have come to manifest elements of nativism in their tribal association as a response to the perceived threat that other, more numerous, ethnic groups will usurp their favorable position (Plotnicov 1964).

I am not sure what Epstein means by his fourth type of tribal association (p. 257), that which "approximates more to the type of exclusive social club." All such groups that I am aware of are not based in tribalism, but, on the contrary, are self-consciously anti-parochial, recruiting members on a basis of common interest and a common lifestyle rather than ethnic origin. These groups are modern elite or incipient modern elite who energetically pursue policies of national integration.

Epstein's hypothesis that it is "in the ports and great commercial centres rather than around the mines that variegated interest groups may be expected to emerge and political associations and trade unions to develop and flourish" (p. 250) has much promise. His argument is plausible, and the data, while few, are supportive. The hypothesis certainly merits testing and can be applied to various mono-industry settlements. Epstein spells out the social and political implications of this type of settlement convincingly (pp. 251–52), and the comparison he suggests of West African towns built around extractive industries with Copperbelt mining areas would be useful; but I question his choice of Enugu in eastern Nigeria as a possible unit for comparison. Enugu is the capital of the Eastern Region, and coal-mining has been declining in importance while varied commercial enterprises and communications activities have been expanding. Jos, in northern Nigeria, like Enugu, initially developed from mining activity (tin ore), but it too presents problems for comparison because of a diversity of economic and administrative activities. Some of the very recently developed mining areas of Sierra Leone and Liberia may well be the only places in West Africa suitable for comparison with the Copperbelt.

Epstein calls our attention to the important problem of determining "to what extent the growth of towns gives rise to a system of cross-cutting ties and allegiances" .... He suggests that in the Copperbelt municipal allegiances are developing, but I wonder how, given the transiency of the urban populations there, this can be anything but superficial. Nontraditional, nonparochial ties have developed in the urban area of my firsthand experience (Jos) between status peers, co-religionists, and neighbors, but a loyalty to one's urban location can hardly be said to exist.

Where the author speaks of the effects of colonial racial segregation in the new towns and cities ... his discussion might have more clearly distinguished the effects of black-white social and political relations from other aspects that have analytically different dimensions. For example, he says that the effect of a segregated residential pattern has been "to exclude the [African] residents from full participation in the life of the town and the enjoyment of its amenities." In complex social systems, no one enjoys *full* participation, and with independence achieved African town residents will continue to suffer amenity deprivations based on economic and class distinctions.

I am particularly pleased to note Epstein's use of indigenous authors of fiction (e.g., Ekwensi), which I think may be employed more extensively in the future, obviously not as sources of empirical data, but as sources of insight into modern African social life as communicated by sensitive and articulate insiders.

Epstein's paper is a good contribution to modern urban African studies, for it presents many stimulating ideas and hypotheses that merit close attention for their promise. Because the paper is so vast an undertaking, containing so many germinal

thoughts in a brief space, I often wished that the author might pause, delve more deeply, and further develop some of his ideas. He should be congratulated for this attempt to deal with an extremely complex and challenging area.

by W. B. Schwab

Possibly the most severe problem facing anthropologists studying towns in Africa has been the absence of a pertinent and systematic theoretical framework within which one could formulate questions and assess findings. In many ways this is a unique situation. Anthropologists studying religion, kinship, political systems, etc., have, despite many differences in outlook, a common frame of reference; but none of us seems to be very clear about what we mean by urbanism or urbanization. Approaches based on demographic criteria, sociologists, dependings as they do on Western models, are inadequate and sometimes misleading in dealing with the towns of Africa. There is a need for a long, hard look at African towns in terms of the empirical data that are available. One starting point that has been suggested (Balandier 1956; Southall 1961; Schwab 1965) is an analysis of town life in terms of the differences between towns. Epstein, by focusing on the variations in social and economic determinants of African towns, has taken an important step in this direction. He has, moreover, made an admirable effort to bring together extremely diverse materials from many parts of the continent. Whether or not he has provided a general framework which is appropriate for the study of urbanization in Africa is a further question.

It is difficult to know just what it is that Epstein means by "urbanization." We are told that it is not industrialization, Westernization, the growth of settler communities, etc.; that it involves movement and change; and that its essence is the possibility of some discontinuity with some pre-existing set of conditions. It is difficult to assess these statements, because it is not clear what kind of change, or what kind of movement, is critical. There are many kinds of changes in the life of any individual; we must select certain sets of changes in behavior or values which are pertinent to urbanization. If the movement in question is physical movement from rural to urban areas, then migration becomes a necessary part of urbanization. Further, it appears to me that the discontinuities have been overstressed in the study of urbanization in Africa and that continuity, whether in terms of values, social relationships, or roles, is equally essential. The imposition of migrancy and discontinuity on urbanization produces certain contradictions and inconsistencies. Thus, according to these restrictions, those of us who have lived all of our lives in American cities are not urbanized, and, more to the point, neither is any African born and reared in town. To be sure, people born and reared in town may have become urbanized as part of their early socialization process, but they have made adjustments and adaptations to certain sets of town conditions and have learned to solve their problems within an urban frame of reference. Surely this is a process which, whether it happens early or late in life, to a child or to a migrant, is essential to urbanization. Epstein distinguishes between urbanism and urbanization and makes the point that while the "way of life" of the Yoruba is urbanism, urbanization has not occurred. This conclusion, I think, is based upon the fact that neither migration nor cultural discontinuity are important factors in Yoruba towns. I am not certain that the Yoruba way of life is urban (see Schwab 1965); but if it is, then Yoruba townsmen somehow, somewhere, have been through a process of urbanization.

In discussing the physical environment of towns, Epstein has raised some interesting points and has shown that physical limitations and restrictions have broad impli-cations for the social relationships of the Africans. This is, as he points out, very evident in the towns of Central and Southern Africa. However, I think he misses a point when he states that, "In the countries of West Africa, physical segregation was not built into the legal code, but the social pattern has often been broadly similar." The differences between West and Central and Southern Africa are much more than legal. In West African towns there has been spatial differentiation based on ethnic differences, cultural antagonisms, or social or economic stratification; but it is not equivalent to the physical segregation in Central and Southern Africa, which is a reflection of a pervasive and rigid class and racial system.

The question of the structural determinants of urban social systems is an extremely important one. When Africans come to town they meet certain sets of conditions, varying from place to place, with which they must come to terms if they are to remain in town. Housing conditions, influx policies, access to economic opportunities, and the like are part of a particular urban matrix. Certain relationships are clearly derived from these determinants. For example, the viability of the extended family unit within a town is directly related to housing policy. However, I think that the correlations suggested by Epstein between structural determinants and broader aspects of behavior are unwarranted. For example, we read that people tend to develop a more "independent outlook" (whatever that may be) in commercial towns than in the more structured, paternalistic mining communities. People's attitudes, their adaptability, their creativity, and their independence are determined by many complex and interrelated social, economic, and psychological factors, and it seems to me that we need a lot more empirical data to draw such a conclusion.

Associational life is another factor which Epstein relates, separately, to both civic and industrial determinants. He concludes first that associational life is more likely to develop in commercial centers than in mining towns. The facts that we have thus far indicate that associations flourish in the commercial centers of West Africa and have little significance in the commercial centers of Central Africa. If these data are correct, then the industrial structure of a community by itself is not the primary factor in associational life. Other factors (e.g., age, the strength of kin ties, religion, occupation, cultural background, etc.) may together or separately have as much or more influence in determining participation in associations. Dawson's (1964) analysis of the associational participation of the Mende and Temne in Free Town supports this view. The data he presents suggest very clearly that, within this one urban environment, association participation depends largely on cultural antecedents. Epstein himself alludes to the differential participation in associations in the latter part of his paper.

I am confused by Epstein's analysis of the relationship between tribal associations and civic structures. He seems to be saying that associations tend to develop when there are no tribal elders in the formal administrative framework or no indigenous urban courts (as in Dar-es-Salaam and West Africa); and, conversely, that associations are absent where (as on the Copperbelt) there is indigenous urban and tribal leadership. If these are his points, I am in complete disagreement. To begin with, among the Yoruba, for example, there were urban courts, a highly developed indigenous leadership, and many associations. In Free Town, certainly, as he notes, there were associations together with an acknowledged and developed indigenous leadership. In fact, this was generally the situation, as far as I know, throughout West Africa. Further, in Gwelo, Rhodesia, there were no indigenous leaders, no traditional urban courts, and few associations.

It seems to me that the primary difficulty with Epstein's approach is his failure to take into account the differential response of people to any particular set of urban conditions. Although he refers to it on occasion throughout the paper, he has not come to terms with the fact that in any given urban environment there may be many intervening variables determining the impact of town life and the adaptations made to it. An urban environment is a datum imposed upon a townsman, but his adjustments and his assessments are his own, and an understanding of what is happening in towns must take this consideration into account.

Epstein has chosen to limit his discussion of the social structure of the town to tribalism and tribal associations. He accepts the views of Mitchell and Wallerstein and differentiates between urban and rural tribalism. He argues that tribalism in the urban community is one of the major factors regulating relationships between townsmen, and that most frequently a man tends to limit his relationships, where he has choice, to fellow tribesmen. While this is important for understanding urban behavior, an equally important consideration is the fact that tribalism may be breaking down in town. For example, my data from Gwelo (Schwab n.d.) indicate that about 1/4 of the marriages in Gwelo are tribally mixed. Marriage is one of the most important indices of social evaluation in any society. Mixed marriages are a strong indication that traditional tribal loyalties are being put aside, at least by some of the people, for new values and standards which do not include tribal affiliation as a basic criterion. Hellmann (1956) has made a similar point about South African towns.

I do not understand Epstein's apparent quarrel with Little's interpretation of the adaptive role of associations in West African towns. Epstein argues that the vast majority of recent immigrants to town are not "joiners." This appears to be a valid assessment for Central Africa but certainly is not for West Africa. There, all evidence indicates that associations are very important in facilitating the adjustment of new migrants to town and that they perform varied and important functions for many segments of the population. This interpretation, from my point of view, does not cloud sociological issues. On the contrary, it clarifies them. There is still room for the other analyses that Epstein suggests.

Finally, I do not agree that camaraderie, ebullience, and gusto are characteristics common to all African towns. It is my impression that in many Rhodesian towns, for example, passivity, repression, and lack of gusto are the most striking characteristics of these African people. Perhaps it would be best if we did not stereotype African town-dwellers in any way.

by William A. Shack

Epstein's paper is important not only in that it calls attention to the oversimplified view frequently apparent in studies of urbanization and social change in Africa, but also in that it stresses the need to develop new conceptual tools for understanding both the forms and variations in patterns of African urbanization. This need increases as demographic and sociological data from urban centers in Liberia and Ethiopia, heretofore neglected by social anthropologists, are reported.

In contrast to Epstein's general demographic picture of African towns (p. 254), a striking feature of the urban population of Addis Ababa, capital of Ethiopia, is the marked excess of females over males within the age groups 15 to 49; the over-all sex ratio is 90/100 (*Social Survey* 1960: 63). This data suggests that Southall's (1961: 6) Type A category of African towns—the old, established, and slowly growing—could be further refined to account for urban centers like Addis Ababa, which lack significant industrialization or wage-labor markets. The relative scarcity of skilled or semi-skilled employment opportunities for men, as against such wage-earning activities for women as domestic service, beer-selling, and even prostitution, gives rise to an excess of females over males in nonindustrial African cities.

My own evidence from Addis Ababa would support Epstein's contention that urban tribal associations are to be understood in terms of the over-all status system within the community. Moreover, I would suggest that "self-help" associations among urban Gurage tribesmen in Addis Ababa (and no doubt among other townsmen as well), whose aims are directed primarily toward improving the welfare of kinsmen in the hinterland, express two interrelated aspects of urban tribalism: (1) a degree of social and psychological detachment from the urban community within which maximum sociocultural integration is yet to be attained; and (2) an idealization of the social and economic security that most urban tribesmen endeavor to achieve (Shack 1966).

Westernization, or "Europeanization," as a model denoting processes of change in urban Africa must be re-examined in the light of developing national cultural systems in newly independent African states. Where a particular tribal (or ethnic) group is dominant in the national system, the over-all process of change is very often shaped by that group's own political-cultural model; the Americo-Liberian and Amhara national cultural systems in Liberia and Ethiopia, respectively, are two cases in point. New conceptual formulations of social change in Africa might profitably take account of the long-established patterns of urbanization in the old independent African states.

Reply

by A. L. Epstein

I should like to thank all those who kindly offered comment on and criticism of my article. Since I regard the paper as a contribution to a discussion which is likely to continue, I do not feel it necessary to defend the argument at every point and will therefore reply fairly briefly.

Since a number of comments touch on the scope of the paper, in terms of its theoretical perspective as well as its coverage of particular topics, I think I ought to begin by noting some of its self-imposed limitations. Firstly, in preparing the article I was acutely aware that a number of analyses with broadly similar aims had appeared over the past few years. In these circumstances it seemed to me unnecessary to retrace ground that had already been well covered by my colleagues, save where this was important for the development of my argument. Hence, for example, to take one of Plotnicov's points, I did not spell out the notion of the "demographic imperative" because, as Miner rightly observes, the matter has already been treated extensively by Mitchell and others. Secondly, as I pointed out in my first footnote, the paper in its original form was shaped to fit into a more general discussion of political development. In revising it, I decided to allow the original bias to remain as providing a convenient peg on which to hang the argument. (I find it interesting that this aspect of the paper evoked so little comment.) This explains the failure, referred to by Little and others, to deal with such topics as kinship and marriage, religious movements and cults, and other features of the urban scene. The paper was not intended as a definitive treatment of the subject, but as a skeletal outline of an approach to it with illustrations of particular points.

Some doubts have been raised about the value of the framework suggested. Indeed, Gutkind takes the view that we still do not know enough to be in position to develop such a framework, and argues that our approach to the study of urban systems should be more eclectic. There can be few

phenomena of any degree of complexity that do not throw up problems of concern to different disciplines; and urbanization is no exception. I would be very surprised if an economist or an urban geographer were to cast his inquiries and subsequent data into the same kind of mould as I would, since each discipline is likely to be concerned with different sets of interconnexions or regularities. The question is what the distinctive contribution of the social anthropologist is or should be. The way in which the anthropologist conceptualizes the process of urbanization is likely to have been considerably influenced by the situation in which he conducted his own field-research. Because of the way research is organized, and the heavy personal investment it involves, few are able to work in more than one area. The result is a tendency towards a kind of regional divide. When we read the reports of our colleagues who have worked in areas other than our own, we are often uncertain how far they are describing different situations, how far the differences are really the expression of alternative modes of approach. The aim in formulating a single framework is not to reduce everything to a common denominator, but to obviate this difficulty and to provide the means whereby the relations between variables can be examined in a number of different combinations and hypotheses put forward to be tested by further research.

The basic concern of this approach is with the examination of systems of social relationship in towns, and it therefore seems sound sense to focus analytical attention on the towns themselves. Here, as Bruner observes, I follow the line of attack advocated by Gluckman; but I do not, as he claims, see "urbanization processes as a function of factors intrinsic to the city itself." In the first place, I thought I had made it clear that the kind of urban growth with which I was concerned was a product of colonialism. Secondly, while it might appear as though I treat the variables of industrial structure, civic structure, and demographic structure as purely intrinsic, it is plain that they may also be regarded as external factors. Where one places the stress is a question of analytical context. (Incidentally, since Miner raises the point about the history of ideas, I should note that I attempted to formulate a framework along these lines in a paper written in 1959 [published in 1961] in which I used the expression "environmental constants." The term "environment" here is a relative concept: its bounds are not set, but vary according to the social units isolated for purposes of analysis [Epstein 1961: 42]. Thus factors which for one purpose may be regarded as external may for another purpose or in a different context be regarded as internal.) The main point I wanted to make was that the social structure of the town is a product of the complex interplay of a number of factors, some of them located within the town, some of them outside it (hence the discussion of rural-urban relations in the latter part of the paper). I would therefore certainly accept Bruner's comment about the importance of the region.

Bruner and Schwab argue that I have placed too much emphasis on discontinuity in the definition of urbanization. This criticism seems to me to rest on a misconception. In my view, urbanization refers to a social process involving people in social relationships within a new kind of physical environment. It is in this sense that I speak of urbanization as requiring departure from some pre-existing set of conditions. I would have thought that the case of a child growing up in an American city was adequately covered by speaking of his being socialized or enculturated to an urban way of life. Would Schwab speak of an African child growing up in the tribal or rural areas of Africa as being "tribalized" or "ruralized?" The more important point, however, is that to place the initial stress

on discontinuity is not to deny the importance of continuity. Discontinuity rarely involves a complete break with the past, but varies along a continuum. This was noted many years ago by Godfrey Wilson when he showed how grants of five-acre plots to Africans in Broken Hill affected their adjustment to life in the town and in some contexts produced a different response from that of Africans on the Copperbelt. The degree of discontinuity present in any given situation is to be established empirically and its further implications traced out.

My discussion of industrial and civic structure was evidently not as clear as I had hoped. Miner is of course quite correct when he points out that administration has political as well as economic functions. My aim, however, was to separate out these functions so that given, for example, the economic character of the town, we could go on to make inferences about other aspects of the urban system. In the same way, one could, I would have thought, speak of the "industrial structure" of a University town; certainly, in a sociological study one would presumably want to do more than treat it simply in terms of its educational functions. But I can perhaps make my position clearer here if I take up one of Schwab's comments about the relationship between associational life and the industrial or civic structure. Schwab ascribes to me the view that the industrial structure is the primary factor in the development of voluntary association. This is not my contention. I am not seeking to establish simple one-to-one correlations. What I suggested in the paper was that when confronted with a problem of the kind specified by Schwab, we should look first at the civic institutions to see what provision is made for handling those difficulties that people are likely to encounter when they move into the towns. For example, where coffins are provided by the local authority (as they once were in the Copperbelt), there is clearly less need for a burial society. As Schwab himself observes later, an urban environment is a datum imposed upon the townsman. My major concern has been to break up this environment into a number of variables so that we may examine what each entails and in this way discover problems for further inquiry. For example, provision has sometimes been made within the civic structure for the setting up of urban courts. In Gwelo, where Schwab worked, there were no such courts. What implications follow from this? How were disputes handled in Gwelo? Did they all go before a European magistrate, or had other informal mechanisms of adjudication been developed? Was the incidence of crimes of violence greater in Gwelo than in places where formal courts did exist? The framework I have proposed was designed not so much to provide a set of ready-made answers, but to suggest questions for further investigation and to advance the search for regularity in urban social life. It seems to me that Schwab contradicts himself when he argues that the townsman's adjustments and assessments are his own but at the same time complains that my discussion of associational life ignores the strength of kin ties, religion, occupation, and cultural background.

For reasons already indicated, my discussion of urban social relationships was necessarily uneven. Hence in dealing with categorical relationships I said little about stratification but concentrated on tribalism. In regard to the latter Schwab appears to attribute to me the view that we are dealing with unchanging categories and with processes that operate uniformly throughout urban Africa. I subscribe to no such view. More than a decade ago Southall (1956b: 580) indicated that the accurate assessment of what tribalism counts for was a fundamental requirement of urban studies in Africa. Here questions obviously arise as to the particular expression ethnicity takes in different urban communities (one of Mayer's comments and Horowitz's reference to landsmannschaft are very relevant here) and the forces that maintain it or lead to its decline. If the high proportion of tribally mixed marriages may be taken as an indication of the breaking down of tribalism in Gwelo, as Schwab maintains, I would find in this situation not a point to be contended, but a problem I hope Schwab will go on to analyze. To what extent are these mixed marriages inter-tribal marriages (using "tribe" in the narrow sense), and to what extent are they intra-ethnic group or intra-district marriages (see Mitchell 1957)? And if significant differences do emerge between the pattern in Gwelo and that reported elsewhere, how do these relate to other aspects of Gwelo's social system? Is it possible, for example, that in Rhodesia, with its major division between Ndebele- and Shona-speaking groups, region or district is more relevant to the definition of categorical relationships than is ethnic group or tribe? It is, incidentally, in addressing ourselves to problems of this kind that the value of repeating a study at regular intervals, advocated by a number of people, becomes most apparent, since changes for example in the patterns of marriage can then be directly measured.

Plotnicov raises a question in this context about the "tribal" basis of certain exclusive social clubs. Plotnicov is probably correct that most clubs of this type are self-consciously parochial, recruiting their membership amongst the modern elite. What I had in mind was the situation referred to by Leslie in his account of Dar-es-Salaam. It appears in some cases that, for historical reasons, a particular group may receive a headstart over other groups in matters of education. When members of the group are posted to "elite" jobs in areas where they are a "stranger" minority, they may form their own exclusive social club.

Plotnicov makes a number of other comments with which I am in substantial agreement. He questions my choice of Enugu as a possible unit for comparison with the mining towns of the Copperbelt. I would defer to his judgment on this; my suggestion perhaps illustrates that regional divide to which I referred earlier. However, we do at least agree on the main point at issue: the need for comparative studies of this kind where at least some of the variables can be held constant. I agree too with his observation that no one enjoys *full* participation in the social life of a town, and that what he calls amenity deprivations rest on bases other than residential segregation. The passage in question was redrafted before I received Plotnicov's comment, and I hope the analogy I have drawn between African location and Western city slum may go some way to meeting his point and a similar one raised by Schwab.

One final comment: Bruner says I state that Gluckman treats all towns as if they were alike. If I had said this, it would seem to me a gross misrepresentation of Gluckman's position. What Gluckman was arguing, when he first addressed himself to the question of urbanization, was that African towns should be regarded sociologically as being of the same order as towns elsewhere; the focus of comparison was on towns and not the contrast between town and country. This is very different from treating all towns as though they were alike. Gluckman's formulations have provided the starting point for my own and others' work, but where his most recent discussions seem to stress the study of what is common in urban development, it seems to me that we must now also address ourselves to the question of variation in urban social systems. By laying equal stress on both these aspects we may hope to advance towards a more complete theory of urbanization in Africa and elsewhere.

REFERENCES CITED

ALMOND, G., and J. S. COLEMAN. Editors. 1960. *The politics of the developing areas.* Princeton: Princeton University Press.

BALANDIER, G. 1956, "Urbanism in West and Central Africa: The scope and aims of research," in *Social implications of industrialization and urbanization in Africa south of the Sahara.* Edited by D. Forde. Paris: Unesco.

BANTON, M. 1957. *West African city.* London: Oxford University Press for the International African Institute.

——. 1966. "Social alignment and identity in a West African city," in *Urbanization and migration in West Africa.* Edited by Hilda Kuper. Berkeley: University of California Press.

BASCOM, W. R. 1955. Urbanization among the Yoruba. *American Journal of Sociology* 60: 446—54.

——. 1958. Yoruba urbanism: A summary. *Man* 58: 253.

——. 1962. Some aspects of Yoruba urbanism. *American Anthropologist* 64: 699—709.

BATES, M. L. 1962. "Tanganyika," in *African one-party states.* Edited by Gwendolen Carter. Ithaca: Cornell University Press.

BOTTOMORE, T. 1954. "Social stratification in voluntary organizations," in *Social mobility in Britain.* Edited by D. V. Glass. London: Routledge & Kegan Paul.

BUTCHER, D. 1965. The role of the Fulbe in the economic and social life of Lunsar, Sierra Leone. Unpublished Ph. D. thesis, University of Edinburgh.

COLEMAN, J. S. 1958. *Nigeria: Background to nationalism.* Berkeley: University of California Press.

——. 1960. "The politics of Sub-Saharan Africa," in *The politics of the developing areas.* Edited by G. Almond and J. S. Coleman. Princeton: Princeton University Press.

DAWSON, J. 1964. "Urbanization and mental health in a West African community," in *Magic, faith, and healing.* Edited by A. Kiev. Glencoe: The Free Press.

DOTSON, F. 1951. Patterns of voluntary associations among urban working-class families. *American Sociological Review* 16: 687–93.

DOUCY, A., and P. FELDHEIM. 1956. "Some effects of industrialization in two districts of Equatoria Province (Belgian Congo)," in *Social implications of industrialization and urbanization in Africa south of the Sahara*. Edited by D. Forde. Paris: Unesco.

EKWENSI, C. 1954. *People of the city*. London: Andrew Dakers.

ENGELS, F. 1950. *The condition of the working class in England in 1844*. London: Allen & Unwin.

EPSTEIN, A. L. 1953a. The role of African courts in urban communities of the Northern Rhodesia Copperbelt. *Rhodes-Livingstone Journal* 13: 1–16.

———. 1953b. *The administration of justice and the urban African*. Colonial Research Series 7. London: H.M.S.O.

———. 1958. *Politics in an urban African community*. Manchester: Manchester University Press.

———. 1959. Linguistic innovation and culture on the Copperbelt. *Southwestern Journal of Anthropology* 15: 235–53.

———. 1961. The network and urban social organization. *Rhodes-Livingstone Journal* 29: 29–62.

FORDE, C. D. Editor. 1956. *Efik traders of old Calabar*. London: Oxford University Press.

FRAENKEL, M. 1964. *Tribe and class in Monrovia*. London: Oxford University Press for the International African Institute.

FRIEDLAND, W. H. 1964. "Basic social trends," in *African socialism*. Edited by W. H. Friedland and C. G. Rosberg. Stanford: Stanford University Press.

GIBBS, J. 1965. *Peoples of Africa*. Edited by J. Gibbs. New York: Holt, Rinehart and Winston.

GLUCKMAN, M. 1945. The seven year research plan of the Rhodes-Livingstone Institute. *Rhodes-Livingstone Journal* 4: 1–32.

———. 1960. Tribalism in modern British Central Africa. *Cahiers d'Études Africaines* 1: 55–70.

HELLMANN, ELLEN. 1937. "The native in the towns," in *The Bantu-speaking tribes of South Africa*. Edited by I. Schapera. London: Routledge.

———. 1948. *Rooiyard*. Rhodes-Livingstone Paper 13.

———. 1956. "The development of social groupings among urban Africans in the Union of South Africa," in *Social implications of industrialization and urbanization in Africa south of the Sahara*. Edited by D. Forde. Paris: Unesco.

HODGKIN, T. 1956. *Nationalism in colonial Africa*. London: Muller.

KOMAROVSKY, M. 1946. The voluntary associations of urban dwellers. *American Sociological Review* 11: 686–98.

LEMARCHAND, R. 1964. *Political awakening in the Congo*. Berkeley: University of California Press.

LESLIE, J. A. K. 1963. *A social survey of Dar es Salaam*. London: Oxford University Press for the East African Institute.

LITTLE, K. 1957. The role of voluntary associations in West African urbanization. *American Anthropologist* 59: 579–96.

———. 1965. *West African urbanization*. London: Cambridge University Press.

LLOYD, P. C. 1959. The Yoruba town today. *The Sociological Review* 7: 45–63.

LORRIMER, F., W. BRASS, and E. VAN DE WALLE. 1965. "Demography," in *The African world*. Edited by R. Lystad. New York: Praeger.

McCULLOUGH, M. 1956. *A social survey of the African population of Livingstone*. Rhodes-Livingstone Paper 26.

MARRIS, P. 1961. *Family and social change in an African city*. London: Routledge & Kegan Paul.

MAYER, P. 1961. *Townsmen or tribesmen*. Cape Town: Oxford University Press.

———. 1962. "Migrancy and the study of Africans in town." *American Anthropologist* 64: 576–92.

———. 1964. "Labour migrancy and the social network," in *Problems of transition*. Edited by J. F. Holleman *et al*. Pietermaritzberg: Natal University Press.

MERCIER, P. 1965. "On the meaning of 'tribalism' in Black Africa," in *Africa: Social problems of change and conflict*. Edited by P. van den Berghe. San Francisco: Chandler.

MINER, HORACE. 1953. *The primitive city of Timbuctu.* Princeton: Princeton University Press.

——. 1967. "The city and modernization," in *The city in modern Africa.* Edited by H. Miner. New York: Praeger.

MITCHELL, J. C. 1953. A note on the urbanization of Africans on the Copperbelt. *Rhodes-Livingstone Journal* 12: 20–27.

——. 1956a. *The Kalela Dance.* Rhodes-Livingstone Paper 27.

——. 1956b. "Urbanization, detribalization and stabilization in Southern Africa: A problem of definition and measurement," in *Social implications of industrialization and urbanization in Africa south of the Sahara.* Edited by D. Forde. Paris: Unesco.

——. 1957. Aspects of African marriage on the Copperbelt of Northern Rhodesia. *Rhodes-Livingstone Journal* 22: 1–29.

——. 1959. The study of African urban social structure. Unpublished paper for CCTA Conference on Housing and Urbanization, Nairobi.

——. 1960. The anthropological study of urban communities. *African Studies* 19: 169–72.

——. 1961. "Wage labour and African population movements in Central Africa," in *Essays on African population.* Edited by K. M. Barbour and R. M. Prothero. London: Routledge & Kegan Paul.

——. 1965. "The meaning of misfortune for urban Africans," in *African systems of thought.* Edited by M. Fortes and O. Dieterlen. London: Oxford University Press.

——. 1966. "Theoretical orientations in African urban studies," in *The social anthropology of complex societies.* Edited by M. Banton. A.S.A. Monographs 4. London: Tavistock.

MITCHELL, J. C. and A. L. EPSTEIN. 1957. Power and prestige among Africans in Northern Rhodesia: An experiment. *Southern Rhodesian Journal of Science* 45: 13–26.

——. 1959. Occupational prestige and social status among urban Africans in Northern Rhodesia. *Africa* 29: 22–39.

MITCHELL, J. C. and J. R. H. SHAUL. 1963. An approach to the measurement of commitment to urban residence. Paper presented to the Second Central Africa Scientific and Medical Congress, Lusaka.

MONTEIL, C. 1932. *Un cité sudanaise: Djénné, métropole du delta central du Niger.* Paris: Société d'éditions géographiques, maritimes et coloniales.

PARKIN, D. 1965. The social structure of two African housing estates in Kampala. Unpublished Ph. D. thesis, University of London (S.O.A.S.).

PLOTNICOV, L. 1964. "Nativism" in contemporary Nigeria. *Anthropological Quarterly* 37: 121–37.

——. 1965. Going home again—Nigerians: The dream is unfulfilled. *Trans-Action* 3(1): 18–22.

——. 1966. Rural-urban communication in Nigeria. MS.

——. 1967. *Strangers to the city.* Pittsburgh: University of Pittsburgh Press. In press.

PONS, V. G. 1956. "The growth of Stanleyville and the composition of its African population," in *Social implications of industrialization and urbanization in Africa south of the Sahara.* Edited by D. Forde. Paris: Unesco.

——. 1961. "Two small groups in Avenue 21," in *Social change in modern Africa.* Edited by A. Southall. London: Oxford University Press.

——. 1965. *Stanleyville: A study of an African urban community under colonial administration.* In press.

POWDERMAKER, H. 1962. *Copper Town: Changing Africa.* New York: Harper & Row.

READER, D. H. 1961. *The Black Man's portion.* Cape Town: Oxford University Press.

REISS, A., JR. 1956. "Functional specialization of cities," in *Cities and society.* Edited by P. Hatt and A. Reiss, Jr. Glencoe: The Free Press.

ROUCH, J. 1956. Migration on the Gold

Coast. *Journal de la Société des Africanistes* 26: 33–196.

ROUX, E. 1948. *Time longer than rope.* London: Gollancz.

SAMPSON, A. 1956. *Drum.* London: Collins.

SANSOM, B. 1965. The social system of the Pedi. MS.

SCHWAB, W. 1961. "Social stratification in Gwelo," in *Social change in modern Africa.* Edited by A. Southall. London: Oxford University Press for the International African Institute.

———. 1966. "Oshogbo—an urban community?" in *Urbanization and migration in West Africa.* Edited by Hilda Kuper. Berkeley: University of California Press.

———. *n.d.* Differential urbanization in Gwelo, Rhodesia. MS.

SHACK, W. A. 1966. "Urban tribalism and the cultural process of urbanization in Ethiopia," in *Urban anthropology.* Edited by A. W. Southall and E. Bruner. Chicago: Aldine Press. In press.

Social Survey of Addis Ababa. 1960. Addis Ababa: University College of Addis Ababa and United Nations Economic Commission to Africa.

SOFER, C., and R. SOFER. 1955. *Jinja transformed.* East African Studies No. 4. Kampala: East African Institute of Social Research.

SOUTHALL, A. 1956a. "Determinants of the social structure of African urban populations with special reference to Kampala," in *Social implications of industrialization and urbanization in Africa south of the Sahara.* Edited by D. Forde. Paris: Unesco.

———. 1956b. "Some problems of statistical analysis in community studies, illustrated from Kampala," in *Social implications of industrialization and urbanization in Africa south of the Sahara.* Edited by D. Forde. Paris: Unesco.

———. 1961. "Introductory summary," in *Social change in modern Africa.* Edited

by A. Southall. London: Oxford University Press.

SOUTHALL, A., and P. C. W. GUTKIND. 1957. *Townsmen in the making.* East African Studies 9.

STACEY, M. 1960. *Tradition and change: A study of Banbury.* London: Oxford University Press.

VAN VELSEN, J. 1960. Labor migration as a positive factor in the continuity of Tonga tribal society. *Economic Development and Culture Change* 8: 265—78. (Reprinted in *Social change in modern Africa,* edited by Aidan Southall. London: Oxford University Press for the International African Institute. 1961.)

WALLERSTEIN, L. 1960. Ethnicity and national integration in West Africa. *Cahiers d'Études Africaines* 3: 129–39.

WATSON, W. 1958. *Tribal cohesion in a money economy.* Manchester: Manchester University Press.

WHYTE, WILLIAM F. 1943. *Street corner society.* Chicago: University of Chicago Press.

WILSON, G. 1941–42. *The economics of detribalization.* Rhodes-Livingstone Papers 5 & 6.

WILSON, G., and M. WILSON. 1954. *The analysis of social change.* Cambridge: Cambridge University Press.

WILSON, M., and A. MAFEJE. 1963. *Langa: A Study of social groups in an African township.* Cape Town: Oxford University Press.

WIRTH, LOUIS. 1938. Urbanism as a way of life. *American Journal of Sociology* 44: 1–24.

WORSLEY, P. 1964. *The third world.* London: Weidenfeld & Nicholson.

XYDIAS, N. 1956. "Social effects of urbanization in Stanleyville, Belgian Congo," in *Social implications of industrialization and urbanization in Africa south of the Sahara.* Edited by D. Forde. Paris: Unesco.

22. Some Generalizations Concerning Primate Cities

ARNOLD S. LINSKY

ABSTRACT

Six hypotheses are formulated and tested on the conditions under which primate cities occur. Using worldwide data, it was found that high urban primacy occurs most frequently in countries with small areal extent of dense population, low per capita income, export-oriented and agricultural economies, a colonial history, and rapid rates of population growth.

The purpose of this paper is to report on the formulation and testing of a set of hypotheses concerning primate cities.[1] The primate city concept refers to the relationship in size between the largest city in a country and the other cities in that same country. When Mark Jefferson introduced the concept in his classic article, he noted that in twenty-eight of the leading countries of the world the largest city was more than twice as large as the next, whereas in eighteen of these countries it was more than three times as large as the next city.[2] Jefferson stated that there were many reasons why one city might exceed its neighbors in size originally but that once it did, "This mere fact gives it an impetus to grow that cannot affect any other city, and it draws away from all of them in character as well as in size . . . it becomes the primate city."[3] Wherever high primacy failed to occur, Jefferson explained the absence by citing unusual local circumstances, such as the effect of foreigners on Shanghai, the newness of Brazil, and the regionalism of Russia, Italy, and Spain.[4]

The primate city concept has not received a great deal of attention since

Reproduced from the Annals *of the Association of American Geographers, Volume 55, (September 1965), 506–13. Reprinted by permission of author and publisher.*

[1] A revised version of a paper read at the annual meeting of the Pacific Sociological Association, Sacramento, California, April, 1962. I wish to thank Roy I. Wolfe, Ontario Department of Highways, and Calvin F. Schmid and Joseph Cohen of the University of Washington for their valuable advice on an earlier form of the manuscript.

[2] M. Jefferson, "The Law of the Primate City," *Geographical Review*, Vol. 29 (1939), pp. 226–32.

[3] Jefferson, *op. cit.*, footnote 2, p. 227.

[4] Two classical works dealing with the relationship in size of leading cities are G. K. Zipf, *National Unity and Disunity* (Bloomington, Indiana: The Principia Press, 1941); and E. Ullman, "A Theory of Location for Cities," *American Journal of Sociology*, Vol. 46 (1941), pp. 853–64. According to Zipf's "rank–size rule" we would expect the largest city in most nations to be approximately twice as large as the second city. We would expect it to be three times as large as the second-ranked city according to Christaller's formulation as described by Ullman. There is little support for either of these hypotheses for the countries listed in Table 7.

Jefferson's article.[5] Several recent papers, however, have dealt peripherally with this concept or have applied it to selected regions of the globe. Stewart has dealt with patterns of primacy in Western European nations and Australia.[6] Ginsburg has pointed out that, "A major characteristic of urbanization in Southeast Asia is the functional dominance, with two major exceptions, of one great metropolis in each of the countries of the region."[7] Browning, in his recent paper on urban trends in Latin America, noted that urban primacy is more common in Latin America than in any other region of the world.[8]

Jefferson's paper suggested that primacy is connected with specific social and geographic factors, but his hypotheses were stated in a loosely descriptive manner which precludes rigorous testing.[9] Both Browning[10] and Ginsburg[11] discussed the development of primacy in Latin America and Southeast Asia, respectively; their discussions were largely in terms of unique regional and historical factors. Browning's discussion created the impression that primacy is independent of particular identifiable conditions. He reported that primacy is found both inland and on the coast, in both large and small countries at different stages of economic development and under very different political systems.[12]

My own investigation is based upon quite different assumptions than those reported above. I have assumed that high primacy wherever it occurs is related to the same identifiable conditions. This paper reports on the testing of six hypotheses about conditions under which primacy occurs. The six hypotheses are tested against the widest possible universe using worldwide social, economic, and demographic data that have become available in the last decade.

HYPOTHESES

1. Areal Extent of Dense Population

It is almost a truism that most large cities are integrated with the rest of their nation or region by the reciprocal exchange of services. There tends to be only one very large city in a country where distinct primacy occurs. All "large city" services required by the entire country would have to be provided from the principal center. It is clear that the servicing task of that city would be comparatively greater in a territorially extensive country because of transportation and communication problems, than it would be in a country that was areally compact. Accordingly, we would predict that areal extent of a country and degree of primacy would be negatively associated. Since unpopulated or sparsely settled areas would

[5] A recent exception to this statement is S. K. Mehta, "Some Demographic and Economic Correlates of Primate Cities: A Case for Re-evaluation," *Demography*, Vol. 1 (1964), pp. 136–47, which explores the question of whether primate cities have a parasitic effect on the economy of the remainder of a country and some of the correlates of the "primate city" urban structure. The use of different operational definitions of urban primacy and a different universe of countries, makes cross-comparison of the findings of Mehta's paper and this paper difficult.

[6] C. T. Stewart, "Migration as a Function of Population and Distance," *American Sociological Review*, Vol. 25 (1960), pp. 347–56.

[7] N. S. Ginsburg, "The Great City in Southeast Asia," *American Journal of Sociology*, Vol. 60 (1955), pp. 455–62.

[8] H. L. Browning, "Recent Trends in Latin American Urbanization," *The Annals of the American Association of Political and Social Science*, Vol. 316 (March, 1958), p. 114.

[9] Jefferson, *op. cit.*, footnote 2, pp. 226–32.

[10] Browning, *op. cit.*, footnote 8, pp. 114–16.

[11] Ginsburg, *op. cit.*, footnote 7, p. 356.

[12] Browning, *op. cit.*, footnote 8, pp. 114–16.

be largely irrelevant from the stand-point of demand for urban services, the hypothesis was qualified to read: *The areal extent of dense population in a country will be negatively associated with the degree of primacy of the leading city.*

2. Per Capita Income

It was suggested above that the degree of urban primacy possible was limited by the areal extent of the population of a country for which services were provided. If we assume that a higher volume of services would be required by a wealthy population, it would appear unfeasible to provide these services from a single center because of the inconvenience of frequently obtaining goods and services from a great distance. Demands for urban services in more affluent countries would encourage the growth of local cities capable of meeting this demand. In the case of poorer countries, as Ginsburg pointed out:[13]

There are in effect only a limited number of services to be performed by cities within a predominantly village and folk society, although it may be industrializing slowly, and the great cities continue to possess a virtual monopoly of those services.[13]

For this reason we would predict that *average per capita income in a country will be negatively associated with the degree of primacy of the leading city.*

3. Export-Oriented Economies

It has been argued that high primacy would be encouraged by both an areally compact population, and by a poorer country as both of these factors would ease the problem of distributing large city services. The distribution problem would also be minimized if the consumers of these services lived in the primate city itself rather than in

[13]Ginsburg, *op. cit.*, footnote 7, p. 457.

other parts of the country. Stewart pointed out that when the commercial development of an economy is based upon a plantation system geared to foreign markets:[14]

The gain from commercialization, accruing mainly to a small landowner class will be spent in the capital and abroad, whereas if the gain were widely distributed in the first instance, its expenditure would stimulate the growth of regional market towns with many complementary amenities.[14]

Likewise Browning cited the "peculiar nature of the export economies . . . which had the effect of concentrating the control of wealth and power in relatively few hands," as being instrumental in the development of high primacy.[15] He pointed out that absentee owners of the mines, estates, and plantations preferred to live in the capital and concentrated their wealth and power there. On this basis we would predict that *dependence of the economy of a country on exports will be positively associated with the degree of primacy of the leading city.*

4. Colonial History

The hypotheses above tacitly assume that natural trade areas correspond to political divisions. It must be recognized that the population of a country may in fact obtain urban services from beyond its national borders. We would expect that countries formerly involved in a colonial system would remain, to some degree, economically interdependent. What effect would this have on degree of primacy in these ex-colonial countries?

Stewart stated that the country that provides the administrative capital and security for areas beyond its borders would be expected to have, according

[14]Stewart, *op. cit.*, footnote 6, p. 356.
[15]Browning, *op. cit.*, footnote 8, pp. 114–16.

to the rank–size rule, a high primacy pattern whereas the largest city in a colonial or otherwise dependent country will have lower primacy.[16] The opposite view is held by D. W. Fryer, who pointed out that colonial systems facilitated the growth of primate cities by centralizing the administration of these countries and improving the communication and transportation networks that focus upon them to make them easier to administer.[17] Ginsburg also pointed out that growth of capitals of ex-colonial countries has been spurred by the accelerated rise of nationalism and increased centralization of political functions in the capitals.[18]

Because of the difference of opinion regarding the direction of the relation between primacy and ex-colonial status, our hypothesis in this case is a nondirectional one. We would predict that *the ex-colonial status of a country will be either positively or negatively associated with the degree of primacy of the leading city.*

5. Agricultural Economies

Industrial centers often locate close to the source of raw material and power, thus providing a basis for alternative population centers in other parts of a country. In heavily agricultural countries, this dispersive tendency of industry would not be operating to a high degree. Also, countries with a high proportion of their labor force engaged in agriculture would tend to have higher primacy because they would be typically poorer countries and export countries, each of which we have

argued is associated with primacy. Therefore, we would predict that *the proportion of a nation's work force engaged in agriculture will be positively associated with the degree of primacy of the leading city.*

6. Rate of National Population Growth

There are several reasons for expecting that a rapid rate of national population growth would be associated with primacy. Such growth is most often the result of an interruption in the demographic balance of high birth and high death rates by a sharp decline in the death rate with little or no immediate decline in the birth rate. This is most characteristic of underdeveloped countries which are moving toward a more urbanized industrialized society. Such development would create an expanding demand for the type of services that would be provided by large centers; but this demand would not necessarily be so great that it could not be met by a single center. Rapid population growth also would provide surplus population for the expansion of the primate city itself, particularly if the revolution in death control were accompanied by mechanization of agriculture. Therefore we would predict that *a rapid rate of national population growth will be positively associated with high primacy of the leading city.*

PROCEDURES

The degree of primacy as used in this paper refers to the ratio of the population of the largest metropolitan area to the second largest in the same country. Other possible dimensions and connotations of the degree of primacy and the primate city were ignored here in favor of the population ratio of the two leading cities for operational simplicity.

The universe was defined as all countries in the world which contained

[16]C. T. Stewart, "The size and Spacing of Cities," *Geographical Review*, Vol. 48 (1958), p. 223.

[17]D. W. Fryer, "The Million City in Southeast Asia," *Geographical Review*, Vol. 43 (1953), p. 479.

[18]Ginsburg, *op. cit.*, footnote 7, p. 455.

at least one metropolitan area with over 1,000,000 population. Thirty-nine countries met this criterion. (Hong Kong and Singapore, which were city-states during the period for which the data were obtained, were not included.) Countries were placed in rank order from one to thirty-nine according to how many times the primate city was larger than the second city. (See Table 7). The range extended from Saigon–Cholon, which was 16.3 times larger than the second city in Viet-Nam, to Montreal which was virtually the same size as Canada's second largest city, Toronto. This array of thirty-nine countries was then dichotomized at the midpoint. The nineteen countries above this point were classified as high-primacy countries and the nineteen falling below were classified as low-primacy countries. The twentieth or middle country was dropped from the computations to keep the totals even. The nineteen countries with high and the nineteen countries with low primacy patterns were then cross-classified with their rating on each of the other six variables in turn.

When the tables were first constructed, a fairly strong negative relation was observed between degree of primacy and areal extent of dense population, but the degree of association with each of the five other variables was disappointingly small. It was observed that the relation between primacy and each other variable was present in the case of small-sized countries, but that in countries with extensive populated areas, the relationship with the other variables was practically nonexistent. It was felt that the influence of territorial size was operating so strongly in the larger countries that the effect of all other variables on degree of primacy was masked. For this reason it was decided to statis-

tically remove the effect of territorial size by measuring the relation between primacy and the other five variables within smaller countries only. These are the relationships reported in this paper in Tables 2–6.

Countries were classified as large if their densely populated area (fifty persons or more per square mile) extended over 700 miles in length. This definition resulted in nine large and twenty-nine small countries.[19] Cutting points for income, export economies, agricultural economies, and rate of population growth were obtained by dichotomizing the ranking of all countries on indexes of these variables at the midpoint.[20] The nine countries which won their independence after 1800 were classified as ex-colonies.[21]

[19]If the distribution of countries by size was cut at the midpoint, there would not have been enough smaller countries left for the subsequent analysis in Tables 2–6, which are based on smaller countries only. Also it was reasoned that a primate city located roughly in the center of a 700-mile stretch of densely populated area probably could provide services to persons living 300 to 400 miles distant. Distance estimates were made from an isometric population density map with the aid of a rule. Hence, these measurements may be regarded only as approximations.

[20]High-income countries had average per capita income of $200.00 annually or over. High-export countries were those in which the total value of exports amounted to forty percent of the total national income or over. Countries with forty-five percent or more of the male labor force engaged in agriculture were classified as agricultural countries, and countries in which population increase amounted to 1.8 percent or more per annum were classified as fast growing.

[21]Countries which became independent from territorially adjacent countries during the period were not considered to be ex-colonies. Although the year 1800 may seem somewhat early, it is consistent with the logic of the argument expressed in the hypothesis. Moreover, taking a later date as the cutting point would not have left a sufficient number of ex-colonies to analyze.

Koppa, or small "q" (for quadrant measure), was used as the measure of association for all six of the two-by-two tables in the study.[22] No test of significance is employed in this paper since hypotheses were tested on consideration of an entire universe rather than on a sample.

Since published statistical series were not complete for all countries, it was sometimes necessary to use more than one source or to combine information from different years.[23] In some cases the necessary statistics were not available for a few countries, and estimates were made providing that there was enough additional information upon which to base them, and that the estimates would place the country clearly in the upper or lower half of the continuum on the variable in question. Countries are omitted from the tabulations where information was not available and estimates were not possible.

[22]W. H. Kruskal, "Ordinal Measures of Association," *Journal of the American Statistical Association*, Vol. 53 (1958), pp. 815–61. Koppa is a measure of association for two-by-two tables which is calculated by subtracting the sum in one set of diagonals of the table from the sum of the other diagonals and then dividing by the sum of all four cells. The values of koppa are fairly close in magnitude to phi coefficients computed for the same tables. However, Yule's "Q" computed for the tables yields values ranging from 40 to 300 percent higher.

[23]All population estimates for cities were obtained from: K. Davis, International Urban Research, *World's Metropolitan Areas* (Berkeley and Los Angeles: University of California Press, 1959). Data for the indexes of the independent variables in Tables 3 through 7 were obtained from the following sources: W. S. Woytinski and E. S. Woytinski, *World Commerce and Governments: Trends and Outlooks* (New York: The Twentieth Century Fund, 1955); United Nations *Statistical Year Book* (New York: 1956 and 1957); United Nations *Demographic Year Book* (New York: 1957); and *Stateman's Year Book* (New York: St. Martin's Press, 1960).

Consequently, totals vary between tables.

FINDINGS

The first hypothesis predicted that areal extent of dense population and primacy would be negatively associated. In Table 1 we find that this is in fact the case (koppa, −0.37). Size appears to be a definite limiting condition in the development of primacy. Eight out of the nine large countries had a low degree of primacy.

Table 1

Degree of Primacy and Areal Extent of Dense Population: Circa 1955 (No. of Countries)

Extent of dense population	Primacy		
	High[a]	Low	Totals
Large[b]	1	8	9
Small	18	11	29
Totals	19	19	38
			$q = -0.37$

[a] A population ratio of the first to the second metropolitan area of a country of 2.4 or greater.
[b] Countries with dense population (50 persons or over per square mile) extended over 700 miles in length.
Source: Computed by author.

Hypothesis two predicted that per capita income would be negatively associated with primacy. In Table 2 we find some support for this hypothesis (koppa, −0.22). The relationship is not symmetrical however. Whereas eight of the ten poorer nations manifested high primacy, wealthier nations are almost evenly divided between high and low primacy. Our findings indicate a wider scope for Ginsburg's generalization concerning the relation between

Table 2

Degree of Primacy and Per Capita Income: Circa 1955 (No. of Countries)

Per capita income	Primacy		
	High	Low	Totals
High[a]	7	6	13
Low	8	2	10
Totals	15	8	23

$q = -0.22$

[a] Average per capita income of $200.00 annually or over.
Source: Computed by author.

Table 3

Degree of Primacy and Export-Oriented Economies: Circa 1955 (No. of Countries)

Export-oriented economies	Primacy		
	High	Low	Totals
High[a]	10	4	14
Low	5	4	9
Totals	15	8	23

$q = +0.22$

[a] Value of exports 40 percent of national income or over.
Source: Computed by author.

economic development and urban primacy in Southeast Asia.[24]

Hypothesis three predicted that export-oriented economies would be positively related to primacy. We find in Table 3 some support for this hypothesis (koppa, +0.22). Ten of the fourteen countries with export-oriented economies had high primacy, whereas the economically self-contained countries were more evenly distributed between the high- and low-primacy categories.

Hypothesis four was a nondirectional hypothesis because of contradictory opinions in the literature as to whether colonial history would be associated with high or low primacy. We find in Table 4 that ex-colonial countries tend to have high primacy (koppa, +0.21). Here again the relationship is nonsymmetrical. Eight of the nine countries with a colonial history had high primacy whereas countries without a colonial history were almost evenly divided between high and low primacy.

Hypothesis five predicted that agricultural economies would be positively related to primacy. We find in Table 5

[24]Ginsburg, *op. cit.*, footnote 7.

Table 4

Degree of Primacy and Ex-Colonial Status: Circa 1955 (No. of Countries)

Ex-colonial status	Primacy		
	High	Low	Totals
Yes[a]	8	1	9
No	10	9	19
Totals	18	10	28

$q = +0.21$

[a] Countries achieving political independence after 1800.
Source: Computed by author.

Table 5

Degree of Primacy and Type of Economy: Circa 1955 (No. of Countries)

Economy	Primacy		
	High	Low	Totals
Agricultural[a]	10	5	15
Nonagricultural	7	6	13
Totals	17	11	28

$q = +0.14$

[a] Forty-five percent or more of the male labor force employed in agriculture.
Source: Computed by author.

a slight tendency in this direction (koppa, +0.14). Agricultural countries were twice as likely to have high primate cities as low primate cities but nonagricultural countries were almost evenly divided between high- and low-primacy categories.

Hypothesis six predicted that rate of population growth of a country would be positively related to high primacy of the leading city. In Table 6 we find that this relationship is in the direction predicted (koppa, +0.33). This association, like several of the others reported above, appears to be nonsymmetrical.

Table 6

Primacy and Rate of Population Growth in Country: Circa 1955 (No. of Countries)

Growth rate	Primacy		
	High	Low	Totals
Fast[a]	8	1	9
Slow	8	10	18
Totals	16	11	27
			$q = +0.33$

[a] Population increase of 1.8 percent per annum or over.

Source: Computed by author.

The overall pattern which emerges is that high primacy is precluded in large countries but is not characteristic of all small countries. However, primacy is characteristic of those small countries which have low per capita income, are highly dependent upon exports, have a colonial history, an agricultural economy, and a fast rate of population growth. These are all attributes of underdeveloped countries, particularly those in the transitional or emergent phase of social and economic development. The situation with respect to wealthier, economically self-sufficient countries, with no recent colonial history, with nonagricultural economies, and a slower rate of population growth, is not as clear as half of the countries in these categories have high primacy and half have low primacy. (See Table 7.) Thus, cases of high primacy occur in such fully developed countries as France (7.5), Denmark (7.7), and Austria (7.3) as well as in such underdeveloped countries as South Vietnam (16.3), Mexico (7.4), and Cuba (7.3), although the proportion of high primates is smaller among the highly developed countries. This raises questions concerning the validity of our original assumption that high primacy would be related to the same identifiable conditions wherever it occurs. This study has revealed at least two patterns of high primacy. The major pattern was characteristic of almost all countries in this study with geographically limited densely settled areas, low income, export-oriented and agricultural economies, a colonial history, and fast population growth; a less marked pattern was characteristic of approximately half of the smaller highly developed countries. Within this latter group, further knowledge is needed as to why primacy developed in some of these countries but not others.

An important limitation of this study was its dependence on current cross-sectional data to test several hypotheses concerned with conditions under which primacy develops. The concept of development implies an historical process. It suggests the need for studies systematically relating changes in degree of primacy with changes in the social, economic, and geopolitical conditions within countries.

For instance, what has been the effect of the dissolution of empires on the degree of primacy of the leading city in the former mother country? What has been the consequences of political partition of national states upon the patterns of primacy in both of the new political units? Similarly what are the consequences for the primacy pattern of some of the various forms of political and economic union which are now occurring? At what point in the economic development of emerging nations are primate cities seriously challenged by other population centers? Such longitudinal studies would help clarify our understanding of the conditions relating to the development of primate cities.

Table 7

Primacy of World's Metropolitan Areas Over 1,000,000 in Population, 1955

No.	Metropolitan area	Country	Population of primate	Ratio of first to 2nd Met. area
1.	Saigon–Cholon	Viet-Nam	2,000,000	16.3
	Hue		123,000	
2.	Bangkok	Thailand	1,484,000	15[a]
3.	Budapest	Hungary	1,783,000	13.2
	Miskok		135,200	
4.	Manila	Philippines	2,348,000	9.8
	Cebu		240,000	
5.	Buenos Aires	Argentina	5,750,000	9.1
	Rosario		630,000	
6.	Bucharest	Rumania	1,236,905	8.0
	Cluj		154,752	
7.	Copenhagen	Denmark	1,292,915	7.7
	Aarhus		168,700	
8.	Paris	France	6,736,836	7.5
	Lille-Tourcoing		898,524	
9.	Mexico City	Mexico	3,900,000	7.4
	Guadalajara		530,000	
10.	Havana	Cuba	1,315,000	7.3
	Santiago de Cuba		180,000	
11.	Lima	Peru	1,169,000	7.3
	Arequipa		160,300	
12.	Vienna	Austria	1,865,000	7.3
	Linz		255,000	
13.	Tehran	Iran	1,513,164	5.2
	Tabriz		290,195	
14.	Athens	Greece	1,490,000	4.9
	Salonika		305,000	
15.	Santiago	Chile	1,600,000	4.8
	Valparaiso		335,000	
16.	London	Great Britain	10,490,690	4.1
	Birmingham		2,575,840	
17.	Istanbul	Turkey	1,365,363	3.3
	Ankara		408,029	

No.	Metropolitan area	Country	Population of primate	Ratio of first to 2nd Met. area
18.	Caracas	Venezuela	1,000,000	2.8
	Maracaibo		355,000	
19.	Cairo	Egypt	2,770,000	2.4
	Alexandria		1,170,000	
20.	Johannesburg	South Africa	1,825,000	2.4
	Cape Town		760,000	
21.	New York	U.S.	14,280,500	2.3
	Chicago		6,121,600	
22.	Shanghai	China	6,204,417	2.2
	Peking		2,768,149	
23.	Stockholm	Sweden	1,021,068	2.2
	Göteborg		458,400	
24.	Moscow	Russia	7,300,000	2.1
	Leningrad		3,500,000	
25.	Djakarta	Indonesia	1,871,200	2.0
	Surabaja		935,700	
26.	Tokyo–Yokohama	Japan	11,349,339	1.8
	Osaka–Kobe		6,404,749	
27.	Lisbon	Portugal	1,130,000	1.8
	Oporto		640,000	
28.	Brussels	Belgium	1,371,816	1.6
	Antwerp		833,177	
29.	Karachi	Pakistan	1,318,000	1.5
	Lahore		864,000	
30.	Seoul	South Korea	1,574,868	1.5
	Pusan		1,049,363	
31.	Sydney	Australia	1,869,000	1.3
	Melbourne		1,470,000	
32.	Essen–Dortmund–Duisburg	West Germany	5,353,100	1.3
	Berlin		4,244,600	
33.	Calcutta	India	5,700,000	1.3
	Bombay		4,400,000	
34.	Katowice–Zabrze–Bytom	Poland	1,921,000	1.2
	Warsaw		1,595,000	
35.	Amsterdam	Netherlands	1,017,042	1.1
	Rotterdam		935,710	
36.	Madrid	Spain	1,840,000	1.1
	Barcelona		1,655,000	
37.	Milan	Italy	2,153,700	1.1
	Rome		1,958,600	
38.	Rio de Janeiro	Brazil	3,750,000	1.1
	São Paulo		3,300,000	
39.	Montreal	Canada	1,713,662	1.0
	Toronto		1,632,149	

ᵃ Bangkok is the only metropolitan area listed for Thailand. The correct ratio is fifteen or greater.
Source: Population Estimates from International Urban Research, *The World's Metropolitan Areas* (Berkeley and Los Angeles: University of California Press, 1959).

23. Some Demographic and Economic Correlates of Primate Cities: A Case for Revaluation

SURINDER K. MEHTA

INTRODUCTION

In the recent literature, a number of social scientists have maintained that many of the underdeveloped countries are overurbanized relative to their stage of economic development, i.e., much higher proportions of their populations live in urban areas than would be justified by the level of national economic development.[1]

Aside from the phenomenon of overurbanization, it has been maintained that many of these colonial, ex-colonial, or quasi-colonial underdeveloped countries, especially those of Asia and Latin America, show a peculiar urban structure, namely, the presence of one very large city that greatly overshadows the next largest city in each country. The growth of these "great cities" has not been due primarily to industrial expansion but to extraindustrial factors.[2] It has been proposed by Fryer, Ginsburg, and other writers that in Burma, Thailand, South Vietnam, the Philippines, Malaya, Indonesia, etc., such cities as Rangoon, Bangkok, Saigon-Cholon, Manila, Singapore, and Jakarta, each of which is many times the size of the second largest city in each country, are "Primate Cities," each

Demography, 1 (1964), 136–47, with supplementary extended footnote 21 and Appendix supplied by author in November 1967. Reprinted by permission of author and publisher.

Otis Dudley Duncan, Thomas A. Reiner, Leroy O. Stone, Donald V. McGranahan, and especially Richard W. Redick are thanked for reading the preliminary version of this paper and critically commenting on it.

[1] On overurbanization in underdeveloped countries see the following: Kingsley Davis and Hilda Hertz Golden, "Urbanization and the Development of Preindustrial Areas," *Economic Development and Cultural Change*, 3 (October, 1954), 6–26; Eric E. Lampard, "The History of Cities in the Economically Advanced Areas," *Economic Development and Cultural Change*, 3 (January, 1955), 81–136; United Nations, *Report on the World Social Situation—Including Studies of Urbanization in Underdeveloped Areas* (New York: 1957), Part II; Philip M. Hauser (ed.), *Urbanization in Latin America*, a UNESCO survey (New York: International Documents Service, Columbia University Press, 1961); Philip M. Hauser (ed.), *Urbanization in Asia*

and the Far East (Calcutta: UNESCO, 1957); Shanti Tangri, "Urbanization, Political Stability, and Economic Growth," in Roy Turner (ed.), *India's Urban Future* (Berkeley: University of California Press, 1962), pp. 192–212; Arthur F. Raper *et al.*, *Urban and Industrial Taiwan—Crowded and Resourceful*, Foreign Operation Administration Mutual Security Mission to China, and National Taiwan University (Taipei: September, 1954); R. M. Sundrum, "Urbanization: The Burmese Experience," Economic Paper No. 16, Economic Research Project, Departments of Economics, Statistics and Commerce, University of Rangoon (Rangoon: March, 1957).

[2] Philip M. Hauser, "Summary Report of the General Rapporteur," in Hauser (ed.), *Urbanization in Asia and the Far East, op. cit.*, pp. 3–32; also see "Conclusions of the Seminar," chapter ii in *ibid*. The present author himself took this position in an earlier study; see his "The Labor Force of Urban Burma and Rangoon, 1953, A Comparative Study" (unpublished Ph. D. dissertation, Department of Sociology, University of Chicago, 1959), *passim*.

dominating their nation's economy and political life.[3]

In the literature the "primate city" phenomenon has been contrasted to what has been called a regular urban hierarchy, or "system of cities," which is supposedly a characteristic of only highly advanced industrial economies. This "system of cities" refers to the fact that when the cities of certain countries are ordered by rank and size, one ob-

tains a distribution which "is in accordance with Pareto's law;"[4] that is, the largest city is roughly twice as large as the next largest city in the given country.[5]

THE ARGUMENT

We often come across statements, implicitly or most emphatically made, that the "primate cities" of such countries as Thailand, Burma, Paraguay, Guatemala, etc., are "parasitic,"

[3] D. W. Fryer, "The Million City in Southeast Asia," *Geographical Review*, 43 (October, 1953), 474–94; Norton S. Ginsburg, "The Great City in Southeast Asia," *American Journal of Sociology*, 60 (March, 1955), 455–62; Bert F. Hoselitz, "Generative and Parasitic Cities," *Economic Development and Cultural Change*, 3 (April, 1955), 278–94; Eric E. Lampard, "The History of Cities in the Economically Advanced Areas," *Economic Development and Cultural Change*, 3 (January, 1955), 81–136; O. H. K. Spate, "Factors in the Development of Capital Cities," *Geographical Review*, 32 (October, 1942), 622–31. Hauser (ed.), *Urbanization in Asia and the Far East, op. cit.* For an extended discussion of this topic and additional literature, see Surinder K. Mehta, "The 'Primate City'—Rangoon . . . ," Chapter VII, pp. 232–51, in *op. cit.* The concept of the Primate City was proposed by Mark Jefferson, "The Law of the Primate City," *Geographical Review*, 29 (April, 1939), 226–32. Jefferson's concept of the "primate city" differs from the meaning given it by more recent writers. To Jefferson, New York, Tokyo, and other similar cities "supereminent" in national influence were "primate cities" irrespective of the fact that they were only about twice the size of the second largest city in the country.

[4] Hoselitz, *op. cit.*, p. 291. For some literature on this subject see Carl H. Madden, "On Some Indications of Stability in the Growth of Cities in the United States," *Economic Development and Cultural Change*, 4 (April, 1956), 236–52; George Kingsley Zipf, *National Unity and Disunity* (Bloomington, 1941); George Kingsley Zipf, *Human Behavior and the Principle of Least Effort: An Introduction to Human Ecology* (Cambridge: Addison-Wesley, 1949); Brian J. L. Berry, "City Size Distributions and Economic Development," *Economic Development and Cultural Change*, 9 (July, 1961), 573–88; Brian J. L. Berry and William L. Garrison,

"Alternate Explanations of Urban Rank-Size Relationships," *Annals, Association of American Geographers*, 48 (1958), 83–91; Martin J. Beckman, "City Hierarchies and the Distribution of City Size," *Economic Development and Cultural Change*, 6 (1958), 243–48; Otis Dudley Duncan, "Population Distribution and Community Structure," *Cold Spring Harbor Symposia on Quantitative Biology*, 22 (1957), 357–71, especially pp. 364–67; and Rutledge Vining, "A Description of Certain Spatial Aspects of an Economic System," *Economic Development and Cultural Change*, 3 (January, 1955), 147–95. For certain insightful comments on the implications of the rank-size rule, consult Edgar M. Hoover, "The Concept of a System of Cities: A Comment on Rutledge Vining's Paper," *Economic Development and Cultural Change*, 3 (January, 1955), 196–98: John Q. Stewart, "Empirical Mathematical Rules concerning the Distribution and Equilibrium of Population," *Geographical Review*, 37 (July, 1947), 461–85, shows the application of Pareto's distribution to various sociological and ecological data.

[5] This is really an over-simplified statement. The largest city of the system is twice the size of the next largest city when the exponent n in the following relationship is unity or very close to it: $R^n S_r = M$, where M and n are constants; S_r stands for the population of the Rth city in the group, and R is the rank in the group of that city (see Stewart, *op. cit.*, p. 462). Or, alternatively, consider the form of the Pareto curve, "$y = Ax^{-a}$, where x is the size (number of inhabitants) of a community, y is the number of communities of size n or larger, and A and a are parameters estimated from the data. It frequently is the case that a has a value close to unity. . . . If a is exactly unity, the equation simplifies to

rather than "generative."[6] Hauser writing about these cities says:

These cities tend to be "parasitic" in the sense that they tended to obstruct economic growth in their country of location by retarding the development of other cities in the nation, by contributing little to the development of their own hinterland, by being oriented primarily toward the contribution of services to the colonial power abroad or the colonial or indigenous elite in the great city itself.[7]

In a similar vein, Lampard writes:

Thus the presence of an overly large city in a preindustrial society may act as a curb rather than a stimulus to wider economic growth. Its growth and maintenance have been somewhat parasitical in the sense that profits of trade, capital accumulated in agricultural and other primary pursuits have been dissipated in grandiose urban construction, servicing, and consuming by a "colonial" elite. The labor and enterprise which might otherwise have been invested in some form of manufacture or material processing in the interior are

drawn off to the great city by the attractive dazzle of a million lights.[8]

Again, Stolper writes:

In developed countries, cities are on the whole generative in Hoselitz's sense, in that they perform functions not only for themselves and their like but also for their hinterland on which they depend for supplies and markets. In underdeveloped countries cities are apt to be "parasitic" in Hoselitz's terminology, in the sense that their physical hinterland is neither their market nor their supply area, that for all practical purposes their physical hinterland might just as well be on the moon. Batavia [Jakarta], Rio de Janeiro, etc., are examples of what I am talking about. They drain off a few supplies for export, but little of the imports filters back into the hinterland.[9]

Although the views of these authors can in some measure be justified, it seems that they have overstated the case in regard to the "parasitic" in contrast to the "generative" impact of these "primate cities." Some of the positive factors involved are described here. First of all, with the coming of national independence, these "primate cities" more and more are looking inward to their own hinterlands rather than

---

$xy = A$, A becomes the estimated size of the largest community, and the estimated size of the nth ranking community is A/n (the so-called 'rank-size rule')." Duncan, *op. cit.*, pp. 364–65. "Elsewhere it has been argued that these J-shaped distributions are Yule distributions, the steady-states of stochastic growth processes." Brian J. L. Berry, "Some Relations of Urbanization and Basic Patterns of Economic Development," in Forrest R. Pitts (ed.), *Urban Systems and Economic Development*, Papers and Proceedings of a Conference on Urban Systems Research in Underdeveloped and Advanced Economies (Eugene, Oregon: University of Oregon, 1962), p. 21. For further discussion of the J-shaped distributions see Herbert A. Simon, "On a Class of Skew Distribution Functions," *Biometrika*, 62 (December, 1955), reprinted as Chapter 9 in Simon's *Models of Man* (New York: John Wiley & Sons, 1957).

[6] Hoselitz's terms, *op. cit.*

[7] Philip M. Hauser, "World and Asian Urbanization in Relation to Economic Development and Social Change," in Hauser (ed.), *Urbanization in Asia and the Far East, op. cit.*, p. 87.

[8] Lampard, *op. cit.*, p. 131. For somewhat similar viewpoints see Ginsburg, *op. cit.*; Noel P. Gist and L. A. Halbert, *Urban Society* (4th ed.; New York: Thomas Y. Crowell, 1956), pp. 68–71; and Clyde E. Browning, "Primate Cities and Related Concepts," in Forrest R. Pitts (ed.), *op. cit.*, pp. 16–27.

[9] Wolfgang Stolper, "Spatial Order and the Economic Growth of Cities: A Comment on Eric Lampard's Paper," *Economic Development and Cultural Change*, 3 (January, 1955), 141. In the same place Stolper indicates that even in regard to the Western countries this city and countryside integration into a functioning whole is a recent phenomenon. He writes: "This is true to a much greater degree than romantically inclined economists seem to believe, who talk about organic interrelations which may or may not have existed in the Middle Ages."

outward to the colonial motherland. They not only are becoming administrative, trade, educational, and cultural centers servicing the indigenous population, but also are probably stimulating the growth of cities in their own hinterlands.[10] Second, although the mushrooming growth of these "primate cities" places a heavy burden of expenditure on the national and municipal governments to meet infrastructure requirements of more housing and other building construction, power, sewage disposal, and other essential municipal services, it is also true that these cities are usually very favorably located at the confluence of waterways, rail and air transport lines. Hence additional investment in these cities is perhaps more justified than building new cities or investing in cities that are not so favorably located as the "primate cities."[11] With regard to a third factor, Lampard points out that in these great cities there is, "at least, some tradition of urban life, and constant pressure to secure a livelihood from non-farming."[12] The populations of these cities for some time have been exposed to a market economy and are being made more and more aware of rational economic considerations. The inhabitants of these cities are becoming urbanites to some extent and are certainly much more urbanized than those who remain in villages or small towns. These metropolis dwellers[13] are faced with the requirements of urban living that force "innovations which those in the countryside, if left to themselves, would

[10]As the "primate city" becomes more and more indigenous rather than foreign in ethnic composition and character, it generates a greater demand for indigenously produced goods both for reasons of nationalism and preference for local products satisfying indigenous cultural tastes and fashions. For example, the demand for Burmese slippers and *longyis* in Rangoon is certain to be much greater at present than formerly now that Burma is an independent country and highly nationalistic. Rangoon's population is predominantly indigenous rather than foreign as in the past, with many of the remaining foreigners having gone "native" in dress and identity. This greater demand for indigenously produced articles in lieu of imported goods—Western shoes and dress copies of Paris fashions or European style men's suits, for instance—encourages the growth of native industries in Rangoon itself and in other towns, such as Mandalay, Bassein, and Henzada.

[11]Furthermore, it should be noted that such "primate cities" as Bangkok, Montevideo, Saigon, and Rangoon are located in the most densely populated regions of their countries and therefore, investments made in these cities can service with less operating and "friction"

costs a larger proportion of the total population of the country than would be the case if equal investments were to be made in cities such as Uttaradit, Durazno, Dalat, and Mandalay which are not similarly situated. Of course, it is not argued that all new investments should be poured into the "primate cities." It is merely pointed out that perhaps much of the investment being made in these cities is justifiable and should not outrightly be condemned as wasteful. Certain writers, such as Hauser, *Urbanization in Asia . . . , op. cit.,* chaps. i, ii, and iii; Shanti Tangri, *op. cit.,* Catherine Bauer Wurster, "Urban Living Conditions, Overhead Costs, and the Development Pattern," in Roy Turner (ed.), *op. cit.,* pp. 277–98; and Clyde E. Browning, *op. cit.,* believe that governments of underdeveloped countries should allocate a larger share of their inputs toward the development of smaller cities and towns and a smaller share of the inputs for the "primate cities" than they have hitherto. Any decisions in this regard on the part of the governments concerned, however, must rely on better evidence than has been presented to date. For some additional material on this topic, see: Sachin Chaudhuri, "Centralization and the Alternate Forms of Decentralization: A Key Issue," in Roy Turner (ed.), *op. cit.,* pp. 213–39: and Britton Harris, "Urban Centralization and Planned Development," in *ibid.,* pp. 261–76.

[12]Lampard, *op. cit.,* p. 130.

[13]The reader should be cautioned that many of these metropolis "dwellers" in the "primate cities" in Burma, Malaya, and the Philippines, for example, are not to be thought of as being like the typical "metropolis dwellers" of Berlin,

never make."[14] Finally, it seems that the writers who focus on the "parasitic" aspects of the "primate cities" either neglect or unduly de-emphasize a very important "generative" aspect of the city, especially the large city. Generally speaking, the city is the only efficient locale for non-agricultural production, both manufacturing and specialized services. This is because it has the advantages of a large and concentrated labor and consumer market; it is the focus of transportation routes; it has the economies of scale and juxtaposition of industries and specialists;[15] it is a fertile ground for social and cultural change

---

Paris, Philadelphia, Boston, New York, or Chicago. As one scholar points out, and with some justification: ". . . many of the characteristics of the great cities of Asia and Southeast Asia are at variance with the patterns observed in the West. For example, although they have large size, high density, and often heterogeneous populations, these characteristics of the urban environment have not produced the basic changes in interpersonal relations, the nature of human nature, and the social institutions as in their Western context.

"Although the large cities in Asia have great size, their pluralistic composition and characteristic dual economies have enabled indigenous groups to live under essentially 'folk' conditions within the boundaries of the city. Despite their relatively high densities, life has not necessarily become largely secularized, great differentiation of functions has not taken place, and the way of life has not changed markedly for many of the indigenous population groups. Finally, despite the great heterogeneity of the population in many of these cities, both exogenous and indigenous ethnic groups, little has occurred in the way of increased sophistication, rationality in behavior, cosmopolitanism of outlook, or innovation and social change. . . ." Philip M. Hauser, "World and Asian Urbanization in Relation to Economic Development . . . ," *op. cit.*, pp. 87–88.

[14]Davis and Golden, *op. cit.*, p. 25.

[15]For a discussion of the disadvantages of regional decentralization of industry and technical and managerial manpower see Albert Mayer, "Social Analysis and National Economic Development in India," *Ekistics*, 15 (June, 1963), 326–30, especially, p. 329.

necessary for economic development; it is a center from which these innovations or new adaptations, artifacts and technologies introduced from the outside or of local origin spread and diffuse into the countryside and to other towns; and it is an area that receives migrants from the countryside thus relieving the farming areas of the burden of excess populations.[16] Furthermore, the great city "makes possible a greater accumulation of capital and personnel for purposes of formal education, public health, science, art, etc.";[17] in addition, "the possibility of specialization in different branches of knowledge, of the accumulation of libraries and the exchange of ideas, exists because of the character of the city."[18] These and many more advantages accruing from a large city cannot be denied, even though it may be "parasitic." Of course, there are heavy economic and social costs involved and much wealth is wasted, but it is not certain that the balance sheets always show red for countries harboring "primate cities" in

---

[16]Shanti Tangri argues that it is cheaper to raise per capita income in the rural areas than in the cities. For instance, he writes: "The possibilities of asset creation without prior or concomitant savings are quite extensive and impressive in rural areas and insignificant in urban areas." *Op. cit.*, p. 194. In this paper Tangri also holds that the rural social system as well as the urban will be less disrupted if the policy of investment for rural development is pursued in contrast to the sinking of capital in cities. For a detailed analysis of the rural-urban capital formation in underdeveloped countries see Tangri's "Patterns of Investment and Rates of Growth, with Special Reference to India" (unpublished Ph. D. dissertation, University of California, Berkeley, 1960).

[17]Davis and Golden, *op. cit.*, p. 26.

[18]*Ibid.* For a cogent argument in defense of the "primate cities" of Latin America see Harley L. Browning, "Recent Trends in Latin American Urbanization," *The Annals of the American Academy of Political and Social Science*, 316 (March, 1958), 111–20.

their midst. Furthermore, even if one grants that these cites may be "parasitic" at the present time, their impact on the social and economic development of their countries may very well be "generative" in the long run.[19]

As already pointed out, the recent literature, in a rather general way, is concerned with the characteristic dominance and economic role of these cities and how they differ in their economic impact from the cities of the industrialized West. However, this literature is for the most part speculative, with little or no concrete data being presented or specifically taken into consideration.

SOME RESULTS OF AN EXPLORATORY STUDY

The means for testing the hypothesis of the parasitic effect of the "primate city" present a series of difficult problems. What is needed are studies that will enable one to evaluate given inputs of capital and labor in the "primate city" and the resultant output, compared with the output resulting from a similar input in smaller cities. One extremely serious problem is that not all intra-city inputs and outputs are tangible. The problem is compounded because in many instances the given inputs in the "primate city" when compared to similar investments in non-primate cities may have extremely important differential impact on the *rest of the economy of the country* but are somewhat intangible. There is the additional problem of evaluating short-run versus long-run effects. At any rate, the necessary data for such studies

are lacking, particularly for the underdeveloped countries.

What is to be presented here are some results of an exploratory study of the correlates of the degree of "primate city" urban structure in relation to various socioeconomic and demographic variables.[20] Eighty-seven countries, for which at least two sets of data—degree of primacy and per capita gross national product—were available, have been studied.

The study had two broad objectives: first, to examine the relationship between the degree of primacy and certain demographic and ecological characteristics of these countries; second, to be able to indicate tentatively whether or not "primate cities" have a deleterious effect on the national economies.

Table 1 shows the primacy values and rank of the 87 countries. The measure of primacy employed is explained in the note to the table. In Table 2 these countries are allocated to three equal-sized groups according to value and rank in per capita gross national product. Also shown is their rank in primacy within each group and among the 87 countries. Rank order coefficients of correlation between primacy and per capita GNP are given in row (1) of Table 3. The 87 countries were divided into three groups according to per capita GNP since in the literature it has been implied that, generally speaking, the "primate city" phenomenon is found primarily in the underdeveloped countries, and not in the economically advanced.

From these data it is clear that overall there is no relationship between the level of economic development and

---

[19]Hoselitz is himself aware of this possibility —see his paper cited earlier. Also see Bert F. Hoselitz, *Sociological Aspects of Economic Growth* (New York: The Free Press of Glencoe, 1960), chapters vii and ix.

[20]For a closely related study see Berry, "City Size Distributions and Economic Development," *op. cit.*

Table 1
Primacy of Urban Structure and Rank in Primacy
87 Selected Countries, ca. 1955[a]

Country	Rank	Value	Country	Rank	Value
Thailand	1	94.2	Israel	45	58.3
Uruguay	2	86.7	Sweden	46	57.1
Hungary	3	84.7	Czechoslovakia	47	56.0
Guatemala	4	83.9	Belgian Congo	49	55.9
South Vietnam	5	83.7	Iraq	49	55.9
Paraguay	6	83.3	Turkey	49	55.9
Philippines	7	82.0	Morocco	51	55.2
Peru	8	81.7	U.S.S.R.	52	54.8
Argentina	9	79.4	Japan	53	54.7
Costa Rica	10	78.9	French W. Africa	54	52.1
Ceylon	11	78.0	Algeria	55	51.1
Haiti	12	77.8	Cyprus	56	50.0
Cuba	13	77.3	Belgium	57.5	49.7
Austria	14	76.8	Taiwan	57.5	49.7
Denmark	15	76.2	United States	59	49.6
Ireland	16	75.8	French Eq. Africa	60	49.4
Tunisia	17	75.6	Ecuador	61	48.5
Greece	18	75.2	South Korea	62	47.9
France	19	74.7	Ghana	63	47.8
Mexico	20	74.3	Union of So. Africa	64	47.2
Nepal	21	73.9	Afghanistan	65	46.5
Rumania	22	73.8	West Germany	66	46.4
Panama	23	72.4	Indonesia	67	45.6
Dominican Republic	24	72.0	Jordan	68	45.3
Chile	25	71.4	Pakistan	69	45.2
Lebanon	26	70.6	China	70	44.8
Puerto Rico	27	70.2	Brazil	71	44.7
El Salvador	28	69.0	Fed. of Rhodesia		
Burma	29	68.1	and Nyasaland	72	44.5
Honduras	30	67.7	India	73.5	44.4
Ethiopia	31	67.2	Luxembourg	73.5	44.4
Nicaragua	32	66.9	Switzerland	75	43.6
Iran	33	66.1	New Zealand	76.5	43.0
Bulgaria	34	65.6	Netherlands	76.5	43.0
Sudan	35	63.7	Yugoslavia	78	42.2
Bolivia	36	63.0	Australia	79	42.0
Egypt	37	62.0	Columbia	80	41.8
Venezuela	38	61.4	Nigeria	81	41.0
Finland	39	61.3	Spain	82	40.3
Malaya & Singapore	40	60.8	Canada	83	40.1
Portugal	41	60.7	Poland	84	39.7
United Kingdom	42	60.3	Syria	85	37.8
Libya	43	60.2	Saudi Arabia	86	32.8
Norway	44	60.0	Italy	87	32.1

[a] The data for the primacy measure are 1955 population estimates of cities or metropolitan areas or for years as close to 1955 as possible. The measure of primacy used here is the percentage of the population of the four largest cities residing in the largest city of the country. In some cases the unit is the metropolitan area rather than the city.

Source: Norton Ginsburg, *Atlas of Economic Development* (Chicago: University of Chicago Press, 1961), Table 12, p. 36.

Table 2

Group I Countries (High PCGNP)[a, b]
Group II Countries (Medium PCGNP),
Group III Countries (Low PCGNP) by Value and Rank in PCGNP
and Rank in Primacy of Urban Structure[c]

Group I Countries (High PCGNP)	Within 87 Countries			Within Group	
	PCGNP Rank	Value ($)	Primacy Rank	PCGNP Rank	Primacy Rank
United States	1	2,343	59	1	19
Canada	2	1,667	83	2	27
New Zealand	3	1,249	76.5	3	24.5
Switzerland	4	1,229	75	4	23
Australia	5	1,215	79	5	26
Luxembourg	6	1,194	73.5	6	22
Sweden	7	1,165	46	7	14
France	8	1,046	19	8	7
Belgium	9	1,015	57.5	9	18
United Kingdom	10	998	42	10	11
Norway	11	969	44	11	12
Finland	12	941	39	12	10
Denmark	13	913	15	13	5
West Germany	14.5	762	66	14.5	21
Venezuela	14.5	762	38	14.5	9
Netherlands	16	708	76.5	16	24.5
U.S.S.R.	17	682	52	17	16
Uruguay	18	569	2	18	1
Czechoslovakia	19	543	47	19	15
Israel	20	540	45	20	13
Austria	21	532	14	21	4
Puerto Rico	22	511	27	22	8
Ireland	23	509	16	23	6
Poland	24	468	84	24	28
Italy	25	442	87	25	29
Hungary	26	387	3	26	2
U. of South Africa	27	381	64	27	20
Argentina	28.5	374	9	28.5	3
Cyprus	28.5	374	56	28.5	17
Cuba	30	361	13	1	5
Panama	31	350	23	2	9
Colombia	32	330	80	3	27
Rumania	33	320	22	4	8
Costa Rica	34	307	10	5	4
Malaya & Singapore	35	298	40	6	17
Yugoslavia	36	297	78	7	26
Bulgaria	37	285	34	8	16
Turkey	38	276	49	9	19.5

[a] Per capita gross national product.

[b] Of the 87 countries, Group I consists of 29 countries ranking from 1 through 29 in value of PCGNP; Group II consists of 29 countries ranking in value of PCGNP from 30 through 58; and Group III consists of 29 countries ranking from 59 to 87 in PCGNP. Data are for *circa* 1955.

[c] Source of data: Norton Ginsburg, *Atlas of Economic Development* (Chicago: University of Chicago Press, 1961), Table 3, p. 18; and Table 12, p. 36.

Group II Countries (Medium PCGNP)	Within 87 Countries			Within Group	
	PCGNp Rank	Value ($)	Primacy Rank	PCGNP Rank	Primacy Rank
Lebanon	39	269	26	10	12
Brazil	40	262	71	11	25
Nicaragua	41.5	254	32	12.5	15
Spain	41.5	254	82	12.5	28
El Salvador	43	244	28	14	13
Japan	44	240	53	15	22
Greece	45	239	18	16	6
Dominican Republic	46	205	24	17	10
Ecuador	47	204	61	18	24
Philippines	48.5	201	7	19.5	2
Portugal	48.5	201	41	19.5	18
Iraq	50	195	49	21	19.5
Mexico	51	187	20	22	7
Chile	52	180	25	23	11
Guatemala	53	179	4	24	1
Algeria	54	176	55	25	23
Saudi Arabia	55	166	86	26	29
Morocco	56	159	51	27	21
Peru	57	140	8	28	3
Honduras	58	137	30	29	14
Ghana	59	135	63	1	20
Federation of Rhodesia and Nyasaland	60	134	72	2	26
Egypt	61.5	133	37	3.5	13
South Vietnam	61.5	133	5	3.5	2
Tunisia	63	131	17	5	6
Indonesia	64	127	67	6	22
Ceylon	65	122	11	7	4
Syria	66	111	85	8	29
Paraguay	67	108	6	9	3
Taiwan	68	102	57.5	10	17
Thailand	70	100	1	12	1
Iran	70	100	33	12	10
Sudan	70	100	35	12	11
Belgian Congo	72	98	49	14	15
Jordan	73	96	68	15	23
Libya	74	90	43	16	14
South Korea	75	80	62	17	19
Haiti	76	75	12	18	5
India	77	72	73.5	19	27
Nigeria	78	70	81	20	28
Bolivia	79	66	36	21	12
French West Africa	80.5	58	54	22.5	16
French Equat. Africa	80.5	58	60	22.5	18
China	82.5	56	70	24.5	25
Pakistan	82.5	56	69	24.5	24
Afghanistan	84.5	54	65	26.5	21
Ethiopia	84.5	54	31	26.5	9
Burma	86	52	29	28	8
Nepal	87	40	21	29	7

Table 3

**The Relationship by Countries Between Primacy of
Urban Structure and Selected Ecological and
Demographic Characteristics**

Characteristic	All Countries N	All Countries Rho	Group I Countries N	Group I Countries Rho	Group II Countries N	Group II Countries Rho	Group III Countries N	Group III Countries Rho
(1) Per capita gross national product (*circa* 1955)[a]	87	−.08	29	−.33*	29	−.01	29	+.09
(2) Per capita gross energy consumption (1952)[b]	85	−.12	29	−.33*	29	−.04	27	−.16
(3) % of econ. active pop. in non-agriculture (*circa* 1950)[c]	75	−.14	29	−.30	26	+.06	20	−.15
(4) % of pop. in urban places of 20,000+ (*circa* 1955)[d]	82	−.12	28	−.11	28	−.07	26	−.20
(5) Per capita international mail flow (*circa* 1955)[e]	81	−.04	28	−.14	29	+.17	24	−.02
(6) Per capita international trade (*circa* 1955)[f]	81	+.05	26	−.17	29	+.18	26	+.22
(7) % of exports classified as raw materials (*circa* 1955)[g]	77	+.19*	24	+.12	27	+.06	26	+.32
(8) Population size (mid-year estimates, *circa* 1959)[h]	85	−.29*	29	−.25	29	−.34*	27	−.28
(9) Area[i]	85	−.28*	29	−.13	29	−.44*	27	−.34*
(10) Population density (*circa* 1959)[j]	85	+.02	29	−.06	29	+.19	27	.00

* Significant at the .05 level (one-tailed test). The significance test used for N> 30 is given in Maurice G. Kendall, *Rank Correlation Methods* (London: Charles Griffin & Co., 1948), pp. 46–47. For N≤ 30, see Sidney Siegel, *Nonparametric Statistics for the Behavioral Sciences* (New York: McGraw-Hill Book Co., 1956), Table P, p. 284.

[a] Source of raw data: Norton Ginsburg, *Atlas of Economic Development* (Chicago: University of Chicago Press, 1961), Table 3, p. 18.

[b] Source of raw data: *Ibid.*, Table 34, p. 80.

[c] The data are for varying years from 1941 to 1957. For Indonesia the datum was for 1930. For most countries, however, the data are for 1949–51. Source of raw data: *Ibid.*, Table 10, p. 32.

[d] Source of raw data: *Ibid.*, Table 11, p. 34.

[e] Source of raw data: *Ibid.*, Table 44, p. 100.

[f] Source of raw data: *Ibid.*, Table 46, p. 104. The data refer to value of export-import trade per capita.

[g] Source of raw data: *Ibid.*, Table 47, p. 106. The data are expressed in terms of value.

[h] Source of raw data: United Nations, *Statistical Yearbook, 1960* (New York, 1961), Table 1, pp. 21–40.

[i] Source of raw data: *Ibid.*

[j] Source of raw data: *Ibid.*

degree of primacy—Spearman's *rho* is −.08 for degree of primacy and per capita GNP. The mean rank in primacy for the 87 countries is 44. The mean rank in primacy of Group I countries is 51.7; the range is 85 with rankings from 2 to 87. The mean rank for Group III countries is 48.6; the range is 84 with rankings from 1 to 85. Thus, it is clear that the underdeveloped countries are no more likely to have a "primate city" urban structure than are the economically developed countries of the world.

Reference to characteristics (1), (2),

and (3) in Table 3, shows that only within Group I countries, i.e., the economically advanced countries, is there any significant negative association between the level of economic development and primacy. Further interpretations of the data of Table 3 may be briefly summarized as follows:

a) There is little or no indication that primacy is associated with the level of urbanization.[21]

b) If per capita international mail flow is taken as an index of the extent to which countries are ecologically and culturally bound with other countries, there is no indication that countries with the more developed bonds of this nature are either more or less likely to have a "primate city" urban structure.

c) There is some slight indication that countries, especially the least developed ones, that have an export dependency on raw materials are more likely to have a "primate city" than countries whose export trade is composed of a larger proportion of processed and manufactured goods. In addition there is some evidence that among Group III countries, those with higher per capita international trade are somewhat more likely to have higher primacy values.

d) The most salient characteristics related to the primacy of urban structure are size of population and area of the countries.[22] It would appear that countries that are large in terms of population and area have hinterlands that are regional in character rather than national.[23] Conversely, smaller countries tend to have a "primate city" urban structure since the largest city can have the whole country for its economic hinterland with a virtual monopoly over numerous functions. The economies of scale and juxtaposition of industries, services, and specialists is such that the largest city tends to be the most advantageous location

---

[21]Berry in *ibid.* arrived at the same conclusion. We might mention in passing that the "primate city" phenomenon is by no means only a modern phenomenon. For example, it has been noted for quite an extended period of history in England and France where London and Paris still hold their primate stature. See Hoselitz, "Generative and Parastic Cities," *op. cit.;* Lampard, *op. cit.;* and Mehta, *op. cit.,* pp. 239–42. Conversely, the "rank-size rule" has held for the United States throughout its history, from the first census of 1790 to the latest census of 1960. See Vining, *op. cit.;* John Q. Stewart, *op. cit.;* and Madden, *op. cit.* This should suffice to indicate that it is hazardous to generalize that "rank-size" and "primate city" urban structures are associated with level of urbanization or degree of economic development. In relation to this point see G. R. Allen, "The 'Courbe des Populations': A Further Analysis," *Bulletin of the Oxford University Institute of Statistics,* 16 pp. 179–89. Allen basing his work on H. W. Singer's, "Courbes des Populations: A Parallel to Pareto's Law," *Economic Journal,* 1936, pp. 254–63, proposed anew the use of the ∝ parameter of the Pareto distribution as a measure of the degree of urbanization. It seems to us that such a use of ∝ which Allen proposes, leads at times to certain absurdities, and at best it leads to inconclusiveness and obfuscation regarding differences in the degree of urbanization between countries for a given date, or change in level of urbanization over time. See for example, the values for England and Wales, the United States, and other countries given by Allen. Note the rather absurd conclusions one would be forced to draw if one follows his proposal in interpreting these ∝ values as indices of the relative degree of urbanization in these countries.

[22]For a study that provides some support for this finding see Charles T. Stewart, Jr., "The Size and Spacing of Cities," in Harold M. Mayer and Clyde F. Kohn (eds.), *Readings in Urban Geography* (Chicago: University of Chicago Press, 1959), pp. 240–56.

[23]To the extent that the largest city in these large countries has, in addition to its regional functions, a monopoly of some national functions, these functions are either not numerous or not important enough to give it an exceptionally larger economic base compared to the economic base of the other regionally dominant centers.

Table 4

The Relationship by Countries Between Primacy of Urban Structure and Selected Socio-economic Characteristics

Characteristic	All Countries		Group I Countries		Group II Countries		Group III Countries	
	N	Rho	N	Rho	N	Rho	N	Rho
(1) Index of industrial production (change over 1953–58)[a]	44	−.16	23	−.09	14	−.39	7	−.39
(2) Index of agricultural production (change over time)[b]	47	−.06	20	−.24	16	−.01	11	+.38
(3) Index of per capita product at constant prices (change over 1953–58)[c]	55	−.07	24	−.08	19	−.08	12	−.12
(4) Consumer expenditures as % of GNP (3 year average circa 1957–59)[d]	29	+.26	17	+.36	6	+.09	6	−.54
(5) Domestic capital formation as % of GNP (3 year average circa 1957–59)[e]	40	−.24	20	−.51*	12	+.12	8	+.08
(6) Intensity of railway use (circa 1955)[f]	76	−.35*	27	−.27	25	−.41*	24	−.37*
(7) Daily newspaper circulation per 1,000 pop. (early and middle 1950's)[g]	83	−.04	29	−.14	28	+.13	26	.00

* Significant at the .05 level (one-tailed test).

[a] For most countries the data refer to the United Nations International Standard Industrial Classification—Mining, Manufacturing, Electricity and Gas. In the case of a few countries, however, the data pertain to manufacturing alone, or to manufacturing and mining. Source of raw data: United Nations, *Statistical Yearbook, 1960* (New York, 1961), Table 12, pp. 78–88.

[b] The index is for all crops and livestock products for human consumption, and fibers, tobacco, industrial oilseeds, and rubber. The value of the index is 100 for each country's production averaged over the years 1952–53 to 1956–57. The change over time refers to the change in the index, 100, over this period to the value for 1958–59. Source of raw data: *Ibid.*, Table 13, pp. 89–90.

[c] Source of raw data: *Ibid.*, Table 163, p. 459 (and footnotes to Table on p. 458).

[d] Source of raw data: *Ibid.*, Table 165, pp. 467–70.

[e] Source of raw data: *Ibid.*, Table 166, pp. 471–75.

[f] The data are primarily for 1955, although in some instances somewhat earlier figures are used. The data pertain to ton-kilometers of railway freight moved per kilometer of existing railroad. Source of raw data: Norton Ginsburg, *Atlas of Economic Development* (Chicago: University of Chicago Press, 1961), Table 27, p. 66.

[g] A daily newspaper is defined as "a publication containing general news and appearing at least four times a week." Source of raw data: *Ibid.*, Table 14, p. 40.

for various social and economic institutions.

e) Finally, it may be noted that population density of countries is not at all related to the degree to which primacy of urban structure is developed.

Table 4 shows the association between primacy and a few socio-economic characteristics. An exploratory analysis was made of available data with some hope of diminishing the vast lacuna in our knowledge regarding the "parasitic" or "generative" impact of "primate cities." On the basis of the "parasitic" effect hypothesis, the association between degree of primacy and characteristics (1), (2), (3), and (5) would be expected to be negative, while the association between primacy and characteristic (4)[24] would be expected to be positive. This does in fact turn out to be the case for all countries taken together. However, the magnitudes of the *rhos* range only from low to very low. When the *rhos* for the three groups of countries are examined, little can be said about association, and little or no inference can be made regarding the "parasitic" or "generative" impact of "primate cities."

The rank correlation between primacy and the intensity of railway use was shown to be negative and significantly high. Thus, if intensity of railway use is taken as a measure of the efficiency with which existing transportation lines are used, it may be said that countries whose urban structures tend to be primate use their existing means of transportation less efficiently than other countries. However, since rail transport is generally less economical than other modes of transportation on the short-haul, the inverse relationship between intensity of railway use and primacy may be a function of the areal size of the country, a characteristic which is inversely associated with primacy.

There appears to be no consistent relationship between the flow of information and news, as measured by the relative extent of daily newspaper circulation, and primate urban structure. It appears that a number of regionally dominant urban centers in the urban complex of countries is no more likely to lead to a greater over-all distribution of newspapers than an urban structure characterized by primacy.

In summary, the "primate city" urban structure does not appear to be a function of the level of economic development, industrialization or urbanization. It is a phenomenon by no means limited to or characteristic of the underdeveloped countries of the world. Primacy appears to be to some significant extent a function of small areal and population size. To the extent that we were able to explore the hypothesis of the "parasitic" effect of "primate cities," the results do not warrant a clear negative judgment of primacy. In light of the great importance of the question for governmental policy considerations, particularly in underdeveloped countries, we plan to do further research on the subject and hope others will join in the effort.

Appendix—
A Note on the Measurement of Primacy

The data for the primacy measure are *circa* 1955 population census figures or estimates for "urban or metropolitan areas." Most appear in Kingsley Davis, Richard L. Forstall, *et al.*, *The World's Metropolitan Areas* (Berkeley: University of California Press, 1959). The data utilized in this paper are published in Norton Ginsburg, *Atlas of Economic Development* (Chicago: University of Chicago Press, 1961), Table 12, p. 36, and were supplied to Ginsburg by Richard L. Forstall.

---

[24]We realize that the time periods to which these data pertain are really too short for the purpose at hand. However, this is the best that could be done in view of the lack of relevant data for extended time periods for most countries.

The measure of primacy used is the percentage of a given country's four largest metropolitan areas' population that is claimed by the largest metropolitan area.[25] Thus, in the case of Italy, the estimated population (for 1956) of the country's four largest metropolitan areas was as follows: Milan, 2,153,700; Rome, 1,958,600; Naples, 1,565,100; Turin, 1,028,300 (source: *The World's Metropolitan Areas*, p. 56). The primacy value for Italy is, therefore: 2,153,700 ÷ (2,153,700 + 1,958,600 + 1,565,100 + 1,028,300) = 32.1.

It should be pointed out that in checking the primacy data appearing in the *Atlas of Economic Development* against those calculated from the data in *The World's Metropolitan Areas*, some discrepancies were found. For example, the primacy values of Canada, Union of South Africa, Algeria, and Egypt given in the *Atlas of Economic Development* are 40.1, 47.2, 51.1, and 62.0 respectively: Our calculations of primacy values based on data in *The World's Metropolitan Areas* produced the values 37.1, 49.4, 50.6, and 64.3 respectively for these four countries. This is not too serious a matter for, in general, the rank-ordering of the countries by primacy remains relatively unchanged. In this paper we used primacy values as given in the *Atlas of Economic Development* rather than using those derived from the data in *The World's Metropolitan Areas* for two main reasons. Firstly, for some countries it was not possible to compute the primacy value from the data in the latter volume as data for metropolitan areas with less than 100,000 inhabitants are not given. In the case of many countries it was necessary that such data be available before primacy values could be computed. Secondly, presumably Forstall had available to him certain revised and better data than those given in *The World's Metropolitan Areas*.

The measure of primacy employed in this paper is admittedly arbitrary. One could have used the two, three, or the five largest metropolitan areas of countries in computing an index of primacy rather than the four largest. It is possible that had one of these other measures of primacy been employed, the findings of the study reported here would need some revision. However, we computed primacy values for 81 countries where primacy was defined as the ratio of the first largest metropolitan area's population of a given country to the population of the country's second largest metropolitan area.[26] The two sets of primacy measures for the 81 countries were highly correlated—the rank correlation coefficient being +.86. This is some indication of the fact that if a measure of primacy different than the one used in this study had been employed, the findings reported would probably be substantially the same.

[25]For some countries the primacy values given in the *Atlas of Economic Development* are presumably based on administratively defined urban areas rather than ecologically delimited urban or metropolitan areas. The incomparability introduced by this fact, however, would not be too serious. For any given country the primacy value in the first instance, i.e., where the units employed are administratively defined, is not likely to radically differ from the primacy value derived from ecologically delimited areas.

[26]We were able to compute such primacy values for only 81 countries as opposed to 87 countries which have been dealt with hitherto. For six countries we were unable to get the necessary data. Furthermore, for one-half of the countries the primacy measure computed had to be based on cities rather than metropolitan area data for these countries. The sources for the data were: U.N., *United Nations Yearbook*, 1960, Vol. 12 (New York, 1961); *Encyclopaedia Britannica World Atlas* (Chicago, 1961); and *The World's Metropolitan Areas*. The search for the data and the computations for the rank-correlation coefficient reported below were done by Robert M. Figlio.

24. Urbanization, Technology, and the Division of Labor: International Patterns*

JACK P. GIBBS AND

WALTER T. MARTIN

In a previous paper[1] the authors advanced a theory which links the degree of urbanization in a society to the spatial dispersion of objects consumed by the population. A series of tests based on pre-World War II data yielded strong supporting evidence.[2]

The theory does not assume a simple cause and effect relationship; on the contrary, it recognizes that a high degree of urbanization depends on widely scattered materials and represents the type of spatial organization necessary for acquiring them. The present paper seeks to identify those factors which underlie both urbanization and the dispersion of objects of consumption.

American Sociological Review, 27 (October 1962), 667–677. Reprinted by permission of authors and publisher.

*Revision of a paper presented at the annual meeting of the American Sociological Association, Washington, D. C., 1962. Certain portions of the research reported here were made possible by support from the Office of Scientific and Scholarly Research, University of Oregon, and the Population Research Center, Department of Sociology, The University of Texas.

[1] Jack P. Gibbs and Walter T. Martin, "Urbanization and Natural Resources: A Study in Organizational Ecology," American Sociological Review, 23 (June, 1958), pp. 266–277.

[2] Additional tests for a larger number of countries and with improved measures of urbanization and dispersion of resources also provided strong support. See Walter T. Martin, "Urbanization and National Power to Requisition External Resources." (Scheduled for publication in Pacific Sociological Review, 5 [Fall, 1962]).

It is helpful to begin by recognizing that a city, as a large population settled in a small area, cannot possibly develop, within its own limits, the materials necessary for its inhabitants to survive. Stated otherwise, a city depends on the acquisition of objects of consumption originating outside of its boundaries. However, as we shall see, it is only through the division of labor and an advanced technology that a population is able to bring material from great distances. It is in this particular connection that the relationship between urbanization and the spatial dispersion of objects of consumption can best be understood. For if large-scale urbanization requires that materials be brought from great distances, and if a high degree of division of labor and technological development are necessary for this, then the level of urbanization is contingent, at least in part, on the division of labor and technology.

DISPERSION OF OBJECTS OF CONSUMPTION, DIVISION OF LABOR, AND LEVEL OF TECHNOLOGY

For purposes of discussion two types of dispersion of objects of consumption are distinguished. The degree of "internal dispersion" in a society refers to the average distance between the points of origin of raw materials and the points at which the materials are consumed, with both points being within the society's boundaries. The degree of "external dispersion," on the other hand, is the average distance between the points when the origin is outside the society.

A high degree of internal dispersion immediately suggests that the society is characterized by territorial specialization and a certain minimal level of technology. As a rule, objects are not imported unless they are derived from raw materials that are not a natural resource of the area. Speaking colloquially, one does not take coal to Newcastle. It is this exchange among different geographical areas of a society that forms one dimension of the division of labor. The very fact of exchange means that different objects are being produced. This is a basic factor in occupational differentiation. Further division of labor is suggested by the fact that movement of materials necessitates the development of specialized occupations related to transportation and communication. The movement of materials also requires the establishment of commercial institutions and related occupations to facilitate the exchange. In addition, the flow of raw materials often calls for processing to reduce their bulk or to preserve them. This activity forms the basis for numerous occupations and industries. In each of these instances, the development of specialized occupations and industries goes hand in hand with technological advances.

The development of specialized occupations and industries, for whatever reason, leads to the use of greater varieties and amounts of raw materials. On a probabilistic basis, this makes for a greater dispersion of objects of consumption. Moreover, occupational specialization plays a major role in the creation of new objects of consumption. For example, unlike certain food items, rubber in its raw state is relatively useless. However, given occupational specialization and a certain type of technological system, raw rubber can be processed and put to many uses, and it is sought over the world as a consequence.

Still another consideration is the fact that different kinds of raw materials may be combined in a way that increases the demand for each. Thus, the automobile has increased the demand for both rubber and steel. As a consequence, these materials travel great distances between their raw material states and points of acceptance as parts on an automobile. Such combinations, needless to say, are not possible without an elaborate division of labor and an advanced technology.

Most of what has been said about the relationship of internal dispersion to technology and occupational specialization applies equally well to external dispersion. The establishment of trade with countries throughout the world requires, as a rule, the production and processing of a variety of different objects for exchange. Even if a country can establish extensive trade relations on the basis of one natural resource, it is still necessary to have transportation, communication, and commercial industries to process the export and handle the flow of imports.

The line of reasoning pursued in the earlier paper led to the following proposition: *The degree of urbanization in a society varies directly with the dispersion of objects of consumption.*[3] This generalization, even when strongly supported by empirical data, does not explain the relationship. However, the additional observations expressed above generate four propositions which link urbaniza-

[3] Gibbs and Martin, *op. cit.*, p. 270; Martin, *op. cit.*

tion to dispersion. In propositions IA and IB the division of labor serves as the connecting link:

IA. *The degree of urbanization in a society varies directly with the division of labor;*
IB. *The division of labor in a society varies directly with the dispersion of objects of consumption.*

In propositions IIA and IIB the connecting link is the level of technological development:

IIA. *The degree of urbanization in a society varies directy with technological development;*
IIB. *Technological development in a society varies directly with the dispersion of objects of consumption.*

Note that if these statements are treated as postulates, the proposition advanced in the earlier paper can then be stated as a derived theorem. In addition, there is an important corollary proposition: III. *The degree of the division of labor in a society varies directly with technological development.* Thus, it can be seen that all of the propositions are logically interrelated in such a way that evidence supporting any one of the propositions can be regarded as lending credence to all of them. Specifically, propositions IA, IB, and IIA, IIB, if supported by the data, will show that the direct relationship between urbanization and dispersion of objects of consumption is neither fortuitous nor inexplicable.

THE DIVISION OF LABOR AND ITS MEASUREMENT AT THE SOCIETAL LEVEL

The concept of division of labor has had a somewhat strange career in the history of sociology. On the one hand, the concept has achieved wide accep-

tance, particularly since Durkheim's classic treatment.[4] On the other hand, it is rarely employed in the generation of testable hypotheses. This is even true for the field of human ecology where, like competition,[5] the concept is often invoked in pure theory but remains in the background as far as research is concerned.

The empirical referents of the division of labor have yet to be specified in any rigorous fashion, but there are two general ideas associated with the concept. First, there is the suggestion of occupational differentiation. However, more is involved than individuals "doing different things." In addition to differentiation there is functional interdependence. Occupational groups do something more than produce different goods and services. They also exchange goods and services and it is this exchange which underlies occupational differentiation.

A second idea associated with the concept is often confused with the first. In the process of differentiation a person's occupational status may be determined, more or less, by biological characteristics, ethnic-caste status, or territorial location. These distinctions may be called the bases of the division of labor, but they are not to be confused with the degree of the division of labor. Occupations in a society may be closely correlated with non-occupational distinctions, but, at the same time, the number of different occupations may be small. This means a low degree of division of labor.

[4] Emile Durkheim, *The Division of Labor in Society*, translated by George Simpson, Glencoe, Illinois: The Free Press, 1949. Durkheim suggests a direct relationship between division of labor and urbanization in this work (pp. 256–260).
[5] Amos H. Hawley, "Ecology and Human Ecology," *Social Forces*, 22 (May, 1944), p. 401.

Table 1

Illustrations of the Measurement of Industry Diversification

Industries	Hypothetical Society A	Hypothetical Society B	United States 1950[a]	New Zealand 1951[a]
Agriculture, forestry, hunting and fishing	500,000	2,000,000	7,331,353	135,889
Mining and quarrying	......	2,000,000	968,702	7,807
Manufacturing	......	2,000,000	16,113,479	177,430
Construction	......	2,000,000	3,743,183	62,314
Electricity, gas, water, and sanitary services	......	2,000,000	797,528	8,298
Commerce	......	2,000,000	11,082,470	121,681
Transport, storage, and communication	......	2,000,000	4,184,123	78,066
Services	......	2,000,000	14,221,018	143,936
Not classifiable elsewhere	......	2,000,000	1,595,591	5,075
$\sum X$	500,000	18,000,000	60,037,447	740,496
$\sum X^2$	25,000,000,000	3,600,000,000,000	674,090,085,916,761	95,603,959,708
$1 - [\sum X^2 / (\sum X^2)]$	.0000	.8889	.8130	.8256

[a] Source of data: *Demographic Yearbook, 1956*, Table 12.

If one is concerned, as we are here, with the degree and not the basis of the division of labor, then the most relevant data pertain to occupations and industries. The distinction between occupation and industry in the analysis of the degree of the division of labor has evidently not been determined, conceptually or empirically. For present purposes, however, it makes little difference since the only data available for a large number of countries pertain to the industry composition of the labor force (i.e., the economically active population). The data consist of the number of persons in nine industry categories by countries and territories, as reported by the United Nation's Statistical Office.[6] Only autonomous countries have been considered in this study, and many of these could not be included because data on them were either not available or not reported in a way comparable to other countries.

The industry categories employed in the Statistical Office's report are shown in Table 1, with the United States and New Zealand serving as examples.

Regardless of the type of measure considered, there are certain obvious shortcomings in the industry statistics. The categories, for one thing, are far too gross, particularly manufacturing, commerce, and services. In addition, they do not directly take occupational differentiation into account. Furthermore, the data at best only indicate differentiation and not the degree of functional interdependence.

Certain technical deficiencies are also present in the data. There are reasons to believe that the industry categories

[6] United Nations, *Demographic Yearbook, 1956*, New York: 1956, Table 12, pp. 344–387. Some data on occupations by countries are also reported in this source (Table 13), but they are not nearly as complete and comparable as is the case for industry data.

are not applied in an absolutely uniform way from one country to the next. This is particularly true for the category "Not classifiable elsewhere." This category was retained only after experimentation revealed that its exclusion had no appreciable effect on the adopted measure. A more detailed discussion of limitations as to reliability and comparability is provided in the Statistical Office's report.[7]

Measurement of the degree of division of labor

The statistics at hand make possible only a measure of industry diversification, and it is used on the assumption that it would bear a close relationship to a more refined measure of the division of labor. In columns 1 and 2 of Table 1, two hypothetical societies are considered—one (Society A) in which industry diversification is at a minimum and the other (Society B) in which it is at a maximum. To measure the deviation of countries from these polar types a formula has been developed which differentiates between the two. With "X" as the number of persons in each of the nine industry categories, this formula is: $1 - [\sum X^2 / (\sum X)^2]$. Where all of the economically active are concentrated in one industry, the measure would be .0000; and for a population with an even distribution throughout the nine industries the measure would be .8889. Measures of industry diversification for 45 countries are shown in column 2 of Table 2.

A problem in measurement is posed with regard to one of the polar types, the society in which industry diversification is at a maximum (.8889). For a population to reach this point the number of economically active in what is usually considered a minor industry

[7] *Ibid.*, p. 38.

Table 2

Percentage of Population in Metropolitan Areas and Measures of Industrial Diversification, Technological Development, and the External Dispersion of Objects of Consumption, for 45 Countries, Circa 1950

Country	Percentage of Population in Metro-politan Areas[a]	Measure of Industrial Diversification (MID)[b]	Measure of Technological Development (MTD)[c]	Measure of External Dispersion (MED)[d]
Argentina, 1947	44.6	.8147	0.76	604
Australia, 1947	55.4	.8348	3.12	1457
Austria, 1951	37.7	.7911	1.54	237
Belgium, 1947	41.4	.7969	0.28	793
Canada, 1951	42.7	.8197	6.47	1373
Ceylon, 1946	9.5	.6723	0.08	197
Colombia, 1951	19.3	.6624	0.27	119
Costa Rica, 1950	19.9	.6565	0.24	224
Cuba, 1953	26.1	.7420	0.48	248
Denmark, 1950	37.3	.8007	2.09	464
Dominican Republic, 1950	11.2	.6293	0.09	100
Ecuador, 1950	14.9	.6793	0.12	81
Egypt, 1947	19.6	.6394	0.22	143
El Salvador, 1950	11.9	.5689	0.09	134
Finland, 1950	17.0	.7193	1.17	509
France, 1954	34.7	.8100	2.03	360
Greece, 1951	22.0	.7114	0.22	235
Guatemala, 1950	10.5	.5086	0.14	82
Haiti, 1950	6.0	.3010	0.02	46
Honduras, 1950	7.3	.3029	0.15	73
India, 1951	7.8	.4788	0.10	34
Ireland, 1951	27.5	.7631	1.10	504
Israel, 1948–52	55.8	.8187	0.80	919
Japan, 1950	36.6	.7055	0.78	164
Malaya, 1947	12.7	.5500	0.28	846
Mexico, 1950	20.6	.6303	0.60	95
Netherlands, 1947	45.5	.8132	1.96	655
New Zealand, 1951	43.6	.8256	2.43	3310
Nicaragua, 1950	13.3	.5140	0.09	51
Norway, 1950	21.8	.8098	4.37	738
Pakistan, 1951	5.1	.4033	0.04	42
Panama, 1950	23.9	.6956	0.30	234
Paraguay, 1950	15.6	.6549	0.02	104
Peru, 1940	11.0	.5816	0.19	58
Philippines, 1948	10.3	.5418	0.09	235

[a] Source: Data prepared by International Urban Research. These percentages supersede earlier provisional figures reported by Gibbs and Davis in the *American Sociological Review*, 23 (October, 1958), pp. 504–514.

[b] Source: *Demographic Yearbook*. See text for a description of the measure.

[c] Source: *Statistical Yearbook*. Commercial consumption of energy expressed in metric tons of coal per capita.

[d] Source: United Nations, *Statistical Papers*, Series T, Vol. 6, No. 10. See text for a description of the measure.

Country	Percentage of Population in Metropolitan Areas[a]	Measure of Industrial Diversification (MID)[b]	Measure of Technological Development (MTD)[c]	Measure of External Dispersion (MED)[d]
Portugal, 1950	19.6	.7073	0.26	129
Spain, 1950	25.5	.7014	0.57	41
Sweden, 1950	22.4	.8007	3.22	873
Switzerland, 1950	28.9	.7762	2.15	882
Thailand, 1947	6.8	.2735	0.02	35
Turkey, 1950	9.5	.4082	0.26	82
Union of So. Africa, 1951	29.9	.7059	1.89	796
United Kingdom, 1951	71.5	.7687	4.42	1188
United States, 1950	55.9	.8130	7.74	381
Venezuela, 1950	25.2	.7597	0.77	420

(public utilities, for example) would have to equal the number in a major industry (agriculture and manufacturing). This suggests that the polar type is unrealistic in that it is virtually impossible for a society to resemble it. The objection is made less serious by the fact that 14 of the 45 countries are within .1000 of the maximum value, while none of the countries is this close to the lowest possible value. There would appear to be little doubt, however, that numerous historical societies and non-literate peoples closely resembled the polar type in which the measure is at a minimum.

LEVEL OF TECHNOLOGICAL DEVELOPMENT AND ITS MEASUREMENT AT THE SOCIETAL LEVEL

Technology, like division of labor, is a concept frequently utilized in sociological discourse, especially in observations on the location, growth, development, and physical structure of individual cities.[8] Less attention has been given to the relationship between

[8] See, e.g., William Fielding Ogburn, "Technology and Cities: The Dilemma of the Modern Metropolis," *The Sociological Quarterly*, 1 (July, 1960), pp. 139–153.

technological development and the amount or rate of urbanization, but observations and research findings do suggest that the two are closely related.[9]

Among sociologists, at least, there appears to be a general consensus as to the meaning of technology.[10] In some cases there is an emphasis on technology as material culture, a conception which is rejected by those who stress the ideational content, i.e., the application of knowledge and beliefs.[11] Despite the differing emphases, however, there is general recognition that technology involves the application of knowledge and beliefs in carrying out tasks and includes the artifacts developed to reduce the amount of labor or to accomplish what cannot be achieved by manpower alone. In societies where

[9] Kingsley Davis, "The Origin and Growth of Urbanization in the World," *American Journal of Sociology*, 60 (March, 1955), pp. 431–432; and Jack P. Gibbs and Leo F. Schnore, "Metropolitan Growth: An International Study," *American Journal of Sociology*, 66 (September, 1960), pp. 160–170.

[10] Francis R. Allen, *et al.*, *Technology and Social Change*, New York: Appleton-Century-Crofts, Inc., 1957, Chapter 1.

[11] Kingsley Davis, *Human Society*, New York: Macmillan Company, 1949, pp. 435–436; Robin M. Williams, Jr., *American Society*, New York: Alfred A. Knopf, 1960, p. 24.

technical knowledge is primitive, the utilitarian artifacts are simple and operate with little or no use of inorganic energy; where technical knowledge is highly advanced there is a great complex of utilitarian artifacts that operate largely through inorganic energy. Stated otherwise, societies with primitive technologies are low-energy societies, those with advanced technologies are high-energy societies.[12] Thus, the best indicator of the level of technological development would appear to be the per capita consumption of energy.[13] In this study the data used are for the estimated consumption of commercial sources of energy expressed in metric tons of coal per capita reported in the *Statistical Yearbook*.[14] These data are shown in column 3 of Table 2 for 45 countries.

MEASURES OF THE DEGREE OF URBANIZATION

Census reports and publications of the United Nation's Statistical Office make possible a variety of measures of urbanization at the national level. However, the most reliable and comparable measure is the percentage of the total population who reside in the Metropolitan Areas delimited by International Urban Research.[15] The percentage is shown for 45 countries in column 1 of Table 2.

MEASUREMENT OF EXTERNAL DISPERSION OF OBJECTS OF CONSUMPTION

The measure of the external dispersion of objects of consumption (MED) used in the present research is considerably improved over the one employed in the earlier study,[16] although still necessarily far from precise. It considers the amount of materials (expressed in dollar value) imported by a given country from all other countries and the distance the materials are transported in each instance. For example, in the case of Switzerland, the dollar value of imports in 1951 was obtained for each country exporting to Switzerland. The value of each country's shipments[17] was then multiplied by the distance between the center of that country and the center of Switzerland following usual traffic lanes as closely as . possible.[18] The resulting products were summed and the total divided by the 1950 population of Switzerland to give a per capita

---

[12]See Fred Cottrell, *Energy and Society*, New York: McGraw-Hill Book Company, Inc., 1955.

[13]See William F. Ogburn and Francis R. Allen, "Technological Development and Per Capita Income," *American Journal of Sociology*, 65 (September, 1959), pp. 127–131; William F. Ogburn, "Technology and the Standard of Living in the United States," *American Journal of Sociology*, 60 (January, 1955), pp. 380–386; William F. Ogburn, "Population, Private Ownership, Technology, and the Standard of Living," *American Journal of Sociology*, 56 (January, 1951), pp. 314–319.

[14]United Nations, *Statistical Yearbook, 1953*, New York: 1953, Table 127, pp. 276–278.

[15]See Jack P. Gibbs and Kingsley Davis, "Conventional Versus Metropolitan Data in the International Study of Urbanization," *American Sociological Review*, 23 (October, 1958), pp. 505–514; and International Urban Research, *The World's Metropolitan Areas*, Berkeley and Los Angeles: University of California Press, 1959.

[16]Gibbs and Martin, *op. cit.*

[17]Statistical Office of the United Nations, "Direction of International Trade," in *Statistical Papers*, Series T, Vol. 6, No. 10.

[18]This figure was calculated in most cases by taking sea-lane mileage between major ports and adding the approximate mileage from the two ports to the center of their respective countries.

figure.[19] This per capita figure is thus a gauge of the extent to which the Swiss nation acquired globally dispersed objects. MED's for 45 countries are shown in column 4 of Table 2. There are clearly many deficiencies in this measure, e.g., (1) the weight of goods imported is not considered; (2) the measure assumes that all goods originate at the geographic center of the exporting country and are consumed at the approximate geographic center of the importing country, an assumption that obviously distorts the situation;[20] and (3) the measure necessarily assumes that the movement of all goods between any two countries follows a single route. These deficiencies appear to influence the preciseness of the measure rather than its general ability to rank countries in terms of the external dispersion of their objects of consumption. Thus there appears to be no doubt that objects of consumption in New Zealand and Canada are much more externally dispersed than are those in Thailand, Pakistan, and even the United States. Note, however, that in no instance does MED reveal the "internal dispersion" of objects of consumption, and a

[19]The operations can be summarized as follows:

$$\frac{\sum_i^n (X_i)(Y_i) + (X_j)(Y_j) + \ldots (X_n)(Y_n)}{Pa} \times 1000$$

Where: $i \ldots n$ countries from which imports are received.

X_i: \$ value of imports from country i.

Y_i: estimated average miles imports from i were transported.

Pa: population of the importing country.

[20]In a few extreme cases an adjustment was made to take into account the fact that the heavy concentration of population near the port of entry made it very unlikely that on the average the imported materials were transported as far as the center of the country.

truly adequate test of any theory pertaining to dispersion of objects of consumption cannot be conducted without considering both external and internal dispersion. Since international data on internal dispersion are not available, it has been necessary to assume that there is a fairly close relation between the two kinds of dispersion. However, this may not be true for certain countries (particularly the large ones), and therefore some exceptions to the predicted relationship between dispersion and other variables are not unexpected.

TESTS OF THE PROPOSITIONS

According to proposition IA, there is a direct relationship at the societal level between the degree of urbanization and the division of labor. On this basis we should find a high positive correlation between the percentage of the population in Metropolitan Areas and the measures of industrial diversification. A rank-order correlation coefficient of $+.91$ between the values in columns 1 and 2 of Table 2 provides strong support for the proposition.

Proposition IB anticipates a direct relationship between the division of labor and the dispersion of objects of consumption. The two variables used to test the proposition are the measures of industrial diversification and the measures of external dispersion in columns 2 and 4 of Table 2. *Rho* in this instance is $+.83$ and, accordingly, consistent with the proposition.

On the basis of proposition IIA, a direct relationship should hold between the percentage of the population in Metropolitan Areas and the measures of technological development shown in column 3 of Table 2. A *rho* value of

+.84 indicates that the relationship is substantially as predicted.

The prediction in the case of proposition IIB is the existence of a direct relationship between the measures of technological development and the measures of external dispersion of objects of consumption. A *rho* value of +.79 is thus consistent with the proposition.

Finally, proposition III leads to the prediction of a direct relationship between the measures of industrial diversification and the measures of technological development. A *rho* of +.85 represents supporting evidence.[21]

Another Aspect of the Relationships

If both the division of labor and technological development are closely linked to the dispersion of objects of consumption, then their relationship to urbanization should conform to a particular pattern. The earlier study[22] revealed that dispersion of objects of consumption bears the closest relationship to large-scale urbanization,[23] the percentage of the total population in urban places of 100,000 population or more, and the least relationship to small-scale urbanization, the percentage of the total population in urban places of 5,000–9,999 inhabitants. Similar findings based on more recent data have also been reported elsewhere.[24] These differential relationships were antici-

pated on the grounds that large-scale urbanization makes it necessary for the inhabitants of the large cities to draw their objects of consumption from a great distance. A large proportion of the population in small urban places, however, does not necessitate a high degree of dispersion of objects of consumption, since the inhabitants of such places can live off their immediate environs. In short, the percentage in small urban places varies independently of the dispersion of objects of consumption because a high degree of dispersion is not a necessity for survival.

Just as it is necessary for the populations of large cities to draw objects of consumption from great distances so is it equally necessary for them to have a high degree of division of labor and technological development to accomplish the task. Conversely, small urban places can survive with or without a high degree of division of labor and technological development. If this is the case, the MID and MTD should be more closely associated with large-scale urbanization than with small-scale urbanization.

The data in Table 3 provide a basis for a test of the hypothesis stated above. They show for each of 41 countries the percentage of the population who reside in urban localities by size range of localities.[25] Variation in census practices makes it necessary to consider two types of localities. Type A localities are agglomerations delimited without

---

[21]*Rho* was used in this series of tests rather than *r* because of the existence of non-linear relationships in all cases. In each instance, an increase in one variable beyond a certain point is associated with progressively greater or smaller increase in the other variable. Although *rho* is applicable in such cases, it probably underestimates the degree of association. The relationships should eventually be expressed as a correlation ratio (*eta*).

[22]Gibbs and Martin, *op. cit.*

[23]Referred to in the earlier study as "metropolitanization."

[24]Martin, *op. cit.*

[25]Five of the countries in Table 2 (Austria, Belgium, Egypt, Spain, and Switzerland) are not included in Table 3 because their locality statistics in the *Demographic Yearbook* are based on minor civil divisions (Type C localities) rather than Type A or Type B localities. Yugoslavia is the only country in Table 3 which is not also in Table 2. It was excluded from Table 2 because data relating to Metropolitan Areas and imports could not be obtained. MID for Yugoslavia is .5250, and its MTD is 0.41.

Table 3

Percentage of Population in Urban Localities for 41 Countries, Circa 1950

Countries by Type of Locality	\multicolumn{6}{c}{Percentage of Population in Localities by Size}
	2,000–4,999	5,000–9,999	10,000–19,999	20,000–49,999	50,000–99,999	100,000+
Type A						
Argentina, 1947	5.6	4.2	4.4	6.2	4.9	37.2
Australia, 1947	7.8	4.8	4.3	4.9	1.0	51.4
Cuba, 1953	5.9	4.1	4.4	8.0	6.6	21.9
Denmark, 1950	3.1	4.3	6.6	8.1	3.2	33.5
France, 1954	7.8	5.6	7.0	8.6	6.2	15.0
India, 1951	16.6	5.8	3.3	3.3	2.1	6.6
Ireland, 1951	5.0	3.3	3.9	4.6	6.1	17.6
Israel, 1949	7.4	4.3	10.6	5.7	0.0	45.6
Netherlands, 1947	9.0	7.5	6.3	8.5	8.6	32.7
Norway, 1950	3.8	1.9	5.7	6.7	6.2	19.8
Pakistan, 1951	0.2	0.9	1.1	2.1	0.8	5.1
Portugal, 1950	6.6	5.2	3.0	3.7	0.0	12.7
Sweden, 1950	6.5	5.1	7.3	7.5	6.1	19.4
United States, 1950	4.8	4.1	4.2	5.2	2.9	43.9
Type B						
Canada, 1951	5.4	5.1	5.1	7.6	4.2	23.3
Ceylon, 1946	0.4	0.8	2.6	2.7	3.3	5.4
Colombia, 1951	5.6	3.6	3.1	4.2	3.5	14.7
Costa Rica, 1950	4.9	4.9	7.9	0.0	10.9	0.0
Dominican Republic, 1950	3.0	2.5	4.9	0.0	2.6	8.5
Ecuador, 1950	3.7	2.7	3.5	3.2	0.0	14.6
El Salvador, 1950	5.9	4.4	4.4	1.4	2.8	8.7
Finland, 1950	3.5	3.4	6.0	8.0	0.0	14.2
Greece, 1951	11.4	4.4	7.1	10.8	3.3	12.7
Guatemala, 1950	7.1	4.3	1.3	1.0	0.0	10.2
Haiti, 1950	1.8	1.9	1.2	0.8	0.0	4.3
Honduras, 1950	5.4	2.0	3.0	1.5	5.3	0.0
Japan, 1950	1.6	7.3	8.6	8.9	7.6	25.6
Malaya, 1947	3.1	2.2	1.9	6.9	2.8	7.4
Mexico, 1950	10.9	5.7	4.9	5.3	3.6	15.1
New Zealand, 1951	5.5	3.2	2.8	12.6	8.8	32.8
Nicaragua, 1950	6.3	2.7	3.8	4.9	0.0	10.3
Panama, 1950	8.7	6.0	5.4	0.0	6.5	15.9
Paraguay, 1950	7.9	1.8	3.2	0.0	0.0	15.2
Peru, 1940	5.1	2.9	3.6	3.4	2.1	8.4
Philippines, 1948	7.2	4.9	2.6	2.2	0.7	3.4
Thailand, 1947	0.1	0.9	2.2	2.2	0.0	4.5
Turkey, 1950	6.3	3.7	4.2	4.4	1.9	8.2
Union of So. Africa, 1951	3.6	3.0	2.5	2.5	4.2	24.0
United Kingdom, 1951	2.1	3.6	7.1	16.1	14.7	36.1
Venezuela, 1950	7.3	5.6	4.6	7.5	4.1	20.6
Yugoslavia, 1948	0.0	1.0	3.1	4.1	1.9	6.3

^a See text for a description of the two types of localities.
Sources: Demographic Yearbook and census reports.

regard to political boundaries. They therefore correspond to an urban area as a physical entity, in much the same sense as the Urbanized Areas delimited by the Bureau of the Census. Type B localities, in contrast, have definite administrative limits and thereby correspond to cities as political entities.

According to the hypothesis in question, we should find that the magnitude of the correlation coefficients between MID or MTD and component measures of urbanization increase directly with the size range of the urban localities. Thus, the coefficient of correlation should be at a minimum for urban localities of 2,000–4,999 inhabitants and at a maximum where the size of the localities is 100,000 or more. Tables 4 and 5 show that the correlation coefficients do vary in substantially the way predicted.

Complete conformity to the predicted pattern would prevail if each coefficient were of greater magnitude than all coefficients below it on the urbanization

scale and of less magnitude than all coefficients above it on the urbanization scale. Among the Type B countries in Table 4 (which considers the relationship between MTD and component measures of urbanization) there are only six exceptions to the expected pattern in a total of 30 comparisons, and the corresponding figures for Types A and B combined are two and 30. On the basis of chance we would expect to find 30 exceptions in 60 comparisons, but there are in fact only eight.

The coefficients of correlation between MID and the component measures of urbanization in Table 5 also conform closely to the predicted pattern. There is no exception in a total of 30 comparisons for Type B countries, and only six exceptions in the 30 comparisons for Types A and B combined. Thus, whereas 30 exceptions in 60 comparisons would be expected on the basis of chance, there are actually only six.

These findings leave little doubt that both the division of labor and technological development are, as anticipated,

Table 4

Rank-Order Coefficients of Correlation by Countries Between Measures of Technological Development and the Percentage of the Population in Urban Localities[a]

| | Countries Grouped by Type of Locality[b] | |
Urban Localities by Size Range	Type B (N=27)	Types A and B (N=41)
100,000+	.652	.79
50,000–99,999	.648	.56
20,000–49,999	.67	.72
10,000–19,999	.43	.55
5,000– 9,999	.51	.40
2,000– 4,999	.01	.07

[a] Sources of data on percentage of population in urban localities: *Demographic Yearbook* and census reports on individual countries.

[b] See text for a description of the locality types.

Table 5

Rank-Order Coefficients of Correlation by Countries Between Measures of Industrial Diversification and the Percentage of the Population in Urban Localities[a]

| | Countries Grouped by Type of Locality | |
Urban Localities by Size Range	Type B (N=27)	Types A and B (N=41)
100,000+	.77	.87
50,000–99,999	.58	.47
20,000–49,999	.537	.66
10,000–19,999	.536	.58
5,000– 9,999	.43	.29
2,000– 4,999	−.11	.22

[a] See footnotes for Table 4.

more closely related to large-scale urbanization than to small-scale urbanization.

OTHER CONSIDERATIONS AND CONCLUSIONS

The findings of this study and those presented in earlier papers demonstrate consistent relationships among urbanization, the division of labor, the level of technological development, and the dispersion of objects of consumption. The relationships are obviously not so close as to preclude exceptions. Exceptions do occur, and some of them are probably "real" exceptions, that is, not subject to explanation in terms of inadequate data or crude measures. We do not deny the possibility of exceptions, but we do maintain that societies can deviate only within certain limits and, in any case, there are certain identifiable consequences of deviation. For example, some societies may have a much higher degree of urbanization than would be anticipated on the basis of the present propositions. There is, however, a limit as to how high urbanization can go without increases in the division of labor, in technological efficiency, and in the dispersion of objects of consumption. And, with regard to consequences of deviation, one effect of over-urbanization is likely to be a low standard of living.

The explanation of deviant cases and the identification of the consequences of deviation must await improvements in the scope and quality of international statistics, particularly data pertaining to the degree of the internal dispersion of objects of consumption and to the division of labor. Even before this, however, we can anticipate alternative explanations of urbanization and the relationships reported here. Of the various alternative explanations, there is a certain type which particularly deserves consideration, because it is traditionally viewed in opposition to the theoretical orientation which characterizes the present paper.

One could argue that a high or low degree of urbanization and the relationship of urbanization to other variables is largely a matter of socio-cultural values and ideologies. We reject such an interpretation and emphasize that a high degree of urbanization depends on the division of labor, technology, and organization to requisition dispersed materials. The value systems of some societies may in fact favor a high degree of urbanization, but there is no particular set of values that is a sufficient condition for a high degree of urbanization. It makes no great difference whether the population professes socialism or capitalism, liberalism or conservatism, Buddhism or Free Methodism; for if a high degree of urbanization is to be maintained, widely dispersed materials must be requisitioned, and this can be accomplished only through the division of labor and technological efficiency.

Note, however, that the writers do not deny that values and ideologies may largely determine certain types of behavior. It may even be true that, *within* certain limits, socio-cultural values and ideologies influence urbanization. But we do reject these phenomena as possible explanations of the particular relationships observed in this study. This would be the case even if a spatial association between urbanization and certain types of values could be demonstrated. It is entirely possible that as urbanization occurs certain values will come to prevail. Unfortunately, this opens the door to future confusion by making it possible at some later date for observers to conclude that the presence of these values explains urbanization.

25. The Analysis of "Over-Urbanization"

N. V. SOVANI

The rapid rate of urbanization in the underdeveloped areas of the world during the last two decades has attracted widespread attention and has evoked quite a considerable body of analytical writing from social scientists. Out of this discussion a broad structure of analysis seems to be taking shape. I would conveniently describe it as analysis bottomed on the concept of "over-urbanization." The ground work is laid by defining "over-urbanization," and the upper structure is provided by the discussion of its causes and consequences. Asia, for example, is said to be over-urbanized at present, in the sense that "at comparable levels of urbanization, the developed countries of today had a correspondingly greater proportion of their labor force engaged in non-agricultural occupations."[1] This over-urbanization is supposed to have come about because rural migrants have been "pushed" rather than "pulled" into the urban areas in these countries, as a result of great and mounting population pressure in the rural areas. In over-urbanized countries "urban misery and rural poverty exist side by side with the result that the city can hardly be called 'dynamic,' as social historians of developed countries generally described the process of urbanization."[2] The purpose of this paper is to examine critically these three propositions. The first, dealing with the definition of "over-urbanization," is mainly methodological, while the other two are empirical in character. I will consider them in the same order as above.

I. DEFINITION OF "OVER-URBANIZATION"

In defining over-urbanization, two indices are being related to one another, the percentage of population living in urban areas, and the distribution of the total labor force in the country as between agricultural and non-agricultural occupations. The first is a spatial index without being an occupational one, and the second is the opposite. As modern urbanization is associated with industrialization, we may generally agree that there is justification for such a comparison.

The next question is what should be regarded as the normal relationship between the two indices so compared. In this context, two kinds of norms have been suggested. One is based on cross-section analysis of data for a large number of countries in the world, in and near 1950, and is proposed and used

Economic Development and Cultural Change, 12, No. 2 (*January 1964*), 113–22. *Reprinted by permission of the University of Chicago Press and the author.*

[1] *Urbanization in Asia and the Far East*, Proceedings of the Joint UN/UNESCO Seminar, Bangkok, 8–18 August 1956 (Calcutta: UNESCO Research Center on the Social Implications of Industrialization in Southern Asia, 1957), p. 8.

[2] *Ibid.*, p. 10.

by Davis and Golden;[3] another based on historical analogy is suggested and used by the UNESCO Seminar Report quoted earlier.

Davis and Golden take the percentage of economically active males not engaged in agriculture and the percentage of population in cities of 100,000[4] and above in a large number of the countries in the world in and near 1950 and find a correlation coefficient of 0.86 between the degree of industrialization and the degree of urbanization. When the "relationship between the two variables is represented in the form of a regression curve, certain

[3] Kingsley Davis and Hilda H. Golden, "Urbanization and the Development of Pre-Industrial Areas," *Economic Development and Cultural Change*, 3, No. 1 (October 1954).

[4] The index of urbanization used by Davis and Golden is the percentage of the total population of a country living in cities of 100,000 and more. In maintaining that this index is valid for comparative purposes, they observe:

"Actually, since there is a certain regularity about the pyramid of cities by size, the proportion in any major size-class tends to bear a systematic relation to the proportion in other size-classes. Thus the percentage of a population living in places above 100,000 has a ratio to the percentage in places above 5,000 which is roughly similar from one country to another. An index of urbanization is therefore quite feasible for comparative purposes (*ibid.*, p. 7, fn. 1)."

Unfortunately, this is not so. A tabulation of the ratio between the percentages of population in places of 5,000 and more (P1) and those of population in cities of 100,000 and more (P2) for countries from the 1952 *Demographic Year Book* of the UN reveals the following:

Range of the Ratio P2/P1	Number of Countries
.10 to .30	8
.31 to .40	11
.41 to .50	14
.51 to .60	12
.61 to .70	7
.10 to .70	52

countries are found to be off the line to a significant extent."[5] Egypt, Greece, Korea, and possibly Lebanon are found to be off the line, i.e., in them the degree of urbanization is much more than would be expected from the level of industrialization they have achieved.[6]

This criterion has been derived from a correlation found to exist between two variables at a point or over a short stretch of time. It may be considered, as a first approximation, a fairly useful criterion for identifying cases of urbanization that do not conform to the broad pattern found to be prevailing at or around a point of time and which therefore need special attention or

---

Thus the validity of the index of urbanization used by Davis and Golden is rather questionable. Their observation is probably based on the rank-size rule or the Pareto distribution that characterizes the sizes of cities in many countries. In the first place, this rule is not universal, and in several countries, particularly those dominated by single large or primate cities, the size distribution of cities does not conform to it. Secondly, even if the rule were universal, the slope of the Pareto curve will differ from country to country, and the ratio between the percentages of population in different size classes of towns will therefore differ. The value of α ranges from 0.93 to 1.59 in the case of six countries for which Singer gives the values. Cf. H. W. Singer, "Courbes des Populations: A Parallel to Pareto's Law," *Economic Journal* [1936], 254–63. The necessary and sufficient condition for the Davis-Golden observation to be valid would be (a) that the rank-size rule is universal, and (b) that the slope of the distribution curve is either the same everywhere or varies only slightly as between different countries.

I will go no further here than to indicate the questionable assumptions underlying one of the variables used by Davis and Golden, and in the rest of the paper, I will treat their index as valid.

[5] Davis and Golden, *op. cit.*, p. 8.

[6] Correspondingly, on the other side of the regression line there would be cases of "under-urbanization." If one is considered abnormal in some sense those on the other side of the regression line also are abnormal.

study. But before proceeding further, it would be necessary to examine the correlation iself, to test its stability through different stages of industrialization and through time in the different countries. For the first, we can examine how it works for subgroups of countries that are in similar stages of industrialization. For the second, we can examine whether the cross-section analysis is also borne out by the time-series analysis.

As a first step towards this I tried to work out the correlation coefficient for countries for which data on urbanization and occupational distribution were available from the same year and in the period from 1946 to 1951 in the UN's *Demographic Year Books* of 1952 and 1956. These data were available for a total of 41 countries, excluding countries or geographical units that had no cities of 100,000 and more. The correlation coefficient was found to be 0.70.[7] In order to see how the correlation holds in highly industrialized countries as against the rest, I worked out the correlation coefficient for a group consisting of the U.S., Canada, and 15 European countries for which data were available, and another for the remaining group of 24 countries in my original list. Surprisingly, the correlation coefficient between urbanization and industrialization for the group of highly industrialized countries was 0.395, and that for the remainder was 0.85. These results indicate that the association between the two variables is much more close in the underdeveloped countries than in the highly industrialized countries or, by implication, that the pace of urbanization in

the underdeveloped countries is much more closely dependent on the pace of industrialization than in the highly industrialized areas. This flies in the face of the entire over-urbanization thesis, at least in the way it has been formulated up to now.

Yet the results obtained above make sense, because what they bring to light is the non-homogeneous character of the two groups of countries and the invalidity of deriving correlation coefficients for all countries together in one lump. An analogy should make this clear. That there is a strong correlation between the height and weight of human beings is well known. But if this correlation is considered for persons of different age groups it will be certainly far stronger in the age groups below 20 than in those above 20 years, in which persons have approached or are approaching the asymptotic limit of their height. The same is true of countries at advanced and early stages of industrialization and urbanization.

This is supported by a similar correlation analysis done for U.S., Canada, and eleven Western European countries for the year 1891,[8] which gives a correlation coefficient of 0.84. The occupational data are for the entire labor force and not for males alone as in the analysis of recent data. But that would mean that the correlation coefficient here is slightly smaller than what it would be if data for males alone were used. The indication, however, is clearly that in the earlier stages of

[7] The higher value of r and r² that Davis and Golden obtained might have been due to the use of data for more countries than I have been able to get together.

[8] Urban population data are from A. Weber, *The Growth of Cities in the Nineteenth Century, A Study in Statistics* (New York: Columbia University, 1899). Labor force data are from S. Kuznets, "Quantitative Aspects of the Economic Growth of Nations. II. Industrial Distribution of National Product and Labor Force," *Economic Development and Cultural Change*, 5, No. 4, Part II (July 1957).

industrialization and urbanization in these countries, the correlation was much stronger than now, when both the processes have gone much further.

I tried to test this further by studying time-series data for these variables in England and Wales, the U.S., Canada, France, and Sweden. Data for other countries was not easily available to me, but that for the few countries I could study gave significant results. When the two variables are plotted for each country separately and compared over periods varying from 80 to 100 years, the two curves are found to be broadly of similar shape but to differ considerably with regard to the distance between them at different times, as well as in the way they develop or grow with time.

The conclusion that emerges from this is that the correlation worked out by Davis and Golden varies at different stages of industrialization and is not stable through time. They are therefore clearly in the wrong when they apply their correlation historically to Egypt. They calculate the expected levels of urbanization in Egypt in 1907, 1917, 1927, 1937, and 1947 from the regression equation and compare the expected to the actual levels of urbanization, concluding that there was "over-urbanization" in Egypt at these points in time. If the case of Egypt in 1947 is judged from the regression equation worked out by me for the 24 countries, outside Europe and excluding the U.S. and Canada, it is found to conform very much to the general pattern.

The other criterion based on historical experience elevates the course of urbanization and industrialization in some developed countries, namely, the U.S., France, Germany, and Canada, into a norm and regards the proportions subsisting between the two indices at different times in their evolution as a measure of normality. If the proportion of population living in cities of 100,000 and above is used as an index of urbanization,

... it can be said that roughly one in twelve in Asia is a city-dweller as against one in eight in the world as a whole, approximately one in three in North America, and one in five in Europe (including U.S.S.R.).

Such a degree of urbanization is associated in Asia with a degree of industrialization corresponding to 30 percent of the labor force engaged in non-agricultural activities. At comparable periods of urbanization levels the United States (1850's), France (1860's), Germany (1880's), and Canada (1890's) had roughly 55 percent of their labor force engaged in non-agricultural occupations. Thus Asia can be said to be comparatively over-urbanized in relation to its degree of economic development.[9]

An implicit assumption here is that the course of industrialization and urbanization in all countries should radiate more or less in close conformity to the path taken by them in the four countries mentioned, if it is not to be classed as abnormal. When stated in this way, few will be disposed to regard it as in any way decisive or valid. The only reason for regarding the situation in a

[9] UNESCO Seminar Report, *op. cit.*, p. 133. Not that it is materially important for the subsequent argument, but to set the record straight this statement appears to be true of Canada and Germany in the respective periods noted, but not of the U.S. and France. In the U.S. the comparable level of urbanization was reached in the 1850's, but the proportion of the labor force in non-agricultural occupations varied between 35 and 46 percent between 1850 and 1870; see Colin Clark, *Conditions of Economic Progress*, 2nd ed. (London, 1951), p. 404. In France the comparable level of urbanization was attained in the 1860's, but the proportion of the labor force in non-agricultural occupations was around 48 per cent between 1856 and 1876; see F. Simiand, *La Salaire, L'Évolution Sociale et La Monnaie* (Paris, 1932), quoted by Kuznets, *op. cit.*

few developed countries as the norm for the rest of the world seems to be nothing better than the fact that they are today developed economies. But even if we judge other developed countries at some period of their development, we will find that they did not conform to this standard. For example, when in 1895 the degree of urbanization in Sweden was comparable to that of Asia today (8.2 percent in cities of 100,000 or more), the proportion of the labor force in non-agricultural occupations there was less than 45 percent. Even in 1910, though urbanization had increased slightly to 9.3 percent, this proportion was only 51 percent. Conversely, in Switzerland, though the proportion of the labor force in non-agricultural occupations was 60 percent in 1888, there was no city with a population of 100,00 or more in the entire country at that time. In fact, if we logically pursue the analysis based on this norm, the whole of South and Central America would have to be classified as over-urbanized, and for that matter, the whole of Africa and so too the world! One can turn around and say that, compared to the world outside, these four countries are really over-industrialized or under-urbanized with equal justification!

It may be noted, if it has not already become obvious, that the two criteria of over-urbanization discussed above conflict with one another. Eight to nine percent of the population living in cities of 100,000 and more will be associated, in the Davis-Golden regression, with 30.5 percent of the labor force engaged in non-agricultural occupations, and not 55 percent as under the second criterion; conversely, 50–55 percent of the labor force would be associated with about 18 to 20 percent of the population in cities of 100,000 or more. Several cases can be cited

where over-urbanization exists according to the second criterion but not according to the first.

It is surely unnecessary to further labor the obvious—that the definitions of "over-urbanization" developed so far are chimerical and so unusable.

II. CAUSES OF "OVER-URBANIZATION"

From the criteria of over-urbanization, let us now pass to the alleged causes of this phenomenon. The main one, according to the current analysis, is the pressure of population on land in the rural areas in these countries. Economic pressure or "push" in the countryside mounts continuously and pushes out people to the cities in search of employment and livelihood. The rural-urban migration that leads to over-urbanization is mainly a consequence of this "push" from the countryside, rather than the demand for labor by developing economic activity in the towns and the cities, or what is called their "pull." Consequently, these migrants can only get employment in activities with very low productivity or swell the ranks of the unemployed.

Thus the recent rapid rate of urbanization visible in Asian countries does not bespeak of a corresponding growth of industry but a shift of people from low productive agricultural employment to yet another section marked by low productivity employment, namely, handicraft production, retail trading, domestic services in urban areas.[10]

This statement describes only a part of the reality, and its suggestive implications are darker far than they are in actuality. It is true that migrants to towns are absorbed in low productivity employment, but even so, this urban employment is found to be by and large

[10]UNESCO Seminar Report, *op. cit.*, p. 133.

more productive than the pre-migration rural employment of the in-migrants. The urban per capita incomes are almost universally found to be higher than per capita rural incomes in most of the countries. That there is unemployment in the urban areas is true, but can the towns and cities remain dry islands of full employment and very high labor productivity in a sea of rural unemployment and underemployment? A rate of industrial development much greater than that witnessed in these countries in recent years would not be able to change this over-all picture materially because of the enormous backlog of unemployment and underemployment in these countries. A little examination of the relevant data can easily bring this out. That urbanization in these countries does not bespeak of industrialization has been shown to be a questionable inference in section I above.

It should next be noted that over-urbanization according to the first or the second criterion is also found in countries and areas where there is little or no pressure on land in the rural countryside. Most of the countries of Central and South America and many in Africa are in this category. There seems to be no invariant correlation between rural pressure and over-urbanization.[11]

Moreover, the Asian countries referred to in the quotation above

have historically (under colonial rule) experienced increasing pressure on land for at least the last century. Yet it is only in the last two decades that the rate of urbanization in them has accelerated. Before 1939, most of them were noted for their very small degree of urbanization. Rural pressure, therefore, is no new factor in their situation, and if it is such a potent force in furthering urbanization, as is alleged, then why it did not formerly result in "over-" instead of "under-urbanization" has not been satisfactorily explained. On the other hand, if it is to be maintained that this pressure only reached the critical level necessary for resulting in rapid urban growth only during the last two decades, then again it will be necessary to define this critical level of rural pressure and the factors that determine it. This begs the whole question.

Information regarding the causes of rural-urban migration in underdeveloped countries of Asia and elsewhere is very meager. An ILO report furnishes an authoritative recent analysis in this field. It concludes:

The main push factor causing workers to leave agriculture is the lower level of incomes. In almost all countries incomes in agriculture are lower than in other sectors of the economy. The main factor determining the rate of outward movement is the expansion of employment in other occupations. It is this factor which explains the high rate of movement in recent years in the advanced countries (among which Sweden, the United States, and Canada are outstanding) and in rapidly developing countries in Latin America, the Middle East, and Africa. Although the push factors of falling incomes and underemployment in agriculture in most of the less developed countries are now very strong, they do not, in the absence of strong pull factors, suffice to cause large shifts in manpower between occupations. High rates of movement indicate rapid growth and high rates of

[11]Davis and Golden also did not find any correlation between the degree of urbanization in a country and the average density of population there. See *op. cit.*, p. 10. There is, however, they claim, a negative relationship between urbanization and agricultural density defined as the number of males occupied with agriculture, hunting, and forestry per square mile of cultivated land. It can be easily seen that this goes against the whole thesis of rural pressure being the main factor bringing about rapid urbanization.

investment, either in the economy as a whole, including agriculture, or in the industrial or urban sector, as is the case in almost all of the less developed countries which are now in the process of very rapid development.[12]

This indicates that the causal relationship underlying rural-urban migration is quite complicated and cannot be completely explained by the rural push factor.[13] The phenomenon of a rural "push" resulting in urban growth is highly questionable.

III. CONSEQUENCES OF "OVER-URBANIZATION"

Let us now turn to the absence of dynamism in the urban centers which is supposed to be the consequence of over-urbanization. The argument is that because this urban growth is abnormal, in the sense that it is not based on sufficient industrial development, the urban centers are not likely to be such

dynamic centers of social and cultural change as, for example, they had been in Europe and other developed areas. This assumes that urbanization based on industrial development was mainly responsible for the social and cultural changes associated with urbanism or the urban way of life. This analysis is linked with the name of Wirth. Wirth's urban way of life, however, was a theoretical concept of a polar type that was hardly universal even in the Western industrialized countries. Wirth himself had become doubtful about his "ideal typical polar concept" towards the end of his life.[14]

Moreover, this line of thought regards the city as a key variable for explaining certain social phenomena and completely neglects the fact, emphasized by writers like Max Weber, that urbanization itself is a culture-bound phenomenon. Cities in various cultures diverge in some facets of their ecological and social structures. An interplay of these forces produces several types of urban communities even within the broad class of pre-industrial and industrial cities. Urbanization has its own universal structurals, but they are not capable of influencing all social structures in the same way or with the same effectiveness. It is unrealistic to expect the same kind of social developments in underdeveloped countries as in the polar type of Western city. An infinite variety is possible.[15]

. . . it is a highly debatable matter as to whether Western outlook, so characterized, is an antecedent or a consequent of industrialization and urbanization, or something of both, and also whether this outlook, or

---

[12]ILO, *Why Labor Leaves the Land, A Comparative Study of the Movement of Labor out of Agriculture*, Studies and Reports, New Series No. 59 (Geneva, 1960), p. 209. The report goes on to point out that lower levels of income are a universal reason for movement. But different causes operate to reduce the level of incomes in agriculture in relation to other incomes as between the advanced and the less developed countries. In the former, labor leaves the land because agriculture is growing in efficiency, and in the latter, because it is an underprivileged sector of the economy (p. 210).

[13]With the available Indian data I have argued elsewhere that rural pressure exploding into urban growth is a phenomenon rarely met with in India. The migrants to urban areas form only a small percentage of the total unemployed and underemployed in the rural areas. There is also no reason to believe that the economically worse off in the rural areas only migrate. Rural economic conditions are bad, but they are not a necessary nor a sufficient condition for rural-urban migration. N. V. Sovani, "Urban Social Situation in India," *Artha Vijnana* [Journal of the Gokhale Institute of Politics and Economics, Poona, India] (June-September 1961).

[14]Passage quoted by Hauser from the posthumus collection of Wirth's writings in the UNESCO Seminar Report, *op. cit.*, p. 93.

[15]Cf. Gideon Sjoberg, *The Pre-Industrial City: Past and Present* (Glencoe: Free Press, 1960), p. 16.

each element of it, really is an essential ingredient of economic development. It is conceivable that the differences between Asian and Western outlook may produce somewhat different types of industrialization and urbanization or interpersonal and social relations arising therefrom. It is also conceivable that much of what has been written on the subject is the product of premature generalization based on limited observation of the Western experience.[16]

So far as the cultural role of the cities is concerned, there seems to be enough ground to believe that if viewed in relation to the rural areas that surround them, they do play a dynamic role. Hoselitz observes:

The primate cities of Asia are the most important centers of cultural change, especially in those fields which vitally affect economic development: advanced education, new forms of business organization, new administrative practices, and last but not least, new technologies find a fertile soil in them, their intermediate position between East and West, their contact with world markets of commodities and ideas, their land of many traditional bonds make them into eminently suitable vehicles for the introduction of new ideas and new techniques. If economic development is associated with modernization, the mediation of new, "more modern" forms of social action through the primate cities of Asia is an indispensable part of this process.[17]

Rapid urbanization in underdeveloped countries is said to hamper economic development. Because of rapid urbanization the demand for provision of economic and social infrastructure investment increases much more rapidly than do several other sectors. "This means that demand for less productive projects (in the imme-

diate sense) will be made on the scarce capital resources of these economies in the early stages of their development."[18]

This would be so if the available capital resources in underdeveloped countries would be wholly or mainly devoted to more immediately productive investments. In regard to most of the underdeveloped areas, the infrastructure investments are necessary both in rural and urban sectors, and a large part of the available capital resources has to go into them anyway. It is only a question of the relative share of the urban and the rural portions of the economy, with respect to the total investment to be devoted to it. In many ways, because of the earlier start in the cities in these countries, it is vastly more productive to make much of this kind of investment in the cities than in the less developed rural areas. They are likely to come to fruition much more quickly in the urban than in the rural sectors. Even apart from this, the greater advantages of quickly maturing as against slowly maturing capital investments in promoting economic growth are quite questionable. On the whole, therefore, the argument regarding the economic burden of rapid urbanization, as hampering economic growth in underdeveloped areas through the misallocation of scarce capital resources, is not impressive.

I have tried to show that the definition of over-urbanization that has emerged in the current discussion is unsatisfactory and vague; that the analysis of causes and consequences of over-urbanization developed so far is tenuous and oversimplified. Granted, however, that this is so, I am unwilling to end this discussion on a negative note by saying that this line of analysis,

---

[16]*Ibid.*, p. 93.

[17]Bert F. Hoselitz, "Urbanization and Economic Growth in Asia," *Economic Development and Cultural Change*, VI, No. 1 (October 1957), 43.

[18]UNESCO Seminar Report, *op. cit.*, p. 8.

like that of overpopulation before it, is likely to end in a bog and to not prove very fruitful. I think that the time for drawing such a conclusion is not yet here. The subject needs to be investigated further, perhaps by trying to go behind this analysis and to discern and then formulate in concrete, testable terms what it seeks to convey. I can imagine a few ideas that together or separately it struggles to express. The basic thought underlying the concept of over-urbanization seems to be some kind of undesirability of rapid urbanization in the underdeveloped countries. Perhaps it is felt that such a development is inimical to economic growth. In that case, it will have to be proved that in the absence of rapid urbanization, or at a slower pace of urbanization, these areas would have been able to progress more rapidly than they actually have so far. Without prejudging the issue it seems to me *prima facie* that this will be difficult to prove.

Secondly, perhaps over-urbanization is felt to lead to the rise of new urban centers that are parasitical and also that the character of old urban centers becomes more parasitical because of over-urbanization. As a result, urbanization is not as creative as it should be. This will be difficult to verify but should be investigated, if this is what the present analysis seeks to convey. Thirdly, there seems to be implied some kind of norm of the tolerable density limits in rural and urban areas beyond which the resulting social situation is somehow abnormal. If this is what is meant, then it will have to be much more concretely put, bearing in mind all the while how elastic in time and space such tolerable levels can be. There might be many other ideas behind the concept. Whatever they are, they should be formulated clearly and precisely before the concept and analysis of over-urbanization can be more solidly based and put to greater use.

It is not only the role of cities that is important. It is also important to understand the inhabitants of such cities.[1]

Since the growth of urban areas in newly developing countries depends heavily on in-migration, it is essential to perceive just how this is likely to take place. Case studies of in-migration in two widely separated places—Elizaga's for Santiago (26) and Zachariah's for Bombay (27)—are presented here as revealing not only certain differences between Latin America and Asia, but also as embracing otherwise most of the features of such population movement in newly developing countries.

Much of the adjustment of these migrants to their new environment is similar throughout newly developing countries, although there are some differences from place to place. One example of such differences is examined by Janet Abu-Lughod (28), whose attention focuses primarily on Cairo.

Fortunately for our understanding of what actually takes place in the adjustment of in-migrants to their new environment, to other migrants, and to their larger society, several monographs on particular cities and particular segments of the city population are beginning to appear and their number seems likely to be multiplied. The broad features of the context of adjustment are noted by Peter C. W. Gutkind (29) in his analysis of social network phenomena.

Lucien W. Pye (30) calls attention to the great significance of the move to cities for political participation. This is a subject that merits fuller discussion than can be accommodated here. If it is agreed that, in newly developing countries as well as elsewhere, it is in the city that we find the theatre for, and many times the roots of, social change, then the potentialities of these enlarged channels for action are indeed great, not only for city folk but for all inhabitants of the country concerned.

[1] Part III of this reader is most directly related to pp. 73–100 in Breese, *Urbanization in Newly Developing Countries*.

PART THREE

THE INHABITANTS

26. A Study on Immigrations to Greater Santiago (Chile)

JUAN C. ELIZAGA

I. INTRODUCTION

In 1962 the Latin American Demographic Center (CELADE) conducted a survey which covered 2,000 households or more of the urban area of Greater Santiago, the main objectives of which were to obtain statistical information on the migratory stream to that area and of the differential characteristics of the in-migrants. In a more specific way the objectives could be stated as follows:

1. To establish and measure the demographic and socioeconomic differentials of the in-migrants, with respect to the natives of the area.
2. To measure the level and historical trends of the migratory stream.
3. To disclose the subjective and objective factors of this migration.
4. To investigate the adaption of the in-migrants to the environment of the city.

This survey is the first of a series of analogous investigations which CELADE will conduct in important cities of Latin America.[1] This article is a summary of the most interesting results, in the opinion of the author, obtained

Demography, *3, No. 2 (1966), 353–77. Reprinted by permission of author and publisher.*

[1] This research originated in the recommendations formulated by the Department of Economic and Social Affairs and the Population Commission of the United Nations in their tenth period of meetings, to study interior migratory movements, especially regarding the problems which arise from industrialization and urbanization in the underdeveloped

in that investigation. Where possible, those events which display definite trends were included.

Greater Santiago is made up of 11 smaller administrative units (*comunas*) with a total surface of 1,850 sq. kms. and an estimated population of 2,054,000 inhabitants in mid-1962. Not less than 98 percent of this population was urban.

Since 1920 the population of Greater Santiago has been growing at an annual rate close to, or higher than, 3 percent. During the last intercensal period (1952–60) the rate was 3.9 percent. This information alone was more than enough to show that the growth due to migration would be about 1.5 and 2 percent annually. A first important conclusion to affect the selection of the sample was that a high proportion (of the order of 50 percent or more) of the adult population was in all likelihood in-migrants. Consequently, it would be expected that one of every two heads of households was an in-migrant.

The latter circumstance, jointly with the objectives of the research, gave rise to the decision to use a random sample of about 2,000 households, using the results of the 1960 census as a frame. Through a sample of 2,319 households,

countries. A first report was published at the end of 1964 (CELADE, "Survey on Inmigrations to Greater Santiago: General Report, Part I [provisional ed., A/15, 1964]).

A similar survey has been conducted in the metropolitan areas of Lima (Peru), and at present the information is being tabulated. A third survey to be conducted in Greater Buenos Aires is in its preliminary stages.

it was possible to collect information on 10,836 people of all ages, of which 3,701 (34.1 percent) were in-migrants (born in places other than Greater Santiago). The population studies were taken to be representative of the population of Greater Santiago.

The information was collected in two types of questionnaires. A general questionnaire, used in order to obtain information on all members of the households, referred to the demographic, educational, economic, and dwelling characteristics, and to their migratory status. A second questionnaire was used in order to interview personally those who had arrived after the age of 14. In the latter questionnaire, the migratory history was investigated in detail: the reason declared by the in-migrant for migration to Greater Santiago; the occupational situation in the place of last previous residence; diverse circumstances connected to the first occupation held in the city; and other questions regarding social participation, opinions, and attitudes of the in-migrants. Finally, it must be stated that there was a 92.6 percent rate of answers in the general questionnaire and also in the personal interviews of those established as in-migrants in the general questionnaire.

II. THE MIGRATORY STREAM: SEX, AGE, AND TREND

The immigrant population of Greater Santiago, at the time of the survey, is the final result of a process of arrivals and departures (deaths and remigrations) throughout time. Consequently, the distribution of that population by periods of arrival does not represent the stream of migration for such periods. It is distorted by mortality and by emigrations (remigrations), both of which movements affect the immigrants in a direct relation to the time elapsed since their arrival. It can be thought, then, that the immigrants which correspond to the less-recent periods are underrepresented.

Despite the latter fact, about 40 percent of the immigrants arrived before 1942 and the remainder during the last twenty years. These figures show the importance of the migratory movement during the decades 1920–30 and 1930–40.

On the other hand, it seems true that the stream increased in volume during the last two five-year periods. Between the five-year period 1941–47 and the five-year period 1952–56, there was an increase of approximately 20 percent; from 1952–56 to 1957–62, of 30 percent. However, in relative figures (rates), there is no definite evidence of growth during the last twenty years but rather of a relatively constant level, which reveals the regularity of the phenomenon.

Women surpass men, as shown by the masculinity index of 72.0. This is a feature which is to be encountered frequently in the immigrants of the large cities of Latin America. That figure could be adjusted on account of masculine overmortality, but still the masculinity index would be low. On the other hand, the differential behavior by sex became sharper in more recent years, to the extent that the index for immigrants for the last five-year period is 67; for the immediately preceding decade, it is 72; and for the immigrants who arrived before 1942, it is 76. This means that in recent years the differential by sex increased.

The masculinity rate is lower in the young-adult ages, that is, at the ages when at least half of the immigrants arrived, as can be seen from the following figures:

Age of Arrival	Masculinity Index
Less than 15	85
15–29	62
30–49	75
50 and over	57

The low index (57) for people who emigrated at age 50 or more could be ascribed to the decisive effect of masculine overmortality, which is stronger even in people who arrived in recent periods. On the contrary, the relatively low index for those under the age of 15 has no immediate explanation, if it is remembered that it is even lower (50.0) for people who arrived during the last decade and who at the time of the survey were under 25 years of age. Finally, the index for immigrants between 15–29 years during the last decade, and not older than 39 at the time of the survey, is also 55.0, quite below the general index for all the periods. These results confirm, in general, the increasing importance of feminine migrations.

The age structure of the immigrants has the shape frequently found in statistics of this type. The greatest frequencies occur in the age interval between 15 and 29. Of the immigrants of the last decade, about half arrived at those ages (44.0 and 50.7 percent, respectively, of men and women). Analogous figures correspond to immigrants of the decade 1942–51. The age structure of the immigrants who arrived before 1942 is notoriously distorted by mortality (see Table 1).

The age group with the highest density is, for both sexes, 15–19, followed in order of importance by the group 20–24. Children under 10 years of age represent 17.7 of the immigrants of the last decade, a number higher than that of immigrants over 40 years old (14.7 percent).

The features mentioned, particularly

Table 1

In-Migrants to Greater Santiago, by Periods and Age at Arrival

Age at Arrival	Males			Females		
	All Periods	1952–1962	1942–1951	All Periods	1952–1962	1942–1951
Percentages						
Total	100.0	100.0	100.0	100.0	100.0	100.0
0–4	12.3	11.3	13.5	10.0	7.3	9.6
5–9	12.5	9.6	9.8	9.9	8.2	7.4
10–14	14.2	10.3	14.1	13.1	10.4	12.4
15–19	16.6	18.2	17.3	21.5	24.0	21.6
20–24	15.8	16.4	15.0	14.7	15.7	14.6
25–29	8.7	9.4	11.0	11.2	11.0	12.2
30–34	5.9	5.7	6.9	5.2	4.7	6.6
35–39	4.2	4.4	4.0	4.2	4.1	4.6
40–49	5.7	8.8	3.8	5.3	7.4	5.8
50–59	1.9	3.1	3.5	2.6	4.1	4.0
60 and more	1.4	2.8	1.1	1.6	3.1	1.2
Unknown	0.8	...	...	0.7	...	...
Number	1,549[a]	523	347	2,152	782	500

[a] Includes in-migrants having last residence abroad and of unknown last residence.

Table 2

In-Migrants by Place of Last Residence and Age at Arrival (Period 1942–62)

Age at Arrival	Males Nuclei with: 20,000 or More Inhabitants	900 to 19,999 Inhabitants	Rural Area	Females Nuclei with: 20,000 or More Inhabitants	900 to 19,999 Inhabitants	Rural Area
Percentages						
Total	100.0	100.0	100.0	100.0	100.0	100.0
0–4	13.0	11.1	4.0	8.5	6.8	4.4
5–9	11.3	8.1	8.0	9.4	6.8	8.9
10–14	10.1	9.4	16.0	8.8	11.4	12.2
15–19	15.1	20.1	24.0	18.8	26.7	33.3
20–24	13.4	20.5	12.0	13.8	17.6	15.6
25–29	7.9	9.8	14.0	12.4	10.0	10.0
30–39	10.5	10.3	8.0	13.3	5.9	3.3
40–49	12.1	6.0	6.0	8.8	7.1	3.3
50 and more	6.6	4.7	8.0	6.2	7.7	9.0
Number	239	234	50	340	352	90

the concentration in the young-adult ages, are more marked in immigrants from small nuclei and from the rural area. Table 2 shows the distribution by age of immigrants in three categories of places of departure: nuclei of 20,000 and more inhabitants; nuclei of 900–19,999 inhabitants; and the remaining population, or rural. The frequencies for women between 15 and 19 years of age are, respectively, 18.8, 26.7, and 33.3. Among men they are 15.1, 20.1, and 24.0 percent.

The results in Table 2 suggest that immigrants from relatively large nuclei move with a larger number of children, at least in part, in all likelihood because they arrive at a slightly higher average age. Their greater previous mobility contributes to the increase of the average age of adult immigrants from the larger nuclei. Of the immigrants from these nuclei about half (53.5 and 45.8 percent, respectively, for men and women) had previous movements (one or more). This proportion becomes

smaller when smaller nuclei are considered, to the extent that, for instance, for immigrants from nuclei of 900–4,999 inhabitants it is 43.0 percent (men) and 31.7 percent (women) and for immigrants from the rural area it is 25.0 percent (men) and 20.9 percent (women). The fact that the average age of adult immigrants with no previous movements is lower that that of immigrants with one or more previous movements is implied in these observations.[2]

The "rates" of immigration by age complete the analysis of these characteristics. The rates aim at two objectives of importance: first, to furnish a measure of the differential character by age of migration, indispensable for referring

[2] The percentages for in-migrants in the age group 15–24 with no previous movement were, in the case of in-migrants 15 and more years of age in an equal situation, 67.4 for men and 68.8 for women. For the in-migrants with one or more previous movements, the corresponding percentages were 50.3 and 53.6.

Table 3

Average Annual Rates of In-Migration to Greater Santiago, by Sex and Age: 1942–62 (Rates Per 100 Inhabitants)[a]

Age at Arrival	Periods					
	1957–1962		1952–1956		1942–1951	
	Males	Females	Males	Females	Males	Females
0–4	0.9	0.9	1.3	1.3	1.3	1.2
5–9	1.0	0.9	1.2	1.4	1.3	1.1
10–14	1.6	1.9	1.4	2.0	1.8	2.0
15–19	2.7	4.4	2.0	3.5	2.2	3.5
20–24	2.3	3.4	2.5	3.0	2.4	2.9
25–29	1.5	1.8	1.6	1.8	1.9	2.0
30–34	1.2	1.4	1.1	1.1	1.3	1.4
35–39	1.2	1.2	0.9	0.8	1.1	1.2
40–44	1.2	1.2	0.8	0.7	0.8	1.1
45–49	1.2	1.2	0.9	0.9	...	...

[a] For an explanation of the method used to reckon the rates, see Note 3.

the immigrants to the corresponding population of Greater Santiago, and, second, to obtain values which, if applied to that same population, will yield a projection of volume of migration in the near future.

If the immigrants had, at the time of arrival, a similar age structure to that of the population of Greater Santiago, the rates would be the same for all ages. In Table 3 it can be observed that, for instance, the rates for women between 15 and 19 years of age, for the period 1957–62, are about 5 times higher than those for girls between 5 and 9 years of age, and the proportion for those same ages is 2.7 times that of men. The rates confirm the greater importance of immigration in the young-adult ages, now in relative figures with regard to childhood and middle, and advanced ages. It must be observed that, for instance, there is a fall in the rates at such an early age as 25.

Another interesting observation is the upward trend of rates between 15 and 19 and between 20 and 24 years of age, in the twenty-year period considered (1942–62). In the remaining ages there would be practically no trend to change, with the exception of changes that are probably accidental.

Even though the size of the figures and the method used to reckon them compel us to consider with reserve the results obtained, these are fairly coherent and could be used as an expression of the tendencies of migration to Greater Santiago.[3]

[3] The denominator of the rate was estimated in an approximate way, by deducting from the population at June 30, 1962, and by age cohorts, the corresponding in-migrants for the half of the corresponding period, or, in other words, by deducting half of the in-migrants of the cohort that arrived in each period. No correction with respect to death has been made, on the basis that the survival of in-migrants was equal to the survival of the population of the denominator. Before calculating the rates, the information was smoothed.

III. PLACE OF EMIGRATION
(LAST RESIDENCE)

If it is accepted that, in general, the nuclei of more than 5,000 inhabitants display relatively well-defined urban characteristics in Chile,[4] it is concluded that two-thirds of the immigrants of Greater Santiago already had experienced urban life before arrival. With the limit of urban population set for nuclei with more than 20,000 inhabitants, the proportion would still be important: 42.2 percent. Only 12.7 percent moved from the rural area (disperse rural areas and nuclei with less than 900 inhabitants). The distribution of the immigrants who emigrated after the age of 15 is practically the same as that observed in the case of immigrants in general.

These results confirm that the mass of immigrants came from places with urban characteristics. It could be suspected that the situation would be quite different if the place of birth were taken into account instead of the place of emigration, on the basis of the assumption that the population moves in stages. However, as can be seen in the preceding paragraph, the conclusion does not lose validity even if this mobility is taken into consideration.

It would seem logical that the magnitude of the migratory stream should be related to the population from which it proceeds; nor can it be overlooked that the size of the latter is a conditioning factor. To this end, the relative importance of immigrants from each zone is related to the corresponding importance of the population of the zone itself (excluding the population of Greater Santiago). The corresponding results are as shown in the accompanying tabulations:

[4] Number of inhabitants in the 1952 census of population.

Zones of Emigration (Last Residence)	Relative Importance of Immigrants from Each Zone (A)	Population of Each Zone[a] (B)	Relation A/B
Nuclei of 20,000 or more	42.4%	23.5%	1.8
Nuclei of 5,000–19,999	25.6	8.8	2.9
Nuclei of 900–4,999	19.3	16.2	1.2
Rural area	12.7	51.5	0.25
Total	100.0%[b]	100.0%	1.00

[a] Population of 1952, excluding the population of Greater Santiago.

[b] Excluding immigrants who arrived directly from abroad (4.6 percent) and those with no information about place of immigration (1.2 percent).

The relation for the rural population (0.25) clearly indicates that, in spite of a range of 51.5 percent, it is poorly represented in the stream to Greater Santiago. The populations which seem to be best represented are those of the intermediate nuclei (2.9) and those of the relatively large nuclei (1.8).

It is to be observed also that the rural population, and the population of the smaller nuclei, were relatively more important in the past, and consequently the previous relation would be even more antagonistic.

The distribution of immigrants by zones of emigration underwent slight changes during the last decades, judging from the figures in Table 4. It would be venturesome to draw conclusions from the variations observed, especially if they are fluctuations which have no definite tendency. The comparison of the last two decades serves the purpose of this analysis more adequately.

In the first place, in each of these decades there is a great similarity in the distribution of men and women.

Table 4

In-Migrants by Place of Last Residence and by Periods of Arrival

Zones of Emigration	Males (%)			Females (%)		
	1952–1962	1942–1951		1952–1962	1942–1951	
Percentages						
Total	100.0	100.0	100.0	100.0	100.0	100.0
Nuclei with 20,000 or more	40.2	43.3	35.6	39.8	42.0	37.3
Nuclei with 5,000 to 19,999	24.8	22.1	28.8	23.7	22.2	27.2
Nuclei with 900 to 4,999	17.0	20.3	17.0	19.0	21.2	17.0
Rural area	10.9	9.1	21.1	12.8	11.1	15.1
Other countries	5.9	5.2	6.2	3.6	3.0	3.1
Unknown	1.2	...	0.3	1.1	0.5	0.3
Number	1,549	552	371	2,152	810	518

Second, some changes are to be mentioned with respect to the contribution of the different zones of emigration; of special importance is the fact that the proportion which immigrates from the nuclei of 20,000 and more inhabitants increases, and this is the most significant change (5 to 6 points); there is an almost equivalent decrease in the nuclei with 5,000–19,999 inhabitants; and, finally, there occurs a similar compensation between the nuclei with 900–4,999 inhabitants (the contribution of which increased) and the rural area. It could be added that immigration from abroad fluctuated slightly (5–6 for men and 3–4 for women).

Even though it is true, as stated, that distribution by zones of emigration for immigrants over 15 years of age (three-fifths of the total) greatly resembles the distribution of all immigrants irrespective of age, there are some differences worth pointing out in short intervals of age. Thus, the proportion of immigrants from nuclei of 20,000 or more inhabitants varies according to age; that proportion is lower in the young-adult ages, especially between 15 and 24 years of age. The opposite is observed in the other zones of emigration, as the maximum value is reached at about the age of 20 and such behavior is more marked the less urban the zone, and is more marked among men than women. The following figures refer to men. The proportion ascribed to the nuclei with 20,000 or more inhabitants varied from 52.1 percent (age 0–4) to 32.7 percent (age 20–24); the one ascribed to nuclei with 900–4,999 inhabitants varied, in turn, between 12.6 and 21.6 percent, respectively, for the ages mentioned.

IV. PREVIOUS MOBILITY

It has been seen that a high proportion of the immigrants arrived in Greater Santiago before the age of 30. This fact leads to the assumption that previous mobility, that is, the existence of one or several migratory stages, should not be, on the average, high.

Before examining the results, it is necessary to state that this mobility was measured taking into consideration movements occurring after the age of 14, although some results which consider all the movements since birth are included. That limitation, 14 years of age, would be justified because all the movements during childhood are, in general, the result of movements made by adults. Besides, it is most likely that in the case of a child, who changes residence one or more times, only the last place of residence has an important meaning, while the place of birth and other eventual places of residence during childhood lose all meaning.

Table 5, like all the tables included in this section, refers to immigrants arrived in Greater Santiago after the age of 14, the only ones whose migratory history was investigated. It shows the proportion of immigrants who did not have any previous movement, as of their birth, from different zones of birth.

A higher proportion of women (55 percent) than of men (51 percent) arrived directly from the place of birth, and accordingly their previous mobility was nil. If the movements which took place before the age of 14 were excluded, then the proportions with nil previous mobility increase to 65 (men) and to 72 (women) percent. Always in the case of the latter type of mobility, the immigrants with one or with two or more previous movements are evenly distributed: 16 and 19 percent (men) and 14 and 16 percent (women).

The proportion of cases with nil previous mobility decreases when, instead of urban, rural places of birth are considered; this means, in other words, that the immigrants of rural origin and of small towns had greater mobility. Such a decrease is stronger for women, varying from 62.2 percent, if the origin was a nuclei of more than 20,000 inhabitants, to 52.8 percent, if that origin was a nuclei of less than 5,000 inhabitants or a rural area. These figures consider all the movements from

Table 5

Percentage of In-Migrants by Number of Previous Movements and Place of Birth

	In-migrants (%)[b] Arrived at Age of:		
	14 and more		**14–29**
Sex, Number of Previous Movements, and Birthplace[a]	**Movements as of Birth**	**Movements as of Age 14**	**Movements as of Age 14**
Males			
Zero movement[c]	50.8	64.8	63.0
20,000 and more	54.7	67.6	65.4
5,000 to 19,999	52.2	62.9	62.9
Less than 5,000	51.6	62.6	60.8
One movement[c]	20.7	15.9	16.0
20,000 and more	17.4	14.2	14.7
5,000 to 19,999	20.2	17.3	16.5
Less than 5,000	20.4	16.2	16.9
Two or more movements[c]	28.5	19.3	21.0
20,000 and more	27.9	18.2	19.9
5,000 to 19,999	27.6	19.8	20.6
Less than 5,000	28.0	21.2	22.3
Females			
Zero movement[c]	55.1	71.6	70.5
20,000 and more	62.6	72.5	71.2
5,000 to 19,999	53.6	69.3	68.9
Less than 5,000	52.8	73.2	72.4
One movement[c]	22.6	14.4	15.0
20,000 and more	13.4	11.2	11.2
5,000 to 19,999	23.2	17.1	18.2
Less than 5,000	28.0	14.9	15.3
Two or more movements[c]	22.3	14.0	14.5
20,000 and more	24.0	16.3	17.6
5,000 to 19,999	23.2	13.6	12.9
Less than 5,000	19.2	11.9	12.3

[a] Birthplace according to size of nuclei.
[b] Excludes the in-migrants whose number of movements is unknown.
[c] Includes the in-migrants whose birthplace is unknown.
[d] Includes rural areas.

birth. By eliminating movements before the age of 14 years, the differentials of nil mobility disappear with respect to the zone of birth for women but persist for men. It would seem, then, that the greater mobility of women of small nuclei and rural areas with regard to more urban zones occurs during ages below 15 years.

The greater mobility of immigrants of rural origin and from small nuclei is observed for men who had a previous movement as well as for those who had more than one. For women, on the contrary, this is only observed in the figures for immigrants with one previous movement as the relation would be in the inverse sense considering the immigrants with more than one previous movement. In the latter case, in fact, the most mobile immigrants would be those born in the nuclei with 20,000 or more inhabitants (see Table 5).

It is always interesting to know the behavior of immigrants from 14 to 29 years of age, which constitute half of the adult immigrants. The results of Table 5, which render all remarks unnecessary, are very similar to those obtained by immigrants of more than 14 years of age, with no limitation as to age.

If now the mobility of immigrants classified by place of last residence is considered, instead of place of birth, the most mobile are those who came from urban places. This greater mean mobility stems from the people of rural origin and of semiurban origin who completed one or more stages in urban places before their arrival in Greater Santiago.

The accompanying tabulation contains proportions of immigrants with none, one, or two or more previous movements after 14 years of age, with respect to those who arrived in Greater Santiago between 14 and 29 years of age.

Place of Last Residence[a]	Previous Movements of Immigrants Arriving in Greater Santiago Between Ages 14 and 29 (after 14 Years of Age)		
	None	One	Two or More
Men:			
Urban	53.5%	20.5%	26.0%
Semiurban	60.2	15.8	24.0
Rural	73.0	10.0	17.0
Women:			
Urban	63.0	19.0	18.0
Semiurban	70.0	14.0	16.0
Rural	79.0	9.0	12.0

[a] Urban: nuclei with 20,000 or more; semiurban: nuclei with 5,000–19,999; rural: nuclei with less than 5,000 and scattered population.

The above figures require few comments. Differentials by the last place of residence are more marked among men, the differences by sex occurring, according to such figures, at the level of two or more previous movements; the proportions with one previous movement are also fairly equal. The fact that approximately one-fourth of the male immigrants between 14 and 29 who arrived from urban and semiurban places had made two or more previous movements before their arrival in Greater Santiago stands out; the figure for women is approximately one-sixth.

The analysis can be carried further by establishing how the migratory stages have been completed by those immigrants with one or more previous movements—in other words, whether these stages involved places of equal, higher, or lower standing from the standpoint of the size of the nuclei. Thus, two main classes of movements were distinguished: (1) intraclass, when a movement occurred between two places of equal standing—for instance, between urban places; (2) interclass, when movement occurred between two places of different standing —for instance, between a semiurban and an urban place. The interclass movement can be a rising one (rural-urban) or a falling one (semiurban-rural).

The figures available involve all movements starting from birth and, as is obvious, refer to immigrants with one or more previous movements. Table 6 shows the percent distribution with respect to the last place of origin of immigrants for each category of birthplace. When the case involved immigrants with only one previous movement, the interpretation is direct; the relative importance of intraclass movement varies according to the place of birth. If the latter place is urban, 55 out of every 100 made intra-

class movements; if it is rural, the proportion is 35 in the case of men and 41 in the case of women; and if it is semiurban the proportion is lower still (less than 30). The behavior of the immigrant of semiurban origin can be accounted for by a marked tendency to move interclass to urban places (approximately 50 out of every 100). In general, the trend of the interclass movement is oriented to the category of higher standing so, for instance, the immigrants of rural origin moved more frequently to an urban rather than to a semiurban place.

The results for immigrants with two or more previous movements have an important limitation. In Table 6 the

Table 6

In-Migrants Arrived at Age 14 and More, by Place of Birth and Last Residence. In-Migrants with Two or More Movements in Their Life-Spans

Sex and Place of Emigration	Birthplace (percentages)							
	Urban		Semi-urban		Rural		Total[a]	
	One previous movement							
Males	100.0	(43)	100.0	(41)	100.0	(62)	100.0	(163)
Urban	55.8		46.3		37.1		45.4	
Semi-urban	27.9		22.0		27.4		28.2	
Rural	16.3		31.7		35.5		26.4	
Females	100.0	(57)	100.0	(81)	100.0	(149)	100.0	(302)
Urban	54.4		53.1		34.2		45.4	
Semi-urban	28.1		29.6		24.9		26.5	
Rural	17.5		17.3		40.9		28.1	
	Two or more previous movements							
Males	100.0	(69)	100.0	(56)	100.0	(85)	100.0	(224)
Urban	58.0		46.5		40.0		48.7	
Semi-urban	27.5		37.5		16.5		25.9	
Rural	14.5		16.0		43.5		25.4	
Females	100.0	(102)	100.0	(81)	100.0	(101)	100.0	(298)
Urban	67.7		43.2		42.6		51.7	
Semi-urban	18.6		35.8		16.8		23.8	
Rural	13.7		21.0		40.6		24.5	

[a] Includes in-migrants whose place of birth is unknown.
Note: Within brackets ( ), number of cases observed.

place of birth and the place of last residence are identified; at least one movement is not recorded. As a characteristic feature it is observed that the intraclass movement of immigrants born in urban places is stronger than in the case of only one movement. This could be interpreted in the sense that some interclass movements were canceled (people who emigrate to a semiurban place, then return to an urban place). The same thing occurs with immigrants born in rural and semiurban places, though with less intensity than in the case of immigrants of urban origin. As these movements include those which occurred before the age of 14, it is likely that there are a number of movements which cancel those occurring in childhood.

V. INITIAL AGE OF MIGRATORY HISTORY

The initial age of migratory history is an interesting characteristic of the mobility of the population from several standpoints. It furnishes information about the time in life in which the process of adaptation to the social and economic environment begins, is in itself an important condition for obtaining an effective adaptation, and, finally, is a factor having influence on the composition and natural growth of the populations involved.

The simple consideration of the age of arrival in Greater Santiago is a clear indication of the fact that a high proportion of immigrants to Greater Santiago made their first movement at an early age. Of the immigrants of any age in the last decade, about 66 out of every 100 arrived before the age of 25 (both men and women); before the age of 15 the proportion was already high—31 and 26, respectively, for men and women. In a more general way, considering any previous movement, it

can be said that approximately 39 out of every 100 immigrants, of either sex, started their migratory history before reaching age 15.

Excluding movements before the age of 14, for reasons given at the beginning of this article, there would remain an estimated 65 cases out of each 100 whose initial migratory age is interesting to know in greater detail. Of the latter, 84 percent made their first movement between 14 and 29 years of age. The greater density corresponds to the age interval between 15 and 19—44 percent. Above the age of 40, there is only a 5 percent density.

The above percentage of 84 for the age interval 14–29 varies very slightly, either in the total or in each of the three categories of place of birth given in Table 7. Within each sex there is a slight variation according to the place of birth, in the sense that it decreases with the level of urbanization. The similarity of the figures, however, may lead one to think that, when the age of 30 is taken as the highest limit, there is practically no variation by sex or by place of birth.

Considering narrower limits, certain differences appear that are worth pointing out. Such differences tend to compensate themselves in the totals by sex but are relatively conspicuous when sex is combined with place of birth. Strictly speaking, those differences refer in the main to women. The most conspicuous one shows in the percentage which corresponds to the ages 14–19 in which the span is from 40.7 (urban) to 50.1 (rural). These figures are compensated especially in the age group 25–29—17.0 (urban) and 13.0 (rural).

Above the age of 30, the trend is of a greater proportion in immigrants born in urban places, even though the size of the figures gives scarce stability to the results.

Table 7

In-Migrants Arrived at Age 14 and More, by Initial Age of the Migratory History (after Age 14) and by Place of Birth

Initial Migra-tory Age (after Age 14)	Males				Females			
	Urban	Semi-urban	Rural	Total	Urban	Semi-urban	Rural	Total[a]
Percentages								
Total[b]	100.0	100.0	100.0	100.0	100.0	100.0	100.0	100.0
14–19	45.0	44.1	45.9	43.4	40.7	48.6	50.1	45.1
20–24	28.5	28.9	29.5	28.0	25.6	25.4	23.1	24.7
25–29	9.9	12.8	11.5	12.2	17.0	12.9	13.0	14.2
14–29	83.4	85.8	86.9	83.6	83.3	86.9	86.2	84.0
30–39	11.5	8.3	8.5	10.6	10.7	8.6	6.2	8.9
40 and more	5.1	4.9	3.6	5.2	5.8	3.7	6.1	6.1
Number	253	204	305	844	430	350	537	1,398

[a] Includes in-migrants whose place of birth is unknown.
[b] Includes in-migrants whose initial migratory age is unknown.

The above results are strongly determined by the immigrants whose first movement after the age of 14 was to Greater Santiago. In Section IV it was stated that these immigrants represented 65 and 72 percent, respectively, of men and women. It could be assumed reasonably that the initial age should be the lower, the more the number of previous movements increases. However, the data contradict this assumption, at least when comparisons are made by means of a relatively wide interval of ages, such as 14–29 years. The accompanying tabulation indicates an analogous percentage among the immigrants starting their first movement between 14 and 29 years of age who moved directly to Greater Santi-

Number of Previous Movements

	Percentage	
	Men	Women
None	82.5	82.9
One	82.0	83.9
Two	70.1	70.1

Age at the time of the first movement after the age of 14. Percentage from 14 to 29 years of age.

ago (no previous movements) than among those immigrants with one previous movement.

It is surprising to find that immigrants with two previous movements have made their first movement within the age interval of 14–29 in a smaller proportion than immigrants with no and one movement, as 30 percent began after age 30. It is worth asking whether those who begin to move after the age of 30 comprise a certain class of immigrants who, for special reasons, have a high mobility (for instance, civil servants, technicians in enterprises operating on a nation-wide scale, etc.). A separate examination according to categories of place of birth gives similar results with respect to immigrants with two movements.

It is possible that differences arise among immigrants with no and one movement, subdividing in smaller groups the age interval 14–29. For instance, a difference should be expected in the age group 15–19, in the sense of finding a higher proportion with no movement than with one movement.

Table 8

**In-Migrants Arrived at Age 14 and More, by Age and
by Present Level of Education**

Sex and Age at Arrival	Level of education[a] [%]					Total[b]	
	0	1	2	3	4		
Males	6.8	14.6	37.9	19.7	20.1	100.0	(844)[c]
14–19	6.0	12.3	37.4	21.3	22.7	100.0	(366)
20–24	6.3	14.8	44.1	19.1	15.7	100.0	(236)
25–29	4.8	17.5	37.9	21.4	16.5	100.0	(103)
30–39	10.0	18.9	31.1	14.5	23.3	100.0	(90)
40 and more	13.6	15.9	20.4	15.9	27.3	100.0	(44)
Females	12.8	20.7	35.7	17.2	13.1	100.0	(1,398)
14–19	11.9	23.9	35.2	16.0	12.7	100.0	(631)
20–24	8.7	19.4	36.8	20.0	13.6	100.0	(345)
25–29	14.6	16.7	36.4	18.2	14.1	100.0	(198)
30–39	15.3	17.7	37.1	15.3	14.5	100.0	(124)
40 and more	25.9	17.6	31.8	15.3	9.4	100.0	(85)

[a] Level 0: No formal schooling.
Level 1: One to three years.
Level 2: Four to six years.
Level 3: Seven to nine years.
Level 4: Ten and more years.
[b] Includes cases whose level of education is unknown.
[c] Includes cases whose age is unknown.
Note: Within brackets ( ), number of cases observed.

The purpose of the study was to establish if initial age is correlated with education. As level of education is not known at arrival in Greater Santiago and even less at the time of the first movement, the information about the level of education at the time of the survey is used. In the case of immigrants who arrived in Greater Santiago after the age of 14, it could be assumed that a great majority had completed their education,[5] as shown in Table 8. Taking this limitation into account, the data indicate, in the case of men, against expectation, that a lower level of education corresponds to a higher initial age.

[5] More than half of the in-migrants considered initiated their migratory history after the age of 20. Approximately two-thirds of the in-migrants had a level of education under the secondary cycle (six years of primary school or less).

Thus, of those who made their first move at the ages of 15–19, approximately 18 percent had less than four years of primary instruction; for ages 25–29 the proportion rises to 22 percent, and for ages 30–39 it is 29 percent. As for the women, a similar behavior is observed after the age of 29. Of the female immigrants who arrived at ages 15–19, the proportion—36 percent —which had less than four years of primary education was similar to those who arrived at ages 30–39. This leads one to believe that, among the women immigrants 15–19 years of age, there is a very particular group (probably young women who will be domestic servants) of a low level of education which has no counterpart among men of the same age.

At the other end of the educational ladder, that is, at least four years of

secondary education, the same phenomenon occurs. The proportion at that
level of education increases with the
initial age, save for the fact that for
men of initial ages 15–19 that proportion is higher than in the next age
groups. Probably in this group there
are many who had the opportunity to
continue their education after arrival in
Greater Santiago.

The behavior mentioned at both ends
of the educational ladder is not contradictory. The proportion with either type
of education increases with age, with
the exception noted. They are, however,
two different groups of immigrants,
groups to be found in many migratory
movements. It would seem, then, that
immigrants having an intermediate
level of education are those who started
their first movement slightly earlier.

There is a factor which could have
had an influence on the relation between the initial age and a low educational level. For cross-sections in time,
it is possible to imagine that the people
who started their migratory history
during them at a relatively high age are
obviously older than those who did so
at an earlier age. If they belong to older
generations in a country in which the
level of education has been raised progressively, it is likely that their level of
education is lower than that of more
recent generations.

VI. FACTORS OF EMIGRATION

The information used for this analysis
of factors consists of (1) the motives for
emigration to Greater Santiago, reported by the immigrants, and (2) the
characteristics regarding employment
of the same in their place of previous
residence. Universal experience indicates that occupational opportunities
account for most of the movements,
though there are other causes which

deserve attention. The declared motives
and the characteristics of employment
are factors which complement and
clarify each other.

The data of arriving immigrants, 14
years of age and over, in the last 20
years previous to the survey, are used.
With this limit as for the past, the aim
is to obtain representative results of
a relatively recent period, at the same
time keeping the number of cases
adequately high. The latter requirement prevents a more detailed analysis
with respect to period and age of
arrival, both of which variables would
be interesting to control.

The motives declared with greater
frequency were situations related to
labor, such as "looking for work,"
"to obtain a better salary," and "transfer or new contract." In order of
quantitative importance, the reason
"education of the immigrant or his
relatives or dependents" comes next,
and "heterogeneous group of reasons
termed family problems" (including
health problems, death of a member
of the family). It must be pointed out
that these statements always correspond to immigrants who did not
depend on other people at the time of
their arrival in Greater Santiago and
that therefore they do not include the
married women who arrived with their
husbands or the children who emigrated
with their parents, among other cases.

As can be seen in Table 9, approximately 60 out of every 100 immigrants
declared reasons connected with "work"
and 10 per cent "education."[6] The
"family problems" were more frequent

[6] It is likely that an important proportion of
the in-migrants classified under the item
"education" was, in fact, made up of dependent persons and consequently should not have
been included in Table 9. There were difficulties regarding the correct classification in
dependents and non-dependents.

Table 9

**In-Migrants (Non-dependent) of the Period 1942–62,
According to Main Reason Declared for Move to Greater
Santiago, by Place of Last Residence**[a]

Reason for Moving	Males			Females		
	Last residence (nuclei of)			Last residence (nuclei of)		
	5,000 and More	Less than 5,000 (Including Rural)	Total[b]	5,000 and More	Less than 5,000 (Including Rural)	Total[b]
Percentages						
Total	100.0	100.0	100.0	100.0	100.0	100.0
Work	64.3	62.7	62.0	49.2	67.2	55.9
Education	13.2	3.3	9.5	12.6	7.0	10.4
Family problems	6.3	8.7	7.6	16.3	12.7	14.9
Other reasons and insufficient information	16.2	25.3	20.9	21.9	13.1	18.8
Number	303	150	484	374	213	596

[a] In-migrants of more than 14 years at arrival in Greater Santiago.
[b] Includes in-migrants having last residence abroad or of unknown last residence.

as a factor of emigration among women (14.9 percent) than among men (7.6 percent).

A significant proportion of cases of the order of 20 percent had to be classified under the heading "other reasons and insufficient information." The open form of the question included in the questionnaire is, probably, responsible in part for the lack of precision in the answers. The fact that 22 out of every 100 women who departed from relatively large nuclei (5,000 or more inhabitants) fall under that heading leads one to think also of a great range of different reasons difficult to classify. Among the men, however, the highest proportion of indefinite cases (25 percent) was found in the emigrants from relatively small nuclei (less than 5,000 inhabitants).

Comparing the reasons declared according to the two categories of place of last residence considered in Table 9, it is necessary to point out at least two aspects. The first has bearing on the reason "education," significantly more frequent in the immigrants from relatively large nuclei. The second refers to the differences with regard to the reason "work," to be seen among women, according to which this motivation is stronger, or at least more conscious, among non-dependent women who arrived from relatively small nuclei and from the rural area. If the women who are dependents were taken into account, then the difference among the proportions of non-dependents with the reason "work" would be even greater yet: 50 and 30 percent, respectively, for the nuclei with less than 5,000 inhabitants and for those with more than 5,000 inhabitants.

The degree of employment in the place of last residence is a fact that

Table 10
**In-Migrants (Non-dependents) of the Period 1942–62
According to Main Reason Declared for Emigration to Greater
Santiago and Degree of Employment in Previous Place of Residence[a]**

	Reason				
	Work		Education	Others and Insuffi-	
Sex and Degree of Employment	Total	Looking for Work	and Family Problems	cient In- formation	Total
Percentages					
Males					
Total	100.0	100.0	100.0	100.0	100.0
Employed	84.7	76.0	86.8	97.7	87.4
Not looking for work	59.4	46.3	71.1	81.4	65.5
Looking for work	25.3	29.7	15.7	16.3	21.9
Unemployed[b]	14.0	22.3	9.6	2.3	11.1
Other situations	1.3	1.7	3.6	...	1.5
Number	300	175	83	86	469
Females					
Total	100.0	100.0	100.0	100.0	100.0
Employed	47.1	34.3	82.7	91.1	60.3
Not looking for work	35.1	23.3	69.9	68.9	47.2
Looking for work	12.0	10.0	12.8	22.2	13.1
Unemployed[b]	52.6	65.3	15.0	8.9	38.9
Other situations	0.3	0.4	2.3	...	0.8
Number	333	245	133	45	511

[a] In-migrants of more than 14 years at time of arrival in Greater Santiago, with professional experience in last place of residence. Includes people lacking that previous experience (not economically active) whose declared reason was "looking for work."

[b] Includes people without professional experience in last place of residence whose declared reason was "looking for work."

can be useful to qualify the reason declared. It is likely that frequently the reason declared will conceal the real cause, such as unemployment or disguised underemployment. Table 10 shows information regarding immigrants with professional experience in the place of last residence. It also includes people who do not have professional experience but whose declared reason was "looking for work." In short, the table contains 96 percent of the men of Table 9 and 86 percent of the women.

From Table 10 it follows that not all immigrants whose declared reason was "looking for work" were actually in search of an occupation. In fact, only 52 men out of every 100 and only 76 women out of every 100, were looking for a position (employed and unemployed). On the other hand, a portion of the immigrants who declared a reason other than "looking for work" was also looking for an occupation. Now, if it is admitted that both the unemployed and those who wanted an occupation had reasons (not always declared) to emigrate for that cause, by that criterion 21.9 percent of the men and 52.0 percent of the women have emigrated to Greater Santiago "looking for work" (see last column of Table 10), whereas, on the basis of the reason declared only, those proportions are, respectively, 37.3 and 47.9 percent.

These seeming contradictions show the need to cross-examine the reason with the degree of employment and also the convenience of considering, additionally, secondary reasons declared by the immigrants.

The fact that only 52 percent of the men whose declared reason was "looking for work" were actually looking for an occupation (employed or unemployed) would be evidence of the fact that almost half of them did not do so because they did not expect to obtain a position with better conditions (salary, etc.); even though that percentage rises to 76 in the case of women, it was due simply to the decision of including among the unemployed the women who declared their reason for having emigrated "looking for work" as though they were not working in their place of previous residence.[7] Such people did not consider themselves as unemployed or in search of a position, as there was no opportunity for employment within their villages.

VII. WHERE AND HOW THE IMMIGRANTS LIVE IN THE CITY: DIFFERENTIAL ASPECTS

A. Areas of Residence

The distribution of immigrants in the area of Greater Santiago, at the time of the survey, was approximately equal to the distribution of the natives of the city. However, it is likely that there was a greater density of immigrants in some areas where living conditions are particularly low (slums, shanty-towns, and others), as would follow from the infor-

mation regarding dwelling, even though these conditions have hardly any importance with regard to the entire population.

This similarity in regard to the position of the dwelling is logical if it is considered that the immigrants represent more than half of the adult population of the city; that a relatively large part came from urban places of certain importance; and that the social characteristics of the immigrants and natives do not offer, in general, remarkable differences, as shall be seen later on.

The results are presented by dividing the city into four sections: central, eastern, southern, and northwestern. This division aims at grouping, though in an imperfect fashion, segments of population of different average levels of living. The central section comprises the commercial and administrative center and the older quarters of the city. The eastern section is modern and residential. The southern and northwestern sections are densely inhabited and have achieved the greater part of their growth in the last three decades.[8]

Contrary to expectation, in the central section (35 percent) and in the eastern section (33 percent), a much higher proportion of male immigrants was found than in the popular sections, the southern and northwestern (28 percent). The difference is greater yet with respect to the female population, the extreme cases being the eastern section (42 percent) and the northwestern section (29 percent). A great part of these differences disappears if the population under 15 years of age is

---

[7] They represent the 35.4 percent of those who arrived for reasons connected with work (333 cases).

[8] The areas were formed by grouping neighboring districts (*comunas*) as follows: central: Santiago; eastern: Providencia, Las Condes, Nuñõa; southern: San Miguel, La Cisterna, La Granja; northwestern: Conchali, Barrancas, Renca, and Quinta Normal.

excluded. It is likely, then, that the average number of children (natives) of immigrant parents is higher in the popular sections. Some differences prevail, however, even if the population under 15 is excluded, as shown by the following results with respect to people between 15 and 39 years of age: (a) the proportion of male immigrants is lower in the northwestern section (35 percent), probably the poorest if compared with the other sections (approximately 40 percent); (b) the proportion of female immigrants in the eastern section is very high (53 percent), probably because of the presence of domestic servants, and very low in the northwestern section (39 percent).

The present distribution of the immigrants is the result of initial accommodation and of changes of residence during their lives in the city. The information obtained regarding the first dwelling of immigrants arriving in different periods of time and the comparison, on the one hand, with the present dwelling and, on the other, with changes in the distribution of the entire population of the city in the last twenty years lead to the approximate conclusion that the immigrants, both in first accommodation and in subsequent

mobility, have followed the trends of numerical growth and area of the city.

The table below contains the relative distribution by section of immigrants in the period 1942–62, according to the first dwelling and the present dwelling. The same information is given for immigrants of shorter periods within the last twenty years.

The distribution of immigrants of the period 1942–52 according to first dwelling closely reflects the distribution in equal sections of all the population toward the half of the period (1952). Observe that the distribution of the present dwelling differs less among immigrants arriving in different periods of time than the distribution of the present dwelling of immigrants who arrived in the decade before last. Finally, the distribution of the present dwelling of the immigrants of the period 1942–62 is closely comparable to the distribution of the population counted in the 1960 census.

A marked selectivity on the basis of the place of last residence was not observed. In the popular sections—the southern and northwestern—one-fourth of the immigrants who emigrated from nuclei with 20,000 or more inhabitants had their residence; practically the

In-Migrants by Sections in Which They Had Their Dwelling[a]

Sections of Greater Santiago	In-migrants of the Period					
	1942–1962		1942–1951		1957–1962	
	First Dwelling	Present Dwelling	First Dwelling	Present Dwelling	First Dwelling	Present Dwelling
Central	52.6	34.3	63.8	33.5	43.7	37.7
Eastern	15.5	17.4	12.6	15.3	17.0	18.0
Southern	15.5	24.4	10.1	26.4	20.7	19.7
Northwestern	16.4	23.9	13.5	24.8	18.6	24.6
Total	100.0	100.0	100.0	100.0	100.0	100.0

[a] In-migrants arrived in Greater Santiago with more than 14 years of age.

same fraction from nuclei with less than 5,000 inhabitants and from the rural area lived in each of those sections. In the eastern section, the proportion of emigrants from the places mentioned in first place practically double the proportion of emigrants from the places mentioned in second place (approximately 19 and 12). As a logical consequence, in the central section there was a smaller proportion of emigrants from nuclei with 20,000 or more inhabitants (33 percent) than of emigrants from small nuclei and from the rural area (40 percent).

B. Dwelling

In order to investigate the existence and the importance of the differentials with respect to conditions of the dwelling, we considered the "class" of the dwelling, the basic services (water, light, etc.), tenancy, and average number of persons per room. These data are referred to the head of the family, who is classified according to his migratory status.

It is convenient to clarify here that the denomination "native heads" also comprises immigrants arrived before the age of 14 and that the same criterion was used with respect to all the information in which the statistical unit is the dwelling or household. The immigrant heads who arrived during the last decade will be called henceforth, for the sake of brevity, "recent immigrants" and those who arrived previously "senior immigrants."

The class of dwelling takes into account physical characteristics (main material in roofing and walls) and forms of coexistence. According to these criteria, the conditions of the dwelling would be worse for the households of recent immigrants. Of these families, 45 percent lived in dwellings which could be classified as not satisfactory, half of them on account of the type of coexistence ("conventillo," "rooms in boarding houses") and the other half on account of building materials of a temporary nature (shanties, wooden huts, etc.). In the households of the native heads and of the senior immigrants, the proportion of unsatisfactory

Table 11

Class of Dwelling According to Migratory Status of Head of Household[a]

Class of Dwelling	Natives	In-migrants	
		"Senior" (Before 1952)	"Recent" (1952–1962)
Percentages			
Total	100.0	100.0	100.0
Independent dwelling in building of solid material[b]	65.6	68.0	53.0
Rooms in "multifamily" dwelling[c]	15.2	13.1	22.4
Dwelling of semisolid material and nonpermanent material[d]	18.5	17.5	23.1
Others and unknown	0.7	1.4	1.5
Number	1,210	645	281

[a] Excludes "collective" dwellings: hotels, convents, regiments, etc., and boarding houses with more than 6 boarders.

[b] "Unifamily" type of house, apartment in apartment building.

[c] Slums ("conventillos"), boarding houses, rooms in houses with two or more households.

[d] Shanties, huts, etc.

dwellings would be only one-third. Consider that the qualification of inadequate, which results from the information available, underestimates real shortcomings. Table 11 furnishes more detailed information.

The availability of basic services in the dwelling confirms the previous results. Approximately 30 percent of the households of recent immigrants lack either partially or altogether the basic services (water, light, drainage) (see Table 12). In the remaining households, about 23 percent were in those conditions.

The tenancy of the dwelling could be interpreted as an index of rooting and of the capability to solve the problem of his own dwelling. Only one-fifth of the recent immigrant heads are owners as compared to two-fifths of the other heads. The number of owners probably leads to an overestimation of the situation, because it includes occu-

pants of dwellings of non-permanent material who possibly do not own the plot of ground. In fact, the proportion of leasers and users is, in fact, low compared to the figures in the table relative to the class of dwelling.

The last characteristic to be mentioned is the average number of persons per room to be used as dwelling. The resulting average number of 1.4 people could be considered moderately low. However, this simple average is inadequate to report the conditions in which some groups must live.

In the first place, the density varies in direct relation with the number of members of the household. The average density corresponds approximately to that of households of 5 members. In the case of households with 7 members, the density exceeds 2 people per room, reaching densities as high as 4 people in the more numerous households. Table 13 is a summary of average densities

Table 12

Services Available in the Dwelling, According to the Migratory Status of Head of Household[a]

| | | In-migrants | |
| | | "Senior" (Before 1952) | "Recent" (1952–1962) |
Services[b]	Natives		
Percentages Total	100.0	100.0	100.0
Water, light and drainage	77.4	77.7	69.7
Water and light[c]	11.2	12.1	13.2
Light only	3.9	4.0	6.8
No information[d]	7.5	6.2	10.3
Number	1,210	645	281

[a] See footnote[a] of Table 11.
[b] Water and/or drainage in the dwelling, and out of the dwelling, but within the building.
[c] Ten percent of this figure with water only.
[d] Primarily dwellings without services and with very limited services.

Table 13

Density Per Room Used as Dwelling, According to Number of Members of Household and Migratory Status of Head[a]

| | Average Number of Members Per Room[b] | | |
| | | In-migrants | |
Number of Members	Natives	"Senior" (Before 1952)	"Recent" (1952–1962)
All households	1.5	1.4	1.4
2	0.6	0.7	0.6
5	1.4	1.3	1.5
6	1.7	1.5	1.5
7	1.9	1.9	2.5
8	2.1	2.3	3.1
9	2.7	2.7	4.5
10	2.8	2.6	3.6

[a] Excludes: kitchen, bath, corridors, and storage or commercial and industrial purpose rooms, etc.
[b] Domestic servants not counted.

according to the number of members of the household, in households of heads with different migratory status. According to that information, the households of recent immigrants displayed, in households of 7 or more members, densities higher than those of other groups.

In the second place, density varies inversely to the number of rooms available. It is important to observe dwellings with one and two rooms. The dwellings with one room represent 15 percent of the total (it hardly varies according to the migratory status of the head), and in them the density reaches 4.3 people, when the head is a native and, in the most favorable case, 3.2 people when the head is a senior immigrant.

Dwellings with two rooms represent 23 percent of the total (very similar according to the migratory status of the head). The density was, in these dwellings, 2.3 people, no differentials being noticeable. In short, in 38 percent of the homes investigated, the density is higher in those that have only one or two rooms, but in a sense in which the density is favorable to the immigrants.

It is possible to individualize dwellings in which overcrowding is even greater—dwellings with one, two, and three rooms, in which there are 2 or more people per room. Such dwellings represent 26 percent of all investigated —10, 11, and 5 percent, respectively, according to whether they have one, two, or three rooms. The densities per room were, in approximate terms, 5 people in the dwellings with one room, 3.3 people in those with two rooms, and 2.9 people in the dwellings with three rooms. In short, one-fourth of the dwellings had a density of 3 or more people per room. The general trend was an average slightly lower in dwellings whose heads were recent immigrants.

C. Size and Composition of the Dwelling

The average size of the households investigated was 4.9 people.[9] This figure reflects the situation of native heads and of senior immigrant heads. The average of the households of recent immigrants was lower, 4.4. people. More than 55 percent of these households had 3, 4, and 5 people.

The difference for the households of senior immigrants could be found in the higher average age of these heads; such an explanation cannot hold true for the households of native heads.

The distribution of households according to size, as well as to the average size, depends on the composition of the household. To classify them according to the latter characteristic, the composition of the family nucleus of the head of the household was taken into account (see Table 14). There it is seen that a high proportion (85.1 percent) of the households of recent immigrants is made up basically of a couple with no children or with unmarried children, or by the head and unmarried children. On the other hand, there are comparatively fewer households made up of a couple and married children (3.2 percent) and of households where there is no spouse or children of the head (5.7 percent) with regard to the households of native heads or of senior immigrants. The last three columns of Table 14 suggest that within each class there are some differences in average size with respect to the migratory status of the head of the household, but in any case these differences do not account for all the differences in the general averages, which are due mainly to the proportions of households with different compositions. In fact, by

[9] It does not include domestic servants, who were not taken into account for statistics on households.

Table 14

Composition of Household, According to Migratory Status of Head. Average Number of Members Per Household

Composition of the Household	Migratory Status (Percentages)			Average Number of Members		
		In-migrants			In-migrants	
	Natives	"Senior"	"Recent"	Natives	"Senior"	"Recent"
Total	100.0	100.0	100.0	5.0	4.4	4.8
Head and his wife, without children or with unmarried children	73.9	67.3	75.1	5.3	4.8	5.1
Head (women) with unmarried children	5.7	8.2	10.0	4.1	3.6	3.7
Head and his wife (or without wife) with married sons and/or daughters	6.5	10.5	3.2	7.4	7.3[a]	6.6
Head with other people	9.3	7.0	5.7	3.5	3.4	3.3
Head alone	4.5	6.8	6.0	1.0	1.0	1.0
Others and not well established	0.1	0.2	...	...	...	...
Number	2,136	645	281			

[a] Only 9 households.

applying the averages corresponding to recent immigrants to the proportions according to the composition of native households, a general average of 4.6 is obtained instead of 5.0.

Approximately 43 out of every 100 households had a head who was an immigrant who arrived after the age of 14. In the other households, 25 out of every 100 spouses of the head were immigrants (arrived at any age).

The number of immigrants in the household (with no restrictions as to age of arrival) varies with the migratory status of the head. This stands to reason not only because the head is an immigrant but also because there is a moderate association with the migratory status of the spouse (0.67 ± 0.03) and because a certain association must be expected as to the status of the children and relatives who live in the same house-hold. On the other hand, on account of the correlation between the size of household and number of children, the relative number of immigrants per household decreases as the number of members increases.

Seventy immigrants out of every 100 people were found in homes of recent immigrant heads. This relation, which was 85 in households of 2 members, is still high—55 in households of 8 members. In the households of senior immigrant heads, the proportion drops to 45 immigrants out of every 100 people (81 in households with 2 members, 33 in households with 8 members), and it is even lower in the households of native heads—18 out of every 100 (36 in households with 2 members and 13 in households with 8 members).

If the head is native, the typical

household contains no immigrants; if the head is an immigrant, the typical household contains 2 immigrants, even though this is more frequent or more typical when the head is a senior immigrant (see Table 15).

Table 15

Households by Number of In-migrant Members, According to Migratory Status of Head

Number of In-migrants in Household[a]	Percentages of Households in Which Head Is:		
		In-migrant[b]	
	Native	"Senior"	"Recent"
Total	100.0	100.0	100.0
0	41.0	. . .	. . .
1	35.1	30.7	19.6
2	16.9	42.2	25.3
3	5.0	15.8	18.9
4	1.6	6.0	16.0
5	0.2	2.5	9.9
6 and more	0.2	2.8	10.3
Number	1,210	645	281

[a] In-migrants regardless of age at arrival.
[b] In-migrants arrived at age of 14 or more.
In-migrants arrived before age 14 were added to the natives.

D. Level of Education

The level of education of the immigrants is, as a rule, somewhat lower than that of the natives, with greater difference among women than among men. These observations arise from the figures in Table 16. In these, in order to make comparisons easier, three levels of education have been considered, and the figures indicate the percentage that the level indicated reaches, or a higher one.

On the other hand, when age increases, the level of education becomes lower in the different groups considered, with one exception. This can be accounted for by the improvement of education which favored the younger generations. This situation favors the average educational level of the natives, as they are the younger group, and is unfavorable to the senior immigrants, as [they are] the older one. However, by observing the level of education by ages, the same conclusion is reached. The most important differences occur at level 1 (7 and more years of education). Of native males 15–29 years of age, 57.6 percent correspond to level 1, against 51.5 and 47.4 percent, respectively, of the senior and recent immigrants. In the case of the women in the same age group, the percentage of natives in level 1 was 53.7 against 47.1 and 30.8 percent, respectively, for senior and recent immigrants. It is to be observed that differences of level of education according to migratory status occur more sharply in the case of women at level 2 and even at level 3, an event which does not occur in the case of men. Also, among the women and at levels 1 and 2, differences according to migratory status are observed markedly in the ages over 30.

When the situation between senior and recent immigrants is compared, it is striking that, in both sexes, while the level of education is higher among the former in the age group 15–29, the opposite occurs in the age group 30–49. This is to be seen among men at level 1 and among women at levels 1 and 2. This behavior can be accounted for, with respect to the age group 15–29, by the fact that the senior immigrants arrived, in most cases, as children and consequently were afforded educational opportunities in the city. The recent immigrants (1952–62) arrived at a higher average age. With respect to the age group 30–49, it could be thought that the recent female immigrants

Table 16
Level of Education, According to the Migratory Status by Age

Migratory Status and Age	Males				Females			
	Level of Education[a]				Level of Education[a]			
	1	2	3	X	1	2	3	X
Natives								
15 and more	53.0	85.6	94.9	1.6	48.6	84.4	93.6	2.4
15–29	57.6	87.8	96.4	1.6	53.7	87.1	94.5	3.1
30–49	49.3	85.1	94.5	1.4	45.4	84.3	93.9	2.3
50 and more	41.9	77.0	89.1	1.7	39.1	76.1	90.0	0.4
"Senior" in-migrants								
15 and more	42.7	77.3	91.5	1.4	34.1	68.5	86.9	1.5
15–29	51.5	85.4	93.3	1.8	47.1	79.9	92.6	3.2
30–49	42.0	81.1	93.5	0.9	33.4	72.8	89.3	1.1
50 and more	39.7	68.9	88.2	1.9	30.2	58.5	81.5	1.4
"Recent" in-migrants								
15 and more	47.2	82.1	94.8	0.5	31.3	68.3	87.2	1.8
15–29	47.4	85.2	96.5	0.9	30.8	68.4	89.5	2.5
30–49	46.9	78.0	95.2	...	38.8	75.3	88.2	1.1
50 and more	46.9	79.6	85.7	...	17.5	52.5	72.5	...

[a] Present level: 1. Seven years of schooling or more.
                2. Four years of schooling or more.
                3. One year of schooling or more.
                x. Other types of schooling (vocational for women, etc.) and without information.

(whose average age of arrival would be slightly over 30 years) would have a higher average level of education than the young-adult immigrants who arrived before 1952 and who, at the time of the survey, were in the age group 30–49. The results for people over the age of 50, on account of their low number, are less reliable.

E. Employment

The data of the survey made the study of several economic characteristics possible; among these are level of participation, degree of employment, income, and socioprofessional status.

In the following paragraphs of this section, unless otherwise specified, the figures for natives and the figures for recent immigrants (1952–62) are compared, without considering, as a rule, the age of the latter at the time of the movement. The people dealt with are over the age of 15 at the time of the survey.

a) Rates of participation. The results for men show that the global rate of the immigrants (83.7) is higher than that of the natives (77.9). This difference was determined by the participation of people in the age group 14–29, an interval in which the differential is remarkable: 73.5 (immigrants) against 60.7 (natives). As for women, the differential is even greater than that observed for men (45.5 and 31.2 percent), determined again by the levels of the age group 15–29: 57.0 (immigrants) and 30.3 (natives).

If the results obtained for those immigrants who arrived before 1962 were to be given, it would be seen that rates of participation for men and women are similar to those of natives.

These results suggest that immigrants with few years of residence are compelled to work at an earlier age, on an average, than the rest of the population. This could be due to lack of support from the family and to the fact that, frequently, the reason to emigrate was to find an occupation. The differentials which arise from this survey were confirmed a year later by the results of a survey on occupation.

b) Degree of employment. Under this heading the period of time worked—up to the week before the survey was conducted—is considered, including unemployment. Additionally, a distinction was made in the degree of employment of full-time workers, according to whether they sought employment or not. Those seeking employment, added to those employed on a half-time basis, and those unemployed will provide a measure of the degree of underemployment.

With regard to men, the immigrants were employed full time (88 percent) in a greater proportion than the natives (84 percent). The difference given becomes lower if the proportions of those employed full time, and who were not seeking an occupation, are considered. In the latter case, there is practically no difference in the age group 15–29 (72 percent). In other words, underemployment, as defined in Table 17, should equal 28 percent in the age group 15–29.

On the other hand, and always with respect to the all-important age group 15–29, even though the immigrants display more full-time employment, there is a much higher proportion seeking employment (including those unemployed): 24.6 against 17.2 percent. The extent to which this reflects a difference in the stability of the employment cannot be ventured here.

The female population displays more marked differentials than the men. The higher proportion of immigrants who work full time is compensated by the inverse situation at the level of part-time employment, due to the fact that unemployment lacks quantitative

Table 17

Degree of Employment of the Economically Active Population[a]

	Males				Females			
	Natives		"Senior" In-migrants		Natives		"Recent" In-migrants	
Degree of Employment	15 Years and More	15-24	15 Years and More	15-24	15 Years and More	15-24	15 Years and More	15-24
Percentages								
Total	100.0	100.0	100.0	100.0	100.0	100.0	100.0	100.0
Full time	84.8	83.7	88.1	87.7	82.0	88.2	91.4	94.9
Not looking for work	74.0	72.1	76.3	71.9	75.5	79.8	84.4	90.3
Looking for work	10.8	11.6	11.8	15.8	6.5	8.4	7.0	4.6
Part time	9.2	10.1	6.5	3.5	16.4	9.8	7.3	4.5
Unemployed	6.0	6.2	5.4	8.8	1.6	2.0	1.3	0.6
Underemployed (1b + 2 + 3)	26.0	27.9	23.7	28.1	24.5	20.2	15.6	9.7

[a] Excludes people looking for work for the first time.

significance. These differentials are greater over the age of 30 than in the age group 15–29, showing the relation between age and part-time employment. In short, 9 out of 10 immigrants in the age group 15–29 are employed full time (without seeking employment); the relation was 8 out of 10 among native women. It follows from this fact that underemployment would be at the rate of 2 to 1 higher among the native women in the age group 15–29.

c) *Income.* Part-time employment, in terms of hours worked during the week previous to the survey, did not reveal the existence of important visible underemployment. Employment can be disguised with respect to many factors, such as the way in which the total occupational market operates, as well as the acceptance of low salaries with a normal schedule. This should be reflected in the amount of income derived from personal work.

The data examined correspond to the income derived from a month's work. For the purpose of establishing comparisons of income according to the migratory status of the worker, 70 escudos—about $47 at the time of the survey—for reference, is an amount nearly equal to the vital net salary of a clerk.

The comparison is restricted to establishing the proportion of workers obtaining less than 70 escudos per month. Of the immigrant males, 49.7 percent were in this category; of the natives, 44.9 percent. By taking into account the workers between 30 and 54 years of age, the interval in which they are supposed to obtain their highest incomes, the differences pointed in the same direction, though they are more marked in relative figures—immigrants, 37.9 percent; natives, 30.8 percent.

With respect to female workers, the differences are better understood by comparing the percentages that received less than 30 escudos per month, as the proportion that earned from 30 to 70 escudos was very similar in all the groups considered. Of the immigrants 54.3 percent earned less than 30 escudos per month; only 20.0 percent of the natives earned that amount.

In short, judging from the incomes derived from personal work, the situation of the native workers was favored as compared to that of immigrant workers. However, the importance of such a differential can hardly be stressed.

d) *Socioprofessional status.* Basically, two categories were used to define the socioprofessional status: "manual" workers and "non-manual" workers.

1. The manual workers represented practically two-thirds of male labor in Greater Santiago, with almost no difference for immigrants and natives (63–64 per cent).

The situation is different in the case of female labor. Of the immigrants, 80 percent were manual workers, whereas only 56 percent of the natives were. This difference is due to the high incidence of domestic servants among immigrant female workers (64 percent) as compared to natives (12 percent).

A feature of immigrant labor is the importance of the area of "personal services." In the male immigrants this area involves 21 percent of the manual workers and only 8 percent in the case of native males. For women, the figures are 87 (immigrants) and 39 (natives) percent.

As among manual workers there is a greater proportion of immigrants involved in the area of personal services; the non-manual immigrant workers are also more greatly represented in the higher area of the "professionals and technicians"—22 and 46 percent for men and women, respectively. In the case of the natives, the figures are, respectively, 17 and 27 percent.

The proportion of manual workers is higher in young labor. In the age group 15–24 the proportion of males is 74 percent for immigrants and 60 percent for natives, that is to say, there is a remarkable difference which was not detected when all the ages were taken as a whole. In the age group 25–29 the situation is clearly the opposite but with a less marked differential—54 (immigrants) and 58 (natives) percent.

With respect to women, when age groups are considered, the differential already pointed out in general becomes sharper in the young workers and prevails in those of greater age: 90 against 60 percent in the age group 15–29, 66 against 51 in the age group 25–59 years.

2. The age of the immigrant at the time of arrival and the length of the period of residence in the city affect his professional mobility. In terms of the length of the period of residence, the immigrant increases his possibilities for improving his condition by adapting himself to the environment. Additionally, if he is young, it is thought that he is going through a period of natural lack of stability, with respect to his economic activity, as would also be the case if he were a native.

The mobility of immigrants in the two categories established—manual and non-manual workers—would be relatively low if the first occupation held in Greater Santiago and the occupation at the time of the survey are compared. The remarks that follow are applicable to male immigrants who were more than 14 years of age on arrival and who moved in the period 1942–62.

The classification according to the first occupation gave a percentage of non-manuals (31.9 percent) slightly lower than that of the last occupation (33.8 percent). Even though it could be concluded from these figures that mobility was slight, when the information, according to the age of immigrants on arrival in Greater Santiago, is examined, it was moderately high among people over 40 years of age and, as a rule, increases with age. In fact, in the immigrants who arrived between the ages of 15 and 24, the percentage of non-manuals was about the same in the first and last occupations (26 percent); among those between 25 and 39, the proportion changed from 35 to 37, and it could not be said that the difference is significant. Finally, among immigrants of 40 and more years of age, the change was from 48 to 59 percent.

A direct analysis of 434 immigrants (males) shows that 9 out of 10 manual workers remained in the same category and that 9 out of 10 non-manual workers also remained in the category of their first occupations. In a table of contingency, it was estimated that the index of "departure" from the manual category was 0.24; the index of "departure" from the non-manual category was 0.19. In both cases, then, the index is low and shows hardly any mobility (0 would indicate no mobility at all).

There was, logically, greater mobility within each socioprofessional category. Thus 75 out of every 100 "artisans and skilled workers" remained in the same occupation. In the subgroup "clerks and salesmen," 70 out of every 100 did not move. In workers in the area of personal services, mobility was greater, only 52 out of every 100 remaining in that occupational area.

F. Fertility of Women

A question on the number of sons born alive was included in the survey. The question was put to all women over the age of 12, except those who had declared that their civil status was unmarried.

The women between 20 and 49 years of age had an average of 3.32 sons in the case of married natives. The corresponding average was slightly lower for the immigrants, 3.12 (average adjusted to the age structure of the natives).

Considering the fertility of married women whose husbands are present, the average number of sons of natives and immigrants were, respectively, 3.38 and 3.19. Such results would indicate, against an assumption frequently established, that the fertility of immigrant women was not higher than the fertility of native women. The average number of sons of women of different age groups systematically indicate higher values for the natives, with the exception, accidental in all

likelihood, of the group 40–49, as seen in the accompanying tabulation.

Average Number of Sons (Born Alive) Borne by Married Women Whose Husbands Are Present (Including Those United Consensually)

Age	Average Number of Sons	
	Natives	Immigrants
20–24	2.10	1.91
25–29	2.90	2.75
30–34	3.81	3.56
35–39	4.36	3.85
40–49	3.72[a]	3.79
50 and more	4.26	4.46[b]
20–49	3.38	3.19[a]

[a] Observe that this value does not agree with the trend. In the column "Immigrants," a similar irregularity, though only slightly marked, is observed.
[b] Adjusted to the age structure of natives.

27. Bombay Migration Study: A Pilot Analysis of Migration to an Asian Metropolis

K. C. ZACHARIAH

I. INTRODUCTION

In response to a recommendation of the Population Commission of the United Nations, the Demographic Training and Research Centre at Chembur (India) early in 1960 worked out a comprehensive research program on migration to Greater Bombay. The program envisaged analysis of the 1961 census data pertaining to migrants in Greater Bombay, sample surveys in selected rural areas around the city, and sample surveys in the city itself. In the first part of the program, with which the present paper is concerned, the Centre collaborated with the Census Commissioner of India and with the Superintendent of Census Operations, Government of Maharashtra,[1] who prepared special tables on migrants in Greater Bombay from the 1961 Census of India. The detailed results of analysis of these data are being published as a research monograph of the Centre.[2] The present paper summarizes the major substantive and methodological findings of the study.

The data for the study were obtained from published census tables and also from a set of ten special migration tables. Migrants were defined in terms of birthplace, cross-classified by dura-

tion of residence in Bombay. Inasmuch as the various procedures involved in the collection and compilation of the basic data did not include any operations which could not be repeated in any of the other countries in Asia, the present study should demonstrate not only in substance but also in method how basic information on migration to cities could be obtained by the inclusion of a few simple questions in the national census. In this context, the Bombay study may be considered a pilot analysis and should provide guidelines for comparable studies of other Asian cities.

The recommendation of the Population Commission for intensive research on migration to Bombay and to other cities in developing countries was occasioned by a widely held notion that in these counties urbanization is progressing more rapidly than urban development. It is, therefore, important to explore the extent to which rural-urban migration is actually a help or hindrance to economic and social development. The present analysis is, of course, limited by the form in which the census questions were cast and is not adequate to fulfil such a broad objective. Nevertheless, it gives useful information on migration trends, differentials, selectivity, and the assimilation of migrants, which when taken together contribute substantially to one's understanding of the interrelations between cityward migration and socio-economic changes.

Demography, 3, No. 2 (1966), pp. 378–92. Reprinted by permission of author and publisher.

[1] Bombay is located in the state of Maharashtra.
[2] K. C. Zachariah, Migrants in Greater Bombay (to be published by Asia Publishing House, Bombay and New York, early in 1969).

360

II. MIGRATION TRENDS

The census data on the age-sex composition of Bombay City's population, supplemented by the vital registration data, give reasonably accurate information on the trend of *net* migration to the city. During the sixty-year period 1901–61, there has been, in general, an upward trend in the volume and rate of migration to the city accompanied by a downward trend in the relative contribution of migration to the total intercensal growth of population. The upward trend in migration was interrupted by sharp downward swings during the depression of the 1930's and again during the 1950's. These aberrations in the over-all trend, inasmuch as they are responses both to the "pull" of the city and also to the concomitant "push" of the hinterland, help to explain the relative importance of the various factors associated with migration to Bombay City. The 1931 Census Report of Bombay City documents an unprecedented exodus from Bombay to rural areas, as indicated by the falling-off in the estimated net migration for 1921–31. The immediate cause was, unquestionably, the Great Depression, the impact of which was felt in Bombay with severity during the spring and summer of 1930 and was therefore reflected in the census returns of 1931. Textile mills closed down, unemployment became widespread, and many former in-migrants were said to have returned with their dependents to their native villages. That the depression must have hit these villages, as well as Bombay, is also evident from documentary accounts, but the "push" element in the disadvantaged rural areas was apparently not operative, effectively, in the absence of the "pull" of opportunities in the metropolis.

The decade 1951–61 is of special interest from the point of view of the relative importance of "push" and "pull" factors. The intercensal rate of population increase in India as a whole was up by 8 percentage points to 21 for this decade; the density of population in rural areas increased from 284 per square mile to 297; the literacy level of the rural population aged 15 and over increased from 15 to 22 percent; and the transportation and communication system in the country had improved enormously. Moreover, the two Five-Year Plans for the economic and social development of the country met with a considerable measure of success, and per capita income increased by nearly one-fourth from Rs. 266/- in 1951 to Rs. 326/- in 1961. All these changes favored an increase in rural-urban migration, particularly migration to major cities like Bombay. In the Berkeley Seminar on Urbanization in India, held a few months before the 1961 census, the general opinion was that India was "in the midst of a gigantic urban increase" and that "there is a very rapidly rising tempo of rural to urban migration under way throughout India." However, the census tabulations showed that in Bombay net migration decreased from about 950,000 during 1941–51 to less than 600,000 during 1951–61. In other metropolises, decreases were also notable. An accelerating rate of rural population growth, increasing rural density, and rural unemployment had not pushed out a larger number of migrants from rural areas to cities. The fact that the expected exodus had not occurred may indicate that sufficient "pull" from the cities was lacking and that these "pulls" may, in general, be more important to cityward migration than the "pushes" at the origin.

For Bombay, the decrease in net migration is probably to be attributed in large part to a slowing-down in the creation of new employment opportunities within the city limits. A decrease of 350,000 migrants, however, does not necessarily mean a correspondingly large decrease in the number of employment opportunities, since workers coming into the city were often accompanied by non-working dependents. Moreover, during the decade of 1941–51 there had been a wartime inflation in economic opportunities. New industrial establishments and commercial concerns had sprung up, giving employment to a large number of migrants and providing means of livelihood for their dependents. In addition, some 80,000 displaced persons had come from Pakistan between 1947 and the census year of 1951. The new industries established between 1951 and 1961 were, in general, more capital-intensive and therefore created fewer jobs than those established during the 1940's. Concomitantly, some of the older factories rationalized their production processes and freed workers for other industries. Thus, a shift in the industrial structure of the city, from less-organized to more-organized and capital-intensive industries, seems to have been a major cause of the decrease in net migration to Bombay.

There are, of course, a number of other factors associated with the decrease in migration to Greater Bombay. The policy of the State Government of Maharashtra regarding the location of new industries might also have affected the pace of migration to Greater Bombay. The general policy of the government is to decentralize industrial establishments in the State, to discourage the establishment of new industries and to encourage the removal of existing industrial plants from large cities, and to develop satellite towns and industrial areas at convenient distances

from metropolitan cities. The rapid industrial expansion in some of the adjoining areas of Greater Bombay (for example, Thana and Kalyan) was partly at the cost of the industrial growth within the city limits.

The increase in the number of commuters is another factor which might have contributed to the deceleration of in-migration. The improvement in local transportation facilities has made it possible for a larger number of workers to reside outside the city and work within it on a regular basis. Commuting thus tends to be a substitute for migration.

III. RETURN MIGRATION

One of the unexpected results of the study was evidence of the existence of appreciable reverse migration. Out-migration of former migrants was quite heavy, particularly during the first few years of their stay in the city and especially among those who were above 35 years of age.

Among persons enumerated in Bombay in 1951, the rate of out-migration during the decade 1951–61 was about 18 percent for males and 13 percent for females. There was variation with age, the rate being low for very young males but rising to about 30 percent per decade among those aged 30 years and over. The rates among females did not, in general, rise to the level of those among males, being about 23 percent at ages 35 and over but somewhat higher at ages 15–19, thus suggesting the importance of the marriage factor in their out-migration. Large-scale out-migration was also revealed by the analysis of net intercensal migration by age and sex. In general, Bombay experienced heavy net out-migration at ages 35 and over, relatively higher among males than among females, and relatively more than in the previous decade.

Among recent migrants, the rates of reverse migration were higher than among those with long duration of residence. About 30 percent of the male migrants and 20 percent of the females moved out of Greater Bombay during the first three to four years of their stay. Of the male migrants who moved out nearly one-fifth were aged 25–29 when they in-migrated and about one-eighth were under 5 years of age. Among migrants who moved into the city at ages above 30–34 years, more than 60 percent left within three to four years of their arrival. The rate of reverse migration was as high as 76 percent (among males) for those who came after 55 years of age. Moreover, rates were relatively higher for migrants born in neighboring states of Maharashtra and Gujarat than for those who were born in more distant states, such as Uttar Pradesh or Andhra Pradesh.

The age-sex characteristics of reverse migration clearly indicate that it was not confined to economically inactive persons but suggest that it was heavily weighted with (1) visitors to the city; (2) government servants and other workers on transfer of service; (3) mill workers and other unskilled laborers returning after ten to fifteen years of service in the city to their villages to take up the cultivation of ancestral land; (4) retired workers going "home"; (5) wives and children of low-income workers who decided to bring up their children in the cheaper and more congenial villages; and (6) those who came to the city looking for work but who failed to find suitable jobs.

Comparative analysis in other metropolitan cities of Asia is not available; it is therefore difficult to conclude whether the pattern of heavy return migration observed for Bombay is typical of Asian cities. It is, however, possible, in view of the similarity of cultures and levels of development, that return migration is more frequent in Asia than in Europe or North America.

IV. ECONOMIC CHARACTERISTICS OF MIGRANTS

A commonly mentioned reason for the alleged lack of balance between urbanization and urban development in Asian countries is the inability of the urban industries in these countries to absorb the ever increasing migrant labor force. Compared with European countries during a corresponding period of economic development, the urban labor force in these countries consists of a relatively small proportion of factory workers and a large proportion of workers employed in occupations classified as "miscellaneous, usually menial, unskilled services."[3]

Nearly 648,000 or 40 percent of the working migrants in Bombay are employed in manufacturing; the remainder are in commerce (18 percent), services (24 percent), transport (11 percent), and agriculture, mining, utilities, and construction (6 percent). Similarly, about 655,000 of all migrants or 46 percent of the working migrants are categorized as "craftsmen, production process workers and labourers not elsewhere classified." The proportions of workers in "services," "sales," and "clerical" occupations are each about one-eighth of the total, whereas "professional," "administrative," and "transport" occupations each have about 4 percent of all workers. These broad industrial and occupational *divisions* indicate that the majority of the

[3] B. F. Hoselitz, "Urbanization: International Comparisons," in *India's Urban Future*, ed. Roy Turner. (Berkeley and Los Angeles: University of California Press, 1962), p. 168.

migrants are employed in nation-building activities. However, it is not impossible that each of these *divisions*, including as they do large numbers of occupational or industrial *groups*, may have varying numbers of "miscellaneous, usually menial, unskilled service" workers and that divisions like "services" may include much more than a proportional share of such workers. For example, of the 655,000 "craftsmen, production process workers and labourers not elsewhere classified," nearly 215,000, or one-third, are "labourers not elsewhere classified." This is the major migrant-employing occupational *group* and includes all the casual laborers among the migrants. "Services," another not very clearly defined division, includes about 93,000 "housekeepers, cooks, maids, and related workers" and 31,000 "waiters, bartenders, and related workers." In the "clerical" division, about 35,000 are "unskilled office workers." "Sales" division includes a large number (estimated to be about 25,000) of "hawkers, peddlers, and street vendors." It thus appears that one out of every four migrant workers in Bombay is a casual laborer or a "peon," a cook, a waiter, a hawker, or a petty trader.

Comparison with the situation in Western metropolitan cities is difficult because of conceptual problems related to occupational classification. It is, however, likely that the relative number of manual laborers and low-level service personnel will be small in Western cities in comparison with Bombay. However, at the present stage of technological development in India, it is doubtful whether these so-called "miscellaneous, usually menial, unskilled service" personnel are nonessential. The large number of laborers engaged in loading and unloading trucks, railway cars, and ships, included in the occupational group "labourers not elsewhere classified," for example, can in no way be considered nonessential in a port city like Bombay.

V. MIGRATION DIFFERENTIALS

The migrants in Bombay were a selected group with respect to age, sex, marital status, and family status. They included an excess of adolescents and young adults as compared with non-migrants at destination and with the general population at origin. About 43 percent of the migrants were between the ages of 20 and 35 (compared with 24 percent in the all-India population), and over 80 percent were in the working ages 15–59 (compared with 53 percent in the all-India population). The age of maximum in-migration was close to 20 years.

The sex composition of migrants favored males, with the excess of males exceeding 800 for every 1,000 females. The ratio of males per 1,000 females was almost normal (1,045) at ages 0–4 but increased to 2,367 at ages 40–44. Distance from origin to Bombay was an important factor in determining the sex composition of a migration stream: the greater the distance, the greater the proportion of males. Migrants born in rural areas had higher sex ratios than those born in urban areas.

In each age-sex group, the proportion single was found to be less among migrants than among nonmigrants in the metropolis but greater than in the general population of the states of origin. As a consequence, the proportion single decreased in areas of origin as well as at destination. The high sex ratio among migrants was due not only to high rates of in-migration of single males as compared to single females but also to migration of married males unaccompanied by wives and children. Though it is not possible to give a precise estimate, there is no doubt that at least four out of every ten of the married migrant males were not living with their wives in Bombay at the time of the census, and the proportion may indeed be as high as five or even six out of ten. However, even the low estimate shows how different the migrants were in this respect compared with the nonmigrants resident in the city and the population in the states of origin.

The social attributes of the migrants did not receive adequate coverage in the present study. Analysis of religious composition (in which demographic controls could not be adequately introduced) showed that the propensity to migrate was relatively greater among minority religious groups. This suggests fairly definitely that social "push" factors may also have been operative in cityward migration.

Migrants in Bombay City have much higher levels of educational attainment than the general population of the states from which they are drawn and lower levels than the population to which they migrated (nonmigrants in Bombay). Thus, cityward migration in India deprives the villages of the better-educated and may be an important reason why villages have not shown more social and economic advancement. On the other hand, the talents and skills of these persons might well have been wasted in the rural areas. Migration may thus have helped in bringing skills to areas where they could most profitably be utilized and in contributing to a better utilization of the human resources of the country as a whole.

The work participation ratios of migrants in Greater Bombay were higher than those of nonmigrants in the city in each age group. The over-all difference at ages 15 and above was of

the order of 19 percentage points among males. Though it is difficult to estimate from these ratios whether unemployment was greater among migrants or nonmigrants, they at least show that the combined effect of economic inactivity and unemployment was greater among nonmigrants. Therefore, if migration contributed to the increase in the rate of unemployment in the city, it was probably because of the displacement of nonmigrants by migrants.

In general, the proportions of employers and family workers were greater among nonmigrants and the proportions of employees and single workers greater among migrants. We might assume that single workers and family workers were engaged in small-scale operations and therefore the higher the proportion of these classes of workers, the lower the scale of operation. These two classes together formed 16.2 percent among migrants and 17.7 percent among nonmigrants. The ratio of employees to employers was 17 to 1 among migrants but only 5 to 1 among nonmigrants. Thus, these data do not indicate that migration has contributed to the decrease in the scale of operation of industries in Bombay but, on the contrary, suggest that the opposite may have been true.

A matter of greater importance from the point of view of economic consequences of migration is the differentials in the industrial and occupational composition of the groups. Compared with nonmigrants in Bombay, migrants to the city were more likely to be employed in industries and occupations which required less skill, less education, and less capital. Consequently, they were relatively more numerous in textile manufacturing, services, construction, and mining industries. Similarly, they were more highly represented among craftsmen, production process workers, laborers, and service occupations. There were relatively few migrants in clerical and related occupations. Migrants predominated among "leather cutters, lasters, sewers and related workers," among "chemical and related process workers," among "waiters, bartenders, and related workers," and among "launderers, dry cleaners, and pressers." On the other hand, nonmigrants had significantly higher proportions among "architects, engineers and surveyors," among "directors and managers, wholesale and retail trade," among "stenographers and typists," among "office machine operators," among "clerical workers, miscellaneous," among "telephone, telegraph and related telecommunication operators," and among similar categories.

An interesting aspect of the migrant–nonmigrant differentials was brought out when comparisons were made between the two groups when educational level was held constant. Among illiterates (who formed 30 percent of the male migrants and 14 percent of the male nonmigrants over 15 years of age), the occupational distributions showed marked differences. About 58 percent of illiterate nonmigrants were employed as "clerical and related workers" (being, of course, unskilled office workers) but only 2 percent of the illiterate migrants were so employed. Conversely, about 63 percent of illiterate migrants were employed as "craftsmen, production process workers and labourers not elsewhere classified" as against 31 percent of the nonmigrants. Among literate workers, however, there was a moderate predominance of nonmigrants in white-collar occupations. The over-representation of migrants in blue-collar and unskilled manual jobs and of nonmigrants in white-collar occupations was mainly a result of the difference in educational attainment. This also ex-

plains the relative preponderance of urban-born migrants in white-collar occupations as compared with their rural-born counterparts.

Though the differences in educational attainment accounted for a significant part of the variations in industrial and occupational composition, there were differences which could not be so readily explained, for example, those observed among migrants born in different states. To give a few examples, more than 40 percent of nearby Gujarat-born migrants were in commerce while the over-all proportion for all migration streams was only 18 percent; 16 percent of distant Andhra-born migrants were in construction while the over-all average was only 3 percent. The average educational level of migrants from Madras in the South was almost the same as that of Rajasthan-Punjab in the North, but the proportion of workers in commerce among the Madras-born was less than half that of the migrants from Rajasthan-Punjab. It follows that, though education is important in determining industrial and occupational attachment, there are other important but unmeasured factors which affect the distribution of workers coming from a particular origin.

The difference between the occupational and industrial composition of migrant subgroups classified by religion also confirms the importance of cultural factors other than education. While about 44 percent of Buddhists were employed in manufacturing, only 17 percent of Jains were so engaged, but only 4 percent of Buddhists were in trade and commerce as compared with 72 percent of Jains. Transport industries also showed considerable variation from one religious group to another. Twenty-five percent of Sikhs and 21 percent of Buddhists were thus engaged but only 2 percent of Jains and 10 percent of Hindus. Christians and Zoroastrians predominated in service industries, while Jains and Muslims had the lowest percentages in that category. Differences of this magnitude cannot entirely be explained by unmeasured differences in educational attainment of the different religious groups.

The prevalence of systematic differences in the industrial and occupational distributions between nonmigrants and migrants and among migrants between subgroups classified by rural-urban character of the area of birth, state of birth, religion, educational attainment, and traditionally acquired skills shows the existence of a sort of division of labor among the various migration streams and between the migrants and nonmigrants themselves, each group being engaged in activities most suited to them on the basis of the skills and abilities which they acquired not only by formal education but also through tradition and precept. The intermingling of diverse skills increases the efficiency of the economic organization and provides a better economic base for the city. The fact that Gujarati migrants who are adept in trade and commerce, Punjabi migrants who are experienced in transport, and Kerala migrants who are trained for clerical and related occupations take up these occupations in the city is evidence of a tendency toward rational utilization of human resources.

VI. MIGRATION, AN INSTRUMENT OF SOCIAL CHANGE

Rural-urban migration is not only an integral part of industrialization and economic development, but it may also become a major instrument of social change. The urban setting is a fertile ground for the generation of social and economic changes, and these are spread to rural areas by the process of migration. In Western countries there is abundant evidence that migration between villages and towns has played an important role in bringing change to rural areas. In India, however, it is frequently claimed that migration has had only negligible effects and is, therefore, unimportant as a tool for social change.

As mentioned earlier, the present study revealed the existence of an appreciable amount of reverse migration from the city. About 30 percent of the males and 20 percent of the females left Bombay within three or four years after entering the city. The peculiar age distribution of intercensal net migration corroborates large-scale return migration. These return migrations must have substantial effect on the population of the areas from which the migrants were drawn as well as significant effects on the migrants themselves.

Return migration of workers after retirement and the regular to-and-fro movements between villages and city while working provide many contacts between the migrants and the rural population. Every time a migrant goes to his village, he takes back with him some urban ideas or customs—the discipline of the factory, the concept of a job with a fair wage, the advantages of trade union organization, ideas on health and hygiene, the convenience of piped water supply and of electricity, the usefulness of books and newspapers, the radio and the cinema, the bicycle and the bus service, and the needs for education of children, both boys and girls.[4] The rural population is thus exposed to urban ways of life. But

[4] Asoka Mehta, Convocation Address at the Demographic Training and Research Centre, 1964, *passim.*

one may wonder why the net effect on the Indian villages seems to have been so slight. This is more a problem of the relative dimensions of city and village populations and the subsistence-existence of the villagers than of the "buffers" to which references are usually made.

The constant movements between villages and cities are significant from the point of view of the economic efficiency of migrants. The return migration of a large number of workers involves retraining part of the industrial labor force, and it also results in a labor supply less committed to the industries. In addition, as a result of repeated contacts with villages, the migrants in the cities are able to retain to a larger extent and for a longer period their rural way of life.

The analysis of the characteristics of migrants by duration of residence helps in understanding the manner in which the newcomers are influenced by the city way of life and indicates that slowly, but nonetheless surely, changes take place. If such changes occur on a large scale, they may, indeed, lead the country to a better social and economic order.

With characteristics such as year of birth, sex, and, to some extent, even religion being fixed, residence in the city, however long it may be, has no effect. However, this is not the case with marital status, educational attainment, economic characteristics, and so on.

Under present conditions in India a rise in the age at marriage is viewed favorably, not only because of its effect on the birth rate but also from the point of view of the over-all social development of the rural population. Analysis of the marital status of migrants in Bombay suggests that migration may bring about substantial increases in age at marriage. The proportion single among young migrants lies between that of Bombay nonmigrants and the general population in the states of origin. And among migrant categories, the proportion single increases with increase in the length of residence in the city. For example, among females aged 15–19, the proportion single is 26 percent in the general population of Maharashtra, 28 percent for migrants to Bombay with duration of residence less than one year, 31 percent for those whose duration of residence lies between 1 and 5 years, 50 percent for durations of 5–9 years, 79 percent for durations of 10–14 years, 78 percent for durations 15+ years, and 81 percent among the nonmigrants born and enumerated in Bombay City itself. Comparable systematic and consistent increases are observed for other categories of young migrants also.[5] In part, the increase may be attributed to selective out-migration of married females. But it is also possible that these changes indicate adjustment of the in-migrants' marital pattern to that of city-born persons. The effects of these large changes are hardly felt at the national level because of the relatively small number of migrants involved and because many of them were already married before migrating to the city. But the direction of these changes indicates the potentialities of migration as a significant tool for social changes.

Educational opportunities in a city like Bombay are enormously greater than those in the areas from which migrants are drawn; and the economic returns from investments of money and time in education are correspondingly

[5] At older ages there is very little scope for changes inasmuch as almost all the migrants of these ages were already married when they came to the city.

greater. At the same time, employment opportunities are greater in Bombay, and this factor may prompt some of the persons who otherwise would have continued in school to join the labor force and discontinue their studies. Moreover, the educational system and the language of instruction vary from one area of the country to another, and some migrants may therefore find it difficult to complete their schooling. Migration may therefore act as a stimulant for higher educational attainment for some, whereas it hinders others. Data on educational attainment show that the longer the duration of residence, the higher the educational attainment. The proportion of illiterates among migrant workers decreases with increasing residence-duration intervals, from 44 to 29 percent for males; from 75 to 59 percent for females. Correspondingly, at higher educational levels there were increases. Estimated average number of years of schooling increased from 3.5 for duration 0–1 years to 4.4 for duration 10–14 years among male migrants and correspondingly among females from 1.9 to 3.4. Thus, as a result of the combined effect of return migration of the less educated, delayed employment of educated persons, and improvement in educational attainment subsequent to in-migration, the group of migrants who remained in the city for a longer period of time had a much higher level of educational attainment than those who had been in the city for a short period. However, there was also some indication that those who migrated at certain critical years of their life, as, for example, just before completing requirements for primary or junior basic certificate or matriculation, were adversely affected by the transfer of residence. The large positive effect of migration on educational attainment was partly offset by this smaller negative effect.

Migration of adult males is on the whole economically motivated, and many such migrants come to the city to take up work or to look for jobs. Some migrants take the first job that comes their way, while others wait for a more suitable opening. Even those who take stop-gap jobs are probably on the alert for better opportunities. Since the migrant's knowledge of job openings and his general skill increase with increasing length of residence in Bombay, he should become more and more successful in getting a better job. This adjustment process is confirmed in the economic characteristics of migrants with different durations of residence.

Increase in duration of residence tends to increase the work participation ratios of male migrants and to decrease those of females. Similarly, the proportion of employers increased and the proportion of employees decreased. The effect of duration on the industrial affiliation of migrants varied by industrial division. In primary industries, though the overall proportions were small, there was a tendency for a decrease in the proportion with increase in duration of residence. In secondary industries, particularly in textile manufacturing but also in commerce, there were sharp increases with duration of residence, suggesting lesser opportunities for recent migrants in these industries. These secondary industries were established long ago in Bombay, and their relative importance has decreased in recent years. Consequently, newcomers have found relatively few openings in textile manufacturing and in commerce.

The effect of duration of residence on the proportion of workers in metal and chemical-based manufacturing was somewhat complex. The over-all ratio for all migration streams was almost constant, but this was mainly a result of conflicting trends among the various migration streams. While about 41 percent of the recent (0–1 year duration) migrants born in Gujarat State were engaged in this industry, the proportion dropped to 22 percent for the same stream for residence duration of 1–4 years and fell further to 15 percent by duration 15 years or more. Quite contrary trends were observed in this industry for migrants born in Mysore, Kerala, Madras, and West Bengal. Insofar as the construction industry is concerned, the proportion of workers decreased with increase in duration of residence. A large number of recent migrants were employed in this industry; but with increase in duration of residence the percentage decreased, presumably as a result of return migration and the shifting of workers from this to other industries.

As noted above, state of origin was an important intervening variable affecting the relation between duration of residence and the proportion of workers in an industrial division. This has important implications. If variations in the proportion of workers in a particular industrial division were entirely due to changes in the industrial structure of Greater Bombay, this should affect *all* migration streams equally; but this was not the case. Metal and chemical-based manufacturing, for example, is relatively new in Bombay; therefore, recent migrants from all states should have high proportions in this industrial division. But the proportion of workers in this industry decreased for longer durations among migrants from Gujarat and Uttar Pradesh; increased among those from Mysore, Kerala, Madras, West Bengal, and Madhya Pradesh;

and remained fairly constant among those from Maharashtra and Rajasthan-Punjab.

Similar contrasting trends were noticed in other industries, and, taken as a whole, they suggest that Gujarat-born migrants in Greater Bombay are not entering commerce and services but are presumably entering metal and chemical-based manufacturing and transport. This transition is perhaps assisted by the Gujarati ownership of manufacturing industries and transport undertakings. Evidently most migrants, except the predominant streams from neighboring Gujarat and Maharashtra, found it increasingly difficult in recent years to enter manufacturing industries. For the more-distant migrants from Kerala, Madras, West Bengal, and Rajasthan-Punjab, the major opening was "service." Indeed, more than half of the working migrants from Kerala and West Bengal who came after 1960 were employed in "service" industries. But for the new migrants from Andhra Pradesh, "construction" industry was still the major entering wedge, while Mysore-born migrants found openings in transport, storage, and communications.

The pattern of variation in occupational composition by duration of residence was related to that of industrial distribution. As duration of residence increased, there were declines in the proportion in service occupations and in unskilled labor. On the other hand, the proportion in crafts and white-collar occupations increased with duration of residence. Between duration of residence of less than 1 year, and 15 years or over, the percentages employed in unskilled occupations and in service were nearly halved, while the percentages of craftsmen and those in clerical occupations were nearly doubled.

Proportions in sales, administrative, professional, and technical occupations changed insignificantly, as did occupations in transport and communications. However, drastic declines in the proportion of workers in occupations related to textile manufacturing were noted among recent migrants and reflected decline in the relative importance of this industry.

Comparisons of the demographic, social, and economic characteristics of migrants who have been in the city for varying periods of time show that the longer the exposure to city life the greater the resemblance to city-born persons and the greater the dissimilarity with populations in states of origin. This observation was found to hold true for each of the characteristics examined—marital status, educational attainment, industrial attachment, and occupational composition. However, only a part of the observed "improvements" can be attributed to "real" changes in the migrants' characteristics. The differences between the characteristics of migrants who have just arrived and those who have been in the city for a long time are partly due to attrition of "undesirables" through out-migration and replenishing of "desirables" through delayed employment and only partly to changes in characteristics of individuals. How much of the total change reflects changes in individual characteristics cannot be shown from the present analysis, but indirect evidence suggests that the "real" changes are significant. These effects on characteristics of migrants, especially when considered along with possible effects on their children and on the rural population from which the migrants are drawn, do not suggest a gloomy picture of the social and economic

consequences of migration to Bombay City. On the contrary, they suggest that migration is a major instrument of social and economic change.

VII. METHODOLOGICAL CONSIDERATIONS

A major objective of this pilot study has been to evaluate the potentialities and defects of census data for studies of cityward migration in developing countries. The techniques of using place-of-birth data are well documented in several recent works on migration. These are therefore not reproduced in this study. Not so thoroughly discussed are the techniques of using the data on duration of residence. There are few comprehensive studies that analyze the data obtained by the cross-tabulations of place of birth by duration of residence.

The data on migrants to Greater Bombay show that, as in the case of place of birth, duration of residence is often misreported, in this case because of failure to recall correctly the date of arrival in the city. The possibility of incorrect reporting is enhanced because in India census information on all members of a household is usually given by the head, who may not know these details for all the other members. For people who make frequent "visits" before actually "migrating" to the city, it may be nearly impossible to fix the actual date of taking up residence.

The inaccuracy in reporting duration of residence is manifested, as in the case of age, by definite patterns of digit preference, the preferred digits being 0 and 5. It is therefore necessary to use duration data in broad class intervals such as 0–4, 5–9, and so forth. There are advantages in using class intervals in which 0 and 5 come in the middle, but, since the duration data are to be used in conjunction with age data, it is necessary that the class interval for age be used for tabulating duration data as well. In the case of the Bombay tabulations, the duration interval 15 years and over is not wholly satisfactory, inasmuch as more than a third of the migrants are in this single class interval. It is therefore suggested that, at least up to 25 years, data in future studies be tabulated in closed class intervals.

The adequacy of duration-of-residence data should be examined in the context of the uses to which these data are put. One of the main uses of migration data is in the analysis of population growth. How much of intercensal growth of an area is due to migration, and how much is due to natural increase? This requires an estimate of intercensal migration. It may appear that the number of migrants with duration of residence less than ten years in 1961 approximates the number of in-migrants during 1951–61. But this estimate is inadequate in several ways. In the first place, duration of residence refers to the *place* of enumeration. If the place refers to Greater Bombay, the data for this areal unit can at best be used to estimate intercensal in-migration to Greater Bombay. Such data for all districts of Maharashtra State, of which Greater Bombay is a part, cannot be added to get an estimate of in-migration to the State as a whole. This is because duration of residence of a person in Maharashtra may be very much longer than his duration of residence in Greater Bombay itself. It is only in cases of direct movement between place of birth and place of enumeration (in 1961) that duration of residence is helpful in identifying intercensal migration in terms of larger units than those for which tabulations are made. With the scheme of tabula-

tion adopted in India in 1961 (the district of birth of persons born outside the state of enumeration not being indicated), out-migration estimates can be obtained only for states and not for component areal units.

Another difficulty in using duration data for estimating in-migration or net migration to Greater Bombay is that tabulations are made only for persons born outside the city. But in-migrants are composed of two groups—those born within the city and those born outside. The former are missed completely; therefore, return migration of Bombay-born persons does not appear in estimates obtained from duration-of-residence data.

In brief, we do not recommend the use of duration-of-residence data for estimating intercensal in-migration or net migration. Nor are they useful for studying trends in in-migration during the intercensal period, as the data are affected by return migration. In countries such as India, where the vital statistics are highly defective and interstate variations in mortality levels are great, the usual place-of-birth data without any cross-tabulation by duration of residence seem to be the best source for estimating net migration during an intercensal period. The procedure is described in detail in an earlier study.[6] The tabulation of out-of-state-born persons by age permits better estimates of mortality among migrants enumerated in the first census, and, if tabulations are available for two consecutive censuses, further improvements can be made by using separate survival ratios for different migration streams.

Another major objective in migration

[6] K. C. Zachariah, *A Historical Study of Internal Migration in the Indian Sub-Continent, 1901–1931* (Bombay and New York: Asia Publishing House, 1964).

analysis is measurement of selectivity and differentials. The present data for Bombay are fairly satisfactory for studying migration differentials, and, where they are deficient, they can be remedied by extending the tabulation. For analyzing selectivity, Bombay data are satisfactory for those characteristics (age, sex, religion, language, and to a lesser extent marital status and educational level) that do not undergo drastic changes with migration but are deficient for those that undergo considerable change with migration (industry, occupation, etc.). This deficiency of the data for studying migration selectivity in industry and occupation cannot be remedied by more elaborate tabulations but only by including additional questions in the census on industry and occupation at the time of migration.

The pilot study reported here has emphasized a few points, with regard to both selectivity and differentials, which merit recapitulation. *First,* in the tabulation of migration data, it should be possible to separate recent migrants from total migrants, for the characteristics of migrants at the time of migration are usually different from those after some years of residence in the city. For example, the age of a migrant increases with his duration of residence in the city. As a consequence, the age distribution of lifetime migrants depends considerably on their distribution by duration of residence. If we compare nonmigrants with migrants who came fifteen years ago, the results are quite different from those obtained through comparisons with migrants who arrived a year or so ago. Therefore, information on duration of residence is essential to the analysis of migration selectivity and differentials. *Second,* it is necessary that there be comparable cross-tabulations for mi-

grants and for nonmigrants. If cross-tabulations are made only for migrants, comparisons are not possible. In the present study, for example, occupations of migrants are cross-tabulated by age, sex, duration of residence, state of birth, and rural-urban origin, but those of nonmigrants are not cross-tabulated by age. For education, age-sex cross-classification is available for the general population, but such information is available only for the working segment of the migrant group. Such lack of correspondence makes the comparison of migrants and nonmigrants less exact than is desirable.[7] *Third,* it is necessary to reiterate the need for age controls in all studies of migration selectivity. Marital status data, for example, should be tabulated by five-year age groups at all ages, but for certain other characteristics—education, industry, occupation, and so forth—five-year age groups up to 30 or 35 years and thereafter ten-year age groups may be adequate.

Another important objective of a migration study utilizing data of this kind is to estimate the effect of cityward migration on the characteristics of migrants. The type of data that are obtained in the present study is not satisfactory for this purpose; even the indirect method of comparing the characteristics of migrants with different durations of residence to get information on the probable effect of city life is beset with difficulties. The major problem with the indirect approach is that changes in characteristics are often confounded with the effects of (*a*) multistage migration, (*b*) return migra-

[7] This problem of correspondence cannot be easily solved, as the solution involves detailed tabulation for the entire population of the country. The census authorities may be willing to make special tabulation for cities and yet be unwilling to extend them to rural areas. In such cases, comparisons should be made valid by the method of indirect standardization.

tion, and (c) the time trend. A migrant's duration of residence in the city is considered as an approximation to his period of exposure to the urban way of life. This is true only for those who came to Bombay directly from rural areas and not for those who came after living for a number of years in other cities. Thus, depending on the extent of such multistage movements, duration of residence may not be at all adequate as an index of the degree of exposure to city life. In a city like Bombay, where large numbers of employees may be transferred from one administrative center to another, this factor is of considerable importance. Return migration is often selective, and, therefore, the characteristics of migrants with long durations of residence would be affected by return migration even if there were no change in the individual characteristics of those who remained. In Bombay, return migration was heavy, and it affected most of the comparisons among cohorts.

The trend factor might also affect comparisons of different duration cohorts, that is, migrants who came to Bombay earlier may have had a different set of characteristics from those who came recently. The effect of the trend factor can, however, be eliminated if data are available from more than one census. Inasmuch as these are not available in the present study and since the effect of the other two factors cannot be assessed without more elaborate questions on migration history, it is difficult to estimate the relative importance of the various factors. Consequently, it is frequently impossible to state precisely the extent to which the characteristics of migrants have changed since they came to the city.

An outcome of the present study that has considerable analytical significance is the demonstration of the use of cross-classification of age by duration of residence in estimating the extent and pattern of return migration during the first few years of the migrant's stay in Greater Bombay. The method uses five-year are distributions by five-year duration-of-residence categories. The estimates could have been improved considerably if the actual date of birth and actual date of arrival in the city were known. If these data were available, it would also have been possible to classify migrants by age at the time of arrival in the city.

There are many other questions in migration analysis for which one would like answers, but census data are not adequate for all purposes, and at best census data must, perforce, be supplemented by information from sample surveys. Place-of-birth data with due corrections for mortality yield fairly satisfactory estimates of net migration during intercensal periods. They are also satisfactory for analyses by spatial and by rural-urban origins. Where more detailed information on spatial origins of recent migrants is required, the place-of-birth question can be supplemented by a census question on the place of residence five years (or some other short interval) before the census. The census data are excellent for studying a number of migration differentials, but they have to be supplemented by surveys for determining selectivity in many economic characteristics. The duration-of-residence data are poor for studying assimilation. However, classification of migrants by duration of residence is necessary for the analysis of migration differentials and also for the estimation of the age pattern of return migration. None of these data on migrants is helpful in studying the effect of cityward migration on the rural population. They give no direct information useful for inferences about causes and motives for migration to cities. It is therefore clear that census data cannot cover all aspects of migration analysis and that the major gaps in these data bear on: (1) the extent and characteristics of return migration; (2) the extent and patterns of multistage migration and pendulum movement between city and village (migration history); (3) information on changes in the characteristics of migrants after migration to the city; (4) inferences as to causes and motives for cityward migration; and (5) the effects of cityward migration on economic and social conditions in the rural areas. In a comprehensive study of cityward migration, the analysis of census data must be supplemented by sample surveys on these topics.

28. Migrant Adjustment to City Life:
The Egyptian Case

JANET ABU-LUGHOD

ABSTRACT

One third of Cairo's population are village migrants. Their pattern of settlement within the city is explored to reveal significant differences between types of migrants and to identify the kinds of adjustment they are called upon to make to the new physical, economic, social, and ideological requirements of city life. Certain anticipated difficulties in adjustment are found not to materialize, whereas others, often ignored by sociologists, assume greater importance.[1]

One of the most dramatic phenomena of recent decades has been the urbanization of large segments of the world's peasant folk, particularly in rapidly industrializing countries. In few places has this urban growth been as vigorous as in Egypt—at first spasmodically in the 1940's stimulated by a war economy, then more gradually in the 1950's in response to the indigenous demands of a developing economy[2]—until, at present, one out of every three Egyptians lives in an urban place having 20,000 or more persons.

Migration from rural areas has been chiefly responsible for Egypt's soaring rate of urbanization, even though natural increase, still as high in cities as in rural areas, accounts for half the annual rate of urban growth. This migration has favored the very largest cities of the country, bypassing those of moderate and small size. Therefore there has been a tendency for cities to conform to the principle of allometric growth, with high growth rates correlated positively with rank as to size.[3] Indeed, for the last three decades, cities of highest rank size have sustained average rates of growth which are more than twice the rate of natural increase, while smaller towns, of between 20,000 to 30,000, have failed to keep pace with rates of natural increase, i.e., have actually experienced net losses of population.

Migration, then, has had its prime impact on the largest cities, and the towering giant of Cairo, with a present population of close to three and one-half million, has been the most important recipient of the newly urbanizing population. This paper, therefore, concentrates on the adjustment of

American Journal of Sociology, 67 (July 1961), 22–32. Reprinted by permission of The University of Chicago Press and the author.

[1] This article is a revised summary version of a paper presented to a conference on "The Emerging Arab Metropolis" (Congress for Cultural Freedom and the Egyptian Society of Engineers, co-sponsors) in Cairo, December, 1960.

[2] Expulsion from supersaturated rural environment ranks as an equally important element in this growth.

[3] See Charles Stewart, Jr., "Migration as a Function of Population and Distance," *American Sociological Review*, 25 (June, 1960), 347–56; George Zipf, *Human Behavior and the Principle of the Least Effort* (Cambridge, Mass.: Addison-Wesley Press, 1949). Application of hypothesis to Egyptian data prepared by present writer.

Egyptian villagers to life in Cairo, inquiring into its nature and exploring the elements which mediate any dramatic transition between rural and urban life.

I. THE RURAL AND THE URBAN IN CAIRO

Sociologists studying the adjustment of rural migrants to city life have been trapped in a dilemma of their own making. Even after the replacement of the rural-urban dichotomy by the more reasonable continuum, the sequence and dynamics of adjustment have still been deduced as though the dichotomy were valid; the unconscious assumptions have led many students to an oversimplified image of a one-way adjustment of rural man to a "stable" urban culture, despite lip service paid to feedback and mutual assimilation.

This adjustment is assumed to be disorganizing in the extreme. Physically, it is envisioned as drastically altering the dwelling, changing the accouterments within the home as well as the neighborhood surrounding it, transforming the appearance and dress of the migrant himself. Economically, the migrant is seen as adjusting to changed occupations and rhythms of work, to a new division of labor within the family, and to different relationships between work associates. Socially, it is hypothesized that the migrant weans himself from the intimacy of the village to the harsh superficial relationships inherent in urban life, adapts himself from the homogeneous peer group to the diversified reference groups of the city, and suffers a reduction in proximity-centered social life and neighboring. Culturally, he is assumed to undergo a revolution in motivation, values, and ideology. In short, according to the rural-urban dichotomy, a hypothetical

villager is to be dropped, unarmed, into the heart of urban Cairo to assimilate or perish. He is to be granted no cushions to soften his fall.

It is our contention here that the dichotomy is as invalid in Egypt and in many other newly awakening nations as it is in the Western nations, but for a somewhat different reason. In these cases the dichotomy has not yet sharpened due to the continual ruralization of the cities.[4]

Only one fact need be cited to support this allegation: More than one-third the permanent residents of Cairo have been born outside the city, that is, one out of every three Cairenes is a migrant of one sort or another, and the overwhelming majority are from the rural hinterlands within Egypt.[5] To speak about one-way assimilation to a stable urban culture when so large a minority comes equipped with needs and customs of rural origin is folly. Numbers alone should alert us to the probability that migrants are shaping the culture of the city as much as they are adjusting to it.

These rural migrants are drawn from two extreme types which face basically different problems of adjustment. One type, qualitatively the cream but numerically the less significant, consists of bright youths who migrate in search of education or wider

[4] It probably *never* will sharpen to the same extent as it did in the West because simultaneously with this ruralization of the cities is occurring an urbanization of rural areas (extension of roads, education, and social services). These processes were temporarily distinct in Western development.

[5] The *1947 Census of the Governorate of Cairo* shows that, of a total population of little more than 2 million, only 1.3 million had been born within the city; 51,000 were born in other governorates (large cities); 59,000 were born outside Egypt. Thus more than 630,000 residents of Cairo came from more or less rural sections of Egypt.

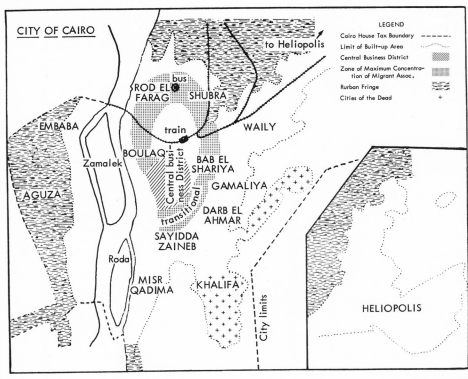

FIGURE 1

Map of Cairo Showing Major Districts and Location of Migrant Associations Within the City

opportunities. These have both the drive and the facility for rapid assimilation into the culture of the city. This paper ignores their real but different problems. The second type, referred to here as the "non-selective" migrants, are drawn primarily from the have-nots of the village. Numerically dominant, they are as much driven from the village by dearth of land and opportunity as they are attracted to the city.[6] With a lower capacity for assimilation, they tend to build for themselves within the city a replica of the culture they left

[6] See the unpublished findings of two American sociologists, Karen and Gene Petersen, who have made a sample study of 1,250 migrant families from five Delta villages.

behind. They are the subject of this article.

A second circumstance which has kept Cairo more rural than would be expected is the continual incorporation into the built-up metropolitan region of pre-existing villages. While some of these villages go back into history, such as Mataria, the pharaonic town of On (Greek, Heliopolis), some are of fairly recent origin. It would take a keen observer indeed to distinguish between a village within Cairo and one located miles beyond its fringes. In fact, the city of Cairo contains within its boundaries an extensive rural-urban fringe which stands juxtaposed against modern villas on the west, intervenes on the alluvial flats between urban Misr Qadima and suburban Maadi on the south, dips deep into the very heart of the city from the north, and, in somewhat different fashion, encircles Medieval Cairo on its eastern border. As can be seen from Figure 1, there are vast quarters within the mosaic of Cairo where, physically and socially, the way of life and the characteristics of residents resemble rural Egypt.

While full proof of this contention lies outside the scope of this paper,[7] a few figures may illustrate this point. High literacy is associated in Egypt with urbanism. In the largest urban centers, literacy rates in 1947 ranged between 40 and 45 per cent, while smaller towns and villages had literacy rates of under 25 per cent. Yet, in one out of eight census tracts in Cairo, the literacy rate was less than 25 per cent. As might be expected, the rural-urban fringe had the lowest literacy rates (5 and 7 per cent), but, surprisingly enough, even some of the more inlying zones contained populations no more literate than the rural. Similar comparisons made for other urban variables, such as refined fertility rates, religious and ethnic homogeneity, and condition and type of building, reveal the same inescapable fact that within the city of Cairo there exist numerous sub-areas whose physical and social characteristics closely approximate the villages of the countryside.

II. WHERE MIGRANTS SETTLE IN CAIRO

It is therefore possible for migrants to live in any of the large sections of the city which retain basic similarities to

the village. To what extent do they actually select such areas as their ports of entry into the city's structure? Since our hypothesis is that one of the major cushions in the assimilation of rural migrants is the nature of the subcommunity to which they gravitate, our concern will be with the areas of first settlement of "non-selective" migrants.

Direct evidence of where migrants settle in the city is not available in the Cairo census.[8] In our attempt to approximate their ecological distribution, however, we are aided by several circumstances: First, small sample studies made in Egypt and other industrializing countries indicate that a fairly typical pattern of initial settlement is followed by many rural immigrants.[9] The typical migrant, here as elsewhere, is a young man whose first contact in the city is often with a friend or relative from his original village, with whom he may even spend the first few nights. Later, more permanent lodgings are found, usually within the same neighborhood. This process, in the aggregate, results in a concentration of migrants from particular villages within small subsections of the city, far beyond what would be expected by chance. Second, migration to Cairo has tended to occur in major spurts, the most important of recent times occurring in the early 1940's. Therefore, not only did the

---

[7] It is presented in full detail in a book on Cairo, prepared by the writer, to be published by the Social Research Center of the American University at Cairo.

[8] A table showing place of birth by census tract of current residence has, unfortunately, never been included in any Cairo census.

[9] See H. Saaty and G. Hirabayashi, *Industrialization in Alexandria* (Cairo: Social Research Center, 1959); "Demographic Aspects of Urbanization in the ECAFE Region," in *Urbanization in Asia and the Far East* (Calcutta: Research Center on the Social Implications of Industrialization in Southern Asia, 1957); a variety of papers in UNESCO, *Social Implications of Industrialization and Urbanization in Africa South of the Sahara* (Paris: United Nations, 1956), among others.

typical migrant gravitate to a small area of the city already containing persons from his home village, but he was not the only newcomer at the time of his arrival.

These two factors, operating together, resulted in the formation of small conclaves of ex-villagers sharing a common past in the village and a similar and often simultaneous history of adaptation to the city. A parallel between this and the ethnic ghettos of large American cities at the turn of the century readily suggests itself. While the congregations of villagers from Kafr Bagour and Garawan are smaller than were the Little Sicilies and although villagers are segregated (and segregate themselves) from the main stream of urban life by less powerful barriers than language and Old World customs, they also have developed the protective pattern of physical proximity and certain social institutions which help mitigate the difficulties of transition.

The formal associations founded for and developed by migrants are important, directly, in the dynamics of rural to urban adaptation, but are even more important indirectly, since their location and distribution in the city offer the *only* evidence as to where migrants settle in Cairo. Before analyzing the locational pattern of these institutions, however, some explanation of their nature is essential.

The *Directory of Social Agencies in Cairo*[10] lists more than 110 village benevolent associations. The Garawan Benevolent Society is typical. Garawan, a village of 8,000, is located in the heart of the Egyptian Delta some forty miles northwest of Cairo. Population pressure resulted first in the formation of several daughter villages, but eventually many

of the men had to seek work in Cairo. (The village has a heavy excess of females.) The Garawan Benevolent Society was founded in 1944 to "extend aid to members" and to "provide burial facilities." Self-supporting, it sustains its activities through the dues contributed by "320 Egyptian Muslim adult males from Garawan," according to the directory's entry. Using a most conservative estimate of size of family (two dependents per adult male), one estimates that approximately 1,000 persons are to some extent involved in the core community of ex-Garawan residents.

One must make two basic assumptions if the locations of these societies are to be used as indirect evidence of migrant settlements. First, it must be assumed that migrants from specific villages are not distributed randomly throughout the city but that the processes described above result in aggregate settlements of persons from the same village.[11] Second, it must be assumed that the office of the migrant association is located in or near the subarea of the city which contains the maximum concentration of members. While this would not be true in every case, one might reasonably expect some relationship between office and clientele.

Even if these assumptions were absolutely beyond question (which they are not), an analysis of the locations of the associations would be irrelevant if they were scattered capriciously throughout the entire city. This, however, is fortunately not the case. When

---

[10]Prepared by Isis Istiphan and published by the Social Research Center, American University at Cairo, 1956.

[11]Obviously, not all ex-residents would be found in the Cairo settlement of maximum concentration, since some, probably the most successful economically, may have already moved to other sections of the city, while others never did follow the typical pattern, for example, the selective migrants or those with intervening experiences, such as army service.

the addresses listed in the directory are located on a spot map, a definite, although not simple, pattern emerges which indicates in rough fashion the areas where rural migrants seem to be concentrated. Most associations fall within the elliptical belt around but never within the central business district. The arc contracts both east and west to a bare quarter of a mile from central business district and expands north and south to more than a mile from city center, thus conforming to the general contours of the city.

Northern Settlement

One-third of the migrant associations cluster in the segment of the city which radiates northward from the central business district, circumscribed south and east by major rail lines, and bounded by the Nile to the west and an agricultural zone to the north. This section contains two subareas of densest concentration: the first in the vicinity of the Khazindar bus station; the other in Al Sharabiya, northeast of the main train terminal.

The Khazindar bus station has served since the twenties as the terminus of bus lines connecting Lower Egyptian provinces (the Delta) with Cairo. Within a radius of one-fourth of a mile of this station are eight village associations, all representing Delta villages; within half a mile are sixteen associations, ten actually concentrated in a four-by-six-block area just northeast of the station. This area has a strange mixture of urban and rural features. Behind the main street on which the station stands, narrow unpaved streets and alleys harbor prematurely aged, badly deteriorated, urban housing interspersed with the rural type of structure. The two- and three-story buildings contrast markedly with the six- to eight-story structures which dominate the main street. A cluster of black-garbed women squat to gossip; old men sit in doorways; a sheep bleats; children swarm in packs. When this area received its major influx of migrants, it was an outpost of urban settlement. As recently as 1940 there were farms just to the north. By now, however, the city has swept beyond it.

The second concentration of migrant associations is located in the tiny quarter of Al Sharabiya, where seven associations almost all from Delta villages are located within four blocks. Occupationally, many residents are bound to the rail yards that virtually surround it. Despite its geographically central location, this section presents a distinctly rural aspect and retains a close functional tie to the rural fringe, since farms bound it where rail lines do not. Lower buildings, some of mud brick, predominate. Commercial establishments are those of the large village or small town. Al Sharabiya and Khazindar areas contain most of the migrant associations of the city's northern quadrant. (The remainder are scattered within the belt shown on Figure 1.)

Most of the associations in this quadrant represent Lower Egyptian villages. Hence many migrants have presumably settled close not only to their point of origin but, even more specifically, to their point of entry into the city, i.e., the bus terminal. Moreover, the migrants settling in this part of the city selected areas which were, at the time of settlement at least, on the outer edge of the built-up city.

Southern Settlement

Another third or more of the migrant associations are clustered directly south of the central business district, quite distant from the southern rural-urban fringe. The densest concentration is found in the transitional business district—a curved interstitial belt buffering the Western-style commercial zone north and west of it from the native market and residential quarters to its south and east. Twenty-five associations are located in this zone, while the remainder are scattered farther south toward Old Cairo.

Most striking is the fact that the majority of these associations represent villages of Upper Egypt. Thus the principle of least effort seems to determine migrant distribution. Villagers coming from north of the city favor the northern quadrant of the city, while those coming from the south prefer location in the southern quadrant. But, whereas the former have their associations in family residential zones near the city's fringe, the latter have theirs in a marginal commercial district characterized by a heavy excess of unmarried males.[12] Further examination reveals that the latter are primarily in rented offices, whereas the former are frequently in the home of the association's president.

What accounts for the remarkable difference? One hypothesis can be offered here. Migrants from Delta villages follow a different pattern of migration and hence make a different type of adjustment to the city than do migrants from Upper Egyptian villages. First, migrants from the Delta move primarily in family groups, while those from the south either remain single or leave their wives and children in their home villages. In Cairo in 1947,

of the 400,000 migrants from Lower Egypt, half were males and half females, but 200,000 out of the 250,000 migrants from Upper Egypt were males. Thus the sex ratio of Delta migrants was remarkably well balanced, while there were four men for every woman among Upper Egyptian migrants in Cairo.

Second, significant occupational differences between the two migrant groups affect both adjustment patterns and spatial distribution. Upper Egyptian migrants go primarily into domestic and other personal services or work in unskilled labor gangs, while the occupations followed by Lower Egyptian migrants are both more varied and less likely to include housing as a part of wages.[13]

In the light of this the major differences between the location of migrant associations representing Upper and Lower Egyptian villages become more comprehensible. The associations of Upper Egyptians are located in an area which serves as a leisure-time focal point as well as a residential area catering to single men. This is both cause and effect of the character of Upper Egyptian migrants. The associations play a more active role in their lives, in part because their members are denied access to the alternative social unit, the family.

Central Zone, East and West of the Central Business District

The remaining associations are divided between Boulaq, which forms

---

[12]The sex ratio here is 129 in the ages most likely to be imbalanced by migration, 15 to 49; in the northern section it is only 104. Forty per cent of males of marriageable age are unmarried here, while only 25 per cent are unmarried in the northern section (computed from 1947 census).

[13]The *Directory of Social Agencies* lists the dominant occupations of members of each association. Government and manual workers are listed most frequently for Lower Egyptian associations, while servants, porters, and messengers are the most frequently mentioned occupations for Upper Egyptian associations.

the western quadrant of the ellipse, and Bab al-Shariya and Waily, the eastern portion of the belt. Ten associations are located within the former zone, while twenty have addresses in the latter. Just as the ecological position of these areas is midway between the northern concentration of Delta village associations and the southern concentration of Upper Egyptian associations, so, sociologically, they lie midway, containing associations from both regions of the country in roughly equal proportions. They share still other similarities. Both are close to the central business district; both rank low in socioeconomic status (below both Shubra and the transitional business zone); both are primarily family areas; and both contain the densest slums of the city: densities of up to 900,000 persons per square mile are recorded for small subsections of Boulaq, and the over-all density of the community area of Bab al-Shariya is the highest in the city. Of the two, Boulaq is the older and hence the one retaining more rural qualities in its buildings and streets, but even Bab al-Shariya, despite its uniformly high apartment buildings looming above narrow access alleys, contains a population more rural than urban in its ways.

These, then, are the areas to which migrants have gravitated within the city. That they are relatively scarce in the highest rental zones of the city is attributable to their low socioeconomic status. Migrants are relatively absent, also, from the rural-urban fringe proper which would, as we have seen, provide them with the most familiar and protective environment. The lack of rental housing in these areas (privately owned farms with villages for laborers only), the death of public transportation, and their desire to live close to their new jobs are undoubtedly impor-

tant reasons for their rejection of these areas. A second area surprisingly overlooked in the search for "near-the-fringe" living is Medieval Cairo, that rectangular belt of oldest structures toward the eastern edge of the city. The complete absence of new housing in these districts, coupled with a low turnover rate (the population works at traditional crafts and trades where production, selling, and living quarters are often in the same structure), have probably prevented mass invasions by new migrants.

III. HYPOTHESES CONCERNING MIGRANT ADJUSTMENT

Earlier, the hypotheses of migrant adjustment were broken down into four classes: physical, economic, social, and ideological. In light of the locational material presented above, plus observations of both rural and city life in Egypt,[14] these will be defined here in an attempt to describe the peculiarities of migrant adjustment in Egypt.

Physical

We have already suggested that many migrants gravitate to areas lying close to the rural-urban fringe, while others settle in areas which have at least a cultural resemblance to semirural areas. In these sections, interior streets and alleyways are seldom used for wheeled traffic, leaving undisturbed the rural functions of the street as pathway, meeting place, playground, and tethering area for animals.

[14]The author has spent more than three years in Egypt, one and a half at a UNESCO project in a village area and two years in Cairo studying the structure of that city. Many observations have been further authenticated by anthropologists and social workers with longer and more intimate experience in both areas, to whom the author expresses gratitude.

Greater adjustments are required with respect to both the dwelling and the physical neighborhood. Housing occupied by the majority of migrants is more urban than rural in style. This results in functional overcrowding more severe than in the villages. The village home minimizes the number of enclosed rooms in order to maximize private open space (a ground-level interior courtyard or a protected roof courtyard in a more commodious two-story home). This cherished space is eliminated in the multifamily flats of the city. While many of the tasks assigned to the courtyard are no longer performed in the city (drying dung cakes, storing crops, tethering animals), other social uses such as cooking, eating, and just sitting are driven indoors or to the streets in the city.

Not only is the home compressed due to the loss of outdoor "overspill" space, but the neighborhood is also more concentrated. While residential densities in Egyptian villages are surprisingly high, they nowhere approach the densities of Cairo's poorer districts. Many families using a common stairwell and public utilities means, paradoxically, more intensive contact with neighbors than in the village; and adjusting to the inadvertent intimacy may be extremely difficult for people new to the city, particularly for women.

Within the home itself are other changes, of which the loss of the oven-room is perhaps the most important. In the rural home one full room is devoted to the massive flat-topped oven in which bread is baked daily and which, during the winter months, heats the adjacent areas and provides a snug bed for a blanketless family. That its loss is viewed with distress by at least some migrants is evidenced by the fact that some seek the top floor of an urban

dwelling to construct a village oven and advise newcomers from their village to do the same.[15]

Other changes in the home are viewed more favorably, since they conform to the aspirations of villagers. Among the objects high in status found in the most prosperous rural homes are small kerosene burners instead of dung-cake fires for cooking, wardrobes and china closets to store a growing stock of consumption items, and the high four-poster bed with its black wrought-iron frame embellished with gilt, which remains, in the city as in the village, the *most* important sign of status. These are items with which migrants tend to crowd their urban homes, as soon as they can afford them.

The dress of migrants changes little in the city. Only the selective migrants change completely from the *galabiya* (long loose robe) to pants and shirts; for non-selective migrants the change is rarely required to conform to the urban pattern, and it is occupation rather than status per se or place of birth which dictates appropriate attire. It is perhaps because of this that the change is more frequently attempted by Delta than by Upper Egyptian migrants.

Change in dress presents more difficult problems for the women. The universal dress of village women is a high-necked, long-sleeved printed gown which is then covered by a black one of similar cut. A kerchief and then a black mantilla completely cover the hair. While many village women retain this attire in the city (as do many old city residents), some of the younger of them first discard the black garment and later may adopt a modified urban version of the printed gown with

[15]Reported by Hind Abu el Seoud, an anthropologist studying a small Delta village and its exresidents in Cairo.

cutout neckline and daring three-quarter-length sleeves.

The foregoing remarks apply best to Delta families making a relatively permanent adjustment to the city. They do not apply with equal force to upper Egyptian migrants working as domestic servants or in other occupations where housing is provided or to those who remain unmarried or leave their families in the village. Paradoxically, this group, exposed most intensively to a completely new physical environment, is least assimilated to Cairo. A lifetime spent in sections of the city which contrast sharply with the village environment affects a superficial sophistication unmatched by the manual laborer from the Delta living in a quasi-rural district. It seems, however, that the very lack of gradual transition and of the mediating influences of family and neighborhood has the reverse effect of prolonging the period when one is a stranger. This type of migrant often completely rejects urban life, confining his periodic social contacts to covillagers often in his own profession and his "real" life to infrequent sojourns to his village family.

Economic

In their villages of origin, migrants were engaged almost exclusively in agriculture. Men worked long and hard during the three sowing and harvesting periods in the Delta and the two crop-change periods in Upper Egypt, these periods of intense activity being followed by slower seasons of maintenance and community sociality. The basic rhythm of rural life thus dictated large finite jobs alternating with lighter routine work. The length of the work day varied with the stage of the cycle.

Women's work was more evenly distributed, with child care, the prep-aration of food and bread, the making of dung cakes, and the tending of livestock performed daily. Work in the fields was done during the early morning hours, except during the busy seasons, when it absorbed a greater portion of the day. Labor was communal within the extended family home and, when outdoors, was usually performed in company.

Laundry is a case in point. In the village, washing is done in the canal or now, increasingly, at the communal water taps. It is never a solitary activity. Contrast this with how laundry is done in Al Sharabiya, a migrant area described above.[16] Water is also secured from communal taps, but a man guards the tap, effectively discouraging women from washing at the site. Women carry their water home to wash in solitude within their dwellings. Other functions are similarly driven indoors or eliminated altogether. Thus the ex-village woman experiences a reduction in her work load (except where outside employment is taken), but, at the same time, she experiences an even greater reduction in the social life which formerly attended her labors.

The experience of migrant men, on the other hand, is often the reverse. The work of a city manual laborer is probably more taxing, certainly more evenly distributed over time, and usually *less* solitary than rural work. Exceptions must be made for migrants working as itinerant peddlers, shoe-shiners, tea-makers, etc., and, of course, for those working as domestic servants. These occupations are both more independently regulated and somewhat more isolating from contacts of a primary nature.

To what extent do migrants working

[16]Account provided by Abdel Monem Shawky, former social worker in the district for fourteen years.

at steady jobs in the company of others come into contact with associates from different backgrounds? Social heterogeneity is one of the distinguishing characteristics of urbanism, but for this to create the mental counterpart—cultural relativity—heterogeneous persons must come into intimate contact with each other. While in large-scale factories the mixing of diverse people undoubtedly occurs, the overwhelming majority of commercial and industrial firms in Cairo employ only a few persons, often within the same family. Furthermore, migrants often depend upon their compatriots to guide them to their first jobs. Sometimes, migrants seek out well-known "successes" from their village to give them employment. Thus migrants cluster together not only residentially but also on the job as well. In the smaller firms of Cairo, then, a far greater homogeneity of the work force exists than would have been expected by chance. Far from isolating the migrant from his fellow villagers, his job may actually consolidate his village ties.

Social

The hypotheses presented by Louis Wirth in his logical statement[17] of the differences between the rural and urban ways of life have been misused, as if they were facts, and many of the concepts almost self-evident to sociologists studying American cities have proved less valid when applied to the growing body of data about non-Western and preindustrial cities. While isolated

refutations have appeared,[18] as yet there has been no major reformulation of the theory.

Wirth hypothesized that the ecological determinants of a city (large numbers of heterogeneous people in dense, permanent settlement) would have certain social consequences, notably anonymity, dependence upon impersonal relations and sanctions, sophistication, and tolerance of change. To what extent do the social relationships in Cairo conform to these predicated types, and, further, how much does the rural migrant really have to adjust his personality to become a functioning member of urban society?

While these questions are too ambitious to be answered here, two propositions are suggested. First, the culture of Cairo fails to be characterized chiefly by anonymity, secondary contacts, and the other attributes of urban life. Second, migrants to Cairo are active creators of a variety of social institutions whose major function is to protect migrants from the shock of anomie.

Middle Eastern culture places a high value on personal relationships, even at a sacrifice of privacy and internal development. This, combined with a system of relationships based on the extended kinship group, serves to increase the number of primary ties far beyond what Western sociologists, reasoning from their own experience, dare to assume possible.[19] This network

[17]Louis Wirth, "Urbanism as a Way of Life," *American Journal of Sociology*, 44 (July, 1938), 1–24, which essentially reformulates the work of earlier German scholars, such as Max Weber, *The City*, ed. and trans. D. Martindale and G. Neuwirth (Glencoe, Ill.: Free Press, 1958); and Georg Simmel, "The Metropolis and Mental Life," in *The Sociology of Georg Simmel*, trans. Kurt Wolff (Glencoe, Ill.: Free Press, 1950), pp. 409–24.

[18]See, e.g., Gideon Sjoberg, "The Preindustrial City," *American Journal of Sociology*, 60 (March, 1955), 438–45; Horace Miner, *The Primitive City of Timbuctoo* (Princeton, N.J.: Princeton University Press, 1953).

[19]Weber himself rejected impersonal relations as a useful part of the city's definition, noting that "various cultural factors determine the size at which 'impersonality' tends to appear" (*op. cit.*, p. 65). See also Richard Dewey, "The Rural-Urban Continuum," *American Journal of Sociology*, 66 (July, 1960), 60–66.

of personal associations enmeshes not hundreds but thousands of individuals.

Were Cairo merely an amorphous mass of individuals, this network, large as it is, might account for but a small fraction of the individual's contacts. However, Cairo is not one community but, rather, many separate social communities. Functional sections of each community may be geographically separated—residence in one section, business in another, recreation in still another. A member of one community may pass daily through the physical site of communities other than his own, neither "seeing" them nor admitting their relevance to his own life. But, within his own community, there is little if any anonymity.

It is within this context of "urbanism" that the Egyptian migrant is called upon to adjust. His adjustment is further facilitated by the formal and informal institutions he develops within his small community, one of which has already been mentioned— the village benevolent society. Through it many migrants receive moral support from their compatriots as well as insurance against the insecurities of urban life, that is, isolation in poverty, sickness, and death.[20] It is unlikely, however, that more than 100,000 migrants are involved in these associations, while it will be recalled that their number exceeded 600,000 in 1947. Thus, even if these associations are important to the persons they serve, they fall short of absorbing most migrants.

Other formal institutions play a relatively minor role in providing social groups for migrant identification. Labor unions (except for craft guilds), civic associations, charitable organizations,

[20]Burial services, offered by almost all associations, parallel the burial-insurance organizations of Negro rural migrants to northern cities.

and political groups are all relatively undeveloped social institutions in Cairo. One must look, then, to the informal social institutions for a fuller understanding of patterns of adjustment. Unfortunately, documentation in this area is totally lacking. While a few may be singled out as playing important roles, no estimate of their magnitude can be offered.

First in importance is undoubtedly the coffee shop in which Middle Eastern males conduct their social and often their business lives. The comparable Western institution is probably the old style of British pub which, with its set of steady patrons and its intimate atmosphere, served as a social focus for the individual's life. Many an Egyptian coffee shop is run by a villager to serve men from that particular village. News of the village is exchanged, mutual assistance for employment is given, and the venture more resembles a closed club than a commercial enterprise.

For the women no such informal association is available. While within the village there are also no purely female informal associations, religious festivals, births, deaths, marriages, circumcisions, etc., are all village-wide events in which women have important roles to play. Within the city, however, these events become more private, and the role of women as full participants is probably reduced. Social life in the city is confined more and more to the immediate neighborhood.

It is this immediate neighborhood, however, which constitutes, after the family, the most important informal social institution for migrants in the city. The cohesiveness of the neighborhood is strengthened by the tendency of persons from the same village to settle together. Similar to the situation elsewhere, it is the women, children, and very old persons who are the most active participants in neighborhood-centered social life.

Motivations and Ideology

The Weltanschauung of the city man is presumed to differ from the peasant's in several significant ways. First, relaxation of the heavy hand of personal social control in the village is assumed to give greater latitude for individual differentiation. Second, cities are assumed to foster a more secular, rational, and mechanistic ordering of activities. Third, cities are gateways to a more sophisticated knowledge of the outside world. Finally, cities have traditionally been the centers of movements of social change, from new religions to new political ideologies and transfers of power.

While these statements are valid premises, data on Cairo are lacking which would permit us to place rural migrants along the continuum from the sacred, conformist, isolated, and relatively static state of the ideal folk society to the extreme of urbanism outlined above. For one thing, the Egyptian village hardly conforms to the ideal prototype of a folk society. Where farmers raise cash crops tied to international markets (cotton and sugar), listen to radios, travel often to market towns, have relatives or friends in the cities, and send their children to schools following a national curriculum, the magic ring of isolation has already been broken. On the other hand, as already demonstrated, it is possible within Cairo to lead a fairly circumscribed existence outside the main stream of urban life. Therefore, while there may be a wide gap between the least-sophisticated villager and the most-sophisticated urbanite, there is certainly no indication that migrants necessarily pass from one pole to the other.

29. African Urbanism, Mobility and the Social Network

PETER C. W. GUTKIND

In recent years African urban studies have changed from the survey type,[1] the documentation and description of basic demographic and social characteristics, to a more analytical type of inquiry and presentation. Thus a number of conceptual schemes are now being tested. Southall[2] and Banton[3] have tried to apply basic sociological concepts, such as analysis of role relationships, to African urban systems. Southall,[4] too, has raised questions regarding macro

and micro analysis both as to approach and method of investigation. Mayer,[5] and Wilson and Mafeje[6] have used group and social network analysis, as has Epstein[7] in a particularly lucid presentation. Both Forde[8] and Mitchell[9] have summarized past approaches and suggested new lines of inquiry. While most of these new studies have been penned by social anthropologists and sociologists, geographers,[10] demogra-

From K. Ishwaran and Ralph Piddington, eds. "Kinship and Geographical Mobility," special number of International Journal of Comparative Sociology (Leiden), 6, No. 1 (1965), 48–60. Reprinted by permission of author and publisher.

[1] For example: The Social Implications of Urbanization and Industrialization in Africa South of the Sahara, Paris: UNESCO, 1956. Acquah, I., Accra Survey, London, University of London Press, 1958. Leslie, J.A.K., A Survey of Dar es Salaam, Oxford University Press (for East African Institute of Social Research), 1963. Southall, A. W. and Gutkind, P. C. W., Townsmen in the Making, East African Studies No. 9, Kampala, East African Institute, 1957.

[2] Southall, A. W., The Theory of Urban Sociology, typed Ms., n.d. (about 1956) and "An Operational Theory of Role", Human Relations, Vol. 12, No. 1, 1959, pp. 17–34.

[3] Banton, M., Role Congruence and Social Differentiation Under Urban Conditions, Seminar on Social Structure, Stratification and Mobility With Special Reference to Latin America, Rio de Janeiro, June 1962, Pan American Union, Document 5 and "Role Theory and Urbanization", Paper presented at Symposium 26, Werner-Gren Foundation for Anthropological Research, Burg Wartenstein, Austria, August-September 1964, pp. 14.

[4] Southall, A. W., Introductory Summary, in Social Change in Modern Africa, A. W. Southall (Ed.), London, Oxford University Press (for

International African Institute), 1961, pp. 25–30.

[5] Mayer, P., Townsmen or Tribesmen, Cape Town, Oxford University Press (for Institute of Social and Economic Research, Rhodes University), 1961.

[6] Wilson, M. and Mafeje, A., Langa: A Study of Social Groups in an African Township, Cape Town: Oxford University Press, 1963.

[7] Epstein, A. L., "The Network and Urban Social Organization", The Rhodes-Livingstone Journal, No. 29, June 1961, pp. 29–62.

[8] Forde D., "Background and Approaches", in Urbanization in African Social Change, Edinburgh, Centre of African Studies, 1963, pp. 1–6.

[9] Mitchell, J. C., Theoretical Orientations in African Urban Studies, Paper presented at the seminar on The Anthropology of Complex Societies, Association of Social Anthropologists, Cambridge, June 1963, 27 pp.

[10]Steel, R. W., "The Towns of Tropical Africa", in Essays on African Population, Barbour, K. M. and Prothero, R. M. (Eds.), London, Routledge and Kegan Paul, 1961, pp. 249–78; Hamdan, G., "Capitals of the New Africa", Economic Geography, Vol. 40, No. 3, July 1964, pp. 239–53, "The Growth and Functional Structure of Khartoum", The Geographical Review, Vol. 50, No. 1, Jan. 1960, pp. 21–40; De Blij, H.J., "The Functional Structure and Central Business District of Lourenco Marques, Mozambique", Economic Geography, Vol. 38, No. 1, Jan. 1962, pp. 56–77; Mabogunje,

phers and planners[11] have also shown an interest in comparative African urban studies.

African urban studies have achieved a place in comparative African sociology in part because an ever larger number of Africans have decided to seek alternative ways of making a living. This almost always means leaving the rural areas for a short or prolonged residence in town. While Africa remains the least urbanized of the continents, an urban environment has become the social and economic habitat for possibly 9%—11% of the continent's population. In political terms, and as social pace setters, the influence of the larger African urban centers is considerable.[12] The growth of modern facilities in such towns is turning them into the showpieces of the new African nations.

Thus Peter Marris writes:

"With the approach of independence, the people of Nigeria began to look more critically at their Federal capital, and saw in its congested lanes of ramshackle houses a poor reflection of their aspirations. As the Minister of Lagos Affairs remarked, 'It is the mirror through which foreigners make their initial appraisal of Nigeria'.

The condition of central Lagos, he said, was 'humiliating to any person with a sense of national pride' ".[13]

While it is not always easy to obtain reliable statistics on urban growth and rural-urban migration, particularly since independence, observers are generally agreed that the annual post-independence increase is considerably above that of previous years. What is also said to be a significant and new development is the larger number of Africans, particularly those with some years of urban residence, even if broken by frequent visits to kin and friends in the rural areas, who are staying for a longer period and will, probably, make the urban areas their permanent home. Thus Plotnicov has shown for his Jos (Northern Nigeria) data that Africans are increasingly reluctant to maintain close rural ties and even more reluctant to retire to the rural areas.[14]

If this is so then there is clearly developing an African urban way of life—an urban system. It will then have to be approached and studied as such.[15] To do so we have to be mindful of Gluckman's solid guidance:

"Urban life exhibits sufficient regularities for us to extract systematic inter-connexions which we can arrange to exhibit a structure and we can study how this structure changes."[16]

A.L., "Yoruba Towns", Ibadan, University Press, 1962, "The Growth of Residential Districts in Ibadan", Geographical Review, Vol. 52, No. 1 Jan. 1962, pp. 56–77; Morgan, W.B., "The 'Grassland Towns' of the Eastern Region of Nigeria", Transactions and Papers 1957, Publication 23, Institute of British Geographers, London, Philip, 1957, pp. 213–224.

[11]Zaremba, P., "The Urban Development of West and Equatorial Africa", Africana Bulletin, No. 1, 1964, pp. 105–134; Georgulas, N., "An Approach To Urban Analysis for East African Towns With Particular Reference to the African Population", Ekistics, Vol. 18, No. 109, December 1964, pp. 236–440.

[12]Gutkind, P. C. W., "The African Urban Milieu: A Force in Rapid Change", Civilizations, Vol. 12, No. 2, 1962, pp. 167–195; Sklar R.L., "A Note on the Study of Community Power in Nigeria", Paper Presented at the Annual Conference of the African Studies Association, Washington, October 1962, pp. 11.

[13]Marris, P., Family and Social Change in an African City, London, Routledge, 1961, p. vii.

[14]Plotnicov, L., "Modern Urban Population Formation in Nigeria", Paper Presented at the Annual Meeting of the American Anthropological Association, Detroit, 1964, 8 pp.

[15]Gutkind, P. C. W., "African Urban Family Life and the Urban System", Journal of Asian and African Studies, Vol. 1, No. 1, 1966. pp. 35–42.

[16]Gluckman, M., "Anthropological Problems Arising from the African Industrial Revolution", in Social Change in Modern Africa, A. W. Southall (Ed.), London, Oxford University Press, 1961, p. 68.

He goes on to point out that:

"The starting-point for analysis of urbanization must be an urban system of relations . . . We have to start with a theory about urban social systems; but these systems are to be seen as made up of loose, semi-independent, to some extent isolated, sub systems."[17]

While we can expect a considerable increase in urban population,[18] largely of those individuals who are engaged in a futile search for wage employment, it remains to be seen what ties Africans will maintain with the rural areas. Mitchell has pointed out that the cycle of rural-urban-rural migration can perhaps be best understood in terms of centrifugal and centripetal forces.[19] However, what keeps a man in town and what draws him back (*pro tem*) to his rural home will be increasingly determined by economic rather than social ties. Even where cash crops are under cultivation, as in Buganda Province or in Ghana's cocoa belt, providing a steady if uncertain return, it is increasingly the fashion for the owners to employ migrants while they seek additional wage employment.[20] Should an agrarian revolution develop in Africa, i.e., a major shift from subsistence to surplus cropping, cash cropping on small or large units, an ever increasing number of Africans will seek employment in nonagricultural activities. Then for a large number of urban Africans the break with the

land and rural traditions is likely to be complete and final.

Of course, it is probably far too early to indicate exactly the salient characteristics of African urban society in the years ahead. At present, urban life in Africa is marked by certain well-known characteristics which were shaped in the immediate pre-independence period. In East Africa's urban areas, particularly since the second World War, the population is usually composed of many tribal groups living in either peri-urban areas or on designated housing estates within the towns. Demographically, the urban population is composed primarily of unmarried young men and few women. Africans come as "target workers" to acquire money and perhaps some new skills but return to their rural areas when it suits them or when their agricultural activities demand it. But more stay longer in town and fewer return to the rural areas.

If these characteristics are a correct assessment of the situation, then *urbanism as a way of life* will become an increasingly distinctive feature in the transformation of Africa. I think it is unsatisfactory to use the convenient label of "transitional societies" to describe the present total social system of African societies as passing through an intermediate phase from being less rural to being more urban. Many complex and yet unidentified processes are at work which may occur at different times and in different contexts from one society to another. The key issue is to find out how change and modernization take place. Central to this discussion is the fact that change and modernization often radically alter the patterns of social relations to bring about a different network of individual and group relations. This transformation is viewed by some observers as productive of negative and anomic characteristics.

---

[17] Ibid., p. 80.

[18] Hance, W.A., "The Economic Location and Functions of Tropical African Cities", *Human Organization*, Vol. 19, No. 3, Fall 1960, pp. 135–136; *The Geography of Modern Africa*, N. Y., Columbia University Press, 1964, pp. 52–57.

[19] Mitchell, J. C., "The Causes of Labour Migration", *Inter-African Labour Institute Bulletin*, Vol. 6, No. 1, Jan. 1959, pp. 12–46.

[20] Richards, A.I. (Ed.), *Economic Development and Tribal Change*, Cambridge, Heffer, 1954, pp. 119–140, 161–223.

The individual and the group have been lifted out of the matrix of a complex system which was dominated by primary relations shaped by kinship, close interdependence and group reciprocity. The break with rural life is sharp and abrupt. However, this view ignores "how fluid the traditional (tribal) situation was" and that "individuals and groups were constantly on the move, communities dissolving and crystallizing again in new patterns".[21] Thus quite obviously it is false to pose the rural tribal system as a system of clearly understood reciprocal relations marked by maximum integration and the urban system as one of maximum fluidity, amorphousness or unbridled individualism. A closer and more analytical presentation would reveal that an urban society is as integrated as any other type of community but that integration takes place around different variables.

Thus extended kinship is not necessarily incompatible with African urban society; nor does the mobility of Africans invariably weaken *all* traditional kin and group ties. The question really is what aspects of traditional social organization are both useful and adaptable to new conditions? In what follows I hope to indicate some of the characteristics of urban social networks[22] and to suggest how such networks are shaped by the extent and type of rural-urban-rural mobility. My data is taken from the all-African parish of Mulago, one of a number of parishes which make up the peri-urban area of Kampala, Uganda, East Africa.[23]

the analysis of mixed and complex groupings. The concept of social structure postulates numerous but interdependent enduring groups and highly specific categories, groups and classes. Srinivas and Béteille suggest that the distinction between social structure (enduring groups—those with "a high degree of consistency and constancy") and networks "is primarily one of boundaries. A group is a bounded unit. A network, on the other hand, ramifies in every direction, and for all practical purposes, stretches out indefinitely . . . The character of a network . . . varies from one individual to another". (p. 166)

Such a formulation allows more adequately for a description and analysis of many semi-independent social situations which result from disturbances and struggles, so much the mark of African urban life. In this sense a network "has a dynamic character. New relations are forged, and old ones discarded or modified. This is particularly true of rapidly changing societies in which individual choice plays an important role". (Srinivas and Béteille, p. 166). The objective, then, of network analysis is to "chart the type and the channels of interaction between persons and the extent of regularities which give a minimum of order and coherence to social life in communities which have no clear structure of discrete groups". (Southall, 1961, p. 25.)

The concept of social structure sprang from the work of social anthropologists working in relatively static and ethnically homogeneous communities. Few such communities are now being studied by anthropologists. As societies change they take on a new and different kind of complexity—a complexity which is increasingly the outcome of the way individuals, as individuals, manipulate a variety of situations and social relations. This in turn is the result of an ever widening field of choices which the individual can make in social, economic and political life. This is the essence of change and modernization which gives rise to new networks which cut across and involve change over the entire system (See: Mair, L., *New Nations*, London, Weidenfeld and Nicolson, 1963, pp. 11–31).

[21]Southall, A. W., *op. cit.*, 1961, p. 2.

[22]The concept of network has received considerable attention in recent years by Barnes ("Class and Committees in a Norwegian Island Parish", *Human Relations*, Vol. 7, 1954, pp. 39–58), Bott ("Conjugal Roles and Social Networks", *Human Relations*, Vol. 8, 1955, pp. 345–84), Jay ("The Concepts of 'Field' and 'Network' in Anthropological Research", *Man*, Vol. 64, September-October 1964, pp. 137–39), Srinivas and Béteille ("Networks in Indian Social Structure", *Man*, Vol. 64, Nov.-Dec. 1964, pp. 165–168).

As a model the concept of social networks has been suggested as particularly suitable for

[23]Fieldwork was carried out between April

The area from which my data is taken contains an extremely heterogeneous African community representative of some twenty-five tribes. The parish of Mulago, which borders on Kampala, is one of about twelve parishes (*muluka*) which are part of the *kibuga*, the headquarters or capital of the Kingdom of Buganda. The *kibuga* in turn is a sub-county (*gombolola*), a number of which make up a county (*saza*). On the south, Mulago borders on the predominantly non-African and modern commercial capital of Uganda. To the northwest and east, Mulago is part of a larger sub-county. In 1948 the population of the *kibuga* as a whole was 34,337 and the parish of Mulago 2,500 (estimated). That part of the population of Mulago which was surveyed between 1953 and 1958 amounted to 1339 people, i.e., about 53% of the estimated total. Almost 75% of the African residents of the *kibuga* are Ganda, while the rest come from other parts of East Africa. Over the years the parish has steadily become more congested with all the characteristics and features of a slum area. Many of those who live in the parish work in Government and business offices in Kampala; others work at the large and nearby Mulago Hospital and others operate shops and services in Mulago itself.

There is considerable mobility in and out of the parish and also from one part of Mulago to another. Firstly, there is a steady stream of Africans

settling in the parish from outside Buganda Province. Likewise many people leave Mulago to return to the rural areas. Secondly, due to the fact that the parish is part of Buganda Province, many Ganda constantly move in or out of the parish. Thus between November 1953 and March 1954 slightly over 10% had left Mulago while just short of 17% were newcomers and 8% had returned to the parish for the second or third time.

Thirdly, there was a good deal of mobility within the parish. Almost 11% of the residents, most of whom had been in Mulago from 9 to 30 months, had moved once since their first arrival; 6% had moved twice and 4% more than twice. Over 61% of those who moved within the parish were non-Ganda. When further interviews were carried out between November 1957 and March 1958, the intake into the parish amounted to 31% (17% newcomers and 14% returnees), whereas only 12% of those who had been interviewed between November 1953 and March 1954 had left Mulago. This intake into the parish was reflected in an overall increase of the population of the *kibuga* to 52,673 by 1959 and of Mulago (now enumerated separately in the 1959 Uganda Census) to 3767; an increase in eleven years, over the 1948 estimate, of 66%. The estimated population of the *kibuga* in 1964 is 65,000 (up by 23%) and of Mulago 4,200 (up by 13%).

These broad characteristics of mobility and population growth are closely linked, particularly the former, to the types of social networks in Mulago which are either kin-based networks or association-based networks. This distinction turned out to be useful when analysing certain characteristics of those more permanently resident (i.e. primarily Ganda) in Mulago (although

1953 and July 1955 and August 1956 to August 1958, while on the staff of the East African Institute of Social Research, Kampala, Uganda. For a description of the peri-urban area of Kampala see: Southall, A. W. and Gutkind, P. C. W., *Townsmen in the Making: Kampala and Its Suburbs*, East African Studies No. 9, East African Institute of Social Research, Kampala, 1957. Second Edition.

Table 1

**Frequency of Visits to Rural Areas[a] (50 Miles and Further)
of Non-Ganda Males 18 Years and Over**

1953–1954 Sample

After Every 3 Months of Residence	After Every 6 Months of Residence	After Every 12 Months of Residence	After Every 24 Months of Residence		Sample Total
41%	49%	8%	2%	100%	100

Table 2

1957–1958 Sample

30%	26%	38%	6%	100%	100

[a] Of at least 2 weeks but no more than 3 months.

frequently interrupted by *brief* visits to nearby rural areas) and those (primarily non-Ganda) who moved in and out of the parish, often staying away many months before returning to village or town. Thus Table 1 indicates that non-Ganda, who have been in and out of Mulago over a period of up to 8 years, up to March 1954, frequently return to their rural homes. While Ganda can see their kin and friends virtually whenever they wish, and rural kin and friends come to see them in Mulago, non-Ganda must make a special effort to return home. This they do often, although Table 2 indicates that compared with the 1953–54 sample, the 1957–58 group had moved less frequently.

For a Ganda to visit the rural areas does not mean that he must give up his employment or otherwise, significantly, pull up his roots. Non-Ganda ties with urban life are thus frequently broken and on each return they must find new lodgings, new jobs and perhaps new friends. While they are not necessarily rural-oriented, the fact that they come without their families continues to tie them to a kin-based network which forces them back to their rural homes. However,

while living and working in an urban area they are tied to a non-kin associational network which has resulted from their contact with members of the same tribe, or their work or neighbourhood associations. Each one of these contacts produces a set of network relations which are operative at different times and under different conditions. At times these networks overlap when tribe and composition of the residential neighbourhood are the same,[24] or when members of the same tribe are employed together. However, association-based networks need not be linked to common tribal background.

Perhaps the most outstanding example of a non-tribal network is the beer bar.[25] There are anywhere from six to ten bars in Mulago. At weekends and at the end of the month small rooms are crowded with customers. Various varieties of African beers are brewed by women, a number of whom have developed a reputation for their excellent beer—beer which has body and gives the drinker the feeling that he is

[24]Gutkind, P.C.W., "Urban Conditions in Africa", *The Town Planning Review*, Vol. 32, No. 1, April 1961, pp. 20–31.

[25]Southall, A. W. and Gutkind, P.C.W., 1957, op. cit., pp. 57–63.

consuming more than mere liquid. Each bar may be filled with 5–25 people and on a really crowded day many more sit outside the room on benches placed in the courtyard. On such occasions men and women of every tribe represented in the parish will sit together and jostle and joke with one another. It is a favourite place to pick up a woman and make whatever arrangements are desired. Friends made at work or in Mulago will frequent the bar as a group. At the start of an afternoon or an evening out, men can be seen playing a card game or any number of other African games. Some beer sellers set aside a little corner or open place for such regular customers. There is much coming and going, much joking and shouting and occasionally dancing. Europeans and Asians are often mocked in informal and spontaneous mime. Men and women discuss the affairs and personalities of the parish. They make cutting remarks about other tribes; they debate on a high moral plane thieves and prostitutes. Men give money to help out those who plead special needs in casual conversation. Newcomers use the occasion to make contacts, to seek lodgings and jobs.

As the afternoon and evening wear on, and as men and women drift in and out of the bars, the excitement and commotion heighten. Minor fights and bottle smashing occur. Those more sober will try to restrain those more excitable and persuade them to go home. Casual contacts and friendships made earlier will dissolve in anger, accusations and sudden violence. Property might be smashed and heads broken. Thieves and confidence tricksters will then ply their successful trades. Tribal feelings will be expressed more bitterly, and factions will line up. But when it is all over the same people will return the next day and the next

weekend seeking companionship and friends.

These informal associational networks extend into the community as a whole. Drinking clubs and credit societies are often born in beer bars. They may last for months until they break up to be re-formed at a later date. For the newcomers a beer bar is a central point of contact. For men it is a place to find a woman; for the down and out it is a way to pick up a drink and some money. For many more it is a way of recreation, of showing off and a debating union where personal and group problems are discussed—but never resolved.

Another common feature of Mulago's non-Ganda is to belong to small credit societies, of perhaps 4–8 members, which allows each participant in turn to receive a share of the wages of all other members at the end of each month. As the penalty for absconding with the money is likely to be a severe beating, should the culprit be found, members of such credit societies tend to be linked in mutual aid and close association. The composition of three such groups was based on friendships made at work rather than on tribalism. Yet another non-tribally based form of association are groups of young men who join together to employ a young girl or older woman to cook for them. Towards this end they pool their resources. Such groupings are very loosely knitted types of association. Yet they should be seen as a particularly suitable structure as men can enter and join such groups without complex contractual and obligatory commitments. The existence of such groups is often attractive to newcomers who do not know their way about but through a friend can join a "supper club".

Other networks are based on residence in a tribal enclave whose members, usually non-kin, aid each other in many ways. Such enclaves often give a strong emphasis to a "we-group" feeling which is expressed in the manner in which they refer to other groups. Not infrequently they appoint one among them as a leader and spokesman. In doing so, members of such tribal settlements have developed a more structured type of associational network which supports the individual in meeting virtually every contingency he might face. An example of this would be how members of a Luo settlement, comprising 8 men, two of whom had their wives and small children living with them, came to the aid of one of their number who had been arrested and fined in the sub-county court. His fine was paid by others of his settlement. In turn he was asked to find employment for a newly-arrived Luo because he was a minor foreman in the Public Works Department. As this request was made to him during a period of economic recession he was not able to locate employment. The other Luo of his settlement accused him of wanting to be paid for his services. A mock court was established, and he was asked to move elsewhere—a step he finally took after having fallen ill and believing this to be due to witchcraft.

This event also illustrates that ethnicity is not always a sufficiently strong bond even under conditions of extreme heterogeneity in urban areas where ethnicity acts as a protective measure *vis-à-vis* the politically and socially dominant Ganda.[26]

Association-based networks are adaptable. They provide the non-Ganda from far away, and resident in a foreign setting, with friendship, mutual aid and support. To stand

alone is impossible. The need for a supportive structure for a non-Ganda immigrant is on the mind of many. Out of several hundred interviews, virtually all of which make the same points, the following two are typical examples:

A

When I first arrived in Mulago I looked for any person of my tribe I knew. I was lucky to find a friend and I stayed with him for three weeks before I found a place for myself. I had a little money when I arrived but after four days in Mulago almost half of it was stolen. My friend introduced me to his friends (not all of whom were of the same tribe) to ask for jobs. Eventually I found work as a sweeper in a big office.

I now live with a group of young men only one of whom is a member of my tribe but two others work in the same office as messengers. We go to work together because one of them has a bicycle and I can ride with him. We cook for each other because we cannot pay for help. When a member of my tribe goes home I give him messages for my wife and if I have any money I will give some of that too.

I am now trying to get better work where I can get more money. So I went to see a Ganda friend of mine. He likes me because I can speak his language. But I do not really like the Ganda people because they treat us all with contempt.

On Sunday I play football. I have joined a club and pay one shilling every three months. There are people from many different tribes in my club but we get on well together. I sometimes get tired of living here and having to buy all my food. If I get tired of work I go home but I always come back.[27]

B

I have lived in Mulago for almost one year. It is the longest time that I have been

[26]Gutkind, P. C. W., "Accommodation and Conflict in an African Peri-Urban Area," *Anthropologica*, N. S. Vol. 4, No. 1, 1962, pp. 163–173.

[27]From my unpublished field notes, October 1954.

away from my country. But I expect to go home for leave next month. The first time I came to Mulago I only stayed two months before I went home. But I came back again and stayed longer. I came back to Mulago because I had friends here and I knew that they would let me sleep with them.

I sometimes go with women but there are not many here in Mulago. I have never been with a Ganda woman because I do not have money to pay them.

Not long ago I was beaten up by another man and I took a complaint to the parish chief. I took a friend along with me to help to introduce me to the chief. The Ganda chiefs are not like our chiefs so I knew that he might not listen to me.

Whenever a friend of mine goes home I give him money for my wife. I get this money from my friends but I always pay them back.

I have some friends but they are not like the friends at home. They are just friends. You cannot trust your friends because they might spoil your name or beat you. In my home I am not beaten and if that should happen I will go to the chief and he will punish the culprit.[28]

What appears to be significant about these accounts is the fact that associationally-based networks provide a migrant non-Ganda with the instrumentalities to obtain a home and a job. Some networks are really class networks. As a migrant repeatedly returns to Mulago, or elsewhere in the *kibuga*, he gradually selects his friends according to similar skills, wealth and education. Such relations generally cut right across tribal background. Thus in Mulago there was a "Monday Night Club" composed of 4–10 members representing five different tribes. Most of the members were foremen, on public works, junior medical orderlies, junior clerks or small-scale artisans. When they met, usually on a rotating basis at a

[28]*Ibid.*, February 1957.

member's house, they just talked about anything that came into their minds. They aided each other both financially and with their labour, such as on the occasion when two members had help from the others to build extensions to their houses. When they met, which was irregular, they were always well dressed and in conversation they would debate the failures of other people, their bad habits and manners and the aspirations they had for themselves.

As his field of contacts extends, the migrant shifts from one kind of network to another. Friends become enemies and enemies friends. Much of the internal mobility within Mulago could be traced to acts of violence or accusations of theft or uncertain love affairs which badly disrupted the individual's relations with neighbours, fellow tribesmen or friends.

Participation in many different associations, such as credit clubs, recreational associations or beer drinking clubs, does not provide the individual with a set of clearly defined relationships which have predictability and regularity over time. Such relationships can be broken by all manner of means. Having visited his rural home means, in most cases, that on his return to Mulago he will have to start all over again the complex process of finding a home and a job. His past friends have gone; his job has been taken by another. Under such conditions men latch on to any type of organization and relationship which they consider suitable for their immediate and short-range needs. An associationally-based network in this sense is a particular kind of structure which lacks the formalness and cohesiveness of kin-based networks. Association networks must provide the individual member with concrete benefits of assistance and protection. Yet at the same time the unique feature

Table 3

Frequency of Visits to Buganda Rural Areas (Within 70 Mile Radius[a]) of Ganda Men[b]

	1 Visit to Rural Area	2 Visits	3–5 Visits	6–8 Visits	8 or More Visits	Total
Per month	6	11	14	–	–	31
Every 2 months	3	11	16	4	2	36
Every 3 months	1	10	14	4	4	33
	10	32	44	8	6	100

[a] Exclusive of those visiting within a 10 mile radius of Kampala.
[b] Both single and married men over 18 years.

of these networks is that they are constantly manipulated by their participants; this means that they are ever shifting and possess an amorphous quality which is reduced to a more structured situation only by the fact that such networks always exist. They can best be isolated by means of following the activities of specific individuals rather than by tracing collective activities.

If we now turn to kin-based networks we shall see that they are associated with quite different characteristics. In the first case kin-based networks are only established when either mobility is low or when circumstances favour their establishment, despite rural-urban-rural mobility. The latter is illustrated by the Ganda residents in Mulago, the vast majority of whom move frequently and easily in and out of Mulago. This is clearly indicated in Table 3. Thirty-one per cent visited their kin and friends from once to five times per month; 36% up to 8 times every two months and 33% between 2 and 8 times every three months. This is in strong contrast with non-Ganda migrants.

Those Ganda who were married, but had left their wives at home, had frequent visits from them and other kin and friends when they found it difficult or inconvenient to leave Mulago. Weekend visiting in both directions was very common. Food was generally brought to Mulago by a rural visitor or a parish resident brought some back to his urban home. It was also very common for a parish resident to bring back a young child, perhaps his brother's child, to look after for a short or prolonged time. Not infrequently a steady stream of kin and friends would visit a Mulago resident and stay with him for a few days or weeks. Such visitors would expect hospitality which involved the host in considerable extra expenditure. This was, not infrequently, resented and formed the basis of bitterness and strained relations.

Most Ganda occupy higher economic and status levels than non-Ganda. This gives them better and more secure employment. In addition many Mulago Ganda own cotton and coffee gardens, looked after by kin or friends or non-Ganda migrants, which give them further incomes. In the parish virtually all shops are owned by Ganda, a fact which is resented by non-Ganda who claim that the former cheat them.

Thus economically and politically the Ganda dominate the parish. Few of them extend their contacts socially to non-Ganda. Most Ganda live on or near the "main street" running north-south through the parish. Non-Ganda live in close proximity but avoid close contact with Ganda. Between December 1953 and July 1954 one Ganda houseowner evicted three non-Ganda tenants to make room for Ganda renters. Ganda women who have too frequent contact with non-Ganda men are criticized and made to feel inferior. At the same time most beer brewers are Ganda women whose clientele are predominantly non-Ganda. In this way and through the authority of the Ganda chief, Ganda and non-Ganda residents are tied into overlapping association-based networks, politically and economically.

Ganda society in Mulago rests on kin-based networks. Although a Ganda lives away from his home he is never far away from its influence. Indeed, the village, via its individuals, extends into Mulago. The basic Ganda social unit in Mulago is, typically, a man and his wife and children or a man and his older children. Numerous other combinations also exist, such as two brothers whose sister cooks for them or a brother and sister, both employed in Kampala, sharing a household. It is less usual for a man to share his household with any of his wife's relatives although there are some cases of an older sister-in-law helping a Ganda shopkeeper. Few Ganda live alone.

When ceremonial and ritual occasions arise, birth, marriage or death, Mulago Ganda invariably return to their rural homes to participate. Shops are then closed and those employed in Kampala seek leave for a day or two. It is true that such easy urban-rural-urban movement is made possible because of the proximity of Mulago to the Ganda rural-interland. But it is also possible because of the substantially greater wealth of the Ganda who can

afford to maintain a town house and a country estate. Non-Ganda, who generally hold inferior jobs, cannot move back and forth as easily although their tribal home may not be substantially further away than that of many Ganda.

In addition the Ganda have imported into the urban areas not only a network of kin-based relations but also those corporate institutions which make up the total structure of Ganda society. Thus in the peri-urban area of Kampala, Ganda own land in exactly the same manner as they do in the rural areas although they use their urban land for different purposes. Some land in the *kibuga* is held by virtue of the official offices held by the owners. The way the land is administered in the urban area has something in common with its administration in the rural area. Land disputes are handled by the judicial institutions of the Ganda.

Furthermore, the fact that most Ganda in Mulago and elsewhere in the *kibuga*, are never far removed from others who are of the same clan (whatever the operational importance of this grouping is at present), reproduces the basic structural categories of Ganda society in town. For Ganda, therefore, urbanism as a new and distinct way of life becomes simply an extension of the structure, operation, and the values of Ganda society as a whole. In this sense urban Ganda, while anchored in a kin-based network, are also part of an association-based urban network. Such a network is fashioned by new opportunities and demands, by new forms of differentiation, stratification and competition resulting from economic, political and social transformation.

For the Ganda, urbanization and urbanism as a way of life have not resulted in an abrupt break with the past. For urban Ganda, the model of the desirable society continues to be the traditions of the main features of Ganda life and culture. The urban non-Ganda, however, must construct for himself a pattern of social life and organization designed specifically for urban, and thus non-traditional, conditions. To achieve his ends he must participate in a network of contacts and associations which are radically different from those of his kin-based rural environment. As he progressively stays for longer periods in town, urban life presents itself as a more desirable social model and, presumably, a more clearly structured social order.

In this paper I have tried to point to a distinction between kin-based and association-based networks. These two models of social organization should not, however, be seen as mutually exclusive. They meet and overlap at numerous points. They are designed to meet different conditions. A kin-based network is designed to meet the demands of reciprocal roles; an association-based network is designed to meet, flexibly, new situations to which role responses are yet uncertain. Southall, I believe, is one of the first to attempt an analysis of comparative rural (kin-based) and urban (association-based) role functions. He writes:

Our hypothesis is that the empirical, commonsense distribution between town and country life may be given sociological precision by determining certain features of role structure in each case. In general, town life is characterized by role-relationships that are more narrowly defined, more specific, more unequally distributed between persons, more extensively developed in latent role structure, more numerous as a whole in relations to persons who are themselves living at a high spatial density, and more fleeting in their duration over time. In short, the passage from rural to urban conditions is marked by a rise in the density of role texture.[29]

While this might be a fruitful way of analysing a complex system of behaviour, I believe that the social network concept allows for the documentation of how in practice the individual and the group manipulate various roles both simultaneously and separately. In this respect social network analysis points to the way in which role performance is a part of the operation of a system, or a series of systems. To achieve a better understanding of how participation in various types of networks determines and structures specific roles, i.e., ethnic, kin, political, economic or recreational roles, micro-analysis is likely to point the way.[30]

[29]Southall, A. W., 1959, op. cit., p. 24.
[30]Southall, A. W., 1961, op. cit., pp. 25–30. In a forthcoming publication on Neighbourhood Units in Mulago, Kampala, I hope to apply some of the suggestions put forward by Southall.

30. The Political Implications of Urbanization and the Development Process

LUCIAN W. PYE

1. Urbanization is a critical process in the development of the modern nation-state. Historically all complex and advanced civilizations have sprung from the city, and in the contemporary world urban life is the dynamic basis for most of the activities and processes we associate with modernity and economic progress. Therefore any systematic effort to transform traditional societies into modern nations must envisage the development of cities and modern urban societies.

2. Urbanization is also a profoundly disruptive process. In nearly all transitional societies the early emergence of urban centers has produced a fundamental cleavage between the separate worlds of the more modernized elites and the more traditional and village-based people. This bifurcation of the social structure is usually matched in the economic realm by the development of dual economies. In the psychological sphere the rapid transition from the compact and intimate world of the village to the highly impersonal and anonymous world of the city can leave people with deep personal insecurities. Thus in a multitude of ways rapid urbanization can cause social, economic, and psychological divisions and

Social Problems of Development and Urbanization (*Volume 7 in series on "Science, Technology and Development," being U.S. papers prepared for a U.N. Conference on the Application of Science and Technology for the Benefit of the Less Developed Areas, Geneva, 1963*), *pp. 84–89. Reprinted by permission of author and publisher.*

tensions which, translated into the political realm, become sources of instability and obstacles to effective nation building.

3. Both the vital role of urbanization and its potentially disruptive consequences create perplexing problems of public policy. Of all the various aspects of economic and social development, there are few areas calling for more delicate and sensitively conceived policies. The simple formula of allocating more energy and resources may be appropriate for coping with most problems of development, but no such intellectually easy solutions are possible with respect to the issues related to urbanization. Effective policies must depend upon a wise blending of controls and sanctions with administrative and welfare programs.

4. Unfortunately it is peculiarly difficult to achieve sound and enlightened policies because there is so little accurate information and knowledge about both the dynamics of the urbanization process and the character and motivations of the migrants who swell the cities and become the objects of public concern. The lack of reliable information often leads to confused and contradictory impressions about such migrants. Policy makers in many such situations will vacillate between viewing the new arrivals as rustics and simple souls who require little attention and few public services, and seeing them as an anonymous mass, capable of being an unexpectedly explosive force, and

needing to be constantly controlled and isolated from the rest of the society. Uncertainty about the nature of the problem and the character of the people thus breeds unsure policies.

5. For general purposes of analysis and policy planning, it is useful to distinguish three distinctive patterns of urban growth common to developing societies.

6. The first, and generally most benign, is the shuttle pattern common to cultures with extended families in which there is a fairly constant movement back and forth between family establishments in rural and urban areas. The movement is frequently highly seasonal, following the agricultural cycle, and composed largely of able-bodied males. In such cultures both the urban and rural poles usually show remarkable absorptive capacity, as even sudden and severe influxes are readily handled with almost no demands being made on public institutions. The ties of family and relatives can provide all necessary minimum support, and a tradition of sharing poverty and enjoying even enforced leisure makes the pattern emotionally tolerable and even welcomed by some.

7. Economically and socially this shuttle pattern usually has many advantages. This is particularly the case if it coincides with a dual economy in which the urban sector represents modern, industrialized activities and the rural is still traditional agriculture. In such situations the apparently less developed side of the society can provide many of the social overhead and welfare services for the more developed side without the need for extensive new investments. Policy might well be designed to maximize the possibility of each side of the society or economy serving as a cushion for the other as each has its separate fluctuations and

rhythms of requiring more or less people. Often, however, we observe authorities striving to break this pattern of population movement either from a misplaced fear of the possible political and social consequences of what may appear to be unreasoned mass mobility or from an incorrect understanding of the conditions in which the sentiments basic to extended families can retard and inhibit industrial growth.

8. A second pattern of isolated individuals moving more or less permanently into psychologically and socially unprepared urban settings is likely to be far more politically dangerous. Whether the people are primarily pushed off the land or attracted to the promises of the city the result is a sense of rootlessness which provides a seed-bed for all manner of anomic movements. Urbanization which is built upon such disorganization lacks firm foundations and is not likely to develop into a creative urban civilization. This is particularly true if the rate of population increase in the cities is not linked to a rise in industry. That is to say, if lonely people come to the cities in search of a better existence and cannot even find the satisfactions of employment, they are likely in time to turn to increasingly antisocial activities in order to find a sense of belonging and becoming again a member of a community. In the past, extremist political movements have generally been most successful in recruiting their followings from precisely such populations.

9. A third pattern of urban migration is based upon communal groupings in which people of a common ethnic, religious, or regional background band together in moving to the cities. Often such people assume that they will be periodically returning to their rural origins, as in the shuttle pattern, but in fact movement tends to be permanent

and, except in the realm of sentiment, most ties with the old location are broken. Such people tend to cling together in the urban setting; and, committed to mutual support, they often appear to present a united front in opposition to the rest of the society. In some cases this pattern of migration crosses national lines, as with the Chinese in Southeast Asia; but in most transitional societies the pattern is also to be found in terms of domestic divisions as with tribes in Africa, caste and region in India, minority peoples in Burma, and regional cultures in Indonesia and the Philippines.

10. Politically and socially the communal pattern of migration can be disturbing to responsible national authorities because it appears to perpetuate and even strengthen potential divisive tendencies in fragile societies. Often there is genuine anxiety over the loyalty of the minority, and its conspicuous presence in the cities readily becomes a constant reminder that national unity is still to be fully established. Yet often these anxieties are excessive and based more on myth than reality. Indeed, frequently aggressive policies designed to break up such communal associations can be counterproductive in that they may in fact drive the minority groups into greater isolation and hostility toward the main society. It calls for truly wise statesmanship to be able to measure the point at which a communal grouping becomes more than an association of human beings seeking the security of collective identity and becomes a threat to the larger community.

11. The significance of these three patterns is that they remind us that no uniform or generalized policy can be advanced for handling the problems of rapid urbanization; different patterns of development call for quite different approaches, and not all signs of even disorderly growth need to be classified as a threat to stable political development.

12. Policywise the political problems of rapid urban growth call for two types of activities. There are first all the problems related to public administration and the need to provide social services for crowded populations. There is secondly the inherently political problem of providing such populations with a sense of participation in the larger polity. It is important to distinguish the limits and the utilities of each of these aspects of policy.

13. Modern governmental bureaucratic institutions have emerged from the needs of industrializing societies to cope with the problems of rising urban populations. And certainly every department of government has a role to play in dealing with the swelling urban populations of most transitional societies. Unfortunately there are no easy solutions to such problems, and the compelling need is only for governments to recognize their responsibilities and try patiently to carry out effective programs to the best of their abilities and in line with their resources.

14. Often governments have had the illusion that they could handle all the problems relating to urban growth by administrative measures. Colonial governments frequently believed that by providing a wide range of social services they could overcome the frustrations and tensions generated by the urbanization process; and many newly-independent governments have sought to cope with social and incipient political problems inherent in urban growth by introducing general administrative programs and opposing spontaneous political activities which may be potentially disruptive to their plans. In such situations the governments tend

to fail to realize that effective administrative programs are a necessary but not a sufficient condition for stable political development.

15. In most situations of rapid urban growth there is a fundamental need for the swelling populations to be given new channels of political participation so that they may come to feel that the national policy is responsive to their needs, aspirations, and anxieties. If explicit channels do not exist there is the danger that essentially political activities will creep into the administrative realm, and in time the rational and authoritative institutions of government may become heavily politicized. The result would then be a drastic decline in the possibilities for effective administration without a saving increase in satisfaction over having opportunities for collective and political associations.

16. It would be highly irresponsible to advance the general diagnosis that most transitional systems need more political activities. In some countries the teeming urban populations are so highly politicized that they have become in a sense loaded revolvers pointed at the responsible governments and on the verge of being triggered off at the slightest provocation. What is needed is more stable and predictable forms of political activity in which there is a greater consistency in the relationship between power and values. This necessary degree of consistency can hardly exist when (a) political action does not carry with it a need for responsibility, not in terms of some vaguely defined national interest or public good, but in terms of some clearly personal costs and risks for the individual; and (b) the values sought are intensely personal ones which cannot be maximized by public policy.

17. Taking up these points separately,

we may note first that whenever there is not some element of sacrifice, some sense of costs, some need to risk something in order to gain something else, political action tends to become frivolous, erratic and lacking in any consistent commitments. Whenever it is possible for people to enter and leave the political arena without having to calculate the personal consequences, their actions tend to become highly unpredictable and those with more serious intentions are left with few guides as to how they should rationally seek their objectives. It would seem that in many societies it is possible for large elements of the newly-urbanized population to rush into the political scene with little need for calculated commitment, and in a nearly spontaneous fashion disrupt the finer political relationships of the ongoing process. Then they can withdraw just as suddenly, leaving behind only confusion and uncertainty. Also, it seems that individuals can proclaim political demands, attract a personal following, and change their political views by personal whim with such ease that others are left in doubt as to what they really represent and how seriously they should be taken. The relations between these aspiring leaders and their followings are not defined in terms that can provide a clear basis for predicting their probable responses to foreseeable political issues.

18. With respect to the second point, it is clear that whenever political behavior is primarily motivated by intensely personal and private considerations there is no logic that can relate the specific needs of the individual to any specific goals of public policy. One policy program becomes as good as another. It is, of course, true that in all cultures one of the basic functions of politics is to provide an

outlet through which people can resolve personal crises. The therapeutic powers of politics are enormous for through it people can find a sense of identity and break the bonds of loneliness; discover new and less confining roles to play and overcome the grip of emotional inhibition; learn respectable ways to express aggressiveness and hostility; and actively seek respect and deference, power and adoration, the security of subservience or the elation of command; as well as a host of other forms of gratification. However, once these goals come to dominate political behavior, then any rational relationship between articulated policy objectives and personal motivation is broken, and meaning can only be found in the act of participation and not in the objectives of policy. It would seem that many of the restless urban elements in underdeveloped societies are unable to comprehend, or find quaint and unrealistic, the notion that one's political acts should be guided by predictions and evaluations of the possible consequences of various courses of policy.

19. The problem of stabilizing and giving rationality to the emerging urban politics in many transitional societies is thus nearly identical with the larger problem of establishing a responsive and responsible national political process in societies experiencing deep disruptions. The prospect of a more rational ends-means related system of politics thus rests upon the resolution of many emotional issues which arise from the rootless character of the new urban environments. The result is a paradox which is not fully appreciated by many sincere policymakers; namely, the prospects for stable modernization can frequently require that effort be made to give legitimacy and respect to essentially parochial elements in a transitional culture. That is to say,

people can often perform more effectively in the modern world if they are able to fuse in their own lives elements of their traditional identities with components of the modern world culture.

20. With reference to the specific problem of urban growth, it thus appears that some of the patterns of migration contain within them some stabilizing elements which should be respected during the difficult phases of the transitional period. In both the shuttle pattern and the communal one mechanisms exist for reducing psychic strain, and the task for policymakers should be one of devising ways to permit the degree of parochialism necessary for preserving the sense of community to be maintained while at the same time exposing to people new opportunities and new ideas of loyalty.

21. The problem is thus essentially one of assisting people as they are inducted into a new society so that they can emerge from the experience as constructive citizens and not frustrated subjects. To bring large numbers of people into urban life always means inducting them into some form of politics. The question is only whether they will turn to some constructive and legitimate form of politics or whether they will become an antisocial force. Historically, the experience of all modern industrial societies has involved the critical issue of inducting the urban population into the political system. If this process can be carried out without alienation and damaging consequences the polity can rapidly gain in benefits of an enlarged citizenry; but if the process is marred by tension and conflict permanent scars can be left on the polity which will be a continuous source of trouble for the effective operation of the political process.

22. It is worth noting that American

history provides a distinctive example of how large numbers of newly urbanized people, with culturally differing backgrounds, can be inducted into a political system, and strengthen rather than weaken the sense of national unity of that system. The essence of the American experience is the point we would make in closing, and that is that the heart of the problem lies in the area of handling the problem of effective political participation. If the new members of the urban community can be made to feel that they are also new members of a national community, and that they can occupy a place of respect and dignity in the larger community, then most of the problems of adjusting to rapid urbanization can be dealt with by routine administrative procedures. If instead of participation there is alien-ation, then an explosive situation can quickly build up which can only be constrained by the most severe forms of control.

23. Thus the phenomenon of rapid urbanization can either increase the dangerous gap between rulers and masses, which is so characteristic of transitional systems, or it can become a process in which this gap is greatly closed. For the latter pattern to occur it is essential for the authorities to demonstrate that they fully appreciate the problems, the sentiments, and even the parochial inclinations of the new urban masses. If the people feel that this is the attitude of those in power, they in turn may come to appreciate and be more tolerant of the problems and limitations of government.

The permutations and combinations of growth and structure patterns in the cities of newly developing countries defy brief description, let alone simple generalization.[1]

Urban geographers, human ecologists, and urban sociologists, not to mention urban planners, continue to apply their perspectives to these phenomena and are gradually beginning to discern generalizable relationships among what at first—and still to all except the most skilled observer—appear to be completely unique variations on the urban theme.

It would require at least one additional book of readings to sample fully the growing number of city-specific monographs on various features of these phenomena now appearing. Such casebooks will doubtless be published, but in the meantime only a token sample can be introduced here.

Norton S. Ginsburg (31) presents a most perceptive analysis of non-Western urban areas and incorporates extremely useful references to city studies for those interested in pursuing the subject further.

A comparison of Lagos and Leopoldville (32) investigates similarities and differences of a major Nigerian city and a major Congolese city.

The discussion of Kuala Lumpur by Hamzah Sendut (33) permits comparisons with urbanization in Southeast Asia—an area recently examined in detail by T. G. McGee.[2]

An introduction to major features of Latin American urbanization is available in the selection by Richard M. Morse (34), who also includes numerous leads to related literature for further study.[3]

[1] The readings comprising this part are most closely related to pp. 101–132, and in the case of Meier (35), pp. 135–145 in Breese, *Urbanization in Newly Developing Countries.*
[2] Introduction to Part I of this book.
[3] Cf. Leo F. Schnore, "On the Spatial Structure of Cities in the Two Americas," *The Study of Urbanization*, ed. P. M. Hauser and L. F. Schnore (New York: John Wiley and Sons, Inc., 1965), Chapter 10.

PART FOUR

THE DEVELOPING CITY

If it were to become necessary to select the single most pressing problem in cities of newly developing countries, the choice would probably fall between the problem of providing appropriate employment opportunities, and, the "squatter" settlements that invariably characterize such cities. These settlements have been discussed incidentally in other selections in this reader, but the magnitude and universality of their existence merits their being given special attention, as is ably undertaken by John F. C. Turner (35).[4]

Urban planning has by no means come of age in newly developing countries. The dimensions of the planning problem in urban areas is colossal in every respect in view of not only the existing and expected urbanization,[5] but also the necessity of tackling such massive problems with crippling shortages of both official commitment to the task and of professional staff, and perhaps most of all, financial resources. Yet some significant planning is already completed and in use; more is in prospect, in spite of the difficulties. Some of the more perceptive observers of the urban scene and urban planning problems in newly developing countries predict that because of the conditions that pertain, quite new solutions will have to be created. It is likely, for example, that technological developments may open the way to such possibilities. Richard L. Meier (36) continues to excite the imagination with his prognoses in this direction and concludes this book with its only selection on the subject of urban planning, which is sufficiently complex as to require an additional reader.[6]

---

[4] Cf. William Mangin, "Latin American Squatter Settlements: A Problem and a Solution," *Latin American Research Review* 2(3): 65–98 (Summer 1967). Excellent analysis and useful bibliography.

[5] Projection of urban population in newly developing countries encounters more than the usual handicaps, and is by no means yet refined. Some systematic effort to cope with the difficulties involved is being made by the United Nations' professional staff and others. In the interim the following materials may be found helpful:

Jack P. Gibbs, "Growth of Individual Metropolitan Areas: A Global View," *Annals of the Association of American Geographers*, 51 (4): 380–391 (December 1961).

Homer Hoyt, "The Growth of Cities from 1800 to 1960 and Forecasts to Year 2000," *Land Economics*, 39 (2): 167–173 (May 1963).

"World Population Trends," prepared by United Nations, Population Division, as Working Paper No. 17, October 1967; to be published as a chapter in the *1967 Report on the World Social Situation*. Originally prepared for fourteenth session of the Population Commission.

"Urban and Rural Population Growth, 1920–1960, with Projections," United Nations, Population Division, Working Paper No. 15, September 1967. Interim version, 144 pp. mimeo.

For general background considerations: United Nations, Department of Social Affairs, Population Division, *The Determinants and Consequences of Population Trends*, Population Studies No. 17 (ST/SOA/Ser. A/17), January 1953.

[6] In preparation by the Editor. For recent contributions to this Subject by Richard L. Meier, see his *Resource-Conserving Urbanism for South Asia* (Ann Arbor, Mich. Regional Development Studies VII, Department of Resource Planning and Conservation, School of Natural Resources, University of Michigan, January 1968).

31. Urban Geography and "Non-Western" Areas

NORTON S. GINSBURG

There is a considerable urban geographical literature on cities outside North America and Western Europe.[1] For the most part, such geographical studies traditionally have dealt either with the distribution of cities in countries or regions, frequently as an aspect of settlement distributions in general, or with the internal characteristics of the cities, in which morphology, sequent occupance, and urban genesis have loomed large. Since the middle 1930's, increasing attention has been given to studies of the relationships between cities and their hinterlands, to various associated aspects of nodality or centrality, and to comparative studies of morphology and function. In addition, fundamental questions are being raised concerning the nature of the urbanization process.

Specifically, as a result of a considerable literature on "non-Western" cities, there is reason to ask whether the urbanization process is unidimensional or multidimensional and whether it is culturally and areally, as well as temporally, differentiated. There is agreement, of course, that all cities bear certain resemblances to each other in both landscape and function, and that "systems" of cities have developed in all countries, evolving out of the socio-economic conditions that characterize them. The controversial issue, one that intrigues geographer, sociologist, and historian alike, turns to a considerable degree on the relationships between value systems and social organization, on the one hand, and the development of city systems and various types of urban morphological patterns, on the other. It also involves levels of living and rates of economic development as they influence the nature of cities in various societies and countries. In other words, if types of urban hierarchy or urban morphology are taken as "dependent variables," to what extent is "culture" as an "independent variable" significant in "explaining" the differentiation among them? Some light may be cast on some of these matters by a discussion of the urban geographical literature pertaining to certain major regions or countries, Africa briefly, and then southern and eastern Asia.

The Study of Urbanization, *ed. Philip M. Hauser and Leo P. Schnore (New York: John Wiley and Sons, Inc., 1965), Chapter 9, pp. 311–46. Reprinted by permission of author and publisher.*

[1] This essay focuses on the urban geographical literature as it pertains to Asia and, to a lesser extent, Africa, thus reflecting the author's scholarly interests. It is intended to be in the nature of a selected annotated bibliography, with such commentary as is necessary to point out the significance of some of the contributions cited. No attempt has been made to include all the relevant geographical literature, and only occasional reference made to the wealth of materials by nongeographers.

THE SUB-SAHARAN AFRICAN CASE

The earlier urban geographical literature on Sub-Saharan Africa is exemplified by studies of individual cities such as Whittlesey's studies of

Kano[2] or Jarrett's on Freetown,[3] in which the development of the town is examined historically, and attempts are made to deal with changing patterns of occupance as reflected in the changing urban landscape, or to use Smaile's phrase, "townscape." Such studies as these still make a major contribution to knowledge concerning urbanism in Africa, since they provide many basic data for purposes of general comparative morphological and functional study. Other studies, such as R. W. Steel's on Ashanti, have attempted to deal with the distribution of cities in various countries and relate it to their functions and size.[4]

Since the Second World War, greater concern with African city-hinterland relations and functional organization has been evidenced. The primary subjects for research have been the functions that a city performs for its hinterland and the effects different "sets" of functions have had on the creation of hinterlands and on modifying those hinterlands that developed when prior sets of functions predominated. The emphasis, in short, has been on the *process of urbanization*, broadly interpreted, and on the effects of modernization and political change upon urban functions, morphology, hinterlands, and city systems.

As an example of this perspective, Edwin Munger states: "Outgoing relationships . . . give an understanding of [city] functions and provide criteria by which the town can be distinguished functionally from others and by which changes in the functions of the town over various periods of time can be recognized."[5] He also asks: "To what extent do . . . varied geographic relationships [focusing on East African cities] coincide with existing political boundaries?"[6]

Similarly, growing preoccupation with culture contact, diffusion, and modernization is reflected in Larimore's assertion that:

Urbanism has been introduced into East Africa by British colonialism. . . . The impact of British colonial and political activity upon the subsistence polities of Busoga has reformed Busoga's patterns of spatial organization. The immigration of alien cultural groups to perform functions now necessary to Busoga's changing spatial organization has introduced cultural features of clustered settlement and Western urbanism to Busoga.[7]

Both Larimore and Munger deal with the hierarchical nature of spatial relationships in East Africa and with the role of the city as a center of change and as an organizer of area. Larimore especially observes the significance of racial segregation on urban morphology and the distribution of

[2] D. W. Whittlesey, "Kano, a Sudanese Metropolis," *Geographical Review* (April 1937), pp. 177–199.

[3] H. R. Jarrett, "Some Aspects of the Urban Geography of Freetown, Sierra Leone," *Geographical Review* (July 1956), pp. 334–354.

[4] R. W. Steel, "The Towns of Ashanti," *Compte Rendus du Congres International de Geographie* (Lisbon, 1949), Tome IV, pp. 81–93; and his "The Geography of Urban Problems in Tropical Africa," International Geographical Union, *Abstracts of Papers* (Stockholm, 1960), pp. 276–277, in which Steel pleads for fresh approaches to types of cities presumably unique to the region.

[5] E. S. Munger, *Relational Patterns of Kampala, Uganda*, Research Paper No. 21 (Chicago: University of Chicago, Department of Geography, 1951), p. 5.

[6] *Ibid.*, p. 3.

[7] Ann E. Larimore, *The Alien Town: Pattern of Settlement in Busoga, Uganda*, Research Paper No. 55 (Chicago: University of Chicago, Department of Geography, 1958), p. 6. To the extent that alien groups have provided a major impetus to urban growth, one might argue, however, that the East African case is more "Asian" than "Western."

urban activities and functions.[8] Both also note the relationships between multi-ethnicism and urban structure. As is true in most studies of this sort, as well as others noted later, field work was essential to research, since adequate published data are not available, and the mapping of field data provided the bases for raising significant hypotheses.

Other studies have dealt especially with the demarcation of hinterlands, as well as with the functional transformations that underlie the growth of cities in Africa. Some have taken the rather traditional form of descriptive port and port-hinterland studies, such as those by Hance and his collaborators, which do not overtly test general propositions about port-hinterland relationships.[9] Others, perhaps more sophisticated but also based on field work, are exemplified by the work of Manshard on hinterland and "urban-field" delimitation in western Africa, using techniques developed by Green and Smailes in England and Godlund in Sweden.[10] Manshard provides an excellent bibliography in his study of West African towns, in which he discusses the hierarchy of settlement and functional differentiation of cities. Like Steel, he is concerned with the relevance of changing cultural and political conditions upon centers of exchange in West Africa, and he experiments with techniques of central-place study used elsewhere.

In addition, there are a few studies that discuss the areal aspects of urbanization over large parts of Africa, among which Harrison-Church's paper on West Africa provides a good example.[11]

Similarly, Hamdan presents a thoughtful appraisal of the characteristics of political capitals in Africa, in which he notes the exceptional role that so-called "colonial capitals" now play on the African scene, and the marked peripherality, relatively small size, and primacy that characterize all but a very few of the capitals of the African states. Implicit in his argument

[8] For another sample study of these fundamental relationships, see H. C. Brookfield and M. A. Tatham, "The Distribution of Racial Groups in Durban," *Geographical Review* (January 1957), pp. 44–65. In this case, census-tract data were employed. The authors observe that ethnic pluralism in Durban extends even to the creation of two central business districts in that city. See also G. Hamdan, "The Growth and Functional Structure of Khartoum," *Geographical Review* (January 1960), pp. 21–40.

[9] See, for example, W. A. Hance and I. S. van Dongen, "Dar Es Salaam, the Port and Tributary Area," *Annals*, Association of American Geographers (December 1958), pp. 419–435. The specialized character of most African port hinterlands is in striking contrast to those in more developed regions or in others, such as China, where overseas trade and highly complex civilizations have resulted in port-focused hinterlands characterized by great functional diversity. Also their "Beira, Mozambique, Gateway to Central Africa," *Annals*, Association of American Geographers (December 1957), pp. 307–335. In each of these the authors use commodity-flow data as the basis for determining the tributary area or hinterland of the port. In the Beira study they also distinguish between the port's "national" and "extra-national" hinterlands and examine the implications of this "dualism" on its future.

[10] W. Manshard, "Die Stadt Kumasi (Ghana): Stadt und Umland in ihren funktionalen Beziehugen," *Erdkunde*, Vol. 15, No. 3 (1961), pp. 162–180. See also his "A Simple Teaching Model Explaining the Spatial Differentiation of Urban Functions," *Bulletin of the Ghana Geographical Association*, 1 (1960), pp. 21ff.; and his "Verstadterungsercheinungen in West Africa," *Sonderdruck aus Raumforschung und Raumordnung* (1961), Heft 1 (Berlin: Carl Heymanns Verlag, 1961). For references to the work of Green, Smailes, and Godlund, see the essays by Mayer and Berry in Hauser and Schnore (eds), *op. cit.*

[11] R. J. Harrison-Church, "West African Urbanization: A Geographical View," *The Sociological Review*, 7, No. 1 (1959), pp. 15–28. Steel's second paper (1960) cited above also fits into this category.

is the proposition that, with the exception of North Africa, and even to some extent there, the new African states, to a far greater extent than in Asia, are the consequences of colonialism and the products of new types of spatial economic, as well as political, systems, which have transformed the map of Africa in the past two centuries.[12]

A. K. Mabogunje expresses this theme explicitly in an as yet unpublished paper on Nigeria, a region in which a system of trading centers, albeit influenced by foreign, that is, Arab culture, preceded and laid the foundation for the existing distributional and functional pattern of cities. Mabogunje argues that "economic conditions call into being a system of cities. As such conditions undergo dramatic changes, the role of the cities is affected not uniformly but differentially," both in time and in space. He further concludes that cultural differences, even within countries, will lead to different urban functional patterns, and compares eastern with northern Nigeria as evidence, ingeniously using a sophisticated factor analysis of demographic data from the 1952 Census of Nigeria as his method. His statement of problem raises issues similar to, though more highly economically oriented than, those proposed at the beginning of this chapter, and perhaps even more relevant to the Asian case than to the overall African:

What happens when, on a system of cities developed under one set of market and transportation conditions, a new, faster, more effective, more capacious transportation system is imposed; what happens when this is done in a rather selective manner as to the area served; what happens when the new spatial economic integration which is achieved by this new transportation system focusses the flow of commodities within the system to a few selected points, with a view to facilitating the export of these commodities . . . ; what is the nature of the adjustments that can be postulated as taking place within the system in consequence of this new development; and what effects would these adjustments have on the efficiency of the system and the growth of the country?[13]

As interpreted in these materials, urbanization in most of Sub-Saharan Africa seems to be, for the most part, a modern phenomenon. Most African cities have grown out of Western contact and arisen either *de novo* or from village or small-town origins, although it appears that in West Africa indigenous cities, or at least high-density population agglomerations, of considerable size existed prior to the period of European domination. Possibly for these reasons, none of the studies cited makes a special distinction between "preindustrial" and "industrial" cities, although several emphasize the distinction between "precolonial" and "colonial." This is in part because Sub-Saharan cities appear to be such recent phenomena, even "alien"; in part because industrialization was not, with few exceptions, a concomitant of African colonialism; in part, because ingredients associated with traditional patterns of settlement appear to have been incorporated directly into the growing new towns and form part of the integral contemporary townscape. With few exceptions, the "preindustrial-industrial" dichotomy appears,

[12] G. Hamdan, "Capitals of the New Africa," *Economic Geography* (July 1964), pp. 239–253.

[13] Akin L. Mabogunje, "Urbanization in Nigeria—A Constraint on Economic Development" (Unpublished paper, mimeographed. Available from the author at the Department of Geography, University of Ibadan, Ibadan. March 1964). See also his "The Residential Structure of Ibadan, Nigeria," *Geographical Review* (January 1962), and his "The Evolution and Analysis of the Retail Structure of Lagos, Nigeria," *Economic Geography* (October 1964), pp. 304–323.

historically at least, to cast little light on the changing character of urban settlement in Sub-Saharan Africa. What appears to offer greater promise by far for further study is the impact of colonially derived administrative and transportation networks on the landscape and the consequence of areally differentiated economic development policies on urban structure, pattern, and hierarchy.

THE ASIATIC TRIANGLE— PAKISTAN TO JAPAN

Of perhaps even greater significance for the problem of "non-Western" urbanization is the great region of relatively dense settlement along the southern and eastern margins of Asia, not only because of the scale of the phenomenon there, but also because in these areas city-building and maintenance have stronger indigenous and historical roots. In fact, in countries like China, Japan, and India, most of the larger cities have their origins in sizable towns which have long had multifunctional characteristics. Since. this is the case in most of the Asiatic Triangle, other than Southeast Asia proper, locational inertia and deeply rooted concepts of what urban living means have substantially affected the contemporary urban landscapes, and, with them, the areal arrangements of functions and occupance patterns in general.[14]

Certainly, Asian cities, other than those founded and/or developed by Europeans, and even those in many

cases, display characteristics or morphology and functional organization that differ from those of the modern Western city. Some resemblance to the "preindustrial city" of the West lends credence to the proposition, as developed by Sjoberg, that many societies, given a certain degree of "urbanness," develop within them cities of a broadly "preindustrial type." On the other hand, the issue as to what sorts of cities are evolving from the older forms remains open. In fact, in Japan the larger and more modern cities display patterns that suggest both high inertial values and distinctive "non-Western" societal settings, which in turn may produce distinctive types of urban and metropolitan organization.

India

The morphology of the Indian city has been well described by Brush,[15] and his description is substantiated by at least two-score articles in the major Indian geographical periodicals dealing with townscapes.[16] Most Indian cities

[14] Although, as Brush points out, some foreign-developed port cities (in India) "exhibit a remarkable blending of Indian and European urban traditions, producing a modified kind of European townscape in which Indo-British culture evolved and still continues to flourish." J. E. Brush in R. Turner (Ed.), *India's Urban Future* (Berkeley: University of California Press, 1962), p. 58.

[15] J. E. Brush, "The Morphology of Indian Cities," Chap. 3 in R. Turner, *op. cit.*, pp. 57–70. This volume contains a number of valuable articles on Indian urbanization in general.

[16] See, for example, O. H. K. Spate and E. Ahmad, "Five Cities of the Gangetic Plain," *Geographical Review* (April 1950), pp. 260–278; R. V. Joshi, "Urban Structure in Western India," *Geographical Review of India* (March 1956), pp. 7–19; A. K. Sen, "Techniques of Classifying the Functional Zones of a City," *Geographical Review of India* (March 1959), pp. 37–42; U. Singh, "The Cultural Zones of Allahabad," *National Geographical Journal of India* (June 1960), pp. 67–104; A. B. Tuvari, "The Urban Regions of Agra," *Agra University Journal of Research (Letters)* (January 1958), pp. 101–113; M. N. Nigam, "Evolution of Lucknow," *National Geographic Journal of India* (March 1960), pp. 30–46. Many such studies are strongly historical in nature, and, as Janaki has observed, some may be concerned with the identification of functional zones "to the extent of finding zones where they do not exist." See note 19 below.

are the product of both indigenous and foreign traditions, but the melding of these traditions, with the partial exception of the great, European-developed port cities, has tended toward the creation of not one, but two cities, side by side, each with its own morphological and functional patterns, and rather poorly interrelated. Delhi-New Delhi is such an example. In such cases, dispersion of functions or of people from the older centers is proceeding slowly if at all, although dispersion from the "new towns" may be proceeding rapidly.

On the other hand, several of the larger cities of India are essentially foreign in origin. Nevertheless, even Bombay and Calcutta, for example, which are predominantly foreign creations, display only in highly modified form the hypothesized functional patterns of the Western city (for example, circular zones or sectors focusing on one central location, or a highly developed areal differentiation of functions). In fact, most are multinucleated, show only a modest development of a Central Business District, display little suburban development (and when they do, most socioeconomic characteristics of the suburbs differ from those in most Western cities), and in general either do not display the Western stellate pattern or display it in singularly embryonic form. In addition, most large Indian cities show the impress of British rule in the form of special districts for foreign residents, cantonments, housing estates for certain types of government employees, and the like. Furthermore, caste and ethnolinguistic differences serve to fragment even the relatively cosmopolitan and "postindustrial" cities into cells among which spatial interaction tends to be low. To some extent, these may be identified as "postindustrial" cities developing

in predominantly "preindustrial" societies, and the slow rate of transformation from "pre-" to "postindustrial" forms might be associated with lags in economic development. Nevertheless, the significance of cultural values and social organization in determining this slow rate of change remains unclear.

The general literature on Indian cities is admirably reviewed by B. F. Hoselitz, who appends a substantial bibliography to his review article.[17] Hoselitz notes the various types of social surveys of individual cities which have been done under the auspices of the Programmes Committee of the Planning Commission, but he prefers the type of treatment given Banaras by Singh in his important prototypical work on that city.[18] In that study, Singh is concerned not only with the townscape, but also with the functional relations among the several land use subregions within the city and those between the city and its "umland" or immediate hinterland. A more recent and somewhat similar study, dependent again on field work, is that of V. A. Janaki and Z. A. Sayed on Padra, a pioneering attempt to deal with the internal and external patterns of a small Indian town, and to document the relevance of caste and religion to the morphology of such a town.[19]

[17] B. F. Hoselitz, "The Cities of India and Their Problems," *Annals*, Association of American Geographers (June 1959), pp. 223–231. Reprinted with modifications in R. Turner (Ed.), *op. cit.*, pp. 425–443. Another useful bibliography which casts light on the type of literature considered important to at least one Indian urban geographer is found in A. Lal, "Review of Bibliography on Urban Geography," *National Geographical Journal of India* (September 1961), pp. 206–226.

[18] R. L. Singh, *Banaras: A Study in Urban Geography* (Banaras: Nand Kishore, 1955).

[19] V. A. Janaki and Z. A. Sayed, *The Geography of Padra Town*, M. Sayajiro University

Among the numerous studies of "urban fields" or "umlands," one of the more interesting is Reddy's on Hyderabad, which describes the evolution of vegetable marketing patterns; defines two vegetable hinterlands, one based on carts, the second on trucks; and observes the dominance of personal preference over distance and apparent convenience in the marketing structure.[20] An equally thoughtful study of Dacca also has identified key indices to the measurement of its "umland" and utilizes them to define it. The delimitation is tested by a formula based on nonagricultural employment in Dacca and other cities nearby.[21]

In addition, various attempts have been made to classify Indian cities according to their functions as measured by occupations and employment, of which Lal's method, an adaptation of the P. E. P.'s "location quotient" technique, is perhaps most useful.[22] Pakistan's cities also have been classified in similar ways by Kureshy and N. Ahmad.[23] On the other hand, V. L. S. Prakasa Rao, in his stimulating presidential address to the Council of Geographers (India), suggests a more sophisticated method of classification, which involves regression analysis and takes into account city-size differences.[24] Prakasa Rao also discusses methods for studying regional differences in the nature of the urban hierarchy and urban concentration and growth, including use of the centroid method and graphic correlations, which help

Geographical Series No. 1 (Baroda, 1962). A similar study, but on a less ambitious scale, is that of R. L. Singh and S. M. Singh, "Mungrabadshahpur: A Rurban Settlement in the Ganga-Ghaghara Doab West," *National Geographic Journal of India* (December 1960), pp. 199–206. Janaki and M. H. Ajwani also have produced an interesting study of the impact of urban influences on a nearby village: "Urban Influence and the Changing Face of a Gujarat Village," *Journal of the M. Sayajiro University of Baroda (Science)* (November 1961), pp. 59–87. Miss Janaki and M. C. Ghia argue, as does Mabogunje, that hinterlands vary over time with the introduction of improved and areally selective transportation facilities in their "The Tributary Area of Baroda," *Journal of the M. Sayajiro University of Baroda (Science)* (November 1962), pp. 81–99.

[20] S. N. Reddy, "Vegetable Markets and Regional Relationships of Hyderabad City," *Geographical Review of India* (September 1961), pp. 24–40. On the last-named point, see Mayfield's article cited in note 31.

[21] F. K. Khan and Mo. H. Khan, "Delimitation of Greater Dacca," *Oriental Geographer*, Vol. 5, No. 2 (1961), pp. 95–120. The formula is as follows: Dacca's proportional Range of Influence (as compared with city A) =

$$\frac{\text{Dacca's nonagricultural labor force} \times 100}{\text{DNALF} \times \text{City A's NALF}}$$

[22] A. Lal, "Some Characteristics of Indian Cities of over 100,000 Inhabitants in 1951 with Special Reference to Their Occupational Structure and Functional Specialization" (Unpublished Ph. D. dissertation, Department of Geography, Indiana University, 1958); also, "Some Aspects of the Functional Classification of Cities and a Proposed Scheme for Classifying Indian Cities," *National Geographical Journal of India* (March 1959), pp. 12–24.

[23] K. V. Kureshy, "Urban Development in West Pakistan" (unpublished Ph. D. dissertation, Department of Geography, University of London, 1957), pp. 271–278; and N. Ahmad, "The Urban Pattern in East Pakistan," *Oriental Geographer* (January 1957), pp. 37–39. A more refined typology, based on occupation data in the 1961 Census of Pakistan, has been developed by Q. S. Ahmad, Lecturer in Geography at University of Sind, Hyderabad. Q. S. Ahmad also used the statistical technique known as "nearest-neighbor analysis" in analyzing the distribution of cities in Pakistan, and presents a graphic model of the internal structure of these cities. Unfortunately, his study is not widely available. Q. S. Ahmad, "Urbanization in Pakistan" (unpublished Master's thesis, Department of Geography, University of Chicago, March 1963). Available on interlibrary loan.

[24] V. L. Prakasa Rao, "Macro-urban Analysis: Geographers' Contribution," Presidential Address to the Council of Geographers (India), *Annual Proceedings* (Cuttack, 1962) (mimeographed).

identify relations between population concentrations, size of city, and occupation. These techniques have been employed by him and others in studies of Mysore State and South India which are just becoming available.[25]

N. R. Kar also has pioneered in applying contemporary methods of areal analysis to Calcutta and West Bengal and combining them with more traditional historical and taxonomic techniques. With regard to Calcutta, Kar concludes:

Though the general trend of urban growth in Calcutta is in line with that of Western cities, its spatial character does not conform to the standard pattern or "norm" of urban and metropolitan growth . . . in the West. The smallness of the built-up areas, the absence of spread of . . . modern traffic nets over the Umland, the absence of a centrifugal drift of population into the fringe areas, and the low standard of suburbanization in the peripheral zones are some of the features of Calcutta and other Indian cities, which often pose problems of a gigantic nature. . . .[26]

In the course of his study Kar also observes: "that the spatial distribution of population in Calcutta shows a concentric pattern. . . . This pattern is of methodological interest because it conforms to the usual . . . pattern found in most Western . . . cities";[27] on the

other hand, with regard to the central business district, he states: "The very small area of this zone, in comparison with any Western city of its magnitude, the gigantic volume of administrative, commercial, and other activities and services carried on daily in this area, and the comparatively little urban renewal, building activity, and vertical extension, are features of strong contrast with those of Western Metropolises."[28] He further emphasizes, *inter alia*, the "mono-functional" character of Calcutta's zones of occupance and the absence of large "neighborhoods . . . having a multi-functional character and acting as 'quasi-cities,' as in big American and European cities, [which] are totally absent in Calcutta";[29] and, in recognizing the existence of an urban hierarchy in the Calcutta metropolitan region, he notes the "underdevelopment" of centralized services in the smaller towns in that hierarchy.[30] In another context, Mayfield has observed in the Punjab that Christaller's "space-preference" of the consumer is a culturally relative phenomenon which inevitably affects the size, location, and "service-mixes" of central places.[31]

Kar also has employed concepts developed by von Thünen, Lösch, Christaller, Platt, Carol, and Smailes to compare the urban hierarchy in West Bengal with that in parts of Germany and Britain, and to provide an introductory study of the process by which the urban pattern he calls "preindustrial," characterized by small regional service centers of approximately equal size, is transformed into

[25] V. L. S. Prakasa Rao and A. T. A. Learmonth, "Trends in Urbanization in Mysore State, India," an unpublished paper prepared for the 1960 Seminar on Urbanization in India, University of California. See also Maps 77–85 and 100–104 and accompanying text in A. T. A. Learmonth and L. S. Bhat, *Mysore State: An Atlas of Resources* (Calcutta: Indian Statistical Institute, 1960), Vol. I. On Map 81, "urbanism" is measured by an "index of concentration" based on the relations between population numbers and densities.

[26] N. R. Kar, "Urban Characteristics of the City of Calcutta," *Indian Population Bulletin* (April 1960), p. 36.

[27] *Ibid.*, p. 54, though socioeconomic characteristics may differ.

[28] *Ibid.*, p. 55.

[29] *Ibid.*, p. 57.

[30] *Ibid.*, p. 65.

[31] R. Mayfield, "The Range of a Good in the Indian Punjab," *Annals*, Association of American Geographers (March 1963), pp. 38–49.

an elaborate hierarchical structure with Calcutta primate, resulting from industrialization, locational specialization, and technological innovation. In this connection, he observes that although cities have been a part of Indian life for centuries, "there has hardly been a continuity of large-scale urban way of life in India since ancient [times], and 'urbanism,' as we see it in modern India, is of recent date, only about a century old."[32] This assertion is at variance with the commonly held argument that large-scale urbanization is part of India's continuous cultural tradition. It implies also (1) that the cities of Mogul India were in some ways alien to Indian society, and (2) that modern Indian urbanization is a process triggered by the Western impact on India.

The voluminous Indian urban geographical literature, stimulated by the contemporary enthusiasm for urban planning, is in part concerned with the morphology of landscape, but more important, with the application to the Indian city by a few competent practitioners of concepts developed in a Western context. In effect, this will mean stronger comparative studies and the modification of theories to fit different regional circumstances. Studies such as Kar's suggest major differences in both morphology and functional organization between Indian cities and models of spatial arrangements hypothesized for Western cities. The nature, causes, and longevity of

[32] N. S. Kar, "Urban Hierarchy and Central Functions around Calcutta, in Lower West Bengal, India, and Their Significance," in K. Norborg (Ed.), *Proceedings of the I.G.U. Symposium in Urban Geography, Lund, 1960, Lund Studies in Geography, Ser. B. Human Geography No. 24* (Lund: C. W. K. Gleerup, 1962). This volume contains 32 papers which form an admirable cross-section of contemporary urban geographic thought.

these differences provide an admirable field for both theoretical and applied research. One can speculate that technology, levels of living, capital available for urban improvements, caste and ethnolinguistic and religious diversity, and other cultural concomitants are involved, but to what extent and for how long?

Clearly, here is support for raising once again perhaps the most important question in cross-cultural urban research: To what extent are basic differences in culture, even given the spread of "modern Western" technology and values, likely to give rise to different urbanization processes and the creation of cities as artifacts that differ from culture to culture? Or, to phrase the problem another way: What kinds of cities can be expected to evolve in different societies as these societies make their decisions to select, adopt, and modify those elements that characterize Western city-building, functions, and structure?

Japan

The same questions can be applied to urban development in Japan, but there are a number of significant differences that bear upon a comparison of the two. First, Japan is a highly developed country economically as compared with India, and its rate of economic growth also has been high, despite lapses, for the past eighty years or so. Second, the growth of Japan's cities has been largely an indigenous phenomenon, one not substantially stimulated by foreign enterprise, political or economic. (Sticklers may cite Kobe here and perhaps Yokohama as exceptions, but these do not substantially alter the generalization.) Third, Japan, even more than India, has long been a highly urbanized country, not so much in terms of the proportion of population living in sizable towns, but in terms of the role of the city in regional and national life and the awareness among rural dwellers of the existence and nature of an urban way of life. The "insular-cellular" ideal-type of social-areal organization so often applied to the Sinitic world, including Japan, probably has less applicability there than in the Indic world.

Recognizing the importance of urban studies in Japanese geography, the Association of Japanese Geographers (*Nihon Chirigakkai*) established a Committee on Urban Studies in 1958. In 1959, this Committee, under the chairmanship of Professor Seiji Yamaga, published a report entitled *Research Materials on Urbanization* (*Toshika Kenkyū Shiryō*), much of which is devoted to a selected bibliography of materials on Japanese cities.[33] About 250 citations are given, all but a handful in Japanese, and only a dozen or so by non-Japanese. The organization of this bibliography is helpful in understanding the ways in which urban geographical studies are viewed by Japanese scholars themselves. The report is divided into five major sections, with a number of subsections:

Part   I. Theoretical Research on Urbanization
    a. General Theory
    b. History of Research and Research Methodology

Part II. Empirical Research on Urbanization in General
Part III. Urban Research Focussing upon Special Topics
    a. Land Use and Agriculture
    b. Population
    c. Residences
    d. Transportation
    e. Commerce and Industry
    f. Cultural Facilities
    g. Land Values
    h. Other Indices (to Urbanization)
Part IV. Special Research Themes Related to Urbanization
    a. The Great City and the Overgrown City
    b. Satellite Cities and Belt Cities
    c. Urban Fields
    d. Urban Planning
Part V. Other Literature

In this literature, every type of problem described by Professor Mayer in his chapter in this book [Hauser and Schnore (eds.), *op. cit.—Ed.*] is dealt with. Studies of land-use patterns, of urban structure and functions, of the spread of urbanized areas, of intra-metropolitan structure, of economic base, and of the functional classification of cities are included. Special attention has been given to the ways in which the metropolis extends its influence into rural areas. From the Japanese point of view, urbanization is intimately associated with the absorption of long-established towns and villages, and studies directed toward understanding the changes in form and function that have taken place under such conditions are numerous.[34]

---

[33] S. Yamaga et al., *Toshika Kenkyū Shiryō* (Tokyo: Nihon Chiri Gakkai, 1959). Since then, a member of the A. J. G. Committee has prepared an updated account of developments in Japanese geography which is based on and supplements this bibliographic report: S. Kiuchi, "Recent Developments in Japanese Urban Geography," *Annals*, Association of American Geographers (March 1963), pp. 93–102; and a volume by eighteen authors has just appeared in Japanese on the same topic: S. Kiuchi, S. Yamaga, K. Shimizu, and S. Inanaga (Eds.), *Nihon no Toshika* (*Urbanization in Japan*) (Tokyo: Kokon Shōin, 1964).

[34] For example, see S. Yamaga, "The Urbanization of Kiyose, A Hospital Town in the Suburbs of Tokyo," *Chirigaku Hyōron* (*Geographical Review of Japan*) (January 1959), pp. 35–41; F. Suzuki, "The Functions of a Small City in a Metropolitan Area: A Case Study of Mobara, Chiba," *Geographical Review of Japan*, 33, No. 3 (1960), pp. 187–199; N. Kato, "A Geographical Study of Tajimi, A Satellite Town," *Chirigaku*

The A. J. G. report reflects the interest in general methodology of Japanese geographers, who have long been familiar with major organizational concepts in settlement geography, such as those of von Thünen and Christaller, but their problem has been to fit them into the Japanese scene for which the basic assumption of "an undifferentiated unoccupied plain" seems incongruous. A recent exemplary article by Professor Kiuchi discusses the necessity for cross-cultural studies, the differences between deductive and inductive approaches to urban studies, and, as an illustration, some structural differences between Japanese and European and American cities.[35] He suggests that many of the same forces are at work in all of these cases (for example, short-run centrifugal forces leading to the dispersion of urban functions and so-called "urban sprawl"), but he also observes that the historical and contemporary cultural and economic circumstances in different societies, such as the higher premium placed in Japan on certain types of relict structures or land uses, may be making for the long-term differentiation of urban structures among nations.

Although the Japanese methodological literature indicates understanding of its Western equivalent, there appears to be semantic difficulty among Japanese geographers in comprehending the meanings of terms such as "urbanization" and "urbanism" as they appear in the geographical and sociological literature in the United States.[36] They reject the definition of "urbanization," for example, as meaning simply a certain level of population density, and point out that in some areas urban densities and agglomerations of rural populations are as high as they are in cities.

Hōkoku, Aichi Gakugeidaigaku Chirigakkai (*Geographical Reports*, Geographical Society, Aichi Gakugei University) (May 1959), pp. 13–19. Each of these stresses the duality of pluralism of functions associated with older central places incorporated into a metropolitan system. Since many official cities have come into being in Japan since 1935, and especially between 1953 and 1956, numerous other studies examine their processes of urbanization and metropolitanization as part of a large metropolitan system. See also the series of articles on the changing character of Kasugai, a satellite in the Nagoya or Chūkyō metropolitan system founded in 1943, in *Chirigaku Hōkoku* (*Geographical Reports*, Geographical Society, Aichi University), No. 14 (1960) (entire volume). For an appraisal of the recent policy of administrative area reorganization, see H. Masami, *Shi-chō-son Ikino Kaihen no Kenkyū* (*The Administration of Cities-Towns-Villages: A Study of Areal Reorganization*) (Tokyo: Kokon Shōin, 1961). All references, unless otherwise specified, are in Japanese. Where available, English translations of titles that appear in the original volumes are used, but in some instances they have been modified for clarity, in which cases the phrase "title modified" is inserted in the citation.

[35] S. Kiuchi, "Problems of Comparative Urban Geography," in *Tsujimura, Taro Sensei Koki Kinen, Chirigaku Rombunshū* (*Geographical Essays: A volume Commemorating the 70th Birthday of Professor Tsujimura*) (Tokyo, 1961), pp. 557–573. Kiuchi's standard work on cities, though now somewhat outdated, presents most clearly the catholic nature of Japanese geographers' approach to urban research: *Toshi Chirigaku Kenkyū* (*Studies in Urban Geography*) (Tokyo: Kokon Shōin, 1951; rev. ed., 1956).

[36] One section of the Association of Japanese Geographers' report contains a discussion of the meanings of these terms, based in fact on questionaires sent to various European and American urban geographers. Another discussion of the same problem appears in F. Takano, "A Typology of Urbanization and Definitions of Terms," *Geographical Review of Japan* (December 1959), pp. 629–642. Takano defines four types of urbanization as defined in terms of land uses and occupations: (1) a metropolitan type, (2) a regional center type, (3) a modern industrialization type, and (4) a traditional industrialization type, of which (1) and (3) are most significant in appraising the ways in which Japanese cities are developing today. See also T. Nakano's review of Kiuchi et al. (Eds.), *Nihon no Toshika* in the *Geographical Review of Japan* (May 1964), p. 255.

In another provocative article, T. Ishimizu reviews recent methodological developments and observes that studies of urbanization as a process tend to fall into two major categories, the one concerned with landscape evolution and the other with functional dynamics. He espouses the second group as being potentially the more useful and productive and believes that functional analysis can be best pursued by the examination of "ecological processes."[37] Ishimizu also lists a number of problems which have been receiving particular attention from his colleagues. Under the heading "Types and Stages of Urbanization" he notes Takano's distinction between "premodern" and "modern" urbanization, Shimizu's "primary" to "quaternary" stages of industrialization, and the latter's emphasis on the necessity for dealing with consumption and not merely production indices to urbanization. He marks the distinctions made by Kiuchi and Shimizu between centrifugal and centripetal forces in the urbanization process, and he notes the distinction between "contiguous" and "discontinuous" (or "leapfrogging") urbanization, the latter of which has been associated by Yamaguchi, Hama, and Suzuki with contemporary urbanization, but which Kobayashi has identified in the Taishō period as well. Ishimizu also cites the contrasts between scale levels of urbanization as reflected in the urban hierarchy and contrasts a "metropolitan" scale with what might be termed "regional." In this, he concurs with Shimizu who, in the report just cited, graphs the various stages in each of two main urbanization streams

—the "regional" and the "metropolitan." He emphasizes the unity of forces that change the character of the central areas of major cities and the suburbanization that goes on at their outskirts, and in so doing notes the relationships between changing land values and changing patterns of land uses and functional distributions. He then refers to the extensive literature on the changes in Japanese agriculture taking place along the urban-rural fringes of the larger cities, and concludes with Takano's and Shimizu's theses that modern urbanization in Japan is a function of a capitalistic and industrializing economic system, the elements of which interact with preindustrial elements to form urban artifacts enmeshed in systems with varying intensities of spatial interaction.

In contrast to the methodological literature, the empirical literature heavily emphasizes historical studies of urban development. The historical tradition is particularly strong in Japanese urban studies because Japan, among the Asian countries, has had so long a tradition of urbanism as a way of life, at least since the fifteenth century.[38] A wealth of historical data is

[37] Teruo Ishimizu, "The Present Status of Urbanization Studies among Japanese Academic Geographers," *Geographical Review of Japan* (August 1962), pp. 362–373 (title modified).

[38] One of the better examples of this approach is K. Kujioka's *Senshi Chiiki oyobi Toshiiki no Kenkyū: Chirigaku ni Okeru Chiiki Hensenshiteki Kenkyū no Tachiba* (*Prehistoric Regions and Urban Regions: Researches into Regional Evolution in Geography*) (Kyoto: Yanagihara, 1955). Part I includes an excellent introductory essay dealing with concepts in urban geography and ecology that are then applied to the development of urban systems in Japan as related to technological and social changes in the society. Some of his ideas are presented, in highly simplified form, in his "Feudal Traditions in the Forms and Zonal Structures of Japanese Cities," *Proceedings of the I. G. U. Regional Conference in Japan, 1957* (Tokyo: The Science Council of Japan, 1959), pp. 317–319. Interest in historical studies of continental cities also is high. See, for example, K. Yamori, "On the Distribution

available, and many Japanese geographers have had sound training in history as well, all this apart from the strong sense of cultural continuity that characterizes Japanese society and the academic subculture in particular.

There are numerous studies on the so-called "castle-town," or *jōkamachi*, which today forms the basic stratum of medium-sized cities in Japan and which accounts for thirty-four of Japan's forty-six prefectural capitals. These essentially regional capitals are almost always "diversified" cities in the various classifications of Japanese cities such as that of Y. Ogasawara, which apply to Japanese cities, with their excellent official data, taxonomic methods previously utilized in the West.[39] They form an indigenous underlayer to the overlayer of great cities and their industrial satellites, such as Tokyo and Osaka which, themselves castle towns, are more familiar to Western observers. The effects on Japanese urban morphology and structure as a result of these types of origins, as well as others such as temple and shrine towns and postroad stages, also occupy a fair proportion of the literature. One of the better known of such studies is in English,[40] but others, such as that of Matsumoto, are even more revealing of the role of inertia, as well as social change, in the structure of the modern Japanese city and in the creation within many of them of twin nodes, one of them associated with the old castle and its major gate, the other with the commercial quarter which developed after Meiji times.[41] In some cases, this morphological dualism developed even prior to the Restoration, however, as in Shizuoka and Yamaguchi cities.

This historical and evolutionary approach to Japanese city systems and internal morphology is by no means dominant, however, and other types of empirical studies with methodological implications illustrate the ways in which the historical theme is combined with the analysis of contemporary morphology and structural function.[42] More important, the great expansion of the urban population in Japan and the development of great cities to the

---

and Scale of Walled Towns during the Ri Dynasty," *Geographical Review of Japan* (August 1962), pp. 348–361 (title modified).

In general, Japanese urban geography should be viewed as part of a long-time interest in settlement geography. See Chap. 6, "Settlement Geography," in the *K. B. S. Bibliography of Standard Reference Books for Japanese Studies, with Descriptive Notes*, Vol. II, *Geography and Travel* (Tokyo: Kokusai Bunka Shinkokai, 1962) (in English).

[39] Y. Ogasawara, "Industrial Population I, II," Plates 10 and 11 in K. Aki et al., *Nihon Keizai Chizu* (*Economic Atlas of Japan*) (Tokyo: Zenkokukyoikutosho, 1954). For translation of legends, see N. S. Ginsburg and J. D. Eyre (Eds.), *A Translation of The Map Legends in the Economic Atlas of Japan* (Chicago: Department of Geography, University of Chicago, 1959), pp. 22–26.

[40] K. Tanabe, "The Development of Spatial Structure in Japanese Cities, with regard to Castle Towns," *Science Reports of Tōhoku University, Seventh Series, Geography*, No. 8 (1959), pp. 88–105 (in English).

[41] T. Matsumoto, "The Structure of Modern Castle Towns," *Geographical Review of Japan* (March 1962), pp. 97–112 (title modified); and "The Transformation of Modern Castle Towns," *ibid.* (May 1962), pp. 212–223 (title modified). Matsumoto relates the evolution of the castle town to its size and regional functions on the one hand and to Japan's changing social structure after the Meiji period on the other hand. See also his "Feudal Capitals and Their Changing Urban Structure in the Second Half of the 19th Century: The Cases of Yamaguchi and Shizuoka," *Geographical Review of Japan* (September 1960), pp. 473–482.

[42] See T. Murata and S. Kiuchi (Eds.), *A Reconnaissance Geography of Tōkyō* (Tokyo: I. G. U. Regional Conference in Japan, 1957) (in English).

point where these account for 64 per cent and 25 per cent (as included in the so-called "Densely Inhabited Districts" around the great cities) of the national population respectively, have occasioned an increasing number of studies concerned with the metropolitan region and its structure.[43] Many focus on the nature of the urban region and explicitly apply various familiar ideas of hierarchy, central-place functions, and spatial interaction to the Japanese scene.[44]

One of the more interesting and controversial of these appeared late in 1960 and attempted an analysis of the regional structure of Greater Tokyo (within forty kilometers of Tokyo Station), based upon a multiple-factor analysis of sixteen variables considered relevant to the metropolitanization process.[45] As a result of this analysis,

three underlying trend complexes were identified: one associated with forces (Factor 1) termed general "urbanization," which exhibited a high concentration at the cores of the conurbation and along major lines of railroad transportation, and decreasing intensities with distance from them; a second factor called "residentialization"; and a third factor, "industrialization." Factors 2 and 3, significantly, showed no such spatial tendency, but, when mapped, were "clumped" in certain areas widely scattered over the metropolitan region. As a result, the metropolitan region was subdivided into nine composite subregions, each displaying different associations of these complexes and "mixes" of the sixteen variables selected.

Studies of urban fields and city-hinterland relationships, in general, using techniques similar to those employed elsewhere, also have been common. Several, including one in English, have emphasized the importance of topographic restraints upon theoretically derived patterns.[46] Others have

[43] S. Muramatsu, "The Formation of the Hanshin Urban Region," *Toshi Mondai Kenkyū* (*Research on Municipal Problems*) (July 1959), pp. 52–65.

[44] See F. Takano, "The City Region Network as the Structure of Area," *Proceedings of the I.G.U. Regional Conference in Japan* (1957), pp. 486–490; and his "Introduction to Research on the Urban Region," *Chirigaku Hōkoku* (*Geographical Reports*, Aichi Gakugei University), No. 13 (1959), pp. 1–17 and Nos. 15 and 16 (1960), pp. 18–24; and his "Study of the Regional Structure of Metropolitan Area Patterns: The Case of the Tōkai Region," *Geographical Review of Japan* (January 1963), pp. 57–67 (title modified), in which he develops an index of "urban power" based on commutation and shopping patterns.

[45] K. Hattori, K. Kagaya, and S. Inanaga, "The Regional Structure of Tōkyō's Environs," *Geographical Review of Japan* (October 1960), pp. 495–514. This study, perhaps the first to use factor analysis for metropolitan subregional delimitation, utilizes a modification of Hagood's technique as described in *Social Forces*, Vol. 13 (1943), pp. 287–297, and is akin to (1) Berry's study "An Inductive Approach to the Regionalization of Economic Development," in N. S. Ginsburg, *Essays in Geography and Economic Development*, Research Paper No. 62 (Chicago:

University of Chicago, Department of Geography, 1960); and (2) J. H. Thompson et al., "Toward a Geography of Economic Health: The Case of New York State," *Annals*, Association of American Geographers (March 1962), pp. 1–20. The study has been criticized chiefly on the grounds that the variables were arbitrarily selected and are not necessarily significant to understanding forces at work in functionally differentiating the Tokyo metropolitan region.

[46] Y. Watanabe, "Types of Central Places in the Yokote Basin: Topographic Influences on Central-Place Distributions," *Science Reports of Tōhoku University, Seventh Series, Geography*, No. 8 (1959), pp. 68–87 (in English). Watanabe also is author of several papers which apply central-place theory to cities and areas in northeastern Japan. These also have been published in the *Science Reports of Tōhoku University, Seventh Series, Geography*: "The Urban Region of Sendai, A Study of Urban Concentric Zoning in Actual Pattern in Japan" (March 1953), pp. 30–52;

dealt with problems of measuring accessibility as a necessary precondition to the determination of urban fields and influences, and still others have examined the changes in the trade areas of towns that have been undergoing absorption into the growing metropolitan areas.[47]

The literature also contains a variety of specialized studies on the internal organization of the large city. One of these analyses is of the location of manufacturing in the Greater Tokyo area.[48] The authors conclude that locational instability has been greatest with regard to some of the "heavier" industries which require increasing amounts of

space as modernization is taking place, but that locational inertia in general is exceedingly high, especially in industries which follow the widespread Japanese industrial practice of farming out work to small companies which then return the processed raw materials to assembly plants about which they therefore cluster. This clustering, the authors argue, is characteristic of the areal distribution of Japanese industry in general and affects the structure of Japanese cities, large or small. Research also has focused on commuting, and the distribution of and explanation for contrasting nighttime and daytime population ratios.[49]

The distributions of service functions and business districts and their relationships to other urban characteristics have been studied as well. For example, Kitagawa has compared the business districts and retail functions of several cities in western Japan, particularly in terms of the relationships between size of shopping area and land values.[50] Using these variables as indicators, he arrives at a hierarchy of central functions within cities of different sizes that approximates for Japan Carol's ordering for European and American cities, although he notes the particular significance of wartime destruction of central areas in many cities in modifying the size, location, and complexity of their central areas. A related study of Sakai, now a suburb of Osaka but formerly a major commercial city, shows how wartime bombing destroyed the central business area, led to the

---

"The Service Pattern of the Shinjo Basin" (March 1954), pp. 77–90; "The Central Hierarchy in Fukushima Prefecture" (March 1955), pp. 25–46; "Kitakami City: The Study of Functions of a 'Local' City in Japan" (March 1958), pp. 54–69. (All are in English.) The *Tōhoku Science Reports* include a number of other studies by Fujimoto, Tanabe et al., which also deal with central-place functions and distributions.

[47] For examples, see S. Watanabe, "Accessibility Isopleths of a Local City and Their Relation to Its Service Hinterland," *Tōhoku Chiri*, Vol. 12, Nos. 3–4 (1959), pp. 43–48; K. Sawada, "Historical Changes in the Trade Areas of Towns on Tokyo's Northern Fringe," *Chirigaku Kenkyū Hōkoku* (*Geographical Research Reports*, Tōkyō Kyōiku University), 4 (1959), pp. 51–64, a comparison of data for 1932 and 1958 in which the trade areas of higher-order centers are found to be expanding at the expense of lower-order centers; K. Sawada, "Changes in the Trade Areas of Towns in the Tedori Fan Area of Ishikawa Prefecture," *Chirigaku Kenkyū Hōkoku*, 4 (1960), pp. 1–16, in which comparisons with an earlier study (1936) and based on purchases of cloth demonstrate the great expansion of Kanazawa's trade area at the expense of lower-order cities; and H. Kanazaki, "Nanao City's Spheres of Relationships," *Jimbun Chiri* (*Human Geography*) (April 1959), pp. 116–131, a study based on transportation services and the purchase of certain consumers' goods.

[48] Y. Tsujimoto et al., "The Distribution of Industries in Tōkyō," *Geographical Review of Japan* (October 1962), pp. 477–504.

[49] H. Hama, "Daytime and Nighttime Populations in the Tōkyō Metropolitan Area," *Toshi Mondai* (*Municipal Problems*) (December 1960), pp. 1361–1370.

[50] K. Kitagawa, "The Differentiation and Development of Central Districts within Cities," *Geographical Review of Japan* (March 1962), pp. 130–148 (title modified).

development of a second business center, but was followed by the recreation of the old center and the present situation in which two core areas rather than one serve the city.[51] Preoccupation with land values as an important device for urban areal analysis is reflected also in a study of Tokyo in which the author observes the peaking of land values in an exceptionally large (by Western standards) central area, their continuation at a high level along major transport (that is, railway) arteries, and their falling off elsewhere with distance from the core zone.[52] Another study confirms a high relationship between central-area land values and size of city;[53] and a study of Sendai on the relationships between prices of retail goods and the areal differentiation of types of shopping streets or areas concludes that ubiquitous low-cost commodities are poorly related to specialized-function shopping areas, but luxury goods shops clearly cluster in functionally central locations.[54]

Other studies concerned with housing and residential distributions find the classic concentric zonation hypothesis interesting but wanting on a number of counts, even though concentricity of other sorts may be ascertained. Although studies of socioeconomic zonation are numerous in the sociolgocial literature, ethnic or caste differentiation is of minor significance in a country which, despite the Eta and Koreans, is populated by a remarkably homogeneous cultural group.

Suburbanization in Japan, however, has proceeded at a rapid rate since the First World War and has been accelerated by the widespread destruction of the central portions of Japan's cities during the Second World War.[55] Unlike the Western situation, the spread of the city into rural areas has been associated with railways, not with highways and the increased use of the automobile, although the impact of the latter is beginning to be felt.[56] With few exceptions, suburban areas in Japan tend to be associated with lower-income groups, not with higher, and the penalty for being poor among Japanese urbanites means, on the one hand, living either in the shadow of a factory wall often on land subject to inundation from river flood or tidal

[51] K. Inoki, "Changes in Shopping Areas in War-Damaged Sakai," *Osaka Gakugei Daigaku Kiyō* (*Memoirs of the Osaka Gakugei University*), 7 (1959), pp. 124–138.

[52] T. Wakita, "On Changes in Land Values and Their Geographical Consequences in Tōkyō," *Toshi Mondai* (*Municipal Problems*) (April 1960), pp. 447–459. The author based his study on current market values of land and not on assessed valuations, as other students of the subject apparently have done.

[53] N. Sugimura, "The Size of Central Shopping Areas (Streets) and (Their Relation to) Size of City Populations and Major Services," *Geographical Review of Japan* (September 1958), pp. 548–555 (title modified).

[54] K. Kawajima, "Commodity Prices and the Classifications of Shopping Areas (Streets)," *Geographical Review of Japan* (April 1960), pp. 232–237 (title modified). A related study is R. Fujimoto's "The Shopping Street: An Element of City Structure in North Japan," *Science Reports of the Tōhoku University, Seventh Series, Geography* (March 1953), pp. 19–29 (in English).

[55] It is estimated that 40 per cent of the residential units in Osaka proper were destroyed during the war, and about a third of the city as a whole. See K. Inoki, *op. cit.*

[56] It is interesting to note that in a typical Japanese metropolis, Nagoya, nearly 80 per cent of all automotive vehicles in 1960 were either *not* passenger automobiles or were owned by corporative groups (for example, taxis and company cars), not individuals. This is precisely the reverse of the situation in the United States. An extensive literature on transportation problems is illustrated by Y. Kajimoto's "Urban Transport in Osaka and Its Environs," *Toshi Mondai Kenkyū* (*Research on Municipal Problems*) (November 1959), pp. 79–106.

wave,[57] or, on the other, traveling long distances to work.[58] Expansion of the larger metropolises generally has been in directions where drainage is better and conflict with paddy land is less.

Since 1955 or so, expansion also has been associated with the construction of public housing estates, or *danchi*, primarily for lower-middle or middle-class occupants,[59] and with the movement outward of certain kinds of space-demanding industries, which most often locate on the outskirts of sizable villages or satellite towns, some distance removed from the main built-up area of the conurbation. This "leap-frogging" phenomenon has yet to be fully explained, but it reflects partly the organization of Japanese industry, partly legal barriers to the easy conversion of wet-rice land to nonagricultural uses, and partly an agricultural revolu-

tion which has begun to release labor from agriculture for other tasks.[60]

The changing character of agriculture in the urban-rural fringe also has received much attention. Usually, but not always, land uses shift from paddy cultivation to even more intensive truck gardening for urban markets before land passes out of agricultural uses.[61] At the same time, part-time farm households or households only partly dependent on agricultural income near the larger cities have increased rapidly. In fact, nearly 70 per cent of *all* farm households in Japan obtain a substantial portion of their income from nonagricultural sources, chiefly employment in city shops, wholesale enterprises, and industries.[62] The rapid conversion of farmland to urban uses also has its effect on recreational activities and their spatial patterning, as apparently does size of city.[63]

---

[57] The problem of land subsidence in large Japanese cities, with consequent flood hazards, is particularly acute, given the site characteristics of most of them, the increasing proportion of reclaimed land, and expanding withdrawals of groundwater for industrial uses. See Hakaru Takamura, "Chinka suru Deruta chitai: Nishi Ōsaka no Baai" ("Subsiding Delta Areas: The Case of Western Osaka"), *Shizen* (*Nature*) (July 1960), pp. 13–20.

[58] "In Tōkyō, too, slums have been distributed near the city boundary [and] on marshy lands in industrial districts. The greater part of them are not in a deteriorated belt [near the central areas] as the slums in American cities are. They have migrated to [the] outer zones ... with urban development." Murata and Kiuchi, *op. cit.*, p. 69.

[59] Examples of studies of *danchi* are: T. Hara, "A Geographical Study of Housing Estates in Nagoya," *Chirigaku Hōkoku* (*Geographical Reports*, Aichi Gakugei University), No. 13 (1959), pp. 19–23, a study of the rates at which various types of services establish themselves in a new housing development; H. Mizuno, "Retail Trade in a Housing Estate," *Toshi Mondai Kenkyū* (*Research on Municipal Problems*) (September 1960), pp. 78–103, a study of the spatial structure of shopping in a middle to upper-middle class *danchi* on the outskirts of Nagoya.

[60] See T. Ishimizu, "The Present Status ...," *op. cit.*

[61] J. H. Thompson, "Urban Agriculture in Southern Japan," *Economic Geography* (July 1957), pp. 224–237. Of interest also in connection with commodity hinterland problems is J. D. Eyre, "Sources of Tokyo's Fresh Food Supply," *Geographical Review* (October 1959), pp. 455–476. Parenthetically, Eyre remarks, à propos the belief that radical changes are occurring in the Japanese urban diet:

The diets of the wealthier ... groups [in Tōkyō] include bread, Western vegetables and juices, salads, and other non-Japanese foods and food preparations in increasing number. Yet, the general pattern of Tōkyō food preference and consumption resembles that of smaller Japanese cities. Rice remains the basic bulk food around which smaller amounts of fish, noodles, vegetables ... are added for taste, consistency, or nutritional value.

[62] M. Saito, "Urbanization and the Increase in Part-time Farm Households in the Vicinities of Cities," *Geographical Review of Japan* (February 1962), pp. 77–88.

[63] Y. Koike, "Recreation for Urbanites: Types and Patterns," *Geographical Review of Japan* (December 1960), pp. 615–625 (title modified).

Other exogenous factors than the proliferation of housing estates and the transformation of agriculture also are entering into the modification of the urban complex. One of these, which is centripetal in effect, is the heavy emphasis on tidewater land reclamation within or near the larger cities, almost all of which are located on coastal sites. As a result of what is an almost entirely government-controlled policy, virtually the entire shore of Tokyo Bay is expected to be in industrial land uses within the next ten years, and similar developments are taking place near Osaka. This means that the populations of Japan's two largest conurbations will be cut off from direct access to the sea. Even apart from the losses accruing to the destruction of fisheries, the noncommensurable costs resulting from the destruction of potential recreational areas will be high.[64]

Another factor, exogenous to intrametropolitan systems and centrifugal in nature, is the policy of governmental agencies both at the local and national levels to discourage the location of new industries in what are perhaps inappropriately termed the "over-grown cities." This policy is reinforced by the central government's "ten-year income- doubling" program which has as one of its major clauses the development of large industial areas in designated potential "millionth" cities as far removed as reasonable from the larger conurbations.[65] How successful this policy will

be remains uncertain, but it undoubtedly will contribute to the creation of an industrialized-urbanized belt extending from east of Tokyo, through the Nagoya and the Osaka regions, and the Inland Sea to northern Kyushu, where the new "millionth" city called Kita Kyushu (Northern Kyushu) has come into being (1962) as a result of the amalgamation of five previously administratively independent cities— Moji, Kokura, Tobata, Yawata, and Wakamatsu.[66]

As must be apparent by now, a long tradition of urbanism, postwar reconstruction, and an unparalleled expansion of the urban population since 1952, has stimulated an already intense interest in problems of urban planning. There are at least three journals concerned with urban studies and urban planning in general—*Toshi Mondai*, *Toshi Mondai Kenkyū*, and *Shisei*. In addition, almost every city of any size has a planning agency of some sort, and many have been studied with an intensity that has not yet been reached even in the United States, Britain, and Sweden.[67] Geographers' contributions

[64] For a stimulating and even revolutionary proposal to use shallow coastal waters for the redevelopment of a metropolitan area, see the K. Tange Team, *A Plan for Tokyo, 1960: Toward a Structural Reorganization* (Tokyo, 1961) (in English).

[65] For a discussion of some of the urban planning implications of this policy, see N. S. Ginsburg, "The Dispersed Metropolis: The Case of Okayama," *Toshi Mondai* (*Municipal Problems*) (June 1961), pp. 67–76.

[66] The amalgamation question and its political ramifications form a major basis for controversy in planning and academic circles. The history of amalgamation in one highly urbanized area, Ōsaka Prefecture, is examined in K. Inoki, "Special Features and Problems of Amalgamation in Ōsaka Prefecture" (modified title), *Ōsaka Gakugei Daigaku Chirigakuho* (*Geographical Reports of the Ōsaka Gakugei University*), No. 8 (1958), pp. 1–18.

[67] As an English-language example, the reader is referred to *Basic Materials for the Comprehensive Development Plan of the Hanshin Metropolitan Region* (Osaka, 1960), Parts 1 and 2. These volumes were prepared for the use of a United Nations' Technical Assistance Mission to Japan, and unfortunately, only a limited English-language edition was published. A number of generalizations which appear in this chapter and are not otherwise documented are based in part of these materials.

to these volumes are substantial, and in the fall of 1960 the Association of Japanese Geographers and the Association of Human Geographers devoted their entire joint meeting to a conference on contemporary pressing planning problems.[68]

One of the extraordinary characteristics of the geographical literature on Japanese cities and urbanization has been the paucity of studies by non-Japanese. Most of the literature is in Japanese and, despite the English abstracts in the *Geographical Review of Japan*, it is generally not available to scholars without a knowledge of the Japanese language. Among publications in English and other European languages, however, there are the classic studies on cultural origins by R. B. Hall and G. T. Trewartha,[69] Schöller's excellent appraisals of recent metropolitan development,[70] studies of the urban fringe by Eyre and Thompson,[71] which focus more than not on agriculture,

and examination of site conditions and urban locations by Kornhauser.[72]

On the other hand, Japanese scholars are well aware of the work being done elsewhere on cities, and their publications display, as already noted, a commendable familiarity with basic concepts concerning urban functional organization, the dynamics of urban morphological change, centrality and accessibility, cultural inertia and other influences on the urbanization process, and ecological relationships that in the United States tend to be of greater interest to sociologists than to geographers. While arguing for more comparative and cross-cultural studies, they refer back frequently to questions of the cultural relativity of the urbanization process. Out of their work are coming some stimulating applications of Western-derived concepts and techniques and possibly some important modifications, as well as confirmation, of theories concerning the functions, structure, and patterns of cities and urban systems.

China

The vast geographical literature on Japan's cities is in marked contrast to the paucity of the literature on Chinese cities, which contained within them an estimated 105 million persons in 1960.[73] Reference here is to the

[68] See the program of the Autumn 1960 Okayama meetings of the two associations, subtitled "The Competition between Urban and Rural Land Uses," "Modern Cities and Transportation Routes," and "The Formation of Coastal Industrial Districts." A symposium on the "Regional City" at the Autumn 1962 meetings of the A. J. G. also dealt with some of these problems.

[69] R. B. Hall, "The Cities of Japan: Notes on Distribution and Inherited Forms," *Annals*, Association of American Geographers (December 1934), pp. 175–200; G. T. Trewartha, "Japanese Cities: Distribution and Morphology," *Geographical Review* (July 1934), pp. 404–417.

[70] P. Schöller, "Wachstum und Wandlung japanischer Stadtregionen," *Die Erde*, 93, No. 3 (1962), pp. 202–234; and his "Center-shifting and Center-mobility in Japanese Cities," in K. Norborg (Ed.), *op. cit.*

[71] Thompson, *op. cit.* Thompson also has worked on patterns of industrial location, as in his "Manufacturing in the Kita Kyushu Industrial Zone of Japan," *Annals*, Association of American Geographers (December 1959), pp. 420–442.

[72] D. H. Kornhauser, "Reflections on the Physical and Historical Roots of Modern Urbanization in Japan," Working Paper No. 10, New Jersey Seminar on Asian Studies (1962) (unpublished). See also his "Urbanization and Population Pressure in Japan," *Pacific Affairs* (September 1958), pp. 275–285.

[73] Leo A. Orleans, "The Recent Growth of China's Urban Population," *Geographical Review* (January 1959), pp. 43–57. In the 1953 census, 77 million were listed as "urban," but the definition of "urban" has not been made public and apparently no uniform standard was used in previous estimates (p. 44). If Orleans' pro-

contemporary literature, since there is an as yet virtually untapped source of information concerning Chinese cities in the thousands of *hsien* (country) gazetteers (*hsien chih*) which provide information over the last millennium. One recent study on the *hsien* capital, which has utilized some of these materials, illustrates the significance in China of the designated administrative city as a focal point about which the rest of Chinese society traditionally has organized itself spatially.[74] To some extent, these *hsien* cities might be likened to the "castle towns" of Japan, but they differ from the Japanese model in that they were walled, they were far more numerous (about 1900 before 1950), they were separated out at an early period from more important provincial centers (less than fifty), and they were established by fiat of a highly centralized government, or series of governments, which for perhaps two and a half millennia was in the city-planning, or at least city-establishing, business. In fact, the present distribution of urban centers in China was quite well defined by the end of the Han Dynasty (A.D. 221), and later extensions of the distribution

were to frontiers of settlement in the southwest, northwest, and northeast (Manchuria).

Thus, the *hsien* cities, and to a lesser degree the provincial capitals, have acted as the basic stratum of urban settlement, forming a close network (perhaps sixteen miles apart) of roughly comparable types of cities, functionally diversified, and underlying another stratum (somewhat similar again to the Japanese case) composed of treaty ports and great capitals or former capitals—for example, Pei-ching or Peking (northern capital) and Nan-ching or Nanking (southern capital). No systematic studies have as yet been made of the size and spacing of Chinese cities, or of the interrelationships that exist among various levels of what appears to be a clearly distinguishable hierarchy, although Chang associates the *hsien* capital with Christaller's *Kreisstadt*.[75]

It should be noted at this point that the treaty ports, including even Shanghai and T'ien-ching, were all based upon indigenous Chinese cities, usually *hsien* capitals, but their development after the middle of the nineteenth century was substantially as a result of foreign enterprise, despite their predominantly Chinese populations.[76] In this respect, the Chinese treaty port more nearly resembled the often heavily Chinese populated port cities of Southeast Asia than the Japanese

---

jection is correct, China has more people living in cities than any country except the U. S. A. and the U. S. S. R.

[74] S. D. Chang, "Some Aspects of the Urban Geography of the Chinese Hsien Capital," *Annals*, Association of American Geographers (March 1961), pp. 23–45. Chang also has published an illuminating essay on "Historical Trends in Chinese Urbanization," *ibid*. (June 1963), pp. 109–143. The distribution of the *hsien* capitals over the face of China is astonishingly even, especially when China's orographic diversity is taken into account. See map in Chang, "Some Aspects . . . ," p. 28. At sub-urban levels, a similar network appears in the "village fairs" or markets (as in the North Indian *hat*), as described, for example, in J. Spencer's "The Szechwan Village Fair," *Economic Geography* (January 1940), pp. 48–58.

[75] Chang, *ibid*., pp. 42–43. See also Chap. 3 of A. Boyd, *Chinese Architecture and Town Planning 1500 B.C.–A.D. 1911* (Chicago: University of Chicago Press, 1962) for some brief comments on this question.

[76] E. T. Williams, "Open Ports of China," *Geographical Review*, 9 (1920), pp. 306–334. In the year of publication there were 120 treaty ports in China, many of them inland commercial centers. A more elaborate discussion of the treaty port can be found in: "China, The Inspectorate-General of Customs," *Decennial Reports 1922–31* (Shanghai: The Inspectorate-General of Customs, 1933).

port city, albeit also Western-influenced and externally trade-oriented.

One of the few important studies of the "treaty-port" stratum is that of Murphey on Shanghai, the largest and most important of the treaty ports.[77] Murphey's rather traditional historical-geographic study helps clarify the ecological processes which help explain the growth and functional organization of Shanghai, and it makes at least one contribution of far-reaching significance. In a chapter entitled "How the City Is Fed," Murphey demonstrates that, even as a city of some 3.25 million, Shanghai was fed not from abroad but by a hinterland less than 100 miles away, in which a traditional agriculture prevailed and where the transportation system consisted primarily of a network of canals and an enormous fleet of junks and sampans. This finding counters one of the major objections to the possibility of the development of millionth cities in China or elsewhere prior to the Industrial Revolution—that a native technology and a primitive transportation system were congenitally unable to support a city of that size.

Various aspects of the morphology and external relations of several Chinese cities have been explored by Ginsburg, Spencer, and others, each observing the dualism characteristic of the treaty port or of the industrial cities in Manchuria which were partly Japanese creations of the treaty-port type.[78] No strictly functional classification of Chinese cities exists, largely through lack of data, although Trewartha has attempted a classification by location on transportation routes,[79] and Ullman has attempted to classify the contemporary Chinese city according to size and function.[80]

In fact, much of the recent English-language literature on the Chinese city has dealt with the size and rate of growth of the urban population of the country, a kind of exercise in "demographic intelligence," which has given rise to some marked disagreements among experts. The difficulty, of course, lies in the fact that from the 1953 Census few data about cities were made public by the Chinese, and Russian sources of limited scope have had to be relied upon.[81] Moreover, very little systematic information concerning cities has come out of Communist China even apart from the census information. Contemporary Chinese-language sources in urban geography are virtually nonexistent. Geography in Communist China is following a

[77] R. Murphey, *Shanghai: Key to Modern China* (Cambridge: Harvard University Press, 1954). A briefer description of Shanghai is J. E. Orchard's "Shanghai," *Geographical Review* (January 1936), pp. 1–31.

[78] N. S. Ginsburg, "Ch'ang-ch'un," *Economic Geography* (October 1947), pp. 290–307; N. S. Ginsburg, "Ch'ing-tao," *Economic Geography* (July 1948), pp. 181–200; J. E. Spencer, "Changing Chungking: The Rebuilding of an Old Chinese City," *Geographical Review* (January 1939), pp. 46–60.

[79] G. T. Trewartha, "Chinese Cities: Origins and Functions," *Annals*, Association of American Geographers (March 1952), pp. 69–93; and his "Chinese Cities: Numbers and Distribution," *ibid.* (December 1951), pp. 331–347.

[80] M. B. Ullman, "Cities of Mainland China: 1953 and 1958," *International Population Reports*, Series P-95, No. 59 (Washington: Bureau of the Census, 1961). A map of city distributions according to size classes is included.

[81] See *ibid.*; T. Shabad, "The Population of China's Cities," *Geographical Review* (January 1959), pp. 32–42; J. S. Aird, "The Size, Composition, and Growth of the Population of Mainland China," *International Population Statistics Reports*, Series P-90, No. 15 (Washington: Bureau of the Census, 1961); J. P. Emerson, "Manpower Absorption in the Non-Agricultural Branches of the Economy of Communist China," *China Quarterly* (July–September 1961), pp. 69–84; Irene B. Taeuber, "China's Population: An Approach to Research," *Items* (June 1964), pp. 13–19.

Soviet pattern which places highest emphasis on physical geography and economic geography, the second of which focuses primarily on aspects of resource development and the delineation of "physico-economic" regions suitable for planning purposes.

The prewar Chinese geographical literature contains a number of studies of Chinese cities, but the majority of these are conservatively historical and descriptive, if somewhat analytical, and none are primarily methodological.[82] Nevertheless, from this literature a simple descriptive model of the "typical" Chinese city, other than foreign-developed treaty ports such as Shanghai, T'ien-ching, and Ch'ingtao, or the very largest metropolises, can be assayed.

It began about 1000 years ago as a walled *hsien* capital, and developed a strong but small urban field and rather weak formal ties with other cities of similar size and function. Ties with provincial capitals and larger trading centers of *hsien*-capital origin often were rather close, however, and a clearly observable, though only loosely definable, urban hierarchy based on administrative and commercial functions existed. Internally, functional specialization was ill defined, except among administrative buildings, temples and their grounds, and all the rest of the built-up area. Density of the

built-up intramural areas varied markedly. In some instances, buildings huddled eave to eave or shared common walls throughout; in others, there were sizable open spaces, many in cultivation. Typically, the urbanized area had spilled out through one or more of the main gates, forming a "market suburb" and lending to the urban landscape a dualism reminiscent of other Asian dualistic townscapes, but unlike most of them, not based on contrasts between "traditional" and "modern." Although generally an administrative center and "planned" for this purpose, the city was in fact rather markedly multifunctional and acted as residence for a landed gentry possessed of strong attachments to an urban way of life.[83]

To a considerable degree, the provincial city and the indigenous capitals followed a similar pattern, site conditions permitting, but there was a somewhat greater tendency toward specialization, especially in terms of streets devoted to the manufacture and sale of specialized types of products. There was virtually no separation of places of work and residence, and little areal distinction between manufacturing, wholesaling, and retailing activities. The city walls enclosed only part of the total built-up area, although in some instances (for example, Nanching), the wall enclosed large areas of cropland.

The recently founded or developed treaty ports and industrial towns were (or are) of two types. One of these, the more common, displays the ubiquitous dualism observed in Indian cities and

[82] For example, see C. W. Wen, "Chukiang: A Study in Urban Geography," *Ti-li Hsüeh-pao* (*Journal of the Geographical Society of China,* now *Acta Geographica Sinica*) (January 1948), pp. 14–20; J. S. Shen and M. Y. Sun, "Chengtu: A Study in Urban Geography," *Ti-li Hsüeh-pao* (December 1947), pp. 14–30; and C. C. Wang and F. L. Cheng, "The Urban Geography of Paotou," *Ti-li Tsa-chih* (*Geographical Journal*) (March 1937), pp.1–27. Wang and Cheng classified about 25 per cent of the land area of Pao-t'ou as a contiguous commercial area and an equal amount as cultivated land, although the city was walled and a key transportation center.

[83] See H. T. Fei, *China's Gentry: Essays in Rural Urban Relations* (Chicago: University of Chicago Press, 1953), Chap. 5; and R. Murphey, "The City as a Center of Change: Western Europe and China," *Annals,* Association of American Geographers (December 1954), pp. 349–362.

those of Southeast Asia, as between an indigenous town, in the Chinese case, walled, and a new city, the latter often laid out in "planned" fashion. The former was usually small and densely populated (more so than smaller walled towns), with few streets cut through a maze of valleys, and "preindustrial" in personality. The latter contained Western-type buildings or Chinese shophouses (though taller than in the smaller towns), residential districts chiefly for foreigners or compradores, in which houses were set within spacious grounds or tall apartment buildings rose above the generally low roof level of the city; modern factories were located near the margins of the old town. Cities that fit this description to a greater or lesser degree include Shanghai, T'ien-ching, Han-k'ou, Mukden, Ch'ang-ch'un,[84] and, to a lesser degree, Canton. These differ substantially, however, as to the relative proportions of built-up area and population in old and new cities respectively, and as to the amount of change that has been imposed upon the old city (for example, little in Shanghai, despite its size; great in Ch'ang-ch'un where the Japanese created a new capital for Manchukuo).

The second type of city in this broad class is one almost wholly developed as a result of modern industrialization, but there are only a handful of these in China. Such a one would be An-shan in Manchuria, based upon mining and heavy industry, displaying many of the characteristics of a traditional Chinese city, but resembling in some respects also a British Midlands town. Somewhere between this type and the mixed type noted previously would be cases like that of Ch'ing-tao, in which virtually the entire existing city was constructed

by the Germans after the razing of the old Chinese town, which included a new "Chinese" town laid out alongside the "Western" and disconcertingly Teutonic new town.[85]

Variants on these themes are found in T'ai-wan, for which there is a notable descriptive literature, chiefly in Chinese, but partly in English, about Taiwanese cities.[86] These are even more mixed than most, representing elements of earlier Chinese settlement, Japanese urban development and planning, and later postwar occupance by mainland Chinese.

The contemporary Chinese city bears the indelible imprint of its history, but its changing character is obscured by lack of information concerning urban development. One reads of great apartment blocks and administrative buildings going up on the outskirts of Peking; of new industrial towns, reminiscent of the Japanese towns in Manchuria, rising alongside traditional walled cities (for example, Pao-t'ou, site of one of the major heavy industrial developments in mainland China), but detailed studies are lacking.[87]

This is a pity, since China most likely could be the crucial test case for hypotheses concerning the multidi-

[84] Ginsburg, "Ch'ang-ch'un," op. cit.

[85] Ginsburg, "Ch'ing-tao," op. cit.
[86] See, for example, C. S. Chen, "Cities and Rural Towns of Taiwan," Research Report No. 48 (Taipei: National Taiwan University, Institute of Agricultural Geography, 1953) (in Chinese and English); C. S. Chen, "The Port City of Keelung," Research Report No. 83 (Taipei: National Taiwan University, Fu-min Institute of Economic Development, 1958) (in English); and T. H. Sun, "Population Growth and Movement in the T'ai-pei Basin: A Demogeographical Survey and Analysis," Geography and Industries, 6, No. 2 (November 1961), pp. 169–243 (in Chinese with English summary). Chen and his collaborators also have issued a series of descriptive monographs on other cities in Chinese.
[87] J. F. Gellert, "Geographische Beobachtungen in Chineschen Grossstädten," Geographische Berichte (October 1962), pp. 142–152.

mensional courses of urbanization. As the situs of more cities of size, in existence for a longer period than those of any other cultural region, China is blanketed by a long-established city system, poorly integrated as compared with Western countries, but much more highly integrated, through administrative ties, market hierarchies, and indigenous and modern transport facilities, than any country in Asia other than Japan, itself a Sinitic cultural variant. Here lies, perhaps, the greatest, if as yet inaccessible, frontier for urban research outside the Western world.

Southeast Asia

Urbanism appears to be alien to most societies of Southeast Asia. Where cities exist, they are associated with Chinese or Chinese enterprise, with Europeans or European activity, or with combinations of the two. There are virtually no exceptions to these categorical statements, despite the urbaneness (sic) of the Khmer and their architectural achievements at Angkor. In its nonindigenous character, urbanization in Southeast Asia bears a much closer resemblance to that in Africa or Latin America, for example, than it does to neighboring areas where Indic or Sinitic civilizations predominate. There is, of course, a history of Southeast Asia, but it is not, unlike that of China and Japan, an urban history. It was writ on a landscape almost wholly rural, by societies to which urbanism was a strange phenomenon.

In almost every country in Southeast Asia, with its 220 million people of which about 25 million live in cities, there are large cities, but every one of these is the product of a merging of European colonialism with Chinese urbanness (sic). Partial exceptions might be Hanoi, with a small minority

of Chinese and several lesser towns in culturally Chinese Vietnam (for example, Hué); Rangoon, which was more Indian than Chinese until the Japanese occupation during the Pacific War; and Bangkok, which, strictly speaking, was never a center of colonialism, although it was and still is largely populated by Chinese.

In general, cities in Southeast Asia are relatively new creations, although they may have developed at focal points in existence before them. Most of them are ports. There is a poorly developed urban hierarchy, and primacy is common.[88] Thailand is perhaps the best and most extreme example of this phenomenon, and it also is characterized by the largest population size gap between the primate city (Bangkok) and the next stratum of settlement. Modifications of these propositions are most conspicuous in Malaya, where a communications network was relatively highly developed under British rule; they are less so but apparent in Indonesia, or more precisely on Java, where

[88] The "Primate City" concept was first introduced by Mark Jefferson in his "Law of the Primate City," *Geographical Review* (April 1939), pp. 226–232. Recently, Brian Berry has viewed primacy as part of a process of change in urban hierarchies, that is, related, *inter alia*, to economic development, in "City-Size Distributions and Economic Development," *Economic Development and Cultural Change*, Part I (July 1961), pp. 573–588. In general, primacy *in Asia* appears to be associated with low levels of living, a colonial heritage, relatively small size of county and population, and lack of an urban tradition. It may also, as Edward Ullman suggests, be associated with the port function, by which larger and wealthier overseas hinterlands are tied in with less extensive and poorer national hinterlands (e.g., Singapore as the entrepôt for the Malaysian world). In fact, the entrepôt function in particular may stimulate urban growth far beyond expectations based on size of contiguous hinterlands (e.g., Cebu).

Dutch policies of local regionalism created towns or encouraged the enlargement of previously small native towns; and they appear also in the Philippines which were under the firm control of Western powers—Spain and the United States—for a longer period than any other country. As a corollary, the phenomenon of the "hill station," though found elsewhere, is particularly widespread in Southeast Asia.[89]

These circumstances are reflected in the nature of Southeast Asia's larger cities which tend to resemble the China treaty ports or India's larger cities. Most are easily divided into Western and non-Western zones. Most have some sort of recognizable central business district associated with foreign enterprise and display a high degree of ethnic segregation. In fact, much of the urban landscape in the cities of greatest Chinese population (for example, Singapore or Kuala Lumpur) is virtually indistinguishable from that in South China where the ubiquitous shophouse also prevails. Suburbanization is poorly developed on the whole, and commuting is relatively unimportant, although the cities are attracting increasing numbers of immigrants from rural areas who tend to bypass the smaller towns. Functional segregation is moderately developed, less so than in the West, and modern industry has tended to localize either in the port areas or on the outskirts of the urbanized areas. All of these generalizations must be qualified, of course, when

applied to any one country or city. General discussions of them can be found in papers of Fryer, Ginsburg, and Murphey.[90]

For the most part, the urban geographical literature on Southeast Asia is scanty. Except for Malaya, little geographical research of quality is carried on in higher educational institutions within individual countries. The lack of comprehensive census data for most countries (Malaya has the best coverage) makes studies of the sort possible in Japan or even in India, impossible. Thus, many studies must either be field-oriented and covering relatively limited areas, or highly generalized and qualitative.[91]

For these reasons comprehensive studies of city systems in Southeast Asia are virtually nonexistent. One partial exception is Ullman's pioneering study of the Philippines, in which he establishes a hierarchy of cities based on size and functions, and compares it with theoretical hierarchies and those examined elsewhere.[92] He observes,

[89] J. E. Spencer and W. L. Thomas, "The Hill Stations and Summer Resorts of the Orient," *Geographical Review* (October 1948), pp. 637–651; also, W. A. Withington, "Upland Resorts and Tourism in Indonesia; Some Recent Trends," *Geographical Review* (July 1961), pp. 418–423.

[90] D. W. Fryer, "The Million City in Southeast Asia," *Geographical Review* (October 1953), pp. 474–494; N. S. Ginsburg, "The Great City in Southeast Asia," *American Journal of Sociology* (March 1955), pp. 455–462; Rhoads Murphey, "New Capitals of Asia," *Economic Development and Cultural Change* (April 1957), pp. 216–243.

[91] A discussion of data deficiencies and field work difficulties appears in R. J. W. Neville, "An Urban Study of Pontian Kechil, South-West Malaya," *Journal of Tropical Geographical Geography* (October 1962), pp. 32–56.

[92] E. L. Ullman, "Trade Centers and Tributary Areas of the Philippines," *Geographical Review* (April 1960), pp. 203–218. The author notes (p. 205) that an "extensive descriptive table of trade centers and tributary areas is available in mimeographed form upon request to the *Geographical Review*." A supplementary article, which attempts to better define the "real," as opposed to the "census," populations of some 29 cities is J. E. Spencer's "The Cities of the Philippines," *Journal of Geography* (September 1958), pp. 288–294.

however, both that the hierarchy is stunted and that it reflects the relative "stickiness" of Philippine society, as well as the insular character of the country. Even lower levels of spatial interaction and smaller trade areas might be expected in other countries in Southeast Asia, but data are not yet available to make comparative studies. A useful study by Hamzah on Malayan urban patterns casts some light on this problem, as does Withington's paper on Indonesian cities.[93]

Studies of urban morphology, at least for certain of the larger cities, are more common.[94] These tend to be descriptive and historical, but provide insights which point to some of the major problems that need further investigation. Hodder also has delved deeply into the matter of ethnic segregation in his historical study of Singapore,[95] and McIntyre has attempted to analyze the pattern of retailing in Manila.[96] Interest in planning problems

has generated some research into these cities, as in Singapore, Djakarta, and Bangkok, but generally results are not published or only superficially deal with fundamental aspects of spatial organization.[97] A number of nongeographical studies, however, are valuable in understanding the importance of ethnic and class segregation in determining the basic spatial patterns of cities, although few deal directly with this subject.[98]

The little evidence available nonetheless suggests that cities in Southeast Asia may come to resemble Western prototypes somewhat more rapidly than their equivalents in China and even in Japan and India. Without an urban tradition to fall back on, Western models are being followed to a greater or lesser degree, although this emulation appears to be restricted to the already large capital and port cities, and less in others. It is still true that even in the large Indonesian cities, the major form of land use is a *kampong*-type of residential area which physically is virtually indistinguishable except for densities from its rural equivalent. Nevertheless, the transformation of the largest cities from colonial to national capitals has meant an increasing con-

[93] Hamzah Sendut, "Patterns of Urbanization in Malaya," *Journal of Tropical Geography* (October 1962), pp. 114–129; W. A. Withington, "The Kotapradja or 'King Cities' of Indonesia," *Pacific Viewpoint* (March 1963), pp. 87–91. Withington observes that the "rank-size rule" cannot be applied conveniently to Indonesian cities. He also tabulates and maps the proportions of city populations that were Chinese and other foreign in 1930 and 1957.

[94] For example, see O. H. K. Spate and L. Trueblood, "Rangoon: A Study in Urban Geography," *Geographical Review* (January 1942), pp. 56–73; E. H. G. Dobby, "Singapore: Town and Country," *Geographical Review* (January 1940), pp. 84–109; H. J. Heeren, "Urbanization of Jakarta," *Ekonomie dan Kenangan Indonesia* (November 1955), pp. 696–736; W. A. Withington, "Medan: Primary Regional Metropolis of Sumatra," *Journal of Geography* (February 1962), pp. 59–67.

[95] B. W. Hodder, "Racial Groupings of Singapore," *Malayan Journal of Tropical Geography* (October 1953), pp. 25–36.

[96] W. E. McIntrye, "The Retail Pattern of Manila," *Geographical Review* (January 1955), pp. 66–80.

[97] A useful paper, however, is J. M. Fraser's "Town Planning and Housing in Singapore," *Town Planning Review* (January 1953), pp. 5—25. Several other reports on Manila, Saigon, and Jakarta were prepared as working papers for the UN-UNESCO Regional Seminar held at the Indian Institute of Public Administration in New Delhi, December 14–21, 1960. U.N., *Public Administration Problems of New and Rapidly Growing Towns in Asia* (Bangkok, 1962) (62, II, H.1).

[98] Among these are, Barrington Kaye, *Upper Nankin Street, Singapore* (Singapore: University of Malaya Press, 1960); Jacques Amyot, *The Chinese Community of Manila*, Research Series No. 2 (Chicago: Philippine Studies Program, University of Chicago, 1960); Donald Willmot, *The Chinese of Semarang* (Ithaca: Cornell University Press, 1960).

centration of Western-oriented cultural forms, including modern manufacturing, political-administrative offices, higher educational institutions, and mass communication facilities. In Malaya, for example, one finds government housing estates transforming the fringe areas and introducing, as in Japan, administratively derived occupance patterns which are not "natural"; and in Singapore in 1962 new flats were being provided at a rate of one unit every forty-five minutes, some of them well within the city where previously unsuitable land uses were converted (for example, the old airport at Kallang) or in the fringe areas which previously had been unattractive to people accustomed to think only of central areas as being desirable.[99] West of Kuala Lumpur, a continuous urban belt is in the making, extending from the swelling capital of the Federation of Malaya via the new University of Malaya campus and the wholly planned suburb (originally called a satellite) of Petaling Jaya, to the Selangor state capital of Klang, and an expanding Port Swettenham. Similar spectacular modifications of the urban fringe landscape are taking place in most countries in Southeast Asia, especially around Manila and Djakarta, but country differences in the scale and rate of change are predictable, at least roughly, in terms of the relative wealth of the countries concerned. The outcome of fundamentally political policies concerning urban development is unclear. Here again is a major research frontier, but one which, for the most part, is defined by the unpredictable parameters of political decision-making in politically unstable settings.

[99] W. A. Hanna, "Malaysia, A Federation in Prospect; Part VIII: Billets for Ballots," *Southeast Asia Series*, 10, No. 12 (New York: American Universities Field Staff, 1962), pp. 1–2.

32. Leopoldville and Lagos: Comparative Study of Conditions in 1960

UNITED NATIONS ECONOMIC
COMMISSION FOR AFRICA

INTRODUCTION

Since the Second World War, some cities in Tropical Africa have grown fast. Whereas before the War this region had only 5 cities with more than 100,000 inhabitants (Dakar, Lagos, Ibadan, Khartoum, and Addis Ababa), there are today 10 with over 200,000 (those already mentioned, plus Abidjan, Accra, Leopoldville, Luanda and Nairobi) (A-14)[1]. This rapid growth raises problems meriting attention, some of which it is the purpose of the present study to underscore. Leopoldville and Lagos have been selected as being very characteristic, and the comparative method has proved of particular value in emphasizing the existence of a serious basic problem, namely, the lack of coordination in the compilation of African statistics.

These two cities, similar in many respects, differ owing to their geographical situation, Leopoldville being inland and Lagos being a seaport. It is to be noted that the 10 cities mentioned above are divided into two equal groups in the same way. This fact is significant and represents a major consequence of the effects on Africa of the nineteenth century industrial revolution. Most of the great cities in history, especially in Africa, were situated inland (Cairo, Kairouan, Fez, Kumbi,

UN Economic Bulletin for Africa, 1, No. 2 (June 1961), 50–65. Reprinted by permission of publisher.

[1] Those figures refer to the bibliography at the end of the article.

Kangala, Zimbabwe etc. in the Middle Ages; somewhat more recently, Djenné, Kano, Benin, Abomey, Gondar, Tananarive). European expansion, which began in the fifteenth century and culminated with the industrial revolution, invested seaborne trade, and hence seaports, with an importance that they have rarely enjoyed in history (A-22). It may also be noted that Leopoldville is the second capital of Congo, the port of Boma having been the first until 1929. Here again the situation is characteristic; several inland African cities have replaced seaports as capitals (Pretoria for Capetown, Nairobi for Mombasa, Brazzaville for Libreville, Yaoundé for Douala etc.), whereas no example of the opposite movement has yet been noted. It would therefore appear that the status of a seaport as a political capital is more precarious than that of an inland city; that of Leopoldville has been strengthened by the railway, which has made it into a quasi-seaport without destroying the advantages of its inland position (A-13).

HISTORY

From the historical point of view, the main difference between the two cities is that Lagos alone already enjoyed some importance before 1885. From the beginning of the century it was even a flourishing seaport, in which the "merchant princes" built themselves luxury dwellings, especially those who

436

had returned from slavery in Brazil (B-29). However, with its some 20,000 inhabitants, Lagos was merely the modest outlet for the large towns of the Yoruba country, and in particular the metropolis of Abeokuta, which had probably more than 100,000 inhabitants. It was precisely around 1885, the period of the greatest wave of European colonial expansion, that the "merchant princes" began to give way to the large foreign companies, and for a time the population of Lagos declined (from 37,452 in 1881 to 32,508 in 1891), but began growing again on new lines to reach 73,766 in 1911, while Abeokuta, on the other hand, had its population reduced by half, its indigenous textile industry ruined and lost its position as metropolis to Lagos (B-26).

Leopoldville, which was founded in 1881, at first progressed much more slowly than Lagos, before taking a sudden leap forward which gave it almost the same population as Lagos about 1950. After the First World War, the two towns together experienced their first boom. Trade remained flourishing until about 1934; but there was little thought of industrial development. Although Leopoldville always cut a poor figure beside Lagos (32,000 against 99,000 inhabitants), the Congolese centre nevertheless saw important innovations. Reference may be made in this connexion to the unification of river transport services in 1925, the establishment of a textile factory in 1928 and the general expansion of the town of Kinshasa, situated 8 kms. from the station founded by Stanley but administratively attached to it in 1922 in a manner that appeared very artificial at the time. As early as 1914, Lagos was provided with a direct channel to the sea and many public buildings followed.

The world crisis of 1929 had consequences that were the more crucial because the crisis occured shortly before the Second World War. It delayed the economic expansion of the two cities for a time, but it also encouraged, mainly for reasons of economy, the promotion of indigenous personnel. It was also of great help in stabilizing and urbanizing the population, since the more unstable and more isolated elements were the first to return to their villages. Thus the Africans were ready to take the fullest possible advantage of the radical changes induced by the Second World War in colonial policy, particularly as regards industrialization. In Leopoldville what had been a small boatyard became a large factory, while Lagos served as a supply base for British forces isolated in the Middle East and, as such, was granted public works that Nigeria could not have afforded—for example, a complete anti-malaria drainage system (A-18). The movement thus begun was further accelerated in the two cities after the War and largely helped to provide economic support for the political changes which resulted in Congo and Nigeria gaining their independence almost simultaneously, in 1960.

TOWN-PLANNING

Both cities have grown up with no master plan, and there can be distinguished within them built-up areas representing the main phases of their development (A-18). In the Congolese capital an African "cité" and a commercial and an industrial district emerged as offshoots of the station founded by Stanley in 1881, and this part of the city continues to lead its own life as the provincial capital. Some 8 kms. away as we have said, a more modern-looking town has grown up around the port and along the railway, with the same three main divisions as the first, but on a large scale. The intervening area, which was given the name of Kalina, was designated as the seat of the central government as early as 1922, but remained almost desert until after the Second World War; even today a goodly part of it is occupied by the military camp. The year 1952 can be regarded as decisive, because it saw the beginning of a plethora of "cités" that changed the plan of the city. Until the last minute the Belgian colonial authorities did their best to maintain the principle of racial segregation by channelling the expanding white population either to the western limit of the new city, in direct contact with the Stanley station, or to another much smaller and isolated zone situated alongside an extension of the industrial zone at the city's eastern limit.

Lagos has grown in time on similar lines to Leopoldville, but in a different manner. The essential fact was that Lagos was founded on a small island, so that land was difficult to find—a problem that scarcely arose in the Congolese capital. Old Lagos, i.e., the Lagos of the nineteenth century, is still divided into three distinct zones representing the first settlements of the main population groups: 1. the original nucleus, which is almost exclusively inhabited by Yorubas clustered around the palaces of their chiefs and in particular of the "Oba" (king), 2. the "Brazilian" district, situated east of the first, which has continued to attract non-Yoruba Africans, and 3. the zone situ-

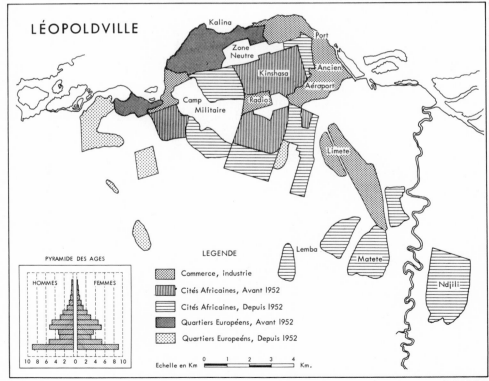

LÉOPOLDVILLE

Kalina
Zone Neutre
Port
Kinshasa
Ancien
Aéroport
Camp Militaire
Radio
Limete
Lemba
Matete
Ndjili

PYRAMIDE DES AGES

HOMMES   FEMMES

10 8 6 4 2 0 2 4 6 8 10

LEGENDE

Commerce, industrie
Cités Africaines, Avant 1952
Cités Africaines, Depuis 1952
Quartiers Européens, Avant 1952
Quartiers Européens, Depuis 1952

Echelle en Km   0 1 2 3 4 Km.

FIGURE 1

ated south of the first two along the southern coast of the island, which was developed by the Europeans and is divided into the shipping and commercial district to the north-west and administrative and cultural centre to the south-east. The railway encouraged the creation of the first suburb, Ebute Metta, which has remained functionally very mixed, while the racial segregation policy introduced by Lord Lugard in 1914 resulted in the creation of a white reserve at Ikoyi, in the east of Old Lagos. It is to be noted that in Lagos, as elsewhere in West Africa, it is the whites who have taken up residence in a special district, while south of the Equator, from Congo to South Africa, they have applied segregation in the opposite manner, i.e. by confining Africans rather than themselves to certain districts (A-20).

After the First World War, an attempt was made to clear the original heart of Old Lagos by creating the residential suburb of Yaba, north of Ebute Metta; but it was not until about 1950 that Lagos took on a really new look, through the extension of a shipping and industrial zone (Ebute

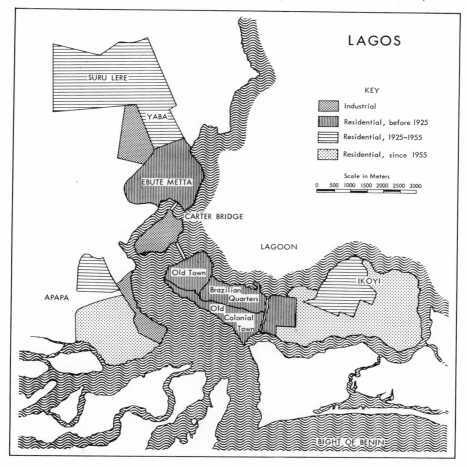

FIGURE 2

Metta, Ijora Island, Apapa) in the center of the town, and of residential suburbs methodically established to the north, south-west and east.

Like almost all modern colonial cities, Leopoldville and Lagos are today typified by untidy planning, waste of land and generally thin population combined with over-population of the older African districts. Leopoldville has now an area of 100 sq. kms. with a density of 3,800 per sq. km., which is low for an urban area; the corresponding figures for Lagos are 27 sq. miles and 14,400 inhabitants per sq. mile, or 5,600 per sq. km.

Attempts have been made to explain this situation by attributing it to the water problem: at Leopoldville, rivers winding through sand making building impossible without an expensive drainage system; at Lagos, the channel to the sea and the lagoon demanding equally costly bridges. However, in the first case the main cause of waste has been the racial segregation policy, which has resulted in the creation of a "neutral zone" with a vast military camp added in the very heart of the city. In both cities the distance to be covered lessens the economic value of urban concentration, which is precisely that it reduces distances to a minimum (A-18).

POPULATION

The most obvious difference between the two cities certainly lies in their populations, Leopoldville having far more non-African inhabitants than Lagos. At the beginning of 1960, Leopoldville had more than 20,000 foreign residents, legally described as "Europeans," including 2,000 in government service and 1,000 employed by transport undertakings. "Native" trading (*traite*) is dominated by 1,000 Portuguese families. Lagos, on the other hand, has no more than 4,000 foreigners, who, while certainly enjoying higher average incomes, have to face competition from Africans in all fields and at all levels.

Moreover, the African population of Leopoldville has increased much faster than that of Lagos, especially over the last two decades. This increase has been accompanied by radical changes in the demographic situation, although the ratio of males to females has stood at between 170 : 100 and 200 : 100 since 1937. The increase has been mainly in the child population, which rose by ten times between 1940 and 1955, against an increase in the adult population over the same period of only six times. It may therefore be assumed that the situation of town-dwellers, and especially of families, has become stabilized. The birth-rate rose from 34 per mile in 1950 to 50 per mile in 1955, while the infantile mortality rate fell from 196 per mile to 140 per mile over the same period and the general death-rate dropped from 12.1 per mile to 9.8 per mile between 1952 and 1955.

The demographic situation in Lagos is different, though less so than might be assumed from the apparent stabilization of population at 118 males for 100 females in 1950. Some relevant figures are given in Table 1.

The death-rate therefore remains fairly high, though it must not be forgotten that it is lower than the rate

Table 1

Vital Statistics, Lagos (B-4)

Year	Births	Infantile Mortality	Deaths
		Per Thousands	
1939	27.6	126.7	21.4
1950	55.9	85.7	16.2
1955	47.6	80.8	12.5
1959	61.2	32.2	13.1

for any capital in the world a mere half-century ago. The birth-rate is the oddest phenomenon accompanying the process of urbanization in Africa. There is no reason to expect a reduction, unless by a forced analogy with western urban societies. It is, however, certain that there is no connexion between this increase in the population through births and the economic situation; hence problems may be expected to arise in the future of which account must be taken.

MIGRATIONS

Despite the high birth-rate, the population of Leopoldville has increased mainly through immigration. Between 1945 and 1955, arrivals amounted on average to 25,000, and departures to 5,000 per year (A23). A survey conducted in 1955 revealed that only 25.9% of the inhabitants had been born in the city, and 80% of these were children under 15 years of age. On the other hand, 38.4% had less than 5 years' residence. As the immigrants were mostly adults, the age pyramid has a characteristic bulge, especially for males between 25 and 35 and for females from 20 to 25. There is a common saying that "the African population comes from all regions of Central Africa." While this is true on the whole, there are well-defined migration flows which serve to show that the city has a specific hinterland. Two thirds of the population come from the province of Leopoldville itself, which is mainly populated by Bakongos. The neighbouring territories of Angola and former French Equatorial Africa merely help to strengthen the Bakongo element, the city being therefore clearly dominated by this ethnic group, which is characterized by the matrilineal family system and contacts (that are much too easily forgotten) with Euro-peans since 1482. Belgian statistics show only the district of origin, never the tribe; but they suffice to demonstrate the growing importance of the Bakongo element, incomers from the province representing 66% in 1955, as against 67.5% in 1950 (C-36).

Only two other provinces besides Leopoldville have made an appreciable contribution to the population of the city: Equateur (8.9% in 1950, 7.6% in 1955) and Kasai (4.2% and 4.5%, respectively). The "Bangalas" come from the former, and their name is sometimes given to all non-Bakongos in the city. The contrast between the two groups is striking; but there are few statistics available to check it. A survey of independent workers conducted in 1954 showed that 3.69% of them came originally from the province of Equateur and 5.6% from abroad, but only 1.83% from the province of Leopoldville itself (C-7). On this point, therefore, the Bakongos are differentiated according as they are of local or foreign origin. However, as the "independents" are much less numerous among those coming from Angola (4.9%) or from French Equatorial Africa (8.5%) than among British nationals (24.6%), it may be assumed that the former find independent careers distasteful. The gradual decline of the Bangalas has destroyed the hopes reposed in them by the Belgian authorities and missionaries, who had imposed their language on the Army and hoped to see it recognized as the national language of the whole Congo, and in particular of the entire urban community of Leopoldville, which would thus have acquired a more intertribal character (2—27).

In the case of Lagos, there is no source of information on length of residence in the city; but the number of inhabitants born in the city fell from 42% in 1931 to 36% in 1950, and censuses show a rate of increase well above the difference between death-rate and birth-rate (B-17). The rate of increase reached an annual maximum of 5.8% in 1901–10, against an annual average of 1.3% over the 30 previous years, and 2.9% for the 30 following years. In recent years. most of the immigrants came from eastern Nigeria, where 11% of the 1950 population had been born, as compared with 4% of the 1931 population. When tribal origins were investigated, it was found that the Ibos of Eastern Nigeria were the only tribe emigrating to Lagos in substantial numbers (25% of the urban population, including 7% born outside their region of origin, and no less than 40% of children under 15 years of age) after the Yorubas, who come not only from the vicinity of Lagos but even from more or less everywhere in Nigeria (Yorubas born in Northern Nigeria represent 14% of the population of Lagos, as against only 4% for tribes native to the region).

This increase in the Ibo element stands in contrast to the decline in Hausa immigration; the Hausas represented 2% of the population in 1950, as against 3% in 1931 and 4.7% in 1921. This change has considerable social and economic repercussions, as up to 95% of the Ibos are Christian, educated (not more than 19.4% illiterate) and keen to work in offices, where there were in 1950 1,698 out of 11,205 employees of Ibo origin, as compared with only 579 business managers or clerks. The Hausas are, on the other hand, Muslims (93%), generally illiterate (66.2%), traders (377 out of 1,691 males) or craftsmen (281), but seldom employed in offices (31). It may be added that immigrants belonging to the small tribes in the south-west (4% of the population) have the same characteristics as the Ibos, and that immigrants

from other countries in Africa are few in number (6% in 1950) and without much influence.

FOREIGN INFLUENCE

The Belgians were far less interested than the French or Portuguese in westernizing their colonial subjects, and they habitually used Lingala to communicate with the Congolese, especially in the Army, where Lingala was compulsory. In a colonial situation it is nevertheless, inevitable that the subject should feel inclined to adopt his masters' customs, and above all their language and symbols of values. The European dress worn by all men reflects this attitude, which will change with time if the history of Lagos is to be repeated in Leopoldville.

Lagos has already experienced the attitudes now still obtaining in Leopoldville, and what is more important, the ruling class in Lagos had a chance to assimilate western culture much more deeply than seems ever likely to be the case with the Congolese. For many families of that class are descended from black Sierra-Leonese or Brazilians who had for some time entirely lost contact with their original environment. Nor is it uncommon to come across whole families that have attended the best English schools for three or four generations. It is therefore wittingly that they have introduced into their preponderantly western culture certain African elements of which they are no longer ashamed, such as dress, birth, marriage and death rites (supplementing western rites) and amusements. In the latter connexion, mention may be made of the "high life" dance as a supreme form of syncretism at which, for the moment, the Congolese balk, preferring to stick to either "western" or purely African dances.

Primary education has for long been much more common in Leopoldville than in Lagos, in accordance with the Belgian policy of educating the masses up to primary level before training *élites*. Since before the Second World War, almost all boys have attended school at least for some time; but it later became impossible to keep building schools at the same rate as the population was increasing. At the end of 1959, Leopoldville had 66,650 attending educational establishments, including 2,217 in secondary schools or seminaries and 247 Africans at Lovanium University. Intruction was given mainly in Lingala, with local programmes, and it was entirely free of charge. A different scholastic policy was followed in Lagos, dominated (as throughout the British Empire) by the principle that children should be prepared for the English Cambridge School Certificate, unadjusted to local conditions. Attendance at school remained low until 1956, when it stood at 38,072. Since that time education has been made compulsory and free of charge, and the number of scholars rose to 63,064 (including 4,798 in secondary and teacher training schools) in 1958 and to some 75,000 in 1959.

Lastly, conversion to new religions may be regarded as the acme of foreign influence (A-19). In 1949, the African population of Leopoldville comprised 58,000 Roman Catholics, 40,000 Protestants, and 1,300 Muslims, leaving 60,000 adherents to the traditional religions. At Lagos, in 1950, there were 35,600 Roman Catholics, 86,600 Protestants, 95,167 Muslims and only 3,500 following African creeds. Islam therefore constitutes a major difference between the two cities that extends far beyond religion. In Lagos, it helps to maintain a gulf between two sections of the population; but the Christians are themselves so divided that this gulf becomes less important. Since the Second World War, most Muslims have accepted the idea of secular education even for girls, while the Christians have emulated them in the cultural syncretism already mentioned. At the ruling-class level, where religious scepticism prevails, the gulf has almost disappeared (B-24).

INTER-TRIBAL ACCULTURATION

Quite apart from any foreign influence, urban life entails changed customs. Unlike village life, it imposes contacts with people of different, and often even unknown, traditions and the consequent need to assimilate a system of impersonal relations that would be of no use in the countryside. It also becomes necessary to substitute formal association (the "Gesellschaft" of the old German sociologists) for obsolete family and customary associations ("Gemeinschaften"). In town even the family or tribal association cannot prosper unless its members elect a management committee and loyally support it financially. In that connexion, it would be wrong to underestimate the force of the cultural change faced by a countryman entering the service of an enterprise, i.e. a formal association to which he gives his labour in exchange for his wages. There need be no surprise at the slow emergence of class-consciousness and the trade union spirit, even in Lagos, which is in that respect more advanced than Leopoldville. What is remarkable rather is the proliferation of all kinds of associations —signs of the desire to organize—and among them associations that have already acquired a considerable degree of stability (C-32).

Most writers describing African cities have emphasized the mixture of tribes found in them as compared with the village, where—so they imagine—only people of the same tribe are to be found. What there is in fact is not so much "mixture" as "coexistence", African towns being no more "melting-pots" than the North-American towns about which the same mistake was made in the past. In Leopoldville, the colonial administration and the missions did their utmost to encourage the tribes to mix, and most of the parcels of land in the old township of Kinshasa are occupied by people of more than one tribe. However, this situation (which goes beyond the administration's intentions since each parcel of land is supposed to be reserved for one family) exists only through necessity; it is the cause of much tension and, characteristically, does not prevent most marriages from taking place within the tribe (C-27). Urban life has nevertheless brought about some unification of cultures, mainly in two directions. First, it has mitigated differences and antagonisms between what may be called "subtribes." Strong organizations have been set up to work, and worked successfully, for the unity of the Bakongos in Leopoldville (the "Abako") (C-3) and of the Yorubas in Lagos (the "Egbe Omo Oduduwa") (B-32) to mention only the foremost. Secondly, people of all tribes seeking solution for the problems of urban life have often come to accept the customs of one particular tribe rather than a western model; this phenomenon is on a par with the cultural predominance of one tribe in each town, though no cause-and-effect sequence can be discerned.

In Leopoldville, the predominance of the Bakongos is incontestable, and colonial officials and missionaries have merely had to regret it, being unable to deny it. It is the more remarkable in that Lingala, the language of the

schools and the Army, is at least understood by most of the population. The main outward sign of it is the trend of the family sytem towards a matrilineal common custom and the adoption of the dowry, even by tribes, like some of Lake Leopold II, to whom it is unknown in their home area (C-28). And the dowry is one of the most vital problems, if not the most vital, since parents' demands are increasing more rapidly than suitors' living standards.

In Lagos, the preponderance of the Yorubas is to be observed particularly in the matter of land, Old Lagos having remained family property of the Yorubas, except for land expropriated by the State. Legally speaking, English common law has been in force in Lagos since 1861; but in actual fact not more than 2,900 out of 15,000 properties have been registered, the remainder being subject to Yoruba custom (B-7). This position may be compared with that in Khartoum-Omdurman, where 47,000 properties are registered for a population of 200,000 inhabitants. Furthermore, families of Sierra-Leonese origin (called "Creoles") and of Brazilian origin have been endeavouring for about fifteen years to eliminate any difference between them and the rest of the population, and it is to the Yoruba element they turn in seeking a local name, a substitute for European dress etc. In summary, however, the Yoruba predominance in Lagos is probably less strong than the Bakongo predominance in Leopoldville, certainly at any rate in the political field.

ECONOMY

Leopoldville and Lagos are poles of development for countries developed on different principles which have nevertheless resulted in giving their inhabitants remarkably similar per capita incomes ($62 in Congo and $67 in Nigeria in 1956) (A-2) and in inducing the same number of people to concentrate in these their capitals (380,000). However, the contrast between the two countries' economies explains that between their capitals. Congo is a thinly populated country (14 million inhabitants) which has been developed by great European Companies, with the help of a large number of foreigners, who receive nearly half of the wages and salaries paid, which reduces the Congolese population's per capita income to $43. Industry there supplies nearly half of the national product. Nigeria, on the other hand, is densely populated (36 millions); indigenous agriculture provides nearly two thirds of the national product, and foreigners are too few in number to have any appreciable effect on the per capita income.

The figures for foreign trade, which is the foundation of the economies of their capitals, are shown in Table 2.

Table 2
Foreign Trade (Million US Dollars) (A-1)

	Exports		Imports	
	Congo	Nigeria	Congo	Nigeria
1950	261	253	188	173
1959	489	458	308	502

Their foreign trade was therefore of about the same order of magnitude until the reduction of Congolese imports from 436 to 360 million dollars in 1957–58.

Against such background, the two capitals stand out as centres of concentrated activity from the points of view of both production and foreign trade. According to estimates for 1957, Leopoldville itself (with $2\frac{1}{2}\%$ of the total population) contributed 7%, and the rest of its province 20%, to Congo's national product, while the province of Katanga contributed 34% (C-31). Hence more than half of the national product came from these two provinces alone, and the Congolese economy appears to be based on two poles of development: Leopoldville with the Lower Congo and Elisabethville with Katanga. Moreover, Belgian colonial policy had favoured Leopoldville by creating a "national highway" (half railway, half waterway) by which about one half of Congo's products was to be exported. Thus the twin ports of Matadi and Leopoldville (river) had become respectively the second and third of Equatorial Africa, coming immediately after Mombasa. Traffic through the river port of Leopoldville in 1959 amounted to 1,739,300 tons of goods, and through the port of Matadi to 1,388,000 tons (C-13). 30% of the goods arriving by the river and 10% of the in-bound freight from overseas carried on the Matadi-Leopoldville railway, are retained in Leopoldville, for consumption or processing, according to a 1955 estimate.

The share of Lagos in Nigeria's national product has been merged in surveys on the subject with that of the whole of Western Nigeria; but the latter's superiority over other regions is well established ($29 per head, against $16 in the North), and Lagos certainly contributes more than the 1% of the population of the country its inhabitants represent (B-2). Electricity consumption is a good indication in this respect: 46% of the total in the commercial and industrial sector, 50% in the domestic sector. As to foreign trade, traffic handled at Lagos in 1959 amounted to 3,457,000 tons and represented 67% of Nigeria's total exports and 53% of its total imports.

ECONOMIC FUNCTION

Despite the importance of their political status, Leopoldville and Lagos are first and foremost business centres that have arisen through shipping activities. The share of the State in the estimated product of the city of Leopoldville in 1957 was 1,700 million francs ($34 million), out of 5,000 million francs ($100 millions) (C-31). There is no corresponding study for Lagos; but the same preponderance of the private sector is borne out by figures such as those for employment in 1959 (Table 3).

Table 3

Employment, Lagos, 1959 (B-6)

	Establishments	Employees	Wages £
Public sector			
Lagos	116	30,400	551,000
Nigeria	3,184	221,400	1,719,000
Private sector			
Lagos	378	65,500	1,041,000
Nigeria	1,621	251,300	3,054,000

A main characteristic of the two cities is the chain reaction that their initial activities have provoked; the existence of a port resulting in the appearance of a variety of workshops and finally of actual factories, then shops, building enterprises and all kinds of services to meet the needs of an ever-growing population. The importance of Lagos in Nigeria's economy can be gauged from such figures as 38% of new car licences, 27% of renewals, 56% of telephone calls, 7 hotels out of 19, 4 daily newspapers out of 20, 18 periodicals out of 19 etc.

The same holds true for Leopoldville, which, according to the *Annuaire du Congo Belge* for 1958, had 15 cinemas out of 88, 13 hotels out of 271, 310 cafés out of approximately 1,000, 3 breweries out of 7, 4 shoe factories out of 8, 92 building enterprises out of 563, 23 metal-working firms out of 67, 2 daily news papers out of 7, 20 periodicals for Europeans out of 67, 11 periodicals for Africans out of 53, etc. (C-14) Yet in all spheres it is to be noted that Elisabethville is on a par with the capital, so that Congo always appears to have two poles of development, while Nigeria has only one.

Despite these resemblances, the two cities are very dissimilar industrially. Apart from the port and the railway, Leopoldville has no less than 100 industrial companies, the activities of more than half of which, with a total capital of some 3,000 million francs ($60 millions) are entirely concentrated in the city. Foremost among the latter are a brewery with a capital of 500 million francs, a spinning-mill with a capital of 486 million francs and an electric power station with a capital of 360 million francs (C-14). Lagos is far from reaching this level of industrialization, and the local capitalists—these do exist, and this makes Lagos very different from Leopoldville—prefer to invest their money in commerce and building rather than to follow the Government's exhortations to invest in industrialization. There do exist a brewery, a metal container factory, a margarine factory and a soap factory etc.—but only one of each, and they are small. North of Lagos, outside Federal territory, the Government of Western Nigeria has developed a rival industrial estate to Apapa; but the two estates taken together are of modest proportions, while the political question has already arisen as to when the Federal territory of Lagos will absorb this competitor.

PUBLIC SERVICES

The progress of a city can be fairly well gauged from the scope of its public services, such as water and electricity supplies, transport etc. In this field, as in others, Leopoldville has long been remarkable for its strict racial segregation. Nevertheless, the Congolese population there had a goodly number of free and permanent public fountains, which enabled the people to maintain their tradition of extreme cleanliness (C-27). Piping to individual dwellings began after the War and reached 7,000 (Africans only) in 1956, and water consumption for that year amounted to 35,000 cubic meters per day for the whole population. In the same year, 1,300 Congolese received an electricity supply. Power consumption rose from 7.5 million kilowatts in 1942 to 20 million in 1945; then it doubled in 5 years and quadrupled in 10, to reach 122 million kilowatts in 1958 (A-23).

There has in principle never been racial discrimination in Lagos, except as regards the Ikoyi residential reserve; nevertheless, the mass of the population has to make do with public fountains, and the water supply problem has been acute since 1898. During the Second World War daily consumption fell to 18 gallons per head, the population having increased much faster than water supplies (3.03 million gallons in 1938, 3.90 million in 1945) (A-18). In 1959, it amounted to 9 million gallons per day, or 25 gallons per head of population. The electricity consumption curve is surprisingly similar to that for Leopoldville; 6.2 million kilowatts in 1935, 18.6 in 1945 and 119.8 in 1959. This is the more remarkable in that indigenous private consumption is infinitesimal in the capital of Congo, while it predominates in Lagos, which has more than 30,000 subscribers (B-1).

The great area of the two cities and the waste of land create serious transport problems. There are 185 kms. of macadamized streets alone in Leopoldville (132 in the European districts) and 161 in Lagos (A-24). The most popular vehicle in the two cities is the bicycle; but it is not suitable for everybody.

Leopoldville had no public transport system for the Congolese before August 1955, when a service was introduced, which had 202 vehicles and carried 33 million passengers in 1959. The two longest routes cover some 70 miles, between Kinshasa and the south and south-west. In Lagos a private service of 32 buses was taken over in 1958 by the municipality, which added 53 more vehicles. The two main lines cover about 6 miles each, from the entrance to Ikoyi to the northern and south-western limits of the city. There are also some 20 privately-owned buses, which the municipality has decided to buy. It should be noted that in Lagos many workers live in the very centre of the city, so that the transport problem is not so acute as in Leopoldville, while there is an African upper class that owns at least half of the 11,000 motor vehicles in the city. Traffic in 1960 nevertheless passed the 40 million mark, with 10,000 regular passengers per day and 5,000 children per school day.

LABOUR

The two cities are about equal as regards total manpower (male): 79,525 in Leopoldville (C-36) and 78,058 (B-17) in Lagos, in 1950 and 114,000

(C-31) and 119,000 (B-6) respectively, at the end of 1959. They differ, however, in the use they make of their available labour.

TYPES OF ENTERPRISES

The public sector is less important in the Congolese capital, where the number of African officials amounted to 4,222 in 1950 and to 12,000 in 1959. The corresponding figures for Lagos were 11,391 in 1950 and 30,400 in 1959. Allowance must be made for the fact that Leopoldville has more than 2000 "European" officials, while Lagos has not even 500 "expatriate" officials, though this does not suffice to equalize the total figures. It is regrettable that no particulars are obtainable at Leopoldville concerning the labour force of the municipal undertakings ("régies"), which employ most transport, electric power and building workers. The latter are lumped together with workers in the private sector. In Lagos the public corporations employ no less than 21,400 workers, whom we include in the private sector for purposes of comparison.

The large enterprise is characteristic of colonial economies. It is predominant in the two cities with which we are here concerned. Leopoldville has 83 firms with more than 100 employees each, amounting to a total of 39,000 men, and 213 other firms with between 20 and 100 employees, making a total of no more than 3,500. There remain 3,500 men employed by small enterprises and 12,000 "independents". Lagos has 175 enterprises with 100 or more employees and 185 with 20–99 employees.

INDUSTRY

There are more people employed in the industrial sector than might be supposed considering production figures, which are still low, especially in Lagos. Leopoldville has 13 mills with 3,364 employees, 2 chemical factories, with 412 employees, 7 power production plants with 2,206, 6 food—processing factories with 3,042 and 9 cotton mills with 5,576 employees—or a total of 37 industrial concerns with 9,600 employees in all. To this figure may be added 8,023 building workers employed by 19 firms and 10,312 employees of 7 transport undertakings (C-31). Lagos has 8,226 workers employed in mills, 2,809 in power production plants, 18,542 in the building industry and 22,178 in transport (B-6).

These figures are not absolutely comparable, since in Leopoldville they are limited to the large enterprises; but it is significant that even so the Congolese capital can show a higher figure (12,664) for mill and factory workers than Lagos (8,226). Industrialization is undeniably more advanced in the former than in the latter, except as regards the power production plants, where the numbers employed are about the same (2,206) in Leopoldville, (2,809) in Lagos). It should also be pointed out that the figures for Leopoldville are affected by the crisis that has been going on since 1958. This is still more true of the figures for the building industry; 8,023 in Leopoldville, 18,542 in Lagos, and for the transport industry; 10,312 in the former, 22,178 in the latter. In this case it may be worth while to recall the figures for 1950, when the economic situation in the two cities was similar (Table 4).

Table 4

Employment in Selected Sectors, 1950

	Leopoldville (C-36)	Lagos (B-17)		
Industry	20,716	15,114 +	3,173	women
Building	10,782	3,142 +	9	″
Transport	12,719	11,908 +	114	″

WAGES AND SALARIES

The visitor to Leopoldville is struck on arrival by the contrast between "European city" and "native cités". This contrast reflects overdifferentiated wage and salaries scales. In 1954, the annual per capita income of the Africans in Leopoldville was estimated at some 4,350 francs ($87) (C-36). This places them well above the national average, which we have already mentioned, but still very far below the average for foreigners, which is estimated for Leopoldville at 250,000 francs ($5,000) per head. The average income without regard to race ($333) has but little practical meaning, unless perhaps to explain how the town in general can have an appearance that favourably impresses the casual visitor.

In Lagos, wages are generally higher for the masses, although it has been considered advisable to grant a rent allowance to 1,300 heads of families earning less than £330 per year ($924). The general average is about £563, but it falls to £81/12/($228.50) for labourers, who account for one third of the total. Foreigners have earnings on a par with those in Leopoldville, even higher; but they are too few in number to have much effect on the average income or the general appearance of the city. When racial segregation was abolished in 1947, the white district of Ikoyi was clearly more opulent than any corresponding district of Leopoldville; but it contained only 290 houses and those so remote that the visitor had already formed a general impression of the city before getting that far (A-20).

SOCIAL CLASSES

The Belgian colonial administration gave a good deal of publicity to the "independents" or "indigenous colonists", i.e., African workers who had set up on their own account or those employed by the latter. It considered them a "middle class" in embryo, satisfied to get out of the low-wage rut and ready to collaborate for many years with the colonial authorities. A scientific survey conducted between 1943 and 1945 analyzed the situation of 3,575 "independents" (including 816 employees) then working in Kinshasa alone (C-27). In 1954, an official survey revealed the presence of 7,070 of them in the whole city, with 850 employees (C-8). Of these 2,572 (36.38%) were Portuguese, French or British nationals. Their enterprises numbered 12,548, only half of them being satisfied with one single activity. Among these enterprises food took first place (51.5%), followed by clothing and footwear (14.54%). Contrary to a popular prejudice, entertainment concerns amounted to no more than 439 (5%), including 315 bars. In 1960, the number of "independents" had risen to 12,000; but the authorities were beginning to be disillusioned about them, having noted that work on their own account had become the only hope of many of the unemployed, and they were beginning to become concerned about the effects of competition which had resulted in the opening in a particular district of one shop per 125 inhabitants, i.e., more than twice too many for each shopkeeper to have enough custom to live decently.

It is quite possible that the group of "independents" is divided into two sections one of which—the most numerous—is very little different from the masses and the other of which has attained the standard of living of the "Europeans". This would appear to be so from certain signs, such as tax declarations (in 1955, 30 Congolese taxpayers declared annual incomes of over 300,000 francs ($6,000)) (C-36).

In Lagos, there is no doubt, on one hand that the emergence of class-consciousness is retarded by the persistence of extended family ties (A-16) and, on the other, that these ties suffer from migration to new districts (B-38). If average wages (B-6) are considered together with certain pointers to standards of living, such as residence in an old over-populated district (73%), electricity consumption below 100 kilowatts per month (75.2%) and illiteracy among women (68%), (B-17) the conclusion must be that between two-thirds and three-quarters of the population have not yet succeeded in improving their standards of living. This figure includes all labourers (34% of all workers, with an average wage of £81/12/– ($228.50) per year) and half of the 54.5% other workers (skilled workers and office-workers) whose average annual income amounts to £180 ($504). On the other hand, we may regard as an upper class the 9.6% (professional men and officials) who earn an average of £1,472 per year ($4,281), or the 7.6% who consume more than 600 kilowatts of electricity per month. Foreigners represent barely more than 1% of the population, so that the African *élite* would thus make up between 6.5 and 8.5% of the total. There would then remain a middle class forming from a quarter to a fifth of the population, characterized by the fact of living in a new district, the consumption of 100-600 kilowatts of electricity per month and the extension of education to women. But this class leads a precarious life owing to low wages and insecurity of employment.

FEMALE LABOUR

In the field of labour the most striking difference between the two cities lies in the fact that women are kept in the background in Leopoldville and are everywhere in Lagos (B-31). Indeed, the situation in Leopoldville would merit study, since the Belgian authorities perhaps underestimated the role of women in Congolese life. The fact is that they played an important part in the renascence of the prophetic sects during the War and in the nationalist movement that followed, despite the inferior type of education they received and, in particular, the fact that they were not allowed to learn to speak French (A-17).

In the 1950 census, 32,026 women registered in Lagos as earning their living in trade, 9,695 as exercising other private activities and 261 as in government service, no distinction being made between female wage-earners and women working on their own account. The surveys of wage-earners conducted in September 1958 and September 1959 at the very least show a considerable increase in the number of women in government service (Table 5).

Table 5

Female Employment. Lagos (B-6)

	1958	1959
Government	1,400	1,800
Private	1,400	2,200

There is a sizeable number of women in the high-salaried professional category (1,376, against 7,404 men), although women generally prefer to continue the market life. It should be added that in Lagos the market-women have always been strongly organized under the *Iyalode* ("queen of the market"), their recognized chief, who comes immediately after the *Oba* ("king"). These market-women play an important role politically, socially and economically (B-33).

HOUSING

In Leopoldville, as in most of the African colonial cities, the housing problem is essentially a financial one, since geographic conditions present no insuperable obstacle and there is plenty of land. Until about 1945, Leopoldville could be said to have no serious housing problem. Two native "cités," popularly known as "Belgians" had been built by the Congolese themselves on 8,000 parcels of land, each 20 × 25 metres, allocated by the Government. Beginning in 1933, a loan fund enabled about 300 Congolese to build on these parcels houses that were both comfortable and to their taste. Unfortunately, the Second World War raised the population of these "cités" from 40,000 to 80,000 and in 1945 the Congolese took their own step to extend their living space by squatting on the land to the south of Kinshasa. This was the first serious act of rebellion against the colonial authorities; but an administrator with political good sense had the new state of affairs accepted, and thus a third "cité" of 4,000 parcels was established (A-18). Despite the revolutionary origins of the new "cité", it remained, like the others, a mere appendage to the European town in which the inhabitants built their shanties ("cases") to the best of their ability with their own hands. The loan fund continued its activities at the rate of 300 loans per year.

In 1949, the population had increased so fast that another idea began to emerge. The first "Office de Cité" was established and built 3,000 houses in three years, let at from 150 to 455 francs per month, at a time when a labourer's monthly wage was 450 francs. Two years later, the Government made a new departure by building a fourth "cité" of 4,500 parcels 15 kms. south-east of the city center, a real "satellite town" in the sense in which this term is used in modern town-planning, with a commercial and civic center. Again, in 1952 the "Office des Cités Africaines" (O.C.A.) was established for the purpose of systematically building such "dormitory towns" in the five main urban centres of Belgian Africa. Between 1952 and 1960 the O.C.A. built five "cités" in Leopoldville, at the same time assuming responsibility for the public works (streets, drains etc.) required for their efficient functioning. Each of these "cités" was technically an improvement on its predecessor, the culminating point being reached at Lemba-Est, a "cité" of 4,433 dwellings built at an average cost of 94,751 francs ($1,895), with an infrastructure that brought the real cost per dwelling up to 131,477 francs ($2,629) (A-6).

The O.C.A. certainly achieved complete success on at least two points. It completely changed the general appearance of the city in a technically satisfactory manner, and demonstrated that the Congolese inhabitant of Leopoldville could adapt himself fairly easily to types of dwellings that were new to him. On the latter point it should be carefully noted that before 1952 almost all the "cases" in Leopoldville were isolated one-storeyed structures. The O.C.A. succeeded in popularizing not only detached houses but blocks of flats. To this technical point must be added that the work of the State organ aroused serious social and economic, and even political, criticisms. One basic fact undoubtedly remains, namely, that the housing problem in Leopoldville has not been solved, as the O.C.A. has not succeeded in building fast enough to meet the needs of a rapidly growing population. Indeed, conditions in the old "cités" have worsened, since they had 245,000 inhabitants (on an area of 1,930 hectares) in 1960, as compared with 222,000 in 1952, the O.C.A. having 135,000 people living on 1,023 hectares (C-12). Furthermore, the inhabitants of the new "cités" are far from satisfied with their lot, especially owing to the cost of rents, transport and living in general, which is beyond their means. Particularly from 1955 on, the O.C.A. resolutely specialized in the building of dwellings which could not be let at less than 300 francs ($60) per month, whereas at the time Leopoldville had at least 20,000 workers earning less than 1,000 francs per month (C-36). To the already heavy burden represented by such rents must be added the cost of public transport and the financial loss to women represented by the distance from the city's central market. It is, indeed, in this distance that lies the most obvious contradiction in the principles behind the work of the States organ. On the one hand, the aim was to follow the European or American style; on the other, the accent was laid on the typically colonial custom of pushing the native population, i.e. those inhabitants who cannot afford to live the suburban life that is so characteristic of the well-off classes in the western world, as far away from the centre as possible. Politically speaking, it can be held that the O.C.A. increased the number of communities from which the Belgians were not only excluded but kept at ever-increasing distance, and in which the future leaders of an independent Congo had their first opportunity of measuring their forces in 1957, when these "cités" were transformed into "communes" with elected administrative bodies. But these bodies are now confronted with the social problems we have mentioned, while pressure in the old "cités" has reached such a point as to provoke another squatters' movement, more extensive still than in 1945.

In Lagos, the housing problem is quite different from that in Leopoldville or even in most of the cities in Tropical Africa. It recalls rather the situation in the rest of the Old World, in so far as it primarily arises from the existence of an old urban centre that time has changed into slums, which have to be demolished before rebuilding is undertaken, particularly as Old Lagos is an island and thus cannot be enlarged to any great extent, although it has been a little by drainage. Unfortunately, every demolition implies the sacrifice of interests which may be very worthy of respect; and the sacrifice is the more difficult to accept in Lagos because it is the very essence of traditional life that is affected when what is destroyed is the palaces of the chiefs, which were built like Roman houses, with their "atrium" and "compluvium", and the homes of their subjects, which were arranged around the palaces in closed circles rather than in streets. What there still is of Old Lagos is, moreover, full of charm and one can but hope that something of that charm will always remain.

It was nevertheless difficult to resist the cold reality of figures that showed 3930 dwellings for 28,518 inhabitants in 1871, and only 12,930 for 126,000 inhabitants in 1931. Spurred on by a plague epidemic, the Government set up an independent public corporation in 1929, the Lagos Executive Development Board, with an initial capital of £200,000, which immediately began operations at the very seat of the plague—an area of 150 acres with 30,000 inhabitants. The complaints of these inhabitants nevertheless put a stop to the works when the project was only one third finished, and the Board thereafter merely collected the rents of the houses it had built, the value of which was three times that of those it had demolished. At the same time the Land Department offered the population 1,800 parcels at Yaba, north of the then existing town. African contractors in less than two years covered these parcels with houses costing on average £300 each. Yaba may be considered a success, though too many more houses were later built there. On the other hand, a loan fund established by the Government in 1926 has been rather a failure, only 325 applications having been submitted in 18 years (A-18).

After the Second World War, the Board came into operation again and began by drawing up a master plan, which it sought in vain to keep secret, in order to avoid criticism and speculation. Over the last 10 years it has developed the three suburbs of Suru Lere, north-west of Yaba; Apapa, south-west of Old Lagos, on the other side of the channel; and Ikoyi, at the eastern end of the city. Suru Lere consists of four "complexes", the first two of which have 987 houses built at an average cost of £633 ($1,772) and let at 25 shillings ($3.50) per room, thanks to a subsidy of 23 shillings, the third 1,300 houses built at an average cost of £733 ($2,052) and let at 16 shillings and 6 pence ($2.31), thanks to a subsidy of 33 shillings 6 pence, and reserved for workers earning less that £330 per year, and the fourth 670 parcels of land of 40 × 110 feet each, mostly sold for £280 each. At Apapa, the Board distributed 1,000 acres of land divided into; (1) in the east, an industrial estate of 230 acres let at £400 per acre per year; (2) in the west, a cheap housing and shopping area, divided into 678 parcels let at £120-170 per acre per year; (3) a residential estate of 444 parcels, let at £75 per

acre. Lastly, at Ikoyi the Board extended the old white district to the south-east and south-west in such a way as to cover almost the whole of the island where it is situated. The first extension comprises 270 acres divided into so many parcels for sale, and the second 278. In the latter development costs have amounted to £766,000, and the parcels will be let rather than sold. Apart from these "complexes", the Board has built 359 houses, sold at from £1,120 (two rooms) to £3,370 (six rooms with garage) (B-3).

Of course, the activities of the Board cover only a small part, perhaps 10%, of the needs of Lagos. This can be judged by comparing with the figure of 3,645 houses built by the Board in 10 years the figure of 4,853 building permits issued during the last 5 years. Moreover, the Board is criticized for treating households as isolated units with the result that families transferred to the new districts feel lost among strangers—a situation that is familiar in the western world but exceptional and particularly unpleasant in Africa, even in towns. Again, there is also the prospect of a politico-social problem that might arise from the fact that a goodly part of Old Lagos is now passing into foreign hands, as the local people cannot afford to buy their enlarged and developed properties on the Boards' terms.

In summary, the housing situation in both cities is therefore disappointing. The authorities seem to be incapable of providing sufficient, or, what is more important, cheap enough housing. But no really practical method of assisting private building has as yet been found either. The situation is undoubtedly aggravated by the freakish manner in which these cities were built, particularly from the point of view of distances; but the basic problem is undoubtedly low wages, which make impossible the purchase and upkeep of decent homes.

MUNICIPAL GOVERNMENT

The existence of great multi-functional capitals raises such serious administrative problems that the world's main metropolises (Paris, London, New York, etc.) have been given special administrative systems unlike those applying to other cities in their respective countries. However, as the cities of Tropical Africa are still very far from having the population and the economic importance of these metropolises, the tendency has been to give them the administrative system common to cities of secondary rank in Europe. This the British, French and Portuguese did systematically, unlike the Belgians, who sought to introduce a new type of municipal administration in their colony, Congo (A-18).

In Leopoldville, the most obvious result of this attempt to find a new system was unfortunately that the municipal institutions were introduced too slowly, and this has been denounced as one reason for the discontent prevailing in the last years of the colonial regime. As early as 1891, the Governor-General proposed the introduction of Belgian municipal institutions in Congo. As this policy was rejected once for all, it was not until 1922 that Leopoldville acquired a system based on the town boards established in Uganda by Lord Lugard, who himself had been inspired by a visit to the "cantonments" in British India. An "Urban Committee" composed entirely of Belgians appointed by the colonial authorities thus functioned in a purely advisory capacity until 1957. The African population had to wait until 1945 before having a "conseil de cité" (town council) also

appointed by the authorities and also advisory; but from that time on the Africans had an advantage over the white population in their "chef de cité", who was the first accredited representative of the urban community, although without clearly defined powers (C-11). In 1957, after endless discussions, the Belgian colonial Government introduced in the colony a municipal administrative system which had been proposed in 1948 in a thesis presented at the University of Oxford (A-18). This system had nothing in common with that existing in Belgium either, apart from the title of "bourgmestre" given to the elected chief of each of the thirteen communes into which the territory of the city was thenceforward divided. The supreme authority remained in the hands of a colonial official, who assumed in his new capacity the title of "premier bourgmestre". This system has been provisionally retained by independent Congo; but it should be noted that the general circumstances in which it was introduced set it on the wrong lines from the start.

Leopoldville had been subjected even more than the colony as a whole to a "paternalist" regime, characterized by abundant subsidies and the absence of political responsibilities of its inhabitants. The 1957 reform itself granted the "bourgmestres" and their councils only very limited powers, while their superior was an official of "district commissioner" grade, as was already the case in 1922, when the population was 21,200. However, as it was the very first time elections were held in the Congo, the leaders of the political parties rightly saw their opportunity to put themselves forward as candidates for future positions at the national level (C-3). Men of the calibre of Mr. Kasavubu therefore stood at these elections, in which they won only to be subsequently removed from their seats by the colonial authorities for their general political activities. Since that time the various communes have been administered by authorities who were appointed at the last minute by the Belgians and who have been temporarily kept in office by the Government of the Republic of the Congo in order to spare the urban population the excitement that an electoral campaign would undoubtedly cause.

Leopoldville's budget is high but artificial. In 1953, it included 78.7 million francs in subsidies ($1,574,000) and only 44 million francs of receipts ($500,000) 20 million francs in loans plus Hand 25 in gift, or a total of 167.7 million francs ($3,354,000) (C-20). There are 22 different taxes, which are imposed not only on all lucrative activities but also on private individuals, in the form of a poll-tax on men and a special tax on spinsters. The city maintains its own police force but has no responsibility for water supplies, transport and housing (which are all controlled by public corporations), electricity (which is operated by a private firm) or education.

In Lagos, the Colonial Government pursued a systematic policy of gradually introducing British municipal institutions, beginning in 1909 by establishing an Advisory Committee and going on, in 1919, to the election of some of the members of a new Municipal Council. In 1950, this policy culminated in the installation of a Council identical with English town councils; but the experiment was not completely satisfactory. Since that time Lagos has been administered by a Council comprising not only 42 elected members but also 4 customary chiefs, as *ex officio* members, under the purely honorary chairmanship of *Oba* Adele II (A-24). The police

force, which is a Federal force, water supplies, electricity and housing, which are controlled by public corporations, are outside municipal jurisdiction, which however, covers education and public transport.

Subsidies represent a little more than 20% of the Lagos budget, and they are always justified by services rendered to the Federation. The 1959–60 budget (taxation year beginning 1 April) amounted to £890.870 ($2,495,000), including 185,410 in contributions from the Government, 540,900 obtained from rates (a tax on tenants and very characteristic of British municipal organization), 74,800 in receipts from municipal services and 89,760 from miscellaneous sources (B-4). In 1952–53, the Lagos budget amounted to £537,000 ($1½ millions), and the International Bank mission did not expect it to exceed £723,000 in 1959–60 (B-2); but rates brought in much more than the £430,000 estimated by the mission. In English administrative law "rates" are the only tax collected by the municipalities. Objections have been raised to their introduction into the colonies, one of them being that landed property does not offer the same basis for taxation there as it does in Europe, and another that rates tend to discourage owners from developing their land in countries where they should rather be encouraged to do so (B-18).

RELATIONS WITH THE CENTRAL GOVERNMENT

In both capitals relations with the central government raise thorny problems. Pending a constitutional reform, Leopoldville is only one of 25 districts in Congo, and this legal status barely reflects its political and economic importance. On the other hand, the central government proves by its subsidies that Leopoldville is not a district like the others. The capital's share of 7% in the national product seems to justify the subsidies; but the question has not been gone into.

In Nigeria, on the contrary, the status of the capital has been the subject of innumerable studies and discussions, which resulted in its recognition in 1954 as a Federal territory independent of all regional jurisdiction but at the same time devoid of powers outside the ordinary competence of local authorities. This situation remains a cause of disputes particularly as regards the "Ministry for Lagos Affairs," which was set up as a guarantee of the whole nation's interest in the capital, but which the local authorities fear may assume quasi-tutelary powers. The question of the payment of subsidies and other moneys by the government to Lagos has been studied by a Fiscal Commission, which found that, far from receiving more than its share, the population of Lagos was at a disadvantage under the existing system. In 1956–57, the Federal Government spent £2.2 million, and in 1957–58, £2.4 million to provide Lagos with services that were elsewhere the responsibility of the regional authorities; but the corresponding taxation brought in £3.4 million and £3.3 million respectively, in these years (B-19). There is therefore a misunderstanding between the urban community of Lagos and the rest of the country, which does not grasp the extent to which development in the capital exceeds the general level.

CONCLUSIONS

Leopoldville and Lagos are not only large towns. They are two communities that have soared in the midst of underdeveloped societies, contrary to the principles of orthodox political economy. Such situations are, however, justified by modern economists, who no longer believe that a country should, or can, develop simultaneously in all its parts. Therefore they regard towns like those we studied as "poles of development" in which basic activities give rise to all kinds of chain reactions, the main characteristic of which is that the rural masses move into the towns without the actual inducement of possible employment.

Although favoured in comparison with other regions in their respective countries, these cities have nevertheless serious tasks to contend with. The corollary to the relative abundance of manpower is wages so low that it becomes difficult to house this manpower decently and find a suitable basis for taxation to meet the cost of public services. The main task of all is to take stock of urban living conditions, which is complicated by the extreme division of responsibilities and the careless attitude of many authorities towards publishing statistics and, especially, towards co-ordinating them with those of other services. This would quite obviously be a fertile field for technical assistance.

As we have already seen from examples given in this study, such stocktaking would reveal the existence of considerable waste of land, capital and manpower, due to the failure to plan and coordinate urban activities. The municipalities would appear to be the authorities most competent to ensure greater harmony of views in the development of these cities; but the strenghtening of their power will no doubt depend on the understanding a majority of the nation shows of the part played by these cities as poles of development.

BIBLIOGRAPHY

A. Articles of general Interest

United Nations

1. Economic Commission for Africa, Economic Bulletin for Africa, January, 1961.
2. Yearbook of National Accounts Statistics, 1960–61.
3. Report on the Economic Situation of Africa since 1950–1959.
4. Report on the World Social Situation, 1957, especially Part II, vii, Social Problems of Urbanization in Economically Under-developed Areas, pp. 111–143, and viii, Urbanization in Africa South of the Sahara, pp. 144–169.
5. Special Study on Social Conditions in Non-Self-Governing Territories, 1958.

C.C.T.A.—C.S.A.

6. Housing and Urbanization, 19–30 January 1959, 267 pages.

Centre International de l'Enfance

7. Le Bien-Etre de l'Enfant en Afrique, Lagos, 1959, 186 pages.
8. Les Problèmes de l'Enfance dans les Pays Tropicaux de l'Afrique, Brazzaville, 8–13 December 1952, 364 pages.

International Labour Office

9. The Development of Wage-earning Employment in Tropical Africa, International Labour Review, September 1956, pp. 239–258.
10. Inter-racial Wage Structure in Certain Parts of Africa, International Labour Review, 1958, p. 20–55.
11. African Labour Survey, 1958, xv, 712 pages.

UNESCO

12. Social Implications of Industrialization and Urbanization in Africa South of the Sahara, 744 pages.

Comhaire, E.

13. Les transports fluviaux au Congo jadis et aujourd'hui, Congo, October 1927.

Comhaire, J.

14. Roles des villes dans la crise africaine, Société belge d'étude et d'expansion, 1959, pp. 849–851.
(repr. Problèmes Sociaux Congolais, Elisabethville, December 1959, pp. 138–141)

15. Das Wachstum der Afrikanischen Staedte, Geopolitik, November 1955, pp. 669–675.
16. Economic Change and the Extended Family, Annals, American Academy of Political and Social Science, May 1956, pp. 45–52.
17. Sociétés secrètes et mouvements prophétiques au Congo Belge, Africa, January, 1955, pp. 54–59.
18. Aspects of Urban Administration in Tropical and Southern Africa, Cape Town, 1953, 100 pages.
19. Religious Trends in African and Afro-American Societies, Anthropological Quarterly, 1953, pp. 95–108.
20. Urban Segregation and Racial Legislation in Africa, American Sociological Review, June 1950, pp. 392–397.
21. Some African Problems of Today, Human Organization, Summer 1951, pp. 15–18.

Comhaire, J., & Cahnman, W.

22. How Cities Grew: the Historical Sociology of Cities, Madison, NJ, 1959, xiv, 141 pages.

Denis, J.

23. Le phénoméne urbain en Afrique centrale, Brussels, 1958, 407 pages.

Edition Encyclopédiques Européennes

24. Les Capitales du Monde, Paris, 1959; Lagos, Vol. I, pp. 478–481; Léopidville, pp. 484–487.

Silberman, Leo

25. The urban Social Survey in the Colonies, Zaïre, March 1954.

B. Bibliography of Lagos

Electricity Corporation of Nigeria

1. Report on Survey of Markets for Electricity Supplies, 1959, 120 pages 7 plates.

International Bank

2. The Economic Development of Nigeria, Baltimore, 1954, xxii, 686 pages, map.

Lagos Executive Development Board

3. Annual Reports.

Lagos Town Council

4. Annual Reports.

Nigeria

5. Report into the Relationship between

the Federal Government and Lagos Town Council, by Sir John Imrie, 1959, 40 pages.

6. Report on Employment and Earnings Enquiry, September 1959, 28 pages.

7. A Report on the Registration of Title to Land in the Federal Territory of Lagos, by S. Browton Simpson, 1957, 45 pages.

8. Report on Educational Development in Lagos, 1957, 10 pages.

9. Report of the Commission of Inquiry into the Retail and Ancillary Trade in the F. T. of Lagos—Kikinde Sojola, Chairman, 1957, 8 pages.

10. Progress Reports on the Economic Programme 1955–1960, Sessional Papers 2, 1957, 34 pages, and 1, 1958, 43 pages.

11. Urban Consumers Surveys in Nigeria . . . Lagos, Enugu, Ibadan, 1957, 70 pages.

12. The Economic Programme . . . of Nigeria 1955–1960, Sessional Paper 2, 1956.

13. Handbook of Commerce and Industry, 1954, 189 pages, plans, and later editions.

14. The Lagos Consumer Price Index– The Lagos Consumers Survey, 1953–1954, Bulletin, 1, Department of Statistics, 1954, 2 pages.

15. Commission of Inquiry into the Administration of the Lagos Town Council—Bernard Storey, 1953, 55 pages.

16. Census of Nigeria, 1952–1953, 3 regional reports, 30 provincial bulletins and summary tables of 13 data.

17. Population Census of Lagos—1950, 1951, 114 pages, map.

18. Your Town Council . . . by Wilfred Powler, 1951, 22 pages.

United Kingdom

19. Nigeria—Report of the Fiscal Commission, July 1958, 70 pages.

20. Development of Local Government in the Colonies, Report of a Conference, Queens' College, Cambridge, 22 August –2 September 1955.

21. A Note on the Lagos Town Council, Journal of African Administration, July 1953, pp. 133–134.

Banney, L.

22. Registration of Title to Land in Lagos–an Appreciation of the Report of S. R. Simpson, Journ. of Afric. Admin., July 1958, pp. 136–143.

Buchanan, K. M. & Puch, J. C.

23. Land and People In Nigeria, University of London Press, London, 1955, 252 pages.

Comhaire, J.

24. La vie religieuse à Lagos, Zaïre, March 1949, pp. 549–556.

25. La délinquence dans les grandes villes d'Afrique britannique, Zaïre.

26. Expériences économiques en Afrique britannique, Zaïre, October 1950, 15 pages.

27. Trois Budgets municipaux, Zaïre, December 1950, pp. 1107–1110.

28. L'administration municipate à Lagos, Revue coloniale belge 1949, pp. 494–496.

29. A propos des "Brésiliens" de Lagos, Grands-Lacs, Namur, Belgium, March 1949, pp. 41–43.

30. Enseignement féminin et mariage a Lagos, Nigéria, Zaïre, March 1955, pp. 261–277.

Comhaire, Sylvain, S.

31. The Position of Women in Lagos, Nigeria, Pi Lambda Theta, Menasha, Wisc., 1949.

32. Associations on the Basis of Origin in Lagos, Nigeria, American Catholic Sociological Review, 1950.

33. Le travail des femmes à Lagos, Nigeria, Zaïre, February 1951, pp. 169–187, & May 1951, pp. 475–502.

34. Le problème du marriage a Lagos, Nigéria, Revue de l'Institut de Sociologie, Brussels, No. 4, 1956, pp. 499–521.

Faulkner, D.

35. Social Welfare and Juvenile Delinquency in Lagos, Nigeria, Howard League for Penal Reform, London, 1952, 7 pages.

Heads, J.

36. Urbanization and Economic Progress, Conference Proceedings, West African Inst. Soc. & Econom. Research, 1958, pp. 65–73.

Marris, P.
37. The Approach of Sociologists and Anthropologists to the Study of Family Relationships, Do., pp. 164–167.
38. Slum Clearance and Family Life in Lagos, Human Organization, 1960.

C. Bibliography of Léopoldville

Banque Centrale du Congo Belge et du Ruanda Urundi
1. Monthly Bulletin.
Belgique
2. Rapport de la commission parlementaire chargée de faire une enquête sur les événements qui se sont produits à Léopoldville en janvier 1959, *Moniteur*, March 1959.
3. Notes pouvant servir à l'étude des groupements politiques à Léopoldville, C. C. De Backer, 1959.
4. Guide du voyageur au Congo Belge et au Ruanda-Urundi, 4th edition, 1958, 800 pages.
5. L'urbanisme au Congo Belge, 1955, 211 pages, plans.
6. Plan décennal pour le dévelopement économique et social du Congo Belge, 1949, 602 pages, plans.
Congo
7. Résultats de l'enquéte démographique entreprise dans la cité indigène de Léopoldville en 1955, 1956, 34 tables.
8. Un recensement des activités indépendantes à la cité indigène de Léopoldville 1956, 78 pages.
9. Congo Belge 1944, 214 pages.
10. Silhouettes indigènes, 20 articles by S. Comhaire-Sylvain, 1944–1945.
11. La vie indigène à Léopoldville, 60 articles by S. & J. Comhaire-Sylvain, 1943–1946.
Office des Cités Africaines,
12. O.C.A., 1952–1960, Brussels, 26 pages.
Office d'Exploitation des Transports Coloniaux
13. Annual reports.
Annuaire du Congo Belge
14. 1959 Edition, Brussels, 1564 pages.
Baeck, L.
15. Economische Ontwikkeling en Social structure in Belgish-Kongo, Louvain, 1959, 331 pages.

Bezy, F.
17. Principes pour l'orientation du développment économique au Congo, Léopoldville, 1959, 56 pages.
Comhaire, J.
18. Die Verstaedterung und die Krise in Belgish-Kongo, Weltwirtschaft dienst, February 1960, pp. 98–101.
19. Some Aspects of Urbanization in the Belgian Congo, American Journal of Sociology, July 1956, pp. 8–13.
20. Evolution politique et sociale du Congo Belge en 1951–1953, Zaïre, January 1954, pp. 45–53.
21. Note sur les Musulmans de Léopoldville, Zaïre, March 1948, pp. 303–304. (repr. Le problëme musulman en Afrique Belge, L. Anciaux, Brussels, 1949).
Comhaire-Sylvain, S.
22. At Home with Congo Children, World Mission, Washington, 1955.
23. Les jeux des enfants noirs de Léopoldville, Zaïre, February 1949, pp. 139–152 & April 1952, pp. 351–362.
24. Proverbes recueillis à Léopoldville, Zaïre, June 1949, pp. 629–647.
25. Le lingala des enfants noirs de Léopoldville, Kongo-Overzee, No. 5-1949, pp. 239–250.
26. Quelques devinettes des enfants noirs de Léopoldville, Africa, January 1949, pp. 40–52.
27. Food and Leisure among the African Youth of Léopoldville, Cape Town, 1950, 124 pages.
Comhaire-Sylvain, S. & J.
28. Kinship Change in the Belgian Congo, African Studies. 1954, pp. 20–24.
Dresch, J.
29. Villes congolaises, Revue de géographie et d'ethnographie, 3, 1949.
Guides Bleus
30. Brazzaville-Léopoldville-Pointe-Noire, Paris, 1958, 96 pages, plans.
Herman, F.
31. Situation économique du Bas-Congo, Bulletin du Centre de Recherche et d'information Socio-Politique, Brussels, 8 April 1960.
Revue Coloniale Belge
32. Numéro spécial sur Léopoldville, No. 258, 1 August, 1956.

Sobchenko, A. I.
33. Etnograficheskaya Kharakteristika go-
    rodskovo naselyeniya Belgishkovo
    Kongo, Sovyetskaya Etnografiya, 3,
    1957, pp. 107–118.
Van Wing, J.
34. Le Congo déraille, Bulletin de l'Institut
    royal colonial belge, 3, 1951, pp. 607–
    626.

Wallis, C.A.G.
35. The Administration of Towns in the
    Belgian Congo, Journal of African
    Administration, April 1958, pp. 95–100.
Zaïre
36. Numéro spécial sur Léopoldville, June
    1956, articles by L. Baeck, L. Denis,
    A. Van Cauwenbergh.

33. The Structure of Kuala Lumpur, Malaysia's Capital City

HAMZAH SENDUT

There is a common pattern of urbanization in South East Asia, where, owing to historical and economic factors, each country has one major town or city dominating political and economic life. Such a city serves as the national capital of the country concerned, and, over the centuries, has been the main centre of relations with other countries of the world. Each capital is a commercial centre of some importance, functioning largely as a distribution centre of manufactured goods imported from overseas and as a collecting point of agricultural and mineral products for export to foreign countries. Rangoon, Bangkok, Saigon, Manila and Djakarta are clear examples of dominant cities of this kind. Hanoi in North Vietnam, because of the size of its population, also falls into this category. Besides being the entrepôt of Singapore, Kuala Lumpur is also one such city. It is the political and administrative capital of two year old Malaysia and, being in the centre of the world's richest tin-mining and rubber growing area, it is the hub of a new nation, performing the functions characteristic of other primary cities. The importance of Kuala Lumpur should be considered against the background of changing political development within this region and the various factors that have given it its present status in Malaysia.

This paper traces only briefly the historical development of Kuala Lumpur but emphasizes other factors which are responsible for its present dominance. An analysis is made of the demographic pattern of employment opportunities and the major economic functions of the city, with particular reference to the central area, because this area, with its concentration of high buildings, forms the heart and centre of the metropolis. Reference is also made to the way in which the radial roads,

Town Planning Review, 36, (*July 1965*), *125–38*.
Reproduced by permission of the editor of the Town Planning Review *and its publishers, Liverpool University Press, Liverpool, England, and with the permission of the author.*

FIGURE 1

The Malaysian Peninsula

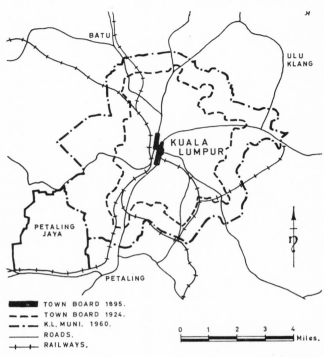

FIGURE 2

Map Showing the Growth of Kuala Lumpur, 1895-1960

lined with buildings, extend out from the central area, joining the parent city with neighbouring urban areas and large villages to form the metropolitan area of Greater Kuala Lumpur. (Figures 1 and 2.)

HISTORICAL BACKGROUND

The city came into being during the nineteenth century at a time when the development of towns in the Malay Peninsula was intensified after the discovery of minerals, when prospectors were attracted from overseas and from the local coastal areas. The success of one of these operations, in the upper reaches of the Klang and Gombak rivers, induced Chinese traders to establish an urban nucleus which was later to become Kuala Lumpur. History,

however, is not clear on its foundation date, although the year 1859 is often quoted in official records.[1] It is known, nevertheless, that because of its strategic location at the confluence of the two rivers, this early settlement assumed control over regular traffic moving up and down-river carrying mining personnel, food supplies, and tin ore. Its break-of-bulk location from whence traders travelled on land to deliver supplies to adjacent mining areas in Ampang and Rasah, gave the city additional impetus for growth as tin-mining activities were intensified. The period from 1862 onwards was especially one

[1] *Kuala Lumpur Municipal Council Annual Report*, 1959, page 9. Additional information is also available from the *Historical Handbook of Kuala Lumpur*, Kuala Lumpur, Municipal Council, 1959, pp. 7–27.

of accelerated expansion, with the economic boom and the rise in price of tin during 1882 to 1884. Many more tin prospectors and traders arrived, and the population increased to 18,000 in 1891. This necessitated the transfer of the political headquarters of the British authorities from the port of Klang on the coast of the Malacca Strait to Kuala Lumpur, situated about twenty-five miles inland. The stable government that followed not only enabled trade and commerce to develop but also marked the introduction of western methods of town building over what had been essentially a 'shanty' town. The British erected permanent buildings which included a police headquarters, and, by clearing Chinese allotments, they made a parade ground for training policemen. Frank Swettenham, a renowned British administrative officer, rebuilt the 'shanty' town with tiled-roofed brick buildings, and replanned the street system on a rectilinear pattern. In addition, disused mining ponds and marshy areas were drained and malarial mosquitos eradicated.

The first wooden bridge was constructed over Sungai Klang in 1883 to allow development on both sides of the river bank and in 1886 a railway was built to connect the city with Klang and to replace the river traffic. With the formation of a railway network over the length of the Malay Peninsula in the early twentieth century, the Kuala-Lumpur-Klang railway was finally linked with Penang in the north and Singapore in the south. Following the establishment of road links with the surrounding tin and rubber areas, the city underwent a further period of expansion.

In 1933 the first city plan was prepared and has remained in force until the present day except for some modifications which have been introduced to suit modern conditions. Recent changes of a physical, social and economic nature have created further problems so that a new master plan for the city had to be prepared in 1959 with the assistance of a United Nations physical planning expert.[2]

Population Characteristics[3]

The city's rapid growth is reflected in its population which rose from 46,718 in 1911 to 316,230 in 1957. Before 1947 the rate of population growth varied according to the fortunes of the rubber and tin industries because these determined the inflow and outflow of alien immigrants. The city's development during the last decade, however, was largely determined by its status as a leading city; and because it was a large enough area to receive surplus population from the countryside. Consequently, its population composition changed and one of the most striking post-war features (also common to many towns in Malaysia) is the increase of indigenous population.

The rate of change of the Malay population is greater than that of any other racial group, although their number is much smaller than the numbers of the non-indigenous groups. The significance of this statement may be emphasized further by the fact that there is an inverse correlation between the fertility ratio and the number of Chinese living in towns; in fact, it has been observed that the fertility ratio of both Chinese and Indians

[2] See *Klang Valley Plans*, Federation of Malaya Federal Department of Town and Country Planning. Summaries of the major recommendations of the United Nations Planning Adviser, Kuala Lumpur, 1962.

[3] Much of the information on population has been derived from the official census of the Federation of Malaya held in 1957. Data for subsequent years are not available.

Table 1

Population Composition and Rates of Increase 1931-1957

Composition/Year	1931	1947	1957
Total Town Population	111,418	175,961	316,230
Index of increase	100	157.6	283.7
Malays	10,769	21,989	47,615
Index of increase	100	204.2	237.9
Chinese	67,929	111,693	195,822
Index of increase	100	164.1	123.6
Indians	26,803	31,607	53,505
Index of increase	100	117.7	81.4
Others	7,378	10,672	19,288
Index of increase	100	1144.6	116.7

is lower than the average for Malays.[4] It follows that the reduction of fertility among the non-indigenous people and the rapid rise of the Malays are the key aspects of the future population of the city.

This rise of the Malay proportion of the population may be explained by a variety of social and economic factors. As government functions (concentrated in Kuala Lumpur) expanded, administrative offices have multiplied to take in an increasing number of government employees of whom a fair proportion are Malays. The concentration of the nation's defence organization in Kuala Lumpur has also been a significant force drawing an increased number of Malay military personnel and policemen into the city. Other Malays have migrated into the city because of poverty and the lack of modern amenities in the surrounding areas. In addition, the city itself acts as a magnet. Being replanned on modern lines with greatly improved standards it naturally attracts population from the poorer areas. The increase of Malay popula-

[4] See McGee, T. G., 'The Cultural Role of Cities, a Case Study of Kuala Lumpur,' *Journal of Tropical Geography*, Vol. 17, May, 1963, pp. 178–196.

tion is also due to the changes in the municipal administration of Kuala Lumpur since the extension of the city boundary in all directions had led to the incorporation of at least one major Malay village at Gombak (with a population of 1202 people in 1957 of whom only eighteen people were non-Malays).

It should not be inferred, however, that the increase in the proportion of Malays has been spectacular. In fact, the ratio increased only from 12.5 per cent in 1947 to 15.0 per cent in 1957. Although the combined percentages of Chinese and Indians decreased from 87.5 per cent in 1947 to 85.0 per cent in 1957, their numerical increase of 114,600 from 1947 to 1957 was more than four times that of the Malay increase.

The increase in the percentage of women in the city is also significant, for, whereas in the past this was due to an increased number of Chinese women from overseas the present decade has seen the inflow of many women from rural areas. This indicates a complete reversal of past tendencies when movement to the towns was predominantly male with the women being restricted to their homes by traditional and economic forces. As a result of this movement the disparity between the sexes tends to even out and the urban sex-ratio is improved. Increased marriages have also resulted in a high percentage of children under fifteen years of age (Table 2).

Table 2

Age Composition of Population, 1957

Age-Group	Percentage
10—4	40.3
15—29	27.7
30—44	17.1
45—59	10.8
60—74	3.4
75 and above	0.9
	100.2

The age-structure, like that of most of the south-east Asian towns, is relatively young. This indicates that within a decade or two more than forty per cent of the population will grow to marriageable age, and the potential increase is therefore very great. In the next few years many children will enter the working age-group. It will be a difficult problem to find employment for them. The immediate requirements of these young people for schools, playing fields, youth clubs and other social services have also to be met.

ECONOMIC POSITION OF KUALA LUMPUR

Because of its special position Kuala Lumpur provides administrative and professional services including a wide range of governmental and private activities. It has an economy heavily weighted in the service sector, and an analysis of the employment structure of the city showed that out of a total population of 176,000 in 1947, 35 per cent were gainfully employed. Of this,

three-quarters were employed in tertiary activities, the rest being in manufacturing, mining and agriculture. Of those engaged in the tertiary services, 40 per cent were in public administration, 15 per cent in transport, and another 15 per cent in commerce and finance. Data on the occupational structure of the city in 1957 and subsequent years are not available. However, the physical concentration alone of banking corporations, clearing houses, the Stock Exchange, business agencies and big departmental stores testifies to the growing importance of the city. Through its function as the capital of Malaysia it is the focus of all administration and as a result has been the venue of a number of international conferences; thereby employment opportunities are increased. This fact is further emphasized by the provision of some 250 acres of land for housing and allied development for the diplomatic community in the country. With the completion of the national university, the national mosque and the teachers' training college, it is not only becoming the intellectual centre but also the religious centre of the nation; also, as a result of increasing demand, it provides a growing number of restaurants, hotels, night clubs, entertainment places and a host of cinemas, both large and small, with the National Art Gallery, and Arts Council providing other forms of recreation.

The city is also the transport centre for primary products, for export, and for consumer goods for distribution to rural areas. Apart from being at an intersection of the north-south and the east-west transportation routes, it also provides for extensive local and foreign air traffic. In addition, it commands an extensive lorry service which links it with all parts of the Malay Peninsula, including Singapore.

While the service industries provided employment in 1947, manufacturing industry accounted for fifteen per cent of the labour force. This made the city the industrial centre of rubber goods, soap and certain goods required by the local population, especially foodstuffs, clothing, furniture and building materials (which are centred in Sungei Besi Road, Brickfields, Sentul and Klang Road). The establishment of Petaling Jaya, Malaysia's first new town, with a population of more than 30,000 people in 1961, and its industrial complex, has given the city's economy an added significance.

Kuala Lumpur also engages directly in the production of tin which industry employed five per cent of the town's total work force in 1947. This activity, however, is declining because of the sterilization of mining land; moreover, the expansion of manufacturing areas and the demand for building sites also compete for space in the city.

Agriculture accounted for only five per cent of the city's gainfully employed population in 1947, and like mining, it is also declining in importance. The scope for agricultural development near the city, other than market gardening, is limited because much of the hinterland has been given over to rubber, and disused mining lands are too poor for any cultivation. Thus, most of the city's vegetable supplies come from the Cameron Highlands, a hill resort specializing in the cultivation of temperate-land vegetables such as cabbage, tomatoes, carrots and green pepper.

Briefly, therefore, the main functions of the city are administration, transportation and communication. Other services such as manufacturing, commerce and finance also bring in revenue. Manufacturing generates more employment (and therefore income) in services closely linked to the industries themselves, for instance, soap-making, plastic products, dry-cell batteries industries.

Because of its multiple functions the city dominates not only its immediate tributary areas, but the whole of Malaysia. But unlike the other primary cities of south-east Asia, which are by far the largest cities in their respective countries, Kuala Lumpur is only the second largest city in Malaysia, and is a third of the size of Singapore. It is only one and a half times bigger than the city of Georgetown (Penang), the third largest town in the country, two and a half times that of Ipoh, four times that of Klang and about five times that of Johore Bahru, the fourth, fifth and sixth towns on the list respectively. In spite of this, the city as a whole may be regarded as being undersized for the functions it performs.

CENTRAL AREA DEVELOPMENT

The major functions of Kuala Lumpur are mainly concentrated in the central area where there are to be found new, modern, tall buildings. Here vehicular traffic, rickshaws, cyclists and pedestrians converge. The land values in this area are high. Enclosed by many short streets the central area occupies about one-third of a square mile; a small portion only of the thirty-seven square miles which form the total administrative area of the city. Although the boundary of the central area is not well defined, the central area is synonymous with the business area and its nucleus coincides with the old section of the city constructed before 1884 (Fig. 3). The position of the central area is more or less defined by the areas reserved for railways and buses that converge upon it. The railway termini represent breaks in transportation and have been associated with the

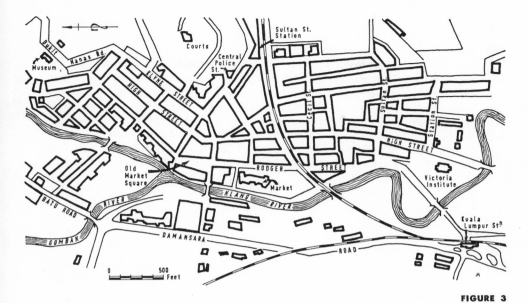

FIGURE 3

The Central Area of Kuala Lumpur in 1895

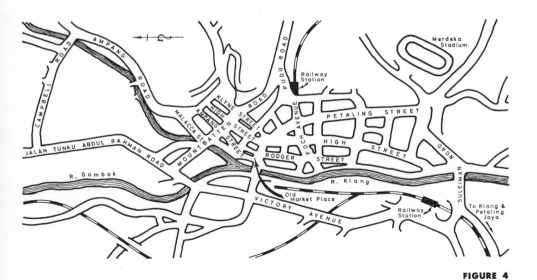

FIGURE 4

The Street Pattern in Present-day Kuala Lumpur

development of the central area ever since it was established. The bus terminus at Foch Avenue is at the main point where traffic converges and, together with the Central Market, it more or less fixes the centre of the city. This, although it is not a geographical centre equidistant from every point on the fringe of the city, marks the approximate position where conditions permit the development of a complex of institutions intended to discharge, with efficiency, the functions of the city. [Figure 4.]

The importance of the central area as a commercial centre is reflected in the heavy traffic that flows in and out of it. Along Jalan Tuanku Abdul Rahman (formerly known as Batu Road) the density of motor traffic of all kinds between the hours of eight o'clock in the morning and six in the evening is more than 1,500 vehicles per hour. Between one o'clock and two o'clock the traffic density is at its peak and approaches 2,000 vehicles per hour. This abnormal traffic flow is attributed to the movement of traffic to northern Malaya, and of commuters residing outside the central area, returning home for lunch and returning to work within the hour. Along Pudu Road the average density between 6.00 a.m. and 6.00 p.m. is about 1,500 vehicles per hour with the maximum density occuring early in the morning, late in the afternoon and during the middle of the day when outstation commercial vehicles arrive and converge on the market and other distribution centres in the central area.[5]

Population density is also highest in the central area. In three census dis-

tricts there are 110.8 persons, 162.7 and 217.4 persons per acre respectively. The population density of census districts fringing the central area varies from 4.0 persons to 97.0 persons per acre, indicating decreasing population density with increasing distance from the central area.[6] In contrast to European and American cities, a high percentage of people (Chinese retailers, for instance) live and work in the central area. (This group, which forms the majority of the central area population, reside on the first floor of their building and establish their business on the ground floor.) Nevertheless, there is evidence to show that some central area residents have moved out to live on the periphery. This is not to suggest that relatively fewer persons have daily business in the central area now than in former years; on the contrary, more people are drawn into it today than ten years ago in spite of the dispersal of some shopping facilities and other employment centres. Land values have risen considerably so that the central area remains a highly priced area in the city and although detailed figures are not available, it is generally estimated that the average value of land is about M$50.00 per square foot as compared with M$15.00 per square foot for land outside it. The highest land value is obtainable in the Old Market Square where the major banks of the country are to be found; speculators in real estate estimate that the price of land at this point is about M$100.00 per square foot.[7]

The existing arrangement of land

Note: 10.00 Malaysian dollars = £11.13.4

[6] I am grateful to T. G. McGee of the Department of Geography, University of Wellington, New Zealand, who has kindly allowed me to incorporate these data which are as yet unpublished.

[7] These figures are estimates obtained through conversation with town-planners and a few speculators in real estate in Kuala Lumpur.

[5] The figures on traffic density were obtained from Rudduck, G., *Town Planning in Kuala Lumpur*: a report to the Kuala Lumpur Municipal Council and the Selangor State and Federal Governments, Kuala Lumpur, 1955, pages 30–64.

Table 3

Approximate Percentage of Central Area Used in Relation to Space Under Chinese Shopbuildings, 1961[8]

Classified Uses	Ground Floor	First Floor	Second Floor
Residential	15.00	75.66	22.48
Wholesale Market and Shops	—	0.20	0.02
Street Stalls	0.17	—	—
Lodging houses, Hotels etc.	—	3.28	—
Guild, Association, Union Offices	—	6.53	19.40
Commercial Offices including Banks	19.31	12.95	57.40
Commercial Warehouses	0.41	1.00	0.70
Special Industrial Use	—	0.30	—
Retail Use	65.12	—	—
Building for civil, cultural and other uses	—	—	—
	100.01	99.92	100.00

uses reflects the functional importance of the central area although it does not necessarily represent the most efficient pattern. With the rise in the population through natural increase and migration, there has been not only peripheral expansion, but also an internal reorganization of land uses. Displacement of one use by another and infilling of vacant sites are common features and as business activities expand the demand for office space also increases. Business executives, life insurance salesmen, accountants, lawyers and doctors require work space in this area and because of its location, the area is also preferred by retailers in cloths, women's dresses, men's apparel, patented medicines and tinned food.

Urban land in central Kuala Lumpur may be classified according to its use. There are, broadly speaking, no less than eighteen dominant types of land use comprising 140 sub-types ranging from pet shops to finance offices. The amount of space occupied by each major type of use is given in Table 3.

[8] Information obtained from a survey carried out under the direction of the author with assistance given by students of the Department of Geography, and Miss Mah Puay Koon and Mr Wong Weng Fatt.

The analysis of this table shows that the central area has a variety of uses of which retailing on the ground floor and residential use on the upper floor form a common mixture; it is not unusual to find a building unit housing residences together with eating stalls and space for an insurance office; in fact, one shop in Petaling Street is used for a dispensary and the retail sale of stationery on the ground floor with space for living on the upper floor. In general, then, the central area contains administrative offices, bank and financial premises, shops for the sale of sundry goods, retail shops for textiles, transportation agencies, night clubs and cinemas. Railway stations, bus termini and warehouses are located on the fringe.

There is a tendency for certain types of uses to be grouped together, although sometimes the uses overlap. With increasing demand for office-space the land on the east side of the river up to Mountbatten Road is almost entirely devoted to government and semi-government offices, except for some space occupied by a printing press. The sector bounded by Mountbatten Road, Ampang Street, Old Market Square and the Central Market is used by banks, business, insurance, travel agents' offices and two large department stores. The strip of land between Ampang Road and Klang River is used for engineering showrooms together with insurance and other business uses. The vicinity of the Central Market area and part of Rodger Street is predominantly a wholesale area for dried fish, preserved Asian foods and rice. The corner area by the Suleiman Bridge circus is mainly a warehouse area. The site by Sungai Klang opposite Ampang Road is occupied by squatters at a density of about 150 persons per acre.

In between these groups (which serve the whole region) are the commonplace business-cum-residential areas that remain busy day and night with hawkers, peddlers, stallholders and their customers; even here, in a seemingly disorganized pattern, grouping of uses along major streets is observable. Klyne Street is the street for rubber dealers, Petaling Street has seen the incoming of shoe and textile shops and the concentration of goldsmiths' shops at the northern end on a triangular area by Pudu Road. There is a growing number of shops selling electrical appliances, photographers' equipment and furniture in High Street, replacing bicycle repair shops which have gone out of fashion with the increasing use of motor cars. Charcoal and plywood traders are leaving the street in favour of guild insurance offices; in Pudu Lane residences give way to eating stalls. Jalan Tuanku Abdul Rahman is famous for its comparatively cheap textile shops and Campbell Road is known for its food stalls.

The city's land uses are in a state of flux and change, especially so in some parts of the central area where offices of all kinds are gradually displacing residential use; the trend is towards the replacement of shop-houses with modern office premises which generally occupy a number of original shop-houses. This change means the transformation of urban landscape scenes from those of the early century to those of the present day although, in the process, a somewhat disturbing number of different building styles results. Apart from face-lifting, in which old shop fronts are renovated and new interior fittings installed, new buildings are much higher (the tallest building being seventeen storeys) but these are not uniformly distributed so that they tend to produce traffic concentrations at particular points thereby causing delays in movement of both goods and people. The road pattern has remained substantially as it was in 1895 when the bullock cart was the customary form of transport, consequently the traffic problem in the central area is serious despite the development of suburban shopping centres in Petaling Jaya and elsewhere. Lack of adequate legislation requiring builders to provide parking space further intensifies the traffic problem in this area.

Ribbon Business

Beyond the central area are dominant ribbons which, as the term implies, are axial to main roads leading in and out of the city. Their functions are observed generally to include those of the central area repeated on a small scale including hotels, restaurants and bars, small private clubs, billiard houses and petrol kiosks. Otherwise they serve both the immediate high and medium density residential areas which merge into low density areas on the outskirts of the town. In other words, these ribbons are sub-centres or service areas which may be regarded as forming the lowest level in the hierarchy of urban units as pos-

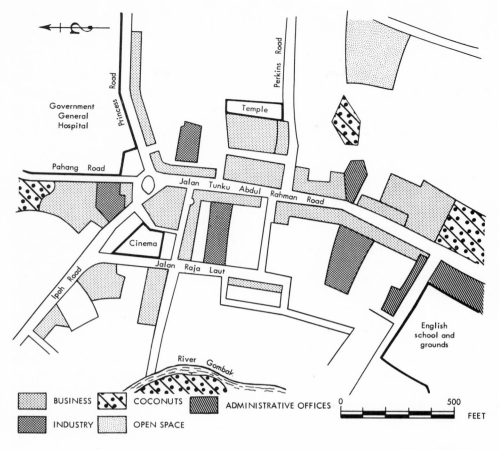

FIGURE 5

Business Ribbon at the Intersection of the Jalan Tunku Abdul Rahman, Ipoh Road, Pahang Road and Princess Road, North of the Central Area of Kuala Lumpur City

tulated in recent central place theory.[9]

The nature of service that each of these centres provides varies with its location, but in general, it appears to depend upon the extent to which it acts as a 'neighbourhood' shopping centre. A study of the business ribbon along Jalan Tuanku Abdul Rahman which is to the north of the central area [Figure 5] suggests that certain business types predominate. These may be identified as groceries, eating shops and textile shops; at the bottom of the road towards the central area motor repair shops are most frequent. But because traffic is funnelled into this road and the ribbon is close to an intersection of major streets, hotels and restaurants are equally common. With its two cinemas, post office and market the entire area functions as the nucleus of a 'neighbourhood' area.

The other business ribbon is the Pudu Road, south of the central area on the road to Singapore and south Malaya. Traffic volumes are as high along this road as on Jalan Tuanku Abdul Rahman so that those types of business

[9] Berry, Brian J. L. and Garrison, William L. Recent developments of the Central Place Theory. *Papers and Proceedings, Regional Science Association*, Vol. 4, 1958, pp. 107–120.

471

occurring in the central area also exist here. Groceries, eating shops and textile shops are grouped together, and where pedestrians are most numerous, beauty parlours, barbers, ice-water stalls and fresh fruit vendors congregate. Where pedestrian density is relatively low there are bicycle repair shops, tinsmiths and general repair shops.

THE EMERGENCE OF THE CONURBATION

One feature of post-war development affecting the central area of the city is that of ribbons of buildings along the road to the south and north; new housing estates have also developed on the west and east sides causing the extension of the municipal boundary in all directions and thereby enveloping some rubber estates and abandoned mining lands. The diplomatic enclave in the north western sector of the city, for instance, recently absorbed 250 acres of land under rubber cultivation. Except for the central area the development of the city is open, in fact, a clear trend is the movement of people from the central area to adjacent areas on the periphery and this trend is gaining momentum. Thus, population density on the fringe areas increases in importance as a factor in the growth of the city as a whole. The conurbation thus becomes apparent for the first time. In 1931 the city's population amounted to only 2.9 per cent of the Malayan population concentrated on an area of eighteen square miles, but since then it has accumulated within its boundary an urbanized area of thirty-seven square miles (1957) containing about 5.3 per cent of the population. Within the last thirteen years or so the re-settlement villages which were created within six miles of the central area, the indus-

trial estate of Old Klang Road and Petaling Jaya, are being amalgamated with the parent town to form one economic unit (Greater Kuala Lumpur) containing a total population of 380,420 or 15.7 per cent of the total Malayan population.

Apart from an increasing suburban population the conurbation has also grown as a result of mutual dependence between joint settlements of population and consumer-orientated industries. It follows, therefore, that the growth of Greater Kuala Lumpur will depend mainly on its industrial composition but whether conurbanization is advantageous or disadvantageous in the Malaysian geographical setting is another matter since it involves a consideration not only of economic factor, but also of sociological factors. It is obvious, however, that a great expanse of land would be required to contain 700,000 people, which is the estimated population in 1975. If the present type of open development persists it will become uneconomic to provide services as well as to build; the cost of street cleaning, garbage collection, street lighting and other annual charges being higher than it would have been in a compact city.

Kuala Lumpur is a city of contrasts; it has half a million people; in it are elements of centralization and dispersal. There exists a degree of specialization of functions and a degree of differentiation. In some respects its functions as a city are dependent on each other. In many ways it accords broadly with American and European cities with similar population size except for the imprints of foreign enterprise that pervade the central area where retail business, financial and adminstrative and other uses generate high land values and compete for space to create tendencies towards specialization of uses along major streets.

Unlike conditions in metropolitan development in other parts of the world, the night time population is the same size as the day time population. However, with intense pressure for expansion to meet changing political, social and economic needs, a gradual decentralization of population to the suburbs has been observed necessitating not only the development of suburban areas but also a re-organization of land uses. This is coupled with accelerated infilling of vacant property, 'face-lifting' of the ubiquitous Chinese shophouses, and urban renewal by street-blocks in the central area of the city. This in turn has resulted in the development of dominant business ribbons along major highways which function as sub-centres or service areas of newly emerging 'neighbourhoods'.

The amalgamation of resettlement villages (established during the anti-terrorist war between 1948 to 1960) with the neighbourhood centres linked to the central area has transformed the whole region into an extensive urbanized zone, the forerunner of another great conurbation in Malaysia, in addition to Singapore city. Greater Kuala Lumpur has the making of a great metropolis, and with its dominant status as a political and administrative centre whose hinterland encompasses the whole of the newly-created Malaysia it is clearly the Washington D.C. of this region with Singapore City serving as an important entrepôt similar to New York City.

The growth of industry has not, however, kept pace with the growth of the city as a whole in spite of active government promotion of industrial development in Petaling Jaya and other industrial estates. Instead of accelerated expansion of many manufacturing industries that usually accompanies the growth of big cities in other parts of the world, there is a preponderance of retail trading, domestic service and other non-generative services. With increasing immigration of population from the rural areas the city has more people than productive employment; this is reflected in increasing under-employment and self-employment. The low per capita income among the majority of its population has led to greater than average dependence on the city's administration for public subsidies on housing and related community facilities. The development of slum and squatter areas in parts of the city is due to insufficient resources at the disposal of the local authority and the low purchasing power of the squatters themselves to afford any alternative accommodation. Taking into account the over-crowding already existing in the city, traffic congestion, competition for land and other problems, the need for a comprehensive policy and programme has become a matter of urgent necessity. Thus, the future of the city depends on the correct approach to these problems.

34. Recent Research on Latin American Urbanization: A Selective Survey with Commentary

RICHARD M. MORSE

A comprehensive survey of recent research on Latin American urbanization would be a large task for a team of specialists, particularly if it were to include local as well as comparative studies, the working papers which circulate through government and academic offices, and all the scholarly disciplines which now contribute to the topic. This paper is no more than a sampling of research on selected aspects of urbanization, interlarded with commentary and a bit of opinion. Except for Section 1, emphasis is upon scholarly output of the past five years. Whatever unity the presentation may have springs from the interests of a historian who is less concerned with physical and social engineering than with identifying cultural and institutional imperatives of the past which shape contemporary social process.

Even with these allowances, the paper will be found to encroach—often fleetingly—upon a great many domains: history, planning and architecture, social anthropology, sociology, political science, economics and ecology. If any

Latin American Research Review, *1, No. 1* (Fall 1965), *35–74. Reprinted by permission of author and publisher.*

Revised version of a paper presented at the Conference on International and Comparative Urban Studies in American Higher Education, Rutgers University, June 6–8, 1965. Research was done under the auspices of a Guggenheim Fellowship, a grant from the Social Sicence Research Council, and a Senior Faculty Fellowship from Yale University.

"integration" occurs, it is produced by the questions raised and not by special skills of the interrogator.

1. THE ANTECEDENTS

The urbanization of modern Latin America received its initial thrust from the Iberian Peninsula and from the forces that made for European commercial capitalism and overseas expansion. If, however, one considers the urban history of the Latin American land mass, one can argue that its most splendid chapters were furnished by several of the pre-Columbian civilizations.

The fact that Spanish settlers were drawn to the sedentary and densely grouped Indian labor of the Middle and South American highlands made for ecological continuity between the pre- and post-conquest eras. Innumerable settlement sites, from rural villages to the imperial capitals of Tenochtitlán and Cuzco, kept their identity or were rebuilt under the European regime. Although frequently thought of as founded *ex nihilo* by the Spaniards, even Lima has a pre-conquest origin:

At Pizarro's arrival, there was one large center at Maranga, and scattered throughout the valley and hills that bound it were legions of other smaller ones. This structural pattern of one principal center and other secondary units loosely connected around and to it, in radial form, was to last throughout the history of the city, and is to this day characteristic of the area in which the metropolis is located.[1]

For large parts of Latin America the urban history from pre-Columbian times to the present is certainly a viable subject. A traumatic break occurs in the 16th century, however, with the mass dislocation of Indian peoples, the replacement of indigenous political and ecclesiastical hierarchies with European, the reorientation of economies to trans-Atlantic trade, and the imposition of European technology and urban forms. Hardoy writes in his recent survey of pre-Columbian cities:

On the ruins and amid disintegration of an age-old heritage the cities of a culture foreign to the continent sprang up within a few decades. This was made necessary by the political, strategic and economic requirements of the conquest. None of the indigenous cities was respected by the conquest or by the colonial administration, and during the first century of independence the governments of the Latin American republics did almost nothing to defend the monuments of the ancient civilizations.[2]

When we look to the late-medieval Iberian Peninsula we find that two classic city types in Spain were the commercial, manufacturing centers that grew up in the north along the east-west pilgrimage routes to Santiago de Compostela, and the agro-military towns of the central *meseta*, which were primary agents for appropriating lands reconquered from Islam. For León and Castile the 12th century has been called

a period of *repoblación concejil*: ". . . it is principally the now-important *Concejos* or *Municipios* which occupy the lands, divide them among the settlers, and promote the colonization of untilled fields."[3] The pilgrimage towns were akin to the towns of Western Europe's urban, commercial renascence. The *meseta* towns were the product of political and military factors of the Reconquest. It was by and large the latter which supplied the model for municipal settlement in Spanish America—not simply because colonists from central Spain had a determinant influence on overseas colonization,[4] but also because the pattern of Spanish New World conquest obeyed forces and circumstances analogous to those of the peninsular Reconquest.

In late-medieval Portugal the representative urban centers were the agro-commercial, maritime towns. They had developed along the seacoast in response to economic possibilities rather than to politico-military design.[5] The settlement of Brazil by the Portuguese appears to reproduce this pattern. Their principal towns are agro-commercial coastal settlements, modest in size and appearance, generally hapha-

[1] Luis Ortiz de Zevallos, "Lima: Rising Metropolis," paper for the 11th Pan American Congress of Architects, Washington, D.C., 15-20 June 1965. The Incaic period is Jorge Basadre's point of departure in *La multitud, la ciudad y el campo en la historia del Perú* (Lima, 1929).

[2] Jorge E. Hardoy, *Ciudades precolombinas* (Buenos Aires, 1964), p. 13. Arq. Hardoy promises two future volumes on colonial and on modern Latin American cities.

[3] Luis García Valdeavellano, *Historia de España de los orígenes a la Baja Edad Media* (3rd ed.; 2 vols., Madrid, 1963), II, 458. Also his *Sobre los burgos y los burgueses de la España medieval* (Madrid, 1960) and José María Lacarra, "Panorama de la historia urbana en la Península Ibérica desde el siglo V al X" in Centro Italiano di Studi sull'Alto Medioevo, *La città nell'Alto Medioevo* (Spoleto, 1959), pp. 319-57.

[4] "[During] the very first years of conquest and settlement in America, in its unplanned aspects conquest culture represented southwest and west-central Spain rather than the north." George M. Foster, *Culture and Conquest, America's Spanish Heritage* (Chicago, 1960), p. 232.

[5] See Jaime Cortesão, *Os factores democráticos na formação de Portugal* (Lisbon, 1964), pp. 58-158; Torquato Brochado de Souza Soares, *Apontamentos para o estudo da origem das instituições municipais portuguesas* (Lisbon, 1931).

zard or "natural" in layout. Portugal had not Spain's resources for large-scale urbanization or widespread settlement of the American hinterland. Unlike the Spaniards, who settled near the sources of Indian labor, the Portuguese recruited their native work force from the interior and brought it to the coastal plantations. Not for two centuries after the discovery of Brazil did mineral strikes cause important displacement of settlers to the interior. The gold rush, moreover, did less to modify than to intensify the "archipelago" pattern of inland colonization. Brazilian settlement has been a leapfrogging process, rather than the systematic advance of a colonizing frontier.[6] Perhaps it is not too much to say that the recent relocation of the national capital at Brasilia has had the effect of creating a new "gold mine" (i.e., of political patronage) in the wilderness, from which development of the hinterland is to flow as a byproduct.

The contrast between the Brazilian and Spanish American city is symbolized in their physical plans. The Spanish chessboard has medieval antecedents; but it reached its classic phase only in the Renaissance, precisely when it was to orient the vast work of urbanization in the New World.[7] Ricard suggests that "a Spanish American city is a *plaza mayor* surrounded by streets and houses, rather than an assemblage of houses and streets around a *plaza mayor*." He then points out the absence of the *plaza mayor* in the Portuguese tradition. The nearest equivalents are:

[6] See Christian Anglade, "Une tentative de répartition territoriale du phénomène de la capitale: le municipe brésilien," *Caravelle*, 3 (1964), 228–40.
[7] Leopoldo Torres Balbás et al., *Resumen histórico del urbanismo en España* (Madrid, 1954), pp. 3–148.

(1) the *rossio*, an unbuilt, generally communal piece of land without special architectural embellishment which is gradually absorbed into the city center as the urban limits expand; and (2) the *largo*, which "is merely a widening of the street with no elevation of its central area."[8]

Even given these differences between Spanish and Portuguese traditions and the respective strategies of colonization, one may still identify features common to the urban history of colonial Latin America as a whole:

(1) Colonization was in large part an urban venture, carried out by urban-minded people. The municipal nucleus was the point of departure for settlement of the land—unlike the West European city, which represented a movement of economic energies away from agriculture toward processing and distribution.

(2) Despite elaborate regulatory precautions, selection of urban sites was frequently arbitrary, ill-advised, or dictated by momentary considerations. Abandonment or transfer of towns was widespread throughout the colonial period.

(3) Firstcomers tended to preempt lands surrounding a new town (even municipal common lands were often alienated to private persons) and to reserve special privileges for their descendants. An initial moment of social democracy was therefore followed by consolidation of an oligarchy

[8] Robert Ricard, "La *Plaza Mayor* en Espagne et en Amérique Espagnole," *Annales, Économie— Sociétés—Civilisations*, 2, 4 (Oct.–Dec. 1947), 433–38. Also Robert C. Smith, "Colonial Towns of Spanish and Portuguese America," *Journal of the Society of Architectural Historians*, 14, 4 (Dec. 1955), 1–12; Erwin Walter Palm, "Los orígenes del urbanismo imperial en América" in Instituto Panamericano de Geografía e Historia, Comisión de Historia, *Contribuciones a la histroria municipal de América* (Mexico City, 1951), pp. 239–68; Luís Silveira, *Ensaio de iconografia das cidades portuguesas do Ultramar* (4 vols., Lisbon, n. d.), vol. IV.

based on land tenure and prior arrival.[9]

(4) In Brazil and much of Spanish America continuity of municipal institutions and processes was threatened by the displacement of city elders to their rural domains. Having radiated energies centrifugally to the land, all but the large commerical or bureaucratic cities tended to become appendages of the country.[10] The substitution of locality groups for kin groups which Weber felt to be so characteristic of the medieval European town often failed to occur in Latin America.[11] This meant that the city was not politically differentiated from the country; it was not a "commune" trying to expand its jurisdiction over a rural area.[12] A municipality in fact included rural lands, and there were no interstices between municipal jurisdictions. More typical than the struggle between burgher and feudal groups was the

conflict between local rural-urban oligarchies and agents of the royal bureaucracy.[13]

(5) Urban networks developed feebly. Geographic barriers to regional transportation were often formidable, while the crown's mercantilist policies did little to encourage centers of complementary economic production. New World cities tended to be related individually to the overseas metropolis and isolated one from another.[14]

[9] Francisco de Toledo, viceroy of Peru (1569–81), wrote to his king: "[The] first settlers of the cities who remained there as magistrates assumed the power of the governors sent to them so as to give and distribute to the settlers the lands they felt to be necessary. This they did more generously than later seemed proper, and they also caused the *cabildos* to give lands to those who asked for them, with so little thought for the common good of the cities that they failed to leave aside *dehesas*, or *ejidos* or *propios* in most cases, as needed to maintain the republics." *Relaciones de los virreyes y audiencias que han gobernado el Perú* (3 vols., Lima and Madrid, 1867–72), I, 14–15.

[10] From a dialogue of 1618 we learn of a wealthy Brazilian sugar planter who amused himself by making a gift to anyone who built a house in the city: 20 milréis for a two-storey house, 10 milréis for a one-storey one. "And he did this for a long time . . . without deriving any benefit other than fulfilling his wish to see the city grow." Brandônio, *Diálogos das grandezas do Brasil* (Recife, 1962), p. 97.

[11] Max Weber, *The City* (Glencoe, 1958), chap. 2.

[12] However, François Chevalier describes a sporadic "free village" movement of the peons and renters on north Mexican haciendas in the late 18th and 19th centuries: "Survivances seigneuriales et présages de la révolution agraire dans le nord du Mexique," *Revue Historique*, 122 (July–Sept. 1959), 1–18.

[13] The attempt of royal officials to make the *encomenderos* of New Granada carry out their municipal obligations caused what one historian calls the revolt of a "Fronde." Indalecio Liévano Aguirre, *Los grandes conflictos sociales y económicos de nuestra historia* (4 vols., Bogotá, n. d.), vol. I.

[14] For bibliography on colonial cities see articles in Instituto Panamericano de Geografía e Historia, *op. cit.* Also: Agustín Millares Carlo, *Los Archivos municipales de Latinoamérica*: Libros de actas y colecciones documentales; apuntes bibliográficos (Maracaibo, 1961); Francisco Domínguez Compañy, "Bibliografía de las instituciones locales de Hispanoamerica (época colonial), *Revista Interamericana de Bibliografía*, 6, 3 (July–Sept. 1956), 209–23. Selected reading: Constantino Bayle, *Los cabildos seculares en la América Española* (Madrid, 1952); Herbert Wilhelmy, *Südamerika im Spiegel seiner Städte* (Hamburg, 1952); R. M. Morse, "Some Characteristics of Latin American Urban History," *American Historical Review*, 67, 2 (Jan. 1962), 317–38; George A. Kubler, *Mexican Architecture of the Sixteenth Century* (2 vols., New Haven, 1948); John P. Moore, *The Cabildo in Peru under the Hapsburgs* (Durham, 1954), and "The Cabildo in Peru under the Bourbons" (unpublished MS); Guillermo Céspedes del Castillo, *Lima y Buenos Aires* (Seville, 1947); Juan A. García, *La ciudad indiana* in his *Obras completas* (2 vols., Buenos Aires, 1955), I, 283–475; Amílcar Razori, *Historia de la ciudad argentina* (3 vols., Buenos Aires, 1945); Julio Alemparte Robles, *El cabildo en Chile colonial* (Santiago, 1940); Edmundo Zenha, *O município no Brasil (1532–1700)* (São Paulo, 1948); Nelson Omegna, *A cidade colonial* (Rio de Janerio, 1961). Thomas Gale (University of Kansas) with the assistance of Bernhard Ansel has collected 8,000 titles referring to "communities" in Latin America with emphasis on the historical aspect. It is in the process of being prepared according to author and area.

Historiography on Latin American cities during the late colonial period and the 19th century does not yet afford sufficient basis for easy generalization. One underlying demographic fact, however, is that the population of Latin America, after holding steady for most of the colonial period, begins to increase at a rate that has accelerated ever since.

Population of Latin America[15]

Year	Population (Millions)	Year	Population (Millions)
1570	10.2	1825	23.1
1650	11.4	1850	33
1750	11.1	1900	63
1800	18.9	1950	160

In many areas the late 18th century population increase was accompanied by economic development, technological modernization, rural colonization movements, and urban improvements for the larger cities. The picture, of course, was not one of unrelieved prosperity. In 1780 a Peruvian viceroy wrote that the backwardness of his realm might lead one to believe that only fifty years had elapsed since the conquest. Rural lands lay idle; the road system was abominable. Towns were widely scattered and scarcely deserved to be called villages. All but two cities outside the capital were losing inhabitants and deteriorating physically. As for Lima: "If this city, capital of the realm, shows more splendor, one soon discovers that its grandeur has no other sources than its rather impermanent buildings and its farms which hardly

produce the most basic staples to sustain its people."[16]

In New Spain, on the other hand, this was a period of mounting prosperity. Liberalization of trade restrictions created a new class of urban merchants and redirected much of the old merchant capital into agrilulture and mining. New Caribbean and European markets for farm products became available, while locally the "possibilities increase because Mexico City and Guadalajara grow, because mining centers like Guanajuato become important and prosperous cities."[17] In Mexico City the annual incomes of the wealthiest family heads were as high as 200,000 pesos in 1800. The equivalent figure in Havana was 35,000 pesos and in Caracas 10,000 pesos. Lima had scarcely a family with an assured income of 6,500 pesos.[18]

In the Viceroyalty of the Río de la Plata Spanish administrators of the 1780's and 1790's founded many new towns designed as outposts against Indian marauding, as centers of economic production, and as assimilation points for scattered rural settlers and new immigrants. Colonization occurred in Patagonia, the Banda Oriental, and the intendancies of Salta and Córdoba. Much was also done to improve the appearance and institutions of existing cities, above all Buenos Aires.[19]

[15] These admittedly sketchy figures include the non-Hispanic Caribbean region and are from Rosenblat and Carr-Saunders in Angel Rosenblat, *La población indígena y el mestizaje en América* (2 vols., Buenos Aires, 1954).

[16] *Relaciones de los virreyes...*, *op. cit.*, III, 18–19.

[17] François Chevalier, "La gran propiedad en México desde el siglo XVI hasta comienzos del siglo XIX," *Desarrollo Económico*, 3, 1–2 (April–Sept. 1963), 51.

[18] Fernando Rosenzweig Hernández, "La economía novo-hispana al comenzar el siglo XIX," *Ciencias Políticas y Sociales*, 9, 33 (July–Sept. 1963), 459.

[19] John Lynch, *Spanish Colonial Administration, 1782–1810* (London, 1958), pp. 154–62. Colonization was not always successful; see Félix de Azara, *Memoria sobre el estado rural del Río de la Plata y otros informes* (Buenos Aires, 1943), pp. 1–25.

Of Brazil Fernando de Azevedo writes that the 17th century was one of territorial expansion, conquest and settlement, while the 18th—the century of gold—saw the development of cities and of "a new bourgeois class anxious to dominate and already sufficiently strong to face the exclusivism of the families of landowners."[20] Three new cities and 118 *vilas* were created in the 18th century as against four cities and only 37 *vilas* in the 17th. In the final years of the colonial period (1800–22) two cities and 44 *vilas* were erected. On the coast Salvador's population doubled and Rio's quadrupled during the 18th century. Urbanization of the interior began in earneast, particularly in Minas. *Bocas de sertão* appeared 300 miles inland, with "sentinel" points at twice that distance or even much farther along the Amazon.[21]

Brito Figueroa documents urbanization in Venezuela [in the table below].

Brito's analysis of the ruling class shows that the Suarezian description of a city in the *De Legibus* and a *civitas* "formed by the coalition of a number of families" was far from archaic.[23] This class was composed principally of:

(1) White landowners. They formed a largely endogamous group of 658 families, proud of their blood "purity." They lived in the cities and left administration of their *haciendas* to foremen who were generally men of color. They monopolized both the productive land and the urban political institutions.

(2) Export merchants. They monopolized the export of farm and ranch products and also employed their capital in usurious loans to small farmers. Often they themselves owned *haciendas* and formed part of group (1).

(3) Import merchants. These were often Spaniards well connected with the royal bureaucracy. Although they might conflict with the first two groups on commercial policy, their dependence on Spanish officialdom scarcely made them a "bourgeoisie."

Period	Urban Population	%	Rural Population	%	Total
1759–72	185,926	29	444,074	71	630,000
1771–84	204,760	29	505,240	71	710,000
1800–10	354,536	34	643,707	66	998,243

Demographic and commercial development, however, failed to produce the social change that one might expect. "Colonial Venezuelan production originated on the plantations, flowed to the mercantile cities connected with the foreign market, and [its profits] returned to the plantations without changing the economic conditions which prevailed there."[22]

[20] Fernado de Azevedo, *Brazilian Culture* (New York, 1950), p. 77.

[21] Aroldo de Azevedo, *Vilas e cidades do Brasil colonial* (São Paulo, 1956), pp. 35–54.

[22] Federico Brito Figueroa, *La estructura económica de Venezuela colonial* (Caracas, 1963), pp. 271, 275.

If economic development diversified the elite, it tended also to produce a coalescence of interests, agricultural-commercial, urban-rural. There appeared in the urban centers a series of socio-occupational categories (*hacendados, comerciantes, mercaderes, dependientes, bodegueros*) which had almost legal, corporate definitions. To describe the lower-class, mixed-blood groups the word *casta* was used in late-colonial Venezuela and in Spanish America generally. The term tells a good deal about the elite as well as about the

[23] Francisco Suárez, *Selections from Three Works* (Oxford, 1944), p. 365.

groups to which it applied. *Casta* does not convey the hermetic, segregative sense of "caste." It is more reminiscent of the Thomist-Aristotelian notion of functional social hierarchy. It refers to a "stratified social group, united by ethnic origin, common juridico-legal status, and a common type of economic-professional occupations and activities."[24]

The point for our purposes is that if the logic of an older order survived as an organizing principle in this period of demographic and economic expansion and wider contact with the world, we might well expect it to survive even today. This would lead us to view the modern Latin American city less as an urban society in "change" (i.e., revolution, self-transcendence, obliteration of the past) than as a society in which the accoutrements and rallying cries of Western industrial civilization are being mediated to an Ibero-Catholic, creole, patrimonial order of life. As a recent ECLA study phrases it, the "traditional structure" of Latin America, "far from having been rigid and impenetrable, has been sufficiently porous to modernize many of its elements, but without achieving swift and radical 'modernization' of a lasting sort."[25]

One may regard Latin America's rural exodus and urban growth of the 20th century as part of a movement which began in 19th-century Europe and has now reached global propor-tions. Or one may place the pheno-menon in historico-cultural perspec-tive. The urban centrifugalism of colo-nial times has become centripetal. The Latin American city now reaps as it once sowed. The rural settlement pat-terns which it long ago created now give their stamp to the process by which millions are drifting and regrouping across the land.

It would be of interest to examine the historical demography of Latin America for the past 200 years and establish the period when urban growth rates began to pull ahead of rural ones for different regions and for different categories of city. A more fundamental job would be to identify the ways in which the 19th century city intensified its control over the country.[26] In my study of São Paulo, a city which is not in every way typical, some of the points brought out are:

—increasingly active political role for the city (this was of still larger importance for new national capitals);

—city now a center for commercial and intellectual contact with foreign countries after removal of colonial mercantilist res-traints;

—attraction of rural aristocracy to urban residence (as in the case of Venezuela cited above) and its participation in commercial and financial activity;

—development of urban credit mechan-isms which cause the commercial "enfeoff-ment" of the rural domain;

—construction of a fan-like railway net centering on the city;

—role of the liberal, "rational" city mind in commercializing, specializing and tech-

[24] Federico Brito Figueroa, *La estructura social y demográfica de Venezuela colonial* (Caracas, 1961), p. 73 n; also his *Ensayos de historia social de Venezuela* (Caracas, 1960).

[25] ECLA (Economic Commission for Latin America), *El desarrollo social de América Latina en la postguerra* (Buenos Aires, 1963), p. 13. The point is developed in my essay "The Heritage of Latin America" in Louis Hartz, *The Founding of New Societies* (New York, 1964), pp. 123–77.

[26] For 19th-century cities see: "Expansión urbana en la América Latina durante el siglo XIX" (symposium), *Estudios Americanos*, 13, 67–68 (April–May 1957), 255–93; William E. Curtis, *The Capitals of Spanish America* (New York, 1888); Razori, *op. cit.*; Gilberto Freyre, *The Mansions and the Shanties* (New York, 1963); Joaquín Capelo, *Sociología de Lima* (4 vols., Lima, 1895–1902).

nifying agriculture and in transforming farm labor into a rural proletariat (abolition of slavery, importation of foreign contract labor, and—in other countries— abolition of tutelary protection for rural Indian communities);

—role of immigrants as entrepreneurs and their eventual absorption into the elite.[27]

George Kubler reminds us that the greater international exposure of Latin American cities after independence made them more provincial rather than more metropolitan. He defines the metropolis as a center of binding decisions that affect networks of other settlements. "Its physical equipment tends towards uniqueness. It is costly, intricate, and exemplary, while that of the provinces is imitative, derivative, and merely typical." Even though colonial Latin America was ruled from Madrid and Lisbon, the margin for autonomy was enough to allow it to develop eight "second-echelon" metropolitan centers by the late 18th century—that is, cities commanding within their own political and regional spheres and not internationally. Kubler identifies them as Mexico City, Lima, Guatemala, Bogotá, Quito, Buenos Aires, Havana and Rio de Janeiro. Today, he claims, only three of them are properly metropolitan: Mexico City, Buenos Aires and Rio. The traveler can scarcely tell one commercial center or upper-class suburb or proletarian slum from another. There has occurred a "diminution in the cultural diversity of Latin American life, and in the range of choices being freely made."[28]

One may argue with Kubler's two

lists, but the point is sound. Political emancipation subjected Latin America to new "colonial" influences, artistic and intellectual as well as others. Present "development" strategies cannot take hold or cast an image as long as they are routine exercises in problem-solving. They need also to be informed by the style, assurance and coherence that only the defiant regionalism (as distinct from provincialism) of a great metropolis can give them.

2. RECENT URBAN GROWTH AND THE ROLE OF MIGRATION[29]

In 1950 39% of the Latin American population, or 61 million people, lived in urban centers of more than 2,000

---

[27] R. M. Morse, *From Community to Metropolis, A Biography of São Paulo, Brazil* (Gainesville, 1958).

[28] George A. Kubler, "Cities and Culture in the Colonial Period in Lain America," *Diogenes,* 47 (Fall 1964), 53–62.

[29] For bibliography on contemporary Latin American cities see: Exchange Bibliographies, Latin American Series (Nos. 1–8, 1962–64), compiled by Francis Violich and distributed by the Council of Planning Librarians, Eugene, Ore.; Angel Rubio y Muñoz-Bocanegra, Bibliografía de geografía urbana de América (Rio de Janeiro, 1961); Waldemiro Bazzanella, *Problemas de urbanização na América a Latina, fontes bibliográficas* (Rio de Janeiro, 1960). Comparative bibliography: William Bicker *et al; Comparative Urban Development: An Annotated Bibliography* (Washington, 1965). General studies or collections of studies: Philip H. Hauser, ed., *Urbanization in Latin America* (New York, 1961); "Actes du Colloque sur le problème des capitales en Amérique Latine," *Caravelle* 3 (1964); Jaime Dorselaer and Alfonso Gregory, *La urbanización en América Latina* (2 vols., Fribourg and Brussels, 1962); Luis Calderón, Arturo Calle and Jaime Dorselaer, *Problemas de urbanización en América Latina* (Fribourg and Bogotá, 1963); R. M. Morse, "Latin American Cities: Aspects of Function and Structure" in John Friedmann and William Alonso, eds., *Regional Development and Planning* (Cambridge, 1964), pp. 361–81; Centro Latino Americano de Pesquisas em Ciências Sociais, *Situação social da América Latina* (Rio de Janeiro, 1965), pp. 50–79; T. Lynn Smith, "Urbanization in Latin America," in Nels Anderson, ed., *Urbanism and Urbanization* (Leiden, 1964), pp. 127–42; John P. Powelson and Anatole A. Solow, "Urban and Rural Development in Latin America," *Annals of the American Academy of Political and Social Science,*

inhabitants, while 61%, or 95 million people, lived in rural areas. In 1960 there were 95 million in towns (46%) and 111 million in the country (54%). The urban growth rate for the decade was 55%, the rural growth rate 12%. Annually, the rate was 4.5% as against 1.4%.

An ECLA projection gives Latin America a population of 291 million for 1975, 54% urban and 46% rural.

In 1960 four countries had an urban population greater than 60% of the total national population (Uruguay was highest with 82%). Four countries were in the 40–60% range. Twelve were below 40% urban (with Haiti lowest at 13%). By 1975 the distribution in these categories will be something like 11 (urban), 7 (equilibrium), 2 (rural).

Until 1930 Buenos Aires was Latin America's only city with more than a million inhabitants. Mexico City, Rio de Janeiro and São Paulo soon joined it. Havana, Lima and Santiago were million-cities by 1950; Bogotá, Caracas and Montevideo were added by 1960. By 1970 there may be 16 million-cities, and 26 by 1980. The million-cities contained 27 million inhabitants in 1960; by 1980 they will have 90 million. The four original million-cities already

present the phenomenon of conurbation.[30]

Half or more of the population increase in the large cities is attributable to migration from the country and smaller towns.[31] From country to country the ratio of migratory to natural increase of urban populations varies appreciably. Although the rural-urban migration had its 19th-century counterpart in the industrial countries, the movement has special implications in modern Latin America:

(1) The flow of people to large cities is out of proportion to fresh opportunities for stable urban employment, especially industrial.

(2) The city has insufficient physical resources to absorb its growing population. This is not merely to say that governments lack the wherewithal to mount vast housing programs. It is also to say that in many cities private enterprise fails to meet the demand for outright slum housing. Therefore many new migrants, along with many who abandon or are dislodged from slums, are forced to *build their own city*.

---

[30] For a case study of "conurbation" see M. T. Segadas Viana, "Nova Iguaçu, absorção de uma célula urbana pelo Grande Rio de Janeiro," *Revista Brasileira de Geografia*, 24, 2 (April–June 1962), 155–250.

[31] See Moysés Poblete Troncoso, "El éxodo rural, sus orígenes, sus repercusiones," *América Latina*, 5, 1–2 (Jan.–June 1962), 41–49; Henry F. Dobyns and Mario C. Vázquez, eds., *Migración e integración en el Perú* (Lima, 1963); José Francisco de Camargo, *Éxodo rural no Brasil* (2nd ed.; Rio de Janeiro, 1960); Instituto Joaquim Nabuco de pesquisas Sociais, *As migrações para o Recife* (4 vols., Recife, 1961); Pan American Union, *Éxodo rural en Venezuela* (Washington, 195?); Nathan L. Whetten and Robert G. Burnight, "Internal Migration in Mexico," *Estadística, Journal of the Inter-American Statistical Institute*, 16, 58 (March 1958), 65–77; Edmundo Flores, *Tratado de economia agrícola* (2nd ed.; Mexico City, 1962), pp. 204–20; Universidad de Chile, Instituto de Economía, *La población del Gran Santiago* (Santiago, 1959), chap. IX; *La Torre* (special no. on Puerto Rican emigration), 4, 13 (Jan.–March 1956).

---

360 (July 1965), 48–62; Mauricio Gómez Mayorga *et al.*, *La superurbanización caótica* (Mexico City, 1963); W. Stanley Rycroft and Myrtle M. Clemmer, *A Study of Urbanization in Latin America* (New York, 1962). Case studies: Jorge E. Hardoy, "The Process of Urbanization in Argentina," paper for the Conference on International and Comparative Urban Studies in American Higher Education, Rutgers University, 6–8 June 1965, and two papers circulated by the Instituto Latinoamericano de Planificación Económica y Social, Santiago: Luis Ratinoff, "La urbanización en América Latina: el caso de Paraguay" (multilith, July 1964) and Suzana Prates, "Algunas consideraciones sobre el proceso de urbanización de El Salvador" (mimeog., Dec. 1964).

(3) The city is deficient in the regime of impersonal organization, voluntary association and administrative services which is accepted as part of the Western urban ethos. Migrants and underprivileged are thrown back upon primary, quasi-rural modes of association which serve: (a) to organize their improvised communities, and (b) to relate these communities, or their component families, to sources of urban patronage by means of "clientage" arrangements.

(4) At the same time that millions of "marginal" Latin Americans are straining for access to urban security and opportunity, their allegiance is being courted by a new stripe of "populist" political leader. Populism is a tricky term. Some define it as politics for a mass society: demagogic, paternalistic, nationalistic, non-ideological —a kind of Bonapartism or democratic Caesarism.[32] Pearse, while accepting this framework, Latin-Americanizes the term by stressing the "informal and non-institutionalized" structures of clientage upon which populist politics rest. This clarifies the distinction between the urban "mass society" of a northern industrial nation and a Latin American urban society which resists "the organization of common interest groups or co-operative groups." Populism is the surrogate for such organization, bridging the gap between city life and "a tradition of rural dependence."[33]

Each of these four points is dealt with more fully later on.

The causes of migration are customarily divided into push and pull factors. Germani minimizes the forces of urban attraction and finds no necessary correlation between degree of rural poverty and tendency to migrate. The so-called objective factors "are filtered through the attitudes and decisions of individuals. . . . Therefore rural-urban migration is not merely a symptom, a demographic fact and a response to a certain economic pressure, but also the expression of a mental change. . . . Thus one can say that migration is a substitute for a social revolution."[34]

Marshall Wolfe also warns against the "oft-repeated generalizations on the 'lure' of the great cities." He then identifies four key factors at the rural end of the migration process:

(1) Resident workers on large estates are uprooted by mechanization of agriculture, shifts in commercial crops, and landowners' fears of future land tenure claims. Typically they move to roadside clusters of shacks or to peripheries of smaller towns.

(2) Nuclei of small owner-cultivators are being squeezed by population increase, land exhaustion, declining demand for seasonal labor on large estates. They may show greater initiative than the landless workers by moving into petty commerce; organizing invasions of large estates; migrating to tropical pioneer zones; becoming temporary wage laborers; or migrating permanently to towns and cities.

(3) Despite population pressures, rural settlement patterns are moving toward dispersal and impermanence. Roadside "line settlements" are increasing in number. The primary neighborhood, or small, loose cluster of families, remains more typical than the large agricultural village, or "community." Hence the difficulties of extending public services, school systems and housing programs to the country.

---

[32] F. C. Weffort distinguishes urban populism from "coronelismo," the old-style, personalized client relationship of the rural Brazilian *município*: "Política de massas" in Octávio Ianni *et al.*, *Política e revolução social no Brasil* (Rio de Janeiro, 1965), pp. 159–98. The classic study of "coronelismo" is Victor Nuñes Leal, *Coronelismo, enxada e voto* (Rio de Janeiro, 1948).

[33] Andrew Pearse, "Some Characteristics of Urbanization in the City of Rio de Janerio" in Hauser, *op. cit.*, p. 202.

[34] Gino Germani, "Emigración del campo a la ciudad y sus causas" in Horacio Giberti *et al.*, *Sociedad, economía y reforma agraria* (Buenos Aires, 1965), pp. 74–75. Charles Rosario emphasizes the imponderables and the sense of personal crisis attending each decision to migrate: "La emigración como experiencia vital," *La Torre*, 4, 13 (Jan.–March 1956), 23–31.

(4) Small towns in Latin America have always been less than effective as administrative, marketing and service centers. Even these few functions are now being eroded away. Small towns tend to grow no faster than the countryside, and they are being "ruralized" by the desertion of leadership elements and their replacement by families of landless farm workers who use the town as a base for job-seeking.[35]

3. EXPANSION OF THE "SERVICES" SECTOR

It is often shown that rural-urban migration in Latin America outruns the possibilities for employment in urban industry. The ratio of the tertiary or "services" sector of employment to the secondary or manufacturing sector is therefore much greater than the ratio prevailing in Western Europe. It even approaches, and for many countries exceeds, the ratio in the United States, where technological multipliers have permitted a heavy growth of "services."

Relation of Tertiary to Secondary Sector in Selected Countries (C. 1950)[36]

Venezuela	2.08	Malaya	2.82
Cuba	2.00	India	2.17
Haiti	1.56	United States	1.48
Argentina	1.51	Canada	1.31
Mexico	1.48	France	1.15
Bolivia	1.40	Spain	1.09
Brazil	1.27	Italy	0.96
Paraguay	1.18	West Germany	0.85

The Latin American and United States tertiary sectors bear little resemblance.

[35] Marshall Wolfe, "Some Implications of Recent Changes in Urban and Rural Settlement Patterns in Latin America," paper for UN World Population Conference, 1965 (A.8/I/E66). Also ECLA, Social Affairs Division, "Rural Settlement Patterns and Social Change in Latin America: Notes for a Strategy of Rural Development" (multilith, April 1964).

[36] Torcuato S. Di Tella, *La teoría del primer impacto del crecimiento económico* (Buenos Aires, n. d.), p. 34.

The former is heavily weighted toward petty commerce. and street vending, domestic service, unskilled and transitory work, and disguised unemployment. Perhaps the most dramatic example is the division of labor frequent among shanty dwellers who comb refuse dumps, specializing in the collection of specific items or materials.[37] The rural exodus is sometimes called a transfer of poverty or unemployment from country to city.

Since the indices for urbanization are outrunning those for industrialization, the two processes do not seem closely linked. In the case of Brazil, Bazzanella has shown industrialization to be an efficient but not a sufficient cause of urbanization. He divides the country into three zones which he calls Retarded, Intermediate and Advanced with respect to socioeconomic development.[38] For each zone he then analyzes the population of cities having more than 10,000 inhabitants for the intercensal period 1940–50. Here are some of his findings:

(1) Urban population growth (i.e., urbanization) over the ten-year period is roughly equal for each zone: 47.6% (Retarded zone), 46.1% (Intermediate), 50.3% (Advanced).

(2) The percentage of the ten-year population increment which was absorbed by industry differs sharply: 5.6% (R), 12.4% (I), 19.5% (A).

(3) In 1940 the Advanced zone had 75% of Brazil's industrial workers in cities over 10,000; in 1950 it had 78%. The cities in zones (I) and (R) *lost ground* slightly during the decade with respect to their share of the urban industrial force.

(4) The increase of persons employed in

[37] *Child of the Dark* (New York, 1962) by Carolina Maria de Jesus is the diary of such a person.

[38] He classifies Brazil south from the state of Rio as advanced; Pernambuco, Bahia and Minas Gerais as intermediate; the rest of Brazil as retarded.

the secondary sector varied with the degree of development. The total rose by 32.7% for zone (R), 59.3% for (I), 74.7% for (A).

(5) The growth of the tertiary sector was much more nearly uniform: 59.4% (R), 65.7% (I), 69.1% (A).

It can therefore be concluded that:

—the urbanization rate is more or less constant for the different socioeconomic zones of Brazil;
—growth of the tertiary sector is a necessary concomitant to urbanization and its rate of growth shows only moderate zonal variation;
—the rate of urbanization is not a function of the degree of industrialization.

Like others, Bazzanella uses the term "modernization" for cases of urbanization without industrialization, where stimuli from the outside industrial world induce changes in style of life and levels of aspiration without being strong enough to provoke structural changes in the economic system. More significant to him than the oft-deplored phenomenon of "overurbanization" is the "overruralization" which produces it.[39]

Having studied the figures for Bra-

zil's most recent intercensal period, 1950–60, Celso Furtado attacks still another "excess": overmechanization. During the decade of the '50's the total population increased by 3.2% a year, while the urban sector increased by almost 6% a year. At the same time the annual increase for agricultural production was 4.5% and for industrial production 9%. Yet owing to "borrowed technology" and "overmechanization," the yearly increment to the industrial labor force was only 2.8% against 3.5% for agriculture.[40]

The debate over whether urbanization, and specifically the growth of the tertiary sector, can be "excessive" is by no means ended. Denis Lambert is apprehensive. He claims that urban unemployment, open or disguised, is more onerous than rural because the minimum resources for survival are fewer in the city, and that it is more "dangerous" because social tensions are more explosive there. He also claims that rural-urban migration does not necessarily raise productivity.[41] Rottenberg, on the other hand, feels that to approve of a high level of tertiary employment in rich countries as an index of progress and to disapprove of it in poor ones as an index of poverty is to argue on a non-intellectual premise. He finds it hard to call manufactured goods superior to services, or to distinguish "petty" from significant services. In rather classical fashion he assumes that people seek out the most advantageous employment open to them and that therefore the reallocation of workers produced by urbanization

[39] Waldemiro Bazzanella, "Industrializaçãoe urbanização no Brasil," *América Latina*, 6, I (Jan.–March 1963), 3–26. The urban style of life may of course extend beyond the confines of a city; see Ruben E. Reina, "The Urban World View of a Tropical Forest Community in the Absence of a City, Peten, Guatemala," *Human Organization*, 23, 4 (Winter 1964), 265–77. For historical and comparative analysis of urbanization without industrialization see Bert F. Hoselitz, "The Role of Cities in the Economic Growth of Underdeveloped Countries," *Journal of Political Economy*, 61, 3 (June 1953), 195–208, and "The City, the Factory, and Economic Growth," *The American Economic Review*, 45, 2 (May 1955), 166–84. Frank Sherwood in an unpublished study on Brazil, "Patterns of urban growth and their political consequences," MS (1965), found there was not as high a correlation between levels of urbanization and voter eligibility and participation as between these latter and industrialization.

[40] Celso Furtado, "Obstáculos políticos ao crescimento econômico do Brasil," *Revista Civilização Brasileira*, I, 1 (March 1965), 133–41.
[41] Denis Lambert, "Urbanisation et développement économique en Amérique Latine," *Caravelle*, 3 (1964), 266–71; also Camilo Torres Restrepo, "La proletarización de Bogotá," *Monografías Sociológicas* (Bogotá), 9 (Nov. 1961).

has narrowed the distance to an optimum employment pattern.[42]

A controversy of this sort seems a little fatuous to the extent that it implies the possibility for substantial planned control over demographic and employment patterns during the next generation. So tidal a population movement must be accepted as a "natural force" on the order of the trans-Atlantic migration or the Industrial Revolution. What we need from the urban theoreticians are several ideal and creative models for the "under-industrialized" Latin American city which will combine the demographic, economic, sociological, historico-cultural and architectural perspectives.

4. THE PRIMATE CITY

"Primate cities" are a subcategory of the "overurbanization" problem. When the "rank-size" rule is applied to each of the Latin American countries, the first city nearly always towers above the other groups of cities which the model establishes. This dominance is usually most striking when the first city is compared to the group that immediately follows it. It is also noted that, except for Brazil, neither the size of a country nor the size of its urban system has any systematic influence on its urban pattern. The chief exceptions to the "primate" rule for Latin America are: Ecuador (bicephalous with Quito and Guayaquil), Colombia (with an almost "normal" pyramidal hierarchy),[43] and Brazil (whose immense territory contains two leading metropolitan systems and several secondary

ones).[44] In only a few cases is the growth rate of the smaller cities approaching or overtaking that of the primate city or "primate pair." In Mexico and Colombia the medium cities have higher growth rates than the primate, while in Brazil and Venezuela rising growth rates are affecting both medium and small cities.[45]

Berry finds "no relationships between type of city size distribution and either relative economic development or the degree of urbanization of countries." He concludes that a "few strong forces" affecting urban growth tend to produce primacy while many complex forces tend to produce lognormal distribution.[46] The ECLA study just cited calls present evidence insufficient to explain "in what manner—through bottlenecks in transportation, administration, distribution of goods, capital or skilled labor force—the present distribution of urban population has been influenced." Two alternate and perhaps mutually reinforcing hypotheses are advanced: (1) Where population is initially distributed evenly among smaller cities none of them has much power of attraction, and only one or two leading cities show strong growth. (2) Where one city acquires early dominance it inhibits the growth of close competitors while not greatly

[42] Simon Rottenberg, "Note on the Economics of Urbanization in Latin America," UN document E/CN.12/URB 6 (30 Sept. 1958).

[43] Colombia is highly regionalized; a city like Medellín might be said to have primacy at the departmental leve.

[44] Pedro Pinchas Geiger, *Evolução da rêde urban brasileira* (Rio de Janeiro, 1963).

[45] ECLA, "Geographic Distribution of the Population of Latin America and Regional Development Priorities," UN document E/CN.12/643 (10 Feb. 1963), pp. 28–33.

[46] Brian J. L. Berry, "City Size Distributions and Economic Development," *Economic Development and Cultural Change*, IX, 4, Part 1 (July 1961), 587. Floyd and Lillian Dotson noted high growth rates for smaller Mexican cities after 1940 and suggested correlation between decentralization and technological-economic development: "Urban Centralization and Decentralization in Mexico," *Rural Sociology*, 21, 1 (March 1956), 41–49.

affecting the growth of smaller cities.[47] Browning leans toward the second hypothesis and offers historical evidence for the colonial period (bureaucratic centralization), early republican period (commercial and cultural concentration, nature of export economies) and contemporary period (central bureaucracy, urban real estate investments, industrialization near labor source, cartwheel rail and road systems).[48]

An example of primacy is Greater Santiago, which has grown from roughly 800,000 in 1930 to nearly 2,500,000 today. It has not grown as fast as some Latin American capitals. Its share of the national population (almost 30%) is not as high as that of Buenos Aires or Montevideo. But it ranks as a typical primate city. Chile's second urban center, Valparaiso-Viña del Mar, had a 1960 population of 368,332 and in effect formed part of the urban complex of the capital. Of particular interest is the fact that Santiago's growth is not always favored by official encouragement or acquiesence.

It is not true that Santiago represents something artificial. It developed spontaneously, against the will of the government itself. . . .

The government had done what it could to hold back Santiago. It has established no important industry in the capital and has located them as far off as possible.

Urban construction, the writer continues, was stimulated by inflation, which diverted domestic capital from economic production into urban real estate. "But even if one sharply limits this sort of abuse . . . Santiago will keep on expanding, and we should entertain

no illusions about being able to hold back that growth."[49]

The Mexican government has deliberately encouraged the growth of Mexico City. Food products, fuel oil, electricity and natural gas have all been subsidized to hold back living costs and to attract industry. There is evidence that freight rates have been managed to encourage shipment of raw materials rather than finished goods to the metropolitan market. While approving any reduction in the amount of sheer political favoritism enjoyed by the capital, Richard Bird warns against egalitarian regionalism for its own sake: ". . . one can make the strong argument that the growing urban center is the leading 'growth pole' in a developing country and should be encouraged, not hampered."[50]

In the writing on urban macrocephalism the primate city is frequently called a parasite, a suction pump, a spreading blotch of oil, or a spider's body with shriveled legs. Browning, however, asks whether concentration of urban services is not a valuable economy for a capital-poor nation, especially a smaller one such as Uruguay.[51] This raises the issue of "optimum size," an exceedingly complex one in light of the many variables involved and the open-ended possibilities of technology. Rama shifts the grounds of the argument by suggesting that the case of Montevideo be regarded not as pathological but as a pioneer "social experiment." He claims that "all of Uruguay forms part of Montevideo's metro-

[47] ECLA, "Geographic Distribution . . . ," *op. cit.*, p. 32.

[48] Harley L. Browning, "Recent Trends in Latin American Urbanization," *Annals of the American Academy of Political and Social Science*, 316 (March 1958), 115–16.

[49] Carlos Keller R. in "Seminario del Gran Santiago," *Boletín Informativo* (Universidad de Chile), 8, 34 (Oct. 1958), 197–98. For Caracas see José V. Montesino Samperio, *La problación del area metropolitana de Caracas* (Caracas, 1956).

[50] Richard Bird, "The Economy of the Mexican Federal District," *Inter-American Economic Affairs*, 17, 2 (Autumn 1963), 50–51.

[51] Browning, *loc. cit.*, p. 116.

politan area," and that the whole country is becoming absorbed into "a rural-urban environment, that is, a way of life which participates in an urbanized society even though the population centers do not strictly constitute cities."[52]

5. "MARGINAL" SETTLEMENTS

For many observers urban shanty towns are the most spectacular visible hallmark of the social composition of a Latin American city (though the mansions of the rich run them a close second). The leader of a squatters' invasion is even becoming a new culture hero. An ECLA study states that "among the so-called 'popular classes' the figure of the *poblador*—probably a mixture of rural tenant and urban worker—has been acquiring undeniable importance alongside the organized minorities of industrial workers."[53] Indeed, he projects a more compelling image than the factory workers who, in Latin America, have rarely generated grass-roots class leadership or seriously challenged the economic system as an urban "proletariat."[54] The *poblador* has no niche in the system. He must be in-

ventive; he must form his own community; he must challenge and force his way into the existing order.

Nomenclature for squatters' settlements varies from country to country. A generic name is *población* or *barrio* "*marginal*." This term connotes many kinds of marginality—geographic (peripheral location), functional (deprivation of urban services), sociological, economic and psychological—not all of which need apply in a given case. The term is slightly ironic in view of the high potential for organization, self-legitimation, and inventive accommodation to urban life which many "marginal" communities exhibit.

Marginal settlements have leaped into prominence since World War II. The *favelas* of Rio, however, date from the 1890's, and one suspects that peripheral clusters of squatters' or rural-type dwellings are a traditional urban feature, particularly in the Indian countries. Kubler describes the Indian sections of 16th century Mexico City as "casual, dense agglomerations of huts and shelters" serving as a labor reservoir for the proud, orderly Spanish city.[55]

The study of another Mexican city, Mérida, shows how its colonial growth steadily displaced the surrounding Indian *barrios* outward from the urban center. The ruling class lived in the center virtually monopolizing its facilities; till 1820 they alone could be baptized and married in the cathedral. In the *barrios* Maya was spoken, indigenous costumes were worn, huts were thatched, streets were impassable for wheeled vehicles. Each *barrio* was a semiautonomous community with its plaza, church and stores, governed by its own *cacique*. Neighborhood loyalties

[52] Carlos M. Rama, "De la singularidad de la urbanización en el Uruguay," *Revista de Ciencias Sociales*, 6, 2 (June 1962), 177–86. Also: David E. Snyder, "Urban Places in Uruguay and the Concept of a Hierarchy" (author's offprint), and "Commercial Passenger Linkages and the Metropolitan Nodality of Montevideo," *Economic Geography*, 38, 2 (April 1962), 95–112. For Uruguay's social discontinuities see Aldo E. Solari, "Impacto político de las diferencias de los países en los grados e índices de modernización y desarrollo económico en América Latina," *América Latina*, 8, 1 (Jan.–March 1965), 5–21.

[53] ECLA, *Desarrollo social . . . , op. cit.*, p. 81.

[54] For a recent inquiry into industrial workers' attitudes, see Guillermo Briones and José Mejía Valera, *El obrero industrial* (Lima, 1964).

[55] Kuber, *Mexican Architecture . . . , op. cit.*, I, 74.

were strong, yet in spite of inter-*barrio* rivalry and gang-fighting the humblest dweller felt superior to persons born outside Mérida. Many Indians worked in the city center, and all patronized its business institutions. The first effect of the 19th century profits from henequen was to intensify the *barrios*-center polarity (c. 1880), but by 1900 the pattern was breaking down. Well-to-do residential sections penetrated the suburbs, and the *barrios* became absorbed, culturally and administratively, into the city.[56]

Current migrations to cities are in some ways reproducing the historic *barrios* phenomenon described for Mérida. The main difference is that the new groups are trying to gain *access* to the city (not infrequently by *forming* communities) while the old groups were *traditional* communities *resisting* the assault of the city. Today the experiences of migration, of exposure to the city, of regional mingling, generally preclude the formation of urban "folk" enclaves. Yet new social polarities and discontinuities indicate that the city is becoming "ruralized" in certain ways. The work of Lewis, Mangin and Butterworth warns us not to dismiss regional origin and culture as a potential binding force for the fortuitous communities of the city.[57]

One reason for placing Latin American urban ecology in a time perspective is to suggest that it may loosely conform to a historic archetype—to a "segmental" structure and growth pattern, for example, rather than to what Caplow calls the "crescive" pattern of North American cities.[58]

Examining contemporary squatters' settlements, we find that the portion of total lower-class housing which they contain varies from city to city, and that their quantitative importance is easily exaggerated. Their significance for our purposes is their rapid growth ratio in many countries and their convenience as laboratories for observing social and political process:

—In Lima the *barriada* population grew from about 100,000 in 1958 (10% of the city population) to about 400,000 in 1964 (20%).[59]

"A Study of the Urbanization Process among Mixtec Migrants from Tilaltongo in Mexico City," *América Indígena*, 22, 3 (July 1962), 257–74; Latin American papers for Symposium No. 26, Wenner-Gren Foundation for Anthropological Research (Aug. 27–Sept. 8, 1964). "Cross-cultural Similarities in the Urbanization Process," for a critique of the folk-urban continuum and comparative bibliography see Francisco Benet, "Sociology Uncertain: The Ideology of the Rural-Urban Continuum," *Comparative Studies in Society and History*, 6, 1 (Oct. 1963), 1–23.

[56] Asael T. Hansen, "The Ecology of a Latin American City" in E. B. Reuter, ed., *Race and Culture Contacts* (New York, 1934), pp. 124–42.

[57] Oscar Lewis, "Urbanization without Breakdown," *The Scientific Monthly*, 75, 1 (July 1952), 31–41, and "Nuevas observaciones sobre el 'continuum' con especial referencia a México," *Ciencias Políticas y Sociales*, IX, 3 (Jan.–March 1963), 13–28; William P. Mangin, "The Role of Regional Associations in the Adaptation of Rural Population in Perú," *Sociologus*, 9, 1 (1959), 23–35, and "Mental Health and Migration to Cities: A Peruvian Case," The New York Academy of Sciences, *Annals*, 84 (Dec. 1960), 911–17; Douglas S. Butterworth,

[58] Theodore Caplow hints at this possibility in "The Social Ecology of Guatemala City," *Social Forces*, 28, 2 (Dec. 1949), 113–33, and "The Modern Latin American City" in Sol Tax, ed., *Acculturation in the Americas* (Chicago, 1952), pp. 255–60.

[59] Junta Nacional de la Vivienda, Lima, mimeog., memo on *barriadas*. José Matos Mar states that in 1961 the percentage of Lima's inhabitants in *barriadas* stood at 26%, and that for the newly developed industrial city of Chimbote the figure reached 70%; "El caso del Perú: consideraciones sobre su situación social como marco de referencia al problema de Lima," *Caravelle*, 3 (1964), 119.

—In Rio de Janeiro the population of the *favelas* grew from about 203,000 in 1950 (8.5% of city pop.) to about 600,000 in 1964 (16%). By 1960 their growth rate was three to four times that of the city as a whole.[60] *Favela* growth has shifted predominantly from the central and southern zones (e.g., Copacabana) to the north and northeast (industrial concentration).

—In twelve communes of Greater Santiago the number of *callampa* family dwellings appeared to hold steady from 1952 (16,502 dwellings) to 1961 (16,042 dwellings). This is explained by (1) the campaign of the government Housing Corporation, greatly accelerated in 1959, to eradicate *callampas*, and (2) the tendency of new *callampas* to be smaller and even more provisional, thus escaping enumeration.[61]

—In Caracas the Pérez Jiménez regime undertook to eradicate the *ranchos* by constructing immense apartment houses. In 1954–58, 85 of these "superblocks" were delivered. When construction was suspended, they housed 160,000 persons in 17,399 apartments, or 12% of the city's population. At that time, however, 30% of the city's inhabitants were still living in *ranchos*.[62]

—In Argentina I was told that perhaps 10% of the population of Greater Buenos Aires live in *villas miserias*, or some 800,000 people. The figure seems high, however,

and in any case the rapid growth period is over. Of the *villa* dwellers some 10% are in dire need, without hope or resources, while some 30% have solid prospects of moving to their own land in five years or less. The rest are in intermediate situations. Enclaves of Paraguayan and Bolivian migrants are a distinctive feature of the *villas*.[63]

—São Paulo has only a small percentage of its poor in *favelas*, a maximum of 200,000 persons in a metropolis of almost 5 million.

—In Mexico City squatters' shacks (*jacales*) are scattered in small nuclei, with larger settlements appearing near the highways west of the city. The dwellings are generally of adobe and in the rural tradition. Obsolete figures (1952) show 11% of the city's population in *jacales*, 14% in *colonias proletarias* (low-density, relatively substantial squatters' huts without urban services), 34% in *tugurios* (traditional slums).[64]

ECLA has made some simplified calculations to show the relation of rate of national population growth to the size of urban "marginal" population.[65] The study assumes a hypothetical country of 10 million people—3 million urban and 7 million rural. It further assumes: (1) a total of one million urban dwellers in a "marginal" category; (2) a 5 per cent annual increase in remunerative urban employment; (3) a net rural population increase of 1.5 per cent a year. Projections are then made for varying rates of over-all national population growth:

---

[60] Figures taken with extrapolations from "As favelas do Estado da Guanabara, segundo o censo de 1960," *Boletim Estatístico* (Instituto Brasileiro de Geografia e Estatística), 84 (Oct.–Dec. 1963).

[61] ECLA, "Urbanization in Latin America, Results of a Field Survey of Living Conditons in an Urban Sector," E/CN.12/662 (13 March 1963), pp. 5–7.

[62] *Architectural Design*, 33, 8 (Aug. 1963), 373–74. For an evaluation of the superblocks and their maladministration by the regime which built them see Banco Obrero, *Proyecto de evaluación de los superbloques* (Caracas, 1961); Rolando Grooscors, "Problemas de vivienda urbana en Venezuela," VI Congreso Latinoamericano de Sociología, *Memoria* (2 vols., Caracas, 1961), II, 47–51.

[63] Two novels about *villas miserias* are: Bernardo Verbitsky, *Villa miseria también es América* (2nd ed., Buenos Aires, 1958), and Rubén Benítez, *Ladrones de luz* (Buenos Aires, 1959).

[64] Claude Bataillon, "Mexico capitale métis," *Caravelle*, 3 (1964), 173–74; Bird, *loc. cit.*, pp. 48–49.

[65] ECLA, "Geographic Distribution . . . ," *op. cit.*, pp. 5–8.

Year	Urban Population Remuneratively Employed, Increasing at 5% Per Year (Thousands)	"Marginal" Urban Population for Varying Annual Rates of National Population Growth (in Thousands and as % of Total Urban Pop.)			
		2.0	2.5	3.0	3.5
0	2000	1000 (33%)	1000 (33)	1000 (33)	1000 (33)
10	3258	808 (20)	1419 (30)	2057 (39)	2724 (46)
20	5307	124 (2)	1651 (24)	3326 (39)	5163 (49)
30	8644	absorbed	1390 (14)	4687 (35)	8482 (50)

For national growth rates of 2.5% and above there occurs an absolute increase in the urban "marginal" population, and for rates of 3.0% and above a relative increase. The calculation is highly schematic. But it is worth noting that the actual growth predicted for all of Latin America for 1965–75 is 2.9% per year. Mexico and Brazil are estimated at 3.0%, with three Central American countries and the Dominican Republic at 3.5%. Cuba on the other hand is at 2.0% and Argentina at 1.7%.[66]

Two opposed hypotheses about the *barrios marginales* are: (1) that they are slums, blighted areas, belts of misery, incubators for disease, crime, social disorganization and personality disorder; and (2) that as semirural enclaves they make available new possibilities for urban social reconstruction on the basis of neighborhood communities, regional and kinship ties, mutual-aid associations, and small-group political activity.[67]

Two studies have tried to ascertain "objective" indices of social cohesion, or neighborliness, for different class levels in Bogotá and in San Juan, Puerto Rico. They find negative or inverse correlation between neighborliness and lower-class status.[68] The validity of these studies may be questioned on several counts. The interview schedules imply a cultural (i.e., North American) definition of neighborliness; this definition is presumed not to vary with social class; interviews are statistically analyzed with no description of the specific kin, association and locality groups from which they emanate. A reader who hungers for the mulligan stew of ethnography is left to gnaw the dry bone of sociometry.[69]

It is difficult to generalize about the social solidarity of the various types of lower-class residence community in

[66] Centro Latino Americano de Pesquisas, *op. cit.*, p. 89.

[67] A sidelight on this question comes from a study of lower-class use of leisure time in Salvador, Brazil, which indicates that the proportion of activities demanding active rather than passive participation is much higher here than in "developed" urban societies: Acácio Ferreira, *Lazer operário, un estudo de organização social das cidades* (Salvador, 1959).

[68] Luis Calderón Alvarado, *Poder retentivo del "area local urbana" en las relaciones sociales* (Fribourg, 1963); Theodore Caplow *et al.*, *The Urban Ambience, A Study of San Juan, Puerto Rico* (Totowa, N. J., 1964).

[69] For an extended critique of the Caplow study see R. M. Morse, "The Sociology of San Juan: An Exegesis of Urban Mythology," *Caribbean Studies*, 5, 2 (July 1965), in press.

the absence of case studies and careful typologies country by country, or even city by city. For Santiago, Rosenblüth identifies no less than 15 varieties of dwellings or communities of the lower economic classes. Among them are: *callampas* (mushrooms), squatters' settlements built of waste materials and having no public services; *poblaciones de erradicación*, or *callampa*-type settlements removed to new sites with land titles and minimum services; *poblaciones de radicación*, the exceptional *callampas* which become permanent with expropriation and improvement of the land; the isolated huts of families who serve as caretakers for residences or construction sites; *conventillos*, or multi-family dwellings where families are distributed one to a room and have common sanitary facilities; self-help settlements in which the residents build their own dwellings with technical assistance, materials and credit facilities from the government Housing Corporation; settlements constructed by private institutions; workers' settlements built by industrial firms and enjoying urban services; and "emergency huts" built for earthquake victims.[70]

These types can even be subdivided. *Callampas*, for example, may be classified by location: on active or abandoned refuse dumps, along the banks of canal and rivers, along roads or railway tracks, on public or private lands which have been invaded, or on private unimproved lands where there is a promise of sale to the squatters.

[70] Guillermo Rosenblüth López, *Problemas socio-económicos de la marginalidad y la integración urbana* (Santiago, 1963) and "La participación de las poblaciones urbanas en el crecimiento urbano," MS (Jan. 1965). Also ECLA, "Urbanization in Latin America . . . ," *op. cit.* Joaquín Edwards Bello, *El roto* (Santiago, 1920) is an early novel of lower-class Santiago life.

Conversely, one may group the basic types under three larger categories:

(1) *Conventillo* type: located in older districts of the city center; access to public utilities; traditional "slum" dwelling for urban proletariat; rental occupancy; structures built as *conventillos* disappearing, being replaced by conversion of houses to multi-family use. Corresponds elsewhere to *vecindad, cortiço, callejón*.

(2) *Callampa* type: segregated urban nucleus; illegal land occupation; waste material used for construction; generally single-room dwelling without sanitary facilities; generally peripheral location with constant displacement by growth of city (though occasional *callampas* are more than 20 years old). Corresponds elsewhere to *favela, villa miseria, rancho, barriada, jacales*.

(3) Suburban settlement: semisegregated urban nucleus; land titles acquired through settlers' initiative or by government intervention; heterogeneous building materials; construction by settlers, government or private firms; generally peripheral location; varying access to public utilities.[71]

With changes of emphasis and detail these three broad categories apply to the underprivileged urban areas of most of the major Latin American cities as well as many smaller ones. One might expect the index of social cohesion to increase as one proceeds from the *conventillo* or slum to the squatters' settlement to the semidetached nucleus, but it seems safer to say that there is greater variety on this score within the categories than among the modal types for each category. A *villa miseria* in Buenos Aires that is subject to frequent floods and whose Peronista population distrusts any overture by a post-Perón government is very different from a Lima *barriada* built on desert land and receptive to public or private assistance. Studies on social aspects of

[71] Rosenblüth, "La participación . . . ," *op. cit.*

public housing projects often raise more questions than they answer. In Caracas the government has built more than 2,500 low-rent apartments since 1959 at the same time that an estimated 13,000 *ranchos* have been constructed (many of them by entrepreneurs who find them more profitable than apartments). The government has had trouble with its tenants. "Some who built their own *ranchos* are reluctant to leave their rent-free accommodations, while others have found apartment living too confining and have moved back to the slums."[72]

For each city there is a constellation of factors which defines its housing problem uniquely. Yet in every case the following questions must be asked:

(1) When is technical and social assistance more efficient and effective than architectural solutions that entail massive relocation of families?

(2) When relocation *is* advisable, how can lessons from existing, spontaneous communities be made available for physical and social planning?[73]

John Turner criticizes the orthodox

"low cost" project "designed to give maximum comfort to the maximum number with the minimum outlay."

Unless the State is prepared to invest its limited capital resources and to restrict its building program to an insignificantly small minority of subsidized dwellings, the family will have to pay for the cost of developed land, for the public utilities as well as the land itself. This means that half or more of what they must pay for goes into installations which, relatively speaking, are luxuries. The result is that they must accept a very small house and wait, in all probability, for schools, market places and so on —the lack of which will be all the more serious for the relatively distant location which the cost of the undeveloped land imposes.[74]

It is well to remember that in San Juan, Puerto Rico, where the government commands relatively generous funds for public housing: "The decline of the slum population has recently averaged less than one-half of one per cent per year—a rate that, if continued, would give the Slum Belt two centuries more of existence."[75]

In Lima one must distinguish between the *corralón* and the *barriada*. The *corralón* is a jumble of small shacks, generally rented, which serve as reception or transit camps for rural migrants. The typical *barriada* originates in a carefully planned invasion by a group of families who are partly educated to the ways of city life and who are taking effective action to acquire—not housing exclusively—but permanent dwelling-space and, with it, the time needed to work out their problems as resources and ingenuity permit.

---

[72] *New York Times*, 15 Dec. 1964.

[73] See G. H. Dietz *et al.*, *Housing in Latin America* (Cambridge, 1965); C. A. Franken-off, "Low-cost Housing in a Latin Economy," *Inter-American Economic Affairs*, 17, 4 (Spring 1964), 79–86. Charles Abrams, *Man's Struggle for Shelter* (Camridge, 1964) provides a comparative context; in chap. 12 he points out difficulties of self-help programs. For Puerto Rico, which has had much experience with public housing, see Kurt W. Back, *Slums, Projects, and People* (Durham, 1962); Helen I. Safa, "From Shanty Town to Public Housing," *Caribbean Studies*, 4, 1 (April 1964), 3–11; A. B. Hollingshead and L. H. Rogler, "Attitudes toward Slums and Public Housing in Puerto Rico" in Leonard J. Duhl, ed., *The Urban Condition* (New York, 1963), pp. 229–45. The last two studies illustrate the frustrations and social disorganization which the move from slums to public housing (*caserios*) may produce.

[74] John C. Turner, "An Interpretation of the Housing Problem in the Light of Popular Experience," mimeog. lecture, Junta Nacional de la Vivienda, Lima.

[75] Caplow *et al.*, *Urban Ambience . . .*, *op. cit.*, p. 228.

The "corralón" has no future; at best it crystallizes out into a typical labyrinth complex of slum courts which can only deteriorate until, eventually, they are eradicated. The "barriada," on the other hand, will develop into a typical working and lower-middle class suburb—although slowly, as it will take the average family about 20 years to complete its house without credit assistance.[76]

The studies which reveal high rates of mental illness and social disorganization among Lima's poor refer largely to the *corralones* and the *callejones* (enclosed patio slums) rather than to the *barriadas*.[77]

An investigation in Santo Domingo relies on type of employment rather than type of residence to determine social structure and mechanisms of acculturation in lower-class *barrios*. Workers are divided into a *traditional* sector (those who are jobless or who have short-term or low-paid permanent jobs) and a *modern* sector (higher-paid permanent jobs). This is felt to be a more empirical classification than into tertiary and secondary sectors. The author asserts that the non-specialized institutional life of the popular *barrios* favors a new structure of "local community" relations. Sample interviews indicate that the proportion of persons in the modern sector having *compadres* in the *barrio* (72%) is larger than in the traditional sector (53%), and that mutual aid is much more frequent in the modern sector (61%) than in the traditional (27%). The study concludes: that (1) acculturation to specifically "urban" ways is not necessarily what facilitates passage from the traditional to the modern sector, and that (2) the "local community" relations which *are* established do not necessarily obstruct the recruitment of urban dwellers to modern economic institutions.[78]

These findings are corroborated and in some ways extended by a study of Puerto Rican migrants to Chicago.[79] In this setting two types of *compadrazgo* are distinguished: the horizontal, largely a nominal relation which arises from the baptismal ceremony and "may serve to unite the kin- and in-group"; and the vertical, a more utilitarian relation between upper- and lower-class Puerto Ricans typically formed at the instance of the lower-class participant and facilitating his

[76] Junta Nacional de la Vivienda, memo on *barriadas, op cit.* Oscar Lewis illustrates differing levels of social cohesion among Mexican *vecindades* in "The Culture of Poverty in Mexico City, Two Case Studies," *The Economic Weekly* (June 1960), 965–72.

[77] Baltazar Caravedo, Humberto Rotondo and Javier Mariátegui, *Estudios de psiquiatría social en el Perú* (Lima, 1963); Richard W. Patch, "Life in a *Callejón*, A Study of Urban Disorganization," AUFS, West Coast South America Series, VIII, 6 (June 1961). For a strategy with respect to such zones Viceroy Manuel de Guirior established a vigorous if paternalistic precedent. In 1780 he wrote of his troubles with Pitipití, a settlement of 2,000 persons of all *castas* near the plaza of Callao that was subject to "grave and continuous disorders." Deserters took shelter there; theft, murder and assault were endemic. The haphazard grouping of shacks made it hard to intervene without risking violence. "*But keeping always in mind the necessity which created this first settlement*, I seized a good opportunity, and without any disturbance or casualties the inhabitants were all moved near the town of San Simón de Villavista, a quarter of a league from Callao. There, *with the streets and facilities that were given to them, they are building houses and ranchos* where they can live more obedient and civilized lives." *Relaciones de los virreyes . . . , op. cit.*, III, 90 (italics added).

[78] André Corten, "Como vive la otra mitad de Santo Domingo: estudio de dualismo estructural," *Caribbean Studies*, 4, 4 (Jan. 1965), 3–19.

[79] Irwin Press, "The Incidence of Compadrazgo among Puerto Ricans in Chicago," *Social and Economic Studies*, 12, 4 (Dec. 1963), 475–80.

accommodation to urban life.[80] Dividing his subjects into four groups, Press finds that *compadrazgo* is relatively weak among the most insecure and least acculturated migrants. The strongest and most extended *compadre* ties exist among migrants who are still at a socioeconomic disadvantage, "yet whose degree of acculturation and urban outlook permits them to cope with the external environment in an independent manner and with at least partial success." In Parsonian terms, the adjustment to "universalism" has activated "particularistic" mechanisms for social solidarity. Within the third group, the middle class, *compadrazgo* is weakest and of least socioeconomic importance; it is little more than a form of close friendship. Among upper-class Puerto Ricans *compadrazgo* again becomes functional as a means of preserving cultural identity (horizontal) and of offering protection to lower-class migrants (vertical).

In a study of Cali, Lima and San Juan, Rogler brings out that recourse to particularistic ties within "marginal" urban groups is not an automatic response to challenges of the city. The comparative analysis of cities and of *barrios* within a given city, leads him to conclude that only strong sociological imperatives in the face of adversity will produce neighborhood or community organization. For him the critical issue is not whether rural community patterns are sometimes imported into the city (a datum proven largely for migrants from Indian backgrounds; see studies cited in footnote 57), but the

conditions under which quasi-rural patterns are sometimes *re-created* in the city as an aggressive response to the progressive limitation of options. Rogler contrasts the effective organization of the Lima *barriadas* in the face of adversity and hostility with the "tossed salad" shanty towns and anomic slum life of San Juan, where the government attitude toward squatter settlements is relatively benevolent.[81]

If this analysis is correct the social planner faces an overwhelming dilemma. Stated in the crudest terms it is that the social integration of "marginal" urban groups gathers momentum under adversity and hostility, and recedes before permissiveness and benevolence. The experience thus far with public housing projects in Latin America gives some support to this hypothesis.[82]

6. "MARGINAL" GROUPS AND THE URBAN CORE

Discussion of the internal structure of "marginal" groups leads inevitably to the question of how these groups are to relate to and participate in urban

[80] In Cali a similar distinction exists between the "traditional" and the "economic" *compadrazgo*. Centro Interamericano de Vivienda y Planeamiento, *Siloé, el proceso de desarrollo comunal aplicado a un proyecto de rehabilitación urbana* (Bogotá, 1958), p. 9.

[81] Lloyd H. Rogler, "Slum Neighborhoods in Latin America," unpublished paper. Ernesto Ruiz reports on anxiety and insecurity in a Puerto Rican slum in "Algunas observaciones e interpretaciones sobre un arrabal puertorriqueño," *Revista de Ciencias Sociales*, 7, 1–2 (March–June 1963), 149–67.

[82] Research by North Americans on Latin American slum and shanty dwellers hums with a war chant against venerated theoretical models for urban society. What the new interpretations prove is not so much the ethnocentrism of Maine or Durkheim or Wirth as the naïveté of contemporary American social science and the inability of its practitioners to deal simultaneously with generalized models and cultural systems. The "culture of poverty" invites the same mischievous inversion which Marx performed for Proudhon's "philosophy of poverty."

life. The cities have been given a short breathing space by the fact that migrant families arrive with relatively low expectancies and with cultural attitudes scarcely conducive to revolution-mongering. Most of them do not form a proletariat. They are not yet reintroduced to society. Their single overwhelming task is simply "to settle" (*poblar*).[83] Of great import for the future, however, are the parents' hopes for their children. Let us assume the optimum case of a migrant who acquires a lot in a peripheral *barrio*, establishes legal title to it, finds more or less steady employment as a construction worker, and over the years manages to convert his shack into a plausible house. What comforts him throughout this travail is the certainty that his children will obtain middle-class schooling, jobs and respectability. In most Latin American cities his hope is today a forlorn one.

A tide of migrants is swirling at the edges of the cities. These human reservoirs are rising rapidly. If they continue to seep into the channels of city life at the present sluggish rate, they will soon begin to move and behave as an independent force. (Witness the political opposition between the *villas miserias* and the "asphalt zone" of Buenos Aires.) Their hybrid rural-urban character, now transitional, will become a fixed identity, dichotomizing the city and causing mutations in the familiar patterns of political action.[84] If urban growth rates are two

or three times rural rates, we must remember that "marginal" growth rates in the city may be three to four times the general urban rates.

Although the situation is partly a result of new population pressures, the ultimate problem is not strictly Malthusian. The ratio of people to habitable land is more favorable than in most major world regions. "Population control" would be less a corrective than a palliative—or as many Latin Americans feel, less a palliative than a counsel of resignation before the challenge of human institutions.[85]

The process of accommodating "marginal" populations to the established urban classes can be considered from at least three points of view.

(1) *Economic.* This takes us beyond the scope of the paper by hooking city planning to national economic planning. The central question is whether future economic development will continue indefinitely to inflate the tertiary sector with disguised unemployment and mendicancy.[86] If so—and in many countries there is every indication that this will be the case—the social planner labors under special imperatives to be inventive. For any given peripheral or satellite community there is also the microeconomic question of whether household crafts or truck-farming and husbandry might

[83] An ironic twist to Alberdi's injunction of the last century: *gobernar es poblar.*

[84] A Peruvian sociologist claims that in his country this social sector is establishing its cultural identity as a *cholo* group, that it is not taking what he feels to have been the Mexican path of total Westernization. Aníbal Quijano O., "La emergencia del grupo 'cholo' y sus implicaciones en la sociedad peruana" (Lima, 1964, mimeog).

[85] "[Many Mexican] economic and political planners consider a rapid population growth as an exciting national challenge, opportunity, or stimulus rather than an obstacle to national progress." Arthur F. Corwin, *Contemporary Mexican Attitudes toward Population. Poverty, and Public Opinion* (Gainesville, 1963), p. 49. Also J. Mayone Stycos, "Opinions of Latin-American Intellectuals on Population Problems and Birth Control," *Annals of the American Academy of Political and Social Science*, 306 (July 1965), 11–26.

[86] See "Creation of Employment Opportunities in Relation to Labour Supply" in Hauser, *op. cit.*, pp. 118–48.

be developed. Such schemes require large, perhaps uneconomic amounts of technical assistance. It may be that they are not feasible in the larger cities, but theoretically they would cushion families against vagaries of the industrial labor market. The large-scale purchase or expropriation of choice, privately owned suburban lands might create possibilities for systematic experimentation along these lines.[87]

(2) *Political*. Bourricaud has studied how conventional party politics become inserted into the Lima *barriadas*. In explaining the strength of rightist General Odria among the "marginal" population in 1962 and 1963 he stresses the ideological apathy of the *barriadas*. He then describes the political machines, which were: (a) set in motion by transactions between the candidates' agents and the local political leaders who can deliver the votes of clienteles of friends and kin, and (b) lubricated by handouts of food, clothing and other necessities. Such a system is precarious. Charity tends to reach only the disinherited and least integrated elements. It creates indifference among local leaders, who wish to show their power by delivering precisely those *community* improvements (water, electricity, sewage disposal) which the highest authorities reserve for allocation by themselves. The key question is whether the local leaders' policy of prudence, ideological indifference and calculated horse-trading will continue; or whether "it will give way, suddenly or gradually, to acute radicalization

and to a sharp revolutionary sensibility. The answer to this question will probably govern the course of Peruvian politics during the next years."[88]

For the Rio *favelas* Medina stresses the lack of organizations mediating between the *favelado* and political life. There is no hierarchy of candidates. The campaign of a *vereador* or *prefeito* is no different from that of a senator or president, and the issues presented to the voter are in no hierarchical arrangement.

While the great topics are being discussed, each voter looks for a personal benefaction each *político* strives to guarantee his constituency. This is where the most important figure in Brazilian elections appears: the *cabo eleitoral*. . . . He fills the gap between what the candidates proclaim and what they will perform. Politics is thus imbued with a highly demagogic content. The candidate presents the voter with a program of action, but to the individual he promises his personal intervention. It is this which counts.[89]

An alternative to drift-and-crisis on the political scene has been proposed by the brains trust responsible for planning the *Promoción Popular* program in Chile. A primary research target is the elaboration of strategies for avoiding the disintegration of urban society, for countering overcentralization by creating and/or giving legal status to grassroots structures for community initiative and action. It has been decided that the strongest mechanisms for reform and reconstruction will be the *comités*

[87] In *Los dueños del Perú* (Lima, 196?), pp. 63–67, Carlos Malpica lists "urbanizable" private landholdings of one million square meters or more in the environs of Lima and Callao, a total of 119 haciendas. These lands, generally held for speculation, are carefully protected against invasions by squatters, who are forced into arid, sandy zones.

[88] François Bourricaud, "La place de Lima dans la vie politique péruvienne," *Caravelle*, 3 (1964), 138–46. Also Torcuato S. Di Tella, *El sistema político argentino y la clase obrera* (Buenos Aires, 1964); Alfonso Trujillo Ferrari, "Atitudes e comportamento político do imigrante nordestino em São Paulo," *Sociologia*, 24, 3 (Sept. 1962), 159–80.

[89] Carlos Alberto de Medina, *A favela e o demagogo* (São Paulo, 1964), pp. 97–98.

and *juntas de vecinos* now so widespread among urban *poblaciones*. Ideally, the *comités* will represent 200–250 families, while the *juntas*, comprised of two to four *comités*, will represent 500–1,000 families. Each *comité* is to have a general assembly and a five-man directorate elected by the assembly.

The specific aim of such mechanisms is to stimulate a change of outlook by which citizens in a marginal situation (*pobladores*) can, through new organizational structures, integrate to the values of the contemporary world which are now shared by only the most privileged sectors of the national society.[90]

The priority given to the traditional, multi-purpose, "neighborhood" *cabildo* structure in a modern urban setting and the overlaying of new structures in lieu of revamping the old speak loudly for a historico-cultural approach to social reform.

(3) *Social.* Knowledge of the total urban social structure is basic to understanding the Latin American city and the processes by which it incorporates new groups. For a long time the view of Latin American urban society was clouded by attempts to apply paradigms for class structure and dynamics extracted from Western industrial scieties. It is now increasingly recognized that in Latin America: (a) the nature of "classes" and their interaction needs special definition; (b) historico-cultural factors contribute importantly to this definition; (c) a much-needed preliminary job is a straightforward description of the principal "actors" (social groups) in urban society to elucidate commitment and motive without theoretical preconceptions.

Some heuristic studies of the past two or three years have directed attention

to the otiose way in which patterns of social action are accommodating to nationalism and economic change. It still appears to be a silent premise of Latin American life that individual or group advancement is more likely to occur through a change in distribution of resources than through dramatic increase in total resources available. Beneath a well-nigh universal ferment of change, Latin American society, urban or rural, seems to retain its corporative structure and patrimonial logic. The "Hoselitz hypothesis," attractive to many Latin American sociologists, finds no positive correlation between economic development and size of the middle class. Maximum economic growth can scarcely be expected in economies where private choice is still important, where conspicuous consumption motivates the upper class, and where redistribution rather than augmentation of the social dividend motivates the middle.

It is sometimes thought that the Latin American middle classes have so far been characterized not only by the dual efforts of "climbers" and "distributors" but also, in some countries, by the tragic weakness of an aimless bourgeoisie, demoralized by the enjoyment of a "white" prosperity, to the dismay of its best intellectuals. This picture may not be correct. But where do we find the self-control and discipline of the true creators of modern capitalism, the energy and austerity of the young *samurai* who built up modern Japan?[91]

[90] Comisión Promoción Popular, *Informe* (4 vols. mimeog. Santiago, Aug. 1964).

[91] José Medina Echavarría, *Consideraciones sociológicas sobre el desarrollo econōmico en América Latina* (Montevideo, 1964), pp. 69–77. Also: ECLA, *Desarrollo social . . . , op. cit.*; Andrew H. Whiteford, *Two Cities of Latin America* (Beloit, 1960); Miguel Othón de Mendizábal *et al.*, *Las clases sociales en México* (Mexico City n. d.); Octávio Ianni, *Industrialização e desenvolvimento no Brasil* (Rio de Janeiro, 1963); José Luis de Imaz, *La clase alta de Buenos Aires* (Buenos Aires, 1962) and *Los que mandan*

The study of entrepreneurship is yielding clues to the social context of the economy, the sociology of urban institutions, and psychological aspects of industrial organization. A four-country ECLA study speaks of the "marginal" nature of capitalism in Latin America and the "ambivalent" attitudes of its entrepreneurs toward the roles of the state and of labor unions in economic development. Successful industrial enterprise often depends upon utilizing political connections to exert pressure upon the central system of power. Many industrialists see their relations with workers as simply "another element of the political and bureaucratic maneuvers" in which they must engage.[92]

(Buenos Aires, 1964). An extended essay which cities interesting literary material is Juan José Sebrelli, *Buenos Aires, vida cotidiana y alienación* (4th ed.; Buenos Aires, 1965). Juan Carlos Argulla studies the impact of recent industrialization on social classes and social process in Córdoba, Argentina, in "Aspectos sociales del proceso de industrialización en una comunidad urbana," *Revista Mexicana de Sociología*, 25, 2 (May–Aug. 1963), 747–72.

[92] ECLA, "El empresario industrial en América Latina," UN document E/CN.12/642 (11 March 1963), with 4 appendices containing case studies of Argentina, Brazil, Chile and Colombia. Also: Louis Kriesberg, "Entrepreneurs in Latin America and the Role of Cultural and Situational Processes," *International Social Science Journal*, 15, 4 (1963), 581–94; Fernando Henrique Cardoso, *Empresário industrial e desenvolvimento econômico* (São Paulo, 1964); Juarez Rubens Brandão Lopes, *Sociedade industrial no Brasil* (São Paulo, 1964); Albert Lauterbach, *Management Attitudes in Chile* (Santiago, 1961); Charles H. Savage, Jr., *Social Reorganization in a Factory in the Andes* (Ithaca, 1964); T. C. Cochran and Ruben E. Reina, *Entrepreneurship in Argentine Culture* (Philadelphia, 1962). Warren K. Dean has done a historical study which shows how the organizational structures of the Brazilian *fazenda* was transferred to industrial management: *São Paulo's Industrial Elite, 1890–1960*, unpublished Ph. D. dissertation, University of Florida, 1964.

Faletto recently marshaled the most promising hypotheses regarding the way in which urban "working sectors" are incorporated into "developing" societies of Latin America. In contrast to France, where the recruitment of an urban "subproletariat" from rural Italy or North Africa does not signify radical change in the working-class structure, urban workers in Latin America are a "class in formation." Here migration means not merely "transition" but also "conforming to" a new situation. The already established industrial proletariat of Latin America is not the *avant-garde* of the workers' movement but a group with diminished channels of communication to the "new masses" —even an eilte which is threatened by them.

Latin America's low-paced industrialization contributes little to the consolidation of a working "class" or a working-class "culture." The scale of the migrations in relation to industrial opportunity means that the populist leader rather than the labor union becomes the agent for political organization. Even those migrants who do obtain industrial employment derive surprisingly low satisfaction from it. The worker seems "to 'use' the industrial firm rather than become integrated with it." Apparently he did not head "toward the city to work in industry but rather the contrary. The primary goal is to live in the city; the means to this end are secondary." Industry, therefore, has not "really signified a deep change in the traditional ways of life." Workers are not engaged in industrialization *as workers*. They view the process as a positive one, yet show a general tendency to abandon industrial work. Since "the system" is more or less accepted, a workers' movement is not felt to be an instrument of change or revolution so much as a pressure group for improving present conditions.[93]

7. SOCIAL BASES FOR URBAN PLANNING[94]

For anyone concerned with how sociology should inform the work of the physical planner nothing could be more suggestive than a stroll through the streets of Santiago de Chile. One should start at the Plaza de Armas, heart of the city's public life for some three and a half centuries. The colonial Plaza was surrounded by the *casas reales*, the *audiencia*, the *ayuntamiento* and the cathedral; the square itself was used for tourneys and bullfights. Later the public market was installed there, only to be replaced by a garden promenade in the 19th century when the well-to-do classes began to venture from their patriarchal houses to enjoy new cosmopolitan pleasures.[95] Today the past century still lingers in the attractive park, in the hum of petty commerce under the *portales*, in some once-elegant French architecture. With some effort we can even evoke colonial times—the pomp of government and worship; the jostle and

clamor of the mixed-race classes. For all the apparent schematism of Spanish city planning, here is a fine example of geometric design become living tissue, a case of functional adaptation and sedimentation which roots us in history while wedding us to a changing present.

From the Plaza de Armas one walks five blocks to the wide, low-squatting *Palacio de la Moneda* with its topheavy balustrade, built in 1788–99 and now serving as the presidential palace. It faces north on the *Plaza de la Constitución* and south on the *Plaza de la Libertad*. Here life and color are gone; movement is matter-of-fact and unobtrusive. The two somber plazas are framed by cement beehives—banks and ministries populated by patronage groups of the power elite, the Hotel Carrera by transient foreign advisers and businessmen. The meager neoclassical elegance of the old *Palacio* is stifled by the grey, massive buildings which glower down upon it. The names of the plazas, Constitution and Liberty, are by no means anachronistic on the Chilean scene; but they lack the realism and familiarity of "*Plaza de Armas.*" They do little to suggest that the squares were carefully designed to lessen the possibility of military attack upon the executive mansion. It is symbolic that the plan to complete the architectural vista across the *Plaza de la Libertad* with a new legislative palace was never carried out.

The vision of Santiago enshrined here dates from the 1920's and '30's. It stands for early recognition of the depressed urban multitudes and of the perils they represent for the old order, if not the implications they hold for a new one. The loci of power, once embellished with neo-Renaissance façades, now seek anonymity in nondescript piles of concrete. The honeycomb windows of the banks and ministries

[93] Enzo Faletto, "Incorporación de los sectores obreros al proceso de desarrollo," Instituto Latinoamericano de Planificación Económica y Social, Santiago, multilithed (Dec. 1964). Also: Alain Touraine, "Industrialisation et conscience ourvrière à São Paulo," ed., "Ouvriers et syndicats d'Amerique Latine," special No. of *Sociologie du Travail*, 3, 4 (Oct.–Dec. 1961), and esp. Touraine's own study (pp. 77–95): Bertram Hutchinson, *Mobilidade e trabalho* (São Paulo, 1960).

[94] For a general statement see Desiderio Graue, "Coordinación de la labor del sociólogo y del urbanista frente al fenómeno citadino y el problema de la vivienda," VI Congreso de Sociología, *op. cit.*, II, 62–75.

[95] See Benjamín Vicuña Mackenna, *Historia crítica y social de la ciudad de Santiago* (2 vols., Valparaiso, 1869).

look out from a Minotaur's labyrinth of sinecures, thrown up by the paternalism of a new state socialism. Yet never can there be one window for each Chilean. Historically necessary, the new plazas were from the start archaic.[96]

What of the future Santiago? If Chile were erratic, fanciful Brazil with the resources of a subcontinent, we might expect plans for a new metropolis. One thinks of Brasília, grown to a third of a million inhabitants in five years. Or the impudent schemes of Sérgio Bernardes to rebuild Rio de Janeiro for an "age of cybernetics" with an enormous pier-bridge across the bay, resting on seven hexagonal islands; ten-level shopping centers interconnected by moving sidewalks; 45 "cultural centers," each structure containing 36 movie houses; 156 "vertical suburbs" built in "helicoidal" form to a height of 600 meters, served by "vertical metros" and housing 20,000 families apiece.[97]

Chileans, however, are sober and conservative. Perched on their shelf between the Andes and the Pacific, shaken regularly by earthquakes, they deploy their modest resources cautiously. In Santiago one looks twice to tell whether an office building is four or forty years old. Adopting the practical view, we will merely underscore two social preconditions for planning: (1) population growth and (2) "populism" with all its connotations. The quantitative index of city growth warns against another centralized, monolithic, architectural solution. Not only must new solutions be "cellular" and spatially extended; they must also solicit the active collaboration of the populace.

The qualitative index of "populism" establishes a cultural and social matrix for physical solutions. It is from such considerations and from a knowledge of available economic resources[98] that planners should triangulate, hopefully in collaboration, upon the familiar problems of housing, transportation, traffic circulation, zoning, public services, facilities for education and hygiene, and municipal government.

This sounds like the counsel of Mumfordian organicism and neotechnics as a corrective to the Spanish legacy of gridiron planning. In a sense, though, the counsel is to revivify that legacy. The elaborate ordinances for planning colonial towns emanated from a broad social and political philosophy to organize the settlement of a hemisphere.[99] Far from being static design, the urban chessboard was a radiating center of energy—visible symbol of an adaptive social structure, an intricate system of acculturation, and a regulated process of territorial appropriation and economic development.

When we associate Spanish urbanism with frozen design and elegant façade, we may be responding to latter-day influences upon it of Haussmann's Paris. It is not far-fetched to say that the Spanish municipal tradition is vigorously perpetuated in today's squatter invasions, which may recapitulate all the ingredients of a town-founding by a conquistador's band: careful staging and role allocation; solicitation of patronage from a powerful political figure; legitimation of the claim by planting of flags and strategic public-

---

[96] These reflections were suggested to me by Luis Ratinoff.

[97] "Rio admirável mundo novo," *Manchete* (17 April 1965), 42–87.

[98] In capital-poor Latin America a fixed investment of $100 generates average annual production of $40–50, but only $10–12 if put into residential building. Hauser, *op. cit.*, p. 37.

[99] Zelia Nuttall, "Royal Ordinances concerning the Laying Out of New Towns," *Hispanic American Historical Review*, IV, 4 (Nov. 1921), 743–53 and V, 2 (May 1922), 249–54.

ity; meticulous distribution of building lots; common resistance to low-echelon police; discrimination against later settlers; formation of a committee of *vecinos*; mutual-aid arrangements; gridiron layout with provision for plaza and common facilities; erection of community chapel, school and council house; priority for legalization of land titles; efforts to create a channel for claims and grievances to the highest political authority, even the president or his wife.[100]

One of Santiago's most fascinating urban laboratories is the José María Caro district. With some 130,000 inhabitants it is the equivalent of Chile's fourth largest city. It contains at least four types of housing: privately built, government-built, self-help with government assistance, and *callampas*. Residents are organized into *Juntas de Vecinos*, collectively represented in an *Agrupación General*. For several years this body has campaigned to have José María Caro erected into a single *comuna*; it now sprawls across four *comunas* of Greater Santiago. In the words of the president of the *Agrupación*:

We want to be a *comuna* because today our people, the 130,000 people of Cardenal Caro, don't want to have anything to do with anyone. They were thrown out of other communities, and all they want is something that is theirs, something of their own, and they're prepared to go after it.

According to this spokesman, José María Caro is Chile's "experimental base." It contains occupational groups of government employees, transport and railway workers, and military; it has ten blocks of migrants from Valdivia, even a few blocks of Indians.[101]

In physical terms, what does it mean for the future that these thousands of one- and two-family dwellings are being built on miniscule plots close to the metropolitan center? Will they become slums? Will they give way to high-rise construction? Or will the proprietary, small-plot mentality become ingrained? Will community and neighborhood pride win out? Or does the portent lie with those residents who take a longer route home simply for the shame of being seen on a Jose Maria Caro bus? Will the community organize to assess and assert its collective needs? Or will it continue to be a passive recipient of intermittent handouts from the uncoordinated agencies and conflicting political groups of the metropolis?

It will perhaps be said that these questions confront the Latin American city planner with three standard options: centralized planning, decentralized planning and laissez-faire. But let us recapitulate some historico-cultural factors that condition the choice:

(1) Latin America's powerful tradition of centralization may today take the guise of state socialism, but it retains overtones of the vegetative mercantilist, patrimonial state.

(2) As a planning strategy laissez-faire leads to even more chaos and confusion here than in most places; as a political and economic philosophy it favors elitism and status quo.

(3) In Latin America decentralization might specifically mean energizing the nuclear groups of society in recognition of the fact that intermediate structures tend to function ineffectively.[102] The small group,

---

[100] See William Mangin's account of a Lima invasion in *Architectural Design*, 33, 8 (Aug. 1963), 368–69; also J. P. Powelson, "The Land-Grabbers of Cali," *The Reporter* (16 Jan. 1964), 30–31.

[101] "Población Cardenal Caro ¿llegará a ser comuna?" *La Voz* (Santiago), 21 March 1965.

[102] A Lima informant told me that a *barriada* of about 450 families is optimum for develop-

like the state or central bureaucracy, has here an intermittently vigorous tradition. The farflung impersonal association will not play the role which Western urban history leads us to expect of it—except as it may be legitimized and utilized from below and from above.

(4) "Populism" is forcing the issue. As we use it, the term means not merely the participation of urban "masses" in politics but also the cultural form of participation. We find paradoxically that (a) the lower classes integrate to city life through informal clientage arrangements at the same time that (b) they show tendencies toward individuality and autonomy (squatter invasions, land ownership, resistance to routinization, preference for owning a taxi or small store to working in a factory).

(5) Judged by economic indices, Latin American cities have sizable middle classes. Yet the cities almost *function* as two-class societies—in the sense that "middle classes" tend to look for accommodation within upper-class clientage systems, or else, under certain pressures, they endorse and even formulate lower-class demands for social justice.[103] The typical instigator of an urban or rural squatter invasion is a middle-class lawyer-*político*. In some ways the situation comes startlingly close to the Marxist model for class "polarization." Be that as it may, *one might expect the Latin American lower classes to perform the role of social innovation and reconstruction which the West historically identifies with its middle classes.*

8. THE REGIONAL HORIZON

The emphasis in this paper is upon the internal adjustment of the Latin American city to modernization and centripetal population movements. However, we should avoid identifying as "critical" merely those problems which have immediate visibility, which seem politically explosive, and which relate to human deprivation. One can argue, for example, that the regional projections and interrelations of cities are as significant as their internal tensions. Although the literature on regionalism and urban networks cannot be reviewed here, mention of one schematic and suggestive study will at least enlarge the focus. It concerns São Paulo, a bellwether city with respect to modernization and industrialism.

In a recent essay on São Paulo the architect and planner Luiz Saia divides the history of the city and its hinterland into a number of ecological phases, each dominated by one or two "principal theses" and several "ancillary theses."[104] The penultimate phase corresponds to the boom years for coffee (1848–1929). Its main theses were:

I. Development of the coffee economy in a framework of "colonial" monoculture.
II. Implanation of a tree-shaped ("dendritic") transport system as a result of the coffee-railway symbiosis.

Some of the subtheses were:

1. occupation of coffee zones by predatory pioneering;
2. rail penetration and linear spacing of urban settlement along interfluvial ridges;
3. polarization of the rural and urban domains;
4. functional coalescence of São Paulo-Santos, the port becoming in effect a *barrio* of the highland city;
5. "abstract," "reticulated" and therefore chaotic management of both rural and urban lands.

---

ment work. Comisión Promoción Popular (*op. cit.*) contains discussions of the ideal size for nuclear urban communities.

[103] Middle-class Chileans who try to assimilate to the upper class and its ways are called *siúticos*. They are analyzed in Frederick B. Pike, "Aspects of Class Relations in Chile, 1850–1960," *Hispanic American Historical Review*, 43, 1 (Feb. 1963), 14–33. For a general statement see A. Pizzorno, "Sviluppo economico e urbanizzazione," *Quaderni di Sociologia*, XI (1962), 21–51.

[104] Luiz Saia, "Notas para a teorização de São Paulo," *Acrópole*, 25, 295–96 (June 1963), 209–21.

These factors were attended by rapid population growth, reflected in an increase in the municipalities of São Paulo state from 29 (1834) to 243 (1929), and in the megalocephalic growth of the state capital from 24,000 inhabitants (1872) to 900,000 (1929). Now that São Paulo city is a metropolis, the definition of its problems requires "a drastic change at the conceptual level."

Saia's principal thesis for the contemporary period is the mounting of an industrial system on a regional scale. This requires a leap from mere "technical" solutions to the plane of "technology" (i.e., choice *among* technical solutions informed from the social, cultural and political orders). Because of inadequate urban services and profiteering in urban real estate, Paulista industry is not necessarily attracted to the city and its outskirts. A broad dispersal pattern has already developed which is eroding the urban-rural polarity. Other ancillary theses are:

1. restoration and reinterpretation of the city's original site under "technological" (implying non-"capitalistic") auspices;

2. rearrangement and integration of haphazard "reticulated" nuclei;

3. reformulation of the problems of public services (elaboration of an integral system of rail, highway and river transportation; long-term regional planning of power resources, etc.).[105]

Above we said that the demographic lines of force of the Latin American city passed from a centrifugal phase in the colonial period to a centripetal one in the modern period. The corollary is that the contemporary city is projecting its image, its scheme of life, its economic imperatives out across the face of the land to a degree unparalleled in the history of the area.

[Significant on-going research in Latin American urbanization is being conducted in Venezuela and Middle America.

CENDES, the Center for development studies in Venezuela, has embarked upon a three year $1,380,000 study of urbanization in that country with support from the United Nations Special Fund. The study will 1) identify the most important aspects of the urban phenomenon; 2) determine the causes and consequences of said phenomenon; 3) arrive at specific recommendations for the resolution of present and future problems and to establish an urbanization policy within the context of national development policy; 4) serve as a prototype in method and perhaps content for similar studies in other developing countries and 5) initiate a permanent program of research on urbanization problems which may keep

---

[105] For Paulista regional ecology see: Pierre Monbeig, *Pionniers et planteurs de São Paulo* (Paris, 1952); Aroldo de Azevedo *et al.*, *A cidade de São Paulo, estudos de geografia urbana* (4 vols., São Paulo, 1958); Caio Prado Júnior, *Evolução política do Brasil e outros estudos* (4th ed.; São Paulo, 1963), pp. 95–146. For regional studies of other cities see: Instituto Brasileiro de Geografia e Estatística, Conselho Nacional de Geografia, *O Rio de Janeiro e sua região* (Rio de Janeiro, 1964); Mary C. Megee, *Monterrey, Mexico: Internal Patterns and External Relations* (Chicago, 1958); Jean Tricart, "Un exemple

du déséquilibre villes—campagnes dans une économie en voie du développement: Le Salvador," *Développement et Civilisations*, 11 (July–Sept. 1962).

ADDENDUM. The following three articles, all by Kingsley Davis, should be appropriately inserted in the footnotes above: "Colonial Expansion and Urban Diffusion in the Americas"; "Las causas y efectos del fenómeno de primacía urbana con referencia especial a América Latina"; "The Place of Latin America in World Demographic History." They appear as Nos. 131, 144 and 145, respectively, of the Reprint Series of the Institute of International Studies, University of California, Berkeley.

the government informed on developments and the consequent policy.

In a joint effort by the Colégio de México, the University of Texas Population Research Center and Universidad de Nuevo León, a large assembly of researchers since late 1963 has been engaged in a study of the nature of mobility, both geographical and social and its effect on the urbanization process. Harley Browning and others are working out a technique for "sampling" the censuses by working on a certain percentage of the total number of completed census forms and processing them in detail to determine the type of correlations that might be possible. *Editor's note.*]

SUPPLEMENTAL BIBLIOGRAPHY (1964-1967)

Bibliographies and Guides

Rabinovitz, F. F.; F. M. Trueblood, and C. J. Savio, *Latin American Political Systems in an Urban Setting: A Preliminary Bibliography.* Gainesville, Fla., 1967.

Sable, Martin H., Latin American Urbanization: A Guide to the Literature, Organizations and Personnel. Los Angeles, 1967.

Street, J. H., and G. G. Weigand, *Urban Planning and Development Centers in Latin America.* New Brunswick, N. J., 1967.

Historical Aspects

Adams, Robert M., *The Evolution of Urban Society: Early Mesopotamia and Prehispanic Mexico.* Chicago, 1966.

Arcaya, Pedro M., *El cabildo de Caracas.* Caracas, 1965.

Arzáns de Ursúa y Vela, Bartolomé, *Historia de la Villa Imperial de Potosí.* Providence, R. I., 1965.

Boxer, C. R., *Portuguese Society in the Tropics, the Municipal Councils of Goa, Macao, Bahia, and Luanda 1510–1800.* Madison, Wisc., 1965.

Dean, Warren, "The Planter as Entrepreneur: The Case of São Paulo,"

The Hispanic American Historical Review, XLVI, 2: 1966, 138–52.

Guarda, Gabriel, *Santo Tomás de Aquino y las fuentes del urbanismo indiano.* Santiago, 1965.

——— *Influencia militar en las ciudandes del Reino de Chile.* Santiago, 1967.

Gutkind, E. A., *Urban Development in Southern Europe: Spain and Portugal.* New York, 1967.

Hanke, Lewis, "Urban Life," *History of Latin American Civilization, Sources and Interpretations.* Boston. 1: 1967, 276–351.

Hardoy, Jorge E., "Centros ceremoniales y ciudades planeadas de la América precolombina," *Ciencia e Investigación.* 20, 9: 1964, 387–404.
"La influencia del urbanismo indígena en la localización y trazado de las ciudades coloniales," *Ciencia e Investigación.* 21, 9: 1965, 386–405.

——— *et al.,* "Conclusions and Evaluation of the Symposium on 'Process of Urbanization in America since its Origins to the Present Time,'" *Latin American Research Review.* 2, 2: 1967, 76–90.

Moore, John P., *The Cabildo in Peru under the Bourbons.* Durham, N. C., 1966.

Sarfatti, Magali, "Patterns of Urbanization and Urban Attitudes," *Spanish Bureaucratic-Patrimonialism in America.* Berkeley, Calif., 1966, pp. 64–92.

Universidad Central de Venezuela, *Estudio de Caracas: Historia, tecnología, economía y trabajo.* Caracas, 1967. Vol. 2 (2 parts) of 8.

Contemporary Aspects

Bataillon, Claude, "La geografía urbana de la Ciudad de México," *América Latina.* 7, 4: 1964, 71–88.

Benko, François, "Traditionalisme et développement: les villes latinoaméricaines," *Psychologie des Peuples.* 20, 1: 1965, 8–27.

Bourricaud, François, "Lima en la vida política peruana," *América Latina.* 7, 4: 1964, 89–96.

Casimir, Jean, 1967 "Duas cidades no Nordeste do Brasil: sua estrutura social e sua importância para a planificação econômica regional," *América Latina*. 10, 1: 3–48.

Díaz, May N., *Tonalá: Conservatism, Responsibility, and Authority in a Mexican Town*. Berkeley and Los Angeles, 1966.

Economic Commission for Latin America (Social Affairs Division), *Los servicios públicos en una población de erradicación*. Santiago (mimeog.), 1965.

Friedman, John, and T. Lackington, *Hyperurbanization and National Development in Chile: Some Hypotheses*. Santiago (mimeog.), 1966.

Geisse Grove, Guillermo, "Información básica de una política de desarrollo urbano-regional," *Cuadernos de Economía*. 2, 6: 1965, 41–71.

Germani, Gino, "Asimilación de inmigrantes en el medio urbano: notas metodológicas," *Revista Latinoamericana de Sociología*. 1, 2: 1965, 158–177.

Gurrieri, Adolfo, *Situación y perspectivas de la juventud en una población urbana popular*. Santiago (UN doc., mimeog.), 1965.

Gutiérrez, Samuel A., *El problema de las "Barriadas Brujas" en la Ciudad de Panamá*. Panamá, 1965. 2nd ed.

Herrick, Bruce H., *Urban Migration and Economic Development in Chile*. Cambridge, Mass, 1965.

Kahl, Joseph A., "Social Stratification and Values in Metropoli and Provinces: Brazil and Mexico," *América Latina*. 8, 1: 1965, 23–35.

Korn, Francis, "Algunos aspectos de la asimiliación de inmigrantes en Buenos Aires," *América Latina*. 8, 2: 1965, 77–96.

Larangeira de Mendonça, Mário, "O plano habitacional e a expansão das áreas urbanas," *Revista de Administração Municipal*. 11, 70: 1965, 155–75.

Lewis, Oscar, "The Culture of Poverty," *Scientific American*. 215, 4: 1966, 19–25.

Lipset, S. M., and Aldo Solari, eds., *Elites in Latin America*. New York, 1967.

Mangin, William, "Latin American Squatter Settlements: A Problem and a Solution," *Latin American Research Review*. 2, 3: 1967, 65–98.

Margulis, Mario, "Estudios de las migraciones en su lugar de origen," *América Latina*. 9, 4: 1966, 41–72.

Morse, Richard M., "Urban Society in Contemporary Latin America," *Ventures*, 7, 2: 1967, 39–48.

Norton, A. V., and G. E. Cumper, "'Peasant,' 'Plantation' and 'Urban' Communities in Rural Jamaica: A Test of the Validity of the Classification," *Social and Economic Studies*. 15, 4: 1966, 338–52.

Quijano, Aníbal, *Urbanización y tendencias de cambio en la sociedad rural en Latinoamérica*. Santiago (mimeog.), 1967.

Quintero, Rodolfo, *Antropología de las ciudades latinoamericanas*. Caracas, 1964.

Rivarola, Domingo, and M. Margulis, "Las migraciones," *Aportes*. 3, 4: 1967, 4–128.

Safa, Helen I., *An Analysis of Upward Mobility in Low Income Families: A Comparison of Family and Community Life among American Negro and Puerto Rican Poor*. Syracuse, N. Y., 1967.

Schnore, Leo F., "On the Spatial Structure of Cities in the Two Americas," *P. M. Hauser and L. F. Schnore, The Study of Urbanization*. New York, 1965, pp. 347–98.

Tricart, J., "Quelques characteristiques générales des villes latino-américaines," *Civilisations*. 15, 1: 1965, 15–26.

Utria, Rubén D., "The Housing Problem in Latin America in Relation to Structural Developmental Factors," *Economic Bulletin for Latin America*. 11, 2: 1966, 81–110.

Valencia, Enrique, *Cali: estudio de los aspectos sociales de su urbanización e industrialización*. Santiago (ECLA doc., mimeog.), 1965.

Violich, F., and J. B. Astica, *Community Development and the Urban Planning Process in Latin America*. Los Angeles, 1967.

Wilheim, Jorge, *São Paulo metrópole 65*. São Paulo, 1965.

35. Uncontrolled Urban Settlement: Problems and Policies

JOHN F. C. TURNER FOR
UNITED NATIONS CENTER FOR
HOUSING, BUILDING AND PLANNING

INTRODUCTION

Limitations and Purpose

There are tens of millions of people in the world today for whom urban settlement is the only hope of bettering an utterly miserable lot. For many it is their only hope of survival. The United Nations has estimated that 200 million people will have moved into cities in Asia, Africa, and Latin America during the nineteen-sixties alone. (5) Even more people are being born within the cities, many as poor as the rural migrants. Hundreds of millions are living through experiences that radically alter their lives and that are revolutionizing two-thirds of the world. The demographers have successfully raised the alarm and have called the world's attention to the facts of the population explosion and to the colossal scale of contemporary urbanization. Planners, too, have begun to recognize that an increasing proportion of urban settlement today is occurring "spontaneously"—in totally unplanned ways, beyond the control of the authorities charged with the regulation of land-uses and building construction. The marginal urban growth of today—the inner rings of tomorrow's

Inter-Regional Seminar on Development Policies and Planning in Relation to Urbanization, Organized by the United Nations Bureau of Technical Assistance Operations and the Bureau of Social Affairs in cooperation with the Government of the United States of America, Selections from Working Paper No. 11, University of Pittsburgh, Pittsburgh, Pennsylvania, USA, October 24–November 7, 1966. Reprinted by permission of the United Nations and the author.

cities—is largely carried out by squatters and illegal developers in many of the world's cities. One-and-a-half million people, over one-third of the population of Mexico City, live in the "colonias proletarias"—known originally as "barrios paracaidistas" or "parachutists' neighbourhoods"; nearly half of Ankara's population of 1,500,000 live in the "gecekondu"—the squatter settlements whose name describes an over-night house-builder; the area of the "villes extracoutumiers" of Kinshasa is greater than that of the city itself. Apart from a relatively abundant literature on the more general demographic and statistical aspects of the urbanization process, there is remarkably little information that is easily available to those who must work on these problems. On the aspects with which this paper deals, that is, the ways in which the urbanizing millions accommodate themselves in the cities, and the consequences of their action, all we have are a few books and several dozen articles. The remainder, which is not generally available to the majority of those that need the information, consists of official documents for limited circulation and of unpublished studies and reports.

As the data on which this paper is based is rather limited compared to the vast subject matter, it is difficult to arrive at any hard conclusions. The most that can be done, until we know much more than we do at present, is to formulate working hypotheses as a basis for a systematic evaluation of the areas concerned, and also to learn through the experience of governments and others directly concerned with the problems. The hypotheses presented in this paper are based more on first-hand observations, on research into field reports and on project evaluation studies than on deductions from rigorous academic investigation. Too much time would be required for this, even if there is enough material for more definite and scientific conclusions. While an attempt has been made to summarize the information that has been obtained and to give a general outline of "autonomous urban settlement" in the urbanizing world, the main object of this paper is to provoke discussion and to precipitate hidden knowledge.

Our first problem in the investigation and discussion of the subject is in its definition. It is assumed, for reasons that are presented in this paper, that the problem has two elements which do not necessarily coincide: urban planlessness or institutional uncontrol, and the "shantytown" environment in itself. There are millions of shacks that are neither built nor occupied by squatters, and there are hundreds of thousands of squatters who do not live in shacks but in solidly built houses. (3) The squatter shantytowns—the kind that are referred to as "provisional squatter settlements" in this paper—will often have far more in common with the traditional downtown slumlord tenements than with the self-improving squatter settlement which is transforming itself into a soundly built neighbourhood. And the "self-improving" settlements often have far more in common with orthodox residential suburbs than they do with shantytowns. *By "autonomous urban settlement" we mean urban settlement, whatever its duration or expectations may be, that takes place independently of the authorities charged with the* *external or institutional control of local building and planning.*[1]

Summary of Main Conclusions

The assumption of two distinct problems of planlessness or anarchy and of the "shantytown" slum conditions points directly to the first hypothesis: that uncontrolled urban settlement is a manifestation of normal urban growth processes under the exceptional condi-

[1] In addition to the confusions that arise from those generally unrecognised facts there is the fact that a "squatter" (except in Australia) is commonly assumed to mean: a "person who settles on new, especially public land without title; a person who takes unauthorized possession of unoccupied premises." This is the definition given in the Concise Oxford Dictionary. So, unless or until it is generally agreed and understood that squatting can also mean in the urban sense what it means in Australia and, until recently anyway, in North America, namely a "person who gets right of pasturage from government on easy terms," the use of the term "squatter settlement" to define our field tends to carry with it a rather narrow legal connotation. This can obscure the issues by lumping together essentially dissimilar "provisional" and "incipient" squatter settlements and separating essentially similar "incipient squatter" and "incipient semi-squatter" or even fully legal settlements. In the original paper from which these extracts are drawn, the phrase "uncontrolled urban settlement" was used; this too is unsatisfactory and misleading as, in the local and perhaps most important sense, they are very much more controlled than the massive anonymous "projects" we are getting so used to. Since writing this paper I have adopted Patrick Crooke's suggestion that the word "autonomous" is the most accurate and the least misleading. An "autonomous settlement" is explicitly self-governing or self-determining and this, together with the implied independence from and even conflict with the authorities that the settlement is independent from, is the most significant common denominator of the phenomena described and analysed in this paper. In spite of its length and awkwardness in comparison with the more commonly used "squatter settlement"—with the "squatterdom" and "squatment" derivatives given by Charles Abrams—I have substituted the phrase "autonomous urban settlement."

tions of rapid urbanization.[2] In other words, *we do not consider the existence of urban settlements to be the problem, but the fact that they are uncontrolled and that their forms are so often distorted.* Unless the process of urbanization can be reversed, unless there are real and immediate alternatives for the millions of migrants and new-born, it cannot be said that urban settlement, even if anarchic, should not exist. Obviously, there must be settlements, people must live somewhere—except for those that are really prepared to live, literally, in the open and on the streets. As one distinguished scholar put it, "the only way of eradicating slums (without eradicating their causes) is to eradicate their inhabitants along with them." Even if new settlements are squalid shantytowns, the common analogy of a plague is questionable. As Charles Abrams has said:

It may have to be conceded that in the formative years of industrialization, the slum will be the inevitable by-product of urban development, like the abdominal

[2] Since this paper was written I have formulated an hypothesis on the relationship between the volume and types of autonomous settlement and stages or levels of demographic and economic development. My data show that the cities with the highest proportion of autonomous settlement are generally (and perhaps always) those of countries with the highest rates of urbanization; the less urbanized and the more urbanized countries, with slower-growing cities therefore, appear to have proportionately less autonomous settlement. There is, I believe, a close parallel between the demographic curve of increasing and decreasing urban growth rates described by Lowdon Wingo in his recent paper (in *Urban Affairs Quarterly*, mid-1967, on demography and urbanization) and the increase and subsequent decrease of the phenomena discussed in this paper. The data also suggest, however, that this parallel is consistently modified by the state of the national economy as indicated by, for example, John Friedmann's "phases of national development" (*in Regional Development Policy, A Case Study of Venezuela*, MIT Press, 1966). My findings will be summarized in my forthcoming book.

distortion that precedes birth and growth. The trouble has been that reformers have always called the swelling cancer to be excised where it appears.

The second hypothesis is implicit in the first: if the processes producing autonomous settlement are essentially normal processes of urban growth then it follows that *autonomous urban settlements are both the product of and the vehicle for activities which are essential in the process of modernization.* In order to justify this statement it is necessary to identify the functions which the settlements perform. These are, naturally, the functions of any dwelling environment. The dwelling is an address—it gives the person and family a place in society and, therefore, an identity. The individual "of no fixed abode" is a vagabond and outcast. The dwelling provides *location*—however long or short the period of residence—and without a location the dwelling cannot exist. But if the dwelling cannot be occupied for the minimum period needed, if there is no *tenure*, it is useless as a dwelling. And, of course, the dwelling must provide a minimum degree of *shelter* for peace of mind and body. The kinds or varieties of location, tenure and shelter are many and they may vary independently. The demands for residential location in the city vary greatly with the social and economic situation of the inhabitant: those who cannot afford to commute, or who must spend every free hour looking for jobs, must live very near their sources of employment. Those whose income depends on their upper-income status may be obliged to live in outlying suburbs. The very poor, the "chômeurs" or unskilled, casually employed with very low and insecure incomes, must be free to change their residence at short notice in order to follow jobs—the next construction labourer's job may be on the other side of the city or in another city. The "chômeur," therefore, needs temporary accomodation at very low cost, within walking distance of his sources of livelihood and he must be free to give it up at very short notice. The regularly employed "blue-collar" worker, on the other hand, he who has a skill for which there is a reasonably steady demand but which does not give him more than a small savings margin, may need permanent tenure of his dwelling. This is especially common in economies where the mass of the wage-earners are uninsured against loss of income; for these, who are in the great majority in most rapidly urbanizing countries, the security provided by home-ownership is one of the principal sources of security open to them. Another important source of social security, the kinship network of an established local community, also requires permanent residence. The higher-income salary earner, or independent business-man or professional, on the other hand, may also demand a form of tenure that enables him to move geographically without difficulty or loss—to follow better opportunities, like the chômeur. But, unlike the blue-collar worker, he is not so dependent on home-ownership for his security (or, as a participant in the more fully institutionalized sector of society, he is more able to liquidate his assets and acquire the equivalent in another area). The kinds and standards of shelter required by such different social groups also varies—from the bed-space and locker of the young bachelor (the typical condition of the recent migrant) to the modern-standard "villa" essential for the upper-income sectors (without which they would lose the status on which they depend to maintain and improve it). The mass of the wage-

earners in a rapidly urbanizing context place secure tenure well above physical comfort in their environmental priorities. For them the principal "vehicle" for social and economic improvement is the ownership (or de facto possession) of land on which to live and, little by little, to build a permanent structure. For the underemployed, the principal vehicle is a location that provides access to opportunities; and for the "middle-classes" the principal vehicle for their progress, in environmental terms, is a house to modern comfort standards.

From the descriptions that follow in this paper it is clear that the inner-city tenements and slums of the very poor, or the interstitial shanty towns, and the peripheral squatter settlements do, in fact, perform the principal functions demanded by their inhabitants. So, in spite of the many and often severe drawbacks, they often act as forward-moving vehicles of social and economic change. On the other hand, many publicly financed housing projects, in spite of improved physical conditions, act in the opposite direction. By dislocating the "chômeur"—by divorcing him from his opportunities—or by loading the wage-earner with a mortgage, the conventional project acts more often as a barrier than as a vehicle for social change.

It should be clear from this argument that the subject matter of this paper is not the physical plant of settlement nor is it the settler and his community. The subject of the discussion is the *relationship between* the inhabitant and his habitat. The word "environment" is used in its literal sense of "surroundings"—a concept that has no meaning without reference to that which is surrounded. The values assumed, therefore, are not the conventional values based on quantitative material standards. A materially poor house may be better than a materially "good" one (i.e. one to high material standards) in a given situation. For instance, the same tenement court with one-room dwellings may be excellent for the very poor young couple, recently arrived from some province to seek their fortune in the big city, and extremely demoralizing for their immediate neighbours with a higher income and young children. The latter family will not only be living in much poorer conditions than are justified by their economic (and even social) status but they will also be living in constant fear of losing their hard-won progress as the result of some emergency (the illness of a child, for instance) leading to eviction as the result of inability to pay rent. Owing to the high competition for a decreasing supply of rental housing it is unlikely that they could find another at the same or better standard for the same rent—and a lowering of their condition may well lead to the collapse of the family. Abandonment is extremely common under these circumstances—and far rarer when the entire family has a stake in jointly occupied and jointly owned (because jointly built) property.

The focus of this paper—the loss of institutional control over urban settlement and its consequences—is seen primarily as an institutional problem and only secondarily as a by-product of poverty. I argue that the values and priorities of the popular sectors are different from those which they are required to adopt by society's institutions. Policy objectives and the institutional framework for their fulfillment are too often geared to one sector of society (the relatively wealthy minority) and are economically and culturally unacceptable to the remainder, the "remainder" being composed of four-fifths of the urban populations. Any family accommodating itself in the city is obliged to do so at modern standards, or, if it cannot afford to do so, to accept urban housing standards that are as low as they ever have been. It is argued that the loss of control over urban settlement—as distinct from the deficit of modern standard housing units—is a consequence of institutional maladjustments which, of course, are at least partly due to erroneous beliefs and social attitudes. But while the "modern housing unit deficit" is only indirectly an institutional problem, the extremely bad physical conditions in which the poor of many cities live are certainly exacerbated by institutional demands and failures. Guided, very often, by erroneous notions of slum clearance and the prohibition of any forms of building which are not considered to be "modern" enough for the city, official policies have frequently contributed directly to the worsening of housing conditions and to the precipitation of squatting and clandestine development as the only alternatives for the masses. The third hypothesis is that *autonomous urban settlement (in the major cities of urbanizing nations) is the product of the difference between the nature of the popular demand for dwellings and those supplied by institutionalized society.*

The idea that a modern city can develop from relatively primitive beginnings, over very short periods in relation to the city's history, seems to be unacceptable to many planners and decision-makers. This is strange, as there is nothing new about the concept of "progressive development." It is only very recently and only in the most developed countries that new towns have been built completely before occupation. The sequence of operations that most squatters attempt to follow—and that many succeed in to a remarkable extent—is wholly traditional and it is also logical and economic.[3] The information and the arguments contained in this paper show that it is economically impractical for governments of urbanizing countries to insist on development procedures designed under totally different circumstances. The costs are far greater than the vast majority of the people can afford and state subsidies on a sufficient scale are out of the question. Modern country standards are socially uncalled-for as well as being economically undesirable. The essential functions of housing for the masses are analysed in the discussion of hypothesis II and, from this, it is clear that the prior needs of the masses in a developing economy are not served well by the housing procedures of a developed economy. These needs are, however, served very much better by the more successful forms of autonomous settlement—which follow traditional procedures with regard to building and physical development. The conclusion is inescapable: if governments are to control urban settlement and development, policies and procedures must be based on the nature of the local demand. Alternatively, it is impossible to obtain the contribution of the mass of the people on whose collective resources development rests. The fourth and last of the principal hypotheses

[3] Particular procedures are determined to some extent by local climatic and economic conditions; in general, however, the first priority for a permanent settler (only exceptionally a newcomer to the city) is for a plot of *building land* with basic *community facilities* such as elementary schools and a market. The initially provisional shelter will be then replaced or modified to become the *nucleus or shell* of a permanent house; subsequently *modern utilities* (domestic water supply and sewerage) are supplied—or sought.

is that *the institutional control of urban settlement depends on the encouragement and support of popular initiative through the government servicing of local resources*. It is concluded that governments, especially those that do not possess or control the resources needed for environmental development, should *not* attempt to substitute for local direct action but that they should support it—in ways that bring it into the institutional framework of the Nation.

THE CHARACTERISTICS OF AUTONOMOUS URBAN SETTLEMENTS[4]

The Traditional Pattern

Gideon Sjoberg, describing the findings at Ur, one of the earliest known cities, writes in *The Pre-Industrial City*:

Houses were jumbled together, forming an irregular mass broken at intervals by open spaces in front of a temple or government building. Streets were narrow, winding and unpaved and lacked adequate drainage. They became the chief repositories of refuse thrown from the houses. . . .

and later in the same book:

The disadvantaged members of the city fan out toward the periphery, with the very poorest and the outcasts living in the suburbs, the farthest removed from the center. Houses toward the city's fringes are small, flimsily constructed, often one-room hovels into which whole families crowd. . . .

Except for the government buildings and temples, these descriptions fit any of thousands of poorer kinds of squatter-settlements today. That we are dealing

[4] Since this paper was written and distributed, an excellent study by William Mangin has been published: "Latin American Squatter Settlements: A Problem and a Solution," *Latin American Research Review*, 2(3): 65–98 (Summer 1967).

with a phenomenon which is new neither in its form nor in the planning problems it creates is illustrated by Stow, a contemporary observer of Sixteenth Century London. Describing suburbs "without the walls" of the City, he writes:

.... both the sides of the street be pestered with cottages and alleys, even up to Whitechapel Church, and almost half a mile beyond it into the common field; all of which ought to be open and free for all men. But this common field, I say, being sometime the beauty of this city on that part, is so encroached upon by building of filthy cottages, and with other purpressors, inclosures and laystalls (notwithstanding all proclamations and acts of Parliament made to the contrary) (sic), that in some places it scarce remaineth a sufficient highway for the meeting of carriages and droves of cattle; much less is there any fair, pleasant, or wholesome way for people to walk on foot; which is no small blemish to so famous a city to have so unsavoury and unseemly an entrance or passage thereunto.

A contemporary drawing of New York Central Park in 1869 shows the following: a disorderly jumble of shacks made from scrap timber and other odds and and ends; goats, poultry and other domestic animals; a table outside a shack with a small quantity of goods for sale set out on it; a fair number of poorly dressed people and a large number of children—playing in the mud, of course. Paris, in 1966, has similar settlements on its periphery, and the authorities seem to be having much the same problems that faced those of Elizabeth I and James I of England though, in this case, on a much smaller scale in relation to the size of the city:

The city of Paris decided recently to move 60 Portuguese workers from the misery of their present slum to a new housing project.

On the appointed day, only six of the Portuguese were willing to make the change. The 54 others preferred to stay in their hovels. They would rather stay among their own people and save money than gain the benefits of sewerage, electricity and water.

The incident underlines one of the many problems being discovered as Paris and France begin their war on provery—a war that takes the form of an assault on the "bidonvilles," squalid camps that house immigrant workers.

The workers—Algerians, Spaniards and now, increasingly Portuguese—are drawn to Paris by job opportunities.

About 40,000 workers and families live in the bidonvilles ringing Paris. Though the Government is pledged to the early elimination of the camps, some Frenchmen suggest that the authorities will be lucky if the problem does not grow even more severe.

Considerable Government interest centers on the project. It arises in large part from the personal interest of Michel Debré, who was Premier until 1961, and who this year re-entered the Government as Minister of Economics and Finance.

Earlier this year, Mr. Debré pledged the Government to get rid of the bidonvilles and announced that the housing budget included plans for 5,000 apartments for families now living in them. A similar rate of construction would be continued until these slums were eliminated, by 1970.

But the more the French come to grips with the problem, the more they are awed by its complexity.

"The problem is actually insoluble," a city official said. "You go through the really difficult business of building an apartment and preparing the family for it, and by the time the process is complete and the family is moved in, four more families have slipped over from Portugal."
.... "It is like a cancer that you cut out from one place only to see that it has reappeared somewhere else" said the French magazine *L'Express*. (*New York Times*, March 27, 1966.)

There is at least one radical difference between the pre-twentieth century cities referred to and the metropolitan areas from which many of our contemporary examples are drawn: most principal modern cities are many times larger than the largest cities before modern industrialization and present urbanization rates began. The very poor of Ur, of sixteenth-century London or of nineteenth-century Manhattan even, had no difficulty in walking to their work places from their marginal settlements. But the very poor of Calcutta or Mexico City—with populations of six million—or of Delhi or Lima, with populations of around two million—cannot live on the periphery and work in the city centre. It is far too far to walk and they cannot afford to use public transport. The traditional location of the "provisional squatter" has changed in many areas and the new peripheral squatter settlements frequently occurring in their stead must not be confused with them.

Typical Stages of Settlement Development

In the paragraphs that follow, different settlements at different stages of development and with different degrees of tenure are described and compared; it is, therefore, necessary to use standardized terms in order to "locate" particular cases. The chart below shows the relationship of the factors and terms used:

ITINERANT transient occupancy with no intention of permanent tenure (E)	"TENTATIVE SQUATTER" occupancy without any legal status or guarantee of continued tenure (D)	"ESTABLISHED SQUATTER" de facto and secure possession but without legal status (C)	"SEMI-SQUATTER" or semi-legal without full recognition but with some rights (B)	LEGAL OCCUPANCY institutionally recognized forms of tenure (eg. freehold, lease, rental) (A)	LEVELS OF PHYSICAL DEVELOPMENT
			complete semi-squatter	complete legal	COMPLETE structure and utilities to modern standards (A)
		incomplete squatter	INCOMPLETE SEMI-SQUATTER	incomplete legal	INCOMPLETE structure or utilities but built to modern standards (B)
	incipient tenative squatter	INCIPIENT SQUATTER	INCIPIENT SEMI-SQUATTER		INCIPIENT construction of potentially modern standard (C)
	PROVISIONAL TENATIVE SQUATTER	PROVISIONAL SQUATTER	PROVISIONAL SEMI-SQUATTER		PROVISIONAL construction of low standard or impermanent materials (D)
nomad	TRANSIENT TENATIVE SQUATTER	transient squatter			TRANSIENT temporary and easily removed shelter (E)

DEGREES OF SECURITY OF TENURE

FIGURE 1

A Typology of Settlements in Terms of Development Levels and Security of Tenure

Note: "Types" noted in capital letters are those common in autonomous urban settlements. Settlements commonly change their status over time and, therefore, describe trajectories on the chart.

Although the information obtained on settlements throughout the urbanizing world (from over 40 major cities and a dozen smaller ones) is too accidental and scattered to be conclusive, it certainly supports the hypothesis that we are dealing with universal urban growth processes and not some marginal and passing peculiarity. It is however, clear from the data so far obtained that there is a correlation between the types and stages of uncontrolled settlement in a given region or city and the income levels of the population.[5] With the partial exception of West and Central Africa—where urbanization has only recently begun—the lower the per capita income levels the greater the preponderance of the "provisional" levels of settlement. Uncontrolled settlements of low-income sectors in India and Pakistan, for instance, appear to be only of the "provisional" varieties. We have no information, so far, to show that *bustees, jhonpris* or *jhuggis* tend to develop into anything approaching an acceptable modern environment. In areas with appreciably higher per capita income levels, on the other hand, the bulk of the autonomous low-income settlement is in the "incipient" or "incomplete" category. This is true of most Latin American countries and, apparently, of the more recently urbanizing countries in the Mediterranean area. There are, of course, important modifying variables—such as government policy and the exercise of police power. The different stages and types of uncontrolled settlement are described in the paragraphs that follow.

"*Tentative Settlements*": "*provisional*" or "*incipient*" settlements of intended permanent squatters. The amount of data

so far obtained is insufficient to allow for any generalizations with regard to the frequency and regional distribution of settlements of this type or, rather, at this particular stage.[6] It is fairly safe to assume, however, that the majority of settlements which are established through organized invasion must pass through it rapidly if there is any effective police opposition. Organized invasions where tenuously held encampments were defended against police action have been reported during the past few years in Chile, Colombia, Mexico, and Peru. An invasion "along the lines of the Lima squatters" has also been reported recently in Manila and Sewell, referring to the establishments of individual holdings in the *gecekondu* of Ankara, describes how temporary structures of new arrivals are torn down by the police.

An initial encampment, however primitive it may be, is not necessarily temporary; if it is the first stage of a future settlement, it may prove to be either a permanent one, a semi-permanent one, or provisional. Settlements at this stage of development show wide differences in the relative wealth of their inhabitants as well as in their locations and in the possibilities which their sites offer. The *bustee* dwellers referred to in "Slums of Old Delhi" (13) are among the poorest. On the other hand, the original invaders and settlers of the Cuevas *barriada*[7] appear to be of the average working-class level of Lima—by no means the poorest sector of the local population and with far higher living standards than the bustee dwellers. These socioeconomic differ-

[6] See footnote 2.

[7] For a description of the development of this *barriada* see my "Barriers and Channels for Housing Development in Modernizing Countries," *Journal of the American Institute of Planning*, Vol. XXXII, No. 3 (May 1967).

[5] The close correlation of per capita income levels and stages of economic development makes my previous footnote 2 relevant here.

ences correlate with location, topo-graphy, and density. In settlements near the central business districts or indus-trial zones, density will tend to be very high—over 12,000 persons per hectare have been reported in Hong Kong. (9) "Safety in numbers" if not offset by the fire hazard (in one night alone 20,000 squatters lost their homes in one of the Hong Kong squatter fires) (9) or excessive over-crowding, can ensure a degree of secu-rity of tenure or, at least, guarantee a degree of consideration for their plight by the political authorities. The facts available suggest that the "transient" settlements that manage to establish themselves become semi-permanent "provisional" settlements if the settlers have very low or unstable incomes (by local standards) or if they are located on land of high or potentially high value and of limited area. Suc-cessful squatter settlements established by relatively stable, urbanized wage-earners on land of low value tend rapidly to become "incipient squatter settlements."

Incipient squatter settlements: Insecure tenure but with a significant degree of fixed capital investment. While we have abundant evidence of *self-improving settlements* throughout Latin America, North Africa, and the Eastern Mediter-ranean, very little has been obtained that shows their existence in the other developing regions. A number of modern standard houses are built in at least some of the Manila settlements. (18) Charles Abrams and Otto Koenigs-berger in their "Report on Housing in the Philippine Islands" list the signs observed in a Davao settlement. (16) These include: "Dental Clinic," "Master Plumber—Licensed," "Abo-gado—Notary Public," and "Wanted: House-maid." The majority, however,

seem unlikely to progress very far owing to the extremely high densities and apparently total lack of street align-ments and open space. The Commis-sioner for Redevelopment reports a similar situation in Hong Kong. (10) While many of the inhabitants of the Lyari settlement in Karachi regard their dwellings as being of a permanent nature, they cannot be considered satisfactory by modern standards. (15) Apparent exceptions found in the less urbanized areas are the Kinshasa (22) and Brazzaville (20) settlements which resemble the peripheral developments of Lima and Mexico City. Self-improv-ing "incipient squatter settlements" occur predominantly in the countries where urbanization is in full swing and where industrialization has made a significant start. The "incipient squat-ter" (and "semi-squatter") settlements in Latin America, North Africa and the Eastern Mediterranean, on which we have useful data, have many charac-teristics in common. To a greater or lesser extent, most of these conflict with the traditional image of the squat-ter settlement. Only in the narrowest and most literal sense are the majority of these "incipiently modern" settle-ments "slums". In many cases, develop-ment is slow enough and conditions are bad enough to justify the label, but in many other cases—in that of the Cuevas settlement in Lima, for example—the word "slum" is no more apt than it would be if applied to any building works in progress. It is, after all, only the wealthy minority—outside the industrialized countries—who have ever been able to afford to finish a dwelling of relatively high standard *before* moving into it.

Internal organization is necessary, though often not sufficient to enable self-improvement to happen. The direct evidence for internal organization among squatter groups is scarce. But even where it is reported, as in the Ankara *gecekondu*, (29) their ability to control physical development to provide material facilities appears to be very limited. In the majority of settlements there are few public squares or recreation areas, or areas set aside for schools, churches, and other community facilities. In sharp contrast are the *villes extra-coutumiers* of Kinshasa, (22) many of the *colonias proletarias* of Mexico City, (45) and the *barriadas* of Lima, Arequipa and other Peruvian cities, and some of the *ranchos* of Venezuela. (66) In these cases squatting has been organized so that layouts are regular and at least some provision is made for public open space and community facilities. This not very surprising coincidence of topographical conditions and physical order supports the deduction that settler organization is more common than is often supposed.

Apart from the cities mentioned above, squatter settlement layouts which indicate some degree of premeditated order can be seen in Panama City (Panama), Buenaventura (Colombia), Buenos Aires (Argentina) and Fortaleza (Brazil). More information would, no doubt, reveal "planned" settlements in many other areas. Initial layout, designating each settler a clearly demarcated and reasonable plot, may be more influential than might be supposed. Many would assume that the squatters have little respect for planning, since the land has been taken illegally and by force in the first place—they expect squatters would take land from one another, especially if, at any time, a plot is left unguarded. However, plans are respected to a surprising degree. Evidence supporting this respect for "properties" among neigh-

bours, is available for both Venezuela and Peru. Talton Ray, referring to settlements in Caracas, writes:

The eagerness with which people seize land for settlement and the extreme formality of the allocation of parcels would seem to indicate that within a community one would have to be continually on guard lest one's own parcel be stolen. Actually the opposite is true. The people have an extraordinary respect for the land and dwellings of other barrio residents. Once a piece of land has a specific "owner" they will not touch it. Evidence of the strength of this rule is seen all over the country. Families reserve choice sites along main roads for years merely by laying the foundation of a house and putting four or five rows of blocks on top. In a barrio in Ciudad Guayana many neighbours wanted to construct a kindergarten, but on the only "vacant" lot there were the remnants of a mud ranchito—just two dilapidated walls. It was said that the owner had left the barrio some ten years before, and nobody had heard of him since. Nevertheless, it finally took the municipal engineer to convince them that they would not be morally wrong to tear down the hut. (66)

Sewell reports in Ankara that squatters take their "rights" so seriously that, when conflicts arise between claimants, they will often turn to government authorities in order to resolve them. The Ankara incident Sewell reports could well have occurred in a Peruvian *barriada*.

The man had "bought" building rights from another person who purported to own some land in the gecekondu. The "purchaser" had waited until a dark night, then had begun to build his house. At this point another claimant to the land appeared, a claimant supported by many neighbouring gecekondu settlers. A pitched battle ensued and the "purchaser" received a gash on his head with a shovel. Police located and arrested the swindler. The author subsequently visited the "purchaser" in the hospital and found him relating his adventures with gusto to visitors packed three deep around his bed. A few weeks later he built his house on another site. (29)

The eleven unplanned but nevertheless developing or already developed settlements on which we have information are all situated on marginal land which, through geological accident, happens to be centrally located. The four relatively well planned squatter or semi-squatter settlements from different areas for which we have detailed information are all situated on more or less level marginal land of little commercial value at the peripheries of the cities. The only settlement of the "incipient squatter" category on which we have some data but which does not fall into either of these groups is the "barriada bruja" Villa de los Reyes of Panama City. This settlement is peripheral and occupies land of poor quality which is flat and relatively extensive—the density is quite low. But, with the exception of two fairly well aligned streets, it does not appear to have been planned. From enquiries made during a recent and unaccompanied visit, there appeared to have been no community organization until the government housing agency (the I.N.V.U.) stepped in to provide technical assistance which resulted in considerable improvements. The correlations observed between the geographic, administrative, and physical planning characteristics of the developing "incipient squatter" settlements in central and peripheral locations are hardly surprising when one takes the local situation of the settlers themselves into consideration.

Incipient and advanced semi-squatter settlements: Settlements with secure but semi-legal tenure and with significant or advanced degrees of material investment. "Incomplete semi-squatter" (or "semi-legal") settlements within the terms

of reference occur frequently in the urbanizing world. The middle-income earners are an emergent class. Relative to their socioeconomic and cultural status, this sector is often badly served for housing as a result of inflated land costs and interest rates. But, because of their standards and status, the middle classes are rarely tempted to take the direct action of the low-income squatter. There are, however, exceptions. In one country of the Far East where there is a "hopelessly inadequate low- to middle-income housing programme" a recent newspaper report on a settlement of 25,000 squatters observes:

What is surprising here is that most of the squatters are moneyed people, including businessmen, lawyers, doctors, teachers, nurses, midwives, army and navy officers . . . A number of the squatters own cars, TV sets, refrigerators, burners and electric stoves. Their houses are made of concrete. . . and other durable materials.

It is more usual for this middle-income group, when it cannot afford to build in accordance with all legal requirements, to build in developments that circumvent cost-inflating regulations, unnecessary from their point of view. It is common to find suburban developments where fair or even good quality dwellings are being built—and often lived in at the same time—in areas which lack all or some public utilities, paved roads and so on. More seriously, these developments are sometimes very badly laid out with quite inadequate lots. Partly because of the difficulties of deciding what is "squatting" and what is "clandestine" (but not squatting) and of knowing just where to draw the line between "clandestine," "customary," and "legal," it is even more difficult to obtain information on settlement areas in this stage than it is of the more spectacular squatter and slum areas. To limit the field to "squatter" settlements in the strict sense, however, would effectively camouflage the processes which must be focussed on if we are to understand the structure of events well enough to predict them.

The world-wide view of "incomplete semi-squatter" settlement shows that its inhabitants are from an extremely wide range of social classes, occurring commonly in areas where the middle class is a very new one. The periphery of Lagos, for instance, which is evidently expanding fast, is very much like the larger *"barriadas"* of Lima and Arequipa, but even the few most highly paid skilled workers of Lagos find it financially difficult to buy and build in such zones, which, according to our informants, are populated almost exclusively by white-collar, middle-income families. The difficulties experienced by the government in transferring those displaced from the slum clearance areas of central Lagos to the Suru Lere project (described in detail by Peter Marris) (21) confirms this. One of the principal areas of new residential growth in the Lagos metropolitan area is actually in the Western Province, where there are few if any building controls. With the exception of Kinshasa we have, so far, no information on suburban residential settlement by average low-income families that can be described as "advanced" in countries where the annual per capita income is around the $100 level. But where incomes are appreciably higher —or where suburban building can be achieved exceptionally cheaply as in Peru—"working class" suburban development is quite common. Where income levels are very low, settlement of much the same kind may often be found but it will generally prove to be that of the "middle" class.

"Provisional   Squatter"   settlements—

Illegal but de facto possession with little or no investment in permanent construction or installations. Squatters are motivated basically by the need for minimum cost—any expenditure for non-essential needs is considered extravagant. The "provisional" settlements are the refuge of many of the un- or under-employed. These will naturally tend to congregate as near as they can to sources of employment. Physical improvement to modern standards tends, therefore, to be incompatible with the raison d'être of the provisional settlement. Few of them are either intended to become permanent modern settlements or do, in fact, achieve anything approaching that status. The "provisional squatter settlements" are refuges of the urban poor, but the poor are also accommodated elsewhere. Neither are all provisional squatter settlers poor. In Hong Kong, it has been reported that some squatter settlement dwellers belie their economic status to the extent that they are apt to blossom out of their shanty chrysalis into the modern house for which they have been saving meanwhile. (8) Where data is available, income levels in the provisional settlements are consistently very low. A detailed analysis of income levels in eight squatter settlements of Manila in 1963 shows that no less than *85% have incomes below subsistence level.* (17) Settlement studies from Caracas (61) and the famous Rooiyard study in Johannesburg confirm that the settlers are from the least prepared urban groups and have the lowest income levels.

Exceptional provisional settlements may nevertheless develop into integrated parts of the city. The Plaka settlement, situated on the northern slope of the Acropolis in Athens, was probably a "provisional" squatter settlement when it started life some 130 years ago. It is now a delightful area where accommodation is sought by writers, artists, and, even, by architects. The La Peria settlement, on the rocky slope between the city walls of old San Juan (Puerto Rico), and the sea, began as a "provisional squatter settlement" at the end of the last century. Though still threatened with demolition a large section has already been improved. Descloitres and Reverdy point out the similarity between the "*bidonvilles urbains*" and the traditional casbah of Algiers (23) and the *gourbivilles* of Tunis, surveyed in detail by Sebag and others (25–27), suggest that the same process is taking place in spite of the intensified pace and demands of modern city life. However, the great majority of "provisional settlements" existing today will be eradicated eventually, if only because they are on land of potentially high value. The old established *bustees* of Howrah (Calcutta) dating back to the 1870's, have turned into typical and, presumably, legalized slum tenements in poor but more or less permanent structures now located well within the downtown area (12). Under the present circumstances it is unlikely that these *bustees* will be torn down in the foreseeable future. The recommendations set out in the final reports of the Calcutta Metropolitan Planning Organization (the Calcutta and Howrah Area Development Plans, 1966 and 1967), summarized by A. Van Huyck and P. Rosser in "An Environmental Approach to Low-income Housing" *International Development Review*, Vol. VIII, No. 3 (September 1966), not only reinforce this view but represent an important contribution to the redefinition of the "housing problem" along the lines sketched out in this paper.

The traditional provisional squatter settlement model persists, but it is no longer always situated on the periphery in the larger cities. The "provisional squatter" settlements in the sixteen major cities on which we have information are near centres of employment for unskilled or semi-skilled labour. If these centres are the central markets or around the central business districts, then provisional settlements will occur on marginal lands nearby—on hillsides or rocky outcrops, as in Lima, Rio de Janeiro, Ankara and Hong Kong; on marshes and areas liable to flooding, or, even, out into the sea itself as in Santiago de Chile, Guayaquil, Karachi, and Davao (Philippines); or filling up the interstices of the cities—ravines, unguarded and unused plots of private land, public land such as parks, the verges of wide streets, railway embankments, and even bombed sites. This has occurred in Caracas, Mexico City, Algiers, Delhi, and Manila. Where provisional settlements do occur on the periphery—as in Istanbul, Cairo, and Paris—they are located near peripherally located industrial areas.

It seems probable that the "transient" settlements in centrally located areas tend to have a higher proportion of recent provincial immigrants than those established on the periphery, since these areas generally provide the cheapest accommodation and locations within walking distance of casual employment centres. Location, as well as the social convenience of living near relatives and friends from the same village who may be depended upon for help in times of acute need, may well balance the lack of privacy, space, and cleanliness. The processes of urban accommodation will also reflect an improvement in economic status although this may not be apparent from the condition of the environment—except, perhaps, where it bristles with TV antennae.

The Polarity of Settlement Types

We have data from cities in seven countries which allow us to compare income levels between squatters or slum dwellers in central locations with squatters or semi-squatters in peripheral areas. In every case the difference is marked: the peripheral settlers are almost always of a higher socio-economic status than central city slum or "provisional settlement" dwellers. And, in every case where we have data, the majority of the settlers—who are building permanent houses—were previously resident in the city. A survey carried out in the San Martin settlement in Lima in 1960, for instance, revealed that only 5% of the then inhabitants of that very large squatter settlement (with a population at that time of approximately 60,000) were recent rural migrants.[8] But, as mentioned in the preceding paragraph, this situation is likely to change in settlement areas that become so large. Two separate settlement areas, initially "peripheral," have populations of well over 100,000 each—one area (Carabayllo-Comas) has already become, in effect, the third largest city of Peru; and Lima has no monopoly of large marginal settlements: Casablanca is reported to have a *bidonville* with a population of 45,000 (53), and many of the *gecekondu* are as large or larger than this. If, as in the latter case, the centres of these areas are distinctly separate from the rest of the city—if they form a species of urban satellite—

[8] In a study carried out in three Lima *barriadas* in 1965, 11 out of 204 heads of families answering the question moved directly to the *barriada* from a previous residence outside the metropolitan area. Only 7 out of 209 immigrant heads of families had lived in Lima less than 5 years while 179 (85%) had lived in the city 9 years or more. In the *barriada* Pampa de Ceuva, established 5 years at the time of the enquiry, 80% arrived in the settlement, during the 4 years previously but 60% had arrived in Lima not less than 9 years previously—and of the three settlements studied, Cueva is the newest and the one with the youngest population.

then they will naturally tend to reproduce many urban functions, such as markets which provide casual labour for the very poor. These settlement areas will, therefore, attract the very poor—especially rural migrants with established settler relatives. The initial differentiation may tend to become obscured with time but it is clearly most important to recognize the distinctly different nature and function which the peripheral settlement has in contrast to centrally located settlements.

The convenience of the centrally located "provisional squatter" settlement or slum for the poorest sectors of the population has already been touched on above. By the same argument (until it provides an independent source of employment) [it] is highly inconvenient for that sector. On the other hand, very cheap or even free-for-the-taking marginal land, within commuting distance of workplaces, is highly convenient for the regular wage-earner. The regular wage-earner is unlikely to be a newcomer to city life, so that it would be surprising to find a large number of recent immigrants from rural areas in distant peripheral settlements. In none of the studies analysed is there any data to contradict this hypothesis. In a number of studies there are statements that explicitly support the deduction which one can hardly avoid when faced with the above facts: that the essential difference between the "provisional squatter settlement" (which is a slum by any definition) and the actively progressing "incipient squatter" (or "semi-squatter") suburban settlement is precisely that between the orthodox central city slum and the orthodox residential suburb. Both are, of course, at much lower material levels than their counterparts in the majority of cities in the industrialized countries, but their relative locations and their relative functions are the same.

Mixed settlements: centrally located out-crop sites provide suitable locations for both immigrant and wage-earner permitting social mobility with geographic stability. The social function and physical nature of the more centrally located "incipient" settlements [are] less clear. The marginal outcrop sites on which they are sited are often equally suitable for the very poor —providing him with a rent-free location for his shack—and for the less poor wage-earner—providing him with an inexpensive or free plot for a permanent dwelling. The very poor shanty-dweller may very well become a wage-earner, quite able to afford a few dollars' worth of building materials every week. *If this change of economic status takes place without a change of location, and if the original shanty site is large enough and sufficiently accessible, the shanty will be replaced by a more solidly built house.* The resultant mixture of shacks and solidly built—and often quite elegant—houses is frequently reported. As settlements with these mixed characteristics are among the most common—and are easily the most visible in the cities where they do occur—it is hardly surprising that they should provoke so many and such contradictory observations.

THE PROBLEMS OF UNCONTROLLED URBAN SETTLEMENT

Points of View: the Problems as Seen from Above and as Seen from Below

To this stage of the argument the positive aspect of uncontrolled urban settlement has been emphasized; to their inhabitants they are steps toward the solution of their problems, they are not problems *per se.* Squatter settlements—especially the self-improving varieties—can act as bootstraps by which families of low and insecure income can pull themselves up. As Nehru once remarked, building self-help homes builds families—it consolidates them as social and economic units. Yet from the government viewpoint, uncontrolled urban settlement is a very serious problem even where they present no serious or immediate problems for their inhabitants. Squatting and clandestine subdivision point up limitations in the existing machinery for planning and reduce the proportion of urban physical growth that can be effectively influenced by the government—that part which is carried out legally within a technical and institutional framework evolved to accommodate a situation of slow social change.

It is, then, quite clear that we are dealing with a situation that has two very different sides to it—a top side and a bottom one—so that which is seen depends on whether one is looking up at it from below (as the inhabitant) or down on it from above (as the administrator). To understand the whole, one must be able to see from both sides at once. Having pointed out the necessity of urban concentration, there is no need to explain that the problem does not lie in the *existence* of settlements—in spite of many recommendations and policies condemning them—but in the distorted growth processes and stunted forms imposed on the settlements by the conditions under which their development takes place.

The Economic and Physical Aspects of Uncontrolled Urban Settlement Problems

From an altitude that eliminates the details but which allows one to see uncontrolled settlement in relation to cities as a whole and, in addition, viewed through time—from 1940 to 1960 say—the settlement process reveals some surprises. Let us imagine that we are looking down at Lima: 25 years back we would have seen a smallish and quite compact city of some 600,000 people. Twenty-five years forward we will probably see a sprawling metropolis of some 6,000,000 inhabitants. Barring world catastrophe, Lima will have grown 1000% or more in less than a modern man's lifetime, and this will be typical of the majority of major cities in urbanizing countries. Let us now look at the area that will have grown during those 50 years. Based on a simple extrapolation of growth trends from 1940 to the present, by 1990, three-quarters of the population of the entire city—4,500,000 people—would be living in areas originally settled by squatters—in *barriadas* or in ex-*barriadas*.[9] In 1940, a quite insignificant proportion of the city population lived in marginal and squatter type settlements—probably less than 5%. Now, in 1966, at least 25% of the population lives in *barriadas* (including those that have since become incorporated municipalities) and the city, meanwhile, has trebled in size. Not only is this situation paralleled by that of many other cities such as Mexico City, Caracas, and Istanbul, but it is emphasized even more in smaller cities that are also swept up in the present flood of urbanization. In secondary cities of Peru, such as Arequipa or Iquitos, the proportion of uncontrolled growth is even larger (50% and over); a disproportionate amount of capital is invested in the primate city, including investment in modern housing. In Peru the total proportion of the urban population living in *barriadas* is over one-third, and the total urban area of the *barriadas* exceeds the total urban area of the cities of Peru in 1940 by between one-third and one-half. Information on typical secondary cities in other countries—

Valencia in Venezuela, (62) Adana in Turkey, (28) and Davao in the Philippines, (18) for instance—indicates that a similar pattern occurs in those countries. Contemporary cities belong to the poor, and it is the poor that are largely responsible for their growth.

The measurement of the effects of uncontrolled urban growth on the economics of urban and industrial development falls outside the scope of this paper. The research carried out by [other] authorities has confirmed the impressions gathered during the work on this paper: that criteria and techniques for such measurements are, as yet, ill-defined and undeveloped and that very little is really known, for sure—especially when it comes to the study of newly urbanizing areas. The only two direct references we have, so far, to this question are both quoted by Charles Abrams who reports that in Cali, Colombia, the scale and violence of the squatter problem "precipitated an emigration of industry." (1) In a report on Ciudad Guayana, the new industrial city in Venezuela, Abrams refers to a study of factory workers' excessive journey to work (from squatter settlement area) which showed that the workers' demands for compensation, when measured in terms of the effect on dividends, reduced profits by 7%. (60) No hard facts or figures are available on the additional costs of providing water mains and other essential utilities to settlements in outlying areas or difficult terrain, but, undoubtedly, these are very considerably in excess of normal costs. It is, therefore, inevitable that these inflated infrastructure and servicing costs will be reflected in the local tax structure and in general increases of overheads at the expense of production and investment in fixed capital. To these costs one must add the losses involved in the non-

[9] See footnote 2.

participation and non-contribution of the administratively unincorporated marginal areas.

Totally uncontrolled and unplanned but largely permanent development occurs in many areas—the cases of Ankara and Istanbul, or of Caracas and Rio de Janeiro have been mentioned. While a small area—such as the Plaka settlement in Athens,[10] or the La Perla settlement in San Juan—can easily integrate fully with the city, and additional costs of development can be absorbed over time without undue economic strain, it is an entirely different matter when the scale is multiplied hundreds of times. Estimates place the proportion of the population of Ankara that are housed in the *gecekondu* near one-half. (28) The population of the *ranchos* of Caracas in 1961 was 21% of the total urban population of 1,330,000. (63) Both the *gecekondu* and the *ranchos* are almost totally lacking in all public utilities and services; the bulk of them are situated on steep hillsides, without plan forms adjusted to the demands of gravity drainage or vehicular access. Large numbers of solidly built dwellings have been erected, especially in the *gecekondu*, and the demands of this increasingly influential sector, politically speaking, are unlikely to diminish as time goes on and as their individual dwellings are completed, except for the services and utilities.

An equally serious problem is illustrated by Arequipa, the second city of Peru with population of approximately 200,000. In 1960 the built-up area of the incorporated city was approximately

[10] In the September 1966 issue of *Ekistics*, Dimitri Philippides published an article on "Ilissos, A Village Community in Athens," which, though much more recent in origin than the Plaka settlement, appears to have (or to have had as it was then threatened with imminent demolition) many of the same characteristics and qualities.

900 hectares. At that time the "*urbanizationes populares*" (barriadas) occupied an area of 1100 hectares with an average gross density of approximately 22 persons per hectare, though it has increased very considerably during the past five years during which the proportion in settlements has grown from between 20 and 25%—an absolute increase of 300%). Even if the area claimed by squatters does not increase there is a considerable amount of waste involved in the extremely low densities during the development period. Construction as well as public transportation costs are bound to be appreciably higher. A more serious and more permanent problem in the Arequipa case, however, is that a large part of the settlement area is beyond the economic limits for the gravitational water supply and sewer lines. Either a large part of the population is going to remain without water and sewers, or the city is going to have to adjust its system and policy—at considerable expense. Similar problems—those arising from scattered and extremely low densities—appear to be common in West and Central Africa. (22)

The costs of these settlements are reflected in depressed land values as well as in the relocation costs involved in their eradication. Provisional squatter settlements often interfere with city development by blocking it. And although most will certainly be eradicated, the damage that such settlements have done already is considerable. Local land values are greatly reduced, and commercial enterprise in the adjacent areas kept at a low level. Eradication, especially when it involves relocation, can be very expensive and can precipitate all manner of conflicts. The eradication and resettlement of the Intramuros settlement in downtown Manila not only involved a very costly relocation project but also caused a great deal of friction between the different authorities involved. (16, 18) Another case is the Lyari settlement area in Karachi which occupied land urgently required for industrial expansion. (15) While very little investment of value had been made by the settlers, it was deemed necessary to build a complete new town for them (Korangi), which, though not built for that particular sector alone, must at least partly be counted as a consequent overhead.

Poor design is a form of built-in blight. Initial standards can be of great importance to the people themselves, especially if they are building with permanent materials. Bad design in the initial layout of the buildings and poor construction greatly reduce the value of what is built. Inadequate design is certainly the more serious and common problem in the Peruvian *barriadas*. Construction, though frequently poor and wasteful of cement and steel, is better than generally assumed, partly because of the high proportion of construction workers who live in *barriadas*—a phenomenon common to many uncontrolled settlement areas. Construction workers have a double motive: they can build for themselves, and they greatly increase their job opportunities by living in the midst of a construction site. A much higher proportion of construction work in settlement areas is carried out by locally employed labour than is often supposed—in the Lima *barriadas* perhaps no more than a quarter of the total

labour value of the permanently built dwellings is provided by the owner-occupiers.[11] The latter will provide a fair amount of the unskilled labour—from that of small children to their grandmothers—but most of the skilled work is usually contracted locally among relatives or those who have migrated from the same villages. While a great deal could be done through properly administered technical assistance in order to improve skills, still more can be effected through the improvement of design. People will build only in accordance with the models that they know, and they frequently lack suitable models for self-help, single-family urban houses. In Peru the vast majority have only known rural dwellings, company town barracks, and central city slum courts, (33) which are not suitable as types for urban building. A large number of well-built houses are planned in ways that eliminate ventilation and daylighting to many of their rooms and which reduce their market value in the future. The house plans and photographs in the unpublished report on the *gecekondu* by B.E.R.U. (28) reveal similar problems in Turkey. The problem posed by the more provisional settlements of very low slum standards are different and even more intractable.

Charles Abrams has emphasized that the most permanent part of settlement is its layout. Referring to the planning of Ciudad Guayana, Abrams has written:

Rancheros will settle where they can if they are not told where they may. They will build what they can afford if they are not helped to build what they should. I am less worried, however, about what they will build than where they will build it and less concerned about initial standards than about initial layout. Rancho houses will improve with time and with better eco-

---

[11] This may be an under-estimate. Of the 223 responses in the 1965 enquiry (in the three *barriadas* of Lima), only 23% made no contribution (other than financial) to the construction or its supervision while 34.5% (77) did everything. This is sufficient, anyway, to prove that a very large proportion of the work is contracted.

nomic conditions if the rancheros are given a stake. (60)

There are city streets today that were laid out several thousand years ago, but the buildings giving on to these streets have changed many times. Drawing proper lines and digging trenches in the raw earth is of greater significance than erecting buildings, because it fixes the layout—the ancients knew all about this as Joseph Rykwert has made clear in his authoritative essay, "The Idea of the City." Anyone who dared abuse the initial planning rites at the city's foundation was apt to lose his head.

That "bridgehead" settlements are necessary and bound to persist as long as no alternatives are available for those whom they serve, is undeniable. The physical planning and development problems which these stagnant or degenerating slum settlements create for the city due to extreme overcrowding can have serious economic and social problems—both physical disorder and disease undoubtedly contribute to city overheads and to reduced productivity. Provisional slum settlements are often located on land liable to flooding —often with water heavily contaminated by sewers. A recently eradicated shanty-town in Lima was built over the smouldering city garbage dump; these people were living in a literal inferno with smoke coming up through the floors of their shacks. Not all such settlements are as Dantesque, however, and many are more like the El Augustino settlement in Lima in which minor physical adjustments—such as the creation of a few street corner open spaces and the installation of latrines, water spigots, and laundering slabs, could make enormous differences. *There are many good reasons for the existence of these slums, and it is inevitable that they will continue as long as the poor remain poor.*

The basic problem of the slums is not how to eradicate them, but how to make them livable.

Socio-economic and Political Aspects of Uncontrolled Urban Settlement Problems

The gap between rich and poor in the developing countries is many times as wide as in the more industrialized nations. There are very great differences between classes of the low-income or "popular" sector of the urban populations: between those at or below subsistence and those who manage to sustain life at levels which are tolerable by local standards. These quantitative differences are relatively subtle in societies where income differentials are so extreme: in the newly urbanizing economies it is usual for the managerial class to earn fifteen to twenty times more than the workers whom they manage. In the United States, for instance, or in the U.S.S.R., the differential is far less. It is understandable that those from the industrialized areas or the wealthy classes overlook the actually vital differences between the semi-employed "bridgeheader" and the more or less regular wage-earning "consolidator." But without an appreciation of these structural differences, it is impossible to see any meaningful patterns in the massive and fast growing popular sector.

Failure to see these differences results in grossly misleading generalizations such as the common but false assumption that settlers are political radicals. While these striking differences of income levels —between rich and poor—have led to many sweeping generalizations and projections of imminent violence, these often tend to be oversimplifications.

All over the world, often long in advance of effective industrialization, the unskilled poor are streaming away from subsistence agriculture to exchange the squalor or rural poverty for the even deeper miseries of the shantytowns, *favelas* and *bidonvilles* that, year by year, grow inexorably on the fringes of the developing cities. They . . . are the core of local despair and disaffection —filling the *Jeunesse* movements of the Congo, swelling the urban mobs of Rio, voting Communist in the ghastly alleys of Calcutta, everywhere undermining the all too frail structure of public order and thus retarding the economic development that can alone help their plight. Unchecked, disregarded, left to grow and fester, there is here enough explosive material to produce in the world at large the pattern of a bitter class conflict finding to an increasing degree a racial bias, erupting in guerrilla warfare, and threatening, ultimately, the security even of the comfortable West.

Myron Wiener, who quotes this statement by a distinguished economist, has dealt with this hypothesis in a paper (14) showing that the inhabitants of the "ghastly alleys" are much less prone to vote against the local system than other, much better-off, sectors. Similar investigations in other areas where squatters are well entrenched also bear this out. The following quotations from G.H. Sewell's monograph suggest why squatters frequently have quite conservative attitudes toward their governments:

Government officials and intellectuals in Turkey have frequently expressed concern that the residents of the *gecekondu* will become dangerous radicals of the left. . . . Despite the substandard living conditions, however, several forces are operating to counter such a trend at this juncture. The migrants are principally villagers with a deep devotion to their religion and a surprisingly powerful sense of Turkish nationalism. . . . Secondly, the vast majority of the *gecekondu* residents have accomplished significant social and economic mobility in a relatively short period of time. . . . Thirdly, these migrants have developed a sense of responsibility towards

their sizable investment in the *gecekondu*, and they seem anxious to avoid any action or suggestion that would jeopardize themselves, their houses or their community. (29)

Referring to a *gecekondu* settler whom he came to know personally, Sewell underlines the point:

Economically, he is faring far better than his family in the village and is deriving considerable prestige from this fact. He feels his ownership of his house is beyond question and acquiring title for the land beneath it is only a matter of time. Politically, Ali is discontented, but his discontent now is that of a self-righteous burgher.

These observations from the Turkish *gecekondu* hold here for Peruvian *barriada* dwellers (who vote more conservatively than the middle classes) and for the *ranchos* of Venezuela only to a slightly lesser degree.

If the larger and more peripheral areas fail to maintain a discernible rate of improvement or if, for other reasons, their inhabitants lose heart and cease to invest their savings and efforts in the improvement of their homes and local community, then the fear that the huge belt of recent city growth is peopled by disaffected slum dwellers —the common middle-and upper-class image of even the best kinds of marginal settlement—might well turn out to be true. If this should happen, it would, partly, be a self-fulfilling prophesy of the upper classes. In the first place, wealth is badly distributed. In the second place, the upper and middle classes, by persisting long enough, can make people become ashamed of living in them. Some young British Volunteers, living and working in Pampa de Comas, a fairly well advanced "*barriada*" in Lima, reported that young women, daughters of original settlers who have done relatively well, are embarrassed to admit that they live in that area. The mud that is thrown at the settlers and their settlements by the national and international press is apt to stick. Similar reactions are reported from Santiago de Chile, in a government-sponsored housing settlement area. Various observers, among them John Friedmann and William Mangin, have expressed their concern about the future of these settlements in view of rising expectations and the continuing unconcern and misunderstanding of the situation and its problems on the part of the authorities.

If the air of hope vanishes, if expectations are frustrated, the predicted uprisings could take place. Alarmist projections of the kind quoted could well be much nearer the truth if settlement dwellers' progress is thwarted and their confidence in present institutions and structures is lost. On the basis of deductions from the information actually available, it would appear that the political attitudes of the settlers fall into two main groups at present: that of the "bridgeheaders" and the "consolidators." The "bridgeheaders" seem too preoccupied with their immediate problems to concern themselves actively with political matters; the "consolidators," having a stake in society, are participating but are naturally conservative. Rather than being a "misery belt" of the dispossessed, waiting only for that revolutionary spark to drive them to the destruction of the citadels of society which they surround (the paranoic vision of the upper classes which has even been taken as the theme of a play written by a Chilean and enacted recently in Lima), the settlements could more accurately be described as social safety belts. Kill the hope, though, and the situation might well change. As long as urbanization and modernization are progressing the slums and

settlements of the cities involved are, in Stokes' terms "slums of hope" rather than "slums of despair." Harlem and Watts have little in common with the "provisional" settlements discussed in this paper and have still less to do with the typical *gecekondu* or *barriadas*. But this will remain true only as long as the settlements are vehicles of social change—and change for the better. As soon as they become traps, like the infamous ghetto slums of the more stable societies, then they are sure to become the "breeding grounds of discontent and violence" that all squatter settlements are so often supposed to be. Stokes' concept emphasizes that one cannot judge the value of an environment by its material standards. The Watts district of Los Angeles is not a physical slum—materially it is obviously superior to the best *barriada* in Lima. The significant difference is very difficult to see with the outer eye: the difference between hope and despair. This is immediately apparent when one speaks and moves among the inhabitants, as any of the many U.S. Peace Corps or British voluntary service organization volunteers who have worked in these areas will confirm.

The problems felt most strongly by the settlers have to do with the frustration of their capacity to work and build:

It is not the discomfort of the physical situation of the people of the villas (the *villas miserias* of Buenos Aires) feel most bitterly. It is the humiliation of being denied the opportunity of doing for themselves what they are quite able to do. (36)

The first step is to secure possession of the land. It is perfectly natural that the demand for titles to land is of high priority. This explains why so many low-income families are prepared to risk their lives for a piece of their own land—and will, thereupon, proceed to invest a very high proportion of their earnings in building on it—while they are extremely reluctant to buy, on easier terms, a mortgaged house built for them by a public authority. The fact that government-built off-the-peg houses may be mortgaged for a long period is certainly one reason why they are so unpopular. A family in secure possession of a plot of land feels free to invest its efforts and resources to create the one concrete symbol of its identity—the dwelling.

Where it is apparent that a house can result from hard work and sacrifice, hidden resources and efforts are revealed. To imagine that life in an incipient settlement is either all thorns or all roses would be equally untrue. From recent surveys in Santiago de Chile, Lima, Arequipa, and other cities in Peru, in Guayaquil, Ecuador, and in Panama City, it is evident that the settlers in these areas are much happier in their present locations than in their former ones, which were rented central city slums for most of them. But this does not mean an absence of serious problems economically and socially as well as physically—just an improvement as a result of settlement location and life. Apart from the discomforts of living in half-built or provisional structures and the lack of public utilities and services, many families suffer even more from economic deprivation than before. This may seem contradictory but the deprivation is generally voluntary, being the result of the extra costs of suburban living—mainly transportation and drinking water—and the voluntary sacrifices made in order to build. The Lima and Arequipa settlers often sacrifice too much. There is the case of one family, servants holding a secure position with a wealthy and

unusually conscientious household which provided them with good living quarters of their own. Even so, they preferred to build their own house in a *barriada* and exhausted themselves to such an extent that the husband died prematurely. And these families are by no means all very poor, inured to great physical hardship. We have a recent newspaper report from Manila about a recent invasion by middle-income people and, from Lima, we have a photograph of an infant being fed on a highchair—a totally foreign object in a peasant household. The child is being fed by a girl, probably a servant, while the family is living in a hole in the ground covered with brushwood and paper waiting until they are allocated their own plot of land. Other photographs, taken in the same area at the same time—in the El Ermitano settlement one month after the initial invasion—show households camping in shelters made from the furniture they brought with them. But the *gecekondu* builders—who build by night rather than invade in groups—are astonishingly fast builders.[12] Sewell

[12] Between the 8th and 10th of January, 1968, *The New York Times* reported on "overnight houses" in Greece:

. . . Authorities estimate that 500,000 illegal dwellings worth some 15 billion drachmas ($500 million) have literally cropped up on the outer fringes of Greek cities over the last 20 years.

These homes, usually built for low income families who cannot afford the costly processes of putting up "approved" homes according to regulations of the Ministry of Public Works, are built by contractors that specialize in slapping up four walls and a roof between nightfall and dawn.

Once the buildings have four walls and a roof—usually brick and corrugated iron—the authorities are powerless to demolish it. Hence the night-time construction.

. . . . .

The authorities feel the overnight building

describes how specialists assist the would-be settlers in erecting a single cell building with a tiled roof overnight. This speed is not only forced by the exigencies of a harsh climate but, also, by the policy of the local authorities, who demolish any temporary or incomplete structures. *Gecekondu* dwellers might well concur with a Lima settler who, when asked "what is the greatest difficulty that you have experienced in the course of building your house," answered, "the police who kept interfering with the building."

Given the risks and sacrifices that are so frequently made, the advantages of settlements are evidently considerable. The basic motive and reward is socio-economic security. A primary reason for moving to a settlement is the satisfaction of not having to pay rent. The next most common reason given is to build (or own) a house. Others are to improve physical conditions—to have more space, light, and air, especially for their children—to have more privacy, and to get away from the often violent life of the city slums. (52) The

---

boom is not only creating slums and serious economic, social and town planning problems, but believe the moonlighting is a waste of capital and manpower.

Authorities in the past have turned a blind eye to the illegal building because of an acute housing shortage in the cities caused by an influx of people from the provinces made homeless by earthquakes, floods, World War II and four years of guerrilla warfare in the late 1940's.

But the police recently were instructed to stop the building of illegal dwellings while the Government attempted to solve the housing problem in other ways.

Further comment is unnecessary—anyone who has seen the settlements surrounding Athens, for example, will be interested to learn about the "other ways" of solving the housing problem that the Government of Greece has in mind.

gravest dangers in Lima *barriadas*, for example, are not from attack by criminals (in spite of the virtual absence of police) but by dogs. One very great advantage expressed in some settlement areas is the security of the settled community and the proximity of blood relatives—perhaps a deeply seated motive for secure tenure and permanent settlement. Typical of these are the *gecekondu* of Ankara, where settlement patterns are closely allied to village origins.

Community organization is needed, but even where it exists, it often cannot overcome the obstacles. The comparative accounts of the development of the Cuevas and El Augustino *barriadas* in Lima have emphasized the actual and potential importance of community organization. Usually community organization is weak—except for obtaining and defending the land which the settlers hope to possess. From the limited evidence available in addition to Peru, settlement organization tends to evaporate as security of tenure rises. Where settlements have grown by accretion there appears to be little or no formal community organization initially, although there are suggestions that some incipient institutions form as a number of community facilities are provided. The most detailed account is contained in a forthcoming book by Talton F. Ray on the politics of the Barrios of Venezuela in national politics. (66)[13] The author's accounts

[13] A number of studies have been carried out recently on this important topic: Daniel Goldrich in Chile and Peru—See Goldrich, Pratt and Schuller: "The Political Integration of Lower-Class Urban Settlements in Chile and Peru," *Studies in Comparative International Development*, Vol. III, No. 1, Washington University, St. Louis, 1967. Anthony Leeds and collaborators have done a great deal of work on the

reveal that the "barrio" organizations, though common, tended to be ineffectual when it came to the carrying out of public works. In Venezuela these organizations are clearly more closely allied to national political parties than in Peru or Chile, for example. Community action is generally less effective

---

favellas of Rio de Janeiro and their papers are to be published by the University of Texas shortly. Thomas Lutz, a student at the University of Washington, Washington, D.C., has carried out studies in Peru, Ecuador and Panamá. All these studies confirm the active participation of the typical *barrio* inhabitants in national political life and the frequently high degree of internal organization. In any case there seems to be little evidence to support the following point of view:

> The most conspicuous symptom of the contemporary disorder is what happened to urbanisation in the developing areas. Every student of development is aware of the global spread of urban slums—from the *ranchos* of Caracas and *favellas* of Rio, to the *geçekôndu* of Ankara, to the *bidonvilles* and 'tin can cities' that infest the metropolitan centres of every developing country from Cairo to Manila.
>
> The point that must be stressed in referring to this suffering mass of humanity displaced from the rural areas to the filthy peripheries of the great cities, is that few of them experience the 'transition' from agricultural to urban-industrial labour called for by the mechanism of development and the model of modernisation. They are neither housed, nor trained, nor employed, nor serviced. They languish on the urban peiphery without entering into any productive relationship with its industrial operations. These are the 'displaced persons,' the DPS, of the developmental process as it now typically occurs in most of the world, a human flotsam and jetsam that has been displaced from traditional agricultural life without being incorporated into modern industrial life.

Daniel Lerner, "Comparative Analysis of Processes of Modernization," *The City in Modern Africa*, ed. Horace Miner (New York: Frederick A. Praeger, Inc., 1967).

than the action of individual households. This does not mean that the potential is poor—on the contrary, this resource should be developed, because it is very considerable even in areas where little has been achieved. For example, in a *gecekondu* studies by Sewell in Turkey:

> A new community organization, the Aktepe Help and Improvement Association, was established in 1962. As its president explained, "The association has nothing to do with the government; the government gave no help in setting it up. It is a result of the social needs of the Aktepe people. We have three hundred registered members, but we hope to include everyone living in Aktepe soon. The Board of Directors has seven members and now meets once a week.
>
> Houses have been built in Aktepe before and after the 6188th law (passed in 1960 and prohibiting extension of services to gecekondu). If the law is to be enforced, let it be enforced properly. Does it say tear down all the houses? Then tear them down! But what happens? The houses are not torn down. The people are taxed, but the municipality does not assume responsibility for Aktepe. Either the law should be enforced or we should be accepted as a part of the city.
>
> The first things we want to accomplish are the construction of a school and a road. We are willing to help the municipality in every way we can. If they say find 20,000 liras ($2000) and we will build a school for you, then we will find the 20,000 liras for them. The association does not depend upon dues from members but is financed by contributions. When we need a certain amount of money for the school, for example, we ask people to give contributions, each according to his ability.
>
> We have already consulted the city electricity and water departments. They came, saw our houses, and told us that the 6188th law prevented them from doing anything. Now we are going to higher authorities, the President if necessary. (29)

Appendix

A SELECTED BIBLIOGRAPHY OF PRINCIPAL SOURCES AND REFERENCES

World

1. ABRAMS, CHARLES: *Man's Struggle for Shelter in an Urbanizing World*, M.I.T., Cambridge, Mass., 1964.

*2. ———: *Squatter Settlements: The Problem and the Opportunity* Special Report to USAID, Department of Housing and Urban Development. New York, Nov. 1965.

3. DUGGAR, G.: *Renewal of Town and Village, A World-Wide Survey of Local and Government Experience*. I.U.L.A. The Hague, 1965.

4. UNITED NATIONS: *Report on the World Social Situation*, New York, 1957.

5. ———: *Report on the World Social Situation*, New York, 1963.

6. ———: *Social Aspects of Housing and Urban Development*, (E/CN.5/392) 1965.

7. ———: *Finance for Housing and Community Facilities in Developing Countries*. (E/C.6/32) 1965.

Hong Kong

8. DWYER, D. J.: *The Problem of Immigration and Squatter Settlement in Asian Cities, Two Case Studies, Manila and Victoria-Kowloon*, article in Asian Studies, Vol. 2, #2, Univ. of Philippines, 1964.

9. *Annual Departmental Reports, of Commissioner for Resettlement*, Government of Hong Kong, 1954–64.

10. GOVERNMENT OF HONG KONG, *Review of Policies for Squatter Control, Resettlement and Government Low Cost Housing* incl. 1963 Working Party Report. 1964.

*11. CALCUTTA METROPOLITAN PLANNING ORGANISATION: *Improvement Programme for Metropolitan Calcutta: 1964–1971*, Vol. 5, 6a, India, 1964.

12. GUHA, UMA: *A Short Sample-survey of the Socio-Economic Conditions of Sahebbagan Bustee, Rajabazaar*, Calcutta, Department of Anthropology, Government of India, 1958.

13. SAMAJ, BHARAT SEVAK: *Slums of Old Delhi*, Atma Ram, Delhi, 1958.

*14. WEINER, M.: *Urbanization & Political Extremism, An Hypothesis Tested*, M.I.T., Cambridge, 1962.

Pakistan

*15. KARACHI DEVELOPMENT AUTHORITY: *Lyari Redevelopment Scheme, Survey of Existing Conditions*, Pakistan, 1961.

Philippines

*16. ABRAMS, C., Koenigsberger, O.: *Report on Housing in the Philippine Islands*. UN/TAA i/59.

17. GOVERNMENT OF PHILIPPINES: *Minimum Standards of Accommodation in Relation to Levels of Living*, National Economic Council, 1963.

*18. JUPPENLATZ, M.: *Urban Squatter Resettlement, Sipang Palay*, UN, New York, 1965.

Singapore

19. KAYE, B.: *Upper Nankin Street, Singapore*, Univ. of Malaya Press, 1960.

Africa

20. BELANDIER, G.: *Sociologie des Brazzavillesnoires*, Paris, 1955.

21. MARRIS, P.: *Family and Social Change in an African City—A Study of Rehousing in Lagos*, London, 1961.

22. RAYMAEKERS, P.: *L'Organisation des Zones de Squatting*, Editions Universitaires, Paris, 1964.

Algeria

23. DESCLOITRES, P.: *L'Algerie des Bidonvilles*, Paris, 1961.

Morocco

*24. B.E.R.U.: *Les Bidonvilles en Marac:* Special Report to U.N., 1965.

* Not generally available to the public.

Tunisia

25. SEBAG, P.: *Le Bidonville de Borgel*, Cahiers de Tunisie 1958, pp. 267–309.
26. ———: *Un Faubourg de Tunis: Saida Manoubia*, Memoirs du Centre d'Etudes de Sciences Sociales, P.U.F. 1960.
27. ———: *Le Faubourg de Sidi Fathallah*, Cahiers de Tunisie 1960, pp. 75–136.

Turkey

*28. B.E.R.U.: *Les Bidonvilles en Turquie*, Special Report to U.N., 1965.
*29. SEWELL, G. H.: *Squatter Settlements in Turkey: Analysis of a Social, Political and Economic Problem*, M.I.T., Cambridge, Mass., 1964.

Latin America

30. HAUSER, P. M.: *Urbanization in Latin America*, International Documents Service, Division of Columbia University Press, New York, 1961.
31. KOTH, M., SILVA, J., DIETZ, A.: *Housing in Latin America*, M.I.T., Cambridge, Mass., 1964.
32. OLIVERO, H., Jr.: *Basic Sanitary Services in Shanty Towns: Migration and Urbanization*, Environmental Determinants of Community Well-Being, PAHO/WHO, Sc. Publ. No. 123, Washington, D.C., Dec. 1965.
33. TURNER, J. C., and Mangin, W.: *Articles on Housing*, "Architectural Design" No. 8, London, August, 1963.
34. VIOLICH, F.: *Problems and Techniques of Land Use Control in Latin American Cities*, University of California, Berkeley, 1958.
35. WOLFE, M.: *Some Implications of Recent Changes in Urban and Rural Settlement Patterns in Latin America*, C.E.P.A.L., Santiago, 1965.

Argentina

36. WILSON, L. A.: *Voice of the Villas, Socio-Economic Analysis of the Residents of Villas in Parque Almirante Brown*, B. A., Argentina, F.C.H. Co. Inc. and Foundation for Cooperative Housing, Inc., Washington, D.C., 1965.

Brazil

37. DOXIADES ASSOCIATES: *Plans for Metropolitan Guanabara*, C.E.D.U.G., 1965.
38. S.A.G.M.A.G.S.: *Aspectos Humanos de Favela Carioca*, 13 Y 15 De Abril, 1960, O Estado de Sao Paulo, Brazil, 1960.

Chile

39. C.E.P.A.L.: *Urbanization in Latin America: Results of a Field Survey of Living Conditions in an Urban Sector*, (E/CN.12/662). Santiago, 1963.
40. ROSENBLUTH, G.: *La Participation de las Poblaciones Marginales en el Crecimento Urbano*, Division de Asuntos Sociales, C.E.P.A.L., Santiago de Chile, 1965.
*41. ———: *Problemas Socio-economicos de la Marginalidad y la Integracion Urbana*, Universidad de Chile, Santiago de Chile, 1963.

Colombia

42. C.I.N.V.A.: *Siloe, el Proceso de Desarrollo Comunal Aplicado a un Proyecto de Rehabilitacion Urbana*, Bogota, 1958.
*43. TURNER, C. B., Jr.: *Squatter Settlements in Bogota*, Centro Interamericano de Vivienda y Planeamiento, Bogota, 1964.

Mexico

44. FRIEDEN, B. J.: *Search for Housing Policy in Mexico City*, Town Planning Review, Vol. 36, No. 2, Liverpool, England, 1965.
45. INSTITUTO NACIONAL DE LA VIVIENDA: *Colonias Proletarias, Problemas y Soluciones*, Mexico, 1958.

Panama

46. GUTIERREZ, S. A.: *El Problema de las "Barriadas Brujas" en la Ciudad de Panama*, Panama, 1965.

Peru

47. *Barriadas de Lima Metropolitana*, Ministerio de Salud Publica y Asist. Social, Lima, 1960.

48. COMISION PARA LA REFORMA AGRARIA Y LA VIVIENDA: *Informe Sobre la Vivienda en el Peru*, Lima, 1958.

*49. CORPORACION NACIONAL DE LA VIVIENDA *Informacion Basica Sobre Barrios Marginales en la Republica del Peru*, Lima, 1962.

*50. COLE, J. P.: *Estudio Geografico de la Gran Lima*, O.N.P.U., Lima, 1957.

51. CARAVEDO, B., ROTONDO, H., MARIATEGUI, J.: *Estudios de Psiquiatria Social en el Peru*, ediciones del Sol, Lima, 1963.

52. MANGIN, W.: *The Role of Social Organization in Improving the Environment*, Environmental Determinants of Community Well-Being, PAHO/WHO, Sc. Publ. No. 123, Washington, D.C., Dec. 1965.

53. PATCH, R.: *Life in a Callejon: A Study of Urban Disorganization*. AUFS, West Coast South America Series, Vol. 8, No. 6, Peru, June, 1961.

*54. TURNER, J. C.: *A New View of the Housing Deficit*, University of Puerto Rico, 1966.

55. ——: *La Autoconstruccion*, Desarrollo-Economico, Vol. 1, No. 3, New York, Sept.–Oct., 1964.

56. ——: *Lima's Barriadas and Corralones: Suburbs vs. Slums*, Ekistics, Vol. 19, No. 112, Greece, 1965.

Puerto Rico

*57. ADMINISTRACION DE RENOVACION URBANA Y VIVIENDA: *Aspectos Sobre Salientes de la Vivienda y Caracteristicas Socio-Economicas*, La Perla, San Juan, Puerto Rico, 1963.

58. BACK, K. W.: *Slums, Projects and People—Puerto Rico*, Duke University Press, Durham, N.C., 1962.

Venezuela

59. J. ABOUHAMAD H.: *Estudio de 'El Pedregal,'* Economia y Ciencias Sociales, Caracas, 1959.

*60. ABRAMS, C.: *Report on the Development of Ciudad Guayana in Venezuela*, M.I.T. and Harvard University, Caracas, 1962.

*61. BANCO OBRERO: *Serie Sobre Estudios e Investigaciones Sociales* (Study of 4 "Barrios")—Folleto No. 1, Caracas, 1962.

62. C.I.N.A.M.: *Plan de Crecimiento del Distrito Valencia*, Concejo Municipal de Valencia, 1963.

*63. COMITE DE REMODELACION DE BARRIOS: *Programa Preliminar Para la Remodelacion de Barrios, Area Metropolitana de Caracas*, O.M.P.U., Caracas, 1963.

*64. PEATTIE, LISA: *A View from the Barrio*, To be published by the Joint Center for Urban Studies of M.I.T. and Harvard University.

*65. ——: *Social Issues in Housing*. Paper for the Catherine Bauer Wurster Memorial Lectures, Cambridge, 1966.

*66. RAY, TALTON: Forthcoming book on *The Politics of the Barrios of Venezuela*, 1966.

67. BANCO OBRERO: *Estudio de Evaluacion de los Superbloques*, Caracas, 1960.

68. CARRADA, R.: *The Housing Development Program for Ciudad Guayana*, Housing Policy Seminar, University of Puerto Rico. April, 1966.

36. Relations of Technology to the Design of Very Large Cities

RICHARD L. MEIER

The problems that must be faced in providing for the massive new urbanization of the future are extraordinary in dimension and unusual in type. Simple calculations based upon capital requirements, traffic congestion, or water supply—to name but a few categories in which these problems arise—demonstrate that the experience gained in building the contemporary Western metropolis fails utterly to meet the minimum needs of the urban aggregates in Asia. Much more powerful tools must be employed if urbanization is to contribute to the economic development process. These tools must incorporate technological advances to an important extent, but they require simultaneous innovations in social organization and planning.

If the urbanization experience in the West has not established procedures suited to the scale of urbanization needed in the East, it must be recognized that the Orient, taken as a whole, cannot assemble adequate tools for urbanization, either. If any leverage on these problems exists at all, it is likely to be based upon the relatively unused portions of the stock of technology and seldom-used concepts that has accumulated in the Occident. Since there has been an acceleration in innovation in most fields affecting urban structure and design, with only a small

India's Urban Future, *ed. Roy Turner* (*Berkeley, Calif.: University of California Press, 1962*), *Chapter XV, pp. 299–323. Reprinted by permission of author and publisher.*

fraction of these innovations achieving widespread use, there is a fair possibility of finding some economic solutions. Also, since a poor society can afford to change only a few factors at a given time, it is evident that we must look for those techniques that combine readily with the old and well-understood building crafts. Our task is one of identifying what fusions of the old with the new may assist in controlling and directing the forces unleashed by the demand for urbanization and its fulfillment.

It is typical of the academic approach that investigators will discuss substance and delineate problems about which something is already known. This tendency is equally true of the analysis of urbanization in India. An *exhaustive* analysis of major problems is not likely to be elicited by such an approach, yet for the planner, the engineer, and the architect the whole development is dependent upon not only identifying, but solving the crucial problems. The process of finding first the crucial limitations and then of suggesting likely solutions has not been formalized. A series of heuristics are involved which change from one set of situations to another. Those that appear to apply to large-scale urbanization will be illustrated by outlining briefly the arguments used in seeking solutions to problems faced in Asia, and more specifically to India, in the course of economic development.

The outcome, a technical solution for

very large-scale urbanization at levels of comfort and convenience for the population that are comparable with those enjoyed in populous European metropolitan complexes, has to a large extent already been described.[1] What has been lacking particularly is a discussion of the bases underlying this proposal. If anyone else is to evaluate and add to these investigations, it is desirable that the process of arriving at an urban form for the Indian context of A.D. 1980–2000 and beyond be reviewed in some detail. The procedures that must be used are not at all routine. They depend to a much greater degree upon data and trends to be found in modern science and technology than do most other approaches.

My first study was completed in 1954, although publication was delayed. Its primary intent was to demonstrate that at least one pattern could be found which permitted an adequate scale of living despite the paucity of natural resources. The capital requirements were compatible with reasonable expectations for the pace of economic development. Since that time, some new material has appeared in the technical journals and many of the previous ideas have been more completely tested in experiment stations and in individual practice. Can the first proposal still be defended? More than that, is it possible to go farther and identify even greater potential economies for organizing urban regions? Perhaps a whole class of options can be delimited, so that some extra leeway may be provided for cultural and aesthetic choice.

Studies upon urban form spend a great deal of effort on the inductive stage, the elaboration of extensive networks of connected hypotheses, which are extremely difficult to present in a cogent and persuasive fashion. The technique that permits one to work rapidly, and cover a great deal of ground, uses order-of-magnitude calculations in such a manner that the crux of the problem can be pin-pointed. Peripheral issues are set aside at this stage in almost a cavalier fashion. Once the core of the problem has been identified, a concentrated survey of the technical literature is called for. Fortunately, this literature is well organized, as compared to social science documentation, so that comprehensive coverage of the accumulated experience can be achieved in a reasonable amount of time. A quick review of the accomplishments and costs associated with relevant new technology usually suggests new systems, thus opening up new strategies for economizing and leading to a redefinition of the core problem. More order-of-magnitude calculations are then required to elucidate limiting factors. One proceeds in this fashion until the redefined problem can be demonstrated to be insoluble (the most common outcome), whereupon the progression of steps must be retraced to take up the most promising peripheral lead; these leads are followed until a satisfactory technical solution is obtained. When that point has been reached, a series of tests for social, cultural, and political consistency must be applied. If the tests are passed without the appearance of disturbing ambiguities, a candidate solution to the problem has been identified. It stands as the central theme of one of the alternatives for city form.

---

[1] R. L. Meier, *Science and Economic Development—New Patterns of Living* (Cambridge, Mass., and New York: Technology Press and John Wiley, 1956), pp. 139–222.

THE PROBLEM RESTATED

In general terms, the problem is that of finding a structure of society, including its distribution over space, that is most likely to be suited to a long period of economic development. More than ten years ago, after extensive review of the literature, I had come to the conclusion that there was no available means for damming up the flow of population to the cities. The "village industries" program that was much discussed in those days[2] offered no logical next step for improving the productivity of labor. Thus, such a program, despite its intentions, could only be the prelude to the kind of large-scale industrialization that is necessarily associated with cities. The densely populated areas of the world would encounter unprecedented problems of congestion in this industrialization process.

The world's heaviest rural-urban flows of population associated with economic development are expected to appear in China—in the direction of the Shanghai, Peking, and Canton areas—if China finds a way to continue its development. But for China the census is not detailed, and no satisfactory set of detailed maps is available, so that quantitative evaluations are out of the question.

In India the prospective scale of urbanization is almost as great. Excellent topographical maps were available,

and the census is reasonably adequate. India offers an appropriate context for analyzing the implications of urban growth.

One could start by making estimates of the labor required for maximum productivity of the land based upon agricultural techniques already employed in Indian agricultural experiment stations or in Japan, where maximum yields were obtained with labor-intensive methods, and then allow the remainder to be urbanized. But what is the total population to be accommodated? *The demographic transition to low birth rate death rate could (optimistically) be assumed to be completed with only a trebling of population.* The present population of India may be set at 400 million, and that of Pakistan in the neighborhood of 100 million persons. Thus, well over a billion persons would have to make their homes in urban environments in the Indian subcontinent eventually.[3] Most of them would be born in rural areas and be forced to make a personal adjustment to the city. How would these urban residents be distributed?

A map of the urbanizable territory of India based upon three minimal criteria —access to fresh-water supplies, access to raw materials, and the availability of relatively flat land other than flood plain—was prepared. Almost 10 per cent of the area qualified. Putting the ultimate aggregate urban population into that space implied an average population density of 8,000 to 10,000 persons per square mile, which is already an urban density by Western

---

[2] A general statement of the thesis is to be found in H. G. Aubrey, "Small Industry in Economic Development," *Social Research,* 18 (1951), 269. The methods employed in organizing such industries are provided by J. E. Stepanek and C. H. Prien, "The Role of Rural Industries . . . , " *Pacific Affairs,* 23 (1950), 65. My own critique is found in "Automation and Economic Development," *Bulletin of the Atomic Scientists,* 10 (1954), 129. A review of the Chinese progress in this direction is to be found in *Small Industry and Handicraft Development in Mainland China, 1952–58* (Misc. Paper No. 2, International Industrial Development Center [Menlo Park, Calif.: Stanford Research Institute, December, 1958]).

[3] It is assumed that relations between India and Pakistan would become as cordial as those between the United States and Canada. The boundaries would not be defended and a relatively free interchange of population would evolve. Almost any alternative would thwart economic development.

standards. Bengal, Orissa, and the whole Eastern slope seemed to be most favorably situated for urbanization. In this projection Delhi encountered water problems[4] and Bombay's growth was impeded by the hills, although it may decide to fill in much of the bay. Bangalore was found to have serious topographical difficulties, and the territories at the foot of the Himalayas were expected to suffer from restricted access to raw materials.

The Calcutta region seemed to invite the severest agglomeration in these projections. Therefore, using the historic growth rates for metropolitan growth during the exponential phase (6 to 8 per cent per year), and gross population densities of 20,000 to 30,000 per square mile, Calcutta's prospective growth was projected upon the map decade by decade, and at each step the attempt was made to envisage the extra urban services that would need to be installed in order to bring the newly settled territories into the urban economy. We soon encountered insuperable difficulties in estimation. The Hoogli River was a barrier to urban circulation that required expensive bridges, tunnels, and subways, whose construction might not be economically feasible at the time the need first arose. Similarly, the cost of building upon the silt and detritus downstream was likely to be variable. Very possibly, economical solutions existed—London and New York also are based upon estuaries —but we could not judge the physical implications for Calcutta. In New York, however, the existence of the

[4] I am told by Britton Harris that solutions to the Delhi regional water problem are available at not too great a cost and will be discussed in the forthcoming Delhi Regional Plan.

relatively unused Jersey marshes across the river from Manhattan served as a warning. There were too many discontinuities and nonlinearities inherent in Calcutta's location to permit forming a picture of the city at the hundred million mark.

Therefore, other locations where the pressures of urbanization were expected to become extraordinary were investigated. Madras was selected as the focus of an urban region that might attract as many as 60 to 80 million persons— possibly more if other cities encountered difficulties in accepting migrants. The terrain was gently sloping and it was cut by no major rivers. In the case of the geography of Madras it was possible to be far more explicit in our projections.

First, a static solution had to be found—a physical pattern which, on the one hand, permitted the fulfillment of basic human needs (especially the distribution of food, clothing, shelter, and services) and, on the other hand, permitted a level of productivity which was sufficiently greater than these requirements, so that the surplus could be devoted to building and reconstructing the *megapolis* (a name that had already been assigned to such large, multinucleated aggregations). A designer calls the relationship between a level of service and physical specifications a *standard*, and it was evident from the start that the standards underlying Western urban settlement were utterly incompatible with the needs of the densely populated regions in the Orient. A unique set of standards for urbanization would have to be invented for such countries as India and China. Therefore, the next task was to place oneself in the shoes of the Indian planners of the future and grope toward a reasonable system of standards that would be relatively impervious to the social changes that were sure to occur.

THE MINIMUM ADEQUATE STANDARD OF LIVING

In the science of man there has been continuing emphasis upon the search for invariant relationships between any individual and his environment. Extreme conditions must be identified which put a stress upon humans and reduce their ability to interact effectively in society and participate in the culture. The findings tend to be species-specific and so must apply equally well to Asiatic and Western peoples, even though the original data have been obtained almost entirely through studies upon the latter. The nutritional needs belong in this category, as well as those associated with thermal comfort.

Superimposed upon such needs are those underlying coöperation with other individuals—nurture of the young, the acquisition of language, security from attack, medicine, and the like. Moreover, the facilities taking the form of dwellings, vehicles, roads, and time-saving equipment must be conveniently assembled so that all of the necessary tasks can be fitted into a twenty-four-hour day.

The standards that were chosen for a *minimum adequate standard of living* were reduced to a basis that was virtually culture-free—so long as the culture retained a commitment to an urban style of life. It was applicable, with indicated adjustment to climate, to any densely settled portion of the world that lived in poverty. It represented a level of living well above subsistence and one which permitted cultural activity as sophisticated as any

that has been achieved up to the present day—so long as such cultural activity renounced conspicuous consumption of material goods or energy.

The components of the *minimum standard of living* are reproduced in Table 1. This set of relationships was arrived at in 1949 and has not been noticeably outmoded in any respect by what has been discovered in the interim. The resistance to obsolescence speaks well for the form in which the standards have been framed. The costs have been restated in terms of current Delhi prices, so that comparisons with the present economic status of urban residents can be made with ease. It should be remembered that the costs of unskilled labor and personal services are much cheaper today than in a city where virtually all the population is maintained at the minimum adequate level. At the same time, however, the costs of shelter, communications, and manufactured products are likely to be reduced in price due to economies of scale.

The capital costs for installing a minimum adequate level of living were estimated in 1954 on the basis of equipment and installation prices then being quoted. Each category (food production, apparel, water, shelter, transport, communications, manufacturing, etc.) was taken conservatively, allowing for no more cost-reducing innovations than had already been described. The conservatism was intentional, because it was still impossible to determine whether the postwar flow of cost-saving innovations was going to do more than counterbalance the increasing scarcity of natural resources. Now we can see a resumption of the trend toward a reduction in the capital required to generate a unit of income.

Table 1

Components of a Minimum Adequate Standard of Living
(Based Upon Population-average Physiological Requirements for Health and Organized Production in a Tropical Urban Environment)

Component	Requirement	Unit Cost (in Rupees)	Yearly Cost (in Rupees)
Food :[a]			
Rice	100 kg/yr	0.75 per kg[b]	75
Wheat flour	60 kg/yr	0.50 per kg	30
Sugar and syrup	30 kg/yr	0.80 per kg	24
Legumes	20 kg/yr	0.75 per kg	15
Vegetables	50 kg/yr	0.20 per kg	10
Cooking oil	20 kg/yr	1.75 per kg	35
Spices, etc.[c]	. . .	. . .	30
Total	. . .	. . .	219
Shelter :			
Rent and furnishings[d]	6 square meters	20.0 per month	240
Electric (cooking, lighting, communications)	12 kw-hr/mo	0.20 per kw-hr	48
Water	2–3 tons/yr	. . .	12
Misc. household expenses.	. . .	. . .	25
Total	. . .	. . .	325
Personal :			
Clothing	20 m/yr	1.25 per meter	25
Shoes	3 prs. sandals	7.0	21
Haircuts	13	0.30	4
Newspapers	1/5 of 400 issues	0.12	10
Postage	30 messages	0.10 average	3
Telephone	50 calls	0.15	8
Local Transport	200 rides	0.20	40
Total		. . .	111
Services :			
Health (enough for life expectancy of 65 years)			
1 professional, 4 technicians/1,000 persons			12
Medicines and Supplies			30
Equipment (1 bed/200 persons, or Rs. 100 investment)			20
Education (7 teachers/1,000)			13
Buildings (Rs. 100 investment)			20
Teaching materials and equipment			20
Professional training			20
Security (police, fire, public health, etc.)			30
Social insurance (disability, old age)			100
Miscellaneous social services			50
Cultural activity, recreation, etc .			50
			c 365
Total for all components[e] (exclusive of national defense items)			Rs., 1,030

[a] This diet would yield about 2,800–2,900 calories per capita per day and could be easily balanced through minor modifications of the local cuisine. It will be noted that no specific allocation is given to milk, meat, or fish. Actually, a purely vegetarian diet of the kind indicated can be made nutritionally adequate, but may not be culturally satisfying. If such items are added, the quantity of pulses can be reduced, but the over-all cost would be increased.

[b] Prices are based upon quotations in New Delhi, April, 1960. I am indebted to Rodman T. Davis for supplying many of these figures.

[c] Including flavorants, preservatives, condiments, and vitamins.

[d] It was presumed that about a quarter of this would apply to furnishings, some of which may be built into the dwelling, and the remainder for roofed, enclosed space. This suggests that the capital cost of a typical dwelling unit would fall in the range of Rs. 5,000–8,000, including the price of land.

[e] The same standard came to $331 (1950 prices), using world prices and internally consistent values for labor. The present per capita income in Madras State is probably less than Rs. 300.

Therefore, the total capital calculated then, $1,800 to 3,500, altogether about five to ten times the per capita income required for an adequate level of living, is almost certainly too high. The economies of scale that come into effect, combined with capital-saving innovations that are now more clearly foreseeable, suggest that a factor of three is more appropriate.

The spatial requirements for urbanization can also be deduced to some extent from these standards. For a fully constructed megapolis, where the birth rate in the population must, of necessity, be brought into equilibrium with the death rate, the family units are likely to be small as compared to the present, the most common sizes being three or four persons. Even if the extended family is retained as an urban institution,[5] the size will not actually be very much increased—the most likely membership might run to four or five. Therefore, something in the neighborhood of 20 to 30 square meters of living space would appear to cover most of the needs for apartments and houses. At least an equal amount of built-up, organized space would be required for the social services, transport, and out-of-the-house activities. The great shortage of capital that may be expected to prevail during the construction phase will prevent widespread use of multi-story structures and high-rise buildings. Thus, it was expected that urbanization would be made up predominantly of single-story buildings, with residential densities in the neighborhood of 75 persons per hectare (allowing 10 per cent of the land to be stream, pond, marsh, tank, or otherwise unusable for building) so long as the congestion problems posed by such high densities could be solved. In the city center and subcenters another ten square meters per employee position would be needed and allocated at the workplace, but office and industrial activities, particularly the ubiquitous lofts needed for low-capitalized light industry, could be conveniently stacked up four stories or more.

The standards helped very little, however, in envisaging the styles of life that might be adopted, or the different ways in which people might choose to spend their nonworking, nonsleeping hours. Nor did they imply very much about the institutions that link together the individuals and households in coöperative large-scale enterprises for the provision of urban services and the organization of meaningful cultural activities. The scarcity of natural resources and the overwhelming magnitude of the flows of persons to the urban areas were expected, however, to impose some unique requirements in the realm of organization.

RULES FOR URBAN ECONOMIZING

The restrictions placed by poverty upon urban design always come as a shock to Western-trained observers. The familiar proportions and relationships that now represent the good and decent life can be made available to, at best, a tiny fraction of the people that must live in cities in India. Commitment of resources according to Western standards would benefit this minority,

[5] There is now considerable concrete evidence that even in southern India families send members out to seek employment. If these members, mainly men, remain in the city, they bring in their families. G. M. Woodruff, "Family Migration into Bangalore," *Economic Weekly*, 12 (January, 1960), 163–172. S. Epstein has shown that in Mysore the ownership of small amounts of village land stands in the way of rapid urbanization (*ibid.*, 11 [July, 1959], 967–972). The evidence suggests that the urban settlements would be made up internally of low-caste families, refugees from disaster, etc.

but would cut off the hopes for improvement on the part of the majority of the population. Such a decision could only lead to political suicide in the long run. Those who were not included in the privileged class could be easily provoked to overrun any pucka apartment blocks and terrace housing that monopolized amenity.

In the early days of these explorations, strenuous attempts were made to discover whether the megapolis in Asia could not take a form similar to that exhibited in the history and the plans of London and Paris. Each modification that was hypothesized, however, fell far short of requirements. Each demanded many times more capital than was likely to be available if operating costs were to be held at a reasonable level. Tokyo experience offered a precedent for urbanization that was much more helpful, but still far from adequate.

Only one excursion of this sort is worth relating, and this one because it explored the implications of recommendations that are tendered today by some administrators and planners. Such people often suggest that there must be an optimum size for a city so that one objective of large-scale urbanization might well be the allocation of as many people as possible to cities of optimum size. The optimum may be discovered by constructing an index of services and amenities available in cities, as a function of size, or by discovering the per capita overhead costs for providing a standard set of amenities and services. The treatment of such recommendations operationally is rather unclear, but verbal reports of cities in partially developed countries suggested that urban aggregations less than a few hundred thousand population could not support all of the services desired, while cities that had grown

beyond a million persons suffered seriously from congestion. Therefore, a half million was taken as a reasonable hypothetical figure for the optimum size.

After that it was a simple exercise to distribute 1,000,000,000 people living at the minimum adequate standard for space utilization over about 120,000 square miles of land otherwise used for intensive agriculture. In order to be economic, these cities would be connected by excellent transport links and the area occupied in such a way that time lost in movement to and from the center of the city would be at a minimum. These assumptions led to 2,000 star-shaped settled areas with the points of the stars coalescing, leaving round blobs of agriculture in a web of urbanism. For 90 per cent of the residents living in urban units of economically ideal size, escape from the urban environment would then be equivalent to that required to get away from a city hundreds of miles in extent and having a population of a billion people. Thus, the aims of the persons recommending cities of reasonable size are defeated by the size of the population expected.

These preliminary unsuccessful explorations did serve to illuminate certain principles underlying urban design that brought about notable reductions in capital requirements and operating costs. A suitable design might be found if it conformed to all of these principles simultaneously. In outline they may be stated as follows:

1. Virtually all the provisions for new migrants, particularly housing and service facilities, must be erected by self-help techniques. The structures and layout must be so simple that untrained labor can put them into place over an extended period of time with a minimum of central control or assistance. Migrants should be settled in satellite communities and tracts at the fringe

of the urban area in order to reduce their contribution to congestion.

2. The automobile as a major means of private transport must be abolished. Automotive vehicles require too much space, too much fuel, and, thus far at least, threaten contamination of the atmosphere. This sacrifice of the private automobile implies that fewer roads are available for trucks, buses, and even bicycles, and that alternative transport services must be supplied. Main routes to communicate on the fringe would be transformed stepwise from roads with buses to transit lines.

3. The morning and evening peak-load phenomenon in the transportation system should be eliminated from the areas of high-density settlement. This can be done by putting all shops, schools, offices, and services on a multiple shift basis. Buildings and equipment are much more efficiently used on two shifts per day, with a third shift reserved for balancing with overtime work, maintenance, and the receiving of supplies. Horticultural labor and construction labor need daylight and therefore constitute an "intershift," making altogether six peaks of movement per day. The users of services, especially students, can be manipulated so as to fill in the valleys that remain. Multiple shift operations are known to be difficult to put into practice. The best hope seems to be that of evolving into such a state by means of a carefully planned transition.

4. The inventory of perishable foods that require refrigeration and special warehousing must be kept to a minimum. Two features promise to make great contributions in this respect. Protein production could become largely microbiological, making direct use of photosynthesis and utilizing the swampy margins of the metropolitan region in a mechanical, high-yield endeavor. Vegetables and garden fruits, grown in intensive horticulture, could be produced immediately to the rear of the settlements of new migrants, so that relatively little transport and storage of perishables would be needed prior to consumption.

5. There must be segregation of heavy manufacturing (which is proportionally much less important to a minimum adequate standard of living than it is to patterns of affluence in Western society) into appropriately serviced areas, and distribution of light manufacturing to sites that are within walking distance of the dwellings or the confluences of movement within the city.

6. Devices must be installed for the maintenance of social order and the prevention of the massive riots that disturb the peace and even overthrow governments. The different ethnic communities must be permitted to make their own laws, but not allowed to invade the territory or take away the privileges of others.

7. The principal investment must be in education, as much at the adult level as in the schools. The various electronic media make it possible for small nuclei of trained teachers to have a much greater effect than formerly. The feedback, especially the questions that arise among the receivers of education, would require the creation of quite a considerable organization. The transition from rural to urban attitudes must be brought about in the shortest possible time. The introduction of family limitation, work habits leading to high productivity, and the organization of community-level welfare services are programs essential to rapid economic development. Each of these requires social contacts that are designed to be educational.

Only with such rules at hand was it possible to propose and evaluate a transportation system and the land-use allocation scheme that is tied to such a system. Simplicity was essential because the engineering and planning capacities of the urban regions would be rudimentary at the time the skeletal network was laid down. The cheapest long-distance movement of passengers was demonstrated by the electric railway (in the neighborhood of 6 cents per mile, including the value of time lost in movement). Short-distance movement away from the termini was most economically handled via bicycle (less than 4 cents per mile, calculated on the same basis). The physical characteristics of a railroad with feeder transportation required high-volume traffic generation from intensely developed centers.

It quickly became apparent that the rate of acceleration and deceleration of rolling equipment on the electric line was a determining factor for the distance from the center or subcenter that could be tolerated in a mass transit system. Surprisingly, the rolling friction of iron upon iron set limits upon the over-all size for the megapolis. The best resolution of these difficulties in the design of appropriate transportation in present and foreseeable technology was offered by some existing additions to the Paris Metro,[6] which employ rubber tires on dry hardwood or concrete. The stops are best put about a mile apart, except in high-density areas, where the distance may be less.

In order to handle the great variety of people and baggage that descends upon a railroad station when no alternative mode of transportation exists, the bicycle must be supplemented by several other vehicles in its general class—pedicabs and pedicarts primarily, but also some electric warehouse-trucks and gyrobuses for the main stations.

[6] Quite a few variations of this approach have been proposed in the last few years. One of the latest to come to my attention ("Pneuways for Rhodesian Transport," in *The New Scientist*, VII [1960], 384) has estimated costs for construction of ways that run less than 10 per cent of monorail, although cruising speed is set at only 40–50 mph. For the scale of urbanism considered here, high rates of acceleration would be advantageous. They would correspond to cruising speeds of 60 mph or more and demand more capital than was indicated for the "pneuway" above. Even more recently, it has been concluded that similar equipment is best suited to conditions in Los Angeles.

THE URBAN MODULE

The *module*, like the standard, is a simplifying device for the designer. He notes that certain features of an organized structure, such as a city, are unique, complex, indivisible, and subject to rapid and continuous change, while others are iterative and subject to occasional discrete change. The module can be applied to the relatively permanent elements that repeat themselves. It is a form of building block for design —having quite constant dimensions, some assigned structural specifications, and a few fixed functions, yet still permitting differentiation and individuation in many other directions—that can be established as a matter of convenience to designers and builders. For large-scale urbanism, the *communities* of recent migrants from rural areas offer the best opportunity for simplification and rationalization by applying a modular form.[7]

[7] Modules may also be used in the centers and subcenters of new urban regions, but in those instances the dimensions of the appropriate module are smaller in scale and more precise in their other specifications. The basic module for central districts would not contain a community, but might constitute only a block of buildings, or perhaps even a standard plot of land together with the airspace above it. The international styles of elevator buildings may be applied effectively in these central places, and the most educated and urbanized segment of the population may be expected to live in contiguous residential areas. Therefore, modules for high-density central areas can very likely be successfully borrowed from overseas, and do not need to be created *de novo* in the developing country itself. The proper choice of module for central districts cannot be decided upon at the present time. One form may be preferred in Delhi, other forms in Bombay and Madras. It is futile to carry a discussion of general problems of generalized city-center designs any further at this time. Serious economic difficulties cannot be foreseen; therefore, no unusual adaptations of technology need to be brought forward at this stage. The normal working of the real estate market seems

The flood of in-migrants, however, introduces a critical problem. We have already ruled them out of the central area and adjoining neighborhoods, because of the effects upon circulation. The best-known alternative—that of permitting migrants to settle in camps, *bidonvilles*, and industrial shack-towns on the urban fringe—wastes precious land through disorder and lack of planning, so that no simple route toward economic advance and the accumulation of capital is left open to the settlers. It must also be ruled out, therefore. The chaos in the physical and social environment checks any sustained program for self-improvement. Accordingly, another alternative has been employed: the concept of an *urban village*, a place with fixed boundaries, speaking one mother tongue and holding to the same general set of customs. (A few villages could be constituted as mixtures of a wide variety of subcultural backgrounds, so that the in-migrant is granted some choice when he arrives.) This is a community that has some bases for coöperation independent of arbitrary authority asserted from the outside.[8] When established, it would be assigned territory along the rail lines that connect with the large employment centers. The land would be surveyed and the water and sewer lines laid down in advance, but the construction would have to be done by the people themselves.

The urban village was proposed primarily as an environment that made possible a rapid adjustment to city life while at the same time it provided a convenient basis for administration. Ambitious young people would have access to technical schools and higher education by taking the train. Many such persons may be expected to move on to better jobs in the factories and offices, and latter take up residences elsewhere—primarily adjacent to centers and subcenters fitted to an international style of life. The construction of the village dwellings and the preparation of the surface for intensive horticulture, followed by extensive work on the maintenance and improvement of such structures, inculcates an acceptance for modes of organizing work that are better adapted to urban institutions. The growing of garden produce on the site provides a chance for the least adaptable members of the new community to become useful. The next generation, one that has spent the whole of its life in this environment, would be much more educated than the in-migrants and hence able to leave the community if it wished and make a decent living in modern industrial and commercial environments.

The *urban village* may be assigned the following specifications when serving as a module:

Area: 200–400 hectares
Population: 15,000–25,000
Transport: one station on transit line, one connecting path for bicycles
Education: several elementary schools, one high school
Health: one clinic, several bath-washhouse combinations
Commerce: one bazaar or market
Gardening: 100–250 hectares

likely to generate appropriate land uses when present known methods of regulation are employed.

[8] The concept of the *urban village* used here is fully compatible with the detailed descriptions employed by Herbert Gans, of the Institute for Urban Studies, University of Pennsylvania. His studies of the suburbs and immigrant settlements of American cities pay particular attention to the effects of natural, virtually unplanned, ecological forces upon the second generation. ("The Urban Villagers" [1959]; mimeographed, 256 pp.) [Subsequently published (Ed.)]

Madras at its limit could maintain perhaps 3,000 to 4,000 of these urban villages, with an extra 10 to 20 million persons living in residential areas close to the centers. Many of the communities would have the same languages, dialects, and ethnic origins, and exhibit differences due to timing, location, and choice.

In working out patterns for the organization of urban villages, considerable difficulty was encountered in the course of a search for optimum circulation. An urban village could not be established simply by fiat, so that it immediately yielded the minimum adequate level of living. Instead, it was quite certain to be started at levels very close to subsistence, very likely dependent upon various government authorities to help it through emergencies. The climb up to adequate levels of living for the whole community might be expected to require two or three decades, although many households would reach that stage much earlier. An efficient circulation pattern suited to a community living at subsistence, where almost everyone walks to work or at least to the station, becomes much too congested with light vehicle movement well before the time that minimum adequate levels are reached. Yet, valuable space cannot be wasted by holding it in reserve during this period of development. We did not find a neat solution to the bicycle parking problem. We could provide storage at the station, so that the two hectares (5 acres) of parking space that seemed to be required could be telescoped into a tenth of that area, and the bicycles would be stacked as much as 40 feet high, but only at a price. Investment in bicycle storage at the station was estimated to require at least 30 per cent of the average amortized value of the bicycles themselves. It was assumed

that the roads would be metaled in a fashion that is already becoming standard in India. The asphalt and crushed rock necessary for these roads and paths could be financed from a licensing tax on bicycles.

THE GROWTH MODEL

Once the standards and the modules have been chosen, and a view of the long run has been achieved, it is necessary to formulate a program which starts from contemporary conditions and moves step by step toward the desired outcome. At each step the alternative directions for growth can be assessed, the capital and resource requirements be estimated from the standards employed, and the specific difficulties that present themselves be disentangled. Obstacles to growth may require some study. They may be overcome by improved technology, or they may enforce a stunting of the growth that was previously anticipated.

The growth program for the Madras megapolis was set tentatively as follows:

Year	Millions of Population	Year	Millions of Population
1960	2	2010	48
1970	4	2020	64
1980	8	2030	72
1990	16	2040	80
2000	32	2050	80

Thus, exponential growth was anticipated up to an immigration rate of about 1.3 to 1.4 millions of persons per year, a level that would be maintained for about three decades. If we make a necessary assumption for economic growth, namely, that the practice of family limitation has been spread throughout the rural areas in the

1970–1990 period,[9] this migration rate should have removed the surplus population from the rural areas in the hinterland of Madras by 2020.[10] The remaining growth is attributed primarily to the abnormal age distribution created by migration, and so represents children born to recent arrivals that are in excess of deaths registered locally, even though the nation as a whole must have brought the birth rate into equilibrium by that time.

At the time it was first undertaken, the step-by-step programing encountered difficulties when the population reached 30,000,000 persons. It was found impossible then to obtain additional fresh water. The marginal cost of water was estimated to be already at $100 to $150 per acre foot (0.4–0.6 rupees per metric ton). Water from the Himalayas was likely to have been fully claimed by the nearer urban centers, which would no doubt encounter the same difficulties. We were fortunate to have come across at this time the first reports from the University of California Engineering Experiment Station concerning an adaptation of the Claude process. This process was designed to extract energy from sea water, yielding distilled water as a by-product. The California design emphasized the yield of distilled water, and reduced the production of electric power to a level where turbine design no longer posed

any difficulties. This process required a temperature difference in excess of 20°C. between the cold water obtained directly from the ocean depths and the warm surface water in order to obtain the necessary free energy. The crucial factor affecting the cost of water produced was the length of pipe required for moving cold water from the lower levels of the Indian Ocean to shore installations. The maps showed a rather narrow continental shelf in the vicinity of Madras, so the piping requirement was minimal. The amount of distilled water obtainable seems to be large enough to meet the needs of the megapolis if plants are placed on the beaches about a mile apart. In hot weather, when the need for water would be greatest, they should produce enough by-product power to operate themselves. The shallow slough to the north of Madras could be used as a warming basin for sea water and thereby add significantly to the efficiency. Fortunately, the process is contracyclical, since the yield is reduced in rainy periods and raised markedly when rain does not fall and the weather remains sunny. Other methods for obtaining fresh water from sea water are now being developed in the United States, but none of them promises to be any cheaper for a location like that of Madras.[11]

The transportation system posed another preplexing problem at this time: the traffic flowing in and out of the old central city seemed to require a terminus far more complex than the Grand Central Station—Times Square

[9] A. J. Coale and E. M. Hoover, *Population Growth and Economic Development in Low Income Countries* (Princeton, N.J.: Princeton University Press, 1958), and R. L. Meier, *Modern Science and the Human Fertility Problem* (New York: Wiley, 1959).

[10] It will be noted that these assumptions have attributed greater growth to Madras than is indicated by the rank-size employed by Kingsley Davis. The estimates here reflect specific geographical factors affecting cost of urbanization that were left out of account in the demographic study.

[11] Since then much engineering work has been carried out on various other techniques for the desalting of sea water, and standardized cost evaluation has been developed. (Staff report, "Chemists Sum up Water Desalting Progress," *Chemical and Engineering News*, 38 [April 25, 1960], 56–59.)

combination. Was it possible to interchange the population from pedestrian movement and bicycle-class vehicular systems to fast trains, without extravagant terminal costs? It is easy to recommend escalators, moving sidewalks, and automatic shuttles, but these are extravagances in a country with a per capita income still in the neighborhood of 500 rupees per year (projected). The solution appeared to be that of a rental system, very likely with credit cards, which would stock vehicles at convenient points throughout the business and administrative area. The stocks at the central station would be greatest of all, but were still shown to require no more than a fifty-story structure for storage from one working day to the next. Addresses up to three kilometers from the station could be reached within ten minutes after arrival. This simple solution seems most astonishing when it is compared to the present congestion encountered at the major terminals of metropolitan centers much smaller than the megapolis envisaged here. This is one point where multiple benefits derive from the banning of automobiles, the establishment of interlaced multiple daily shifts in offices and services, and the resultant flattening of the peak load.

In these early studies it was already possible to suggest that, when the principal purpose is to transmit information, passenger transportation often represents a waste of time and energy; but the manner by which the advancing technology of information transmission could provide substitutes for such movement was less clear. Now we can see, for example, how teaching-machine programs can be sent to students from a central repository, stored temporarily on tape, and erased later to make way for another lesson. Students still need

to travel, mainly to acquire laboratory techniques not easily reducible to tape, imbibe enthusiasms and observations from picked teachers, and compare experiences with other students at their own level, but this amount of contact does not require daily commutation. Similarly, the routine aspects of finance and market no longer demand face-to-face interaction. The central city, however, and the specialized subcenters, too, would certainly need trained people on hand for the interpretation and analysis of information, for the negotiation of coöperative arrangements between organizations, and for making decisions in the face of unspecified risks. Altogether, the passenger-carrying capacity in the 21st century may be less than has been anticipated at this time, although it must still remain large. A network of small pipes which conduct high-capacity microwave beams would enable the substitutions to be made. They could carry most of the postal flow, the television content, telephone messages, market data and documentation, cultural materials, etc. The network would naturally parallel the rail lines, but the capacity of channels connecting the centers would be many times greater than those connecting the urban villages. By that time the electromechanical switching-equipment used at present, particularly in telephone exchanges, should be displaced by fully electronic equipment requiring much less space and less maintenance.

After the problems of water shortage and traffic congestion were dealt with, the programing of megapolitan growth encountered no critical problems. One could see from the calculations that the costs for the interchange of persons and goods were mounting with added population, so that a city of 100 million population might easily become as inconvenient as New York is today. At the projected per capita income, a single center with subcenters and special communities reaches its limit at around the 100-million mark. The ability to program growth to 80 million on flat terrain does not mean that critical problems do not exist; it only implies that we lack sufficient information at the present time to discover and describe them. This open-ended future has a considerable advantage, nevertheless, over historic paths of development, all of which seem to be blocked, over the long run, by an insufficiency of resources or by the lack of appropriate technology.

PROSPECTS FOR FOOD, FUEL, AND MATERIALS

How has the passage of time dealt with the assumption underlying the projections and the projections themselves? A nonclassical approach had to be adopted in order to find any kind of future that seemed technically and economically feasible. Novel approaches are risky because they may include hidden flaws which have not been detected. The ideas have not had sufficient exposure to criticism. In this brief review we shall proceed from the major to the minor categories.[12]

FOOD

The principal nutritional shortage in India and other societies living at or close to subsistence is in protein foodstuffs. The predicted revolution in

[12] It has been impossible to document the following statements in the standard fashion, due to their brevity. A more detailed evaluation would indicate the technical arguments underlying the conclusions and cite findings to substantiate the conclusions.

protein synthesis has moved closer to realization in Japan, particularly at the Tokugawa Institute for Biological Research, of the University of Tokyo, where most of the practical studies are being carried out. Organisms that fix their own nitrogen and at the same time manage to grow rapidly in warm water have now been found. Methods of controlling predators have been developed. In both Japan and the United States, methods for removing color and original taste have been found. A fillip from an unexpected quarter—the studies on the survival of man in outer space—has brought about a tenfold increase in research upon the technology associated with photosynthesis in continuous-flow systems. The new emphasis is upon the design of reliable fully automatic production systems.[13] The costs of production may be expected to fall to about the same range as soy bean or ground-nut protein in the 1970's, or sooner; the supply is more dependable than that of those crops and the quality of the protein is considerably better.

The intensive gardening procedures based upon the experience of the South Chinese and the Japanese, and the hydroponics experience in Puerto Rican and Indian experiment stations, are most sensitive to plant virus diseases. Some progress has been made in the control of such diseases through the use of antibiotics. A large number of small advances have been made on many fronts which, taken together, do not increase expectations, but offer greater assurance that, despite local mishaps, some kind of crop can be obtained. Even greater flexibility in food supply should derive from develop-

[13] R. G. Tischer, "Nutrition in Space Flight," *Advances in Space Science*, 1 (1959), 341–382.

ments in food processing. Synthetic rice, for example, can be made from whatever bulk starch is in best supply, and has been found to have acceptance in peasant populations.

FUEL

The development of nuclear energy from fission at the technological level has proceeded at a pace very close to the early projections, but costs are high as compared to that of fuel oil on the world market, since extra reserves of petroleum have been found recently. Therefore, most large-scale reactor construction has been postponed for a while.

The fusion process, which aims at obtaining power from the deuterium component in water, is undergoing a thorough researching, but as the details are filled in it appears more and more probable that facilities of economic size would be very large and, therefore, suitable only for the more developed societies where interest rates are comparatively low and the annual increases in demand are large.

The production of liquid hydrocarbon fuels via biological cycles using photosynthesis has now been tested at every step in an engineering experiment station and found to work even more efficiently than had previously been judged. This means that the exhaustion of the reserves of fossil fuels in developing countries need not deal a crippling blow to the development program. The expected cost of using sunlight as an original source of energy sets a ceiling that appears to be equivalent to gasoline at a price no higher than one rupee per liter.

CONSTRUCTION

Building techniques for low-cost, self-help urban housing have not changed very much in the past few years, but the volume of construction undertaken in this category has increased greatly. Perhaps more important than anything else is the evidence, still sketchy and scattered, but nevertheless reassuring, that the organization of self-help construction can be stimulated in such a way that the governmental aid and subsidy is small, compared to the over-all costs. People of rural origin can build houses with their own labor that are really quite decent, and can complete the job within two or three years if they are helped by kinsfolk and friends.

TRANSPORTATION

Although new techniques have appeared in the interim, e.g., hydroplaning, pipelines for solids, "sausage-skin" barges, vertical-take-off aircraft, and guided missiles, there are no striking changes in costs or spatial relationships that must be taken into account. All of these new developments may easily find a niche in the transportation system that is ultimately built into the economy, but they do not promise to do more than extend the plateau of constant unit costs, pushing back somewhat the points where congestion brings about rapidly increasing marginal costs.

MANUFACTURING

The rapid progress that the Japanese have made in mass-producing light, highly engineered articles—a pattern that is now becoming evident in the industrialization of Hong Kong as well —reinforces the earlier conclusion that Asia can develop most rapidly if it rejects the heavy, bulk-ridden, space-wasting features of European and American consumption and concentrates upon using small amounts of material to best advantage.

The scientific and technological reports coming from India in recent years reflect the need to get the basic metallurgical and chemical industries going. Only scattered suggestions can be found that the experience is being accumulated which will be relevant to the light, consumer-oriented industries of the future. Perhaps the labor shortages in Western countries that result in greater dependence upon imports for labor-intensive products will further stimulate the export firms in Madras, Calcutta, and Bombay, laying the foundation for a linking of the great aptitude for aesthetic synthesis and abstract design that exists in Indian culture with the practicalities of production.

Judgments about what may happen to manufacturing cannot be based upon simple extrapolations drawn from India at present, but primarily from the recent histories of territories, Asian and otherwise, such as Japan, China, Puerto Rico, Israel, Jamaica, Mexico, the Philippines, etc. Each of them in some respect has been ahead of India in organizing its industry and has learned through trial and error what is needed to start and maintain that kind of activity.

ORGANIZING THE URBAN COMMUNITY

How can the rural patterns of living be changed most rapidly into new modes which are consonant with urban life? Very likely, Indian cities will never be in a position to apply all the powers they feel they need. The scarcity of capital and adequately trained professional manpower will contribute to the feeling of impotence on the part of the officials. Is there any relatively simple strategy for administration

that seems to be open to the prospective areas of agglomeration?

The principles affecting land use that seem to be an absolute minimum have already been listed. The land and utilities scheme for "planning the slums" so that they could develop over time to a status considerably above that of the typical slum offers a widely used administrative technique. It implies the power to condemn and take over agricultural and other land for residential purposes without paying too much to land speculators. The city would also have to coördinate the railroad lines connecting satellite centers with the public transport that supports the more local circulation. The water and electric utilities, their extension or withholding, offer very simple means for control and guidance of community and neighborhood development. The introduction of the multiple shift system that reduces the peak-load pressures on the transit system and almost doubles the productivity of social overhead capital, will, for example, depend upon the availability of street lighting in the morning and evening hours. Control of the communications systems may rest with the national government, but the local administration of these services should work smoothly enough to enable the police to maintain order and to enable commerce and education to expand rapidly.

Charles Abrams has reviewed the recent experience that is most relevant to the planning of urban metropolitan regions in developing countries.[14] He lists a range of methods that may be drawn upon for the administration of plans, which I shall rearrange and

[14] Charles Abrams, "Regional Planning Legislation in the Underdeveloped Areas," *Land Economics*, 35 (1959), 85–103.

place in order of increasing administrative complexity: (1) compulsion using severe penalties, (2) inducement with subsidies and rewards, (3) education and persuasion, (4) direct operations, (5) joint ventures, (6) planned inevitability. In India, as elsewhere, it seems likely that all of these techniques will need to be employed simultaneously. There is a chance in India, however, that some of the advanced procedures can be used more often than when planning was undertaken before, because it is possible now to transmit information in India at lower relative costs, while the use of the military or the police for enforcement may be expected to become more expensive. The traditions of India foster an open society subject to open criticism and constant revision, so that the political barriers to the flow of information are low. The social and linguistic barriers are diminishing rapidly at the community level, at least, as education increases. (The conflicts between language groups may, however, be exacerbated for a while.)

The communications elements in the undertaking of plans for urban growth have been brought out because they are most subject to revision and improvement over the forthcoming decades. Major advances in communications technology are coming along rapidly and can be quickly adapted to the needs of developing countries.[15] Unit costs for the transmission of messages of various kinds and sizes can be reduced to a striking degree. This means that more complex forms of administration will be possible even at the low income

levels anticipated during the early stages of the urbanization process.

Let us explore some of the possibilities for guiding the evolution of the urban village, using its connections with the centers and subcenters as leverage for bringing about change. At this stage of development the welfare needs of the newcomers cannot be met directly by an urban administration. It must encourage the new groups to elect spokesmen, and it must appoint "caretakers" in some crucial categories.[16] Communications are carried on between these middlemen and the people themselves (whose basic reaction upon experiencing a critical need for a social service is to "see someone whom I know who will himself know where to go and what to do") on a verbal level, mostly informal, with many things remaining unspoken, and between the middlemen and the centers with restated requests translated into more formal language. These middlemen require some daily communication with the centers. Previously, such communication has been established through face-to-face contacts (or through another layer of middlemen), but now it can be handled through two-way communications channels and a set of telephone numbers and addresses.

[16] I am indebted to Dr. Erich Lindemann of Harvard Medical School for this highly economical conception that interrelates the dependent, not-yet-absorbed population with the formally organized elements in the city. An application of this mode of thinking can be found in the "Tenth Anniversary Report of the Wellesley Human Relations Service, Inc., 1948–1958," by R. L. Bragg, W. C. Klein, and E. B. Lindemann (mimeo, 60 pp.). He has recently completed an extended survey of Indian mental health and community organization and may subsequently publish remarks of his own on the applicability of the "caretaker" concept to the Indian scene.

[15] Trade journals such as *Electronics* provide comprehensive news regarding those developments. An excellent nontechnical analysis of recnt origin is to be found in *Business Week*, March 26, 1960, pp. 74–121.

Who are these middlemen? They can be briefly categorized as follows:[17]

The elders, who may serve as a panchayat court and resolve most civil disputes before they become court cases

The salaried administrative group that collects taxes, maintains records, and writes the necessary reports

The police officers, most of whom are, as a matter of policy, drawn from outside the community

The teachers, who will often need to be bilingual

The clinic personnel—nurses, pharmacists, dentists, and doctors

The water-control technicians, who give advice on the economical use of water in horticulture and elsewhere

The transportation agents, who arrange for trips back to the home village and for the delivery of relatives

The produce marketers, who must assess changes in market prices and advise the horticulturist when to harvest

The retailers, who must buy from catalogues or salesmen

The electrical maintenance men, who must service the power distribution system and perhaps make repairs on communication equipment as well

The building artisans, who must show the settlers first how to construct, then repair and maintain, the houses and service buildings needed by the settlers and their families.

The promoters of sports, exhibitions, festivals, and other cultural activities

[17] This list was assembled from experience acquired in the course of observing the urbanization process. It is interesting to compare these roles and functions with those reported for an early nineteenth-century Madras village before British contacts had brought about many changes: headman, accountant, watchman, boundaryman, water superintendent, priest, schoolmaster, astrologer, smith, carpenter, washerman, barber, cowkeeper, doctor, dancing girl, musician, poet. (H. E. Malaviya, *Village Panchayats in India*. [New Delhi; All India Congress Committee, 1956], pp. 88–89, citing Mathai, *Epigraphic India*, 4, 138.)

The secretaries and local committeemen of the major political parties

An estimated 20 to 100 two-way channels are needed to connect the middlemen directly with their respective organizations. They would operate most efficiently nowadays with small, portable radio sets, similar to those now produced in Japan and the United States, which connect with the telephone exchanges if the latter have antennas within a mile or so. The efficiency of a person so equipped when he moves around the community is much greater than if he sits at a desk with a telephone. Indeed, a portable two-way communications instrument with a distinctive antenna could well become a badge of office in the community. The capital investment required per outlet would be no greater than for a telephone and could perhaps be reduced over the next decade.

This is not the only kind of connection with the truly urban culture that the new community could use to advantage. Perhaps a thousand or more one-way instruments (radio, television, teleprinting, etc.) could be accumulated to serve educational, cultural, and recreational purposes simultaneously. Much of adult education can be channeled through the mass media. The questions that are generated, some of which make up the feedbacks to the broadcasters, can be monitored through the two-way connections. With such capacity for speeding interaction with sources of accumulated, specialized experience, it should be possible to create some highly developed institutions. The markets would have stable prices reflecting visible supply-demand relationships, the police would be able to coördinate their efforts in emergencies, the labor force would become differentiated along non-caste lines, involuntary inventory shortages would almost disappear, and current data would be available for the assembly of detailed plans. The principal difficulty that can be foreseen is one that occurs in every developing society—the persons in responsible positions, from the caretakers on up the hierarchy, and including most business administrators and independent professional men as well, would be overworked. The handling of too many messages can be extremely fatiguing, and can lead to actual breakdowns.

The tape recorder can be introduced at the "hot spots" in a message-relaying network. The persons involved can then queue up the flurries of calls that would otherwise overwhelm them. When a lull occurs, they can then review the backlog and, at the very least, take care of the high-priority items. Techniques such as these increase the peak-load capacity of the communications network by a factor of two or three. Institutions in the most advanced urban centers are only now adjusting to the potentials for organization that are inherent in these instruments, so that we may expect that the crucial operations in the construction of a megapolis can be made to work at least as well as their counterparts in advanced societies, though other aspects are likely to remain rather crude and simple for many decades to come.

The following sources were used in preparing selection 3, p. 55:

Afghanistan: U.N. Demographic Yearbook 1966, *Table 6 for 1965 census and 1966 estimates, cities over 100,000.*
　　　　Europa Yearbook 1967, *for 1966 estimate, cities under 100,000.*
Ceylon: U.N. Demographic Yearbook 1966, *for 1963 census for cities over 100,000.*
　　　　Ceylon Census 1953, for cities under 100,000.
India: U.N. Demographic Yearbook 1966, *for 1966 estimate for cities over 100,000.*
　　　　Indian Census 1961, for some cities of 100,000 & over and all cities under 100,000.
Nepal: U.N. Demographic Yearbook 1966, *for 1961 census (prov.) for Kathmandu.*
　　　　Statesman's Yearbook 1965–1966, *for 1964 estimate for Patan and Bhatgaon.*
Pakistan: *Pakistani Census 1961.*

The following sources were used in preparing selection 4:

Burma: Statesman's Yearbook 1965–1966, *p. 854 for 1963 estimate.*
Cambodia: U.N. Demographic Yearbook 1966, *Table 6 for 1962 Census data.*
China (Taiwan): 1965 Demographic Fact Book, *Table 1 for mid-1965 estimate.*
　　　　N.B. Includes "chen" (semi-urbanized townships).
Hong Kong: U.N. Demographic Yearbook 1966, *Table 6 for 1961 Census.*
Indonesia: Europa Yearbook 1967, *p. 569 for Djakarta 1966 estimate only.*
　　　　Republic of Indonesia, Population Census 1961, for preliminary figures. N.B. Includes only political units designated "municipalities."
Laos: U.N. Demographic Yearbook 1966, *Table 6 for 1962 estimate.*
Macau: U.N. Demographic Yearbook 1966, *Table 6 for 1960 Census.*
Malaysia: U.N. Demographic Yearbook 1966, *Table 6 Sarawak, 1960 Census.*
　　　　1957 Population Census of the Federation of Malaya, *Table 3.*
Philippines: U.N. Demographic Yearbook 1966, *Table 6 for 1965 estimate.*
　　　　Census of the Philippines 1960, Population and Housing. *N.B. Includes chartered cities and "municipios" (subdivisions of states) of over 50,000; figures include rural population within political subdivision.*
Portuguese Timor: U.N. Demographic Yearbook 1966, *Table 6 for 1960 Census (prov.).*
Singapore: U.N. Demographic Yearbook 1966, *Table 6 for 1966 estimate.*
Thailand: Thailand Statistical Yearbook 1965, *Table 17 for 1963 estimate.*
Vietnam, North: U.N. Demographic Yearbook 1966, *Table 6 for 1960 Census.*
　　　　Europa Yearbook 1967, *p. 1462, Namdinh only, 1960 Census.*
Vietnam, South: U.N. Demographic Yearbook 1966, *Table 6 for 1964, 1965 estimate. Figures for cities of over 100,000 only.*

The following sources were used in preparing selection 13, p. 162–63.

British West Indies: U.N. Demographic Yearbook 1966, *Table 6 for 1963 Census.*
Note: all references to U.N. Yearbook are to table 6, below.
Costa Rica: U.N. Demographic Yearbook 1966, *for 1965 estimate.*
Cuba: U.N. Demographic Yearbook 1966, *for 1965 estimate, cities 100,000 & over.*
Pan American Union, America en Cifras 1965, *for 1964 estimate, places 50,000–100,000.*
Dominican Republic: U.N. Demographic Yearbook 1966, *for 1966 estimate for cities 100,000 or over.*
Pan American Union, America en Cifras 1965, *for 1960 census for cities 50,000–100,000.*
El Salvador: U.N. Demographic Yearbook 1966, *for 1963 estimate, 100,000 & over.*
Pan American Union, America en Cifras 1965, *for 1961 census, cities of 50,000–100,000.*
French West Indies: U.N. Demographic Yearbook 1966, *for 1954 census.*
Guatemala: *Pan American Union*, America en Cifras 1965, *for 1964 census.*
Haiti: U.N. Demographic Yearbook 1966, *for 1960 estimate.*
Honduras: U.N. Demographic Yearbook 1966, *for 1965 estimate, 100,000 & over.*
Pan American Union, America en Cifras 1965, *for 1961 census, cities of 50,000–100,000.*
Jamaica: *Jamaican Census 1960.*
Mexico: U.N. Demographic Yearbook 1966, *for 1966 estimate for 100,000 & over.*
Pan American Union, America en Cifras 1965, *for 1960 Census, 85,000–100,000.*
Mexican Census 1950, for 40,000–85,000.
Note: Map includes cities of 40,000 & over in 1950.
Netherlands Antilles: U.N. Demographic Yearbook 1966, *for 1960 census.*
Nicaragua: U.N. Demographic Yearbook 1966, *for 1965 estimate.*
Panama: U.N. Demographic Yearbook 1966, *for 1966 estimate, 100,000 & over.*
Pan American Union, America en Cifras 1965, *for 1960 census, cities, 50,000–100,000.*
Puerto Rico: *U.S. Census, 1960.*
Trinidad and Tobago: *Trinidad and Tobago Census 1960.*